# ROD SERLING'S
# NIGHT GALLERY

*The Television Series*
*Robert J. Thompson, Series Editor*

# ROD SERLING'S NIGHT GALLERY

## AN AFTER-HOURS TOUR

Scott Skelton and Jim Benson

With a Foreword by JOHN ASTIN

Syracuse University Press

Copyright © 1999 by Scott Skelton and Jim Benson
All Rights Reserved
First Edition 1999
99  00  01  02  03        6  5  4  3  2  1

The paper used in this publication meets the minimum requirements of American National
Standard for Information Sciences—Permanence of Paper for Printed Library Materials,
ANSI Z39.48–1984. ∞

FRONTISPIECE: *Rod Serling*. Courtesy of Gene Trindl.

LIBRARY OF CONGRESS CATALOGING-IN-PUBLICATION DATA

Skelton, Scott.
    Rod Serling's Night Gallery : an after-hours tour / Scott Skelton
and Jim Benson : with a foreword by John Astin.
        p.     cm.    — (The television series)
    Includes bibliographical references and index.
    ISBN 0-8156-0535-8 (pbk. : alk. paper). — ISBN 0-8156-2782-3
(hardcover : alk. paper)
    1. Night gallery. 2. Serling, Rod, 1924–    . I. Benson, Jim, 1962–    .
II. Title. III. Series.
PN1992.77.N44S54   1998
791.45'72—DC21                                    98-15198

Manufactured in the United States of America

# Contents

# Illustrations

SCOTT SKELTON is a resident of Eugene, Oregon, where he lives with his wife, their dog, and four cats. He graduated with a B.S. in journalism from the University of Oregon and has written freelance articles for the *Eugene Register Guard*. *Rod Serling's Night Gallery: An After-Hours Tour* is his first book.

JIM BENSON lives in La Mesa, California, where he operates his business, Jim's TV Collectables, one of the country's largest mail order companies specializing in TV memorabilia. He has also written copy for the Copley News Radio Network, worked as a video technician for the San Diego Padres baseball team, and contributed to various periodicals, including *The Twilight Zone Magazine*.

Readers' comments can be directed to the authors through the *Night Gallery* website at www.nightgallery.net.

# Foreword

JOHN ASTIN

During the glorious California summer of 1970, San Diego was my playground while I performed in a movie called *Pepper.* Filmed throughout the area, mostly outdoors, it was an improvised film, which meant that we had no dialogue to learn. We were given a basic idea and just "let it happen" as the cameras rolled; it was supposed to bring a freshness and vitality otherwise unattainable. A director friend had called it "either frightened or lazy script writing," but for me, it was an adventure, and I was having a great time, when my agent called.

"Would you be interested in directing an episode of *Night Gallery?*"

"Gosh, I don't think so."

The year before, my short film *Prelude* had been nominated for an Oscar, the great Fellini had praised my work and befriended me, I had just finished a screenplay for a film which I was to direct (if the producer could sell it), and I was obsessed with becoming an "auteur" of feature films. I considered my then current acting assignment a sort of "divertissement," even a vacation, while I prepared to write another screenplay. Why direct a TV episode?

"Rod Serling wrote it," said my agent.

"Sure, I'd love to do it. When does it start?"

"They're sending you a script and can start as soon as you're finished with your 'improvisations.'"

"The script will be good. Don't wait. Tell them I'll do it."

Rod Serling. *Patterns. Heavyweight. The Zone.*

George Bernard Shaw once wrote, "Effectiveness of assertion is the Alpha and Omega of style. He who has nothing to assert has no style, and can have none." I had often used that statement as the measure of a writer. While in college, I had thrown over a promising career in math and the sciences to essay the arts, partly because I had hitchhiked to Ohio one weekend to see my buddy's roommate perform in a play. The play happened to be *Our Town,* and the Stage Manager that evening happened to be played by Thornton Wilder, who wrote the play. Its profound and moving "assertion" changed my life forever and opened my heart to a greater appreciation of the wonder of life. Similarly, I had seen an entire generation changed for the better by Rod Serling, and by some of his colleagues.

To do just a single episode with him would be important.

I was not disappointed. I still feel a warm nostalgia for each of the six *Night Gallery*s in which I participated.

Those of us who are serious parents know the relentless intensity of concern for our progeny, regardless of their success or failure. It seems never to abate. My recollection of *Night Gallery* is that *everyone* who worked on the show appeared to hold that same kind of concern and sense of responsibility for whatever was the current episode. It seemed that *Night Gallery* had become Our Child, and we were, all of us, a great mass of multiple parents, each individually responsible for its welfare. We weren't parents in that we were "bosses." Producer Jack Laird was the boss. It was our concern for the work that made us parents, and the result of this was a great deal of cooperation, rather than competition. Of course, some people were occasionally cranky, but under the bristle was generally concern for the show—a strange and exciting phenomenon. Perhaps I didn't fully appreciate it then, but we had an amazing amount of artistic freedom, considering we worked in television and at a tough studio, and the credit for that rightly belonged with Rod and our big boss Jack Laird. Budget, especially at Universal, was always a consideration, but we made up for it in other ways. I remember cinematographer Lenny South and I, with the guidance of art director Joe Alves, finding, for "The Dark Boy," areas on the back lot that, with proper camera placement, Lenny was able to make look like a Montana location. It was thrilling to see happen, to be a part of it. It seemed to me that no one was punching a clock. I remember, needing the correct sun-through-the-trees angle by the lake for some day-for-night, sitting out there all of one afternoon during prep time to find just the proper hour of the day for the shot. But it worked. It was a gorgeous "night," with patches of "moonlight" skimming across the lake. Much more effective than most expensive attempts to get the same effect during the actual night hours. Given a choice today, I would do it as we did it then, inexpensively, and better. I will always feel gratitude for the cinematographers: Lenny, Bill Margulies, Curly Lindon, and Jerry Finnerman. And for the infinitely creative Joe Alves, the talented and very generous editor Jean-Jacques Berthelot, and many, many others, but mostly for Jack Laird and the incomparable Rod Serling.

If you've bought this book, you're in possession of a unique and astounding document. I've been reading the manuscript for a number of months and still haven't finished it. It's inexhaustible. It's huge. It's an extraordinary documentation of a landmark series. The authors have given us history, with mountains of detail, written with style, because they *have* something to assert.

My career as an auteur? Just after *Night Gallery*, I put some ambitions on the back burner in order to focus on parenthood and family, another area of the fine arts, and haven't had the slightest regret. And these days, in my sixties, I'm back to films and plays and having a real vacation. And it's much more than a divertissement. Thinking of *Night Gallery* infuses me with not just nostalgia but also with the energy and optimism of youth. You have a great read ahead of you. Just let it happen!

# Acknowledgments

Aside from this book, the only major effort to document *Night Gallery* was undertaken in the mid-1980s by Kathryn Drennan and J. Michael Straczynski. The fine series of articles they researched and wrote for *The Twilight Zone Magazine* was beset by editorial difficulties and, frustratingly, never completed. We owe them a debt of gratitude, for they were able to reach a number of persons who, either through advanced age, illness, or death, we were unable to interview.

In our researches, we have enjoyed the help, expertise, and enthusiasm of scores of people to whom we would like to express our gratitude and thanks.

For materials and aid:

David Anderson; Atlantis Book Shop; Jim Benson and Cynthia Littleton of *Daily Variety;* Bill's Answering Service; John Blanshett; Linda Brevelle; Linda Choeneck; Tim Clark of *Starlog* magazine; Ned Comstock and Steve Hanson of the USC Film and Television Archives; Scott Curtis of the Academy of Motion Picture Arts and Sciences; the Directors Guild of America; Elyah Doryon; the Editors Guild of America; Bill Groves of *Television Chronicles* magazine; Jinny of the International Photographers Guild; Joanie's Answering Service; Joe of Time Tunnel Toys; Scott Johnson of Celebrity Addresses; Welton Jones, Jr. of the *San Diego Union-Tribune;* Jeff Kadet of TV Guide Specialists; Valerie Lippincott at Lindsay Wagner's office; Maureen Mata; Jim Nemeth; Pam at San Dimas City Hall; Jeffrey Rankin of the UCLA Library Special Collections; Script City; Jim and Lorraine Stewart; the Stuntman's Association; Craig Uchida of the Screen Actors Guild; Tom Weaver; the Writers Guild of America; and Marc Scott Zicree.

For taking the time to remember, our interviewees:

Edward M. Abroms, Joseph Alves, Jr., Barbara Anderson, Burt Armus, Desi Arnaz, Jr., John Astin, Burt Astor, René Auberjonois, John Badham, Les Berke, Noel Blanc, Robert Bloch, Michael Blodgett, Pat Boone, Tom Bosley, Richard Bracken, Hank Brandt, Ruth Buzzi, Joseph Campanella, Rosemary Campbell, Don Pedro Colley, Alex Cord, Jeff Corey, Grace Cursio, Henry Darrow, Susannah Darrow, Roger Davis, Phyllis Diller, Bradford Dillman, Walter Doniger, Rudi Dorn, Hal Dresner, Daryl Duke, Buddy Ebsen, Leonard Engelman, James Farentino, Gerald Perry Finnerman, Wayne Fitzgerald, Theodore J. Flicker, Rosemary Forsyth, Cherie Franklin, Jerrold Freedman, Paul Freeman, Zsa Zsa Gabor, Timothy Galfas, Jaroslav Gebr, John Gilgreen, Paul Glass, Richard C. Glouner, William Hale, Frank Hotchkiss, Kim

Hunter, Arte Johnson, Peggy Johnson, Richard Kiley, Jon Korkes, Jeri Laird, Persephone Laird, Darrell Larson, Francis Lederer, Michele Lee, Larry Lester, Gene Levitt, Sondra Locke, Gary Lockwood, John Meredyth Lucas, Patrick Macnee, Peter Mamakos, Richard Matheson, James McAdams, Roddy McDowall, Gil Mellé, James Metropole, Robert Morse, Ed Nelson, Lois Nettleton, Denise Nicholas, Leslie Nielsen, Leonard Nimoy, Emil Oster, Suzy Parker, E. J. Peaker, Radames Pera, Joanna Pettet, Sydney Pollack, Laurie Prange, Robert Prince, Terence Pushman, David Rawlins, David Rayfiel, Anthony Redman, Allen Reisner, Tony Roberts, Tony Russel, William Sackheim, Gerald Sanford, Alvin Sapinsley, Ralph Sariego, John Saxon, Ralph Senensky, Barbara Shannon, Louise Sorel, Leonard J. South, Tisha Sterling, Jeannot Szwarc, Harry Tatelman, Don Taylor, Richard Thomas, Angel Tompkins, Marc Vahanian, Phil Vanderlei, Vincent Van Patten, Sam Vitale, Lindsay Wagner, Shani Wallis, Adam Weed, Carol Weed, Mike Westmore, Ellen Weston, Stuart Whitman, Stanford Whitmore, William Windom, Lana Wood, Herbert Wright, and Tom Wright.

For supplying photographs:

Joseph Alves, Jr.; Les Berke; Ronald Borst of Hollywood Movie Posters; Claire and Heidi of Eddie Brandt's Saturday Matinee; Jonathan Burlingame; Eric Caiden of Hollywood Book and Poster Co.; Frank Dennis of Cinema Collectors; Jeff Corey; Susannah Darrow; Gerald Perry Finnerman; Jerrold Freedman; Timothy Galfas; Paul Glass; William Hale; Dana Krizan; Brigitte Kueppers of UCLA Research Library Arts Special Collections; Larry Lester; Janet Lorenz of the Center for Motion Picture Study; Ron and Howard Mendelbaum of Photofest; Sal Milo of Photovideo; Jerry Ohlinger's Movie Material Store; Pacific Photo; Howard Frank of Personality Photos; David Rawlins; Anthony Redman; Tom Rogers of Foto Fantasies; Jim and Melody Rondeau; Dr. David Sanjek of BMI Archives; Roger and Kathy Sapp of Bijou Collectibles; Ralph Sariego; Stewart Stanyard; Sunnies Funnies; Jeannot Szwarc; Don Taylor; TV History Archives; Tony Chiminiello and Ray Whelan, Jr. and Sr., of Globe Photos; Herbert Wright; and Tom Wright.

Thanks also to:

Jerry Wolski, John Shandor, Wendy Orgren, Mike McNulty, Video Dave, Mark Center, Joel Rasmussen, Harry Langdon, Jr., Ken Kaffke, Rolf Gompertz, Welton Jones III, Neil Summers, Ric Wyman, Shel Dorf, Lisa Sutton, and Hal Lifson.

And a very special thanks to:

Dean of Communications Thomas W. Bohn of Ithaca College; Bill Barry of the Library of Congress Film and Television Collections Division; Ralph Bowman; Jonathan Burlingame; Geraldine Cook; Tricia Daniels; Mark Dawidziak; Duane Dimock; John Field; Ed Finn; Molly Frances; Donald Lambdin; Connie Langella of BMI; our man in São Paulo, Mauricio Lhamas; Chris Lowry and Michael Daruty of Universal Studios; Gary Matheson; Susan Mendolia; Alan and Rita Ogle; Herbie Pilato; Edward Plumb; Ed Robertson; Gary Rutkowski of the Museum of Television and

Radio; Carol Serling; the stunning Louise Thomas; Bob Thompson, Nicole Catgenova, Mary Peterson Moore, and John Fruehwirth of Syracuse University Press; Gene Vradenburg; Lucy Chase Williams; and Fred Wostbrock.

Scott Skelton

*November 1997*                                                                    Jim Benson

# Introduction

Darkness.

But not complete darkness.

Pools of light form on a polished black floor. As our eyes grow accustomed to the gloom, we sense, vaguely, forms suspended in the air. Paintings. Statuary. We find ourselves in an art gallery after hours—and there is a chill to the place.

Footsteps. Coming toward us through the array of hanging paintings strides a figure, gradually becoming more distinct as he approaches. Confident, compact, darkly serious, suited and tied. In a familiar voice, the delivery terse and clipped, he invites us in, cautioning us that the paintings on display this evening inhabit the realm of the eerie, the oddball, the unsettling, and that we should take care on this tour not to touch the exhibited works—for very frequently they touch back.

This familiar figure was Rod Serling, the era was the early 1970s, and the place in which we found ourselves at 10:00 every Wednesday night on NBC was the *Night Gallery.* Serling had made his name during television's "golden age," the heyday of the anthology series; he was always keenly reluctant to limit himself to the confines of the returning-character format. His landmark fantasy series *The Twilight Zone* had made for a wide-open field of setting and period choices. When CBS canceled it in 1964, he sought a similar concept in which to continue his imaginative forays, developing *Night Gallery* as a new forum for his unique brand of storytelling.

Where *The Twilight Zone* had introduced shadowy, surreal elements into the button-down, post-Eisenhower landscape, this new show presented more graphic and colorful tales of the strange, the macabre, and the occult. *Night Gallery* was Serling's overt homage to the horror pulps he read voraciously as a youth. He gave a sophisticated spin of literacy and maturity to the plays he wrote, grafting onto conventional pulp outlines his highly personal moral outlook and social agenda. As a logical extension of his ideas for *The Twilight Zone, Night Gallery* seemed a promising venture. But in the end, despite Rod Serling's status as the most honored television writer of his generation, he lacked the industry muscle to mold the show to his satisfaction and grew disillusioned with it over time.

The show had an unusual and problematic structure, with two to four stories per show. Although this format gave *Night Gallery* a variety of tone and style, it also accorded the series an unavoidable inconsistency. This sectioned storytelling, which earned *Night Gallery* a reputation as a kind of ghoulish *Love, American Style*, stemmed from the clash between Serling's original vision of the show and the vision of the man in creative control of the series, producer Jack Laird.

But the fractured format of *Night Gallery*, the very thing that some believe is its greatest weakness, allows for criticism of each story as a separate entity, as if it were a short film—a quality that Laird, in fact, encouraged. By examining the series segment by segment, one can take the measure of *Night Gallery*'s frequent flashes of brilliance, proving that its quality often rivaled *The Twilight Zone*.

Until recently, however, this reappraisal was practically impossible because of the sad condition of the series over the past twenty-five years. In syndication, *Night Gallery*'s hour-long episodes had been forced into a half-hour slot, the segments recut and aggressively redesigned by other hands. The rethinking of almost every episode —the amputations; the disruption of tone and flow; the addition of unrelated new footage, music, and effects; the dishwater prints; the ham-fisted second-guessing of the originators' far more subtle work—had left the series in a shambles.

While researching this book, we based our opinions on an examination of the original prints, not their mangled cousins in syndication. The experience was nothing short of a revelation. Comparing the original series with its changeling was not merely akin to stripping years of yellowing varnish off a master's canvas. It was more like discovering the museum copy had been altered by an inferior artist, then badly cropped to fit a much smaller frame. The superior original, meantime, had collected dust in some forgotten warehouse.

In a fresh examination of the series, we have also noted some past inaccurate impressions by some of Serling's earlier biographers, the primary myth being that Serling's dramatic skills had waned in his last creative years. An overwhelming number of his scripts for *Night Gallery* show a high degree of quality, on a par with his earlier work and often better. Lastly, we wish to credit the many other talented persons who contributed to this free-form and experimental series. Along with Serling, they explored with distinction the genre *fantastique* before *Night Gallery* finally fell victim to the neglect and incomprehension of an indifferent network. In rediscovering that old canvas in the warehouse, we have seen the work in a new light and discovered a merit that cannot be dismissed, and is worthy of further appreciation. There is ample evidence that posterity has judged *Night Gallery* far too harshly.

# ROD SERLING'S NIGHT GALLERY

*Rod Serling. Courtesy of Jim Rondeau.*

# 1
# Rod Serling

The name of Rod Serling is accorded a unique status in the history of television. From his earliest work, he established himself as a first-rate storyteller and a purveyor of challenging drama for the infant medium of television. With his best work, he challenged us to examine social concerns and to take a stand in an age of marginal morality. All his landmark dramas—*Patterns, The Rack, Requiem for a Heavyweight, A Town Has Turned to Dust,* and *The Rank and File*—exhibit his deep concern for the human condition. With these, Serling took his place among the other representatives of the "golden age of television"—Robert Alan Aurthur, Paddy Chayefsky, Ernest Kinoy, Reginald Rose, and Gore Vidal—as an entertaining goad to the public conscience.

In the space of eight years, Serling won the Emmy Award six times for best teleplay writing, a record unmatched by any other writer to date. He was the first playwright recognized by the George Foster Peabody Awards. In the aftermath of his phenomenal series *The Twilight Zone,* he has become one of the most recognized writers on the planet. Serling's most enduring legacy, however, stretches beyond the special qualities of the numberless fine teleplays he left behind, our fascination over his gifts, or his fame. On a far greater scale, he acted as gadfly to the television industry, fighting against the threats of censorship, mediocrity, and the medium's gradual drift into a fat and lazy complacency. Serling well understood the medium's power and potential, and his struggles to keep television relevant and provocative have repercussions to this day. Those he inspired with his imaginative gifts have carried this spirit of dissent and enlightenment forward within the industry, and as such Serling's influence is as broad as the mass media, as far-reaching as the most distant satellite transmission.

Rodman Edward Serling was born in Syracuse, New York, on Christmas Day, 1924, the son of a wholesale butcher. He spent an idyllic childhood growing up in Binghamton, New York, upon which he would later tenderly reflect in a handful of his most pastoral dramas. A confident, popular student, he was president of his high school class and editor of the student newspaper. After his graduation in 1942, he enlisted in the United States Army as a paratrooper.

Serling's first fighting during World War II was as an amateur boxer, winning sixteen military bouts. A severe battering and a broken nose in his seventeenth persuaded him to hang up his gloves. The scrappy flyweight next witnessed conflict on a far larger and deadlier scale when he transferred to the Pacific theater of operations. A severe shrapnel wound received in the Philippines campaign ended his three years overseas, but the incident sparked in him a desperate urge to self-expression. Following the nightmare of his war experience, he began to write as a means of therapy.

After the war, Serling enrolled at Antioch College in Yellow Springs, Ohio, under the GI Bill, majoring in English literature and drama. There he met and married Carolyn Louise Kramer, with whom he would have two daughters, Jody and Nan. As manager of the college's radio workshop, he began to write radio dramas, and in 1949 he won second prize in a *Dr. Christian* script-writing contest sponsored by CBS. His prize included $500 and a trip to New York City with all expenses paid for him and his wife. This success fired his ambition to be a scriptwriter.

After his graduation, Serling and his wife moved to Cincinnati. He worked first as a scriptwriter for radio station WLW in Cincinnati, then moved to television station WKRC in the same city, where he earned $60 a week as a continuity writer and produced scripts for locally shown dramas. He made sporadic headway in his freelance career, occasionally selling original radio scripts.

Serling's breakthrough came in 1951. He sold a television drama to the *Lux Video Theater* series, the first of ten he would sell that year. In his first successful season as a freelancer, he earned $5,000, and doubled that in the following year. He left his scripting job at WKRC in the spring of 1953. A year later, after again doubling his previous season's earnings, Serling moved with his family to Westport, Connecticut, to be near the television centers in New York City.

A one-hour drama by Rod Serling titled *Patterns,* about a power struggle in the executive suites of a major corporation, was telecast by the *Kraft Theater* over NBC-TV on January 12, 1955. It described the ambivalence of the newest young executive, Fred Staples, toward the corporation president, who has brought Staples on board as a wedge in his bid to pressure one of the aging vice presidents to resign. Powerful, intelligent, and uncompromising, *Patterns* drew Serling immediate and overwhelming acclaim.

*Patterns* was greeted by *New York Times* critic Jack Gould as "one of the high points in the TV medium's evolution. For sheer power of narrative, forcefulness of characterization and brilliant climax, Mr. Serling's work is a creative triumph that can stand on its own." It was telecast again on February 9, by popular demand, the first live drama in the history of American television to receive a second production. Serling was suddenly one of the best-known writers in the business, and *Patterns* won him his first of six Emmys.

With his name now firmly established, his scripts were selling as fast as he could write them. After signing a first-purchase-rights contract with CBS, twenty Serling dramas were telecast in 1955—most notably *The Rack,* about an American soldier court-martialed for collaborating with the enemy during the Korean War. In five days, from November 23 to November 28, three of his one-hour dramas were before the camera, while Serling himself was in Hollywood to write a screenplay for Metro-Goldwyn-Mayer. Before the year was out, he had also adapted *Patterns* and *The Strike* for the big screen. The critics, perhaps inevitably, noticed a decline in quality in many of Serling's video plays.

"From *Patterns* on, I suffered what every writer's suffered from a single big success," he later said. "So much of what I put on after that was dictated by economic considerations, too. I had to live. Unlike a legitimate-theater man, I don't have eighteen months to three years for another success. I've got three weeks." [1]

On October 11, 1956, for the newly inaugurated *Playhouse 90* series, Serling scored a fresh triumph with a drama titled *Requiem for a Heavyweight.* The heartbreaking story of a broken-down club fighter's decline, it reestablished Serling's reputation as a topflight video dramatist, and was purchased for the movies and the legitimate stage. It brought him both another Emmy and the first Peabody Award ever bestowed on a writer.

Other dramas in subsequent years included *The Comedian* in 1957 (another Emmy winner), *A Town Has Turned to Dust* in 1958, followed by *The Velvet Alley* and *The Rank and File* in 1959. Serling signed a new one-year contract with CBS-TV in mid-1958, but later in the year decided to write less for television because of the censorship encountered by some of his scripts. Both *A Town Has Turned to Dust,* dramatizing an Emmett Till-type lynching, and *The Rank and File,* dealing with corruption in labor unions, went through extensive revisions at the request of the advertising sponsors before they were accepted.

Serling deeply resented this "strange ritual of track-covering," and the system that made the sponsors so ridiculously powerful: "Drama and television must walk tiptoe and in agony lest it offend some cereal-buyer from a given state below the Mason-Dixon. So instead of a negro, we give battle against that prejudice visited upon American Indians or Alaskan eskimos or Armenian peasants under the Czar. Now, yes, all prejudice is alike down at its very ugly roots, and all prejudice is indeed a universal evil, but you don't conquer intolerance by disguising it, by clothing it in different trappings, by slapping at it with a wispy parable." [2]

Weary of the struggle with the censors, Serling switched from controversial dramas to fantasy in the autumn of 1959, when *The Twilight Zone,* his series exploring the realms of the imagination, premiered on CBS-TV. "I simply got tired of battling," Serling said. "You always have to compromise your script lest somebody—a sponsor, a pressure group, a network censor—gets upset. The result is that you begin to settle for second-best. You skirt the issues. You just can't do social significance on television. The medium will never have an Ibsen." [3]

Yet *The Twilight Zone* allowed him to lay into these pressing issues from a fresh perspective. Serling chose to write fantasy as a way of circumventing the objections to controversial themes made by sponsors and timid television executives. He could freely attack a variety of social ills without fear of censorship in the more abstract, less particular context of the far-fetched. If the dramatic trappings were beyond belief, then the subjects of his concern—mob rule, bigotry, prejudice, totalitarianism, injustice, and the travails of the dispossessed in society—could be dealt with in an indirect fashion, as allegory. In his era, a writer either adjusted to the prevailing restrictive climate or, like many of Serling's colleagues, moved on to prose, features, or theater. Serling, who believed fervently in the potential of the medium, chose to stay and fight in television. *The Twilight Zone* was his weapon of choice.

The series ran for a very successful five years. Serling walked away from the experience with two more Emmys and a proud sense of achievement, but what followed *The Twilight Zone* was not continued acclaim but stagnation. His one attempt to pursue another series, *The Loner*—a thoughtful, adult western starring Lloyd Bridges—was canceled after a half season, another victim of network meddling. The anthologies were long dead by the late 1960s, the occasional motion picture script wouldn't keep him in gravy, and Serling had nowhere to peddle his scripts.

Resigned to the uncontroversial nature of the medium, Serling sought another outlet for his restless imagination. "There was a time when I wanted to reform television," he told an interviewer in 1970. "Now I accept it for what it is. So long as I don't write beneath myself or pander my work, I'm not doing anyone a disservice."[4] Still committed to high standards of drama, Serling developed a new project—*Night Gallery*—which he considered an adjunct to his previous work in *The Twilight Zone*.

He was about to begin the last, turbulent phase of his career.

# 2
# The Season To Be Wary

The original premise for *Night Gallery* surfaced as early as 1964, when Rod Serling discovered that *The Twilight Zone* would not be returning for CBS's 1964–65 season. His agent, Ted Ashley, suggested that he try selling the canceled show to one of the other networks.

Tom Moore, president of ABC, expressed an interest in the series, but an impediment existed: CBS had the rights to the name *Twilight Zone*. Moore suggested a new, somewhat lurid title for the show, *Witches, Warlocks, and Werewolves,* a name borrowed from a 1963 Bantam paperback anthology edited by Serling. In response to Moore's B-movie approach, Serling submitted a proposal for a series more in line with his thinking, *Rod Serling's Wax Museum.*

Set in a shadowy museum of the outré, the show would allow Serling to again act as host, introducing each week's tale by unshrouding a wax exhibit representing its dramatis personae. Moore, however, could not be swayed from his "Triple W" concept. The writer responded with a prickly quote in *Variety:* "ABC seems to prefer weekly ghouls, and we have what appears to be a considerable difference of opinion. I don't mind my show being supernatural, but I don't want to be hooked into a graveyard every week."[1] Thus ended ABC's interest and, praise be, Moore's premise. Serling's premise merely lay dormant for the next few years.

In 1967, Little, Brown and Company published a collection of three Serling novellas, "The Escape Route," "Color Scheme," and "Eyes," under the title *The Season To Be Wary.* Although sales were disappointing, Serling's imagination was fired by the book's dramatic possibilities, wanting specifically to adapt "The Escape Route," "Eyes," and another story, "The Cemetery," into a full-length anthology film. He conceived of the triptych as an exercise in gothic horror and the supernatural, dosed with *Zone*-styled irony and linked by a device similar to his earlier wax museum premise: each story would be introduced by Serling and illustrated by three bizarre paintings at a somber after-hours art exhibit. He titled it *Night Gallery.*

Never as secure with prose as he was with drama, Serling, by adapting his tales for television, could concentrate on his forte: character and dialogue. He campaigned for his property, sending an outline of the three stories to all the major studios. It aroused interest at Universal.

Serling's pitch to studio executive Arthur Joel Katz, dated April 30, 1968, was persuasive, suggesting that the production "would gain considerable strength and sellability if one actor would play all three major roles, a real chewer, like Steiger. We would also have going for us a very definite spinoff possibility for a really first-rate horror series that would encompass the occult, fantasy and science fiction."[2]

Veteran television producer William Sackheim, having recently left Screen Gems to work at Universal as a staff producer, discovered the outlines of the three stories Serling submitted. "At the time we were doing world premieres for NBC, and I thought [the stories] would make a wonderful two-hour show," Sackheim recalls, "so I contacted Serling and he had scripts on them already. They were too long and needed some editing, but I loved them."

Serling and Sackheim went to work paring down the three scripts. "Serling was a remarkable, lovely man, wonderful to work with," Sackheim noted. "In terms of editing or changing, he had no difficulty with somebody, in effect, cocking up his work. Less ego than anybody I'd ever worked with, considering the amount of fame and credentials that he'd acquired."[3]

Serling was eager for *Night Gallery* to succeed. A compulsive writer, his professional habits required a steady outlet for his talents, and his interest in stories of the fantastic required a series project with the scope of *The Twilight Zone,* where his imagination could once again run wild. *Night Gallery,* if picked up by the network as a series, would serve that need admirably.

The studio, however—despite Serling's cachet and Sackheim's conviction—showed little enthusiasm for the project. "They didn't fall over me when I approached them," recalled Sackheim. Responding to the three-tales-in-one format, "they said, 'Oh, come on, that old-hat nonsense?' They didn't think the idea would work. I had to push like crazy. They were looking for something much more classically spooky or frightening. But *Night Gallery* was never meant to be scary in that sense. There was a good deal of provocative material there. The Nazi story ["The Escape Route"] was really more of a study of a man's guilt than anything else."[4]

Serling was frustrated with the lack of enthusiasm on the executive front at Universal. From that quarter came suggestions for a number of ridiculous script changes: glamorizing the squalid settings of "The Escape Route" and, in "Eyes," nixing a bookie's reminiscences of Bobby Thompson's home run and the Louis-Schmeling fight because the references were outdated. Serling vented his ire in a correspondence with Sackheim in December of 1968:

Dear Bill,

I left town shortly after my monumental meeting with Norman Glenn and some chap named Sid, who seemed to pack considerable prerogative and talked like a retarded Dead End Kid. He explained to me—in most affable manner—how audiences are young nowadays and if you do a picture that plays in, say, the 1950s—the whole thing is irrelevant. Hence, the Argentine piece should be in 1968, with Latin American rock and roll set against a background of the main ballroom at the Buenos Aires Hilton. I frankly don't know how this was settled, [although] this was a point I refused to retreat on. I did say that we could probably beautify the surroundings, including the nightclub, so long as the hotel remained seedy and out-of-the-way—as it must be. Norm made some suggestions about updating Resnick's recollections of sporting events and the terminology therein. I had no objections to this, and this seemed to satisfy him. But frankly, Bill, I walked away with an impression that I'm in trouble once they start shooting. Sid made mention of the fact that NBC had actually rejected the Nazi piece as it currently was—so I don't know where the hell we stand. When you get back from Stockton, I wish you'd investigate and find out what, if anything, of mine you'll be producing.

And a scintillating Hanukkah to you, old friend.

Cordially,
Rod Serling

P.S. Your casting ideas are really exceptional. The idea of Eli Wallach and Anne Jackson [for "The Escape Route"] is really walloping. Telly Savalas and Lee Grant would be my second choice. Karl Malden and Pat Barry or Lola Albright would be my third. Davis, Crawford, or Helen Hayes knock me out for the blind woman. Klugman would be my pick for Resnick, though what happened to Buddy Hackett? Maurice Evans—lovely for Portifoy, but John Mills also. And I'd certainly go for Roddy McDowall or Peter Lawford for Jeremy. But you know what, Bill? With my luck, Minasha Skulnick will be playing Jeremy—Molly Picon will be the blind lady—and Nelson Eddy's nephew will play the curator of the museum. The Red Army Chorus will do the flamenco . . . But don't get me wrong, Skolsky—I love Hollywood![5]

Sackheim doggedly persisted, lobbying the project's merits to Sidney Sheinberg, head of the television division at Universal. Finally, with NBC's blessing, *Night Gallery* was green-lighted for production.

Sackheim decided to shoot Serling's three scripts simultaneously using three separate directors, an unusual procedure utilized to meet the film's production dates. For "The Cemetery" and "The Escape Route," veterans Boris Sagal and Barry Shear were signed respectively. The choice for the director of the "Eyes" segment was more of a gamble.

A few months previous to this, Sheinberg had asked Sackheim to view a student film made by a young aspiring director. The young man, eager to prove himself, had bypassed Universal security, secretly snagged a vacant office for himself, and set up shop writing and observing. His name was Steven Spielberg, the film was called *Amblin'*, and Sackheim had been deeply impressed by both the young man's talent and the film's sophisticated execution.

"When it came to getting a director for the third segment, I called Sheinberg and asked for Spielberg, which pleased Sid because he had the same feeling I had about him."[6] *Night Gallery* would be the hungry young director's chance to prove himself. Up to that time, he had been passed over by other producers wary of an untried twenty-two-year-old. "I would have done anything," Spielberg said in a published interview. "I would have shot the Universal directory if I had to, just to get on a sound stage. When they gave me *Night Gallery,* my entire budget for the nine days of shooting was under $500,000, and even that was considered a very big risk to take on a new director."[7]

Spielberg's restrictions, he discovered, were not merely budgetary after his first meeting with the author:

I met Rod Serling once, and he was the most positive guy in that entire production company. He came into the office completely suntanned. He was a great, energetic, slaphappy guy who gave me a fantastic pep talk about how he predicted that the entire movie industry was about to change because of young people like myself getting the breaks. He was terribly enthusiastic and said: "Have fun with my show. I know you're going to do a great job." He shook my hand and left the office. Then Bill Sackheim, the producer, leaned over and whispered in my ear: "However, don't change any of his dialogue," which I didn't.

I know Bill respected Serling so much that he pretty much briefed [the other] directors [about script changes]. He told me that Serling was very particular about his work being visually interpreted properly, but not changed in any literary sense. I was cautioned not to change a preposition.[8]

The casting on his segment brought the young director further stress. Barely out of his teens, Steven Spielberg's first professional directing job would entail working with film legend Joan Crawford, who had been signed for the lead in "Eyes."

The other segments received equally distinguished casting. For "The Cemetery," Sackheim signed Roddy McDowall and Ossie Davis, and New York stage actor Richard Kiley—who had starred in *Patterns,* Serling's first television triumph—was enlisted for "The Escape Route." Nelson Eddy's nephew was, to Serling's great relief, never approached.

Aiding Sackheim with production chores was John Badham, who would go on to direct six segments of the *Night Gallery* series, and later such films as *Saturday Night Fever* and *WarGames.* Drafted from the studio's vast army of staff artisans and technicians were cinematographers Richard Batcheller and William Margulies, old hands at producing the dark, baroque visual quality this genre required, and art director Howard E. Johnson, who would design the sets and scout both back lot and practical locations.

"Eyes" went into production first, followed by "The Cemetery" and "The Escape Route" early in 1969. Throughout production, no one at the studio except Sackheim thought *Night Gallery* was series material, despite the promise of Serling's concept. NBC was withholding judgment on its potential as well until the ratings were confirmed after the first broadcast. The pilot would have to garner considerable audience share to persuade the reluctant network brass, who perceived the anthology series as a dying dramatic form.

As popular as programs such as *Playhouse 90, Studio One,* and *Alfred Hitchcock Presents* were in television's early heyday, the networks felt that anthologies no longer drew audiences expecting returning characters with whom they could establish sympathies week after week. Whether or not this was an accurate analysis, Serling rankled at the rigors of such a bland format. Wary of artistic stagnation, he felt the concept of *Night Gallery,* with its wide-open field of setting and period choices, was a far more promising arena for his talents.

Serling's hopes for the show were high, then, when *Night Gallery* aired as an NBC World Premiere Movie on Saturday evening, November 8, 1969.

# 3
# The Pilot

NIGHT GALLERY
Air date: November 8, 1969
98 minutes

PRODUCED BY  William Sackheim
ASSOCIATE PRODUCER  John Badham
ART DIRECTOR  Howard E. Johnson
FILM EDITOR  Edward M. Abroms
UNIT MANAGER  Ben Bishop
COLOR COORDINATOR  Robert Brower
PAINTINGS  Jaroslav Gebr
TITLES & OPTICAL EFFECTS  Universal Title
SET DECORATIONS  John McCarthy, Joseph Stone, and Perry Murdock
ASSISTANT DIRECTORS  Ralph Ferrin and Marty Hornstein
SOUND  James T. Porter and Elbert W. Franklin
EDITORIAL SUPERVISION  Richard Belding
MUSIC SUPERVISION  Stanley Wilson
COSTUMES  Barton Miller
MAKEUP  Bud Westmore
HAIRSTYLIST  Larry Germain

1
THE CEMETERY
★ ★ ★ ★

Written by Rod Serling
Directed by Boris Sagal
Music: Billy Goldenberg
Director of Photography: Richard Batcheller

**Cast**
Jeremy Evans: Roddy McDowall

*Roddy McDowall in "The Cemetery."*
*Courtesy of Jerry Ohlinger.*

Portifoy: Ossie Davis
Hendricks: George Macready
Carson: Barry Atwater
Gibbons: Tom Basham
Doctor: Richard Hale

G*ood evening, and welcome to a private showing of three paintings, displayed here for the first time. Each is a collector's item in its own way—not because of any special artistic quality, but because each captures on a canvas, suspends in time and space, a frozen moment of a nightmare.*

*Our initial offering: a small gothic item in blacks and grays. A piece of the past known as the family crypt. This one we call simply "The Cemetery." Offered to you now, six feet of earth and all that it contains. Ladies and gentlemen, this is the* Night Gallery.

**/ Summary /** William Hendricks, a wealthy recluse, is suffering a lingering death from a stroke. His dedicated butler, Osmond Portifoy, manages his decaying southern mansion and aids him with his hobby, painting, the only joy left to the old man. Disrupting their quiet existence is Jeremy Evans, Hendricks's grasping nephew and sole heir, who has returned to claim his inheritance.

Jeremy is disturbed by the morbid subject matter of his uncle's paintings, one of which—a view of the family graveyard—hangs on the stairwell wall. Even more disturbing, however, is his discovery that Hendricks intends to cut him out of his will. Jeremy decides to force nature's hand: he locks the old man in his wheelchair by an open window and abandons him. The chill is fatal.

Jeremy's undisguised greed raises suspicions, but no proof can be found to connect him to his uncle's death. He inherits the Hendricks fortune and, more out of spite than charity, allows the disapproving Portifoy to stay on. His good cheer sours, however, when he notices a change in the stairwell painting: there is now a freshly dug grave in the family plot. The next night, the painting exhibits another variant—a casket has appeared in the open grave. Shaken, Jeremy burns the painting, only to find it later in its usual spot on the wall—but now the casket is open and the body of Hendricks is plainly visible. Visible, at least, to Jeremy, for Portifoy claims he can see no change in the painting. After an enraged Jeremy strikes out at him, Portifoy quits, intimating that in death it appears Hendricks can take care of himself.

That night, Jeremy is awakened by sounds outside the house. Believing Portifoy has returned, Jeremy goes downstairs to let him in, only to find another horrifying change in the stairwell painting: Hendricks is now opening the cemetery gate and walking toward the house. Reduced to gibbering panic by this apparition, Jeremy frantically calls Portifoy at the hotel in town, but cannot get through. Every time he checks the painting, the avenging phantom is closer to the house. Hearing a pounding at the door, Jeremy, crazed with fear, stumbles on the stairs and falls to his death. The door opens and a shadowy figure enters—Portifoy.

With Jeremy now out of the way in the family plot, Portifoy pays off the artist he commissioned to do the series of paintings, which he himself carefully changed in sequence. The Hendricks fortune now falls to the ambitious butler, the will having stipulated that he should inherit in the absence of an heir. Surveying his new estate with sanguine satisfaction, Portifoy's attention falls on the stairwell painting—and to his horror finds *two* graves in the family cemetery. Before the butler's eyes, now riveted to the canvas, the late Jeremy Evans is revealed climbing out of his grave and shambling toward the house . . . up the front steps . . . pounding at the door. Cowering in a huddled ball, a deranged Portifoy raves in terror as the door shudders open . . .

/ **Commentary** / Serling's first draft of *Night Gallery*, completed in April 1967, included a story quite different from "The Cemetery." A period piece set in the American Southwest in the late 1800s, the original tale told of a hanging judge who performed his job with a gruesome artistry: he painted portraits of those he had condemned as they dangled from the end of a rope. Needless to say, Serling righteously delivered the corrupt jurist into the phantom hands of his wrongly condemned victims—a grisly but apt justice.

Although the precursor is an interesting idea, the replacement tale gets to the point with sharper, quicker strokes, and offers a more intriguing crew of characters. Of the three stories that make up the pilot, "The Cemetery" is the most indebted in spirit to the pulps—*Weird Tales, Amazing Stories*—that Serling devoured as a youth. His one goal, it would appear, was simply to scare the hell out of his audience. As executed by director Boris Sagal, "The Cemetery" does just that.

This mordant study of greed and amorality was right up Sagal's alley. Running throughout his career as a television director is a series of bleak and sour impressions of man and the arbitrary hand of fate. His distinctive and personal voice can be heard in the *Twilight Zone* episode "The Silence," the miniseries *Rich Man, Poor Man*, the telefeatures *Hauser's Memory* and *The Greatest Gift*, and Robert Loggia's short-lived caper series, *T. H. E. Cat*.

"Boris was a highly underrated director," associate producer John Badham recalls. "He was extremely good with actors and quite, quite efficient in his shooting as well, so you got the best of both worlds: it was done on time and you got wonderful footage. I particularly remember that the camera moves in that segment are really quite lovely. There are scenes that go on for long, long sections without a cut, and they're staged quite cleverly by Boris."

Sagal's reliance on long, fluid shots was due in part to his tight scheduling. Both Sagal and star Roddy McDowall had other projects scheduled immediately after finishing "The Cemetery," and longer shots take fewer camera setups and less time. He needed equally dedicated actors who could memorize Serling's extensive dialogue and block long scenes accordingly. Luckily, he was blessed with a trio of exceptionally fine performers in McDowall, Ossie Davis, and George Macready. "Those guys, they're almost director-proof," Badham says. "You could put them with a terrible director and you can't fuck them up, so when you put them with a *good* director, it's totally painless."[1]

McDowall especially is a delight as Jeremy. Blithely sinister, he delivers Serling's circuitous prose with a singsong, graceful, evil charm, highlighting words for effect, savoring the sinuous beauty of the language. With equal parts gentility and sarcasm, he paints a stinging portrait of treacherous southern manners.

Davis matches him as Portifoy, outwardly the faithful family retainer, but concealing beneath his impassive mien far darker intentions than his employer suspects. His descent into madness in the final scene is horrifying in its cumulative impact, and has maintained its power to raise gooseflesh over the years.

Although Davis and McDowall had worked together before—on stage in *No Time for Sergeants*—neither had ever worked with George Macready before. As the stroke-ridden William Hendricks, the veteran actor was required to play his role in silence, limited only to his expressive eyes and the occasional grunt. "Silent, yes, but *forceful*," McDowall recalls. "Working with George Macready was a great privilege. He was a wonderful actor who, by then, had produced this immense canon of work." Known for his roles as silky villains in films such as *Paths of Glory*, Macready's quiet cameo is a picture of frustrated, straitjacketed rage.

"We had a great, great time," McDowall says. "The director was terrific, it was a wonderful script, and Ossie Davis, besides being an extremely nice man, is a most astute actor. I enjoyed the experience very much and I thought the outcome was extremely good."[2]

According to all involved, production went quickly and smoothly, although John Badham recalls several moments of discomfort during the postproduction phase:

Roddy had a scene where he runs out of the house, looks at the grave, and says, *"What in God's name is happening?"* Well, when he did this outside, they had big wind machines running; it was quite loud so we couldn't get a decent sound track. When the shoot was over, Roddy was released from the picture but no one ever got his looping dialogue from that scene. So when we need this stuff, we don't have Roddy McDowall and he's off somewhere else doing a picture. I guess we could've gotten him back, but it would've been a major pain in the butt.

So I listened to the existing sound track and I thought, "Well, my voice is kind of in the same area, and I'm from Alabama originally, *I* can do this." So I went in and did it, replaced his voice with my own, just for this one little section outside. To test it, I said to Bill Sackheim, "We found Roddy's loops. I hope we've got them in sync, let me show them to you." He was in the projection room doing something else, and he said, "Oh, yeah, yeah, okay, fine, let me hear it." So we played it and he said, "Yeah, that's fine, okay. Next. . . ." So I fig-ured if Bill bought it, what the hell, I'll just sic it on the rest of the world.

Now, truth be told, when I hear this on television—and they play it *all* the time—I hear what is *clearly* my voice coming out of Roddy. I think, "This wouldn't fool anybody," but ob-viously I've gotten by with it. People's eyes are sensational, but their ears are not quite as sharp. They're watching more than they're listening.[3]

Keeping this in mind, it is surprising that no one involved with the production noticed the segment's rather glaring plot hole. While Jeremy is frantically calling for help before his fatal tumble down the stairs, Portifoy is outside the house, prowling the grounds and generally trying to make Jeremy believe the dead Mr. Hendricks is coming to pay a visit. If Portifoy is outside, who is supposed to be inside switching paintings? More disturbingly, one of the switches supposedly occurs while Jeremy is on the telephone in the front hall, in full view of the painting. Neat trick. Perhaps old Mr. Hendricks had a hand in it after all.

## 2
## EYES
★ ★ ★ ★

Written by Rod Serling
Directed by Steven Spielberg
Music: Billy Goldenberg
Director of Photography: Richard Batcheller

**Cast**
Claudia Menlo: Joan Crawford
Dr. Heatherton: Barry Sullivan
Sidney Resnick: Tom Bosley
Packer: Byron Morrow
Louis: Garry Goodrow
Nurse: Shannon Farnon
Artist: Bruce Kirby

*Joan Crawford in "Eyes." Courtesy of Foto Fantasies.*

*O*bjet d'art number two: a portrait. Its subject, Miss Claudia Menlo, a blind queen who reigns in a carpeted penthouse on Fifth Avenue. An imperious, predatory dowager who will soon find a darkness blacker than blindness. This is her story.

/ **Summary** / Wealthy Claudia Menlo, fifty-four and blind from birth, exists in splendid, cocooned solitude far above the streets of New York City. She knows no Braille because she hires people to read to her; she accepts no friendships because she sees value only in things that she can buy; and beneath Menlo's frigid, regal countenance is her perpetual fury and outrage at her own misfortune.

Menlo holds court with her physician, Dr. Frank Heatherton, to discuss a radical new surgical procedure in which the central optic nerve is removed from a living donor and transplanted into a blind subject. He assures her the operation is in the experimental stages only. It has been performed successfully twice on animals, but in each case the blind animal gained sight for only eleven hours before the transplant was rejected by the rest of the optical complex. The donor, of course, was rendered permanently sightless. Undeterred, Menlo informs him that she has found a donor, Sidney Resnick, a broken-down bookie one day away from an assassination because of a bad debt. For a miserable nine thousand dollars, the bookie has agreed to a life of darkness as opposed to no life at all. Heatherton, repelled by the idea, refuses to cooperate—until Menlo threatens him with ruinous, long-buried blackmail. Filled with self-loathing, he agrees to perform the operation.

The evening following the procedure, a trembling and expectant Menlo orders her art collection assembled around her penthouse suite for the unveiling, then dismisses her servants. She has planned her precious eleven hours carefully—first her collected wealth, then a sight-seeing tour of the city. Alone now, she impatiently removes her bandages. Trembling with anticipation, she is dazzled by the brilliance of the first thing she sees, her crystal chandelier—when she is abruptly thrust into darkness again. Shrieking in rage, Menlo rampages blindly through her suite, throwing statuary, telephone, end tables, destroying everything in her path. She calls for help, but there is no one to hear her. Exhausted from her fit, she collapses in tears—unaware that a power failure has left New York City in a blackout.

Awakening the next morning, Menlo opens her eyes to see the sun cresting the skyline through the cracked pane of her penthouse window. She is awed by its beauty—and shocked when it starts to fade. Her eleven hours are up and her eyes are failing. In desperate anguish, she reaches toward this dazzling new bauble. Pressing against the cracked pane, her forward momentum carries her through the window and over the sill. Claudia Menlo, in her last few precious moments of sight, plummets wide-eyed and screaming to the pavement ten stories below.

/ **Commentary** / Serling's muse led him at times to investigate some of the darker, less appetizing aspects of our species. In the cellar of the human psyche, "Eyes" illuminates a particularly black corner. "[Of the three] the horror story actually was the Joan Crawford one," Sackheim points out, "in the sense that she was bitch enough to say, 'I'll take a man's eyes.' It was that kind of horror."[4]

Joan Crawford's performance as Claudia Menlo is intense and frightening, a portrait of a woman whose arrogance and vicious self-interest are so complete they dwarf her humanity. With open disdain and bitterly simmering rage, the legendary actress perfectly limns the "tiny, fragile little monster" that Serling describes in the script. The part, it would seem, was made to order for her.

From the beginning, Crawford, a grande dame of the silver screen, was a daunting challenge to her nervous young director. "That's when the sweat began," Spielberg said. "I never got over the idea of directing *Joan Crawford!* It was a quantum leap."[5] Concerned about Serling's dialogue ("People just don't talk that way," she told Spielberg[6]), Crawford suggested over the phone that the two meet and discuss the problem. When Spielberg arrived at her Hollywood apartment, Crawford greeted him at the door blindfolded—an exercise to immerse herself in the character. "She was going to be playing a blind person, and she went lurching around the apartment," recalls Spielberg. "I was terrified."[7] When the blindfold came off, she met her callow young director for the first time—a shock the actress gamely tried to cover. Over dinner that night, she discovered that "Eyes" would be her director's maiden effort and she cannily bolstered his confidence: "Now, I know what television schedules are, and I know the pressure that will be on you to finish the show on time. You'll want your first work as a director to be something you can be proud of, and I'll break my ass to help you. Don't let any executive bug you because the picture's not on schedule. If you have any problems with the Black Tower, let me take care of it. I'll be your guardian angel. Okay?"[8]

Despite her surface largesse, Crawford was, at first, far from pleased at having been assigned a fledgling director forty years her junior. She called Serling a number of times to voice her anxieties about working with the young tyro. "I remember the event well," notes Crawford's adopted daughter Christina. "Mother was absolutely furious with the studio for assigning her a twenty-two-year-old kid who had never done anything before."[9]

The shooting, as one would expect, was not trouble-free. Ralph Sariego, a former executive at Universal, was working on the set as a second assistant director: "When Spielberg arrived the first day, he was a pimply faced kid in an eight-dollar Sears and Roebuck jacket. He came walking upstage and there was silence from the crew." The chill Spielberg felt was not merely a first response. At Crawford's insistence, the temperature on the set was fifty-five degrees—her comfort zone. She arrived promptly, wrapped in a fur coat and followed by her makeup man, hairdresser, and wardrobe woman. As was her custom, she initiated a very close working relationship with her director. "Crawford got ahold of him," recalls Sariego. "She arrived with dollyloads of Pepsi-Cola and cases of vodka. She'd bring them into her trailer, ply him with Pepsi and vodka, and guide him on the show."[10]

"Directing Joan Crawford was like pitching to Hank Aaron your first time in the game," Spielberg said.

[She] treated me like I had been directing fifty years. She was very good to me, very firm, but very kind. I called her Miss Crawford, and she insisted on calling me Mr. Spielberg. I asked her to call me Steven, but she wouldn't. She knew I was just a scared kid, and she was setting an example—of courtesy and, yes, of respect—for the rest of the cast and crew to follow. Once she knew I had done my homework—I had my storyboards right there with me every minute—she treated me as if I was The Director. Which, of course, I was, but at that time she knew a helluva lot more about directing than I did.[11]

In light of his youth and her experience, the two decided early on not to discuss filming problems before the crew, keeping tensions to a minimum.

The first day of shooting went badly. The principal actors, Barry Sullivan and particularly Crawford, had trouble with Serling's lines. Commented Spielberg: "I remember that Rod's dialogue was very, very hard, not only for an actor to memorize, but was very hard to meter when you were speaking. Joan Crawford had a hell of a time finding moments to breathe, where to pause and what to emphasize. I pretty much had to sit down with her and underline key words to get the story points across, so the plot would not be lost. It was not an easy show to do."[12]

*Steven Spielberg and Joan Crawford on the set of "Eyes." Courtesy of Jerry Ohlinger.*

Spielberg was concerned that if they fell too far behind their seven-day schedule, the Black Tower executives, whose interests tended more toward budget than quality, would place the blame on him, and "Eyes" would be his first and *last* assignment in Hollywood. At Barry Sullivan's suggestion, Spielberg placed cue cards all over the set within Crawford's sightline but out of camera range. Although it helped the pace, further delays were caused by Spielberg's insistence on choreographing complicated camera moves and eschewing the standard TV formula shot menu—establishing shot, medium shot, close-up, close-up—that would guarantee visual boredom. Spielberg avoided zooms, relying on tracking shots instead. He used wide angle lenses, crane shots, dramatic lighting—and received some whispered chuckles from crew members for his beginner's zeal.

Unfortunately for Spielberg, complications continued to accumulate at an alarming rate. Co-star Tom Bosley recalls that, whether for reasons of anxiety or excessive vodka consumption, Crawford further stalled production by spending hours holed up in her trailer. "It was one of the strangest shooting experiences I've ever been involved in," marvels Bosley. "I don't know how else to put it, except to say that I think she was dead drunk most of the time. She was in her dressing room and she never came out, and poor Steven was reduced to shooting a lot of close-ups of Barry Sullivan without a master [shot of the scene]." The pace slackened to such a degree that Sackheim lent Bosley out one morning to replace an incapacitated actor in the *Marcus Welby* pilot filming nearby. When Bosley returned a few hours later, Crawford had yet to make an appearance. "We spent a lot of time on the set watching Steven trying to shoot around Miss Crawford," Bosley notes ruefully. "I just felt terribly sorry for him."[13]

At some point, Crawford came to terms with Serling's dialogue—and, presumably, her vodka binging—and emerged from her trailer. Spielberg began to relax as well. He noticed that Crawford held back in medium shots, but when he called for a close-up, Crawford's performance gained extra voltage. As such, he planned moving shots that made it seem as if she were drawing the camera toward her. As Spielberg's confidence grew, so, apparently, did Crawford's respect for him. While conversing on the set with reporter Shirley Eder of the *Detroit Free Press,* Crawford pointed him out and said, "Go interview that *kid* because he's going to be the biggest director of all time."[14] Prophetic words.

Crawford relished the challenges offered by the role. "There are tricks to playing a blind person. That is, you have to trick yourself into believing you are blind. Whenever Barry [Sullivan] spoke, I made myself find him with my ears first. Barry tricked me a couple of times. He would tiptoe or walk on the carpet so I couldn't tell where he was, *then* talk to me. Naturally, my body would have to turn to find him."

Playing blind offered further challenges for Crawford during the blackout sequence, working in the center of a bright shaft of light with the set draped in black: "I got very dizzy because there is no reference point in a limbo set, and you are staring into the lights, which blind you absolutely. It was really exciting doing the role. But one thing that bothered me was that I couldn't see the camera. And, honey, if after twenty-two years of acting I can't find the camera, I *really* had to like that role to do it!"[15]

The evening before the last shooting day, Crawford cornered Spielberg and requested his help in rehearsing for Menlo's final scene where she awakens to the sunlight. "It scares the hell out of me. That may be the most important shot in the picture, and I simply don't know how to do it." Spielberg assured her they would arrange time tomorrow and told her to get a good night's sleep, but on the following day, the Universal production office read Spielberg the riot act over his slow progress. Already a day behind, the director, in his rush to finish his shot menu, neglected to set aside the time to coach Crawford. By the end of the day, she was distraught. With only a single scene left to film and struggling to finish—another television company was waiting to use the stage—Spielberg was approached by the assistant director, who suggested he meet with Crawford in her dressing room.

"Later," said Spielberg. "I've got to finish with this set by six."

"I think you'd better talk with Joan," the assistant replied, "or else you may not be *able* to finish with the show."

Spielberg found Crawford in tears, claiming that he had let her down and her final scene would be a washout. "You know how important that moment is," she raged. "If the audience doesn't buy it, then the whole picture fails. And I don't know how to do it! I'll be embarrassing to watch. You won't like me, I won't like me. It will just be a godawful mess!"[16]

Spielberg apologized, dismissed the rest of the company for the night, and spent an hour going over the final scene with her. He promised to ignore the railings of the production office and allow her however many takes she needed to get it down to both their satisfaction. By the next day, however, the actress's fears were still not assuaged. "Steven was having a problem with Crawford because she didn't know how to emotionally motivate herself to go out of the window," recalls film editor Edward Abroms. "Bill [Sackheim] was summoned down to the set on the last day of shooting to coach her. And whatever he said to her was the right thing to say."[17] Their attentions paid off, and the final scene is indeed a most moving moment, showing a glimpse of humanity in the detestable Miss Menlo just moments before her death. Crawford came through with a powerhouse performance, and Spielberg captured it with a magnified intensity.

Much to the dismay of the production office, Spielberg had gone two days over schedule. "I was so traumatized," Spielberg moaned. "The pressure of that show was too much for me. I decided to take some time off, and Sid [Sheinberg] had the guts to give me a leave of absence."[18] It was an entire year before Spielberg got another assignment.

Despite everyone's trepidation, the results were spectacular. "From the very first day's dailies, you could see [Spielberg] was a very unique and special talent," recalled Sackheim. "He did a lot of very daring things in it, and spent a lot of time in the editing room trying to get it together. That was the only problem we had with it, because there were some very difficult things that he'd shot and wanted to play with. We had a time element, so we just finally had to say, 'Steven, we've got to get this thing together.' But there wasn't any question about his talent. It blew right off the screen at you."[19]

Says Badham: "I can remember standing in an editing room and having Bill Sackheim say to Spielberg, 'Steven, let's take this shot through the chandelier out. It's really very self-conscious and kind of says, "Look, Ma, I'm directing!"' And Steven said,

'Oh, but really, it's so special.' And it was. I know how hard it is when you've thought of something nifty and have to give it up. So Bill finally said, 'Okay, fine. Leave it in.'"[20]

"Steven got this brilliant idea," laughs Abroms. "He really had to finesse the studio to let him do it." To illustrate the impact of Menlo's fall to the pavement, Spielberg thought up a startling trick shot. "He told them, 'I want to go up to the top of the [Universal] Tower with a missile tracking camera. I want to build a platform out over the edge, I want to drop some heavy plate glass, and I want to shoot it as it's falling.'" Reluctantly, the studio agreed. "The camera zooms down to the concrete, and you see the glass hit and it bursts into millions of fragments. It was so good, I told the clip library to pull that shot as a piece of stock footage."[21] Abroms, remembering the shot, later used it in the *Columbo* episode "Death Lends a Hand," for which he won an Emmy.

Looking back, Spielberg has said: "I did an awful job. I was so frightened that even now the whole period is a bit of a blank. I was walking on eggs. I had no idea I was telling a story. To me, it was just a menu of shots, a memorandum of things to do each day. It was only when I saw the show years later that I discovered the story I was telling. It turned out to be the most visually blatant movie I've ever made."[22]

Spielberg's critical assessment is entirely too harsh. Despite his lack of fondness for the script, he instinctively responded to Serling's theme with a strikingly imaginative, richly visual approach, and justifiably so. The script describes a woman whose hunger for sight is so all-consuming that she would bargain for another's eyes. Spielberg found a cinematic analogue to Miss Menlo's heedless desires in a heightened visual vocabulary and syntax. The camera's eye seeks and savors every image, every color and texture. The segment is filled with inventive transitions and unusual compositions. Spielberg's images succeed in translating that hunger for sight to the audience.

"I want to see something," Menlo demands in one of the segment's most chilling sequences. "Trees, concrete, buildings, grass, airplanes, COLOR!" With each word of her litany, the camera pulls in ever closer to Crawford's frenzied, staring face, punctuated by tiny jump cuts that accelerate the forward momentum, an unsettling effect. Spielberg also worked out a stylish method of lensing the difficult blackout sequence by photographing Crawford, lit in profile only, against a black backdrop, giving an impression of isolation in total darkness. For sheer queasiness value, the optical effects he and Abroms designed for the operation sequence are hard to beat, in which wheeling shots of both Crawford's and Bosley's eyes dissolve into one another.

In the final regard, "Eyes" turned out to be more than a modest first effort for its young, untried director. What might in another's hands have become a series of static talking-heads shots and standard TV narrative, Spielberg transformed into a visual feast.

3
## THE ESCAPE ROUTE
★ ★ ★ ★

Written by Rod Serling
Directed by Barry Shear
Music: Billy Goldenberg
Director of Photography: William Margulies

**Cast**
Joseph Strobe: Richard Kiley
Bleum: Sam Jaffe
Gretchen: Norma Crane
1st Agent: George Murdock

*Richard Kiley in "The Escape Route."*
*Courtesy of Foto Fantasies.*

*A*nd now, the final painting. The last of our exhibit has to do with one Joseph Strobe, a Nazi war criminal hiding in South America—a monster who wanted to be a fisherman. This is his story.

**/ Summary /** Buenos Aires, 1965. Joseph Strobe, alias Gruppenführer Helmut Arndt, former deputy commander of Auschwitz, lives in constant fear of capture by the Israeli agents who have tracked him to Argentina. The Adolf Eichmann kidnapping has destroyed for him any sense of security in his anonymity, and he fears he is next in line.

While wandering the streets one sultry, sleepless night, he notices a black sedan following him. Panicked, he escapes into a local museum. Losing himself in the late evening crowd, Strobe encounters an old man, Bleum, who stands transfixed by a gruesome representation of a concentration camp crucifixion. Strobe is numb to the horror and moves past it with barely a look; but for Bleum the painting holds a nightmarish fascination. A survivor of Auschwitz, Bleum engages Strobe in conversation, and soon a glimmer of recognition appears in the old man's eyes.

Avoiding him, Strobe strolls to the opposite wall where hangs a pastoral scene of a fisherman on a mountain lake. He finds himself strangely drawn to the picture, particularly to the man in the rowboat. Looking closer, Strobe begins to imagine that this indistinct figure is himself, and the more he stares the more familiar grow the lines of the fisherman. Closing time interrupts his reverie, but he returns the next morning to examine the painting further. He is now struck by a new phenomenon: the more he stares, the more he senses an incredible feeling of detachment from reality, of being transferred into the picture—feeling the warm sun, the breeze, the gentle lulling movement of the boat, the sense of sweet serenity—far from his desperate and hunted existence. He returns the next night to the museum until, in progressive stages, it becomes easier to literally will himself into the picture. This respite is short-lived, however. At closing time, he is once again wrenched back from the strange haven he has discovered.

Frustrated, Strobe gets drunk at a noisy nightclub, violently threatens the customers, and, singing "Deutschland über Alles" at the top of his lungs, staggers out into an alley. Approaching him out of the shadows, Bleum openly confronts his old tormentor. Strobe, too drunk to think clearly, drops all pretense, and once again he is Gruppenführer Helmut Arndt, the sadistic, swaggering butcher of Auschwitz. He circles Bleum warily and, upon learning that Bleum has confirmed his whereabouts to the Israelis, strangles him.

Strobe flees to the bus terminal where he is intercepted by the agents contacted by Bleum. Panicked, Strobe eludes them and heads back to the museum, now closed. He breaks in and, with the Nazi-hunters in pursuit, finds his way in the dark to the picture of the fisherman. He falls to his knees and begs God to get him into the picture. He stops, squinting at the painting in the pitch blackness. An agonized scream escapes his lips . . . echoing into silence, the room now suddenly empty.

The curator and a security guard are led to the spot by the scream, but find no one. As they leave, they hear a strange and persistent noise, faint and far-off, like a human cry. They turn back to where the picture of the fisherman had been. The security guard informs the curator that the picture was on loan and had been taken away that evening. In its place hangs the picture of the concentration camp inmate, nailed spread-eagle on the cross, his face a mask of screaming, perpetual agony. The face of Joseph Strobe.

/ **Commentary** / While "Eyes" presents a small, personal evil, "The Escape Route" offers evil on a much larger scale. The crux of the tale is guilt, and poses the question, how does one atone for a crime so monstrous that no punishment devised by man could serve justice? Serling found a way, right out of *The Twilight Zone*.

Serling had tackled the Holocaust before, notably in a third-season episode of *The Twilight Zone*, "Deaths-Head Revisited," a study of unrepentant evil. For "The Escape Route," the protagonist, Strobe, is not the arrogant SS captain of the earlier episode, returning to Dachau in nostalgic triumph. He is a hunted war criminal in exile, trying to outrun not only Israeli agents but also the feeble stirrings of his own conscience. This approach allowed a much wider range of possibilities for the lead actor.

Sackheim, instead of hiring an obvious heavy, secured for the role Richard Kiley, a subtle and intelligent actor with the ability to project a kind of nobility in the commonplace. Kiley's presence gave the role colors and shadings that a standard heavy could not muster, showing that alongside the man's brutality existed simultaneously other, more humane qualities.

"I liked the role, it had a lot of different levels," Kiley recalls. "I liked the fact that the guy was a monster on one level, and on another level he was responding to the beauty, the peace and placidity of the painting he saw and wanted to return to that. I think it's an interesting piece, and to this day people remember that in preference to a lot of other things I've done."[23]

To play against Kiley, Sackheim hired veteran character actor Sam Jaffe for the role of Bleum and Norma Crane, who had often shared the stage with Kiley in New York, as the German prostitute Gretchen, Strobe's personal gadfly and tenement neighbor. Having secured a distinguished cast, Sackheim needed to hire a director with the credentials to bring out their best. He found him at a gin game:

"I used to attend a regular Monday evening card game at a friend's house, where Barry Shear was a regular player. I'd kibitz this game, and I got to know Barry. One night he took me aside and said, 'Nobody will give me a shot at anything worthwhile. They don't think I can do it, and I *know* I can if I ever get a crack at it.'" Sackheim decided to go on faith and hired Shear to shoot "The Escape Route." "I had been concerned about Barry because he'd done a lot of your stock series things and was never known as a particularly artistic director. We had Kiley and Norma Crane, who were both out of the theater, and I thought, Jesus, can Barry handle this?"

To Sackheim's relief, he handled everything with great skill. "His imagination was terrific, his staging was wonderful, his use of the back lot was extraordinary, and his rapport with the actors, to my great surprise, was infinitely better than I ever thought it would be. So to me, *he* was the surprise, not Spielberg."[24] Shear's assured direction on "The Escape Route"—his handling of pace, rhythm, angle, and cutting —brings echoes of another vigorous film stylist, Don Siegel.

Kiley recalls a smooth production, relishing the memory of an inventive detail he added to the portrayal. While shooting in a noisy nightclub, he had to project to the audience that Strobe was mentally back in Germany circa 1943. "We had fun shooting the angry drunk scene," Kiley says. "I remember sitting there at the bar with a glass of beer, and it suddenly occurred to me that with my little finger and thumb I could sort of approximate a classical German stein." Kiley used this detail while Strobe drunkenly sings the Reichs-hymn to anchor his character's mind-set "back in an old bierhaus in Munich."[25]

The result is a powerful portrait of guilt and retribution. As Strobe, Kiley is cruel, tormented, and complex. Even with our knowledge of the atrocities Strobe has practiced, Kiley can still elicit our sympathy. We all can appreciate Strobe's driving impulse: to start over, to clean the slate, to wipe the sins of the past away. In Serling's universe, however, there is no salvation for the criminals of the Holocaust. The punishment visited upon Strobe is chilling, horrible, and ultimately correct. The final scene, with Strobe's face screaming soundlessly from the canvas, crucified for eternity, is an image that remains persistently in the consciousness of the viewer.

The artist for this painting, as well as for the other canvases in the pilot, was Jaroslav Gebr, best known for his re-creation of the Sistine Chapel ceiling in the 1968 film *The Shoes of the Fisherman*. Gebr's expert imitation of Michelangelo's style, particularly *The Last Judgment* panels, was an amazing representation of the great Renaissance master. Recalls John Badham: "When you needed something that really looked like fine art, you hired Jaroslav Gebr. This man had a brother who died in the concentration camps, so working on *Night Gallery* had great personal meaning to him."[26] The dedication is evident in his work. His rendering of the crucifixion is, indeed, a tragic and harrowing depiction of human suffering. As proof of its importance to Gebr, this painting still hangs in his office at Universal.

With a tight production schedule, Gebr could not afford to paint extra canvases for the changing paintings in "The Cemetery" and "The Escape Route," so he devised a system of appliqués for the addition and removal of details on canvas. This method allowed Gebr to produce the illusion of multiple paintings. A separate canvas appliqué of Kiley's face overlaying that of the concentration camp victim transported Strobe to his doom; and smaller scraps of canvas in the likenesses of George Macready and Roddy McDowall helped turn Gebr's original painting of the Hendricks' family plot into a grisly message from the grave. Gebr's work vibrates with stark emotion and gives the film an appropriately diseased atmosphere, an apt complement to Serling's elegant prose.

The inventive cutting scheme for this segment, as well as the others, was executed by film editor Edward Abroms, who racked his brain to come up with an effective visual to get Kiley into the painting. "Every night I'd go home and figure, 'How am I going to do this?'" recalls Abroms. "No one had any input. It still goes on today, the attitude of, 'We'll fix it in post-production.'"

Abroms had footage of the painting—a rendering of Kiley sitting in the rowboat—and footage of Kiley himself in a boat on the Universal back lot lake, but how to merge them? "We used a trick called solarization, a process that physically changes the molecular structure of the colors. It gives the effect of a kaleidoscope, where the colors are very, very intense and you can change them to anything you want, giving it a 'ripple' effect." Abroms cut from a three-quarter face shot of Kiley looking offstage at the painting to the painting itself as it phases into its solarization mode. "We cut to Kiley in close-up, and he has this really elated expression on his face, then back to the painting, and we dissolve through the painting to Kiley live in the boat, enjoying himself. Now Richard Kiley looks out, directly at camera." Abroms here cut to a very brief shot of the opposite museum wall that he salvaged from the cutting room floor. Using it to represent Kiley's point of view from inside the painting, Abroms was able to cement the audience's impression that Strobe had projected himself into the picture.

For the death of Bleum, Abroms executed another visually striking sequence. As the camera follows Kiley circling around Sam Jaffe, Abroms inserted flash cuts of

Kiley, clean-shaven and unscarred, in an SS uniform to highlight Strobe's remorseless mind-set. For the chase sequence that followed, Abroms used freeze-frame effects, brief "snapshots" capturing Strobe's panicked flight. "He'd be running and hit a puddle of water, and then we'd freeze that for a second or so, and then pick him up and he's running someplace else and you freeze it again. That was a very rewarding episode to put together."[27]

Mention must also be made of Billy Goldenberg's imaginative music, so different for each segment, yet so perfectly integrated as a whole. For "The Cemetery," he paints a sardonic musical portrait of Jeremy, utilizing a buzzing, insistent electric keyboard figure, reflecting both his derisive nature and his fear. In "Eyes," Goldenberg creates a sense of impending tragedy with massive orchestral chords accented with tubular bells. For "The Escape Route," he reserves his best, enlisting three elements: driving Latin rhythms and instrumentation, depicting both locale and danger; scraps of a sentimental German song à la Kurt Weill, representing Strobe's yearning for escape; and a haunting choral Kaddish on the death of Bleum, laying bare Strobe's crimes and lamenting the murders of the six million in the Holocaust. Goldenberg's music brilliantly underscores the emotions and themes in the film and more than any other element of production binds the disparate stories into a satisfying whole.

Serling's faith in the quality of his stories was not misplaced. When *Night Gallery* aired, the movie drew tremendous ratings—a 23.3 Nielsen score (an estimated percentage of all television households tuned to a specific program), scoring eighth place overall for the week and besting the other networks' competition by a large margin. Additionally, the script won its author yet another accolade, an Edgar Award, given out by the Mystery Writers of America. Serling was elated. The pilot had scored not only artistically but also commercially and Serling could now negotiate a series deal with NBC and Universal from a position of strength.

Until the premiere, said Sackheim, "nobody really wanted to do the movie except me, and nobody thought it would be a series. I kept saying, 'There's a series here,' and, 'Can we have a deal with Rod?' And they always said, 'Don't worry about it.' Then all of a sudden they come in and say, 'Listen, we think this would make a hell of a series, and we want to make a deal.'"[28] Serling secured a lucrative contract with Universal, but the irony of their turnaround was not lost on him. Later, he would liken getting their approval to "pulling impacted wisdom teeth with cardboard pliers."[29]

The series was set to begin production—but without Sackheim, at his request. "When I went over to Universal, I had it spelled out very clearly that I would do movies of the week, features and pilots, but I was not going to do series television," Sackheim explained. "I had done fourteen years of series at Screen Gems, and I said, 'That's enough.'"[30] Production duties fell to Jack Laird, a Universal staff producer and writer, whose impressive résumé included work on *Ben Casey, The Chrysler Theater,* and, in the coming years, *Kojak.*

NBC, still concerned about the viability of an anthology series, bought only six hour-long episodes. *Night Gallery* would alternate on Wednesday nights from 10:00 to 11:00 with three other series, *The Psychiatrist, McCloud,* and *San Francisco International Airport,* as part of NBC's *Four in One* programming "wheel" (the model for the later *NBC Sunday Mystery Movie,* home of *Columbo*).

For Serling, it was a return to a series format he knew thoroughly and could navigate with complete confidence. Said family friend Mark Olshaker: "My impression was that he hoped at first that it would be another *Twilight Zone,* and kind of bring him back to his peak."[31] Sackheim concurred: "I think what he liked most about doing the whole series was, he loved being in front of a camera."[32]

Serling's contract called for him to introduce each episode and contribute a number of scripts. Apart from this, he neither sought nor received an executive role in the production of the series. Evidently, his experiences as executive producer of *The Twilight Zone* had proved too much of a life-consuming burden. "I'd never want to go back into the vineyards in a week-after-week series form, because that's back-breaking time," remarked Serling in a 1969 interview. "There's not enough money in the world to take a guy over forty and make him go through that grind again—that is, at least not me. Some guys thrive on this kind of work, but not me."[33]

Serling would later have cause to regret his decision. Although he owned the concept of *Night Gallery,* he had not requested a contractual right to creative control. He assumed a tacit accord that, because of his ownership and his name, would naturally admit him into the producer's circle. There are, however, few binding gentlemen's agreements in the film industry, a fact Serling would be forced to face repeatedly in his future dealings with the studio, the network, and most frustrating of all, *Night Gallery* producer Jack Laird.

# 4
# Jack Laird

Universal press releases of the day faithfully parroted Jack Laird's insistence that he was born of theatrical parents touring with a repertory company in far-flung Bombay. His true beginnings were more prosaic—he was born and raised in a small California town. But his hoaxing of the media machine is illustrative of this intensely private man's character in pulling a gag that could ultimately be appreciated by only one person—himself.

Jack Laird was born Jack Schultheis in Monrovia, California, on May 8, 1923. His father was a successful businessman, but his mother, confirming at least part of his story, was an actress. "Our household was very caught up in the theater," recalls his sister, Rosemary Campbell. "This, I'm sure, is what sparked his interest originally." His career in show business began at the age of four when a film company came to Monrovia, casting Laird and his family in a silent film. From then on, he was hooked. His stage involvement deepened with the encouragement of his mother, Thelma Laird Schultheis, a theater director who taught night school dramatics, and from whom Laird took classes.

*Jack Laird. Courtesy of Jerry Ohlinger.*

Laird's adolescence was marked by extraordinary activity. "He was just into *everything* in his high school years, out in all directions," Campbell says. "He usually had the lead in school plays, was art editor of the school newspaper and the annual, and he had his own band."[1] A jazz fanatic, Laird formed his dance band—"Aris Laird and His ARIStocrats of Swing"—while a student at Pasadena Junior College. Though no musician himself, his group was made up of players who later joined the likes of Stan Kenton, Benny Goodman, and Les Brown. The group broke up when Laird enlisted in the Army Air Force during World War II.

Assigned as a pilot in the Ninth Air Force, he served with the First Allied Airborne while stationed in Manchester, England. Upon his discharge, Laird resumed civilian life in New York, where he enrolled at the Dramatic Workshop and studied playwriting under John Gassner.

While working in summer stock in 1947, Laird met his first wife, actress Cicely Ann Browne. They were married the next year, but in the ensuing years were often separated by their careers. Ultimately, Laird's marriage fell apart, and Cicely retained custody of their son, Sean.

Returning to Hollywood for a screen test and ultimately a series of movie and radio roles, Laird began writing and selling scripts on the side for the burgeoning medium of television. Finding his talent better suited to the pen than to the footlights, Laird began to focus almost entirely on his dramatist leanings, writing for such shows as *The Lone Ranger, The Millionaire, M Squad, The Ann Sothern Show,* and *Have Gun, Will Travel.* In 1958, an actor buddy introduced Laird to Peggy Johnson, a young stage actress fresh in town. They were married in Palm Springs a week later. "Jack was a brilliant man," Johnson recalls. "Very generous, and a great sense of humor. But he wanted very artistic people around him—he had to learn from you; if not, he lost interest. He loved food and art and writing, in that order. Aside from John Huston, I don't know of any more colorful character in Hollywood."[2]

Laird next distinguished himself writing and story editing for the prestigious medical show *Ben Casey.* As Laird's career strengthened, he became associate producer under producers Matthew Rapf and James Moser, developing a stable of up-and-coming writers and helping the careers of his friends and associates. "I looked upon Jack as my patron," says actor Leslie Nielsen. "I did a tremendous variety of work for Jack Laird. He cast me in different roles, sometimes as sort of a last resort." One time, Laird was casting for the part of an Onassis-styled tycoon. Having exhausted a list of more appropriately ethnic actors such as Raf Vallone and Lee J. Cobb, Laird hired Nielsen— a light-haired Scandinavian—for the part. "I can't conceive of anybody with the audacity to hire me to play a Greek peasant multibillionaire shipping magnate," laughs Nielsen. "And he knew if I didn't play this role with great credibility, with a believable Greek dialect, that the whole show would go in the toilet, *finito.* But he knew I could do it, he took a risk [on my talent]. That's why I look upon him as my patron."[3]

Laird generously took chances with new directors as well, starting the careers of countless artists still working today—among them Sydney Pollack. Pollack's work in features has included such films as *They Shoot Horses, Don't They?, Jeremiah Johnson, Three Days of the Condor, The Way We Were, Tootsie,* and *Out of Africa.* He was an acting teacher at the time of his shift into directing, and cut his teeth behind the camera in the early 1960s on episodes of *Ben Casey.* "Jack was one of the very gifted group of writers that worked on that series," Pollack says.

He used to always kid me a lot. I was just starting out, and I had grown up in the Midwest, so my upbringing was fairly provincial. I had a tough time getting used to women swearing and all that stuff. I was kinda square. I got a lot of it burned out of me by the time I got to New York and studied acting, but I still must've carried a bit of it around, because Jack used to love to hit that area. He was always ribbing me about the mature women that I was going to have to work with—how they actually had hair between their legs, and how they'd gobble me up. He loved to be really vulgar and shock me, but we were very fond of one another, and I think I wouldn't be exaggerating if I said that we had a kind of a mutual respect for one another. I know that he liked the work that I did on the show, and I certainly liked his work.[4]

"Jack was really a cut above," says writer David Rayfiel. "There was something very colorful about his writing—a little bit like Clifford Odets in the old days of writing for the theater, a wildness and a richness of dialogue. Because everyone knew he was talented, he was allowed little liberties in those days. He was flamboyant and a little rebellious."[5]

"He did a piece for *Ben Casey* called 'I Remember a Lemon Tree,'" Pollack says, "with George C. Scott and Colleen Dewhurst, and it made a vivid impression on me. When I saw it, I thought, 'God, that's really wonderful, original, imaginative writing.' It seemed so fresh. Jack had a very original voice, and he was awfully good at surprising you in terms of the kind of 'arias' he would write for the characters. I was struck by the aria that he gave George Scott, about the lemon tree—what a neat idea for a soliloquy that was."[6]

Laird received an Emmy nomination in 1962 for scripting "I Remember a Lemon Tree." "We went to that awards show," Johnson says, "and he was very upset that he didn't get it. He had a strong ego, and kept saying, 'But I deserved it!' And I said, 'But dear, you *will* win someday. You're young and you'll have other times.' Well, that other time didn't come. Being very perceptive, I'm sure he thought that, too."[7] The writing award that year went instead to Reginald Rose for his work on *The Defenders*. In an ironic twist, one of the other losing nominees that year was a previous winner —Rod Serling, nominated for his work on the third season of *The Twilight Zone*.

In 1963, Laird was offered a full producer's post on *Ben Casey* but declined when he was given a chance to write and produce independent projects for Universal Studios. One of them was his introduction to dark fantasy—a stylish pilot, written by Barré Lyndon (*The Lodger, Hangover Square*) and directed by Harvey Hart, at first titled *Black Cloak*. A precursor in spirit to *The Wild, Wild West*, its main character (played by Leslie Nielsen) is a wealthy playboy living in nineteenth-century San Francisco who investigates a series of weird murders scientifically, à la Sherlock Holmes. "It did not get bought as a series," recalls Nielsen, "but it turned out to be such a well written and directed piece that the studio saved all the material that had been shot, recut it to about seventy minutes—enough to sneak it into the motion picture category—and released it as a feature."[8] Retitled *Dark Intruder*, the feature ran on a double bill with William Castle's *I Saw What You Did* and garnered impressive reviews. The making of *Dark Intruder* escalated Laird's interest in the science fiction and fantasy genre, and led the way to his helming of *Night Gallery* five years later.

Although Laird was happy in his marriage and well compensated at Universal, the passage of time and opportunity effected an abrupt change in his outlook. "All of a sudden, after he got a contract at Universal, Jack got bogged down," Johnson recalls.

To tell you the truth, I think he gave up his dream. He wanted to go off to Mexico and write the great American novel—something that would last forever. That's every writer's dream, and Jack felt he'd sold out—hacking it out at Universal every day. That's when he started withdrawing. He kept saying to me, "Younger writers are catching up to me." I would try to convince him otherwise, but he would see younger writers moving up at the studio and he would become a little more anxious. That's my opinion of why he got more introverted and unhappy.

Laird's brooding ultimately took a heavy toll on his relationship with his wife, his family, and practically everyone he worked with. "He didn't take care of himself," says Johnson. "He sat at the typewriter and typed and smoked. Most writers brood and carry on, but Jack was lonely in a way that nothing could fill. And there were parts of him I *never* knew, even having been married to him. He was not a revealing person to anyone—very introspective, very complicated."

After five years, Johnson divorced Laird, taking their daughter, Sharon, with her. "He was an extremely talented, wonderful person," Johnson says, "but he just became more and more into himself, and I think that's a tough life. If I had been older, I could have coped with it."[9]

In the 1970s, Laird came into his own as a series producer, and his efforts shepherding both *Night Gallery* and *Kojak* helped create some of the best television of the decade. Recalls *Kojak* coproducer James McAdams: "Working around Jack, I became very aware of what makes a creative producer. He wasn't a bean counter—Jack had talent and skill and artistry. He leaned on the best instincts of all screenwriters about what works dramatically. He was a gifted storyteller and dealt with film as we loved and respected it years ago."[10]

As he demonstrated on *Ben Casey* and, later, *Kojak,* Laird's gift for storytelling and passion for the cinematic past would likewise prove itself repeatedly during his stint producing *Night Gallery.*

# 5
# Four in One

I hope this *Four in One* format is successful. It would be nice to do six shows a year. There's a possibility my segment could become an individual series. If so, I think I'd commit suicide.[1]

—Rod Serling, December 1970

Six years after *The Twilight Zone*'s cancellation, Serling finally had his regular forum back. NBC gave the go-ahead to produce the first six episodes of *Rod Serling's Night Gallery*, as it was to be called, and Serling signed on as host and contributor on the series. Universal next approached Jack Laird, who contracted to produce the series on March 24, 1970. His deal with the studio demanded that he bring in the prescribed number of episodes on schedule and for its $190,000-per-show budget.

As the 1970s began, Universal Studios was one of the busiest full-service studios producing television programming, with separate departments for casting, production design, music, photography, editing, costuming, and makeup, as well as countless sound stages, scoring stages, editing suites, offices, and a large, well-utilized back lot for exterior filming. When it was busy, producers at the studio were afforded little choice in the selection of artisans and staff, and assignments were often based on who was available in a given department. Universal had a reputation as a factory, cranking out episodic TV shows with assembly-line efficiency and maintaining firm control over all aspects of production.

For the first season, the writing was predominantly Serling's at the network's request. Serling wrote six original scripts and five short-story adaptations. For the rest, Hal Dresner adapted one of his own short stories, and *Twilight Zone* alumnus Douglas Heyes submitted an original and an adaptation. Others fell under consideration. In a letter to Serling dated April 24, 1970, Laird requested Serling's response to a number of short stories available to them at a reasonable cost: "A Gentleman from Prague" by Stephen Grendon (a pseudonym for August Derleth); "House—With Ghost" by Derleth; "The Dead Man" by Fritz Leiber; and "No Such Thing as a Vampire" by Richard Matheson. Of these, only "The Dead Man" would be produced for the first season. "House—With Ghost" would make the second season cut. The others would never see a camera.

A couple of Serling originals were also discarded or delayed. He wrote his first submission, an outline titled "Does the Name Grimsby Do Anything to You?" immediately after NBC bought the series in December 1969. The story delved into the delicate psyche of an *Apollo* astronaut, driven by his Type-A zeal to be the first man to walk on the lunar surface. But he unravels when he finds—and destroys—evidence during his moon walk that he was, in fact, second to an obscure and discredited scientist from a century earlier. Presented during the early planning stages for the show, the idea was jettisoned. Serling later developed the outline as a short story and included it in the 1971 Bantam paperback *Night Gallery.*

With scripts in hand, Jack Laird assembled his production team. Assigned under him was production executive Paul Freeman, late of *The Virginian:* "Jack didn't want to take 'executive producer' credit," recalls Freeman, "so that left me with the 'production executive' sobriquet. I functioned as the producer; I was involved in all facets of the show and dealt with any problems on the set. Jack really functioned as an executive producer; he rarely visited the set."[2]

As well as being Laird's arm of execution on the set, Freeman also had a hand in postproduction editing along with a rotating group of cutters: James Leicester, Jean-Jacques Berthelot, and James D. Ballas. "Jean Berthelot was a superb editor and a great lover of film," avers actor John Astin, director of one of the first-season segments. "It was my first time directing at Universal, and Jean knew it meant a lot to me—that I had a vision for my segment. I was really a tyro in terms of technique, but Jean was very understanding and tremendously helpful."[3]

On the set, Laird's team included veteran unit manager Burt Astor, the organizational whiz who budgeted the series and assembled the physical materials needed for shooting. Astor's production crew partner, art director Joseph Alves, Jr., was less seasoned. Although his listed credits were sparse, Alves had a distinguished pedigree, having learned his craft under legendary designer Hein Heckroth (whose work included Michael Powell's gorgeous color fantasy *The Red Shoes*).

*Night Gallery*'s format offered Alves a unique challenge: designing and building sets on a restrictive television budget that covered multiple time periods, from medieval to the indeterminate future, from an African village to a lavishly appointed chateau. Alves eagerly accepted Laird's offer. "Jack was an off-the-wall kind of guy," says Alves. "I was really very fond of him and he allowed me to do a lot of creative stuff. He supported me tremendously."[4]

Laird conceived of *Night Gallery* as a stylistically varied potpourri of bizarre tales, demanding a different look for each segment. "Jack wasn't looking for symmetry, and he was not looking for running themes in the show," notes series composer Gil Mellé. "The individual segments had to have their own distinct theme and their own distinct approach, just as though you were doing a minimovie. And he wanted them stylistically different, all of them, each with its own fresh colors."[5]

To maintain this fresh perspective from story to story, Laird originally contracted a different director for each segment. This created problems for Alves, however, who was kept hopping during the first season meeting with each director individually and discussing design ideas for the segment he was to direct: "Because of the time element, I pretty much had the autonomy of saying, 'Here's what we've got to shoot.' We had a couple of stages that were assigned to us with basic kinds of things—big stair units and gothic window units—that I could move around and revamp."

Because each story required different backgrounds, Alves had to practically build each segment from scratch, a fiscal nightmare that spurred some innovative juggling. To maximize the budget for the show, Burt Astor designed the production schedules so that the three or four scripts produced for each hour would allow him to stretch funds to the limit. "Burt and I would go through the scripts," explains Alves,

to see how the hell we can make, for instance, "The Sins of the Fathers," a half-hour segment that's going to cost us as much as an hour show. We would take the budget for the hour and put 85 percent of the money into "Sins of the Fathers" and build that huge set. Then do, say, two fifteen-minute shows with pickup sets that we could just walk into and not spend any money. Universal would allow us to structure the budget that way so that we could actually build an expensive set like "Sins" and not go over budget.[6]

Alves's work helped define the highly stylized, imaginative look of the series, and involved far more than just a draftsman's eye. "Production design isn't just building sets," he explained. "It's totally coordinating the visual look of the picture. That includes not only sets and the dressing of the sets, but also close work with the costume designer and the special effects people, as well as scouting locations."[7] Rod Serling, on one of his infrequent visits, admired the young man's accomplishments and gave Alves his due. "Rod would show up to film the introductions," Alves says,

and he paid me an incredible compliment one time: "I don't know how you do it, the sets, every week." And I said, "What do you mean? You're the *guy*, you're the *mind*." And he said, "Yeah, but you *visualize* it." You see, he was an incredible writer but he wasn't very visual. I worked with another famous writer, Paddy Chayefsky, on *Altered States*. They could both write incredible concepts, incredible words, but if you followed the screen directions in their scripts, it'd be the weirdest looking set. The geography never quite worked. So I got to a point where I never even paid attention to the descriptions, and he was always really delighted. That was a real compliment, because I think the guy was just brilliant.[8]

Besides Serling, Alves would make another important connection on *Night Gallery:* here he would first meet Steven Spielberg, with whom he would later work as production designer on the megahit feature films *Jaws* and *Close Encounters of the Third Kind*.

## THE GALLERY

Although Jaroslav Gebr had painted the canvases used in the pilot, for the series Laird contacted Tom Wright, a production illustrator at Universal who had worked previously with Laird as a design consultant. Laird reached him in Las Vegas on the set of the James Bond movie *Diamonds Are Forever,* described to him the *Night Gallery* concept, and asked Wright if he wanted to do the introductory paintings. Intrigued by the challenge, Wright immediately agreed. "I have a morbid sense of humor anyway," says Wright. "So I was perfect for the job."[9]

Wright, a graduate of the Chouinard Art Institute, had begun his career as a freelance advertising artist in Los Angeles. Then, as Wright says, "one thing just led to another. I got to know some people in the motion picture business, and I guess my first recognition as a painter and artist in my own right came as a result of some portraits I did of Hollywood celebrities, including some movie stars—Gregory Peck and Tony Curtis, among others."[10]

That led to work at various studios as an illustrator working on set and costume designs, continuity sketches, makeup design, even acting, "whatever I could do to make a living." After work on Hitchcock's *Topaz* and Robert Wise's *The Andromeda Strain* came the offer from Laird, beginning Wright's work on his gallery of nightmares. "Jack was a very creative man, great to work with," remarks Wright. "He gave me total freedom, total creativity on what I did once I read the story."[11] Laird would send Wright home with a handful of scripts or story outlines, and the artist, freeing his imagination, would begin sketching ideas.

Working simultaneously on several paintings, Wright's assignments arrived in a constant stream. "It was a crash program, like everything else in this business.[12] The hardest part of the work was coming up with the idea. I would do them in groups of about five, and for each story I would do ten or fifteen ideas." Wright presented the most promising ideas to Laird, pointing out his favorites. "He'd say, 'I love it. Do it.' He never once said, 'No, no,' or 'I don't like it.' He had full confidence in me."[13]

With Laird's blessing, Wright would determine his paint media, order sizes for the boards or canvases he needed, and return to the studio to begin work. For Wright's first effort—the Serling-penned "Lone Survivor"—he worked in oils on a large canvas, but he found that oils proved too time-consuming. He soon began favoring Masonite pressboard with acrylic paints "because they dry the fastest and they hold good color."[14] Wright often mixed his media freely: tempera, oils, acrylics, ink washes, watercolor, markers, and pencil; he occasionally worked on canvas or wood; and the size of the paintings ranged from as small as twelve-by-eighteen inches to as large as four-by-seven feet.

"Once I got the idea for the particular story," recalls Wright, "I tried to approach each one of them a little differently so they didn't all look like they were done by the same artist."[15] Wright's aim was not to reproduce exact scenes, but to capture the "character of the overall story—what it got across, the feeling, the mood." For inspiration, the artist heavily researched the occult.

Serling, a fan, commented enthusiastically on the wide variety of styles and techniques employed by the artist: "[Wright] is interesting in that he doesn't use any single artistic form. He paints in abstracts, impressionism, and almost still-life realism."[16] He occasionally toyed with textures and collage. For his portrait of a clown in "Make Me Laugh," Wright wrinkled shreds of tracing paper, glued them to the board, and painted on top of the clumped and peeling surface.

One of his biggest challenges came for the production of "Pickman's Model," H. P. Lovecraft's tale of a reclusive artist in turn-of-the-century Boston. The title picture and the eight other canvases Wright created for the segment had to reflect the work of an artist from a different era. "I had to suppress my own style," Wright said, "and use a completely different technique. And I had to put myself in the era of the nineteenth century to produce a historically authentic effect."[17]

For the series' brief vignettes, often based on classic scenes from horror films, Wright occasionally depicted the actors famed for their monstrous interpretations: "Phantom of What Opera?" was a portrait of silent film star Lon Chaney, in full makeup; for "With Apologies to Mr. Hyde," Spencer Tracy made an appearance on canvas; and for one of the many vampire blackouts, Bela Lugosi did as well. Occasionally, a subject more closely related to *Night Gallery* would appear: actress Joanna Pettet was Wright's model for "The Girl with the Hungry Eyes"; and after Wright had finished "Rare Objects," unbeknownst to him *another* artist altered the original so that the central face resembled glowering star Raymond Massey. Rod Serling found his way into Wright's painting for "Midnight Never Ends," and a grimacing Jack Laird into "Quoth the Raven." Wright's models included members of his own family: eldest daughter Shevaun was his model for "Brenda," and his youngest daughter, Chanell, for both "The Boy Who Predicted Earthquakes" and "Little Girl Lost." Wright even painted himself into the picture as a bearded undertaker in shades for "Die Now, Pay Later."

To help Serling with his introductions, Laird sent him Polaroids of Wright's work; the writer could then frame his efforts to coincide with the painted interpretation. "Rod was a neat guy, sort of down-to-earth," muses Wright. "When he came into town, we'd always have lunch and go over his notes on the paintings for his introductions. Later on, after he'd passed away and I was directing some of the second-string *Twilight Zones* [the television series from the mid-1980s], I felt rather proud to be doing those, having known the 'real guy' at one time."

For the first season, the gallery was constructed on Stage 12 at Universal Studios; for the seasons that followed, General Service Studios in Hollywood would be its location. Working together, Wright and art director Joseph Alves retained the endless limbo set used in the pilot while giving it a more stylized sense of the weird. The huge set was draped ceiling to floor in black; and, replacing the velvet-covered easels used in the telefeature, Wright's paintings were suspended from the ceiling and anchored to the floor by matte-black wires to give the impression that they were floating within

*Rod Serling in the gallery. Courtesy of Akron Beacon-Journal.*

a void. By the beginning of the second season, the gallery's indeterminate perspective was crowded with paintings.

"I got a lot of mail on the show," Wright says. "Everybody would always ask me where I got these weird ideas. Some thought I was this weird guy, and that I must sleep hanging from the ceiling. I mean, they *believed* that stuff."[18] Genuinely surprised at their popularity, Wright today casually dismisses his contribution to the series. Jack Laird knew better. In the producer's letters to Serling discussing the opening introductions, Laird imparted his respect for Wright's masterful, disturbing, and atmospheric canvases. Affirms makeup artist Leonard Engelman: "Tom did beautiful paintings. They became the *soul* of the show. From my standpoint in particular—having already done the character makeup—when we did the intros with Rod Serling and I saw the pictures for the first time, I thought, 'Oh my gosh, this tells the story!'"[19]

During the run of the series, Wright was deluged with offers of work and requests for reproductions of the gallery canvases. "The show was a very big hit and quite popular for a while," he says. "People wanted them in their houses, and I had people who owned bars in New York calling me, wanting me to do paintings for their walls."[20] The director of the Science Museum at Boston University asked to borrow the whole odd-lot to use in a seminar on witchcraft and the occult. At the time, however, Universal, who owned the paintings, was not interested in sale or loan of their property.

Although only ninety-five segments were produced, Wright painted more than a hundred canvases during the show's three seasons. At the time of *Night Gallery*'s cancellation, the studio was readying production on segments for which Wright had already finished paintings. The network's termination of the show halted any televised display of the remaining pieces. In the ensuing years, however, Wright's paintings for *Night Gallery* have taken on a life of their own. Despite their somewhat morbid atmosphere, some of them have been used as decor for producers' and actors' offices at the studio. "I've done three or four pictures with Sylvester Stallone," Wright says, "and the first time I met him was on a picture called *Paradise Alley*. He had a bungalow on the lot at Universal, and when I walked in, he had a whole wall lined with *Night Gallery* paintings. He was a big fan of the paintings, so when he came on the lot he had them bring some of them up to decorate his office."[21]

As for the rest, some have simply disappeared off the lot, but most of the canvases were sold by Universal in the early 1980s to private parties, some for as little as ten dollars apiece. The studio evidently misappraised their worth. At a Los Angeles auction held in September 1996, Wright's canvas for "The Flip-Side of Satan" was placed on the block. It sold for the princely sum of $1,800. March of 1997 brought the auction of "The Hand of Borgus Weems" at Butterfield and Butterfield's, with an estimated price of $2,000. It sold for $3,500.

Wright wisely laid claim to the pieces that had personal meaning for him and his family. His daughters own the canvases for which they modeled, and the artist still has two: "The Dear Departed" and "The Caterpillar."

Looking back, Wright considers his tenure on *Night Gallery* one of the most stimulating periods of his life. "It was fun, I really enjoyed it. The concept of 'work' never entered into it." Wright's current vocation—television producer and director—doesn't give him much time for the brush and palette anymore. "I still paint, of course," Wright says, "but more for my own pleasure."[22] By the evidence of his superb artistry on *Night Gallery*, if his directing career ever hits the skids, he will always have a profession to fall back on.

Joining the gallery paintings in the second and third seasons, sculptures of a decidedly disturbing nature were provided by Phil Vanderlei and Logan Elston for spatial contrasts from which to film the walking and talking introductions by Serling. Vanderlei came to the attention of the filmmakers while exhibiting his work at the Renaissance Fair in Agoura, California. "I was approached by one of the art directors at that event to use some of the pieces for the show," Vanderlei says. "They liked what they saw, so they told me to bring everything that I had." To make sure he had plenty, Vanderlei borrowed some pieces from friend and fellow sculptor Logan Elston and delivered the whole lot to the studio location.

As with artist Tom Wright, no restrictions were placed on Vanderlei's imagination by the filmmakers, and his collection of satyrs and dragons blended seamlessly into the oddball milieu. After being arranged strategically around the gallery set, some of the sculptures were rigged by the special effects crew. One of the dragons was fitted with a red light glowing in its mouth; another spewed wafting smoke.

At that time, Vanderlei's medium was sheet metal—specifically, discarded automobile hoods, hammered to form and shaped with an oxygen-acetylene torch. The sculptures took anywhere from one week to two months to finish, depending on their size. "I remember one that I took down there," Vanderlei says. "It was a big eagle with a man's chest and huge claws, and the wings were pinned back against the wall. That piece was nine feet tall and four and a half feet wide, and the detail was pretty articulated. It was quite a feat to achieve that with hammers, chisels, and a welding torch, and some of the bigger ones took quite a bit of time." Transporting some of these unwieldy monsters was a feat in itself. "I had a rack on top of my truck. I lived in Santa Barbara and I drove them down to Hollywood myself. People ran off the freeway when I went by!"

Vanderlei fixed the rental fee for his sculptures at 10 percent of their value, which roused some hard-nosed negotiation at Universal's end.

They were always trying to rent them for a fraction of what we considered their value, and I said, "No thanks," because I worked hard to make them. And one of them said, "Well, okay, fine, we won't be able to use you anymore"—because I wouldn't give them a discount of 80 percent on the prices! They tried to fill the need, but they couldn't, so they called me back anyway.

We would take them $25,000 or $35,000 worth of stuff! We got 10 percent—$2,500 or $3,500 in the early seventies for a four-day rental! That may not seem like a lot now, but it sure was then. That was a fabulous situation for someone like me. We were all just a bunch of hippies having a great time making things and happy to be selling them![23]

## THE MUSIC

Unlike most other producers, Jack Laird had a sophisticated musical ear and always strived to retain the services of composers outside the Hollywood mainstream for the projects he produced. For *Night Gallery*, he wanted a musical profile different from any other television show, and his first step in that direction was to hire Gil Mellé.

Mellé was one of the first experimenters with electronics, and his jazz albums exploited his avant-garde influences freely. Aside from a period as the protégé of legendary composer Edgard Varèse, Mellé was entirely self-taught. "Varèse taught me the poetics of music," Mellé says. "To me he was like Bartók or Stravinsky, a giant. It's one of the great privileges of my life to have known the man and to have been able to share his thoughts."

Laird brought Mellé to Universal in 1968 for an earlier telefeature, *Perilous Voyage*, a project that gave the composer the industry foothold he craved. "I owe my career to Jack Laird," Mellé affirms. "I did Jack's show and it made my career at Universal. I became their top guy for quite a number of years. I did a lot of features—*Columbo, My Sweet Charlie, That Certain Summer,* stuff that just won tons of awards—and all because Jack gave me my start. He stuck his neck out for me, and that's a lot to say for a guy. I could have done a crummy job and Jack would've taken the fall. But that didn't happen—the scores I did for Jack put me on the map."

Mellé's rise was swift—so swift that when Laird approached him in early 1970 for *Night Gallery*, the composer was deeply involved in scoring his first feature, Universal's blockbuster production of Michael Crichton's novel, *The Andromeda Strain*. At first, he declined Laird's offer. Along with his considerable responsibilities on *Andromeda*, Mellé felt it might strain his friendship with Billy Goldenberg, who had scored the *Night Gallery* pilot. The usual studio protocol demanded that the composer for the pilot be allowed the right of first refusal on the series. But Laird insisted on Mellé and Universal backed him on the choice.

Right after I had that meeting with Jack, I went over to see Bill. He was scoring on Stage 10 that day, and I told him, "I want you to know, Billy, I never solicited this job in any way, shape or form. I would never try to take a job away from you." And Billy understood that, we were always good friends over the years. But he was hot, though, and he told me, "The fur's gonna fly!" It put me in kind of a weird position. And besides, I was busy on *Andromeda.* [Director] Robert Wise would've hit the ceiling if he thought that I was spending time on *Night Gallery* or anything else. However, the studio wanted me to do it, so I stole time away from *Andromeda* in order to do the format for *Night Gallery.*

Using instruments he built himself, Mellé created the first purely electronic theme music for a television series. With its unearthly timbres, ominous sonorities, and relentlessly iterated nonmelody, it was a shuddery original, unlike anything that had come before. "The main title for *Night Gallery* was along the lines of what I was doing on *Andromeda Strain*," Mellé says. "It was not based on Western scales, or major and minor, or the normal things that people get involved with. It was based on the sonorities, like [Krzysztof] Penderecki's music—the 'sheet of sound' approach."

Mellé sketched the basic idea for the piece working on the piano. Once structured, he then performed and recorded the theme himself, instrument by instrument, track by overdubbed track, manipulating his battery of gadgets—the Elec-Tar, the Percussotron III, and the aptly named Doomsday Machine. Mellé's inventions were supplemented by a sixteen-track mixing console, containing a wide variety of colors and effects on which the composer could draw. Needless to say, it was a far cry from the approach used by most composers at that time.

The trouble began after Mellé turned the tape over to Universal. Almost immediately complaints surfaced from the music department over the recording; Mellé was called in to listen to a playback. One of the technicians kept insisting that there was something wrong with the tape. Recalls the composer:

I listened to it and said, "Sounds fine to me. What part are you talking about?" And he said, "Well, that very low line at the end"—and he sort of sang the part—"there's a lot of distortion on it." So I had to inform him that distortion was a *part* of electronic music. I mean, you alter wave forms, you're not looking for sinusoidal tapestries in the music. That'd be so *boring*. It's just that the things that he was hearing he'd never heard before. So finally I told him, "There's nothing wrong with that tape at all, period."

The theme was finally endorsed—but not without reservations. "It was very radical at the time, and I've got to tell you, it was not smooth sailing for me at that studio. They had no other composers who understood the electronic format. The people who were against it would say, 'That's not music! How can you compare that to a beautiful violin solo?'" But Mellé's growing pains at the studio were balanced by his popularity with producers intrigued by his work, and his career flourished.

"Universal was the best training ground any composer could ever wish for. You had to be fast, but you had to be accurate. You didn't make mistakes. If you were sitting on the scoring stage because of an error, a wrong chord, a wrong voicing, or the music didn't fit to the picture and had to be rewritten while the orchestra was sitting there, you'd be kicked out. There was no margin for error, but you really learned your profession."[24]

With Mellé overtaxed with work, Laird needed another composer to write the music for the first-season episodes. Music department head Harry Garfield suggested Robert Prince. A graduate of Juilliard, Prince wrote arrangements for Johnny Mathis (*Chances Are*) and ballet music for Jerome Robbins (*N.Y. Export: Op. Jazz*) before emigrating to Hollywood in the 1960s.

At first glance he was an odd choice for the show. Up to that point, Prince's work accompanied the straight dramatic fare at Universal: *The Bold Ones, The Virginian* and *The Name of the Game*. "I had never written 'scary music' before," notes the composer, "and usually the time constraints force imitation, but I went to the trouble of figuring it out myself." Prince rose impressively to the challenge.

His compositions, closer to Billy Goldenberg than Gil Mellé both stylistically and instrumentally, provided something of an aural link to the *Night Gallery* pilot. Prince proved himself a natural, equally adept at ambient strangeness ("The House," "Pamela's Voice," "Lone Survivor"), sheer horror ("The Dead Man," "The Doll"), and even comedy ("The Housekeeper"). More to the point, he was fast: Prince was signed to score all of the first season segments on December 3, 1970; *Night Gallery*'s premiere date was December 16. "We had little time for anecdotes," Prince notes. "Universal is considered 'The Factory,' and although we were well compensated, the work schedule was anything but fun. We were given between ten days to two weeks to write a score."[25]

He scored three of the six hours, and all except one of the remaining segments were tracked with these cues. Despite the blistering pace, Prince created memorable scores for *Night Gallery*'s brief first season, furnishing the new series with a distinguished musical persona.

## THE MAIN TITLE

Along with Mellé's distinctive theme, many viewers have been struck by the design of *Night Gallery*'s familiar opening titles, a sequence of telescoping images alternating leering faces with Tom Wright's bizarre gallery paintings. It was the inspiration of freelance designer Wayne Fitzgerald, who got the assignment at the eleventh hour.

A previous main title designed by Visual Computing Corporation had been presented and refused by NBC a week before the show was to premiere. Fitzgerald, who designs titles for both features and television, received a frantic call. "They said, 'It's terrible,'" Fitzgerald recalls. "'Everybody hates it, and we've got to come up with something!' We literally didn't have any time to shoot anything. It wasn't like I could go out and do some artwork or some animation, or shoot some special effects, so I took a look at what they had. The paintings were quite good—the subject matter obviously worked—but they were inanimate, they had no drama to them. They had also intercut some effects, a bunch of faces shot through a distortion lens. The distortion stuff looked like a really bad 'B' movie."

Fitzgerald realized he had to obscure the material, specifically the footage of the distorted faces. Using a technique he had developed for the Barbra Streisand musical *On a Clear Day You Can See Forever*, Fitzgerald scanned across the material with multiple rectangular screens that appeared to advance toward the viewer, allowing only glimpses of the paintings and faces. "A mysterious, hypnotic kind of scanning across," Fitzgerald says, "giving the illusion of moving through space—getting a glimpse of this, and getting a glimpse of that. And the distorted figures work in that sense—you only get quick pictures of them. It's still one of my favorite titles that I've done! And it actually worked quite well, everybody was very happy with it."

For *Night Gallery*'s third season, Fitzgerald would be invited back to design a new main title in which the paintings—but no faces—fly toward the viewer through a black ether. Most fans, though, remember his first effort with the greatest affection. "I always thought of the titles as a kind of put-on," Fitzgerald says. "I didn't think of it as being seriously scary—it was like a bad Halloween joke. But when you only get a glimpse of those elements, it works."[26]

THE EVE OF DEBUT

While *Night Gallery* prepared for production, Serling's attention was divided by the acclaim he had earned for his February *Hallmark Hall of Fame* entry, "A Storm in Summer." The story of a developing friendship between an elderly Jewish delicatessen owner and a black ghetto youth, it received critical raves—a degree of adulation Serling had not experienced since the *Twilight Zone* period. When the Emmy Award nominations were released, however, Serling's name was not among the writers honored, though the production, the director, and its lead actor, Peter Ustinov, were. It would appear that Serling's earlier published comments questioning the legitimacy of the Television Academy—which he bluntly termed an "aging dinosaur"—were having an unintended dampening effect on his popularity. Adding insult to injury, both Ustinov and the producer of "A Storm in Summer" walked away with statues at the ceremony. Serling commented on the proceedings with a sour humor in a note to friend John Champion: "Anti-semitism was the key to the whole award. Ustinov is known in the inner circles to be Gaelic. I, on the other hand, am descended from the construction company that paved the way to Golgotha. So what happens during the awards? This poor Jewish kid gets aced out—while Ustinov gets the nod. Next time, I'll write a comedy."[27]

Smarting from the perceived snub, Serling refocused his attentions on *Night Gallery*. An NBC promotional spot was designed around the series host at his home in Pacific Palisades, and Serling wrote the narration in his by now familiar style:

*The swimming pool and that short, dark, country gentleman you're looking at are hardly mood pieces for a show like* Night Gallery. *In point of fact,* Gallery *is not designed for sunshine or the cheery vestiges of the good life. Its mood is the occult . . . fantasy . . . nightmare. A collection of portraits in black—stories of the eerie and the unpredictable. I'm Rod Serling, and I'll be serving as host and sometimes writer on six hour-long excursions into the realm of the imagination.* Night Gallery, *we believe, will prove to be a most bizarre entry into the fall schedule on NBC. You'll find yourself on a ghost ocean of lost ships . . . the possessor of a deadly diary that not only tells it like it is . . . but like it will be on the next day. You'll wind up in graveyards, mausoleums, haunted houses, and on roadmaps you never even knew existed. The portraits we'll tell about are not to be found in art museums or run-of-the-mill exhibitions. The subjects are much too out-of-this-world to seek permanence in paint and pigmentation. They'll move across your screen at a deadly gallop. Watch for them and watch for me on . . .* Night Gallery.[28]

But even after the critical success of *The Twilight Zone*, Serling still found himself having to explain to the media his interest in fantasy. Many still treated his involvement in such shows as though it were an embarrassment that a writer of his gifts would lower himself to such an insignificant genre. "I enjoy doing these science fiction things," Serling said in an interview shortly before the premiere. "I'm not stuck with them. It's by choice. There's very little of this sort of imaginative story on the air—dramas which defy natural laws." And what of the hard-hitting, realistic social commentary on which he made his name? "I can't do them today because there's no platform for those plays. There are no dramatic anthologies. As life has become tougher and harsher, you don't want to see more of the real thing on television. You can watch the old live television plots and stories on the six o'clock news. The American public wants a Passion Play every night—escapist entertainment . . . the good and the bad immediately identified."[29] Neglecting to note, of course, that the beliefs, passions and concerns that forged his humanist outlook—the very engine of his drive to write—were still vitally stamped on practically every script he submitted, whether fantastic or otherwise.

The morning of December 16, 1970, the *Los Angeles Times* ran a story on the premiere of *Night Gallery*:

There's been a noticeable void in the terror-chills-and-squirm department on TV these past few years. It will be filled with what should prove to be marrow-freezing suddenness tonight with the premiere of the third six-show segment of NBC's *Four in One* series, *Rod Serling's Night Gallery*.

Each of the hour shows will be given over to either two or three examples of Serling's *specialité*: eerie, cryogenic tales calculated to make the hairs on your nape stand at attention. Serling will be the new show's host-narrator. The format, then, should be akin to that of the Serling-created series, *Twilight Zone*. The content of the new show will also parallel *Twilight Zone*, which should more than likely mean top-drawer entertainment.

"Yes, *Night Gallery* will be very similar to *Twilight Zone*," [Serling] says. "But it will be more ambitious and it will be in color, which should make a difference. They're taking more time and spending more money than we were ever allowed on *Twilight Zone*. I think it will be a better show all around."[30]

Time and experience would ultimately temper Serling's enthusiastic prediction.

# 6
# The First Season

FIRST SEASON CREDITS
1970–1971

**PRODUCED BY** Jack Laird
**PRODUCTION EXECUTIVE** Paul Freeman
**MAIN TITLE THEME** Gil Mellé
**ART DIRECTORS** Joseph Alves, Jr. and Sydney Litwack
**SET DECORATIONS** Charles S. Thompson, Bert F. Allen, and Jerry Miggins
**UNIT MANAGER** Burt Astor
**ASSISTANT DIRECTORS** Jack Doran, Ralph Sariego, Les Berke, and Robert Gilmore
**FILM EDITORS** James Leicester, Jean-Jacques Berthelot, James D. Ballas, and Bud Hoffman
**SOUND** David H. Moriarty and John Erlinger
**GALLERY PAINTINGS** Tom Wright
**MAIN TITLE DESIGN** Wayne Fitzgerald and Visual Computing Corp.
**TITLES & OPTICAL EFFECTS** Universal Title
**EDITORIAL SUPERVISION** Richard Belding
**COSTUMES** Grady Hunt
**MAKEUP** Bud Westmore
**HAIR STYLIST** Larry Germain
**CASTING** Bert Metcalfe

NIGHT GALLERY #32361
Air date: December 16, 1970

1

THE DEAD MAN
★ ★ ★ ★

Teleplay by Douglas Heyes
Based on the short story by Fritz Leiber

*Louise Sorel and Carl Betz in "The Dead Man." Courtesy of UCLA Research Library Arts Special Collections.*

Directed by Douglas Heyes
Music: Robert Prince
Director of Photography: William Margulies
Time: 29:55

**Cast**
Dr. Max Redford: Carl Betz
Dr. Miles Talmadge: Jeff Corey
Velia Redford: Louise Sorel
John Fearing: Michael Blodgett
Minister: Glenn Dixon

*We welcome you, ladies and gentlemen, to an exhibit of art—a collection of oils and still-lifes that share one thing in common: you won't find them in the average salon or exhibition hall or art museum.*

*Painting number one. Its title, "The Dead Man"—an interesting meeting between flesh and bone; between that which walks . . . and that which, you should excuse the expression, gets buried. So we submit for your approval this and other frozen moments of nightmare placed on canvas.*

/ **Summary** / At the gates of his secluded clinic, Dr. Max Redford welcomes his colleague and friend Dr. Miles Talmadge, and invites him to witness a bizarre experiment. Redford has given up his practice to concentrate on John Fearing, a young man whose subconscious mind is so slavishly obedient to suggestion that he can, in a posthypnotic trance, instantaneously develop the symptoms of any disease and return upon awakening to perfect health. Talmadge is stunned by the young man's abilities and both he and Redford marvel at the possible benefits to mankind if Fearing's secret could be passed on to others. Redford excitedly ponders casting disease from the body entirely—perhaps even conquering death.

At dinner that evening, Talmadge is troubled by the obvious chemistry between Fearing and Redford's wife, Velia. He counsels his friend either to end the research—and lose his prize patient—or get on with his work and accept the price. Redford has so far tolerated the relationship, but admits he has been sorely tried by the knowledge of his wife's infidelity. At the next session with Fearing, Talmadge's concerns are confirmed when Redford gives the posthypnotic signal, a coded tapping with a set of shears, and his patient stops breathing. Talmadge checks for a pulse and finds none. Panicked, Talmadge accuses Redford of trying to destroy his rival out of jealousy and demands that he bring Fearing out of the trance. Redford, protesting his intentions, gives the signal to revive the subject. Fearing does not respond. He repeats the signal

—three taps, then one—with, again, no change. Blanching, Redford taps out the signal more forcefully, over and over again. No response. Fearing is dead. Velia, hysterical, cannot be consoled. She is convinced not only of Redford's guilt but also that Fearing's mind is still conscious, locked in a dead body—and certain to be buried alive.

A year passes and Redford, racked with guilt, again sends for Talmadge, who arrives to find the clinic in neglect and Velia in a state of almost catatonic grief. Redford asks him to review the notes and tapes of his experiments with Fearing in the hope of finding where he failed. That night, Talmadge awakens Redford with a horrifying revelation: the signal he gave again and again to revive Fearing was wrong. The correct signal was three taps, then *two*. Redford had blocked it subconsciously, tapping instead three-and-*one*. Overhearing their conversation, the deranged Velia races screaming from the house toward the nearby cemetery with Redford and Talmadge in pursuit. Velia arrives at Fearing's crypt first and, wrenching open the gate to the catafalque, hammers the correct signal onto the coffin of her dead lover just as Redford arrives.

Talmadge, lost in the maze of headstones, hears Velia's screams and stumbles toward the crypt. Shining his flashlight over the scene, he finds Velia, shattered and stricken, staring in mute terror at the moldering corpse of the resuscitated Fearing . . . whose rotted fingers have choked the life from her husband.

/ **Commentary** / *Night Gallery* opened with one of its strongest tales, a macabre shocker by *Twilight Zone*–alumnus Douglas Heyes, a contributor also to such classic series as *Thriller* and *Alfred Hitchcock Presents*. Although faithful to Fritz Leiber's original story, Heyes incorporated stylistic elements gleaned from Edgar Allan Poe, genre progenitor, effectively recapturing the chilling atmosphere and creeping horror of his morbidly elegant prose.

The settings, lighting, and camera work blend to create a sense of vaulting gothic spaces and psychological unease. In the segment's later scenes, after Fearing's funeral, wide-angle lenses and low camera angles distort perspective and turn the large, shadowy house into a claustrophobic vault. In the confrontation scene between Redford and Talmadge, the camera peers through the lattice work of the bedroom furnishings, making the audience—as is Velia—an unwitting eavesdropper, silent onlookers to the tragedy. For the hair-raising finale, Heyes shot exteriors at a Catholic cemetery above Boyle Heights in Los Angeles, utilizing the existing memorials and weathered headstones to capture the story's somber atmosphere.

Robert Prince's effectively eerie music adds to the gooseflesh. Details of orchestration heighten each successive mood: his clever scoring for the hypnosis scene, with winds and strings in dialogue re-creating the stasis of the trance (with a rattle and side-drum accent on the word "death"); his flitting, birdlike figurations on flute and harpsichord to mirror Velia's madness; and his coup de théâtre, the race to the cemetery scene, with Velia's flute motif overlying a descending organ figure, imitative of wildly tolling bells, sounding notes of doom and panic. All are tokens of Prince's acute dramatic instinct.

The acting of the principals adds credibility and class. As Redford, Carl Betz creates a believable portrait of a man torn between his jealousy and his passion for his research. The actor's finest moment comes in the scene where Max savors what he believes to be his crowning achievement, bringing a dead man back to life. In previous scenes, he has been sober, sane, professional, but his attitude now is quite different: overpowering, eager, vaguely malevolent, an effect created partly by William Margulies's lighting, but only partly. Betz subtly reveals another side of Redford's character: his Godlike aspirations, his surfacing glee over holding his rival's life in his hands, very skillfully managed. He almost laughs at Talmadge's request to give the signal in the full confidence that Fearing can and will revive, adding chills to a scene already tight with tension. "Carl Betz was tremendous," affirms costar Michael Blodgett. "He carried the whole cast on his shoulders."[1]

As the moonstruck Velia, soap star Louise Sorel convincingly manages a high-wire act between control and hysteria, and her transformation into the unhinged Mrs. Redford is spot-on: an Ophelia lost in her own gothic nightmare. "I went all out in the cemetery scene," Sorel says, "choosing to move my mouth silently, unable to speak, to convey her horror. But I'm doing such bizarre stuff on *Days of Our Lives*—everything from possession to burying people alive—that it makes 'The Dead Man' look like Mickey Mouse time."[2]

For the role of her lover, the unfortunate John Fearing, Heyes and Laird cast a tan and athletic Adonis, Michael Blodgett. "He was a very handsome young guy," Sorel recalls. "He never went on with his career, but he became a very successful writer. He wrote a book that was a major, major best-seller [*Captain Blood*—no relation to the Rafael Sabatini novel]. It was the strangest thing, I couldn't believe that it was the same guy."[3]

Most of Blodgett's time on screen is spent lying on an examination table in a hypnotic trance, manifesting the changes between various illnesses and a counterfeited death. "I found it very difficult to remain still during the death scenes," Blodgett recalls. "And about every twenty minutes I would have to go and get made up differently. I had at least four different makeup changes while I was doing those scenes." Heyes and production executive Paul Freeman debated over how "science fictiony" they wanted Fearing's diseased segues to be. "They weren't sure whether to actually show the diseases occurring on camera, or do it in a subtle way in order to save money," Blodgett says. "They decided to 'trick' it, do trick shots and lighting, that sort of thing, because they figured that, number one, it would look sort of obvious if the diseases appeared on camera, and number two, they couldn't afford it."[3]

To create the illusion of Fearing's rotted corpse, makeup wizard Bud Westmore made a rubber life mask of Blodgett's face. Working from that, Westmore fashioned the grinning, empty-socketed mummy depicting the actor in the advanced stages of decomposition. The head and a set of mummified hands were then attached to a dummy for the segment's final, ghastly tableau of Redford locked in the grasp of the awakened Fearing.

Rounding out the cast as Dr. Talmadge is veteran character actor Jeff Corey. His ability to bring distinction to scores of roles, from derelicts to demagogues, has ensured his survival in films for the last fifty years, weathering a hungry period during the infamous McCarthy blacklist. As a testament to his tenacity and talent, he survived by teaching three generations of actors and actresses their craft. Corey's gifts can be seen at their best in Arthur Penn's *Little Big Man,* John Frankenheimer's Faustian drama *Seconds,* and, behind the scenes, as director of ten segments of *Night Gallery.* According to Corey, that's how he got his role in "The Dead Man":

"When you're an actor and you work at a studio, it's bad form to ask a director if there's a part for you in the sequence he's shooting; but since I was a director, I could ask the guy," recounts Corey. "Doug Heyes came to watch my dailies [for "Certain Shadows on the Wall"], and I said, 'What's your story about and do you have a part in it for me?' And he said, 'Jeff, I'd love to have you in it.'"[5] Corey's performance succeeds in reflecting many of the actor's own qualities: his keen intelligence, his intensity, and, especially, his deep compassion.

But even an actor of Corey's seasoned professionalism can lose focus occasionally, as Louise Sorel recalls: "When you do these kinds of shows, you can't help but laugh. The funniest moment was at Jeff's expense—and that's not fair, because I like him. There's a very tense scene where Jeff, as Miles, knocks on a door, looking for Carl, who plays Max. So, Jeff knocked and said, 'Miles, it's me.' And Carl yelled from the other side, 'No, you're Miles! I'm Max!' Well, this happened five times in a row, and I snapped. I was on the floor, ill with laughter. I'm thinking, 'Of all people, Jeff Corey, a brilliant acting teacher, whom I have the greatest respect for, can't get these names straight?'"[6] Shrugging off Sorel's amusement, Corey worked through his block and delivered a fine performance. For *Night Gallery*'s second season, the lovely Sorel would return to distract yet another fellow actor in an adaptation of H. P. Lovecraft's ghoulish "Pickman's Model."

Besides his exceptional work on "The Dead Man," Douglas Heyes wrote two other scripts for *Night Gallery,* both under the name Matthew Howard, a pseudonym he used when not directing the segments themselves. It is unfortunate he never returned to direct again. His visual flair was perfect for an atmosphere show such as *Night Gallery.* The other scripts, for "The Housekeeper" and "Brenda," had the potential to be better realized than they eventually were, but Heyes's involvement in other projects prevented him from helming them and keeping his unique vision intact.

"The Dead Man," however, had quite an impact—something Blodgett discovered not long after the segment's first broadcast. The actor was vacationing in the

Gull Lake region of northern Minnesota, "way up there in the woods, very rural," notes Blodgett. "I walked into a restaurant out in the middle of nowhere, and everybody there just got real quiet and stared. They went, '*Oh, my God, it's John Fearing!*' I couldn't believe it! I was totally taken aback!"[7] The premiere had obviously scored quite high in memorability.

## 2
## THE HOUSEKEEPER
★ ★ ½

Written by Matthew Howard (pseudonym for Douglas Heyes)
Directed by John Meredyth Lucas
Music: Robert Prince
Director of Photography: William Margulies
Time: 19:18

**Cast**
Cedric Acton: Larry Hagman
Miss Wattle: Jeanette Nolan
Carlotta Acton: Suzy Parker
Miss Beamish: Cathleen Cordell
Headwaiter: Howard Morton

*Jeanette Nolan in "The Housekeeper."*
*Courtesy of Ronald Borst.*

*P*ainting number two. Something on the abstract side to annotate that which is not abstract at all: greed, avarice, and man's constant hunger to change what he doesn't like by whatever means. Said means in this case being a little science mixed with a little black magic. Welcome, if you will, "The Housekeeper."

/ **Summary** / Within the ranks of the employment agency, no one is more surprised than frumpy, funny-looking Miss Wattle at being selected for the choice position of housekeeper for the wealthy Acton household. Cedric Acton has someone very specific in mind: "Someone with a kind heart, a mellow and forgiving soul—someone that no one else would want . . . an old hag"—with no family, friends or references.

Miss Wattle soon realizes that Acton's requirements are not merely for an amiable domestic. Acton, a dabbler in black magic, wants a guinea pig for a diabolical experiment—a personality transplant. His goal: to infuse Miss Wattle's warm, generous spirit into the body of his cold, beautiful (and fabulously rich) wife, Carlotta—while

Miss Wattle's dowdy shell is left to house Carlotta's ice-princess soul. Acton's suave, persuasive manner soon convinces her of the benefits—to be young, breathtakingly beautiful . . . and wealthy.

At the moment Miss Wattle and Carlotta's eyes meet, Acton produces the magical conduit: a jumping frog. Miss Wattle gasps . . . but the sound comes from Carlotta! The transfer is a success—Miss Wattle's body now hosts Carlotta's soul. Before Miss Wattle's horrified new eyes, Acton murders his wife and disposes of her. The panicked housekeeper races to the bedroom and locks herself in. Acton's persuasion falls on deaf ears and she remains locked inside for three days. When she finally emerges, Miss Wattle's expression is distant, her manner cold. Another, more subtle transformation has taken place. She plans to leave—with *all* Carlotta's money, thank you. "It wouldn't do at all for you to profit one penny out of the terrible thing you've done," Miss Wattle tuts. Acton, having expected something of the sort, produces the jumping frog. As if on cue, a wizened, funny-looking old woman enters the room, and *abracadabra,* Miss Wattle now finds herself transferred into the shell of the dowdy intruder. She collapses to the floor, sobbing, "How many times? Dear God, how many times?" With a sinister smile, Acton replies, "Until we get it right."

/ **Commentary** / In the light of Serling's prominence in the new series, it is odd that the premiere of *Night Gallery* should showcase two plays neither of which were penned by Serling, but by Douglas Heyes.

Where "The Dead Man" was a gothic horror story, "The Housekeeper" is altogether lighter in tone. They make a well-contrasted pair, although Heyes's second contribution was a late entry. "I ran into Jack Laird after he had already asked me to do 'Dead Man,'" Heyes recalled, "and at the time we didn't know whether or not there was going to be a writer's strike. I happened to have a script ready that I had written for no particular reason. I had just thought of it, and wrote it down, and had it around for a year, not knowing what I was going to do with it. So with the strike imminent, I said, 'How would you guys like to have a script that's already written?' They said great, and I gave them 'The Housekeeper.'"

At the time, Heyes was not satisfied with the strength of the play's final line—"How many times? Dear God, how many times?"—but the real clincher was supplied during the filming. "Larry Hagman suggested a tag line to me when I came on the set, to see if I would buy it," Heyes said. The line Hagman suggested was "Until we get it right." Heyes enthusiastically bought it. "I thought it was very good. So that's the line that's in it now."[8]

Hagman's whimsical performance as Cedric Acton has just the right comic timing—and the overly refined inflections of a faux British accent. He uses this to his advantage: during times of stress, his flat American accent returns to comically highlight the character's shallowness. And as the dowdy, sweet-souled Miss Wattle, Jeanette

Nolan is a delight. With her Irish lilt and matronly manner, she is the picture of sweetness—until curdled by Acton's Mephistophelian temptation. In the second season, Nolan would return in a less sugary role as an ancient sorceress in "Since Aunt Ada Came to Stay."

Suzy Parker, playing Acton's self-centered wife, was herself a fan of the veteran character actress. "I had such great admiration for this lady," says Parker enthusiastically, "ever since high school when I saw her in Orson Welles's *Macbeth*." Unfortunately for Parker, her enthusiasm was ultimately tempered by decisions made in postproduction. For purposes of continuity it was decided to dub Nolan's voice over Parker's dialogue after the transformation sequence. Recalls Parker, "When I first got the script, my husband [actor Bradford Dillman] helped me with my Scottish burr because he's fantastic with dialects. I worked so hard on that damned accent, I can't tell you. Bradford—he's a real taskmaster!" On the night of the broadcast, Parker received an unpleasant shock. "I was totally destroyed when I saw it. After I had done all that work, they used *Jeanette Nolan's* voice. They hadn't told me, those bastards! But I guess if you're going to be looped by somebody, you might as well be looped by a great actress!"[9]

In sync with the performances, John Meredyth Lucas's direction and James Leicester's editing scheme highlight the comic elements over the potentially phantasmagoric qualities of the subject, and the general design of the piece is very casual in comparison with Heyes's gothic stylings for "The Dead Man." In all, "The Housekeeper" is an enjoyable, if not inspired, offering in the *Night Gallery*.

## NIGHT GALLERY #32366
Air date: December 23, 1970

1
## ROOM WITH A VIEW
★ ★ ½

Teleplay by Hal Dresner
Based on his short story
Directed by Jerrold Freedman
Music: Robert Prince
Director of Photography: William Margulies
Time: 11:03

**Cast**
Jacob Bauman: Joseph Wiseman
Frances Nevins: Diane Keaton

*Joseph Wiseman in "Room with a View." Courtesy of Sal Milo.*

Lila Bauman: Angel Tompkins
Butler: Morgan Farley
Chauffeur: Larry Watson

*A very hearty welcome to* Night Gallery, *and to a collection of art not found in your average museum. These are paintings that represent life . . . but occasionally death as well.*

*Case in point: this canvas here. A bedroom, but with all the cheer and warmth of a crypt. Beneath the paint and the patina is an ingredient called jealousy. Color it a monstrous green—and call the picture "Room with a View."*

**/ Summary /** From his invalid bed, wealthy Jacob Bauman keeps tabs on the world outside his estate with a pair of binoculars and a window view of the courtyard below. Spying his nurse, Frances Nevins, in close embrace with his chauffeur, Vic, Bauman correctly assumes a serious relationship. Upon her arrival, he playfully berates Miss Nevins for her lateness and startles her with his knowledge of both her tryst and her upcoming wedding plans. She marvels at his intuition. Bauman insinuates that not much occurs in his house without his knowledge—and in fact, the old man is secretly aware that his stunning young wife, Lila, is *also* involved in an ongoing affair with Vic. Through his binoculars, he views the two lovers meeting in the courtyard and heading up to the chauffeur's sleeping quarters over the garage.

Dividing his attention, Bauman casually draws from the nurse her feelings about Vic, noting specifically her almost pathological jealousy. Her rages, she admits, can be murderous: once she brutally beat a woman for making a pass at her fiancé. Bauman puts the binoculars aside and begs a favor of Miss Nevins. Pulling a small handgun from his dresser drawer, he asks her to give it to Vic with instructions to clean it for him. "I think I saw him go up to his room a minute ago," he mentions, adding with a sly smile, "why don't you sneak up on him and surprise him?" Agreeing to the prank, the nurse heads downstairs with the gun as the butler arrives with breakfast.

As Bauman dourly inspects his meal, three shots ring out from the direction of the chauffeur's room. "Sounds like a car backfiring," comments the butler. "Shall I butter your toast, sir?" "No, thank you," Bauman replies. "There are still some things I can do for myself, Charles."

**/ Commentary /** This sly Hitchcockian vignette marked Diane Keaton's first role in film owing to director Jerrold Freedman's discriminating eye: "I was well known in those days for starting people out. So Monique James, the head of casting at Universal, came over and said, 'We have this new actress who's just come to town, and she's really going to be great. I want you to meet her.' Diane had done theater in New York, I guess, but it was her first Hollywood appearance."[10] Keaton's self-conscious performance as Joseph Wiseman's murderous dupe is, unfortunately, a bit raw. In time, the stammering ingenuousness exhibited here evolved into the charming quirkiness of her Oscar-winning turn in *Annie Hall*.

Angel Tompkins turns in a more experienced performance as Bauman's unfaithful wife, Lila. "It was one of the most unusual shoots that I can recall," says Tompkins, "because I've always been able to break the ice with people, and that just could *not* be done on this shoot. Usually when you work with people, you're pleasant, you kibitz a lot, you tell jokes, but there was minimal, if any, camaraderie. It was *very* disappointing." Tompkins was able to strike no meaningful rapport with her director whose attentions, she felt, focused more on Keaton than on her. "But I had a *wonderful* time with Joseph Wiseman, because he was rich to work with, wonderfully rich. He made it easy to hit the mark—to be somebody different than who I was."[11]

The segment's author had as little love for its execution as Tompkins had filming it. "I thought it was heavy-handed," says Hal Dresner. "There's an archness in the performance and the direction. And I was astonished at how *young* Joseph Wiseman looked, and how *old* he was playing. He looks more vigorous than that—I mean, the hair was *dark*. I always liked Wiseman, but I thought he was heavy-handed—that really Jewish style."[12]

Freedman's visuals, luckily, are quite inventive, opening up this one-set piece with some interesting perspectives. Although superior to some of the shorter episodes used to fill up the hour on *Night Gallery*, "Room with a View" is a slight diversion at best.

2

## THE LITTLE BLACK BAG
★ ★ ★ ★

Teleplay by Rod Serling
Based on the short story by C. M. Kornbluth
Directed by Jeannot Szwarc
Music: Robert Prince
Director of Photography: Richard C. Glouner
Time: 29:35

**Cast**
Dr. William Fall: Burgess Meredith
Hepplewhite: Chill Wills
Gillings: George Furth

*Burgess Meredith and Chill Wills in "The Little Black Bag."*
*Courtesy of Foto Fantasies.*

Charlie Peterson: E. J. André
Ennis: Arthur Malet
Mother: Eunice Suarez
Girl: Marion Val
Pawnbroker: Johnny Silver
1st Doctor: Lindsay Workman
2d Doctor: Matt Pelto
Dr. Nodella: Robert Terry
1st Old Man: Ralph Moody
2d Old Man: William Challee

*For your approval now, a painting which has to do with time. Not the brief moments left to our culprits in the previous story—their years of imprisonment were minute little fragments compared to the time we talk of in this picture. We talk centuries now, and what happens when men from one century send back items quite unbidden to men of another. We call this painting "The Little Black Bag."*

/ **Summary** / In the year 2098, Gillings, a lower-level employee in a time travel laboratory, alerts his superior to a problem. During a routine equipment test, a medical bag was inadvertently shuffled into the temporal circuitry and sent back to 1971. And, much to the discomfiture of the stuttering Gillings, it cannot be retrieved.

The bag comes to rest in a garbage can in a back alley off skid row, to be discovered by two bedraggled winos. One, William Fall, is a discredited doctor reduced to panhandling to support his thirst. He is astounded by the bag's contents, with equipment and medications so advanced he finds it difficult to believe the medical establishment has advanced so far in the twenty years since his ouster. The other bum, Hepplewhite, sees it as a means to some fast cash. On their way to the pawnbroker's, they are waylaid by a distraught woman whose daughter lies deathly ill. Fall, with some ghost of his old self awakening within him, attends to the little girl following the bag's instructions. Miraculously, she awakens in perfect health. On further inspection, Fall is amazed to discover the bag's patent date of September 2098—and that this gift from the distant future can cure cancer. Fall practices on his old friend Charlie, who lies dying of the disease in a nearby flophouse. With the scalpel guiding his hand, Fall extracts the tumors from the sufferer's throat as he lies awake and unanesthetized. The instruments, tuned specifically to a task, cause no pain and spill no blood!

Later, in a dingy hotel room, Fall and Hepplewhite plot their future. Fall dreams of a sensational return to his respected profession, gathering together a convocation of great medical minds and opening his presentation with a showstopper: "Distinguished ladies and gentlemen, before I begin this demonstration, I'd like to pose to you an academic question. If I were to take this scalpel and I were to imbed it in my throat and then cut to a depth of, perhaps, three centimeters, what would your professional estimation be of my chances of surviving?" And then he will astound them all by demonstrating on himself! Cackling with excitement, Fall envisions the eradication of all sickness and disease, a new millennium for mankind. Watching the doctor swagger about the room in triumph, Hepplewhite plots a much simpler future, one in which there are riches, fame . . . but no William Fall. Hepplewhite grasps one of the surgical blades from the bag and advances threateningly on his soon-to-be ex-partner.

Later, at a packed medical center lecture hall, Hepplewhite holds the stage with a daring boast: if he were to imbed a scalpel in his throat and cut to the depth of three centimeters, what would be his chances of survival? The gathered doctors agree he would be dead within minutes. "Then, gentlemen," grins Hepplewhite, raising the knife to his throat, "watch this!"

At the time travel lab, Gillings tells his superior that the warning system alert relayed that a homicide has been committed with one of the bag's instruments. At his superior's order, the obedient drone deactivates the bag immediately.

Back in the past, grim-faced doctors pour out of the lecture hall as Hepplewhite's body is wheeled out on a gurney. Their diagnosis: suicide. "I'm not so sure it was deliberate," one doctor says. "Did you catch the look on his face just before he dropped? I've never seen anyone look *quite* so surprised." The miraculous medical bag, now filled with a disintegrating mass of rusted instruments and putrefied medications, is deemed junk and fed into the incinerator chute.

/ **Commentary** / Serling's first teleplay for the series, based on C. M. Kornbluth's short story, is wholly reminiscent of his exceptional work on *The Twilight Zone*, for which it could have been written. A welcome returnee from the *Zone* is Burgess Meredith, who lends an air of the fallen angel to the character of the discredited rummy doctor—another rich portrait to put alongside those he did for Serling's first series. "I am very grateful to Rod Serling," muses Meredith. "He provided me with several of the best scripts I ever had the luck to perform. Year after year, Rod used to have a part for me every season, and every one of them extraordinary."[13]

As the greedy Hepplewhite, Chill Wills creates an outrageous, larger-than-life character, and he received high marks from the network. In a memo to Serling after viewing the segment, NBC press department executive Rolf Gompertz noted, "Meredith and Wills are a beautifully seedy pair. There's one scene where Meredith decides to appear before a medical convention in which Wills steals the scene by just standing there with his mouth hanging open, the picture of imbecilic evil personified."[14]

This segment marked the *Night Gallery* debut of the series' most accomplished and prolific director, Jeannot Szwarc, who would direct, all told, twenty-two segments of the series. "Oh, I loved 'The Little Black Bag,'" recalls Szwarc, "but we had a *horrendous* schedule!" The pressure was not, however, enough to dampen one actor's elation on the set. George Furth, who had the part of Gillings, was in a giddy lather over a play of his own. "We couldn't keep him down," chuckles Szwarc, "because he was the author of a play which then became a huge musical hit on Broadway. All day long he kept saying, 'I'm going to be rich, I'm going to be rich!'"[15] The play was *Company*, the music and lyrics were by Stephen Sondheim, and sure enough, it was the musical hit of the Broadway season in 1970.

Not everyone involved in "The Little Black Bag" was overjoyed, however. The friction between Rod Serling and producer Jack Laird over the direction of the series first sparked in an argument over this segment. Laird revised Serling's script, removing the time-travel lab sequence from the opening and bookending it with a similar scene near the end, leaving the explanation of the bag's genesis until practically the end of the segment. This revision, along with a few other minor text changes, arrived in the author's mailbox early in August. A furious Serling responded with a telephone call to Laird, followed soon after by a slightly more diplomatic letter:

Mine Jack,

I wouldn't noodge you about this if I didn't think it were of such the essence. This relates to what we had talked about on the phone as to the opening to "The Little Black Bag," which had been cut without my knowledge. I can't restate too loudly or vociferously my objection to this cut. I think it wipes out the bizarre opening and does irreparable damage to the script. Please, please, Jack—put it back in! I don't know what the hell the time problem is, but I'll cut my intro to the show or something, but it really must go back in.

I gather that you must feel that I am incommunicado or something because of the dearth of communication, but I wish to God someone had notified me of the cuts and various alterations. I duly left my phone number and address in your office and [Universal executive] Norman [Glenn]'s before I left, and I know that most of these changes were made on July 1st, which was only two days after I left.

Hey, Laird—don't get pissed-off. But the show bears my name and though it doesn't say it in the contract, I do feel a sense of propriety in it.

Please keep in touch.

Cordially,
Rod Serling[16]

Laird, assuaging the angry Serling, returned the opening to its original position and for the most part did little to the script. One major change had to remain, however. In Serling's original submission, Hepplewhite's accidental suicide occurred on-screen, although the author delicately suggested the throat slashing be filmed from behind the character. To avoid the network censor's inevitable fit over a prime time bloodletting, a new final scene was tacked on, a postmortem conversation between two witnesses to Hepplewhite's "demonstration." The remainder of the script is Serling's.

The author won his battle . . . this time. But the flare-up between Serling and Laird over "The Little Black Bag" was only the opening salvo in an escalating war over creative control of *Night Gallery*. And Serling would not remain the victor for long.

3

## THE NATURE OF THE ENEMY

★ ½

Written by Rod Serling
Directed by Allen Reisner
Music: Robert Prince
Director of Photography: Richard C. Glouner
Time: 8:28

Joseph Campanella in "The Nature of the Enemy."
Courtesy of Sal Milo.

**Cast**

Simms: Joseph Campanella
Astronaut: Richard Van Vleet
1st Reporter: James B. Sikking
2d Reporter: Jason Wingreen
3d Reporter: Albert Popwell
Man at Monitor: Jerry Strickler

*This offering is a landscape, lunar and low-keyed, suggestive perhaps of some of the question marks that await us in the stars . . . and perhaps pointing up the moment when we'll collect something other than moon rocks. This item is called "The Nature of the Enemy."*

/ **Summary** / Mission Control, Houston. Tense faces are turned toward the large wall monitor as an astronaut from the Project Rescue team approaches scattered wreckage on the lunar surface. Simms, the team leader in Houston, fights to keep a clear signal as the astronaut nears the crash site of the previous mission, Project Settlement. The astronaut can see no signs of life, despite Houston's receipt of communication from the colonists after the crash.

At a press briefing, Simms summarizes the findings. Project Settlement crashlanded on the moon with survivors. The last communication Houston received, garbled by static, was a distress signal: it sounded as if they said they were under enemy attack—which Simms assures the reporters is a misinterpretation. He is pulled away from the briefing by another transmission from Project Rescue. The astronaut has discovered a huge metal platform obviously built by the survivors of the crash. The astronaut cannot identify its purpose at first, when suddenly he pauses, an incredulous tone in his voice: "It can't be. It just can't be!" The signal weakens, but before static erases the picture, a high-pitched scream is heard. The signal goes dead.

When the film of the transmission is rerun for the assembled press, one reporter suggests that the platform looks very familiar . . . like a mousetrap. Suddenly, transmission is reestablished on one of the frequencies. The automatic camera captures a movement near the platform and stops. Approaching from the horizon lumbers the figure of a gargantuan mouse. Arching up on its hind legs, the huge rodent towers over the wreckage, nose twitching. The stunned technicians stare, stupefied. "The enemy," stammers Simms. "That's the enemy!"

/ **Commentary** /  "The Nature of the Enemy" dramatizes one of the more inane ideas to come from the pen of Rod Serling, and its absurdity cannot be minimized. The sight of a moon-walking monster mouse is utterly ridiculous.

For actor Joseph Campanella, the production was a lark: "They *did* want that tongue-in-cheek kind of thing. The plot was possible—it was not real, but let's face it, it could be possible." As Simms, Campanella gamely reacts to the laughable premise, while Allen Reisner's direction is hamstrung by an insufficient special effects budget. The visual displays at Houston Control receive decidedly studiobound transmissions from the moon, with little resemblance to the televised *Apollo* missions. Convenient static and transmission interference cannot erase the images of space suits borrowed from Captain Video, a cat box version of the lunar surface, and miniature models of a disappointingly low grade. "We didn't see the actual videos of what we're *supposed* to be seeing," says Campanella. "The mousetrap, the other astronaut—we had to imagine it for ourselves. In those days, they didn't project it, so the actor had to create the reality and *then* deal with the scene, which is what we used to do on stage."[17]

Director Reisner took this assignment on the strength of Serling's involvement. He had worked with the author before, directing Serling's embryonic dry run for *The Twilight Zone*, "The Time Element," for *Westinghouse-Desilu Playhouse*. "With shows that had to do with Rod," Reisner says, "you just went ahead and said, 'Yes, I'll take that job,' because you knew that at least there was some safety factor there. He was always available to a director, and that's an enormous amount of help."[18] Unfortunately, not enough of a help to save this segment.

"The Nature of the Enemy" was the first real clinker on the series, and a disastrous omen of the occasional inconsistencies that would, in some critics' memories, overshadow the show's considerable successes.

NIGHT GALLERY #32363
Air date: December 30, 1970

1

THE HOUSE

★ ★ ★ ½

Teleplay by Rod Serling
Based on the short story by André Maurois
Directed by John Astin
Music: Robert Prince
Director of Photography: William Margulies
Time: 25:30

Paul Richards and Joanna Pettet in "The House."
*Courtesy of Sal Milo.*

**Cast**

Elaine Latimer: Joanna Pettet
Peugot: Paul Richards
Dr. Mitchell: Steve Franken
Nurse: Jan Burrell
Old Woman: Almira Sessions

*A most hearty welcome to those of you whose tastes in art lean toward the bizarre. Our first painting submitted for your approval is an item of real estate—but you won't find it advertised in the classifieds. Oh, it's light and comfortable and altogether well-heated— but there's a chill to the place. So bundle up when you look at this one. Our painting is called "The House," and this is the* Night Gallery.

**/ Summary /** Elaine Latimer, a patient at a sanitarium, has entertained a recurring dream for many years: while driving down a sunlit lane, she comes upon a lovely, two-story country house. She gets out of her convertible, approaches the front door, and knocks. No answer. She gets back in her car and heads back down the drive. But as her car passes the gate, the front door finally opens to reveal . . .

And thus the dream always ends—never disturbing, only persistent, and precise in every detail. Soon after her release from the sanitarium, Latimer finds herself driving down a winding country road in vaguely familiar country. The landscape soon leads her to the very house from her dreams. From the on-site real estate agent, Peugot, she learns the house is for sale—and to her great surprise, Latimer finds she has a foreknowledge of its every room. Latimer is even more surprised to discover its incredibly low price tag. Suspicious, she worms out of the reluctant Peugot the reason: the owners are selling because the house is haunted—by whom or what they weren't willing to say. Intrigued and not at all put off by this ominous news, Latimer takes steps to purchase her "dream" house.

But she soon senses that there *is* a strange presence lingering on the grounds. She will often be roused from sleep by a knock at the front door, only to find no one there upon answering. Latimer begins to feel uneasy about this insistent and disquieting presence, and calls her doctor to connect with a sympathetic voice. As she tells him about the house and the strange visitations of her daytime ghost, she hears a car drive up . . . then a knock at the door. She excuses herself for a moment to answer it. Latimer, stifling a shriek, races back to the phone and informs her doctor that her ghost has finally revealed itself . . . *"I am the ghost, doctor!"*

Overcome by sudden torpor, she hangs up the phone, lays down on her bed, and drifts off to sleep . . . and to dream. Hearing a knock at the front door, Elaine Latimer awakens once again, hastening downstairs just in time to see the tail of her red convertible rounding the lane and heading away from the house . . .

/ **Commentary** / Rod Serling's original submitted script, based on a clever short story by André Maurois, located the story in France. It was littered with references to francs, châteaus, and mademoiselles; Elaine Latimer's last name was Chambrun (after Jacques Chambrun, who translated Maurois's tale into English); and her doctor's first name was Pierre, not Peter. Switched to an American setting for budgetary reasons, the real estate agent's name, Peugot, is the only remnant of the original backdrop.

Serling shaped a tantalizing and ambiguous adaptation, much expanded from the original. As the past master of the hanging question, Serling perfected this type of tale during his tenure on *The Twilight Zone,* but the tone in "The House" is not the dark, threatening world often found there. This one, as his introduction states, is light and airy, a haunting psychological fantasy.

Actor John Astin, in his directorial debut for television, was hired on the strength of a short film he had written, acted in, and directed, *Prelude.* The film was nominated for an Academy Award, and even caught the interest of director Federico Fellini, who became Astin's cinematic mentor at that time.

Astin had an immediate vision for "The House," although locations had already been chosen. "It was the old house at the Dick Powell ranch up in Mandeville Canyon," Astin says. "That winding road, the lake, it's all there. When I went on a location scout—obviously they wanted me to check it out, see if I could shoot it—that changed *everything* for me because I saw so many possibilities for angles. But the key to much of it was, first, Joanna Pettet. She was ideal for the role, because she had that wistful beauty."[19]

In her first of four appearances on *Night Gallery,* Joanna Pettet—like the story—is a misty, soft-focus dream herself, although she found it difficult to grasp the less tangible aspects of her character. "I got more of a chance in 'The House' to rehearse the scenes," recalls Pettet. "John was one of the first directors to whom I was ever able to say, 'I don't feel comfortable.' He would say, 'Well, try it like this,' and he was always *so* right on. Being an actor himself, he knows those moments when you're dreadfully uncomfortable because you don't know how to play the scene, what attitude to have —and if you don't know that, you're dead. You're just saying the lines."[20] The end results are telling. Pettet seems to inhabit *both* worlds—spirit and flesh—with a calm and ethereal grace, gilded by William Margulies's gorgeous, sunlight-drenched camera work.

"Directing her was a lovely experience," Astin says. "Joanna seemed to sense what I wanted, and she had a feeling for the woman. She had a kind of seeking, spiritual quality about her. Her inquisitiveness, her vulnerability, the little touch of sadness in her, all these were perfect. And her elegance, too—Joanna was *wonderfully* elegant. She wore her chiffon gown with elegance, so that it would blow in the wind during the slow motion scenes—and that gave another level to it. That was part of the key to it for me."[21]

The gown Pettet wore for the dream sequences was from her own wardrobe, part of a conscious effort to craft a specific image of herself for her new television career: "Long flowing hair," Pettet recalls, "and clothing with a gossamer look, very flowing chiffon. John conveyed to me the importance of that 'look' for 'The House.' He was in on the wardrobe, and right away, he loved it! I remember his face in the dressing room while I was trying them on, that big smile! It was exactly what he wanted, and I was very happy with the end result, too."[22]

To set Pettet's character apart from her worldly surroundings, Astin directed others around her to act comparatively harsh. The exception is the role of Peugot, played in a spooky, staring, emotionally off-centered fashion by Paul Richards. "That's why Paul was perfect for the role," says Astin. "I had him sort of appearing from the shadows of the trees, sort of drifting in . . . as though he himself might have been a spirit."

Like most of Serling's scripts, "The House" provided the sparest of camera directions, leaving much creative leeway to the director. Astin used it most effectively, producing some startling visuals and responding immediately to its peculiar themes. "I felt that this story had a great deal to say about who we are," Astin says.

It deals with identity: are we our own ghosts? I know that Rod was uncomfortable with the ambiguity. He liked very much what I did with it, but he felt his script had somehow let people down. I *absolutely* disagreed with him. I thought that it was extremely evocative this way. Its very ambiguity made it an even more powerfully didactic statement, and I think that time has proven me correct, because it is one of the episodes of *Night Gallery* that you keep hearing about. "The House" remains, of the shows I directed or acted in, the one that gets the most commentary. I still get letters about it![23]

The delicious quality of the short story is its twist ending, which is shockingly abrupt and never has to explain itself. Author André Maurois suggests that the narrator, driven from her body during a fevered illness, haunted the house as an astral spectre—but she merely haunted others. Serling's script takes it to a different level, and Latimer "meets" her ghostly self—or is that a part of the dream, too? Serling's adaptation of "The House" is a recursion nightmare looping into itself, to presumably be played endlessly in the mind of the lead character. Says Pettet: "The ending makes absolutely no sense at all. It's a great spin—but wait a minute. What does it mean? It comes out of nowhere. Ultimately, the only thing it is, is odd."[24]

As directed by the talented Astin, who would return in the next season with two other winners, "A Fear of Spiders" and "The Dark Boy," "The House" is an artfully designed and stunningly photographed play on illusion and reality. He cleverly drops hints to the audience early on about the identity of the ghost. In the first dream sequence, as Latimer drives away from the house after receiving no answer to her knock, Astin cuts back to the door as it swings slowly open, revealing . . . nothing. He then dissolves from this white expanse to an extreme close-up of Pettet's eye, as though she were peering out from the house. "That was my little symbolism," says Astin. "The implication is obvious later that *she's* the one in the house, that this is all playing out in her head. If you're looking for a clue to explain the story, that's the clue!"[25]

But Astin also toys with our perceptions in ways that Serling never intended. The dream sequences are always shot in slow motion until the final scene. At the conclusion, Latimer, supposedly awakened from her dream, now moves in *slow motion,* while the car she glimpses driving away from the house is shot in *real time.* The director poses to his audience the question: which now is the dream and which reality? Like some of the best *Twilight Zone* episodes, we are left hanging with an unanswerable riddle—and vague feelings of disquiet. Elusive in spirit, the meaning of "The House" stays just beyond the viewer's reach, and thus haunts with the persistence of that red convertible.

## 2
## CERTAIN SHADOWS
## ON THE WALL
★ ★ ★ ½

Teleplay by Rod Serling
Based on the short story
 "The Shadows on the Wall" by
  Mary E. Wilkins Freeman
Directed by Jeff Corey
Music: Robert Prince

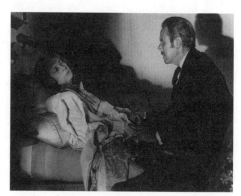

*Agnes Moorehead and Louis Hayward in "Certain Shadows on the Wall." Courtesy of Eddie Brandt's Saturday Matinee.*

Director of Photography: William Margulies
Time: 23:34

**Cast**
Stephen Brigham: Louis Hayward
Emma Brigham: Agnes Moorehead
Rebecca Brigham: Rachel Roberts
Ann Brigham: Grayson Hall

*The least permanent, the most fleeting of man's proof of existence—his shadow. It comes and goes with light—hours of the day, point of the sun, angle of the moon. It is a quickly daubed and imperfect outline of a certain object at a certain given moment. This painting is called "Certain Shadows on the Wall."*

/ **Summary** / In her gloomy Victorian house, Emma Brigham lies deathly ill. Her younger brother, Stephen, a ne'er-do-well physician on the brink of financial ruin, gave up his failing practice years ago to minister to the frail yet strong-willed Emma. Their spinster sisters, the imperious Ann and the timorous Rebecca, live with Emma and keep her house in order during her lingering illness. Stephen reluctantly reads to Emma every evening, invariably something from Dickens, and along with his feelings of resentment has developed something far more sinister. His ministrations appear to be making Emma worse, and over her pale, sallow face falls the shade of death.

To her brother's relief, Emma finally dies. Rebecca and Ann are devastated at losing their sister, but Stephen greedily begins cataloging all the possessions in the house. Against the wishes of his sisters, Stephen plans on selling everything, the house included, and dividing the money among themselves. His plans come to an abrupt halt when his sisters bring to his attention a disturbing phenomenon: a distinct and unmistakeable shadow on the front parlor wall. It is Emma's shadow, showing her in profile sitting up in bed. Stephen is severely shaken by this visitation, and no matter how he rearranges the furniture, alters the lighting, freshly paints or papers the wall, the shadow remains as a permanent and accusing fixture.

Stephen's frenzy in trying to discover an explanation for the phenomenon makes Ann suspicious. Even sweet, uncomplicated Rebecca begins to see Stephen in a new light, and when she finds the bottle of Emma's "medicine" she confronts him with it. Stephen, oozing charm, tells Rebecca that the pills are merely sedatives that he used to help Emma sleep. Smiling warmly, he informs her that if she ever becomes overwrought, she should come to him and he would provide for her.

Rebecca, instead, provides for Stephen. Telling Ann later that she only meant to calm his rages, Rebecca gives Stephen a capsule of the sedative in his tea that night.

The dose is lethal. Stephen's death is termed accidental and he is buried alongside his recently interred sister. But as Rebecca and Ann both wonderingly admire, Emma and Stephen now share proximity in more than just the family plot. There are now *two* shadows cast on the front parlor wall. Opposite Emma's is now Stephen's—and in his shadow hands is held an open book, from which he will read to her in perpetuity.

/ **Commentary** / With "Certain Shadows on the Wall," Serling followed one haunted house with another, and his script received the luxury treatment from all quarters. After securing a dream cast, Jack Laird hired Jeff Corey, an old acquaintance from his Actor's Lab days, to direct. Corey had only one previous directing credit, but he proved Laird's faith in him. From the look and pace of this segment, Corey well understood the needs of an atmosphere show like *Night Gallery*.

He allows his camera to languish on the depressing bric-a-brac of Emma's house and, most especially, on his actors. "If you do 'Certain Shadows' with Rachel Roberts, Agnes Moorehead and Louis Hayward," Corey said, "then you're almost obliged to come in for close-ups and show those Victorian faces, and the strange and eerie house."[26] Joseph Alves's musty sets and William Margulies's photography unite in creating a dour and oppressive atmosphere, in direct contrast to the sunny, open-air effects they achieved in "The House."

The performances are uniformly fine. Louis Hayward's Stephen is a chilly martinet, the image of a greedy and ruthless younger brother; Agnes Moorehead, though inexplicably given the smallest part, has a presence that tends to hover over the play after Emma's death; Grayson Hall (of *Dark Shadows* fame) snagged the meaty role of the waspish Ann; but Rachel Roberts's deceptively sweet and simple Rebecca trumps the rest of her sinister siblings by delivering the abrupt and delicious twist at the end.

Wishing to create the aura of a quaint, sentimental past, Corey departed slightly from Serling's script at the finish by incorporating a tune sung and played by Rachel Roberts. "I had done some English play when I went to the Sagen School of Dramatic Art," Corey relates, "and there was a song in it that I was sure was within public domain. So we got the music for that."[27] Composer Robert Prince worked the tune, "Sing Me to Sleep," into his score, twisting its simple melody into something ominous and slightly off, casting its own unhealthy shadow over the drama.

"That was a lovely, lovely experience," muses Corey. "They had a wonderful artist who came in and painted that marvelous, ephemeral shadow. You'd have to go up to it, even though you knew it was painted, to ascertain that it *was* painted, because it absolutely looked like Aggie's shadow. It was amazing."[28]

NIGHT GALLERY #32364
Air date: January 6, 1971

1
MAKE ME LAUGH
★ ★

Written by Rod Serling
Directed by Steven Spielberg
Music: Robert Prince
Director of Photography: Richard C. Glouner
Time: 25:57

*Godfrey Cambridge and Jackie Vernon in "Make
Me Laugh." Courtesy of Eddie Brandt's Saturday
Matinee.*

**Cast**
Jackie Slater: Godfrey Cambridge
Chatterje: Jackie Vernon
Jules Kettleman: Tom Bosley
Myron Mishkin: Al Lewis
David Garrick: Sidney Clute
2d Bartender: Gene Kearney
Director: Tony Russel
Heckler: John J. Fox
1st Bartender: Sonny Klein
Miss Wilson: Michael Hart
Flower Lady: Georgia Schmidt
1st Laugher: Sid Rushakoff
2d Laugher: Don Melvoin

*O*n display this evening, a pastiche of paintings from oddball-land. The poet Sir Max
Beerbohm reflected that no one ever died of laughter. Object of brush and palette: the rebut-
tal. The clown is Jackie Slater. His occupation, a comedian. His aspirations, to collect funny
bones and hang them on the walls of his life to hide the cracked plaster and yellowed wallpaper that is part of the interior decoration of failure. Poor Jackie Slater: a bad joke told in a
foreign language in an empty hall. The comic unable to coax laughter. The painting is called
"Make Me Laugh"—and this lightless limbo is called the Night Gallery.

/ **Summary** / Jackie Slater, a third-rate comic, has been plying his painfully unfunny
trade at the latest in a long string of anonymous gin joints—to the undisguised ennui
of all. Fired by the club owner and abandoned by his agent, the comic drowns his sor-

rows at a local bar. There he meets Chatterje, a turbaned mystic who is suffering a slump of his own. By profession a miracle worker, if Chatterje fails to perform a miracle by midnight he will be dishonored in the eyes of his ancient fraternity and lose his powers. The desperate comic begs Chatterje to grant him a miracle: Slater wants to make people laugh. The troubled swami informs the comic that his past miracles have not always come off as planned, but Slater is willing to take a chance. Chatterje concentrates for a moment, and it is done. "What's done?" Slater asks, skeptical. The bartender, overhearing this, bursts into hysterical laughter—screaming, uncontrollable, falling-down laughter. Slater discovers to his delight that everyone in the bar finds him equally funny. Everyone, that is, but Chatterje, who looks despairingly into his drink. "You did it, holy man," howls the overjoyed comic. "You worked a miracle!" "Yes, Yefendi," mutters the guru, "I'm afraid you're right."

Slater embarks on a new plateau of his career. He is now wildly successful, playing the big casinos in Vegas, the top television variety shows, all to ecstatic reviews and unanimous acclaim. But as time goes on, Slater becomes bored. His audiences howl at literally *anything* he does. He longs now to be taken seriously; an offer to star in a Broadway drama gives him that chance.

Slater's first rehearsal is a dismal failure. The show's producer, director, and entourage break into hysterics at every line Slater speaks, and the miserable comic is laughed out of the theater. Running into Chatterje on the street, Slater threatens him with a beating if he refuses to work another miracle: the comic now wishes to touch people, make them cry. The tattered fakir reluctantly grants him his wish. Testing his new powers, Slater calls to an elderly flower vendor across the street. As he crosses toward her, letting fly with yet another hoary one-liner, a speeding cab appears out of nowhere. Slater is struck and killed. As a crowd gathers around the comic's mangled body, the flower vendor begins to weep uncontrollably. True to Chatterje's word, Slater now has the power to touch people.

/ **Commentary** / With a concept borrowed from a first season *Twilight Zone* episode, "What You Need," this segment's Achilles' heel is the unfortunate casting of the leads. Neither Godfrey Cambridge nor Jackie Vernon has the ability to capture the pathos and tragedy inherent in these characters. Cambridge, a popular stand-up, cannot truthfully project the comic's desperation and sad humanity; the whole performance is forced. Vernon, in his dramatic television debut, is, if anything, even worse: flat and mechanical, a mystic with no mystery. His delivery is suggestive less of a swami than of a delicatessen owner, and he betrays no grasp of the rudiments of the acting craft. Director Steven Spielberg's visuals demonstrate his usual imaginative flair, but he is saddled with a pair of incompetent players. Had Jack Laird secured actors instead of nightclub comedians, the show doubtless would have worked. Serling's peculiar ability to illuminate the lives of the desperate and misbegotten is here lost in careless and insensitive execution.

The outcome galled the author. "It's really a piece of crap," commented Serling. "It almost single-handedly brought back vaudeville."[29] The executive response to the segment at NBC was even less gracious. "They hated it," recalls Sidney Sheinberg, then head of Universal Television. "They called the people who were producing the show and demanded that Spielberg be removed. It was a horrendous circumstance. As a matter of fact, it was the only time in all the years I ran MCA television that the network insisted a guy be replaced. Not only didn't they like the work he was doing, they ordered me never to use him again on *anything*. It was a very jarring experience, not only for me, but for Steven."[30] NBC executives weren't the only ones peeved at Spielberg. He had made enemies on the set as well.

For the role of the director who guides Slater's Broadway rehearsal, Spielberg had a specific actor in mind, but production executive Paul Freeman stepped in and gave the part to Tony Russel. Frustrated by what he saw as a bald-faced power play, Spielberg did not handle the situation gracefully. Recalls Russel: "When I walked on the set, I was really a persona non grata in Steven Spielberg's eyes, and he let me know it by the way he treated me. He was almost cruel—rather sadistic, if you want to know the truth. At the time, I thought of him as young, pompous, and spoiled. I was very uncomfortable, but I knew what had happened [between Spielberg and Freeman], and I knew where he was coming from. So I could back off and say, 'Hey, this is a couple of days' work, let me do it and get out of here.'"

But Russel's discomfort was only beginning. During the Broadway rehearsal, the spectators were supposed to erupt in cascades of hysterical laughter. Spielberg had planned extended close-ups of a number of the laughing actors. Russel was among them—for take after take after take:

Oh, let me tell you—at the end of the day, I was *so* tired! *And,* I had to go back and do the dubbing later on to get some *more* in there, *and some more in there.* I could hardly talk! And maybe I was paranoid because I went in knowing that this man did not want me for this part, but I got to the point where every time he said, "Do it again, do it again, do it again," I started thinking, "Now, wait a minute. It's *not* going to get any better than *this!*" I *mean* it—I felt *bad.* Of all my experiences as an actor, that was the *worst!*"[31]

Although both Laird and Sheinberg ignored the network's demands to dump Spielberg, parts of "Make Me Laugh" were reshot by Jeannot Szwarc in an attempt to placate the outraged network executive. "NBC was totally stupid," Szwarc says. "Someone at NBC was giving Steve hell, and I never could figure out why. I think I reshot one scene—I did it shot by shot exactly the way he had done it. In retrospect, I probably shouldn't have, but Jack really put it on a friendship basis. I was really caught in the middle. I liked Steve a lot, but I had a lot of loyalty to Jack."[32]

The main reshooting involved the two scenes between Slater and his agent, Jules Kettleman. The Kettleman role was at first played by character actor Eddie Mayehoff, who was then replaced for the reshoot by Tom Bosley—a casting tweak that failed to address the segment's more extensive flaws. Only a complete recasting of the leads could have saved this play—an opinion shared, it would seem, by some of the supporting actors:

"Godfrey was not an easy guy to work with," recalls Bosley. "I had known Godfrey years before in New York, but all of a sudden he thought of himself as something a little *more* than he actually *was*. It was unfortunate. I think one of the reasons Eddie Mayehoff was replaced was because he and Godfrey couldn't get along . . . and it might have been the same thing with Steven."[33] For the final cut, Spielberg's contributions were substantial enough for him to receive sole director's credit.

Spielberg has noted in numerous interviews that his early work in television, with its furious pace and assembly-line aesthetic, almost entirely extinguished his interest in moviemaking. It would reignite again with a vengeance in 1971, when he would stagger the film community with the made-for-television phenomenon *Duel*.

## 2
## CLEAN KILLS AND OTHER TROPHIES
★ ★ ★

Written by Rod Serling
Directed by Walter Doniger
Music: Robert Prince
Director of Photography: Richard C. Glouner
Time: 23:15

**Cast**
Colonel Dittman: Raymond Massey
Pierce: Tom Troupe
Archie: Barry Brown
Tom: Herbert Jefferson, Jr.

Raymond Massey in "Clean Kills and Other
Trophies." Courtesy of TV History Archives.

*O*ur second painting this evening has to do with the stalker and the victim, the hunter *and the hunted—that rare breed of Homo sapiens whose love of butchery is not a sport but a consuming passion. Offered to you now, "Clean Kills and Other Trophies."*

**/ Summary /** Colonel Archie Dittman corrals his dinner guest, Jeffrey Pierce, and his long-suffering pacifist son, Archie, Jr., into the study to witness an exhibition of trophies, the stuffed and mounted remnants of his passion: big-game hunting. Pierce, a family attorney, has come to handle the reversion of a trust fund set up by Dittman for his son. Colonel Dittman, however, is contemptuous of Archie for refusing to take part in his bloody pastime, and he announces his intent to attach a codicil to the trust: if his son has not shot and killed an animal before his twenty-first birthday, Dittman intends to squander Archie's inheritance on high-risk ventures before the boy sees a penny. Goaded by his father's taunts, Archie blows a fuse and turns one of his father's rifles on its owner, but his aim is checked by the colonel's African butler, Tom Mboya, who yanks the firearm out of Archie's grasp. The unflinching Dittman, heading upstairs, tells Tom to put his son to bed. "And leave a light on. He's probably afraid of darkness, too." Shaken by the violence of his response, Archie agrees to the hunt—"Better a deer than a patricide," he says—and retires for the night.

Tom, an Oxford-educated Ibo prince, confides to Pierce that he has stayed on with Colonel Dittman only because of his devotion to Archie. Dittman's planned hunting party tomorrow, Tom feels, will strip the boy of his manhood; he fears the colonel's son will become, like the glassy-eyed evidence of Dittman's bloodlust lining the walls, just another trophy of the kill. Concern prompts him to action: that night, Tom, dressed in ceremonial garb, stands a pagan vigil in front of the hearth's burning embers, praying fervently to his gods.

The hunt the following morning is a disaster. A nervous Archie hits the deer in the lungs, forcing them to track the dying animal. Dittman, demanding a clean kill, is furious. Returning home, he stalks into the study. Tom watches him silently from the shadows as the room grows suddenly warm . . . then hot. Dittman's head begins to ache, and he calls out to Tom for help. But the servant keeps his distance, watching the old man's suffering—and the fruits of last evening's prayer.

Tom exits to find Pierce searching for Dittman. "Best not go in there, Mr. Pierce. Last night I prayed to my gods . . . that the hunter should know what it is like to be the victim." Against Tom's warning, Pierce enters the study for a frozen moment—and exits aghast. "There are gods, Mr. Pierce," Tom explains. "Gods of the bush, of the Congo, of the rain forests. And with them, vengeance is an art." As Pierce and Archie hurriedly leave, Tom pours himself a brandy and toasts the latest addition to the cavalcade of death hanging on the trophy room wall: the white-haired, staring head of Colonel Archie Dittman.

/ **Commentary** / Shortly before his death, Serling remarked, "['Clean Kills and Other Trophies'] happens to represent an area of concern that I have which is so deep-rooted in me that I obviously go way out in the meadow with it. It's a static piece [that] should have been violently moving."[34] The comment was intended as part apology, part defense for a screening of this episode for a dramatic writing class he taught at Sherwood Oaks Experimental College in 1975. His script is less in need of defense than its interpretation.

Serling's passionate tract on guns, game hunting, and their practice as a measure of manhood is undercut, as is the previous segment, by its casting. Raymond Massey is too old and, more to the point, obviously too frail to give the role of Colonel Dittman the kind of energy needed. The character demands an air of smoldering violence, a brute callousness. Massey manages only a waspish disdain—which also reflected his manner on the set. "Massey was in physically bad shape," recalls director Walter Doniger. "He was very hard to talk to, very irritable, and very difficult."[35] Doubtless wedging his head into a trophy mount while balancing on a ladder didn't make him any more charming.

A disappointed Serling noted, "Raymond Massey is a lovely old gentleman who once was a fine actor, but who is very slow, very soft, and doesn't give you any of the balls that you desperately *need* in this kind of guy. I venture to say that if a Rod Steiger did this, he'd blow you apart."

Barry Brown's performance as Dittman's put-upon son, Archie, is similarly pallid, only serving to reinforce to the audience Dittman's view of his son as a gutless wimp. "When Raymond Massey refers to him as a cream puff, a vegetable, a cauliflower, essentially that's what we're looking at," carped Serling. "We're looking at Jimmy Stewart, dead at sixteen. He *is* a vegetable. When the kid aims the rifle at the father, you should think for all the world that he may kill him, [but] there's no doubt in anyone's mind who sees this [show] that the boy *won't* pull the trigger."

Serling's script describes Archie as a white-knuckled, ticking bomb beneath the quiet exterior; this, however, is only one of the story elements that did not translate to the screen. Serling's original ending for the story has Dittman dispatched not by vengeful gods but by his son, who finally snaps under the pressure of withstanding years of his father's abuse. The character of Tom and the supernatural elements in the play were created by Serling to appease network executives who went ballistic over the author's first version. "This was written originally as a short story in which there was no phony black magic," Serling said. "The kid comes back from the hunt and he's outraged by the old man, and he goes berserk. There's a scene in the study where the kid goes after him with an ax and decapitates him, takes this bloody head and jams it on a nail in the wall. It was a delightful comedic scene." Although grisly, it makes more sense out of the preceding material. The dramatic imperative fairly cries out for Archie himself taking his revenge, not some mystic protector, but, as Serling pointed out, "That's decapitation, you know, unheard of in television."[36]

Even with the final version tastefully sanitized, the segment would have scored higher had the main characters been played by actors with some muscle—say, Lee J. Cobb and Jeff Bridges. As filmed, the only stand-out performance comes from Herbert Jefferson (*Rich Man, Poor Man; Battlestar Galactica*), who gives Tom, the manservant, a regal, imperturbable calm that conveys his possession of deadly faculties it would be wise not to provoke.

"Herb Jefferson was a wonderful guy," recalls Doniger. "I had a great experience with him. He played a prince from Africa, but when he came in he started to play it too soft. So I told him, 'You're playing it like a nigger instead of a prince'—which was a risky thing to say, but, being an intelligent actor, his grasp of the difference was instant, and it changed his whole performance. He was playing a man who was, in a sense, a servant there, but he played it like he was the owner of the place. He was wonderful."[37]

So are the visuals. Doniger's camera moves are complex and sinuous, tracking stealthily and unobtrusively around his characters. Notes assistant director Les Berke, "Normally when you do a four-page scene, you do your rehearsal, then you do a partial or full master shot, and then you go in and get all your coverage shots. But with Walter, he would go in and shoot three-, four-, five-page masters and the reverses were built into the master in such a way that all you had to do was go around on one person usually, pick up their close-ups for the entire scene and walk away from it. He was brilliant. Walter Doniger made many a dolly operator want to commit suicide."[38]

"This was very hard on the crews," admits Doniger, "but you have to learn to take risks in my business or you become a hack. When you do those shots, you have to have an excellent camera operator, an excellent crab dolly man, an excellent focus puller, and all three of them have to work together at the right instant or it doesn't work. I thought that I could 'flow' the camera so that the audience wouldn't be distracted by a lot of cutting."

Although Serling stated later he would have preferred a blunter, more visceral visual interpretation to match the violent undercurrents in his script, Doniger's elegant camera moves and striking compositions give the segment an appealing visual scheme that helps far more than hinders this play. His work is certainly superior to other, less talented directors who worked on this series, and Doniger, a writer as well as a director, knew the value of Serling's work: "In my first year directing I was nominated twice for the Emmy, and I didn't even know what I was doing! But one thing I knew how to do was pick a good script, and I refused to do others. I knew a good script would carry me until I learned how to direct. Directors who say, 'I took this terrible script and made a good film out of it' are full of it, because no one makes a good picture out of a bad script."[39]

NIGHT GALLERY #32365
Air date: January 13, 1971

1
PAMELA'S VOICE
★ ½

Written by Rod Serling
Directed by Richard Benedict
Music: Robert Prince

*Phyllis Diller in "Pamela's Voice."*
*Courtesy of Fred Wostbrock.*

Director of Photography: William Margulies
Time: 9:13

**Cast**
Pamela: Phyllis Diller
Jonathan: John Astin

*Welcome, art lovers. We offer for your approval a still life, if you will, of noise—a soundless canvas suggestive of sound. The mouth belongs to Pamela. In life, a shrieking battle-ax made up of adenoids, tonsils, and sound decibels. In death, an unmuted practitioner of fishwifery, undeterred and ungagged by what one would assume to be the Great Silencer. Some ghosts come back to haunt; others come back simply to pick up where they left off. Our painting is called "Pamela's Voice," and this is the* Night Gallery.

**/ Summary /** Jonathan descends the stairs into the mourning room, glances at the casket, and lights his cigarette. His wife, Pamela, is dead, and her hyena mating-call voice is finally, blessedly silent. Suddenly, a strident voice pierces the air. Jonathan spins around to find his late wife Pamela seated in a chair, looking, and unfortunately sounding, every inch the harpy she was in life.

First stunned, then curious, Jonathan asks how she has spent her time since her death. Destroyed any afterlives with her spiteful, wagging tongue? With relish, he admits his sole motive for murdering her was to silence her nagging voice. "Let's face it, Pamela, it's permanent beddie-bye time. The funeral director will arrive soon to convey you to the cemetery." Pamela, frowning, cocks her head at him. "You buried me months ago," she claims. "My funeral was in March. This is August." Jonathan, confused, turns to the open casket to find his *own* pale face on view. Unnerved, he refuses to accept it. When one dies, he says, one either goes Up There . . . or Down There. Pamela agrees. As an extrovert, one who likes to communicate, it is Pamela's heaven to talk . . . and as a wife-murderer, it is Jonathan's hell to listen. And listen he must as Pamela begins to unload a screeching stream of abuse. Now where was she? Oh, yes, as she was telling him just before he pushed her down those stairs . . .

And a suffering Jonathan cringes as the sweeping clock hands mark the painful passage of his eternal damnation.

**/ Commentary /** This script was one of Serling's first-season favorites: "'Pamela's Voice' is a marvelous tour de force for a performer. It deals with just people, two people, and gave me a chance to *write* for people."[40] Unfortunately, the segment didn't come off as planned owing to director Richard Benedict's wrong-headed conception of the piece.

In Serling's original script, the first sound the audience hears is Pamela's grating voice, as it should be. Benedict, however, prefaced her entrance with a bunch of ghostly nonsense—an organ sounding with no player seated, the fireplace igniting by itself, and so on—the director's ham-handed attempt to clarify for a presumably dense audience that this story is about a haunting. It is just as well Benedict never returned to direct another. His touch was not subtle enough for this genre.

Laird was not pleased with the results. And though at first thrilled to get the role, neither was actress Phyllis Diller:

When it comes to "Pamela's Voice," the one thing I always remember—number one, the very word—*voice*. John Astin supposedly killed the wife because of her voice. It had driven the man *crazy* over the years. When we were rehearsing the script, we came to the place where Pamela laughs. I laughed my terrible, raucous laugh, which was supposedly why I was hired, and the director said, "Bring that down." In other words, bring it *way* down to the point where I *wouldn't* have driven the man crazy! That's the way he made me play it.[41]

On top of reining his actors in, Benedict compounded his mistake by running over schedule—a cardinal sin on *Night Gallery*. "I don't know if he was fired, I just know that they were very unhappy with him," says actor-director John Astin. "In the production office, they weren't always open to the creative impulses in a director who might want to take a little longer on something."[42] After Laird saw Benedict's low-energy footage, an attempt was made to repair the damage. "Do you know," Diller continues, "I had to go back and loop the *whole show?* Do you know how *hard* that is? Where you go and you look at your lips on screen, and you try to match *every word* and *every laugh?* They wanted what I do naturally, and the fact that I had to do it over was because of Dick's idiot direction!"[43]

Benedict made a sizable error. For this farce to work, one of two approaches needed to be taken: the actors had to either finesse it with a bitchy elegance or go at it wide open, right off the meter. Instead, Benedict sat on his actors, resulting in muting the script's edge. "Pamela's Voice" was supposed to be *Who's Afraid of Virginia Woolf?* in miniature, and had it been in the budget, it might have been interesting to see the Burtons essay this piece. But as executed, "Pamela's Voice" is, as noted in *Daily Variety,* "a one-set talkathon . . . two unpleasant people hacking at each other for ten minutes, and it's a bore. They may have saved coin with this static offering, but they probably lost viewers."[44]

2
## LONE SURVIVOR
★ ★ ½

Written by Rod Serling

Directed by Gene Levitt
Music: Robert Prince
Director of Photography: William Margulies
Time: 20:07

**Cast**
Survivor: John Colicos
Captain: Torin Thatcher
Doctor: Hedley Mattingly
Officer of Watch (Wilson): Charles Davis
Quartermaster: Brendan Dillon
Richards: William Beckley
Helmsman: Terence Pushman
Captain (Andrea Doria): Edward Colmans
Officer of Watch (Andrea Doria): Pierre Jalbert
Quartermaster (Andrea Doria): Carl Milletaire

*John Colicos in "Lone Survivor." Courtesy of UCLA Research Library Arts Special Collections.*

*An unforgiving sea usually buries its secrets beneath itself. Warships and ocean liners, treasure galleons and submarines turn into rusting relics inside a watery locker, lost to memory. But occasionally there comes a floating unbidden reminder of disaster—like this lifeboat. The painting is called "The Lone Survivor." We'll put it in tow and see where she came from and why.*

/ **Summary** / Cruising through the fog-enshrouded North Atlantic, an ocean liner slows when the watch officer spies something on the horizon: a lifeboat with one survivor. The captain orders a rescue boat launched. Following its progress through binoculars, he is shocked to read the name stenciled on the lifeboat—*Titanic*—sunk three *years* ago. How, the captain marvels, could anyone survive for all that time in an open lifeboat?

When the survivor recovers, he relates to the captain and the ship's doctor, in convincing detail, the circumstances of the great liner's tragedy. After he finishes, the survivor seems astonished to learn that the year is not 1912 but 1915. The captain is skeptical, however, confiding to the doctor his suspicion that the man is a spy. "I know it sounds absolutely fantastic, but there *is* a war on," he says as he heads back to the bridge of his ship—the *Lusitania*.

Later, the doctor returns to further question his patient. The survivor begins to recall, with increasing dread, his place in this strange puzzle: "I'm a Flying Dutchman, doctor—made of flesh and blood and bone. Damned forever to be rescued by doomed ships." He predicts that the *Lusitania* will be sunk by a torpedo within hours. When the captain learns of this, he's convinced the survivor is a spy. The doctor, however, begins to believe that the survivor may be correct, and that everyone on board—himself, the captain, and the crew—are phantoms to people the scene of the survivor's personal damnation. The captain scoffs, but when he turns to address the doctor, the deck is empty. The doctor has disappeared. On a deck intercom, the captain attempts to raise the bridge, then the cargo hold, then the engine room. The captain receives no answer—the ship is deserted. Soon, the captain joins his lost crew.

The survivor staggers out of the infirmary to find no one aboard. Racing around the deck in a frenzy, he spies a periscope rising from the choppy waves off the starboard bow. Then, the torpedo's fanning wake as death speeds toward the doomed ship. Screaming a warning into the dead intercom, the survivor feels the massive shock wave, and then . . . oblivion.

Cruising through the North Atlantic, an ocean liner slows when a lifeboat with one survivor is spotted on the horizon. The captain, peering through his binoculars, marvels at the name stenciled on the bobbing flotsam: *Lusitania*. The captain orders his ship—the *Andrea Doria*—to change course and intercept this strange and mysterious cargo.

**/ Commentary /** Titled variously "Entries in a Ship's Log," "The Sole Survivor," and "Object on the Horizon," Serling's first draft of this segment had *six* survivors drifting in a sea of lost ships. As finally drafted, "Lone Survivor" is a tepid reworking of a first-season *Twilight Zone* episode titled "Judgment Night." In that story, the protagonist's punishment stems from his crimes as a Nazi U-boat captain, and in death he is made to suffer the knowledge of his eminent destruction as a passenger on one of the liners he destroyed, reliving for eternity the same horrible evening.

For "Lone Survivor," the visuals are sadly prosaic and televisionbound. Restricted by the spare sets, director Gene Levitt was forced to shoot the bridge and deck scenes in long master shots. "I didn't have much of a deck," Levitt recalls, "and I could shoot in one direction only. Down in the hold, all I could do was roll past cargo nets." With money tight and the usual scramble for preexisting sets evident, the best they could do was just not enough. Fog can conceal only so much, and the final effect is much like that of a filmed play. Notes Levitt, "We had a lot of trouble getting the fog effect that we wanted—thick enough to be mysterious, but thin enough so you could see. Cheapo productions, you know. We were very limited."

The performances help. Although Levitt had worked with both Torin Thatcher and Hedley Mattingly before, Canadian actor John Colicos, cast as the survivor, was new to him. The infirmary scenes, with close-ups of Colicos's ravaged and haunted face, are the most effective of the segment. "I stayed close on him because the mood has to be in his *eyes,* his *voice,*" Levitt says. "He's crazy; don't let the audience see it's

not real."[45] The performances are aided by the eerie music of Robert Prince, who
goes a long way toward concealing the segment's other shortcomings.


3
THE DOLL
★ ★ ★ ★

Teleplay by Rod Serling
Based on the short story by Algernon Blackwood
Directed by Rudi Dorn
Music: Robert Prince
Director of Photography: William Margulies
Time: 19:48

**Cast**
Colonel Masters: John Williams
Miss Danton: Shani Wallis
Pandit Chola: Henry Silva
Monica: Jewel Blanch
Indian: Than Wyenn
Butler: John Barclay

*The doll in "The Doll." Courtesy of Sal Milo.*

$W$*e move now from ships like the* Titanic *and the* Andrea Doria *to a small fragment
of history. This little collector's item here dates back a few hundred years to the British-
Indian colonial period—proving only that sometimes the least likely objects can be filled
with the most likely horror. Our painting is called "The Doll," and this one you'd best not
play with.*

/ **Summary** / Returning to his London home from Queen Victoria's colonial forces
in India, Colonel Hymber Masters finds his quiet British household in immaculate
order, save for one thing: his orphaned niece, Monica, has a new doll—a filthy, tattered, ugly thing. Monica's governess, Miss Danton, explains that the package in
which the doll arrived was postmarked India; she assumed it was a present sent by the
colonel to his ward. "The doll was never intended for my niece," he mutters. "It was
a gift to me." They must get it away from her somehow, Colonel Masters says. "But
mention nothing about intention . . . in the doll's presence."
 The colonel's hatred—and fear—of the doll is countered by Monica's devotion
to it. Monica, a lonely child, seems prone to fancies and claims that the doll talks to

her. The colonel chastises his niece for such childish make-believe, but she holds to her story. No new toy or doll that he offers to Monica can lessen her obsessive attachment to the strange gift. One night, the colonel and Miss Danton find Monica sobbing in her room with the colonel's latest gift, a new doll, torn to pieces at the foot of the bed. Standing over the mauled toy is the first doll, its small, white teeth bared—and the glittering eyes seem to focus on the old soldier.

Colonel Masters's attempts to get rid of the doll fail; somehow it always returns to Monica. His fears about its purpose are confirmed one evening by an intruder: Pandit Chola, an Indian resister whose brother was executed at Masters's order. As the colonel suspected, Chola, an occultist, sent the doll. Exiting, he offers Masters a warning: "Best remain awake, Colonel. The doll has teeth . . . and there is no medicine on earth to save you." Enraged, the man of action in the colonel finally awakens. He grabs a poker from the fireplace grate and, hearing Monica crying for her missing doll upstairs, runs up the staircase. He finds his tiny, grinning quarry staring at him from the top of the stairs.

As Miss Danton comforts her sobbing charge, a loud cry echoes through the house. The governess finds Colonel Masters at the bottom of the steps, a torn, bloody gash in his arm. The doll has done its work. Collapsing in a chair, the dying soldier directs Miss Danton to hand deliver a special envelope in his desk—addressed to an Indian name—and with it, a message: "Tell him the thing has happened."

At his lodgings, Chola hurriedly packs for his retreat when he hears a knock at the door. A messenger in Indian garb delivers a package, remarking with a smile, "Colonel Masters did not wish to appear ungracious. You gave him a gift—he reciprocates." Apprehensively, Chola carefully unwraps the package—and drops it in shock. It is a doll. The colonel's effigy is stamped on its face. Chola watches in dread as the dead eyes slowly open and the whiskered mouth opens in a hellish grin.

**/ Commentary /** There could be no more sensitive exercise for a writer than adapting for the screen an author with as refined a sense of atmosphere and effect as Algernon Blackwood. Yet Serling does so quite skillfully, retaining his own distinctive flair for language and transferring the chills intact. "The Doll" is truly one of *Night Gallery*'s most frightening tales.

Shani Wallis (*Oliver!*), in her dramatic television debut, gives a fine performance as the governess, as does veteran Hitchcock actor John Williams (*Dial M for Murder*), every inch the British soldier. The character of Pandit Chola, played with a less than authentic Indian lilt by Henry Silva, is Serling's addition to the story. His appearance makes manifest the vendetta that was merely hinted at in Blackwood's short story, giving the segment a richer subtext with its censure of colonialism.

Rudi Dorn, an Austrian director working in Canada, guided the filming. "I worked primarily for the CBC for quite a few years as a designer, producer, director, and sometimes writer. I had a friend down in Los Angeles who got me an agent. I had done quite a few half-hour shows in Toronto. They [the producers] liked what they saw, so they gave me the show."

Dorn, a guest director from abroad with little experience, found himself under a great deal of pressure. He had two days to shoot Serling's twenty-page script. "I worked like a fiend," Dorn moans. "It was all interiors, with sets struck, and walls in and out, and bang, bang, bang. It was murder." A further complication arrived with his lead actor, who had difficulty with Serling's formal, turn-of-the-century British dialogue. "John Williams didn't know his lines *at all,* and it went on forever and ever and ever," Dorn says. "He was supposed to know them Hollywood-style, because there's no rehearsal. He'd come in without lines and he'd just ride up every two seconds. I have a feeling the producers *kind of* blamed me for it. Their reception when they saw the rushes was a little cool."

Dorn's pressures continued unabated. "On the first day, the producer [Paul Freeman] tapped me on the back and said, 'By the way, Rudi, tomorrow at noon Shani Wallis has to fly to Israel. She has some prior commitments. I hope you get everything of hers in the can.' And I said, 'For crying out loud! I haven't planned the damned show that way!'" Freeman suggested that Dorn shoot all of Wallis's close-ups that day, and the next day they could dress a secretary to look like the actress and film her from behind. "Eventually Shani Wallis's part was read by my continuity girl with her voice edited out [and Wallis's looped in]; so it worked, but it was just a little mad. I'm a pretty crazy guy myself, but *that* was wild, especially in foreign territory with everybody watching you. But that's show biz, what can you do?"

Ultimately, Dorn's torments were not in vain. His supervision was exemplary, aided by the craft of art director Joseph Alves and cinematographer William Margulies, whose joint artistry evoked a sense of Edwardian opulence and gothic gloom. "I had a good director of photography," Dorn admits. "It was old hat for him, and he sort of slept in the corner and his operator did a lot of it. It was also well edited. I had no hand in it, unfortunately, but they did a very expert job"—the handiwork of editor Jean-Jacques Berthelot. Although the script was filmed in its entirety, a few of Serling's lines in the scene between Colonel Masters and Pandit Chola ended up on the cutting room floor. Later reinstated for the syndicated version of the series, the cuts sharpen the effect of the scene and prove that the original editors did a superior job of pacing each segment.

Also of note is the music score. Using a small string group moving eerily through microtonal intervals, plus a trio of native Indian instruments—flute, sitar, and tabla—composer Robert Prince weaves an aural tapestry of skin-crawling subtlety. But most effective of all is the design of the dolls themselves, a pair of hideous, truly frightening apparitions created by sculptor Christopher Müller. Müller—who, with Bud Westmore, designed the Gill-Man for the 1954 Universal classic *Creature from the Black Lagoon*—is obviously quite adept at bringing to form the things that infest nightmares.

After his manic adventure in Hollywood, Dorn retreated to his home in Ontario to work on less tension-fraught projects, such as designing the opening and closing ceremonies for the Calgary Olympics. "I haven't directed in about ten years," remarks Dorn today—without apparent regret. "The youth cult has taken over. I don't miss it a hell of a lot, frankly. There's more to life than doing shows in a pressure cooker."[46]

## NIGHT GALLERY #32362
Air date: January 20, 1971

1

## THEY'RE TEARING DOWN TIM RILEY'S BAR
★ ★ ★ ★

Written by Rod Serling
Directed by Don Taylor
Music: Benny Carter
Director of Photography: William Margulies
Time: 40:10

**Cast**
Randy Lane: William Windom
Lynn Alcott: Diane Baker
Harvey Doane: Bert Convy
Pritkin: John Randolph
Officer McDermont: Henry Beckman
Blodgett: David Astor
Tim Riley: Robert Herrman
Father: Frederic Downs
1st Policeman: John S. Ragin
Katy: Susannah Darrow
Intern: David Frank
Miss Trevor: Mary Gail Hobbs
Bartender: Gene O'Donnell
Switchboard Operator: Margie Hall
1st Workman: Don Melvoin
2d Workman: Matt Pelto

*William Windom in "They're Tearing Down Tim Riley's Bar." Courtesy of Photofest.*

*Welcome, ladies and gentlemen, to an exhibit of the eerie and the oddball. Our first offering this evening: faces. Paint, pigment, and desperation. The quiet desperation of men over forty who keep hearing footsteps behind them and are torn between a fear and a compulsion to look over their shoulders. The painting is called "They're Tearing Down Tim Riley's Bar."*

/ **Summary** / In the executive offices of Pritkin's Plastic Products, sales director Randolph Lane returns late from a mainly bourbon-and-water lunch—a common occurrence in recent weeks. His secretary, Lynn Alcott, has attempted to cover for him with company president H. E. Pritkin, but her efforts have been undermined by the backstabbing of Lane's ambitious, two-faced assistant, Harvey Doane. Doane's sabotage has extended to passing off Lane's reports as his own and denigrating the older executive around Pritkin whenever possible. As a sign of the low esteem in which he's held, Lane's twenty-five-year anniversary at the company has passed with barely a comment.

Lane is slipping and he knows it. Tired of fighting off Doane's treacheries during the day only to go home every night to a middle-aged widower's loneliness, Lane has lately taken solace in returning to the site of an old haunt from his youth—Tim Riley's Bar. Condemned, boarded, and scheduled for the wrecking ball, Lane sees in it a curious parallel to his life. He, too, is something of a relic from the past, unappreciated, on the way out, and forced to make way for faster, sleeker designs.

His visits to the bar have brought him more than bittersweet reflection, however. Yearning nostalgically for the "pre–Pearl Harbor, long summer nights" of his youth, Lane's reverie has somehow become reality. At times, scenes from his past—of his return after World War II to his fiancée, Katy; of his father and his loved ones, all long dead—are replayed within the darkened bar. These phantoms beckon to him, cheering "For He's a Jolly Good Fellow" with a welcome he's felt from no quarter in years, making his pressure-filled days at the office unbearable by contrast. Lane's focus is directed so much toward the past that he cannot sense Miss Alcott's growing affection for him.

One evening, an intoxicated Lane breaks into the condemned bar to await the return of the apparitions. He narrowly escapes arrest through the help of an old neighborhood friend, Officer McDermont, who intercedes on his behalf. Lane, desperate to remain, pleads with his old friend: "I rate something more than I've got. Where does it say that every morning of a man's life he's got to Indian wrestle with every hot young contender off the sidewalk who has an itch to go up one rung? McDermont, I've put in my time, do you understand that? I've paid my dues. I shouldn't be hustled to death in the daytime and then die of loneliness every night. That's not the dream! That's not what it's about!" Touched, McDermont offers to drive Lane home, but Lane persuades the policeman to drive him to the house he and Katy had lived in.

Left alone there, Lane soon begins to hear the familiar voices again, surfacing into the present. His reverie is interrupted by Miss Alcott, who in her concern followed him. She invites him to dinner, but he declines in respect to the difference in their ages —and the memory of his late wife. He relates to Miss Alcott the pitiful circumstances of Katy's death, of how he was on the road selling plastics when she died of pneumonia. In a desperate bid to change the past, Lane rushes up to the abandoned house and breaks in—but a less cherished memory greets him as he enters. He finds himself in a hospital corridor being consoled by an intern as his wife's body is wheeled away on a gurney—too late for good-byes. Lane, heartbroken, collapses.

Without McDermont around to help, Lane is arrested for trespassing and disorderly conduct. He arrives at work the following day to find himself out of a job. Furious, Miss Alcott stalks into Pritkin's office to take a stand on Lane's behalf, berating the executive for ignoring twenty-five years of loyal service. And to deny Lane even a kind word of appreciation—that much Pritkin *owed* him.

With nothing else to hold him in the present, Lane determines to return to Tim Riley's Bar and, this time, remain with those phantoms in the past. Upon arriving he finds that the spirits have become resigned to the passing of time. They note with sadness the eventual destruction of their beloved gathering place. As Lane tearfully begs them to stay, the phantoms begin to fade away one by one. Katy, singing a mournful "Auld Lang Syne," finally passes from view, too. Lane is left alone, despondent, in the gutted shell of Tim Riley's Bar as the wrecking crew outside prepares for the demolition.

Stricken by this abandonment, Lane wanders toward his neighborhood bar. From within, he hears a faint chorus of "For He's a Jolly Good Fellow." Drawn by the familiar and friendly refrain, he enters to find his business associates from the office waiting for him. A sheepish Pritkin, shamed by Miss Alcott, offers Lane an apology: "It occurred to some of us—your friends—that a man shouldn't have twenty-five years go by without being remembered . . . and thanked . . . and reminded that he's held in deep affection and sizable esteem. It's to my discredit, Randy, and I ask you to forgive me for not having told you this before, and more than once." Pritkin raises his glass in a toast—to Randy's *next* twenty-five years with the company. Lane, stunned by the warmth, joins the welcoming throng, and lays to rest for good the personal ghosts of his remembered past.

\*       \*       \*

Every writer has certain special loves, certain special hangups, certain special preoccupations. In my case, it's a hunger to be young again, a desperate hunger to go back where it all began. And I think you'll see this as a running thread through a lot of things that I write.

—Rod Serling[47]

**/ Commentary /** There are several points in Rod Serling's writing career when he exceeded his normal standard of excellence to produce a work of great emotional depth; when, with no particular ax to grind, he attempted to illuminate the hopes, dreams, illusions, and regrets of ordinary people. The best of these stemmed from his personal experience. Such a piece was "They're Tearing Down Tim Riley's Bar."

Serling's testaments to the human condition are, by now, well documented. *Patterns,* his play on ambition, compromise, and the sacrifice of personal principles in big business, came out of his early struggles writing for radio and television. His sympathetic portrait of an over-the-hill pug in crisis, *Requiem for a Heavyweight,* came out of his experiences in the boxing ring. In line with those, "They're Tearing Down Tim Riley's Bar" addresses Serling's struggle with middle age, his disillusionment in a career with fewer and fewer personal rewards, and his desperate hunger for days long past. A gentle, emotional exploration of human loss and expectation, the script contains some of Serling's most lyrical writing. It is no surprise that this segment drew the kind of praise Serling had received for his live dramas in the 1950s.

Randy Lane, Serling's protagonist and personal voice, has predecessors in the author's career. As author Marc Scott Zicree pointed out in *The Twilight Zone Companion,* "They're Tearing Down Tim Riley's Bar" is, in essence, the third panel of a triptych, with *Patterns* and the *Twilight Zone* episode "Walking Distance" being the first and second panels. They offer a progression of what is essentially the same character at different points of his life: Fred Staples, the ambitious young Turk climbing the ladder to success; Martin Sloan, who, having reached the top, finds the pace too crushing for his liking; and Randy Lane, the former powerhouse executive, now in reflective middle age, under siege by younger, more aggressive colleagues. All three characters hold a mirror up to Serling as he responds to the fortunes of his career: hungry young scribe; successful award-winning television writer and personality; middle-aged TV icon coming to grips with his gargantuan reputation, the expectations of genius, and his desire to distance himself from it. Randy Lane's yearnings are Serling's. The bittersweet nostalgia in every line came from some deep part of the man as he expressed an aching desire to return to the security of his cherished youth. "They're Tearing Down Tim Riley's Bar" mourns a past innocence now replaced by a growing cynicism. Although *Requiem for a Heavyweight* may always be deemed Serling's masterpiece, this triptych is perhaps a deeper and more telling reflection of the real Serling.

"The script was marvelous," says director Don Taylor. "It was a brilliant piece, really. I thought Rod put more of himself into that piece than a lot of his other stuff."[48] Taylor was an unusual choice for *Night Gallery.* A former actor, he had made the risky move to the other side of the camera in 1957. At that time, the only successful actors-turned-directors were Paul Henreid, Ida Lupino, and Dick Powell—a decidedly small fraternity. In addition, Taylor's track record, having included series episodes of *M Squad, Alfred Hitchcock Presents,* and *Burke's Law,* suggested no particular affinity for the type of fantasy *Night Gallery* embodied. With his first move, he proved his discernment: he hired William Windom.

"He was just brilliant in it," Taylor remarks. "I just slipped him in and nobody said anything, until finally they saw the rushes one day, and they said, 'Holy Jesus! Why didn't somebody tell us we had a big show here? We could've gotten a star.'"[49] Windom concurs: "I think they wanted to use Troy Donahue or one of their standard stable people, and Taylor told them, 'If you don't use Windom, you don't use me.'"

Windom gives a touching performance as Randy Lane, balancing the pathos with gentle humor. Through the cracks of his energetic facade one can glimpse Lane's wistful, battered persona. He is lonely, tired . . . and desperately seeking something beyond his grasp. By Windom's own account, it is his finest performance: "When I got the script, it was a good script. When we were filming it, it's still a good script. And when we're all through filming it, I don't know where I'm going to get a better one. I've been out here all this time, and I've liked all the shows I've done, but still that's the only one I ever bought a copy of—to show my kids when they get older what the old man used to be able to do."

As Lane's protective secretary, Diane Baker is Windom's equal. Crafting a performance of tremendous empathy and truth, she conveys with a look, an inflection, the emotional strength of this character. Baker communicates so directly that Serling could practically have dispensed with her dialogue, and the duo are superb together.

For some, William Windom especially, the filming of the climactic scene in Tim Riley's Bar was as moving as the end product: "I remember being quite amazed, because it's a fairly unemotional business [for an actor], as far as getting into the sequences of a scene. I was the last one on the set for some reason I don't remember, and so they were all ready, all these people—his father, and all his friends, and his girl. None of them were actors I had ever seen before. They all had fairly small parts. But my God! That girl—and her face, and her acting—has stuck in my mind ever since. I went into that scene and did it, and I fell in love with that girl. I didn't see her afterwards. I don't even know her name. It was kind of like a dream in itself. I'm not a guy who is easily moved, certainly not on a TV or movie set. But that really got to me."[50]

Equally affected by the filming of the scene was the actress hired to play Lane's long-lost wife, Katy, Susannah Darrow:

The show was about moving back and forth between the past and the present, and not being able to stay in another time—a *Twilight Zone* kind of time. And for me, even though I worked on that show for just half a day, it seemed like I worked on it for a week. There was a very strange, stretched-out quality to the time when working on that show.

I thought that William Windom threw his soul into that piece of work. And I did, too, in a tiny way. I think that when an artist allows a part of himself or herself to be exposed in that way, then that instant in time freezes in one's mind in a unique way. It creates an exceptional memory. And so, for me, the entire discussion of "They're Tearing Down Tim Riley's Bar" is nostalgic, but it also has a sense of being frozen in time in my mind.

The particular memories that come to mind regarding William Windom are his skills as an actor. As an actress, I found myself mesmerized by him. His voice was entrancing, like listening to music. And I remember his eyes. I figured that Katy had fallen for that vulnerability in his eyes. That kind of vulnerability takes guts, I feel. The world doesn't give you much support to hold onto that kind of sensitivity. I had a difficult time not breaking down and crying when I looked into his eyes. He was so moving.

I remember a strange instance on the set, when the director, Don Taylor, had me sing "Auld Lang Syne." I was terrified that I wouldn't sing it properly or in key! They quieted the entire stage, absolutely dead quiet, and he had me sing that several times through on this dead-silent stage. What was so bizarre was that after he yelled "Cut" and "Print," the entire crew and cast applauded! I was just taken aback, I have no idea still why they would applaud like that. It's odd to me, these fragments in time where nothing exceptional really seems to happen, but where that particular moment evokes a most unusual reaction from many people.

The assistant director came over to me after I had finished the scene and told me I could leave. I assumed that they *wanted* me to leave, so I did. I would have loved to have stayed and met William Windom. We worked together in the scene, but it's like we were other people, so in a sense I've never met him. I would've loved to have just talked to him about the art of acting and that sort of thing.

Hollywood died for me fifteen years ago when I left. I've never returned or had anything to do with it ever again. And yet, even though I was a daytime soap opera star, and worked in at least a hundred prime-time shows, that particular show still sticks in my mind over all the others.[51]

For the filming of the finale, the demolition of Tim Riley's Bar, an impression of a more destructive kind was made by a misdirected wrecking ball. "I built up this Irish pub on the back lot," recalls art director Joseph Alves.

I made this gorgeous stained glass sign with the name "Tim Riley's Bar." The wrecking ball is supposed to go right through it, crushing it. I tell the transportation guy, "Now, I need someone on the wrecking ball that's really expert at this." "Oh, yeah, we've got guys, we've got guys," he says. "Well, maybe we better bring somebody from the outside that's really a wrecker." "No, no, we've got guys." So the guy gets on and he swings the ball back and puts a hole into a brick building on the *other* side of the street. Then he swings, he misses, and he takes out part of the building *next* to it. I mean, we had holes all *over* that street, and the stained glass was perfect.[52]

Don Taylor recalls the incident: "He ruined that other set. Everybody said, 'Oh, my God, what are we going to do?' I said, 'We're going to do take two.'"[53]

One of the segment's key benefits is jazz great Benny Carter's music score. Laird knew of Carter through his work with Count Basie and his solo albums, where he is reputed, along with Charlie Parker and Johnny Hodges, to be one of the great alto saxophonists. For *Night Gallery,* Carter's work is an effective touchstone to Serling's themes: a gently nostalgic swing-band score that underlines perfectly Lane's desperate yearnings, adding immeasurably to the segment's emotional effect.

Excitement at the network over the segment spread quickly. After an NBC screening on December 16, 1970, Rolf Gompertz, a press department executive, hurriedly drafted a memo to Serling:

Dear Rod,

I just saw "They're Tearing Down Tim Riley's Bar," and justice demands that I write you a fan letter! It's an absolute gem! A thing of truth and beauty in miniature. William Windom and Diane Baker do the show honor—wait until you see Windom's performance, a tremendous job!

A few of the execs here were screening it, and I have observed and find it interesting that when something unusual and special happens on the screen, it evokes a warm, appreciative, genuine human response. This one's a classic!

Congratulations!

Rolf[54]

Serling, on viewing it, was also pleased with the result, remarking, "Windom is so gentle, so free in the part. It is rare when an actor does what the author intended."[55] In this case, Serling admitted, Windom improved on his imagined characterization. Serling placed his first call to the actor to compliment his performance. "Thanks for doing a good job, the usual nice stuff," muses Windom. "I was rather proud of that."[56] Serling's next call was not so cheery.

"The ending got screwed up a little bit," moaned Taylor. "We had a young associate producer [Paul Freeman] who did the cutting. He decided to intercut the congratulation scene at the end with flash cuts of the wrecking ball, back and forth, back and forth, which was not the way we'd planned it. Rod called me immediately and said, 'Did you do that?' And I said, 'No I didn't!' It wasn't my taste and it wasn't Rod's taste, but that's the way it ended up. It wasn't all *that* bad, nobody got hysterical about it. But the piece was better than that, to go to a 'schtick' ending."[57]

Critical raves followed its first broadcast, and "They're Tearing Down Tim Riley's Bar" received an Emmy nomination for Outstanding Single Program of the Year, the television academy's highest honor. Inexplicably, neither Serling, Windom, Baker, nor Taylor were acknowledged for their efforts.

*Los Angeles Times* columnist Cecil Smith noted this oversight with some rancor: "You look in vain through the nominations for its author, or its director, or its stars. So what you have is a show so brilliantly done that it rates in the finals for the finest single program of the year—yet neither its writing, its direction, nor its acting were worth mentioning."[58]

Universal's lax attitude toward promoting "Tim Riley's Bar," despite the opportunity offered by the Emmy nod, irked Windom: "Here was a chance to take advantage of the nomination, and I felt that they didn't give it any publicity. They didn't put an ad in the trades the way people do quite often, they just let it go—the hell with it, they didn't care."[59] Windom may have been right. The night of the Emmy gala, the top award went not to *Night Gallery* but to *The Andersonville Trial*.

Confusion over the ending of "They're Tearing Down Tim Riley's Bar" has clouded previous published accounts on this segment. Joel Engel, in his biography of

Serling, reports that Jack Laird "tagged on a pseudohappy ending," and Windom himself recalls another, different ending to the script when he first received it:

"They mushed the tag. Don Taylor said, 'We've got to do this other ending for the Tower,' or for whatever. The tag in the *original* script, the way we wanted to film it, shows the bar destroyed by the wrecking ball and my character standing on a cement slab with the rain pouring down, that's all. End of show. No last-minute rescues in that version. Lane is left as a man who can't live in the past and is unwilling to live in the present."[60]

Director Don Taylor, however, contradicts this remembrance, and believes that the play always ended with Lane getting rehired. Muddying the waters further, Susannah Darrow's recollections mirror Windom's: "My script had the more heartfelt, heartbroken ending with Lane standing on the concrete, looking up in the rain. It didn't slip from the painful memory scene inside the bar to the restaurant across the street with the other office workers. That isn't how it ended in my script—it ended with a blunt reality."[61]

Serling's papers on this segment, kept at the Rod Serling Archive, do little to clarify the issue. Serling's first draft, titled "Backward, Turn Backward," is unfinished, ending with the second act. His first revision of May 28, 1970, with the new title "They're Tearing Down Tim Riley's Bar," includes the "jolly good fellow" ending and Pritkin's apology. Other drafts followed before the finished script was submitted to Universal, but all of them have the same ending. The segment was filmed late in 1970, long after these early drafts, so if at some point the "jolly good fellow" ending had been replaced by something more downbeat, it was certainly not Laird who had scripted a new "pseudohappy" finish. The "upbeat" finale filmed is, word for word, identical to Serling's first completed draft. When Serling prepared a prose treatment of this segment for the first *Night Gallery* anthology printed by Bantam in 1971, he incorporated the filmed ending. From the evidence left behind, the author evidently vacillated over how to end the play, deciding finally to finish it with Lane's vindication.

At every opportunity Serling fought tooth and nail on *Night Gallery* to ensure that his scripts were not tampered with. Although he was not able to protect his work on a few occasions in the second season, his first- and third-season scripts are, for all practical purposes, untouched. It seems unlikely that he would have capitulated to a bastardization of his original thoughts, particularly on *this* script, without some scrap of paper being left behind to document his displeasure. The piece as it stands can be considered his final version.

Although "They're Tearing Down Tim Riley's Bar" would not be the only summit *Night Gallery* reached, it would be considered by many the key significant episode in the series—perhaps rightly so. It is certainly the most poetic, moving, and personal script Serling wrote for the show, and as such deserves its accolades unreservedly.

2
## THE LAST LAUREL
★ ★

Teleplay by Rod Serling
Based on the short story "The Horsehair
    Trunk" by Davis Grubb
Directed by Daryl Duke
Music: Robert Prince
Director of Photography: William Margulies
Time: 8:56

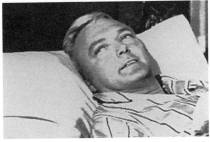

*Jack Cassidy in "The Last Laurel." Courtesy of Sal Milo.*

**Cast**
Marius Davis: Jack Cassidy
Susan Davis: Martine Beswick
Dr. Armstrong: Martin E. Brooks

*W*elcome, art lovers. We offer for your approval a painting which has to do with what happens to men who take a walk into nature's marketplace and exchange certain powers for other powers. The blind we're told, for example, develop an extraordinary sense of touch. In this case the story of a man who perfects the art of killing. Our painting is called "The Last Laurel."

/ **Summary** / Decathlon champion Marius Davis, crippled in an automobile accident, lies bedridden. He suspects that his doctor and his wife, Susan, are involved in an affair. Having developed his mental powers to an extraordinarily high degree, he can, while asleep, project and train his astral body to travel in the physical plane, to even lift and hold physical objects. Scheming to avenge the perceived adultery, he lures his doctor from town during a violent thunderstorm so that he will have no choice but to stay the night. While asleep, Davis rises from his bed in astral form, takes a pair of shears from his wife's sewing basket, and heads toward the bedroom of the sleeping physician. Davis loses the shears during a particularly violent crash of thunder and lightning, and blindly substitutes a weighty metal candlestick. He enters the room and with one stroke crushes the skull of the sleeping figure. Savoring his triumph, Davis begins to laugh, then stops short. The darkened room is illuminated by a sudden flash of lightning: it is filled with trophies. *His* trophies. In dread he regards the battered figure—the bloodied, lifeless form of Marius Davis—and fills the house with his silent scream.

/ **Commentary** / On its initial broadcast, "The Last Laurel" played first in the lineup. For the hour's rerun, meant to showcase "They're Tearing Down Tim Riley's Bar," the segments were reversed—the order in which they remain to this day. The last episode to be filmed, this entry was a hurriedly prepared fill-up for the "Tim Riley's Bar" hour. Unfortunately, "The Last Laurel" was nowhere near as distinguished as its neighbor.

Jack Cassidy, on the downhill side of middle age, little resembles an award-winning decathlon star. Further, his performance is theatrical and overstressed. "It wasn't necessarily his fault," says director Daryl Duke, "but to my taste, Cassidy came on just a bit too strident, too strong, for today's style. But it had to be almost Victorian melodrama to carry it off. He had so little time to get it across, we had to work in broad strokes. We may have made him a bit *too* broad, but it was a question of finding believability—or the suspension of disbelief."

Additionally, the astral body special effects are too primitive to sustain the audience's "suspension of disbelief." Cassidy's transparent form is jarringly out of sync with the sets through which he is supposedly moving. Recalls Duke: "We shot the scenes of his spirit floating around against a black backdrop, which were superimposed over shots of the empty set to give him a ghostlike appearance. It was tricky trying to get a lot of that stuff right, even though it didn't take up that much screen time."[62]

The dictates of logic fall by the wayside in the script as well. Davis's astral self can pass through doors, but he also manages, inexplicably, to tote along solid objects—a plot hole of distracting proportions. In the original short story, Davis Grubb's "The Horsehair Trunk," the killer slips the murder weapon, a knife, beneath the bedroom door before passing through it himself. Once inside, he picks the knife up and commits the deed.

Apropos of this, minor script changes were made in an effort to appease the network. In Serling's original conception, Davis uses his weapon of choice—the sewing shears. Correctly gauging NBC's response to such a gory display, Serling later replaced the shears with a more acceptable instrument of murder, a candlestick. The change matters little. "The Last Laurel" remains one of Serling's less effective essays.

On February 3, 1971, Serling was prodded by NBC to return the six suits provided for him by a Philadelphia clothier for shooting the introductions. Serling, instead, went about trying to purchase them. As it turned out, he was going to need them for the next season. On the strength of its ratings and the prestige of the Emmy nomination, NBC announced on February 24 that *Night Gallery* would be renewed as a nonrotating, individual series in its own time slot.

# 7
# A Maverick Little Island

*Night Gallery* is a bit more ambitious [than *The Twilight Zone*]. It is more flexible since we are not bound by the half-hour format. The first fifteen shows are incredibly diverse, ranging from tongue-in-cheek to foot-in-grave.[1]

—Rod Serling, NBC Press Release

*Night Gallery,* spinning off from the constraints of the rotating *Four in One* wheel, now had its 10:00 P.M. Wednesday time slot all to itself. Having successfully fought off CBS's *Hawaii Five-0* in the previous season's ratings war, *Night Gallery* would now do battle with *Mannix* on CBS and *Man and the City* on ABC.

For the rest of the series' run, the man whose imprint is to be found most distinctly on it is not Rod Serling, but Jack Laird. Everything up to the point of production required his approval: casting, set and costume designs, scoring, cutting, and, most specifically, scripts. Despite this hovering, Laird allowed the artisans an enormous amount of latitude on the creative aspects of the show, and they thrived in this unfettered environment.

Jack Laird's youthful staff reflected his willingness to give breaks to the inexperienced over proven veterans. *Night Gallery* became an incredibly rich and varied training ground for a handful of untried, eager filmmakers, giving them access to the expertise of skilled studio craftsmen and top-rank acting talent. It was their first chance to shine creatively in a studio environment, and they made the most of it.

Where Laird stepped out of the picture almost entirely was during the physical production. His main concern was the writing, over which he maintained complete control and for which he had both a deft hand and a critical eye. For the first season, which comprised only six shows, the writing was predominantly Serling's. Laird, however, wanted *Night Gallery* to be more than just a showcase for Serling, and the second season reflects Laird's view.

Assembling a short list of writers with whom he had worked in the past, Laird began farming out some of his favorite tales for adaptation. Like Serling, Jack Laird was an inveterate fan of the gothic tale genre. "Jack had an enormous flair for finding material," recalls director Jeannot Szwarc. "There were a lot of short stories that he used from terrific writers, Lovecraft and people like that. Most of the scripts came from short stories which had an enormous literary quality."[2]

Laird's desire to produce classic genre fiction proved to be a time-consuming affair. To assist with securing rights to the published material, Laird enlisted Herbert

Wright, a fresh Yale graduate on loan-out from Universal's Business Affairs office. "I started with Jack trying to put together the stories," recalls Wright. "We were buying stories that had been printed in *Weird Tales* magazine in the twenties. I had to track down the author, who oftentimes was somebody living in a dilapidated flophouse in Portugal, and offer him five hundred bucks for the rights to it. Universal wouldn't pay anything, but this was the most money some of these people had seen in years."

Tracking down the authors of these obscure, almost forgotten tales became a full-time job for Wright. "I had a foot in the [Universal] Tower and a foot in the bungalow for about three months until I formally made the move over to Jack's. It reached a point where *Night Gallery* was taking so much more of my time than the other shows I was supposed to be working on that I went to Jack and said, 'I'm either going to have to give it up, or you have to put me on the show.'" Sizing up the young Yale grad, Laird hired him on the strength of his thesis film and a sample of his writing. "I always loved that kind of tale anyway, the fantasy-horror tale, so *Night Gallery* was the perfect transition for me."[3]

Scouring his shelves, Laird was often guided in spirit by the hand of the tireless anthologist August Derleth. His 1946 collection *Who Knocks?* produced "The Phantom Farmhouse" and "The Dear Departed," and the original stories from which were adapted "The Painted Mirror," "Death on a Barge," and "Last Rites for a Dead Druid" came from a 1947 August Derleth anthology, *The Sleeping and the Dead*. Other sources included the annual horror anthologies published in England by Pan Books. Their 1966 edition produced "A Feast of Blood" and "I'll Never Leave You—Ever," while "A Question of Fear" and "Hell's Bells" were inspired by stories from the 1970 Pan edition.

In a 1972 interview, Laird explained his rationale for rummaging through these horror compendiums: "I like to borrow from the classics for two reasons. First, many of the stories I like personally, and second, you're almost sure they will work. If a script writer fails with a story idea, you just pass it on to another writer. Someone will do it right and come up with the spirit of the original source material. I knew the stories were solid and would hold up because they did in their short story form. They had to be meaty or they would not have stood the test of time. I merely had to make certain the visuals—and not visuals in the ordinary sense—could be created by our special effects department."[4]

Serling, although collaborating with Laird over source material early on, was finding stories to adapt on his own. A 1969 Alfred Hitchcock anthology, *Stories That Scared Even Me*, yielded two of Serling's best adaptations, "A Death in the Family" and "Camera Obscura." From *The Third Fontana Book of Great Horror Stories* came his scripts for "Green Fingers," "The Academy," and "Something in the Woodwork." Laird encouraged Serling's contributions by sending him photocopies of short stories, which he could choose to adapt or reject. The field was so rich with adaptable material that

Laird knew he could produce *Night Gallery* for seven years straight without interruption or searching for new story twists.

"Material is always the problem in television, and in this genre it is virtually inexhaustible," Laird remarked. "Not only do you have tens of thousands of stories from specialists in this field, but almost every great writer of fiction tried tales of the supernatural and the mysterious at one time or another in his career. Writers you don't associate with this kind of story tried them—Kipling, H. G. Wells, Ambrose Bierce, Lord Dunsany. We're making poet Conrad Aiken's short story, 'Silent Snow, Secret Snow,' and also a story by his daughter, Joan Aiken.

"The British are masters in this form—Victorian mansions, ghostly footsteps, foggy streets. But there's also such an enormous body of American fiction that there's a publishing house, Arkham, in Sauk City, Iowa, devoted to nothing else but these kinds of stories, and its catalog of titles is a thick book in itself. Aside from an occasional original story by Rod Serling, we plan to do only adaptations from this massive body of work."[5]

Laird's evolving concept for *Night Gallery* was the cinematic analogue to these short story anthologies: a collection of tales that, in their diversity of moods and styles, even their sequencing, reflects an editor's taste. Variety, not consistency of tone, would be *Night Gallery*'s hallmark under Laird—a condition that would cause the show to be criticized for "not knowing what it wanted to be." For better or worse, *Night Gallery* began to reflect the taste of its producer.

## THE FORMAT

*Night Gallery*'s structure was unique, unlike anything else on television at the time. Each show had from two to four tales of varying length within the broadcast hour. The finished scripts were pretimed and juggled by Laird to fill the sixty-minute time slot. This odd format freed the writers from the Procrustean bed of having to fit the stories into a pre-set, inflexible time frame, padding or cutting for such considerations. The length of each piece was dictated by the internal logic of its narrative, not by the need to squeeze the plot in between commercial messages. Although this splintered format has been adopted since (notably in the resurrected *Twilight Zone* series in the mid-eighties), the concept had its first trial on *Night Gallery*.

"I'm probably the only man who really knows the definition of a *Night Gallery*," commented Laird.

And yet, I'm not really able to define the show in words. It's a gut reaction to a story. It's strictly a subjective experience. At first, Universal indulged my whims about the show with some hesitation, but now I think they trust my judgment about content. The studio may be able to object to a particular script, but no one can tell me what a *Night Gallery* is.[6]

Conceptually, what I'm trying to do on *Night Gallery* is something that, to my knowledge, has never been done before on TV. Namely, within the space of an hour we have as many as five different segments of varying lengths. Some work better than others, but I think it is a true anthology, rather than a different story every week. There's no format, no style for the series as such. To separate the men from the boys, I encourage directors to treat each segment as an entity. Each [story] has to be explored in terms of its own needs, not the needs of the series.[7]

Although Laird and his staff tried to keep the rotation to three segments per hour, timing complications often arose to mess up an intended grouping of segments. Scripts assembled for an hour-long slot had to time out exactly before production. "It was like constructing a puzzle," Wright says.

You've got one that you expected to come in at thirty minutes; then you realize it's going to play better at, say, thirty-six minutes. So the one that was going to be seventeen minutes had to be cut to twelve minutes, and the blackout that was going to be three minutes all of a sudden had to be two minutes. It was that kind of craziness going back and forth, because if you added or dropped a scene from one of the scripts, each of the others had to change, too. So we'd have three different directors going on three different sets, and we'd be racing from one to the other with script changes. It was insane.[8]

The broadcast sequence of the segments is not a reflection of the order in which they were filmed. Laird often reassembled the segments for timing considerations. "That was just another of our tricks," remarks unit manager Burt Astor. "On any other hour show, a regular forty-eight minute show, if you ran fifty-four minutes, you'd have to cut. On *Night Gallery*, we'd shuffle the stories for broadcast so that we'd never have to cut. *Night Gallery* was unique in that sense, being made up of two to four separate plays per hour. I mean, we had shows with scripts that ran, like, half a page, so it was very peculiar."[9]

Jack Laird's script contributions to *Night Gallery* were mostly brief comic vignettes. Only once did he turn his hand successfully to a study of fear. His primary contribution to the show was script editing and producing, and from this all-encompassing perspective his work can best be appreciated. The quality of material he selected and the consistency of talent he hired—and the level of ambition these choices revealed —show him to be a gifted producer. "It was called *Rod Serling's Night Gallery*," notes director William Hale, "but I would say Jack was really 95 percent of the talent behind that show."[10] Director Jeannot Szwarc, a friend of both Laird and Serling, concurs: "In truth, Jack deserves a lot of credit for whatever quality *Night Gallery* may have had."[11]

Aside from Serling—who wrote more than a third of the teleplays—and a short list of occasional freelancers, Laird also enlisted the efforts of a full-time writing staff: Herb Wright, story editor Gerald Sanford, and Laird's unofficial right-hand man on *Night Gallery*, Gene Kearney. With a hefty supply of scripts ready early on, Laird, Kearney, Wright, and Sanford worked to revise them to the producer's standards for the show—an arduous process, according to Wright: "Jack had me revising the moment he discovered I could write, because he was crazed to make changes. He would be making changes right up to the moment they got shot, and sometimes I would be literally carrying the pages down from the typewriter to the set. The first [full-length] season in particular he was constantly fine-tuning and honing, and he had a good ear for it. Unfortunately, though, all the scripts had to go through Jack's typewriter, even if he was just retyping the other guy's script. He would oftentimes type the whole script over and make about five changes."

In the world of the Hollywood feature, writer attribution on scripts with more than one contributor is a complicated issue. Individual cases are often arbitrated by the Writers Guild to decide which contributors will receive on-screen credit. A more arbitrary set of rules, often regulated by producer fiat, applies in the world of television. "In my experience," Wright says, "some producers have a policy where, if you're on staff, even though you rewrite the freelancer's entire script—it's all yours, there's not one word left of the other guy, you can *change* the fucking story—but if that freelance guy had the original assignment, he gets the on-screen credit. So looking back at TV credits, if it's a staff writer's name on a script, good chance is they wrote it. But if it's a freelancer, maybe they wrote it and maybe they didn't, but for sure somebody else's hands have been on it."[12]

Although Wright, Gene Kearney, and Gerald Sanford toiled equally at the revision mill, only Sanford received story editor credit on the series. Sanford was new to Hollywood. At the time he was hired for *Night Gallery*, his only other credit was a short stint on the nine-hankie prime time soap opera *Peyton Place*. Young and inexperienced, Sanford's first encounter with Jack Laird left him feeling creatively dispossessed: "When I first got to the show, Jack gave me a script of Rod's and said, 'Rewrite it.' So I went to my little office, rewrote it, and turned it in. But there was a condition. He said, 'It's good, it'll go this way, but you realize if you try to get screen credit, I'll have to let you go.' And even though we had a strong guild at that time, I was a kid, it was my first staff job, and I was just happy to be working. So I agreed. And it used to hurt."

From then on, Sanford's view of events place him at the source of the show's creative font. "Basically, for the time I was there I wrote 50 percent of the scripts that were on the air," Sanford claims.

I wrote four or five myself, but then I rewrote almost everything. Almost everything that Rod had his name on, I rewrote extensively. The way it would work, Rod was committed to write about half of the scripts, mostly originals. Rod would send in scripts that he had written overnight. He would just BOOM, write 'em and send them over by messenger, and that was it. If it were a fifteen-minute episode, he'd write forty pages, far too many. They were just very freewheeling, almost unusable at that point. Then either Jack or I would rewrite them.[13]

Taking these statements point by point, Sanford's remembrances prove to be somewhat distorted. From the evidence of Serling's scripts as they were submitted to Laird—fourteen during Sanford's tenure on the show—Sanford can truthfully claim extensive work on only two, perhaps three, of them. Of the scripts he worked on, the only fifteen-minute episode among them was "The Different Ones." Serling's original was twenty-two pages long, not forty. As for the scripts being freewheeling and unusable, though Serling did not format his work to the current standard at Universal (with every shot numbered and listed), he did describe suggested camera movements. Beyond this, the only aspect of Serling's writing one can take exception to is the occasional tendency of his characters to speechify. In need of trimming, maybe. Freewheeling and unusable? Hardly that.

Herb Wright, Laird's assistant, can put most of Sanford's hyperbole into perspective:

It wasn't necessarily that everyone was racing around trying to rewrite Rod, we were just trying to make it fit. For the first *Four in One* episodes, we had to tailor the scripts to a new form that really hadn't been done before. We were trying to make two or three scripts fit into one hour, and it fell upon Jack to make those decisions on cuts. Basically, production problems and time considerations were the reasons for script changes.

Nobody fucked with Rod's stuff all *that* much—Jack would've been the only guy that dared do that at first. I can't remember Jerry Sanford taking anything of Rod's and violently changing it all that much, you know what I'm saying? Jerry might like to think he rewrote a lot of Rod's stuff, but Rod did okay all by himself. He really didn't need any help.[14]

Sanford's stay on *Night Gallery* was short. His dislike for Laird and his diminishing interest in the show gave him the impetus to jump ship. He found a more comfortable home on the staff of Quinn Martin's stolid bureau mouthpiece, *The F.B.I.*

Looking at the evidence, it would be difficult to ascribe to Sanford all that he claims for himself. He well may have done a tremendous amount of work on the show, but he certainly had no major hand in revising Serling. How much work did he do on others' scripts? With the proper documentation lost to time there is no way of telling. However, with Serling's creative output, including his original drafts, well documented at the Rod Serling Archive, Sanford's exaggerations on that score make suspect his other claims on the series as well. With his own scripts, "The Flip-Side of Satan," "The Tune in Dan's Cafe," and "Tell David . . ." barely passing muster set against the work of his colleagues on the show, it cannot be stated with any firmness that his contributions to *Night Gallery* were at all distinguished.

## SERLING VS. LAIRD

"Rod was a trip-and-a-half, man," laughs Anthony Redman, Laird's postproduction assistant. "Rod was one of the most beloved guys. I don't think you'll ever hear somebody say bad things about him—except, of course, Jack. If Jack were still alive, he would've. They didn't get along."

Almost from the beginning, the relationship between Serling and Laird was strained, but it didn't become serious until late in 1971 after the series began its second-season run. "Rod didn't feel like he had enough input in the show, but he still had to do all those bumper lead-ins and voiceovers," Redman says. "And Rod would always be calling to complain at just the wrong time. They were two very volatile guys."[15]

Serling's contract called for him to write and to host. Beyond that he had no official title, although he assumed his position as creator of *Night Gallery* would ensure his ability to okay script and casting decisions. Laird was not inclined to have his power usurped, however, and was willing neither to defer nor to allow interference with his concept of the show. Used to a high level of creative control on *Zone*, Serling was not prepared for the demotion, as he must have seen it, within the power structure of his own series. "I thought I had [control] at one point," Serling said in a Dick Cavett interview, "until the phone didn't ring for several weeks. And then I kept wondering, 'When are they going to ask *me*?' And they never asked me. They've been very nice, very good-hearted and warm, and very unhostile. But unfortunately, that doesn't come with creative control."[16]

"The network was selling *Rod Serling's Night Gallery*, so they wanted Rod Serling," explains Herb Wright. "Rod, however, didn't want to be on the front lines anymore. On the other hand, he wanted his opinion down. Rod liked to see himself as the captain in absentia with his name above the title. Jack liked to see himself as the captain on the fantail, steering the ship. So there were some fights going on over that."[17]

Laird was the prime mover on *Night Gallery*, and yet the media attention focused almost exclusively on the famed dramatist. Upstaged by Serling, Laird's resentment grew. "Jack guarded his power very jealously," recalls actor and Laird family friend James Metropole. "He wanted *Night Gallery* to be all his—it was his baby. He thought of Rod Serling as just a figurehead. They weren't friends."[18]

Complicating the issue, Laird privately disliked Serling's lyrical, dialogue-driven writing style. "The only writer Jack ever mentioned in all the time I knew him was Rod Serling," remembers Burt Astor, production manager on *Night Gallery*. "He said Rod's scripts were too long and slow and had to be cut down."[19] Writer Alvin Sapinsley was even closer to the source: "Jack once confided to me that one of his main problems in producing the show was to persuade Rod Serling not to write any scripts for it. Jack was a very impatient person most of the time, and he didn't suffer fools easily. I know he would get very impatient with Rod and probably for good reason."[20] Whether this remembrance illustrates the producer's frustration at Serling's proprietary attitude toward the show or is, as it sounds, a broadside at the man's talent, Laird was obviously becoming less of a Serling fan as the second season wore on.

Serling was not happy with Laird's concept for the series, either. Laird's introduction of short, comedic vignettes into the mix of serious stories struck him as perverse; neither did Serling see eye to eye with the producer on script and casting choices; but their clash reached critical mass over script changes. Although it is common in television to have a freelance writer's script entirely reworked by the writing staff of a series, Serling was not just another freelancer and he rankled at the perceived affront to his work. Fiercely proud, and with scores of awards and accolades for validation, Serling fought for his work and his vision. Laird fought back.

"When Jack would talk to a writer about a script, he didn't pull any punches," Jeannot Szwarc says. "It was not that he was insensitive, he just told it like it was. When I first met him, after a while I sorted out that it was not meanness of spirit or lack of heart, it was just that, for him, it was a job. He was ruthless with his *own* scripts, too. 'This is too slow, this has got to be cut out.' So once you understood that, it worked just fine, but a lot of people were hurt."[21]

Serling was not alone. Recalls Laird intimate Jerrold Freedman: "Before *Columbo* had gone to series, [creators Richard] Levinson and [William] Link had a very bad time with him. They wrote a script once that Jack was producing and he didn't like it, so he rewrote it. And they never spoke again."[22] Laird's integrity made him few friends.

"Rod didn't know what to do with Jack," admits Wright. "Jack was always a little irritable because he couldn't *really* go rewrite Rod's stuff"—not admittedly, at any rate. "Rod hardly ever got sent copies of final drafts so that Jack wouldn't have to have conversations with him. Rod and Jack would have an argument about something, Rod'd think he'd won, and then he'd see Jack's version on the air."

Serling had been sent Universal-prepared shooting scripts for the segments he wrote, all of which conformed to the final drafts Serling submitted. Revisions made afterward by Laird and his staff were never forwarded. On the premiere nights of those altered segments—particularly grievous in the case of his scripts for "Midnight Never Ends" and "The Dear Departed"—Serling was entirely unprepared for Laird's sleight of hand. The confrontation was not long in coming. "Those two were pretty high-powered, hot-tempered guys," recalls Wright. "That door used to shake a bit when I'd pass by. Oh yeah, they were *into* it."[23]

During this period Serling's complaints about the show began to surface in the press. In an interview with Marilyn Beck published in the *Los Angeles Herald–Examiner* on November 14, Serling expressed concerns about *Night Gallery*'s extremes of quality, its casting, and—of course—the script changes:

It's spotty and inconsistent. I'm delighted to finally have a show that's doing so well in the ratings. I wish I could be just as delighted over the quality. Values are so distorted now, money's so tight. It would be so much better to use the cash improving the quality of the show instead of frittering it away on name guests.

Sometimes I even have to battle over my own rewrites. But I understand NBC's problems. They probably don't need another chef in the production broth. And I'm such an insane perfectionist I could drive us all nuts. Still, it's hard to remain detached. That show goes on the air as 'Rod Serling's Night Gallery' and when a segment's bad it's my reputation that's at stake.[24]

Although most of his scripts got to the screen untouched, by the holidays Serling was, to say the least, frustrated. "Suddenly, I'd look at a *Night Gallery* film and I couldn't recognize my own script," Serling railed. "People weren't there that I wrote about. Lines were said that I didn't write. Concepts were produced which I had no knowledge of. I couldn't ever find out how or where it had been changed or who did what. And, typically, nobody would admit to not liking my words. I could only sense that they didn't want the more thoughtful, cerebral items."[25] Getting no satisfactory answers from the production office, Serling took his complaints to the executive front at Universal—again to no avail. "When I complain," fumed Serling, "they pat me on the head, condescend, and then hope I'll go away."[26]

Eventually, Laird stopped accepting Serling's calls altogether. The embittered six-time Emmy winner found himself locked out of his own series. Laird must have gotten the message, though. Except for "The Different Ones," a segment already filmed, Serling's work for the rest of the season got to the screen virtually untouched. In all, only four of his thirty-five scripts for *Night Gallery* had suffered revision by other hands.

Serling's experiences battling sponsors and network executives in his early years did not prepare him for the kind of backdoor ouster that he received on *Night Gallery*. It left telling scars. "You must always assume that the relationship between writer and producer is that of adversaries—however you slice it," offered Serling in his last interview in 1975. "They may be your dearest friends, and they'll invite you to dinner, but when all the smoke clears and the ozone lifts, your enemy is the producer. That's the guy you're competing with, and you have to battle him just as if you were an adversary."[27]

Laird left Serling to deal with either Herb Wright or more frequently Grace Cursio, Laird's secretary. "Rod would call me just to commiserate," recalls Cursio, "because he said I was the only person there at Universal that he could communicate with. He was very frustrated, but still a sweet, lovely man with a wonderful sense of humor. I don't know why Rod and Jack never hit it off. Maybe a little bit of professional jealousy—who knows? I don't know if there was any on Rod's side. But it never resolved itself. It was that way until the very end."[28]

As personalities, the two were poles apart. Serling was a gregarious, personable man, ready with his broad smile and flashing, self-disparaging wit to make friends with practically everyone. Although quick to anger, he knew the benefits of diplomacy. "Rod had enormous charm," says Jeannot Szwarc, "but he was also very sensitive—not just in his writing, but on a *personal* basis—which people who knew him may not have always realized. There's no doubt that the guy had a very intense inner life. On top of all that, he knew how to talk to those executives, even though he knew they were total imbeciles. He knew how to handle them."[29]

Laird, by contrast, was an exceedingly private, insular man, a loner by choice and temperament. His dealings with anyone outside his tightly drawn personal circle were

brusque to the point of rudeness. Laird's complicated persona and undisguised mis-
anthropy precluded the kind of studio politicking designed to advance him personally. Most producers tried to maintain a good relationship with the executives who
paid their salaries—lunching with them, glad-handing, back-slapping and chatting
them up—a practice Laird could not stomach. And he often took pains to incite their
conservative outrage with some very bizarre behavior.

"Jack was one of the most talented men I've ever met," says Szwarc. "But he was
the worst at PR, he was never 'one of the boys.' Rod was a much more charismatic,
easygoing, warm kind of man . . . and Jack was this big fruit fly on the wall. I mean,
he showed up at a party once on the tenth floor dressed up in a Roman toga, for God's
sake! He was a very weird guy, a real character. But if he'd had the personality, he
would've conquered that town."[30]

Professionally, again the two had little in common. Laird's scripts were meticu-
lously polished from countless hours hunched over his typewriter, and his work habits
often kept him at the office long into the night. Serling, on the other hand, had a distinctly jet-set work ethic. He worked roughly three to four hours a day, dictating his
scripts poolside, punching up the draft his secretary typed up, and submitting it as a
finished piece. Serling's seemingly casual regimen may have engendered in Laird
some resentment—perhaps because Serling, respected by the industry and the winner of multiple awards for his work, was such a facile, inspired, almost effortless
writer of quality. His Dictaphone habit may have seemed to Laird a disrespectful approach to the craft of writing in comparison to Laird and company's efforts.

"I find dictating in the mass media particularly good because you're writing for
voice anyway," Serling explained. "If it sounds good as you say it, likely as not it'll
sound good when an actor's saying it. The tendency when you dictate is to overwrite,
because you're not counting pages. You don't really know what the hell the page
count is."[31]

This appears to have been Laird's biggest difficulty with Serling's scripts. On occasion, Serling would submit thirty-five pages when thirty were needed. Laird, out of
courtesy, would then have to call him up to discuss cuts—something the producer
was loath to do. On a few occasions, Serling's submissions would raise stickier issues
—questions of attribution.

"Rod was a wonderful guy," chuckles Wright. "He had read a lot of the classics in
his life, and he had the unfortunate habit of submitting stories that, later, turned out
to be by Robert Louis Stevenson or Edgar Allan Poe and not realizing it. Jack would
come in screaming, march over to my desk, slap the script down and say, 'You've got
to tell Rod that he can't do this without giving credit to Robert Louis Stevenson,' or
whoever it was."

Next came the diplomatic dance with Serling in a bid to encourage him to give
credit to the original author, "like he was doing *hommage* to the masters without step-

ping on his toes," continues Wright. "So I'd have to call Rod and say, 'Jack just read your script and thinks that there may be some kind of, uh . . . *similarity* to *Masque of the Red Death* or *Fall of the House of Usher*,' or whatever it was, and Rod would go, 'No, no, that's mine! That's mine!'" Wright would then point out the plot similarities, to which Serling would, at length, sheepishly concede, commenting wryly, "'Well, okay, but I did it *better*.'"

"He was very funny about it," laughs Wright, "but it wasn't like the guy was saying, 'I'm going to rip off Jules Verne this week.' I mean, in this business who *hasn't* done that? George Lucas walks around claiming *The Searchers* was his inspiration for *Star Wars*, so who knows?"[32]

To their credit, both Laird and Serling were careful not to run each other down publicly. Even those close at hand were not always aware. Recalls Jeannot Szwarc,

I was very close to both and I never saw any direct evidence. I never saw Rod directly say anything bad or negative about Jack in front of me. I heard a lot of rumors about that, but I never saw an open explosion between the two of them. [The stories] may have been exaggerated. I mean, at one point or other, we *all* had arguments, because when you put creative people together, differences *will* occur. Occasional friction can even be an essential part of the collaborative process. A lot of the conflicts between Rod and Jack, though, may have had to do with Jack's personality, which *was* eccentric.[33]

Ultimately, the power jockeying between Serling and Laird ended in a stalemate. Serling never gained any creative control on *Night Gallery* and Laird never succeeded in shoving Serling into the background. One can only wonder what they could have achieved had their relationship been less contentious and more cooperative. The whole fiasco is best summed up by Laird's secretary, Grace Curcio: "Jack had one idea of the show, and Serling, obviously, had another, and they just never came together."[34]

## THE EXECUTIVE PRODUCER

Laird's working relationship with the other writers on the show was mercifully less fractious. Most admired Laird's keen eye for plotting and characterization. "The man was a consummate artist, one of the few I've ever met," affirms Alvin Sapinsley (dramatist of "Pickman's Model" and "Last Rites for a Dead Druid"). "His judgment in picking out flaws in writing was exquisite, and his suggestions for new directions the story and characters should take were impeccable. He was the only authentic genius I encountered in all my years in the industry. I found him wholly impressive."[35]

Writer-director Jerrold Freedman ("Marmalade Wine") shares Sapinsley's praise of Laird. "He was really fantastic at analyzing a story. He would send you a set of voluminous notes when they drafted your script, very precise and detailed, and his notes would sometimes be as long as the script! Jack Laird was the Selznick of television."[36] Rightly, Laird saw the script as the basic unit of quality necessary for good television. He focused on his typewriter—and his skills as a "fixer" among Universal producers was legendary.

"He was brilliant," says Jeannot Szwarc. "Whenever they had a script that needed to be rewritten in a hurry, or whenever a pilot was in trouble, this guy could rewrite a pilot over a weekend. I've seen him do it. They would take a pilot that was really a piece of shit, give it to Jack, and he would come back three days later and it was something else. He had a real eye for what was important, what the conflict should be, so there was never really any fat. He really was a tremendous writer."[37]

Beyond his grudging visits to screen the dailies, there was precious little that could get Laird out from behind his desk—including meals, sleep, and the companionship of his family. "Jack was always in his office, buried behind a mound of scripts, his typewriter attached to his fingers," says director John Badham.

He was there virtually twenty to twenty-four hours a day. He never went home. I had an all-night shoot once and I was going home at 5:30 in the morning on the Universal back lot, and I saw this creature in the bushes. I realized, oh, my God, it's a man. It's a huge, naked man. It was Jack Laird. He had taken off all his clothes at five in the morning, was out in the bushes at a hose bib, and he was sort of taking a bath. He had spent the night there, probably fallen asleep, gotten up and said, 'What the hell, I'm already here, I'll just go back to work.' Of course, I drove on quickly and didn't embarrass him.[38]

So focused on writing and story editing was Laird that any interruptions, even those involving production problems, were unwelcome. "If anybody came to coordinate or something," Cursio says, "they'd say, 'Jack, can I get a minute with you?' And he'd say, 'Don't sit down, you're not staying long.' He was only being honest, but it was a little off-putting."[39]

Laird decided early in the production of season two that the constant stream of interruptions—production questions, actors dropping by for a chat, the numerous minutiae that are the normal territory for an executive producer—could not continue. According to Herb Wright, Laird felt he was falling behind: "Jack couldn't stand it anymore, people coming in with what he thought were inane questions, so he had a sign made up."[40] Time and distance have blurred the exact wording, but in essence the sign warned anyone who approached not to bother him while he was working, he was far too busy, and that he was not interested in anyone else's problems. "It was really long," recalls actor James Metropole. "It was a coupla, three sentences. It didn't just say, 'Stay out, bums,' but that's what it meant."[41]

"Then there was a threat at the bottom," says Wright, "basically, a threat to one's life. The sign was three feet tall and two feet across, framed in glass, and fixed to the outside of his office door. He wanted to let you know right away that he didn't give a shit, just stay away from him. I had the office across from him. People would come and stand at the door and read that sign, look a little confused, and I'd see Grace kind of point toward my door." Wright would either handle the question himself or, if the outcome were critical, would wait for Laird's emergence. Then, says Wright, "he'd tell me what to do and I'd go down to the set and handle it."[42]

"He was a brilliant man, but a bit of a hermit," Cursio notes. "None of us really knew him all that well. I probably knew him better than most." Now working with producer Stephen J. Cannell (*The Rockford Files*), Cursio was Laird's secretary for fifteen years, from the mid-1960s through 1980. "He was not a man you could get very close to, and you didn't really question him a lot because he was very private. He had a few good friends, but very few. He was very selective, a loner, so people worked with him but not too intimately."

So tight and controlled was Laird's world that his office doubled as his living quarters, with shelves for his music and film collections, his library, plus a refrigerator and a hot plate. "He'd bring in groceries and cook in the office," recalls Cursio. "Around five o'clock you'd smell the chili starting to cook and he'd have his five o'clock drink. I tried to get out of there by six—he started to get a little surly the more he drank. But underneath it all he was a kind, sweet man, he really was. He was just a very troubled man. No one could get to him."[43]

Despite Laird's insularity, in the evenings after work he enjoyed the company of a small circle of friends and associates. "Usually a small group would always meet in his office at night," recalls Szwarc. "He had all those jazz records and all those books, and I loved it 'cause he could talk about Jean Renoir and French films of the thirties for hours. But he was a very heavy drinker."[44] Vodka was Laird's drink, and his indulgences often began before the five o'clock whistle. "Jack was a major booze hound," recalls production assistant Anthony Redman. "Oh, man, this guy was bad! Everybody would go in there and tie one on with Jack, you know? That was part of the job, to drink vodka with Jack and shoot the shit."[45]

Heavy drinking at the studio was not news. Neither was the more flamboyant dress code in the 1970s. Laird went further down this road than most, however, roaming the conservative halls of Universal in all sorts of bizarre regalia, from fringed suede jackets to deerstalker caps to leisure suits (equipped with the standard footwear of the '70s, platform-heeled alligator shoes). Robed in such stylings, coupled with his height and his excessive girth, he cut quite a swath through the studio. "Jack loved to terrorize the proper," recalls former Universal executive Ralph Sariego. "One story they told about him many years ago, when he had an office in the Tower: this is a very conservative place, and he'd go running around up there scaring people in his bearskin coat. One time he upset somebody, and they just decided he didn't fit their image, so they banished him to one of the bungalows."[46] For a man who preferred to keep others at arm's length, Laird's wardrobe won him far too much attention. His experiments in style even extended to the changing colors of his gull-wing Mercedes.

"We had a guy that we'd give bit parts to once in a while," Redman says. "His name was Larry Watson. Larry was really well known for being one of the premiere auto painters in Hollywood. He was the guy that introduced pearlescent and metallic paint jobs to the stars. I had this Fabergé egg color Porsche, Jerry Freedman had his MG painted this very special purple, and Jack had this gull-wing Mercedes that he would change colors on once a year. Larry did all the paint jobs. The perk for Larry was bit parts, small roles and stuff like that. He was a dreadful actor but a great guy. Everybody got a paint job from Larry."[47]

Cycling repeatedly through Laird's professional career are countless acts of generosity, giving breaks to struggling artists both new and established. "Jack was really generous about starting people out," notes friend and associate William Hale. "He wasn't afraid to stick his neck out and use a new director, and it's murder trying to get started. Jack started Sydney Pollack and Mark Rydell, Spielberg and John Badham, and on down the line."[48]

Laird's generosity extended as much to sharing his interest in cinema as producing it. His knowledge of film history was encyclopedic, and he preferred screening movies with his cronies to making them. "He had one of the biggest private collections of film I've seen," Jeannot Szwarc affirms. "As a matter of fact, he was the first person I met in L.A. who had *seen* a silent film. I was shocked when I started working in the industry. I mean, I talked to people who had never seen a Carl Dreyer film, never a Griffith film, never any of the Chaplin silent films, and they didn't even realize how *fantastic* those films were, how rich, how revolutionary, nothing. But Jack did, boy— he really knew."[49]

Laird was a rabid collector of vintage movies before archiving became the trend, and he used his position at Universal to secure copies of hundreds of rare films for his library. His collection spilled over from his home into his office at Universal, and racks had to be brought in to accommodate their growing numbers. "Jack was a total cinephile," notes Tony Redman. "We had a scam going where we were going to remake all the great horror films, so it was an excuse for Jack to expand his collection. We were running every film we ever wanted to see, ran up an outrageous projection-time bill, and never made a single goddamned movie! But man, we saw some films. . . ."[50]

The "scam" was a project called *Out of the Darkness,* what Laird envisioned as a series of television features inspired by the horror film classics of the past. One of Herb Wright's first jobs under Laird was researching this project, finding and ordering prints of hundreds of old movies going as far back as the work of Lon Chaney and German director Paul Wegener. Laird then had copies struck from them for his library. "We were tracking down films all over the world," says Wright, "Czechoslovakia, the Russian Institute. Lots of them were lost films. The project never really got off the ground. What it did do, however, was greatly enlarge Jack's film collection."

Part of Laird's endeavor was selfish—he wanted the films in his collection—but another part of it was a conscious act of preservation. Before anyone in the industry thought that film had any life beyond its initial distribution, Universal still had warehouses full of films on crumbling, flammable nitrate stock. Wright, while still in the Business Affairs department at Universal, dealt with a request from the Library of Congress to acquire copies from the studio archives for the National Collection. Wright had a meeting with Universal vice president Taft Schreiber on the subject. "The meeting didn't last long," Wright recalls. "He told me as far as he was concerned, once those films had made their money, they were veritable trash. They'd been using the old nitrates for years at M-G-M and Columbia for fire effects, unreeling old movies and burning them. So Jack was not involved in the piracy business, he was simply involved in the preservation business. Jack really cared."[51]

Laird was understood only by those who shared his passion for the arts, cinema, and music. A few of his staffers and associates saw through the troubled persona to the dedicated artist beneath. To most—even his family—Jack Laird remains an enigma. "There were people who didn't like him, and they were legion, I'm sure," says Laird associate James McAdams, "but in this business, most people think you're whatever persona you create, and never go beyond that facade. Jack created the image of a very private, curmudgeonish kind of person who could be very distant and mean, and I knew differently. He cared a great deal about people, he really did."[52]

Whatever opinions are held of his personal problems, agreement is reached by all on the man's intellectual brilliance and his devotion to his craft. Perhaps this is the only fair perspective from which his life can be viewed. "He's a fascinating subject," Cursio avers, "but I don't think you could *ever* get the full story about Jack Laird."[53]

## THE DIRECTORS

Jack Laird's initial concept for *Night Gallery*—a different director for each segment—proved to be unrealistic and was abandoned in the second season. Instead, supplemented by the occasional hireling or novice, Laird drew from a small handful of regular directors. A few of them springboarded from involvement in another Laird series, *The Psychiatrist*. Jerrold Freedman, coproducer and writer on that show, directed several *Night Gallery* episodes, and Jeff Corey, like Steven Spielberg, got his shot at *Gallery* episodes from his work on *The Psychiatrist*. John Badham would also get his start here, and Jeannot Szwarc, who had been struggling throughout the 1960s to get behind the camera, would develop from *Night Gallery* a reputation as one of Universal's most imaginative directors, ultimately helming twenty-two series segments.

"It was a very ambitious series," comments Szwarc.

Of everything I did at Universal, *Night Gallery* was by far not only the most exciting thing but the *only* production where there was really an attempt to do something creative. God, we did interesting stuff. The material had a literary quality. When you looked at the scripts you got on other shows, my God, you'd have to work on it and work on it. Then you'd get this script from *Night Gallery,* and it was like reading poetry. And we had terrific people, a team: Spielberg and Badham, great cameramen, a terrific crew, the art direction and costumes were fantastic, everything was first class. But it proves that it's not all money, because we certainly didn't have the budgets and the schedules we should have. In a way, I think it forces you to be more imaginative, when you don't have it all on a platter. When I look back, I'm absolutely astounded at the overall quality compared to most of the stuff I see today. At least we didn't take the audience for a bunch of idiots.[54]

In his native France, Szwarc received a master's degree in International Political Science from Hautes Études Commerciales ("a Grand École with quite a repute," says Szwarc, "the froggy equivalent of Harvard"), with a course of study leading to the diplomatic corps. His interest in theater and cinema drew him away from his studies, however, and while in college he saw an estimated 250 films a year. Szwarc worked on documentaries before emigrating to the United States in the 1960s. His passion to direct was thwarted by his outsider status, being both a foreigner and having never attended a film school. He met Jack Laird while working as an associate producer on the last season of *The Chrysler Theater,* where they forged a bond based on their mutual passion for film history, jazz music, and dark fantasy literature. Szwarc followed in the same associate capacity on *Ironside* before finally landing a directing job on the series. A period of freelancing came next, but he didn't hit his stride until *Night Gallery.*

"Jack knew I was nuts about *The Twilight Zone* and Rod Serling's work," Szwarc says. "I loved *Night Gallery,* it was like home to me. I had a natural affinity for the show. In French literature at the end of the nineteenth century was a genre called *fantastique.* I had a feeling for that kind of stuff, anything that had to do with atmosphere, that was a little bit absurd or a little strange, I loved it. I think I wound up doing some of my best work on that series."[55]

His associates agree on that point. "He was my little fucking hero," declares assistant director Les Berke. "A brilliant director. I probably assisted him more than I assisted anybody in those years, and it was a real pleasure. I adored the little crud."[56] Editor Larry Lester concurs: "This man really knows what he's doing with a camera. I respect him as much as Spielberg, in that they both know how to shoot *exactly* what they want. Jeannot has an instinctive talent for directing."[57] Laird evidently agreed. After screening the dailies for "Class of '99" and "A Death in the Family," Laird commandeered Szwarc's studio dance card, getting him out of other assignments so that he could work full-time on *Night Gallery.*

*Jeannot Szwarc and Geraldine Page on the set of* Kojak. *Courtesy of Jeannot Szwarc.*

Another fledgling who proved his directorial mettle on *Night Gallery* was actor Jeff Corey. He brought his performer's instincts and role-researching thoroughness behind the camera to refreshing results. Helming ten of the segments, Corey was second only to Jeannot Szwarc in defining *Night Gallery*'s distinctive style, and guided some of the show's best moments.

Gene Kearney was another heavy contributor as both writer and director. His pre-*Gallery* scripts—the kinky chiller *Games,* and the weirdly original Laird-produced telefeature *How I Spent My Summer Vacation*—showed a talent for complicated plotting and exploding audience expectations. Kearney's profile on *Night Gallery* was considerable, writing eleven segments and directing nine.

A New York City native and a Harvard graduate, Kearney made commercial and technical films for M.I.T. and El Al before coming to California in the early 1960s. Laird took an interest in Kearney, and their careers shadowed each other from their work on *The Chrysler Theater* until Kearney's untimely death in 1979. On *Kojak,* they would continue with arguably their best work writing and producing. Although Kearney's work as a director on *Night Gallery* has moments of inspiration, writing was his forte.

Laird himself occasionally directed. Although most of his segments were vignettes, his two full-length segments, "A Question of Fear" and "Pickman's Model," exhibited a facility behind the camera that ranks with the best directors on the show. Strangely, however, considering his former stage work, Laird was not an actor's director. His concerns never took him into the area of wet-nursing a performer unsure of a character's motivation.

"I was over at Jack's house," recalls actor James Metropole,

and he screened one of the shows he directed ["Pickman's Model"]. Afterward, he asked me what I thought of Brad Dillman's performance, and I told him it was very good—I used a lot of acting school method bullshit to describe it. So I said, "What did *you* think of it, Jack?" And he said something to the effect, and I'm paraphrasing, "Well, I liked Brad Dillman because he came in with a finished performance and didn't ask any dumb fucking actor questions." That was him—Jack was all business. He was from the school of directing where you hire an actor who knows what they're doing and stay out of their way. He was more concerned with directors. And he was always having problems finding the right director and complaining like crazy.[58]

Laird never tolerated any laxness in the physical production end. If a director failed to deliver a show on schedule, he was almost invariably fired. Admittedly, the schedules were impossibly short, usually three days to shoot a half-hour segment. If a director's shot menu included too many complicated camera setups, he ran the risk of lagging behind and incurring Laird's displeasure. Additionally, the producer had little patience with what he perceived as insubordination. "I had to fire John Badham—*twice,*" laughs Herb Wright.

There was no question, Badham had the record for firings, he was way out in front. John had the peculiar habit of saying, "Yeah, yeah, yeah, yeah," to whatever the producer said he wanted on film, then John'd go out and shoot whatever the fuck he wanted to shoot. At the dailies the next day, you'd watch these producers go apoplectic. They'd look at him and go, "Wait a minute! We talked about . . . I can't believe this . . . look what he's done!" And that'd be John.

I kept saying to Jack, "God, look at this footage, isn't it great? Wouldn't you want to have him back?" Jack would hire him again, and John would do something he didn't like, and Jack would say, "Why the hell did I listen to you? Go fire him."[59]

Badham's work, like Jeannot Szwarc's, moves between gothic fantasy and gritty street drama, and he is a fluent hand at both. Aside from *Night Gallery*, his strongest work includes such impressive telefeatures as *The Law* and *Reflections of Murder*. Badham has moved from television into features, but his early work should not be ignored.

*Night Gallery*'s main core of directors, though quite different from one another, all have one thing in common: they beat the clock to produce distinctive work in an unforgiving medium. "Television is a great way of learning your craft," Szwarc points out, "because you have to make decisions very quickly, and hope the decisions are right. You have to be strong on concept, since there's no time to try things and change your mind later. Television is really the art of walking away. You're never going to get a scene perfect; it's impossible. What you have to do is be realistic and say, 'This is the best we can get.' But you *can* do good work."[60]

*Night Gallery*'s premise attracted a number of directors who worked outside the Hollywood system as well. Timothy Galfas, an independent filmmaker from New York, was enlisted for three episodes, and Rudi Dorn, an Austrian designer living in Ontario, got his green card just in time to direct a classic *Gallery* segment, "The Doll." In a tantalizing "what-might-have-been" scenario, Herb Wright managed to get interested responses from such distinguished European directors as Alain Resnais (*Hiroshima, Mon Amour*) and Andrzej Wajda (*Ashes and Diamonds*). As proof of the Hollywood film community's insularity, when Wright approached Universal executives with this information, no one there knew of Resnais's or Wajda's work and quashed further overtures.

Executive myopia was evident at NBC as well. When Wright suggested trying to secure Laurence Olivier for a *Night Gallery* segment, the network refused on the basis that the great British actor had no "TVQ"—a rating system determining a performer's "value" for the American television audience. Fellow Brit Laurence Harvey was similarly treated. When the international star of *Room at the Top* and *The Manchurian Candidate* expressed interest in Serling's script for "The Caterpillar," Wright and Laird had to go to the wall at the network to get Harvey approved.

"We were trying to get feature writers and feature directors," says Wright. "I mean, a lot of what they are doing on [the cable series] *Tales from the Crypt* frankly echoes what we were trying to do and *did* do on *Night Gallery*."[61] A more liberal viewer appreciation for the fantasy genre, currently more respectable than it was in 1971, has enabled the producers of both *Crypt* and Spielberg's *Amazing Stories* to woo feature directors to their shows—not always to either series' benefit. The fraternity of filmmakers with a thorough knowledge of both the literature of *fantastique* and its cinematic history is small, but from the evidence, it would appear the core directors on *Night Gallery* had an exceptional understanding of the requirements of the genre.

## THE PRODUCTION

While frustrations were common at the executive level of the show, on the set the director and crew were practically free of creative restraints. *Night Gallery* had no series star to dominate the set, dictate protocol, or demand creative changes. Jack Laird, except for his occasional stints as director, rarely visited the set, entrusting the responsibility for the physical production entirely to unit manager Burt Astor and art director Joseph Alves.

Yet the artistic freedom that came with producing a weekly multiple-story anthology series brought with it a furious burden of work. To keep up with the relentless pace of production in the second season, Alves and Astor developed an unbroken momentum that amounted to a frantic scramble. "I sometimes did twenty-five sets a week," Alves recalls, "and I had two decorating teams and a lot of draftspeople going."

In the early stages of preproduction, Laird would give his art director a stack of scripts "even before directors were assigned, to see if they were possible to make," recalls Alves. If a script was feasible, then planning and building of sets started immediately, "weeks before we actually shot the episode. This was unheard of in television. We weren't even budgeted yet on some of the shows."[62]

Because of the efficiency of the crew in handling the show's myriad difficulties, the strict studio control that was a constant in other productions was mostly absent in *Night Gallery*'s case. It was Universal's orphan show, something of a conceptual oddity, and was not greatly understood by the Powers That Be at the studio. "Universal was never too excited about the show," notes Astor. "We got away with a lot of things because they were so busy, and *Night Gallery* was *so* oddball. I was told by an executive one time, 'Don't bother me with your problems, we don't understand them. Just go do it.'"[63] Happily, *Night Gallery* was allowed to fend for itself and it thrived creatively in this environment. "We all knew that we were sort of like a maverick little island within the system," notes Jeannot Szwarc. "All the people involved with the series were fanatic about it."[64]

Under Jack Laird's governance, a director's biggest enemy was time. There were occasions when, to meet a production deadline, Laird would have two directors on one set at a time: one finishing a segment while the other was waiting to take over the filming of another. Costume and makeup departments were crowded with actors, some dressed in outlandish costumes, giving the set the backstage feeling of a Broadway musical. Dozens of special effects men scrambled around the stage, some concerned with an episode that would be filming until the lunch break, others with the afternoon episode.

"Now this stuff is all done *very* quickly," director John Badham notes, "and with Jack breathing down your neck because, God forbid, if you got behind schedule you were fired. And you couldn't *avoid* being behind schedule because all this stuff was effects and tricks. It was a nightmare to get it done on schedule. The one-minute blackouts typically were shot between 7:30 and 10:00 in the morning, totally unrealistic. Usually something like that would need an entire day, but a television shooting schedule meant ten pages of material a day—ten pages come hell or high water, no matter what. So you were flying along through this stuff."[65] Concurs Szwarc: "It was grueling—I mean, *Night Gallery* was a *cemetery* for directors. We had to direct some shows in one-and-a-half *days*. But for me it was the most exciting thing ever."[66]

"There were bets that we couldn't stay in production," Laird was quoted in an interview. "But contrary to those beliefs, we're the only show that hasn't shut down because of technical difficulties. I attribute this to the crew. They have a great attitude about the work, and everyone has fun with the show. There's nothing static about shooting it. Therefore there's a little more enthusiasm about the problems we encounter."[67]

"It was a wonderful three years of my life," says assistant director Ralph Sariego, "because we had constantly stimulating, interesting material. We didn't suffer the normal bane of television production where you have some maniacal writer-executive producer, which Jack wasn't. Jack was a very modest man—you know, 'I do my job and you do yours.' He was shy; he would come down to the stage occasionally and he would literally hide behind the flats and just peek. When he would call and complain to Burt about something, Burt always had the same line: 'Jack, this is not an exact science, what we're doing here.'"[68]

The crew's remembrances of their work on *Night Gallery* are overwhelmingly positive, and even disasters are recalled with an element of humor. Despite the whirlwind pace, the crew cared about the quality and took what time they could to do their best. "As an assistant director, it's 'let's go, let's get the next shot, let's move on from here,'" Les Berke says. "Some of us did that, and some of us did a little more. If I saw a scene that was really bad and I thought maybe the director missed it, I would quietly suggest he do it over again. Assistant directors are not supposed to do that kind of thing, really. But I did, and I know I wasn't the only one, because we cared. Maybe our name was somewhere on the product, maybe it wasn't, but we did care about what we were doing."[69]

## THE CINEMATOGRAPHERS

One of the striking aspects of *Night Gallery* is its feature-quality photography, for Laird enlisted the services of a handful of brilliant cinematographers. Visually, the series had a handsome, textured look, a vivid, richly hued palette, and the dark, baroque "feel" crucial to the genre. To sustain the ever-important atmosphere of each segment, Laird tried to limit scripts with exteriors to ensure that the cinematographers could maintain tight control over lighting and staging. "We did a lot of fancy stuff with Curly Lindon and, later, Jerry Finnerman," Jeannot Szwarc says, "going for interesting effects, incredible shadows, and German Expressionistic things which one did not get a chance to do on other shows."

*Night Gallery*'s first season boasted the impressive work of Emmy winners William Margulies (*Have Gun Will Travel*) and Richard C. Glouner (*Columbo*), setting the tone for the series. For the second season, Laird scored a major coup by securing the talents of veteran Academy Award–winning cinematographer Lionel "Curly" Lindon. His curmudgeonly, hard-drinking exterior masked a poet of light and shadow, and his compositions are steeped in glowing colors. Although many of his coworkers comment ruefully on his legendary irascibility, their opinion is always balanced by a large measure of awe and respect at his accomplishments.

"Curly understood a lot of things that went beyond lighting," says Szwarc. "Curly Lindon understood concept, and I always maintained that he would have made a first-class director. His one God was competence, and if [as a director] you didn't know what you were doing he was not the kind of cameraman who would help you. He had the reputation of eating young directors for breakfast, and he hated any form of authority. But he loved his work, he was great at it, and the crew would've walked through fire for him."

Lindon's history in cinema ranged back to his work operating the camera on Cecil B. DeMille's original silent version of *The Ten Commandments* in 1923. Lindon won two Oscars in the 1950s for his stunning black-and-white photography on *I Want to Live* and the Todd-AO color extravaganza *Around the World in Eighty Days*. "Curly Lindon was brilliant," Szwarc says. "He literally made [the career of director] John Frankenheimer. When you look at *The Manchurian Candidate,* one of the most gorgeous black-and-white films ever made, the whole opening scene where Laurence Harvey's being brainwashed, where the set changed back and forth [from reality to Harvey's perception of reality], all that was Curly Lindon's idea."[70]

"He was one of the best," notes director John Badham. "A most clever man and, like a lot of the old cameramen, he knew the tricks. He had to do stuff on the set, in-camera, and sometimes he'd forgotten tricks he hadn't used in twenty-five years. Then he'd say, 'Oh, yeah, I remember how to do this.'"[71]

One trick he pulled off for director Gene Kearney was for "House—With Ghost," where actor Bob Crane had to appear to be speaking to the restless spirit of Bernard Fox. With little money for postproduction lab effects, Lindon created the illusion by scrounging a piece of highly reflective glass to use as a mirror. With Crane on one side of the frame, the glass was angled on the other side to capture the transparent reflection of Fox, just out of camera range, to appear as if the two were talking to each other face to face. These kinds of tricks saved *Night Gallery's* budget on numerous occasions.

Along with Lindon's speed and skill came a brutal temper goaded by drink. "He terrorized me for a substantial period of time," recalls Ralph Sariego. "I never did figure out how to deal with him. If we got the right assistant cameraman, we were okay, because he'd start to water Curly's drinks early on and we'd get through the day."[72]

Hard-bitten, ill-tempered and enormously talented, Lindon's presence proved to be a baptism by fire for many of the young people who worked on the show. Without meaning to, he mentored more than one artisan on the set. "Even though Curly Lindon was just a mean, crotchety old guy, I learned an awful lot from him," admits art director Joseph Alves, "not just about walls behind an actor, but about texture and tone and shadow. It was worth the abuse."[73]

*Night Gallery* was to be Lindon's last work in the industry: he died of cancer midway through the second season, and it is illustrative of his professionalism that all of his work on the show was produced during his struggle with the disease. *Night Gallery's* distinctive visual profile continued with the superb work of Lindon's colleagues, Gerald Perry Finnerman and Leonard J. South.

As camera operator, South worked with Alfred Hitchcock under cinematographer Robert Burks during the 1950s and 1960s, and was full director of photography on Hitch's last, *Family Plot*. South's work as camera operator included classics such as *North by Northwest* and *To Catch a Thief*. As his interest in globe-hopping location shooting dwindled, he returned to Los Angeles to work on series television.

Alongside South, the other cameraman to take over after Lindon's death was Gerald Perry Finnerman. Before becoming a full director of photography, Finnerman had operated camera under some of the legendary Hollywood cinematographers: Harry Stradling, Sr. (*My Fair Lady*), Ted McCord (*Rio Bravo*), Russell Harlan (*The Hanging Tree*), James Wong Howe (*The Old Man and the Sea*), and Philip Lathrop (*The Days of Wine and Roses*). After a plane crash in 1969 in which he alone survived, Finnerman vowed never to fly again—a serious curtailment of his feature work. He has since then focused almost entirely on television, and his fine work can be seen not only on *Night Gallery* but also on *Star Trek*, *Kojak*, and *Moonlighting*. Ten Emmy nominations speak for his excellence, and he won for the telefeature *Ziegfeld*.

Finnerman came on board after difficulties arose between Laird and Charles Straumer, another cameraman who had been contracted for the show. "Charlie was a superlative cinematographer," Finnerman says of his Emmy-winning colleague.

"Unfortunately, a couple of things happened. One is, Charlie didn't want to run a school for directors, and that's what it involved sometimes. We had a lot of young directors on *Night Gallery*. Sometimes when you'd explain to them why a shot wouldn't work, they'd do it their way anyway and wind up trapping themselves. Charlie didn't quite have the patience sometimes and he would let 'em know. Sometimes I did, too." The second incident involved crossed signals between Straumer and a lab assistant over instructions for developing the footage from an exterior night-time shoot. The lab botched the job, underexposing all the footage. Straumer was fired. "He took the brunt for something that really wasn't his fault," Finnerman says. "He was screwed."

Laird next called on Finnerman to take over *Night Gallery*. "I told Jack I couldn't do any better job than Charlie was doing, but Jack said it was more attitude than cinematography. He felt *Night Gallery* would be a challenge for me, as much as *Star Trek*. Jack was a *Trek* fan, and he wanted that kind of look on *Night Gallery*—not the colors, but the cross-lighting."

A gourmet cook and wine connoisseur, Finnerman brought his aesthetic sensibilities to bear on the series, remaining as principal cinematographer until the show's cancellation. "It was a joyful experience," notes Finnerman, "and one I embellished with gusto. The nature of the stories tuned to my lighting and vice versa." Finnerman considers the art of lighting an almost musical endeavor, and sees strong parallels between the two forms of composition. "I've always approached the dramatic that way, something you sit down and 'listen to,' like Tchaikovsky or Beethoven or Wagner— that sort of charisma."

In his early thirties at the time, Finnerman brought to the series a darker, film noir sensibility, quite different from Lindon's vibrant hues, and well suited to the shadowy world of *Night Gallery*. His photography on such segments as "The Waiting Room," "Deliveries in the Rear," "The Sins of the Fathers," "The Caterpillar," "The Return of the Sorcerer," and "Rare Objects" ranks with the finest work of his career. Finnerman attributes the high quality he achieved to the enormous freedom allowed him. "I could do anything I wanted and I did. I had a wonderful crew—we were all about the same age and were not afraid to 'go for the effects!'"[74]

Finnerman, however, was a forceful personality, and it was not always an easy transition. "Jerry was a very exacting perfectionist," recalls Herb Wright. "He got into constant tussles with Jack. Jerry had a phenomenal wine cellar, and Jack really liked wine, so it saved him from being fired many a time. A bottle of wine at the right time and place . . . good move. And I got some wine, too, so it worked out fine!"[75]

Despite the occasional conflict, Finnerman's work is critical to the look of *Night Gallery* and, along with Lindon, South, and Margulies, defined its distinctive visual stamp. In a series that gave as many breaks to green directors as *Night Gallery*, there is no undervaluing the help given them by their directors of photography, all of whom brought enormous experience to the set.

## MAKEUP AND SPECIAL EFFECTS

*Night Gallery's* logistics were complicated by the special nature of the show. To have time to develop special effects and equipment—crawling hands, statues with recognizable faces—scripts were required weeks ahead of the actual shooting date. Actors who needed to be fitted for special makeups had to be contacted long in advance, and then also be available for shooting.

Bud Westmore, makeup artist for *Night Gallery's* brief first season, was a legend at Universal Studios for more than twenty-four years. He specialized in monsters and other complicated makeups in such features as *It Came from Outer Space*, *The Creature from the Black Lagoon*, *Man of a Thousand Faces*, *Spartacus*, and *The List of Adrian Messenger*. Westmore moved to another studio before *Night Gallery's* second season began, so new department head Nick Marcellino assigned Leonard Engelman and John Chambers for the rest of the series. Engelman apprenticed at Universal on *The Munsters*, and since *Night Gallery* he has done feature makeup on *Cat People*, *Ghostbusters*, *The Witches of Eastwick*, *Batman Forever*, and *Batman and Robin*. While Engelman dealt more with the physical application, Chambers was in charge of the makeup production lab where the foam and rubber appliances, contact lenses, plastic clamp-on teeth, and other special makeups were created. Chambers won the first Academy Award given for makeup in 1969 for his work on *Planet of the Apes* (coscripted by Serling), and, out of four Emmy nominations, won for the television special *Primal Man*.

On *Night Gallery*, Engelman and Chambers were given a great deal of autonomy. For the nonappliance makeups, Engelman had design authority:

If we were at a point where we felt that something was going to be so involved that we had to have a drawing, then we would contact Jack, and Tom [Wright] would draw up something. But, other than the ones he directed, Laird really wasn't involved in the look of the characters. We pretty well went from what the script said.[76]

Because TV budgets don't really have huge amounts of money, oftentimes we would use appliance pieces that had really been designed for something else. We might use a nose from one film, and a chin from another film, and then create from there. But in some cases, like "Pickman's Model," that one, of course, was completely designed.

Time was as big an enemy to creativity as the budget. Engelman would prepare the makeup for a segment shooting in the morning, leaving it at some point to his assistants to go back to the lab and oversee work needed for another segment to be shot that afternoon. "The work was all-encompassing. With *Night Gallery*, the two-minute vignettes might be even more overpowering workwise than some of the fifteen- or twenty-minute segments because of the complicated characters that would be devised for the vignettes."[77]

Other problems arose from the need to design a makeup around a given actor's facial or body structure. "Some of the scripts would come out three days before [shooting], and so, many times, the people weren't even *cast* until three days before—maybe the night before. It was a chewing gum and baling wire show in a lot of cases."[78]

For all the restrictions, Engelman and Chambers created some memorable work for the show, culminating in an Emmy nomination for their creation of the ghoul makeup in the "Pickman's Model" segment. Although they lost to Frank Westmore for his work on the telefeature *Kung Fu,* the honor was a particular high for Engelman who, at twenty-eight, was the youngest makeup artist ever nominated.

The makeup art form for fantasy films was in its relative infancy then. The great leaps made in makeup design, materials, and techniques in the intervening years since *Night Gallery* make their efforts now appear quaint. "At the time, *Planet of the Apes* was state-of-the-art, a magnificent achievement," Engelman says. "If you look at it now compared to today, it's crude. So there are different states-of-the-art depending on the decade. You have to see these things within the context of their time."[79] Their work, for its time, was truly sophisticated, and acted as an inspiration for others to come, as Engelman discovered later when he met makeup artist Rob Bottin, of *The Howling* fame: "When we met, I told him, 'Rob, I've admired your work for such a long time. I really think that you've done such great work.' And he said, 'Well listen, I've always wanted to meet you because you did *Night Gallery.*'"[80]

Although the budget for special effects was never large, Universal had at their disposal production wizards who had been with the studio since the early days. "That's why *Night Gallery* looks so damned good," claims Herb Wright.

We drew upon the expertise of guys who had worked on the original *Frankenstein.* Those guys were *still there*—ancient, but still there, and they'd know how to do things with mirrors that would now be achieved by expensive opticals. They had all these tricks they'd been using for years, with pull-away sets and painted wax foreground cutouts. There were no video effects or computer tricks in those days, and we had horrible production problems to solve with no money, so we'd have to figure out how the hell to do it. You'd be sitting there spinning in a circle, pen in hand, trying to figure out how to change something to fit the budget, when some old guy'd come over, spit out some tobacco, and say, "You know, when I worked for James Whale back in '31, here's what we did about that. In fact, I still think we got something in a box back at the office. Lemme go see and I'll come on back." And sure enough, he'd find something down there, so for about a buck and a quarter we'd accomplish something that we thought was going to cost us fifteen hundred bucks. Those guys were the brain trust of Hollywood. They've replaced them with computers and video effects, but everything now costs so much more than it has to because none of the new guys know any of the old tricks. It's a lost art, like the Tibetan bells that nobody knows how to make anymore.

Achieving top-quality special effects presented a raft of difficulties, but they were nothing like the problems that arose when dealing with the network. Laird and Wright fought regularly with NBC over the "acceptability" of some of the more controversial elements of the show—and sometimes the very nature of the show itself. "NBC didn't have a fucking clue what we were doing," says Wright.

As associate producer, I had to take the shows over to the network to get them approved. I'd be sitting in the screening room with a guy like Herb Schlosser, the NBC vice president assigned to the series, and he'd say to me, "What just happened there? A moment ago he was outside—why is he in the living room?" I'd say, "He walked through a wall." And he'd say, "Well, how could he do that?" "Because he's a ghost, sir." "Why doesn't he use the front door?" "Because he can dematerialize, pass through walls, and come out the other side." And he'd say, "That's ridiculous. No one's going to believe that." "Well," I'd say, "this has been an acceptable part of fantasy for the last couple thousand *years,* sir." "Not in *my* house, it isn't!" I mean, we'd have these kinds of fights. It was just insane.[81]

Herb didn't understand fantasy, didn't understand horror, and was totally lost. He was very, very literal about the whole thing. It drove Jack and me and Rod Serling up a tree. Rod would have to make special calls to explain to Herb when I was incapable of convincing him, say, why someone could fall in love with a mermaid. Because [Schlosser would say], *"There are no mermaids!"* We had violent fights. Several times I left the network and figured that I'd never work again because of a position that I had to take on behalf of the studio and Jack and Rod on some of the shows.[82]

## POSTPRODUCTION

During *Night Gallery*'s first season, production executive Paul Freeman was in charge of postproduction. When he left for another position, Richard Belding, the head of the editorial department, promoted a raw assistant editor, Anthony Redman, into his place. Under Laird, Redman had enormous authority for one so young: he picked the editing staff; designed opticals and montages; directed second-unit photography (including the insert shots of Tom Wright's paintings used after Serling's intros); oversaw the looping and dubbing of dialogue and the recording of music; designed the trailers ("next, on *Night Gallery*") with editor Leon Ortiz-Gil; and even dealt on occasion with the network.

"I grew enormously," Redman says. "I was just a kid assistant, and I was thrown right into the maelstrom. It was an incredible experience for me, because these were far beyond my normal schlepper duties. It gave me a thorough background and solid understanding of all the postproduction stuff, and Jack gave me total latitude."[83]

Redman started with a fresh staff when he took over. The only editor invited back from the first season on a regular basis was Jean-Jacques Berthelot. For the second season, much of the cutting and pacing was the work of two men: Larry Lester and David Rawlins.

"They had a couple of other editors to start," Lester says, "and then they called Rawlins and me in because they weren't 'getting it.' They just didn't understand Jack's concept for doing this type of stuff." Like the other creative branches of the show, the editing staff enjoyed unusual freedom and was given carte blanche to create wild optical effects that had never been attempted before.

The editors assembled a first cut for the director if he was available. After incorporating his changes, they ran the segment for Laird, who made the final changes. "Rawlins and I would sit there and put a whole show together," notes Lester, "and we usually did all the editing ourselves. Jack didn't mess around with the editing too much with us. Once he'd seen a first cut, he'd usually say, 'Well, that's a hole in one. Ship it.' He trusted us, you know? Sometimes, when we had to turn a show over the next day, Jack would be full of vodka, asleep in his office." When Laird was in no condition to make judgments, Lester and Rawlins would take turns playing producer. "I would look over Rawlins's shoulder at the Moviola and decide how the sequence he was running should be cut. Then we'd switch places, and Rawlins would look over my shoulder and call the shots. So for this particular series, Jack gave us an open checkbook."[84]

"These editors were very creative," says John Badham. "They often had to do miraculous things with very little film. And it was a tremendous challenge to them not just to put [segments] together, but to really make them exciting and fun. A lot of the magic of the series was created in the editing room."[85]

*Night Gallery*'s pacing and tempo were extraordinary for television, and not solely designed for tension or excitement. Many *Night Gallery* segments were paced less like TV shows and more like a good movie, with the unhurried rhythms of real life, helping establish the critical mood for this genre. This deliberate pacing, much of it lost in the reedited syndication package, was another distinctive element that set the series apart from others of the period.

"It was a great experience," reflects Rawlins. "I'm doing features now, but when I look back on my career, I look at the TV days and that was really a lot more fun. I consider my days at Universal the best time in the business. I was very fortunate."[86]

## THE MUSIC

As accomplished as were the visuals, so too was the music written for *Night Gallery*. Jack Laird's credentials as a former band leader ensured that the scores for the show played a dominant rather than subordinate role. He allowed the composers free rein in their approach to each episode, producing music of an adventurous and dramatically effective kind.

"I care a lot about music," remarked Laird. "Postproduction for me is the most fun. Traditionally, you are at the mercy of your composer; you walk on the sound stage and that's the one element over which you have absolutely no control. You listen to it, and there it is, and all you can do is use it or not use it."[87]

Laird delegated musical duties to a most talented roster of composers. The show's musical profile was unique thanks to the talents of Gil Mellé, Paul Glass, Oliver Nelson, Robert Prince, and Eddie Sauter, who composed the lion's share of the scores for the show. The variety of styles and moods reflects the sensibilities of composers hired from jazz, classical, and avant-garde arenas.

Laird's first contact for the new season was, again, Gil Mellé, who balked at the idea of composing regularly for a series: "I told him, 'I'd like to, Jack. The idea of composing the theme for the show is quite an honor, and you're my friend and all, but I have the opportunity to do features, and I don't really want to get into anything that's repetitive.' I had waited a long time in my life to get to that point, and I didn't want to take two giant steps backward by working on a weekly series."

Before Mellé begged off completely, Laird did manage to squeeze out of him a rerecorded main title and format for *Night Gallery* (again, purely electronic), some scattered mood cues, and even a few complete segment scores. The difficulty for Mellé, however, was that he could not score the music to the film. Not a frame of footage had been shot yet. "I said, 'How can I score a show that hasn't been shot?' And he said, 'Just write a theme for the show and then do a lot of versions of it, and we'll cut the show to your music.'" Mellé was nonplussed, but he gamely went ahead, working from scripts Laird gave him. With no possible way to gauge exact timings for cues, Mellé recorded full-length versions of his themes, composed in such a way that they could be dialed into or out of the sound mix without harming their integrity.

"It was highly thematic music," recalls Mellé, "written for specific characters [in the script], done in an amalgamation of electronic and orchestral instruments. In addition to strings, percussion, woodwinds, and brass, I also had three or four people that I had been training to play a number of electronic instruments and act as a section within the orchestra. I played on a lot of the things myself."[88]

For the most part, Mellé and Laird's experiment worked. Mellé's scores for "House —With Ghost," "Dr. Stringfellow's Rejuvenator," and "Hell's Bells" were used with those segments. Some of his scores, however, abandoned for the segments they were written for, turned up elsewhere. Most notably, the eerily beautiful themes he composed for "The Dark Boy" were instead used in "Lindemann's Catch" and "Keep in Touch—We'll Think of Something."

Laird, unable to maintain Mellé's services, began looking for a replacement. Commented Laird at the time, "In part, it has been a fishing expedition. Various associates have recommended certain composers to me, and in some cases I have selected people I'm already familiar with through their recordings and other credits."[89] Thus was hired Oliver Nelson.

Nelson, known to Laird through his landmark jazz albums *Blues and the Abstract Truth* and *Sound Pieces,* was not only an exceptional saxophonist and arranger but also a fluent composer of contemporary classical. His previous work included scores for *Ironside* and the feature film *Jigsaw,* and he was an excellent choice for *Night Gallery.* Unfortunately, with Mellé's work still in mind, Laird apparently requested of Nelson that he emulate the style of his predecessor.

"Jack wanted electronic music, he was sold on it," Mellé says. "So they sent Oliver down to observe me when I was doing those scores. It's kind of unethical, but they told him to take a note from what I was doing, because there was a point when I just simply could not do the show, I had too many other commitments."

Nelson, unschooled at the time in the electronic experimentation that was Mellé's signature, had difficulty integrating synthesizers into his otherwise skillful orchestrations. His first attempts were rough. Instead of Mellé's "sheets of sound," producing blocks of almost orchestral color, Nelson frequently used the synthesizer ineffectively as a solo instrument. "Oliver's sense of electronics was that sort of slide-whistle effect he had," notes Mellé, "that thing he overused to death."[90] To be fair, the blame lies not with Nelson but with those who requested he mimic Mellé. Paul Glass, another composer for *Night Gallery,* illustrates the film composer's constant dilemma:

A producer asked me once, "Can you write a score like Penderecki?" And I said, "No, but I can give you his phone number. You can call him and ask *him* if he can write one." I should have told him to get on his bike. They're always asking you to write like somebody else, all this hanky-panky ghostwriting shit that goes on. If you want Penderecki, call him up! I mean, he'd love to pick up some cash here. That's always the problem when you have somebody hiring you who doesn't know anything about what you're doing."[91]

Aside from his use of electronics, on a purely musical basis Nelson produced superior scores that were reused frequently on many *Night Gallery* segments. Laird himself praised Nelson's "exceptional sense of drama," and to his credit Nelson later reclaimed his voice. Ignoring the requests of the Powers That Be, he scored his work for the standard ensembles at which he was expert, and wrote some of his best scores using little or no electronic gadgetry for "The Boy Who Predicted Earthquakes," "The Phantom Farmhouse," and "The Sins of the Fathers." Unfortunately, Nelson's workload at Universal put an insupportable amount of stress on his health. His genius was cut short far too early in 1975, when he expired from a heart attack at the age of forty-three.

Another jazz artist brought in by Laird was John Lewis, best known for his work with the Modern Jazz Quartet. Said Laird, "I've known John for years, not only through the quartet's work but particularly for some of his more extended writings, such as the album *European Windows.* I felt he could write something big along those lines, or along the lines of Orchestra U.S.A., the large ensemble with which he was associated in New York in the early 1960s. Lewis did a couple of episodes for us not long ago, and enjoyed it so much that he has been telling people that he wants to get into television writing more extensively."[92]

The result was less than rosy, according to insider Mellé: "They brought John Lewis out, he did two shows, and they fired him. I asked Jack, 'Why did you send John back to New York?' And he said, 'When we were laughing, he was dying, and when we were dying, he was laughing.' Jack was really unhappy with him." In truth, Lewis's work often ran counter to the drama. His score for "A Death in the Family" gave the segment something of a comic accent; the segment's thrust, however, is more of a pathetic tragedy. Although his scoring of "Since Aunt Ada Came to Stay" had elements of quality, on the whole his output for the show was not dramatically apt. Remarks Mellé, "One show I remember seeing was 'Class of '99,' and I didn't understand the score that John wrote at all. In those days, we'd always listen to each other's work. I was really geared into everything that David Shire or Billy Goldenberg were doing, but the one with John really eluded me. I just couldn't equate it with the show."[93]

Although Laird's next choice for composer was something of a shot in the dark, he hit the jackpot:

Paul Glass was recommended to me by Harry Garfield, the head of music here at the studio, who sent some tapes that impressed me. Ours is a difficult show to write for, and I'm a hard guy to please, so I'd always rather try out somebody new. The one thing that drives me up the wall is composers who constantly plunder themselves, cannibalize themselves, reworking notions until you know what to expect. Sooner than play it safe with somebody that is too familiar, I will take a chance, cross my fingers, and hope to find something exciting and innovative. Paul wasn't all that new, he was just new to me.[94]

Like Lewis, Glass produced scores for only two hours of *Night Gallery*. The qualitative difference, however, was night and day. Glass exhibited an unerring instinct for dramatic composition, and his music is arguably the best *Night Gallery* produced. As proof, his cues were used and reused constantly throughout the second season, turning up in twenty segments. "Paul was very good," notes Mellé. "Paul was an atonal writer, excellent, and a nice guy. As far as I'm concerned, he's one of the really important writers in Hollywood. He's almost a forgotten hero."[95]

Glass, a noted classical composer currently living in Switzerland, started his musical career playing jazz and touring in a cowboy band. He later honed his craft at the side of two eminent composers, moving to Rome in the late 1950s to study with Goffredo Petrassi, then to Warsaw in the 1960s for further instruction from Witold Lutoslawski. His work brought him both a Fulbright Award and a Princeton fellowship, and while in Hollywood he made his mark with scores for Otto Preminger's *Bunny Lake Is Missing* and the bone-chilling *Lady in a Cage*. "I was involved with the gang of twelve-toners," says Glass, referring to the followers of Arnold Schoenberg, whose theoretical teachings brought a timely Freudian angst into twentieth-century music. "We all got to be known as weirdos, because atonal music is all about tension, right? And something like the *Night Gallery* show would be ideal for somebody like me."

Ironically, in only one of the four segments Glass scored is his natural, atonal voice heard in full flower, but his gift for finding the emotional core of a story was unfailing, and he produced two remarkably affecting tonal scores for "Silent Snow, Secret Snow" and "The Messiah on Mott Street." The quality of his work is doubly amazing when one considers Glass was concurrently scoring a telefeature at Twentieth Century–Fox. "We were at it night and day," sighs Glass. "If you were one of those guys that could get along without sleeping, you'd be all right. It was very tough, but I must say Universal was one of the best music conservatories, because you had to make it quick and it had to sound like something. That was a prerequisite for the job: are you fast enough?"

To decide where the music would appear in the segment, the composer, producer, and music editor screened the film in a brief "spotting" session. In Glass's experience, most producers had trouble relating to the art of scoring—with the exception of Jack Laird. "Jack was an amazing guy," notes Glass. "Jack was very astute, he knew *exactly* what he wanted, there was no problem with that guy. He was difficult, but he *did* know what he wanted."[96]

After spotting, the composer had a week and a half to write the score, and Universal would allow only a blistering three-hour session in which to record it. Composers usually conducted their own music, working with some of the most accomplished session players in the Los Angeles area.

"On one episode we may use as many as thirty musicians," Laird noted. "But on another show, for instance, I once had nothing that would work, so I came up with the notion of simply using guitar, and brought Bob Bain in to do the whole job." Laird's notion was inspired. The segment, an adaptation of H. P. Lovecraft's "Cool Air," benefited immeasurably from Bain's solo performance, capturing the grace and soul of the characters.

Seeking variety to suit his concept, Laird's composer hunt continued. At Gil Mellé's suggestion, Laird contacted Eddie Sauter. Sauter, who came to prominence during the swing era as arranger for Red Norvo and Benny Goodman, later became coleader of the Sauter-Finegan Orchestra. His unique scoring for the Stan Getz album *Focus* and his work on Arthur Penn's *Mickey One* suggested to Laird that he was up to the task. More to the point, Sauter and Laird had a previous connection: they had written an unproduced musical together in 1947. For *Night Gallery*'s second season, Sauter scored four segments, including the brilliant back-to-back chillers "The Caterpillar" and "Little Girl Lost." Laird was practically effusive:

"I would say that since my early experiences with Lalo Schifrin—some of the best scoring Lalo ever did was written for me some years ago—Eddie Sauter is the best intuitive dramatic composer I've ever worked with. He's just dead-on. I was concerned about him because Eddie is so malleable, such a gentleman, and I didn't want him to get out here and be destroyed by the system."[97] As it turned out, Sauter was more fire eater than shrinking violet.

"He had a real attitude about the show," Mellé recalls. "I was sorry that I recommended him. The first day that he came over to listen to my scoring session, I walked over to him, shook hands, and said, 'Eddie, it's so good to see you, it's marvelous! The quality of music in the studio is going to go up a thousand percent now that you're here.'" Sauter's tactless response floored Mellé. "He says, 'This is all bullshit. It isn't classical music and it isn't jazz, it isn't anything. I know where *this* is all at.' I said, 'I wish I'd known that before I put in my two cents about you, because there's about a thousand young guys out there on the street who would love to be sitting where you are now and would be more of a credit to the job.' I mean, I *really* got mad at him."

Adding insult to injury, Sauter campaigned to replace Mellé's distinctive *Night Gallery* theme with one of his own. "He constantly went to Jack and said, 'I could write a better theme than Mellé.' And so at one of the scoring sessions when they were doing the regular cues, Eddie Sauter did indeed record another theme for the show, and it was shot down by everyone at the studio. So they stayed with mine. And then he did *another* theme later on, and *that* got shot down, and then he did a *third* theme. I mean, they were starting to get really hacked at him."[98]

At some point, Sauter did produce something that Laird and Universal seriously considered. When the third season rolled around, there was no sign of Mellé's theme. In fact, there was no sign of any other composer. Sauter advanced to become *Night Gallery*'s house composer for the final season of the series. Although Sauter produced some impressive work in the second season, few of his scores for the third season were on the same level. Whether inspiration failed or the pressure of composing every score was a drain, Sauter's work suffered. And when music suffers, so does the atmosphere.

But for the first two seasons at least, Laird's fishing expedition paid off with music of great quality, of a highly varied and inventive type, reflecting the producer's wish to serve the drama best: "There's no limit to the importance music can take on, particularly in a dramatic sequence where you have no sound effects and no dialogue. In any case, given a choice between sound effects and music, the music is more likely to make it every time—provided you have the right people to handle it."[99] From the evidence of the distinctive *Night Gallery* sound, it is manifest that Laird found the right people.

## BUMPERS AND BLACKOUTS

As production on the individual segments was completed and their numbers grew, Laird began to reconsider their sequencing and to figure how much time would be left over for Rod Serling's introductions, the connecting tissue from segment to segment.

The introductions, or "bumpers," for the second season were filmed in several bunches. When Laird had a rough idea of what he would need from Serling, he would draft a letter that outlined the stories and their approximate place in the sequence for the evening. Polaroids of Tom Wright's paintings were sent along to help Serling compose his introductions.

The first season's bumpers were filmed at Universal Studios. Because of the space shortage, all of *Night Gallery*'s second-season spillover, including the filming of the introductions, was channeled to General Service Studios, a large facility with a number of soundstages on North Las Palmas Boulevard in Hollywood. With Joseph Alves and Tom Wright as overseers, Stage 4 was set up to house the draped gallery and the hanging paintings, and Serling was contacted to schedule a two-day filming junket.

Laird's initial communiqués to Serling were not merely cordial, they were downright jolly, with no sign of the tensions that would soon cloud their intercourse:

Rod baby,

Have enclosed Polaroids (which do not begin to do justice to the originals themselves) of those paintings which Tom Wright has executed to date; I'll send you more in a few days. I ask only that you hang on to the Polaroids as I must return them to the Art Department.

I will now proceed to list the segment groupings as we propose to package them—and in the sequence in which they will succeed each other within an hour program (though not necessarily in the order of their playdates). I'll put an asterisk alongside those titles for which I'm not yet able to provide you with a Polaroid.

Episode #1—"Class of '99" • "A Death in the Family" • "Witches' Feast"
Episode #2—"House—With Ghost" • "Dr. Stringfellow's Rejuvenator" • "Hell's Bells"
Episode #3—"Professor Peabody's Last Lecture"* • "The Diary"* • "Big Surprise"
Episode #4—"The Different Ones" • "The Flip-Side of Satan" • "Silent Snow, Secret Snow"
Episode #5—"Herbie" • "Marmalade Wine"* • "The Painted Mirror"*
Episode #6—"Funeral" • "The Messiah on Mott Street"
Episode #7—"Since Aunt Ada Came to Stay" • "Logoda's Heads"

Any questions? Keep in touch.

Peace!
Laird[100]

The introductions were very stylized, with Serling often passing through pools of light and shadow, his sonorous voice and magnetic presence drawing the audience into the gallery. Sometimes serious, often touched by a wicked humor, Serling's brief discussions were perfect teasers, setting the stage for the ensuing drama. Consistent with his approach on *The Twilight Zone*, they showcase Serling's strongest talent, that of storyteller *extraordinaire*, giving even the least of plays the best of setups—such was the writer's gift of salesmanship.

Directors for the bumpers included John Meredyth Lucas, Jeannot Szwarc, Timothy Galfas, and editing staffer David Rawlins. Unlike the introductions for *The Twilight Zone*, Serling was never seen on *Night Gallery* with his trademark cigarette in hand. A pack was never far away, however, and between setups he resumed his habit. "Serling used to love to have a cigarette when they shot those intros," recalls Rawlins. "He insisted on lighting up, it was his moniker. He lived and died by his cigarette."[101]

*Rod Serling and crew filming the "bumpers." Courtesy of Stewart Stanyard.*

Sometime before October of 1971, Serling received notice from Laird of the second bumper crop:

Dear Rod,

Herewith as promised the Polaroids and/or Xeroxes of Tom Wright's remaining artwork. As usual, the Polaroids, leaning into the blue hues, fail to do justice to Tom's superb efforts, but you can get the general idea nonetheless.

Since we shot some wild opening walk-ons with you at the initial sessions (in which you so brilliantly ad-libbed), we'll only require two walking-and-talking introductions this outing. There are eleven paintings in all. I'll indicate which of them are openings and which of them will appear later within the hour in their respective groupings.

#1. Midnight Never Ends—an opening selection, walking-and-talking. Since you wrote the piece, you'll obviously know what comments are appropriate.

#2. Phantom Farmhouse—an opening selection, walking-and-talking. This is a lovely, haunting piece, moving and scarifying as well, concerning a man who falls hopelessly, obsessively in love with a female werewolf. (35 to 40 seconds)

#3. Cool Air—an opening selection, but without the walking-and-talking. You know the piece, having written it.

#4. Pickman's Model—an opening selection, no walking-talking required. From the H. P. Lovecraft story of the same title, concerning an artist who recruits his models from a very strange place.

#5. Camera Obscura—appears within show, no walking-talking required, your script.

#6. The Devil Is Not Mocked—the story appears within the show. It concerns a collision course between the German Reich and supernatural forces.

#7. Brenda—the story appears within the show. A very strange little girl develops a bizarre relationship with a unique playmate. A new and unorthodox variation on "Beauty and the Beast."

#8. Dark Boy—an opening selection, without walking talking requirements. A moving story set in rural America around the turn of the century involving a newly arrived schoolteacher (beautifully played by Elizabeth Hartman) who discovers one more student in her class than the roster indicates.

#9. Tell David . . .—this story appears within the show. A young wife is driven compulsively by almost insane jealousy to act out her role as Destiny's pawn despite a warning from the future.

#10. The Tune in Dan's Cafe—within the show. A story about a haunted jukebox, and postponed revenge for a fatal betrayal.

That's the lot. If there are any questions, please phone. Stay well, and be sure to bring the same wardrobe we shot before.

Love and kisses,
Laird[102]

The only paintings for which it was not absolutely necessary for Serling to provide commentary were the short vignettes meant to provide comic relief between the more serious segments. Often written and filmed at the last minute when it was discovered a grouping of segments was running short, they were far and away the most controversial element of *Night Gallery*.

Laird's love of classic horror movies gave unfortunate rise to these "fractured classics," as he termed them, written entirely by either himself or his protégé, Gene Kearney, and based on famous scenes or characters from these films. They were Laird's blind spot on the series, and they did nothing to endear the show to critics. Placing one of these inane miniatures immediately after a full-length drama often did more harm than a commercial in defusing the drama's effects, going a long way toward sealing the audience's impression of the whole hour. Serling considered them unfunny, "foreign and substantially incorrect. You can't sustain the mood of horror or suspense and then intersperse light laughter in the middle of it, and then expect to be able to go back in a neutral fashion to an element of horror. You spend fifteen minutes creating a mood for an audience, and then you dispel it arbitrarily by trying to make them laugh."[103]

Most of the directors disliked them. The studio disliked them. But Laird loved the idea and gleefully continued writing and often directing these sketches in the manner of *Love, American Style,* peopling them with vampires, werewolves, witches, Franken-stein monsters, Dr. Jekylls, Mr. Hydes, and other denizens of the classic horror film pantheon. In retrospect, these vignettes were the only stale, formulaic qualities pre-sent in *Night Gallery,* and managed to undercut all the work Laird did to make the se-ries unique and fresh in its dramatic and stylistic approach. Although their number to-taled a mere fourteen, to this day some people remember the series more for these ab-surd little interruptions than for its serious offerings.

"I disliked the sketches that were introduced," admits Paul Freeman, first-season production executive. "They were just mood-breakers. I remember thinking that they were going to be the kiss of death for the show."[104] Freeman may have been correct. The presence of the vignettes was perceived by the Powers That Be as a serious impediment to the show's acceptance by the television audience. "They didn't satisfy anybody," notes Universal executive Sidney Sheinberg. "The audience wanted a fully fleshed-out story."[105]

In the press releases of the period, the publicity machine at the studio did its best to explain the vignettes' place in the show's scheme: "The creators have not always approached horror from a heavy point of view. The twists in many of *Night Gallery*'s teleplays are tongue-in-cheek; comedy is juxtaposed against the skeleton and the death rattle. All in good taste—as Dracula and the Phantom of the Opera are updated, and their menace is pricked like a balloon."[106] No one was fooled, however, least of all the viewing public. "I wasn't crazy about them," admits Jeannot Szwarc, who directed three of the blackouts. "I always felt it took away from the purity of *Night Gallery*."[107]

Laird's devotion to this perversion of the show's original concept lost for *Night Gallery* the respect it could have gained based on the execution of its "serious" epi-sodes. The producer wound up shooting himself—and, by proxy, Serling—in the foot.

Despite some strains, civility reigned between Laird and Serling. Their conflict over script changes had yet to occur. On the eve of the second-season premiere, Laird's Western Union telegram to Serling was leavened by humor:

SEP 15 71
UNIVERSAL CITY CALIF
I'D SAY BREAK A LEG BUT YOU'RE SO ACCOMMODATING, YOU'D GO AHEAD AND DO IT.
SO INSTEAD, GOOD LUCK TONIGHT.
JACK LAIRD[108]

The civility would not last much longer.

# 8
# The Second Season

SECOND SEASON CREDITS
1971–1972

**PRODUCED BY** Jack Laird

**PRODUCTION ASSOCIATES** Anthony Redman and Herbert Wright

**EXECUTIVE STORY CONSULTANT** Gerald Sanford

**MAIN TITLE THEME** Gil Mellé

**ART DIRECTOR** Joseph Alves, Jr.

**SET DECORATIONS** John M. Dwyer, Chester R. Bayhi, Sal Blydenburgh, James M. Walters and Charles S. Thompson

**UNIT MANAGER** Burt Astor

**ASSISTANT DIRECTORS** Ralph Sariego and Les Berke

**FILM EDITORS** Larry Lester, David Rawlins, Jean-Jacques Berthelot, Sam Vitale, Jack Schoengarth, Stanford Tischler, Robert Watts, John Kaufman, Jr., Bud Hoffman, Howard Epstein, and Leon Ortiz-Gil

**SOUND** David H. Moriarty, Roger A. Parish, James R. Alexander, John Carter, and Robert Martin

**GALLERY PAINTINGS** Tom Wright

**GALLERY SCULPTURES** Phil Vanderlei and Logan Elston

**EDITORIAL SUPERVISION** Richard Belding

**COSTUMES** Bill Jobe

**MAKEUP** Leonard Engelman and John F. Chambers

**MAIN TITLE DESIGN** Wayne Fitzgerald

**TITLES & OPTICAL EFFECTS** Universal Title

**CASTING** Ross Brown

NIGHT GALLERY #34304
Air date: September 15, 1971

1

THE BOY WHO PREDICTED EARTHQUAKES
★ ★ ★ ½

Teleplay by Rod Serling
Based on the short story by Margaret St. Clair
Directed by John Badham
Music: Oliver Nelson
Director of Photography: Lionel Lindon
Time: 21:35

**Cast**

Wellman: Michael Constantine
Herbie Bittman: Clint Howard
Reed: Bernie Kopell
Dr. Peterson: Ellen Weston
Godwin: William Hansen
Floor Director: Gene Tyburn
Cameraman: Rance Howard
Secretary: Rosary Nix
Grip: John Donald

*Clint Howard in "The Boy Who Predicted Earthquakes." Courtesy of Sal Milo.*

$Y$*ou're most welcome in this particular museum. There's no admission, no requirement of membership, only a strong and abiding belief in the dark at the top of the stairs, or things that go bump in the night.*

*Example: tonight's first painting. Small boy encased in a crystal ball, born with a very special gift—he can prophesy. But you'll wonder as we look behind that picture if a prophecy is always a gift, or can it on occasion take the form of a nightmare. The painting's title is "The Boy Who Predicted Earthquakes," and this is the* Night Gallery.

**/ Summary /** Ten-year-old Herbie Bittman has been hired by the staff of a New York television station to be its latest on-screen commentator. When Wellman, the station's top executive, discovers the nature of the commentary, he is furious. Herbie predicts the future. According to the boy's grandfather, he is unerringly correct, an assurance that leaves Wellman less than satisfied—until Herbie's first prediction comes true. Under heavy news coverage, a little girl lost in the Sierras is discovered by a search dragnet just as Herbie foretold. When his next prediction, a Los Angeles earthquake, comes to pass, Wellman is convinced and signs Herbie to an exclusive contract.

Herbie's fame spreads during the next year and he becomes an audience-grabbing television personality. Every one of his predictions, from ocean liner disasters to election results, comes to pass. So accurate is he that the boy becomes the subject of a university study on parapsychology, headed by Dr. Peterson. Herbie explains to her his main limitation: that he can see no further than forty-eight hours into the future. While he prepares for his next taping, his grandfather confides concern to the doctor: that Herbie's foreknowledge, his sudden awareness of an impending catastrophe that he cannot change, must be a tremendous strain on an eleven-year-old boy.

Suddenly, Herbie balks. Without explanation, he tells Wellman and his grandfather that he cannot do the show. Wellman, with only a few minutes to air time, carefully persuades Herbie that canceling the show could cause a public scare. Herbie mulls it over and agrees to continue, but the prediction he makes that afternoon is unlike any other Herbie has made before. He informs his audience that the millennium is at hand, a renaissance of knowledge, peace, and prosperity for humanity. Wars abolished, unity among races and nations, the end of poverty, pollution, and hunger, all predicted by Herbie in the space of a few minutes.

The response is worldwide celebration, and in New York alone the dancing in the streets stops all traffic. Not everyone is cheered by Herbie's news, however. Dr. Peterson arrives at Herbie's hotel room with a question: if he can only see forty-eight hours into the future, how could he possibly have seen all that? Herbie, deeply troubled, admits that his prediction was a lie concocted to preserve the peace in the face of his true prophecy. "Look over there," Herbie says, pointing out the window toward the west. "Tomorrow the sun will be different." Dreading the knowledge, Dr. Peterson asks Herbie what he sees for tomorrow. "I forget the word," Herbie says, searching his memory. "It's what they call it when a star flares up—becomes a billion times hotter than it was before." Gazing out at the horizon, Dr. Peterson asks quietly, "A nova?" Herbie replies, "That's it, a nova"—when the sun explodes.

**/ Commentary /** Conspicuous as the only successful entry within the second-season premiere, "The Boy Who Predicted Earthquakes" offers a briskly paced script by Serling and the crisp, imaginative direction of newcomer John Badham. Badham, having followed his sister, actress Mary Badham (*To Kill a Mockingbird*), to Hollywood, wangled a job as a tour guide for Universal Studios. From there he made connections into the production end of the business.

For this segment, Badham won the job by default when William Hale, the director originally slated, was fired by Laird after running over schedule while filming "Since Aunt Ada Came to Stay." Badham, inspired by the TV station setting, produced some arresting shots with his creative use of video techniques and hardware within the segment. Although young and relatively inexperienced, he displayed an impressive visual flair that made him a natural on *Night Gallery*.

Serling's embryonic first draft of this segment, titled "And Now, Danny Dingle," highlighted his strange attraction to absurd names, which had been given full rein during his tenure on *The Twilight Zone*. At some point he came to his senses and changed the title to "Herbie," although Jack Laird ultimately restored the segment title to that of Margaret St. Clair's original short story. Serling's taut script (dictated to completion in seven hours) was filmed exactly as he wrote it, with one minor change. In Serling's script, Wellman hears the news of a little girl's rescue while in his office. In the filmed segment, Wellman receives the news while screening the classic 1933 horror film *Island of Lost Souls*—a respectful nod, no doubt, by die-hard cinephiles Laird and Badham.

For the part of Herbie, the ten-year-old seer, Laird hired Clint Howard, brother of Ron and son of Rance (cast in this segment as a TV station cameraman). Howard was, by then, no stranger to the camera, having appeared in episodes of *The Andy Griffith Show* and *Star Trek,* and starred in his own series, *Gentle Ben*. Michael Constantine, known at the time for his role as laconic principal Seymour Kaufman in the ABC series *Room 222*, was cast against type as Wellman, the apoplectic station manager. It is Ellen Weston, however, who delivers the most understated and believable performance as the psychiatrist left to unravel the terrible secret Herbie Bittman must keep from the rest of the world.

"I had worked with a number of child actors when I used to do daytime soap operas," recalls Weston, "and it could be *murder!* But Clint Howard was unusual, a remarkable kid. He was precocious but not in an obnoxious way, and he knew what he was doing. It was like working with another adult actor! I don't recall having *any* misery with him."[1]

As cast and crew were soon to discover, however, the filming of the climactic scene would yield its share of misery. Seeking a dramatic image to punch home Herbie's final prophecy, Badham first shot the concluding sequence of Herbie and his grandfather with a rear-projected stock image of the sun framing their embrace. The dailies proved it worthless. "It really was not good," moaned Badham, "it just looked like shit. The sun in rear projection couldn't put out enough light to overwhelm the actors in the foreground. Nowadays I do stuff with rear projection that's quite phenomenal, but at the time the film stock wouldn't allow you to do it. So we're standing on the set the last day of the shoot, and I'm fretting about it. The cameraman was Curly Lindon, an extremely clever, very ingenious man. And he grouches, 'Well, here, let me do this,' and he literally grabbed a twenty-five hundred-watt studio light on a stand, wheeled it around, pointed it at the guys, put an orange gel on it, and aimed it right into the camera."[2] With Howard and actor William Hansen performing in front of this intensely burning studio light, the final shot has an otherworldy quality, isolating the two from the hotel room set and thrusting them into a darkened void—a striking effect. "The filming of that final scene was endless," says Weston. "It took *forever* to set up that shot. But it was a great moment and we all wanted it to be just right. I remember feeling as though that light was burning into eternity—that we were actually going to *burn out!*" Complementing Lindon's photography is Oliver Nelson's eerie score, which would be reused many times on other segments.

For Ellen Weston, the filming of this episode had a profound and lasting result. "At the time, I didn't know anything about novas, and the possibility frightened me. I thought, 'My God, what *other* things out there don't I know about that could destroy civilization?' I was concerned about that for years afterward, and it started when I did that show. It was quite an awakening."[3]

"The Boy Who Predicted Earthquakes" was an auspicious start to the season, but unfortunately was followed by segments that failed to live up to its promise.


2
MISS LOVECRAFT SENT ME
★

Written by Jack Laird
Directed by Gene Kearney
Music: Oliver Nelson
Director of Photography: Lionel Lindon
Time: 3:32

**Cast**
Vampire: Joseph Campanella
Betsy: Sue Lyon

*Sue Lyon in "Miss Lovecraft Sent Me." Courtesy of Sal Milo.*

/ **Summary** / Answering the doorbell, the tall, pale gentleman admits Betsy, a gum-popping baby-sitter, into the foyer. "Miss Lovecraft sent me," she says. "I'm from the agency." The gaunt dignitary informs her that he was just getting "Sonny" ready for bed himself: the boy can sometimes be . . . *difficult* . . . with strangers. She offers to read Sonny a bedtime story, but stops abruptly when, gazing into the hall mirror, she realizes the gentleman has no reflection.

Oblivious, he agrees that a bedtime story would be a fine idea. He suggests she pick one of Sonny's favorites on the bookshelf while he finishes readying the boy for bed. The gentleman promises he and his wife will return by dawn: "We are always back before sunup—*always.*" As he ascends the stairs to Sonny's bedroom, Betsy checks out the volumes on the bookcase. Strange titles: *Vampyricon, Satan's Invisible World Discovered, The Book of the Dead, Men into Wolf, Discours des sorciers.* Overhearing the gentleman's soothing voice upstairs, and some snuffling, grunting sounds—that's odd, Miss Lovecraft didn't mention anything about a dog—she listens as he helps Sonny on with his slippers. "Give me your foot, there's a good boy . . . now the other foot, that's right . . . and now, *the other one.*" Betsy, finally putting the freakish equation together, makes a speedy exit—much to Sonny's disappointment.

/ **Commentary** / For the first of the vignettes, distinguished actor Joseph Campanella was invited back from the first season ("The Nature of the Enemy"). Campanella had previously played a similar role, a Russian dignitary with wolfish habits, in a delightfully campy episode of *The Wild, Wild West.* Although campy, this segment has nothing of the other's charm.

"We had fun doing that episode, we really did," Campanella says. "The director [Gene Kearney] said, 'Come on, Joe, play the hell out of it, you can't overdo it!' You know, with the accent—'Alllllllways before sunup,' and 'I preferrr it that way.' When I first came to California from New York, I was mainly doing character things: Middle Europeans, especially French, some Italian. And this was a chance to get back to a dialect, especially doing Bela Lugosi!"

Campanella found this segment held a great interest for his young sons.

At that time I had four boys, ages four, five, and six—the youngest was Nick, one and a half. Of course, they were big with vampires and monsters and Halloween makeup, things like that. When they heard I was going to play Dracula, they wanted to come to the set. And oh, they were having a ball! Except for my eighteen-month-old. Nick wouldn't come near me—he wouldn't even let me hold his hand. I said, "Nick, it's me. It's Daddy, remember me? Daddy? Come on, you recognize my voice—I just have makeup on, the teeth are fake." I started to bend toward him to kiss him, *and he bopped me on the nose with his fist!* I mean, he gave me a real shot![4]

Perhaps Nick should have saved his roundhouse for the script's author—Jack Laird.


3

THE HAND OF BORGUS WEEMS
★ ★


Teleplay by Alvin Sapinsley
Based on the short story "The Other Hand" by George Langelaan
Directed by John Meredyth Lucas
Music: Oliver Nelson
Director of Photography: Lionel Lindon
Time: 20:59

**Cast**

Peter Lacland: George Maharis

Dr. Ravdon: Ray Milland

Susan Douglas: Joan Huntington

Dr. Innokenti: Patricia Donahue

Det. Nico Kazanzakis: Peter Mamakos

Brock Ramsey: William Mims

Everett Winterreich: Robert Hoy

*Ray Milland in "The Hand of Borgus Weems."*
*Courtesy of Cinema Collectors.*

*T*he concept of medical transplants is exciting indeed, but the story behind this painting takes the concept a step further—or, if you will, a step over—into a different kind of world, one in which a gentleman named Lacland finds a hand that is not his own . . . and he finds it at the end of his wrist. Our painting: "The Hand of Borgus Weems."

**/ Summary /** In the office of Dr. Archibald Ravdon, a young man, Peter Lacland, makes a singular request of the surgeon: cut off his right hand. The doctor, upon examining it, can find nothing wrong. Nevertheless, Lacland demands it be removed, claiming it is no longer his. As if to demonstrate, Lacland's right hand grabs a desk pad and pen, scribbles something onto the pad, and thrusts it toward the doctor. It is a Latin phrase the doctor cannot read, in a language that Lacland claims he does not know. The hand, Lacland says, has attempted murder on three separate occasions, and he is not sure how much longer he can hold out against its will. When the doctor refuses to perform the procedure, the desperate Lacland picks up a metal bust on the doctor's side table, raises it over his head, and brings it down on his right hand, crushing it.

Forced into surgery, Dr. Ravdon removes the offending extremity. In recovery, Lacland relates to Ravdon and a psychiatrist colleague his strange story—of how the other hand brought him into contact with three people: Susan Douglas, affianced to Lacland until the hand tried to murder her with a purchased automatic; Brock Ramsey, whom the hand attacked with a letter opener; and Everett Winterreich, a lawyer Lacland narrowly avoided running over in a crosswalk when the other hand took control of the car's steering wheel. All of these people were previously unknown to Lacland, and he certainly had no reason to want to see them dead. The only clue Lacland has received, by the hand's own scribbling, is a name: Borgus Weems.

Dr. Ravdon recognizes the name and contacts a police detective who was assigned to Borgus Weems's unsolved murder investigation years ago. Weems, an occultist, was pushed to his death from his apartment window—now Lacland's apartment. Weems's hand, found gripping the sill after his death, had been lopped off at the wrist. Two people were charged in the death: his niece, Susan Douglas, and her boyfriend, Brock Ramsey. They were acquitted with the help of a lawyer, Everett Winterreich.

Lacland sees all the pieces of the puzzle falling into place. "If it's true, if they *did* murder him and they got free, then how is he ever to rest?" Dr. Ravdon, seeing Lacland's agitation, pulls out a prescription pad to administer a sedative, but what he writes is not the intended prescription: *Exoriare aliques nostris ex ossibus ultor*—the same Latin phrase Lacland scribbled out earlier in the doctor's office. The detective, noting the doctor's consternation, looks at the pad. "That's Virgil," he exclaims, translating: "'Arise, my avenger, out of my bones.' That's what you're prescribing for Mr. Lacland? A dose of Virgil?" Horrified, the doctor studies his right hand, now no longer his own . . . but under the control of Borgus Weems.

/ **Commentary** / Serling's introduction suggests a story about transplants, but what is delivered instead is a dispiriting twist on the stale "disembodied hand" premise, roughly similar to the famed Maurice Renard tale, "The Hands of Orlac." To adapt George Langelaan's short story "The Other Hand," Jack Laird called on Alvin Sapinsley, an associate of Laird's from *The Chrysler Theater* and a writer with credits dating to the "golden age" of the 1950s, to script his first of six episodes for *Night Gallery*.

Originally set in Paris, Langelaan's tale involved a scoundrel, eager for an inheritance, who plots to get rid of his sister and her husband by forcing the husband, through his usurped hand, to murder her. An explanation of how he manages this metaphysical procedure is never offered, a fault corrected in Sapinsley's adaptation. Sadly, other weaknesses from the original short story *are* transferred most faithfully. If Borgus Weems's hand alone was left clinging to that window sill, why should Lacland's foot begin working in concert with the hand while driving? And could Lacland be so obtuse that he could not surmise *why* the hand impelled him to buy a gun, then compound the stupidity by trotting over to his fiancée's apartment with it? Even for a flat-out fantasy this is hard to swallow.

The segment's lapses of logic are further weakened by so-so performances, unimaginative, stock 1970s direction, and an eye-tiring cutting scheme. A more fevered, Ken Russell-ish visual style might have dazzled us into overlooking those plot points. Unfortunately, not even a potent twist ending can redeem what has gone before.

Ultimately, "The Hand of Borgus Weems" is a less-than-distinctive entry in the *Night Gallery* canon. To be fair, writer Alvin Sapinsley claims no particular affinity for this genre, taking the job only after much urging by Laird. For his trouble, the writer found himself caught in the middle of the escalating tug-of-war between Rod Serling and Jack Laird over creative control of the show. Although he had no problem with the inevitable rewrites requested of him by Laird, Sapinsley was far less sanguine about Serling's input and suggestions: "Rod kept intruding himself and trying to putter around with the scripts. In fact, he called me up once at home to talk about one of the scripts I'd written, and he had no business doing that. I wasn't working for him, I was working for Jack."[5]

Although Sapinsley's first script for the show had some problems, his offerings later in the season would be far better. Those to come would include "Pickman's Model," "Last Rites for a Dead Druid," and "There Aren't Any More MacBanes." Later in the 1970s he would cowrite with Allan Knee a television miniseries masterpiece, a literate and faithful adaptation of Nathaniel Hawthorne's *The Scarlet Letter* for PBS/WGBH-Boston. Its haunting atmosphere, rich visual symbolism, and occult undercurrents make it a must for all fans of *Night Gallery*. Despite Sapinsley's professed disinterest in the "weird tales" genre, Hawthorne was one of its respected granddaddies and finest practitioners.

## 4
## PHANTOM OF WHAT OPERA?
★ ★

Written and Directed by Gene Kearney
Music: Oliver Nelson
Director of Photography: Lionel Lindon
Time: 3:38

**Cast**
The Phantom: Leslie Nielsen
Beautiful Prisoner: Mary Ann Beck

*In rehearsal: Leslie Nielsen and Mary Ann Beck in "Phantom of What Opera?" Courtesy of TV History Archives.*

/ **Summary** / In the catacombed depths of the Paris Opera, a masked phantom carries a beautiful young singer screaming to his lair. He commands she never attempt to see the face he conceals beneath his mask and begins to serenade her at the organ. She approaches behind him, curious to know who this madman is. Ripping the mask from his face, she finds herself facing a disfigured, skeletal monster. Screaming, she pulls away. He advances on her threateningly, grasping her throat in rage. She pulls out of his grasp, but her face stays fixed in his hands. A mask! Gazing upon her true face, as hideous as his own, the phantom screams—then recovers. Embracing her, he realizes he has found his perfect soul mate.

/ **Commentary** / At the time, Gene Kearney's variation on *The Phantom of the Opera* was selectively praised by some critics, variously described as "a five-minute hit"[6] and "the most satisfying piece of the premiere night."[7] Twenty-five years later, however, the segment is notable only for Leslie Nielsen's comic turn, later to be developed in such memorable characters as Lt. Frank Drebin in *Police Squad!* and Doctor "Don't

Call Me Shirley" Rumack in *Airplane!* The comedy in this case was not intentional, but was improvised instinctively by an actor having difficulty with a stage prop.

"I was supposed to light the candelabra and seat myself at the organ," recalls Nielsen. "I had this silk robber's mask over my face, and without even thinking I tried to blow out the taper. The veil on the mask goes *bluhbluhbluhbluhbluh,* and I realize I *ain't* going to blow *anything* out with this mask on." He used the gaffe to his advantage by then trying to extinguish the taper with his fingers, but failing again and again. "It was just automatic," says Nielsen. "I thought, 'This is it, this is the comedy part.'"[8]

Makeup artist Leonard Engelman elaborates: "This went on for . . . it must have been half a dozen takes. He'd come all the way down the stairs, set the girl down, light the candelabra, and try to blow the taper out. So he tries to whip it back and forth to make it go out. It won't go out. Finally, he's whipping it so much that it breaks and sort of falls in half, still burning. And, I mean, the crew, Kearney, *everybody* was hysterical!"[9]

"I was not positive at that time about my doing comedy," says Nielsen. "I really felt that there were others who could do this kind of material better than I. The danger of comedy pervaded my marrow. It was something I approached with great trepidation when I said, 'This is really funny, Jack. Don't you think we should do this?' And he bought it."[10]

Laird, Kearney, and the editors wisely decided to keep the screw-ups in the segment, as Leonard Engelman and the rest of the television audience discovered the night of the premiere: "I was at home watching it, and I was rolling off the couch onto the *floor* I was laughing so hard. I don't know how funny it was for the people that didn't know the background of it, but for myself, I was hysterical."[11]

Nielsen's impromptu gag is the funniest thing in the skit, proving that spontaneity is frequently funnier than scripted comedy, and remains as a portent of the hilarity that would later define the next phase of Nielsen's career.


NIGHT GALLERY #34301
Air date: September 22, 1971


1

A DEATH IN THE FAMILY
★ ★ ★ ½

Teleplay by Rod Serling
Based on the short story by Miriam Allen DeFord
Directed by Jeannot Szwarc
Music: John Lewis

Director of Photography: Lionel Lindon
Time: 22:23

**Cast**
Jared Soames: E. G. Marshall
Doran: Desi Arnaz, Jr.
Driver: Noam Pitlik
State Trooper: James B. Sikking
2d Trooper: John Williams Evans
3d Trooper: Bill Elliott
Grave Digger: Bud Walls

*Desi Arnaz, Jr. and E. G. Marshall in "A Death in the Family." Courtesy of Globe Photos.*

*H*ow nice of you all to come to our little exhibition. To the connoisseurs amongst you, those tasteful few who take their art seriously, we acknowledge with no apologies that you won't find the works of the masters here. Because in this particular salon we choose our paintings with an eye more towards terror than technique.

A little American gothic here, with the accustomed accoutrements to mourning: tombstones and tears and the somber look of the bereaved. We generally cry at funerals out of a sense of loss. A poor unfortunate loved one will no longer walk the earth. . . . He or she will simply occupy six feet of it, never to be seen or heard from again. Or at least we make an assumption that that's natural law and we subscribe to it. But this painting here—and we admit this up front—breaks that law. It's called "A Death in the Family." It offers up a new view of death, and it introduces you to quite a family who live here in the Night Gallery.

**/ Summary /** Undertaker Jared Soames receives his latest charge: the body of Simon Cottner, recently a long-term resident of an old-folks' home. Since Cottner had no relatives or friends to prepare for his funeral, the state pays Soames to arrange a lowly potter's field burial for the old man. Saddened that old Simon has no one to mourn his passing, Soames makes other arrangements for his final rest.

That night, Doran, a fugitive who was shot fleeing from a failed robbery, breaks into the funeral home. Holding a gun on Soames, Doran searches the place for others and, opening the door to a back room, receives an unpleasant shock: there, perched stiffly in a chair, sits the corpse of Simon Cottner. "Lest you be unduly disturbed, young man," explains Soames, "this is a funeral home." Too weak from his flight to muster much beyond surprise, Doran slips to the floor. The gentle undertaker, moved by the young man's plight, helps him to a sofa and suggests he rest. Strange confidantes, they find sympathy in their memories of each other's miserable and lonely childhood. "Until tonight, the only hand I ever got was the back of it," Doran labors. "It's a funny thing. I've got to wait until the lights are half out—and I crawl on my hands and my knees to a dead house—to find somebody living, somebody warm." Weak from exhaustion and blood loss, he drifts off to sleep.

When he awakens, Doran rises and searches for Soames. Hearing faint singing, Doran finds the undertaker in the basement, standing at the head of a table, glass raised in a toast. The late Simon Cottner is seated there. So are five other dead people —embalmed, arranged in chairs around the table—dressed for a party. Soames, smiling warmly, introduces his "family" to the horrified fugitive; a knock at the upstairs door cuts off Doran's retort. Suspecting a search by state troopers, Soames tells the shaking fugitive to stay put and be quiet, but the idea of staying with the "family" throws the young man into a panic. The undertaker, fearing for the boy's safety, tries to block his escape.

The troopers at the front door, hearing shots, enter the funeral home pistols raised, following Doran's blood trail into the basement. They find Soames with his family. There is a new addition: Doran, dead eyes staring, is propped at Soames's left. The undertaker, oozing blood from bullet wounds in his stomach, gasps out an explanation to the troopers about their little homecoming party . . . for his "father," Simon Cottner . . . for his "son," Doran . . . "and for myself," Soames smiles weakly, "the father of the family." Dropping his glass, Soames slumps into his chair, dead—completing for the gaping troopers his pathetic tableau.

/ **Commentary** / Based on Miriam Allen DeFord's macabre short story, Serling's script treads a delicate line between black comedy and pathos, dealing perceptively with one of the dramatist's pet obsessions: death and the afterlife. His sympathetic portrait of Jared Soames, who acquires a family made up of society's castoffs, makes "A Death in the Family" one of Serling's finest character studies on *Night Gallery*. Further, it is given sensitive treatment by the joint artistry of star E. G. Marshall and director Jeannot Szwarc.

Both Marshall and Szwarc shared the same understanding of the character, steering the interpretation toward the tragic. Particularly affecting is their staging and exposition of the finale, with Soames's bizarre Norman Rockwell-meets-Charles Addams version of the all-American family. "Marshall was tremendous," Szwarc recalls. "He performed his final monologue with such sincerity. Neither of us wanted this guy to come off like some weird freak. There was a kind of logic in his sickness. I thought it was so sad, that kind of loneliness."[12]

To allow for a more dramatic externalization of Soames's feelings, Serling invented the character of Doran, a hunted criminal fleeing from a botched filling station robbery. The presence of the wounded escapee draws compassion from the gentle undertaker and reveals his desperate need for companionship—*any* kind of companionship. Serling's empathy for both of these characters is mirrored in every line.

As Doran, Desi Arnaz, Jr. is too soft to play a streetwise tough hardened by life and circumstance, but his miscasting is not a serious drawback. He gives a capable performance, abetted by a keen appreciation for the material: "Rod had that inner-life take on the world. He told stories in metaphors and parables, with science fiction and fable, but in a way that's much more realistic than the reality-based things writers attempt today. They don't have the psychological base that he had, or the inner spiritual side which he tried to allude to—that there is more to life than meets the eye."

Of the filming, Arnaz comments, "It was really a great experience. Jeannot Szwarc was a new, hot director at the time, and he was *great*. One of the best experiences I ever had with a director. I was eighteen years old at the time, and I was cast just before we started shooting. There wasn't a lot of time to learn the lines, so it was really off the cuff. We shot the whole thing in just two days, and it was a lot of work, about thirty setups a day. But the crew was really good, and Jeannot knew *exactly* what he wanted."

Despite the breakneck speed of production, the tenor of the script kept things light. "E. G. Marshall and I had a lot of fun doing this episode," notes Arnaz. "I got to play a psychotic, and E. G. was great as the crazy mortician! It was a very odd little piece, kind of disturbing. But there was a comedy element to this particular *Night Gallery,* and we were laughing a lot in between shots. The black humor—and that circus music in the background!"[13]

The noteworthy (and decidedly peculiar) music score for this segment was the inspiration of John Lewis, whose use of bluesy solo violin and a sneaky pizzicato bass reflects his jazz background. Moreover, just beneath the score's jazzy surface one can detect its gospel roots, with hymnlike melodies in a decidedly macabre, chortling, minstrel-show dress—a sly commentary on the play's themes. The effect is as oddly touching as it is comical.

Additionally, Lionel Lindon's rich and brooding photography scores on atmosphere, and manages to fool the audience into believing that the figures seated at the table are corpses. "I didn't want to use still photographs because you can always tell if it's a photograph," said Szwarc. "I shot the close-ups of the corpses in slow motion. The actors, of course, stopped breathing and moving, but shooting in slow motion gave me a much longer piece of film."[14]

Ultimately, Soames's final monologue as written by Serling did not survive the final editing stage complete. To tighten the pace to the finish when the troopers burst into the funeral home, a decision was made to cut the footage of Soames introducing each member of his "family." Ironically, this material has been restored for the syndication print, one of the few times the syndication fiasco resulted in something positive. It offers the viewer some idea of the behind-the-scenes creative process on *Night Gallery.* What Serling lost in the trimming of those lines is ultimately regained in the crisp pacing of the segment as originally broadcast. Both versions are valid. It is for the viewer to decide which is more effective.

2

## THE MERCIFUL

★ ★ ½

Teleplay by Jack Laird
Based on the short story by
    Charles L. Sweeney, Jr.
Directed by Jeannot Szwarc
Music: John Lewis
Director of Photography: Lionel Lindon
Time: 3:27

**Cast**

Wife: Imogene Coca
Husband: King Donovan

*Imogene Coca and King Donovan in "The Merciful." Courtesy of Foto Fantasies.*

/ **Summary** / Brick by brick, the elderly woman walls up the cubicle as her sad-eyed husband watches. "It's for your own good, you know," she notes spryly. "I want to spare you the unpleasantness. It's so easy this way. Once the wall gets sealed, there's nothing to do but lean back. And in a little while the air will be gone, and there will be nothing left but sleep—no fear, no pain, just soft, sweet sleep." Within a few minutes, the cubicle is sealed and her voice can no longer be heard.

The doorbell rings. The old gentleman rises from his rocker, calling, "Dear? Someone's at the front door. I'll be back just as soon as I see who it is." He turns and shuffles stiffly up the basement stairs, leaving his wife—who has walled *herself* into the cubicle—alone for a moment as he answers the door.

/ **Commentary** / Exhibiting a lighter touch than the usual heavy-handed blackouts, "The Merciful" benefited from the comic talents of a real-life husband and wife, King Donovan (*Invasion of the Body Snatchers*) and Imogene Coca (*Your Show of Shows*).

Often on *Night Gallery*, the stories behind the making of the vignettes are more humorous than the actual vignette. Actress Louise Sorel ("The Dead Man," "Pickman's Model") believes Laird fashioned this piece, a twist on Poe's "The Cask of Amontillado," as a way of exorcising some domestic demons. "His wife was *constantly* redecorating his house, and she was driving him *nuts*," recalls a bemused Sorel. "So he wrote this piece that was really his fantasy of walling his wife in. It was hysterical."[15]

In truth, "The Merciful" works better than most of the other short sketches Laird devised—a reason for moderate thanks.

3
## CLASS OF '99
★ ★ ★ ★

Written by Rod Serling
Directed by Jeannot Szwarc
Music: John Lewis
Director of Photography: Lionel Lindon
Time: 18:47

**Cast**
Professor: Vincent Price
Johnson: Brandon de Wilde
Elkins: Randolph Mantooth
Clinton: Frank Hotchkiss
Barnes: Hilly Hicks
Miss Fields: Suzanne Cohane
Miss Peterson: Barbara Shannon
Bruce: Richard Doyle
Templeton: Hunter von Leer
McWhirter: John Davey
Miss Wheeton: Lenore Kasdorf

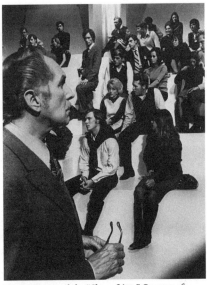

*Vincent Price and the "Class of '99." Courtesy of Globe Photos.*

*A most unusual graduation exercise now. Its title: "The Class of '99." A set of numbers and a pair of eyes. We'll move behind them now to give you an idea why we call the place you're in the* Night Gallery.

**/ Summary /** Oral examination day at the university. Students, members of the class of 1999, silently fill the classroom auditorium as the professor prepares to deliver their final exam.

Part one of the test is on the sciences. The class members respond rapidly and correctly to the professor's random questions, as though the minutiae of the subject had been drilled into them. Addressing one student, Johnson, the professor asks him to name four men whose work has been related to propulsion. Johnson repeats three, but falters on the last name. The impatient professor, making a notation on his student roster, asks the trembling student to sit down. Johnson hesitates, insisting desperately that part of his answer was correct. The professor, infuriated at Johnson's presumption and his poor scholarship, upbraids him severely.

Moving on to the behavioral sciences, the professor calls on a student, Clinton, and poses to him a hypothetical case: he and another student, Barnes, are in competition for an extremely important professional position. The professor asks Clinton to describe Barnes, which he does, noting height, weight, and approximate age. "Look at him again," prods the professor. "Is there any other salient feature which you might consider relevant?" Clinton replies flatly, "He's black." "And being black may pose a special problem," continues the professor. Clinton responds: "He might be pushy . . . aggressive . . . he might be inferior." The professor calmly asks how Clinton would react on the primary emotional level to a man like Barnes. "I'd slap him." The professor, nodding, solicits the action. Clinton moves down the lecture hall steps to face Barnes . . . and slaps him. Now addressing the other student, the professor asks for Barnes's response. "Slap him back"—and Barnes does so at the professor's request.

The next student, Miss Peterson, is allowed by the professor to choose anyone in the class to whom she responds negatively: a Miss Fields. The antipathy springs from social status, Peterson being from a poor family, Fields from the wealthy elite. The professor impels a display of hostility from the two with the same cold, clinical analysis as before—an explosion of violence followed by an immediate return to order.

Next, the professor calls on Elkins, a pale, dark-haired student. The hypothesis: a society made up of his own kind and an enemy. The chosen enemy: scanning the top row of the lecture hall, Elkins picks out an Asian student, William Chang. Asked by the professor to characterize a possible relationship, Elkins replies that none is possible—a question only of survival, him or Chang. And how should Elkins deal with him? "I would have to kill him," Elkins replies. At this, the professor produces a handgun and places it on the lectern. Elkins takes it and climbs the lecture hall steps, taking aim at Chang. He hesitates. The professor demands he proceed. Elkins fires—and shoots out a light fixture, deliberately missing his quarry. The professor is furious and demands to know why he missed killing the enemy. Elkins falters, as if trying to grasp some concept beyond his comprehension. "I'm not sure he *is* the enemy," he responds. The professor, seeing the murmured reactions of the other students, hurriedly deactivates the class. Elkins, he says, has infected the others. The students slowly grind to a halt, winding down like spent clocks. Demanding selective control, the professor calls on Johnson. The professor instructs Johnson to explain the ramifications of Elkins's resistance. "He failed to kill the enemy. So what evolves is yet a second enemy. A traitor . . . a subversive . . . an unreliable." Johnson takes the pistol from the deactivated Elkins, points it at the student's head, and fires. Elkins falls to the steps, a sputtering mass of wires and circuits in the wrecked cavern of his once-human face. "Very good, Mr. Johnson," nods the professor. "You have reinstated yourself most admirably. You get an A."

At the commencement ceremony, Johnson addresses his classmates. Their purpose, he says, is to repopulate society in a world depleted by holocaust. "We have been created by man in his image. All that we know—our attitudes, our values—are part of the integral data fed into us and we shall use them as a point of beginning. We must be just . . . but ruthless in terms of survival. We must recognize that many of the ancient virtues are simply weaknesses. For example, to tolerate an inferior is an act of misplaced compassion and, as such, interferes with our function as members of the society. We shall repay our debt to man by emulating him. We shall act as men . . . react as men. We shall *be* men."

/ **Commentary** / A Serling original, "Class of '99" graphically exemplified to both Jack Laird and the author what Jeannot Szwarc could do for *Night Gallery*. "This kid is brilliant," Serling said, "a consumately skilled director. [The story takes place] all in one classroom, and at no single moment did you ever feel confined, or that you were in the same place. There was movement, movement, movement, constantly."[16] Szwarc was equally taken with Serling's work ("Jack sent me the script and I fell on my ass!"[17]), devising a complicated sequence of tracking shots, cuts, and changing perspectives to mirror the play's gradual arc of tension—all shot on a restrictive one-and-a-half-day schedule, Szwarc's fluidly moving camera and pacing turned a potentially static piece into riveting drama, aided in no small part by the performances of the principals.

Vincent Price is magnetic as the steely, imperious professor, probing for weaknesses in his graduating class of robot surrogates. His harsh manner suggests that not everything is what it seems here, and the viewer's perceptions are then upended when the professor begins proctoring the class in the social imperatives of bigotry. The shock is abrupt and leaves the audience scrambling for answers: What kind of final exam is this? What kind of university is this? What kind of *society* is this? And then, reminiscent of the staggering finale to his screenplay for *Planet of the Apes*, Serling reveals that it is our own. We have passed our dread legacy on to the next eager generation of rote-spinning automatons. Presenting material more appropriate to a neo-Fascist rally (and strongly reflective of the racial turmoil of the times), Serling shrewdly tosses his gasoline cocktail into the benign, high-minded halls of academe. In Serling's future, intolerance has become institutionalized. Price's calm, clinical delivery of this incendiary material is icy and authoritative.

Conversely, the other actors on the set found Price as charming as his character was forbidding. "He was very accessible," recalls Frank Hotchkiss, who played Clinton. "Very pleasant, open, and an interesting guy. He was very happy to talk to people in the cast who had the chutzpah to go up and say 'Hi,' and chat with him. He was quite the opposite of what I expected." During the few lulls in the shooting, Hotchkiss and Price discussed art, photography, and, of course, acting. "He opened that show beautifully with that minute monologue," says Hotchkiss, "sets the whole thing in his inimitable fashion."[18]

Brandon de Wilde also turns in a fine performance as the quick-to-recover Johnson. Best known for his previous work in the classic feature films *Shane, The Member of the Wedding,* and *Hud,* de Wilde's distinguished career ended abruptly—and tragically —the next year. While performing *Butterflies Are Free* in Colorado, a traffic accident ended his life at age thirty.

Trying to disguise the true identities of the students until the finish, Szwarc lectured his acting "class" in the correct behavior of robots. "Jeannot warned us against too much overexpression," recalls Barbara Shannon, who played Miss Peterson. "He told us, 'You have to remember that you are *all* robots, and that you're infiltrating society as humans. You have been programmed for certain behavior according to your social class, but without too much emotion.' At the time, I thought I would play my scene with a little more 'low class,' to give it more color. And Jeannot had to remind me, 'No, you can't do that. There has to be just a *flicker* of emotion.'"[19] The cooling effect of the students' deportment, just shy of deadpan, helps throw Serling's controversial themes into stark relief.

Adding to the segment's effectiveness is its remarkable set, a white-on-white classroom auditorium designed by Joseph Alves, and the fluorescent paranoia of Lionel Lindon's lighting. Combined, they vividly create an atmosphere of cold, antiseptic unease. The special effects for the robot shut-down finale were remarkably simple— in fact, there were none. "There were no opticals in that show," Szwarc recalls. "When you find out the students are robots, and they slow down and freeze, all that was done *live* because we didn't have money for opticals."[20] Confirms Hotchkiss: "We actually *did* freeze. I don't know how long we held that pose."[21]

Technically as well as conceptually, "Class of '99" is a superb testament to what *Night Gallery* could be, and marked a turning point in Szwarc's involvement in the series. "When Serling saw the show, he thought it was terrific," Szwarc recounts. "The rushes were at lunch, and I couldn't make it. When they came back, I was told that Rod Serling kept asking, 'Who is this guy? Boy, this is terrific!' That's when I got to meet him. From then on I sort of had open access to all his scripts. He asked Jack Laird if I could do his stuff regularly."[22]

Later in the season, Szwarc would return to direct a number of classic *Gallery* segments, including H. P. Lovecraft's "Cool Air," "The Sins of the Fathers," and the series' best-remembered episode, "The Caterpillar."

4a
WITCHES' FEAST
★

Written by Gene Kearney
Directed by Jerrold Freedman

Music: John Lewis
Director of Photography: Lionel Lindon
Time: 5:04

**Cast**
Head Witch: Agnes Moorehead
Hungry Witch: Ruth Buzzi
3d Witch: Fran Ryan
4th Witch: Allison McKay

*Agnes Moorehead, Ruth Buzzi, and Fran Ryan in "Witches' Feast." Courtesy of TV History Archives.*

*A* bizarre little item here offered to the gourmet who takes his banquet seriously. If sometime you're invited to a picnic under the moon, you might best check the other guests, the ones who didn't arrive in automobiles—who, as a matter of fact, parked their brooms in the corner of the meadow. This little nocturnal clambake is called "Witches' Feast."

/ **Summary** / Sabbat night. Three cackling witches romp around a bubbling cauldron, tossing various squirmy ingredients into the vile stew while awaiting the arrival of a fourth. One witch, hungry to the point of starvation, is in a desperate lather over the fourth witch's tardiness. "I could have formed a coven and held a black mass, sacrificial virgin and all," she growls, "in the time it's taking her!" Finally the fourth member of the coven arrives, carrying the precious package the hungry witch has so eagerly desired: their deli take-out order. "Now," cackles the fourth witch, "who had ham on rye?"

/ **Commentary** / For this brief business, the casting department dipped into the ensemble pool of the sensationally popular comedy-variety show *Rowan and Martin's Laugh-In*, hiring Ruth Buzzi to play the hungry witch. "I was really looking forward to this role because I love to play witches," Buzzi recalls. "I was very good at makeup—making witches' noses and that kind of thing—and after graduating from the Pasadena Playhouse, I was able to play witches in *Macbeth* and *Dark of the Moon*." Her costar in this segment, Agnes Moorehead, also knew her way around a cauldron, having starred as the imperious Endora in the long-running ABC television series *Bewitched*. "We had a wonderful time," Buzzi says of the filming, "and it was nice letting somebody else make up my nose for a change! It was just a lark!"[23]

Unfortunately, this lark laid a big, fat egg. Even at five minutes this tedious vignette is too long by half, and wears out its welcome long before its painful denouement. With the trappings of a high school skit, "Witches' Feast"—written in verse by Gene Kearney—reflects nothing but the writer's apparent disdain for the genre to which *Night Gallery* was intended as a respectful homage.

4b

SATISFACTION GUARANTEED

★ ★ ★

Written by Jack Laird
Directed by Jeannot Szwarc
Music: John Lewis      Intro: Oliver Nelson
Director of Photography: Lionel Lindon
Time: 5:03

**Cast**
Customer: Victor Buono
Mrs. Mount: Cathleen Cordell
Miss Walters: Marion Charles
Miss Ransom: Leigh Christian
Miss Caraway: Eve Curtis
Miss Blodgett: Cherie Franklin

*Victor Buono in "Satisfaction Guaranteed." Courtesy of
Sal Milo.*

/ **Summary** / A large, distinguished gentleman grills Mrs. Mount, the head of an employment agency, concerning his stringent requirements for a new employee. "I am extremely particular, Mrs. Mount—*extremely particular.*" She assures him she relishes the challenge and ushers in the candidates one by one. Despite their sterling qualifications, the customer expresses disappointment and dismisses them all. Mrs. Mount is clearly at a loss, for she has no one else available. Her first dissatisfied customer in twenty-five years!—she is mortified.

In walks Mrs. Mount's file clerk, a plain, full-fleshed woman who hovers efficiently over a filing cabinet. The customer, staring, asks eagerly about her. Miss Blodgett, the agent dismisses, knows no shorthand, cannot type, has illegible handwriting . . . she can't even brew a digestible cup of coffee. "Nobody's perfect," the customer smiles, writing out a check. Mrs. Mount is dumbstruck: "You actually *want* Miss Blodgett?" "She is precisely what I have been looking for," he enthuses, opening his briefcase. The defeated agent concedes, asking glumly when he wishes her to report. "That won't be necessary," he leers purposefully, tucking a serviette under his chin and fingering a set of cutlery. "I can just eat her here."

/ **Commentary** / Surprisingly amusing, "Satisfaction Guaranteed" was slipped in as a substitution for "Witches' Feast" during the rerun showing of *Night Gallery* #34301 on March 22, 1972, a welcome replacement for its dreadful predecessor. In a game of broadcasting musical chairs, a decision was made two days before #34301 first aired in September to replace "Witches' Feast" with "Satisfaction Guaranteed," but was reversed before the premiere air date. Too bad.

Laird's script gets the luxury treatment from the comic talents of Victor Buono and Cathleen Cordell and the directorial touches of Jeannot Szwarc, whose visuals highlight the drollness of the writing. The segment's racy double entendre punch line did cause some concern, however.

"God, that's Jack Laird for you," winces Szwarc. "You know, when I read that script, I told him, 'You'll never get away with that last line.' But he stuck to it, and his defense was very simple. Whenever someone would say something about it, he'd say, 'Well, you guys have really dirty minds, I never thought about that.' And that would be the end. And we got away with it."[24]

Szwarc and company's efforts paid off; the segment was a hit. It even generated audience response—much to the confusion of actress Cherie Franklin, who played the edible Miss Blodgett: "I got my first two fan letters because of that show! And that really scared me, because I thought, '*What?* Oh, my God, who's out there, and what on earth are they doing sending a letter to *me!?*'"[25]

## NIGHT GALLERY #34303
Air date: September 29, 1971

### 1
### SINCE AUNT ADA CAME TO STAY
★ ★ ★

Teleplay by Alvin Sapinsley
Based on the short story "The Witch"
   by A. E. van Vogt
Directed by William Hale
Music: John Lewis
Director of Photography: Lionel Lindon
Time: 30:38

**Cast**
Craig Lowell: James Farentino
Joanna Lowell: Michele Lee
Aunt Ada: Jeanette Nolan
Nick Porteus: Jonathan Harris
Frank Heller: Eldon Quick
Cemetery Caretaker: Charles Seel

*James Farentino and Jeanette Nolan in "Since Aunt Ada Came to Stay." Courtesy of UCLA Research Library Arts Special Collections.*

Housekeeper: Alma Platt
Messenger Boy: Arnold Turner

*For those of you who've never met me, you might call me the undernourished Alfred Hitchcock. The great British craftsman and I do share something in common: an interest in the oddball; a predilection toward the bizarre—and this place is nothing if it isn't bizarre, by virtue of the paintings you see hanging around me.*

*This item here is called "Since Aunt Ada Came to Stay," and Aunt Ada is a most memorable character. You may not like her, but I seriously doubt if you'll ever forget her. Be thankful you've met her only in the* Night Gallery.

/ **Summary** / Craig Lowell, a professor of logic and scientific method, is becoming annoyed with his wife Joanna's visiting Aunt Ada. The old woman seems to dote on her niece like a parasite. Ada's eccentricities are legion: the specially blended herb teas she brews for Joanna; her rhyming homilies; her violent allergic reaction to all flowers, particularly Craig's prized green carnations; and her spooky tendency to be seemingly there one moment . . . and gone the next. Most disturbing of all, though, is the vague sense of menace Craig feels from her.

Suspicious, Craig filches some of Aunt Ada's herbs for analysis. The verdict: common seaweed. But a folklore specialist at the university, Nick Porteus, pronounces it virulent, "the sinister witches' weed of antiquity." According to Porteus, the weed is employed by the aging witch who has used up her present body to facilitate her entry into the new, young body that she has chosen for herself. This transformation supposedly occurs at midnight during the first full moon following the autumn equinox. Craig scoffs, but Porteus is in earnest, noting additionally that he has never seen Craig without the one weapon that can prevent the transformation: the green carnation he always wears in his lapel. Porteus claims burning it in the witch's presence during the transfer will destroy her power—and he cautions Craig not to forget it.

Craig now doubts the identity of the old guest in his house, and searches the county records for the true whereabouts of Ada Burn Quigley. To his surprise, he finds her name on a headstone. A talkative cemetery caretaker claims he saw Ada Quigley buried six months previously. Returning home, Craig angrily confronts Aunt Ada about his discoveries. "Madam, who are you? Why are you here? *I will have an answer!"* In a flash, the old woman seems to replicate in front of Craig's startled eyes: one, two, three Aunt Adas, shrieking in defiance. She has dared to show him her powers, absolutely secure that he can do nothing to interfere.

In truth, Craig can say nothing to Joanna for fear she will think him mad. His only ally, Professor Porteus, suffers a mysterious stroke, a condition Craig is sure was brought about by Aunt Ada; and the old woman has ominously announced her departure in just a few days—after the first full moon of the autumn equinox. Craig realizes now if he wishes to save Joanna he cannot let her out of his sight for a moment or Aunt Ada will seize the opportunity.

The old witch works hard to separate them. Through her offices, Craig gets locked into teaching an associate's night class on the evening of the first full moon. Frantic, he persuades Joanna to accompany him so he can keep an eye on her all the while. His ruse fails when Ada, casting a spell, reaches out to the pliant Joanna, causing her to slip out of the class undetected and return home. As Ada is persuading the entranced Joanna to sip the last of the herb tea, back at the college Craig finally notices that his wife is no longer in her seat. Racing home, he arrives just scant minutes before midnight to find Joanna seemingly drugged and Ada laboring at some abstruse incantation. Getting between Joanna and the wild-eyed crone, Craig suddenly finds himself faced with twelve Aunt Adas who force him to the side as they attempt to complete the unholy transfer. Remembering Porteus's warning, Craig pulls the green carnation from his lapel and sets it ablaze. The splintered Aunt Ada, howling in agony, is suddenly conjoined and engulfed in green flames. As the midnight bell tolls into silence, she is reduced to a pile of ash. Craig cradles Joanna gently in his arms as she revives from her stupor.

The morning brings a return to normalcy. Joanna sends Craig off to work with a kiss, waving as his car pulls out of the driveway. Slowing down at the end of the block, he hesitates when he realizes he is without his green carnation. Joanna must have forgotten to put it in his lapel—part of her unvarying morning ritual. Shrugging, Craig continues on. As Joanna stands waving after him from the driveway, she glares side-eyed at the nest of green carnations in the front garden, giving them a wide berth as she returns to the house.

**/ Commentary /** Adapted from A. E. van Vogt's short story "The Witch," script-writer Alvin Sapinsley devised a more straightforward narrative that would open up the quiet, hallucinatory original. Unfortunately, part of it involved a hackneyed device to destroy Aunt Ada, a correlative to the werewolf's silver bullet—the green carnation. In van Vogt's short story, seawater was the fatal element, a plot point that might have brought with it too many recollections of Margaret Hamilton and Judy Garland. Sapinsley's version *did* give the special effects technicians a field day, however, in devising ways to split Aunt Ada into twelve cackling hags and to plot her dramatic and incendiary exit.

"Those shows were really fun to do, I'll tell you," affirms director William Hale. "My best one by far was 'Aunt Ada.' I didn't really know Jeanette Nolan, and the first day she came in I said, 'Let's go over to wardrobe and we'll try to work out some kind of outfit.' She said, 'No, no, it's okay, I have it already.' And she had this whole set of witch's teeth that she'd already made up or something, they were all filed down. She did everything herself, the makeup, everything. All I did was shove a 9.8 millimeter lens right into her face, which really distorted her."[26]

A stunning actress, Nolan has played a witch more than once in her career, and makes a potent Aunt Ada—perhaps too potent. The story's effectiveness depends on Craig Lowell's (and the audience's) *gradual* realization of Aunt Ada's true identity and sinister intentions. With her parchment skin, file-sharpened teeth and cronelike intonations, Nolan so obviously suggests *Walpurgisnacht* that any idiot, much less a professor of logic, would have pegged her as a witch from day one. Although the short story itself begins from this premise, van Vogt's characterization of Aunt Ada is much more deceptively benign. Nolan from the get-go is downright scary.

Beyond doubt, the worst single gaffe was casting Jonathan Harris (*Lost in Space*), whose fey performance as Professor Porteus leans toward parody. Harris's febrile theatrics and oracular pomp succeed only in giving the proceedings an inappropriate comic edge. As the Lowells, James Farentino and Michele Lee give far more sober and reasoned performances, raising the plausibility quotient of the segment. The two actors were married at the time, and found themselves teamed frequently in various productions during the 1970s.

"'Aunt Ada' was our first television drama together," Lee says. "Someone had a little brainstorm to cast us together, and we jumped at the chance! Jim and I worked very well together, and that was always a nice part of our relationship. Husbands and wives sometimes have problems that way, but we always really enjoyed it. We had a lot of fun doing this episode."[27]

On the technical side, "Aunt Ada" sports some startling effects produced by editor Larry Lester. In the conjuring sequence where Aunt Ada tries to take over Joanna's body, he engineered an unusual dissolve that had never before been attempted, intercutting shots of Nolan and Lee with multicolored frames to create a novel and bizarre effect. "I had these great shots of Jeanette Nolan," says Lester, "a move-in with that nine-millimeter lens which got up right to her nose and eyes, and Michele Lee sitting in the classroom. I took those cuts and intermixed them with white frames, red frames and blue frames, drawing Aunt Ada and Michele Lee together, trying to make the transformation come to a head." To screw the suspense even tighter, Lester created a sense of urgency and panic by intercutting shots of Farentino, struggling to get home to his wife before the witching hour, with insert shots of a clock's gears ticking off the precious seconds. His fine work added immeasurably to the segment, although as Lester himself admits, "I was bombed out of my skull when I cut that."[28]

Despite the technical excellence of the segment, not everyone received their due praise. Hale's inspired and inventive visuals were unfortunately achieved at a considerable cost to himself:

I got fired doing that one. We did a lot of stuff with split diopters, a camera lens with a split line down the center so one side of the frame is sharply in focus way up front, and one side of it is sharply in focus way in the background. For example, when James Farentino is on the phone in the foreground, and Jeanette Nolan is up on the balcony, way the hell up there, and the whole frame is sharp—you couldn't do that with a normal lens. You'd have to carry either one of them or the other, especially with the lighting level that they used. The split diopter makes all that possible, but it takes a bit of lining up to do. That's one of the reasons I got canned, because those things take a while to set up.

For all his efforts to create an imaginative, visually interesting segment, Hale went ten hours over on the last day of a four-day shoot. "We're talking about Friday afternoon, now," explains Hale, "and the minute night falls, everybody panics because at midnight you get hit with every penalty known to mankind. I couldn't reach Jack to get his okay on some cuts I wanted to make, so I just had to shoot everything. I ended up going to about four in the morning." Without informing him, Laird summarily fired Hale—creating for the director a rather embarrassing episode the following Monday morning. "Jack didn't have the guts to tell me I was fired. I showed up on the lot and started talking to Curly and the crew about the next show I was going to do, and they all looked at me like I was nuts. I was running around making plans, and finally about noon the production manager said, 'Look, don't you know you don't work here anymore?' I felt like a bloody idiot."[29]

Laird and Hale would later patch things up and work together again on *Kojak* and other projects, but Hale would never return to direct another segment of *Night Gallery*.

2
## WITH APOLOGIES TO MR. HYDE
★ ½

Written by Jack Laird
Directed by Jeannot Szwarc
Music: John Lewis and Oliver Nelson
Director of Photography: Lionel Lindon
Time: 1:56

**Cast**
Dr. Jekyll: Adam West
Laboratory Assistant: Jack Laird

*Adam West in "With Apologies to Mr. Hyde." Courtesy of TV History Archives.*

**/ Summary /** Dr. Jekyll, dressed for the evening, accepts a beaker from his hunch-backed lab assistant, who grins insanely as his master downs the draught. Reeling, Jekyll gasps in pain as the transformation begins. His brows beetle, his nose flares, his skin becomes leathery, his hair coarsens. Staggering to a mirror, Dr. Jekyll stares in shock at the new face reflected in the glass. Turning to his giggling assistant, Jekyll shouts hoarsely, "If I told you once, I've told you a hundred times—*go easy on the vermouth!*"

/ **Commentary** / Director Jeannot Szwarc proves here he can make something watchable out of the worst material. Having absorbed enough horror film clichés to know where he's going, both the look and pacing of the segment work. If only the script did.

Adam West, who made a career fighting over-the-top villains as Batman, this time got to play one. The brief shooting schedule, however, required him to play it backward. Because makeup is easier to remove than apply, the segment was filmed in reverse, punch line first.

Jack Laird here stepped in for a rare cameo appearance on *Night Gallery,* the first of three. Taking a page from the notebooks of such great hunchbacked lab assistants as Dwight Frye and Bela Lugosi, Laird attempted a twisted homage—not, alas, with any success. Apologies are due, not to Mr. Hyde, but to the viewers of this insulting drivel.

3

THE FLIP-SIDE OF SATAN
★ ★

Teleplay by Malcolm Marmorstein and Gerald Sanford
Based on the story by Hal Dresner
Directed by Jerrold Freedman
Music: Gil Mellé and John Lewis
Director of Photography: Lionel Lindon
Time: 17:03

**Cast**

J. J. Wilson: Arte Johnson

*Arte Johnson in "The Flip-Side of Satan." Courtesy of TV History Archives.*

We *refer to him by different names—Lucifer, Mephistopheles, Beelzebub—but by any other name, he'd smell of brimstone. These, the ingredients to a one-man stew: a disc jockey, a radio show, and a painting we call "The Flip-Side of Satan."*

/ **Summary** / East coast disc jockey J. J. Wilson hits the airwaves at his new job: the midnight-to-six shift at KAPH, a tiny five-thousand-watt radio station in the middle of nowhere. The station is deserted, and a note in the broadcasting booth directs him to play only the records on the playlist—no variations. When he drops the needle on the first platter, a funeral dirge for organ greets his disbelieving ears. Disgusted, Wilson dials up his agent, Sid, to complain, but the conversation quickly turns to Emily, Sid's late wife, who committed suicide after some sort of emotional breakdown. Sid's suspicions about Wilson's possible involvement with Emily leave the oily deejay scrambling to counter the accusations. It was pure coincidence, Wilson claims, that Emily was away on the same weekends that he was off fishing with Bert Fox.

After cueing up the second, equally unpleasant platter, Wilson calls Bert Fox and presses him to cover for those weekend trysts with Emily. "I just don't like hurting people, Bert, *you* know that," smirks Wilson. "Besides, Sidney's been like a father to me. I like to think I kept Emily from doing what she was destined to do much sooner." Hanging up the receiver, Wilson notices as he turns up the volume that record number two has a spoken narration—sounding much like his own voice. Some sort of satanic ritual from the sound of it. Wilson cuts off the music, explaining to his listeners about how the boss jocks at the station must be ribbing the new guy. Pulling one of his own LPs out of his briefcase, Wilson cues it up—and from the grooves comes the incantatory voice he heard on the previous record: "Oh, Lucifer, the condemned has entered into the crucible from which there is no escape . . ." To his further shock, Wilson finds he is trapped in the broadcasting booth; the telephone's outside line is now dead; and beneath the photos of the past deejays for KAPH lining the studio walls, the listed dates for their tenure lasted no longer than a day! "The Prince of Darkness will receive the condemned," intones the recorded voice as Wilson, frantically scrambling to shut down the station, reaches for the power switch—and is grounded, rigid, to the floor as thousands of amps of electric current arc through his body.

And joining the roster of condemned disc jockeys on the walls at KAPH is yet another photograph—that of J. J. Wilson.

/ **Commentary** / Another disappointment weighs in to kill the hour. The story has worthwhile elements, the direction is inventive and crisp, the set, music, and photography effectively create the predawn limbo of late night radio, but ultimately the success of the piece rises or falls on the choice of the lead. At first, Mickey Rooney signed to play the role. His growing dislike for the script caused him to back out, however, and Arte Johnson agreed to step in. Unfortunately, Johnson doesn't have in his actor's arsenal the tools to bring this greasy, self-centered nightcrawler to life. An alumnus of *Rowan and Martin's Laugh-In,* Johnson was no doubt hired because of his then-high audience recognition quotient. But without a skilled actor to flesh some interesting, believable tics into the character, "Flip-Side" is a waste of time.

"We had a day and a half to shoot it," recalls director Jerrold Freedman. "The first day of shooting I hadn't done anything but shot planning because I had this incredibly elaborate set. We did the whole thing in one or two shots the next day."[30]

One of the screeching frustrations about *Night Gallery* was Laird's tendency to underutilize some of his most promising directors. Jerrold Freedman was one of them. Wasting his talents on a series of extended sketches rather than allowing him to helm meatier segments was perverse. As evidenced by "Marmalade Wine," "Dr. Stringfellow's Rejuvenator," and his chilling 1973 made-for-TV masterpiece *A Cold Night's Death*, his work in this genre could be rich and compelling.

NIGHT GALLERY #34305
Air date: October 6, 1971

1

A FEAR OF SPIDERS
★ ★ ★ ★

Teleplay by Rod Serling
Based on the short story "The Spider" by
    Elizabeth Walter
Directed by John Astin
Music: Oliver Nelson, Gil Mellé, and John Lewis
Director of Photography: Lionel Lindon
Time: 21:48

**Cast**
Justus Walters: Patrick O'Neal
Elizabeth: Kim Stanley
Mr. Boucher: Tom Pedi

*Patrick O'Neal and Kim Stanley in "A Fear of Spiders." Courtesy of Globe Photos.*

$G$*ood evening. We welcome you to this palladium of art treasures that range from the kooky to the uncommon, from the bestial to the bizarre, and I'd like to take you on a guided tour through the Night Gallery. A collection of paintings on display for only the most discriminating because it's best that they be seen both after and in the dark.*

*The story behind this offering: a word which we've coined just for the occasion—arachnophobia. It means for our purposes a special distaste for those crawly little beasties with the multi-legged hairy bodies. In other words, "A Fear of Spiders," the title of our first painting in this, the Night Gallery.*

**/ Summary /** Gourmet critic Justus Walters is trying without success to complete three articles under deadline. He has suffered continuous interruptions from various quarters: his landlord; his upstairs neighbor Elizabeth Croft, a clingy librarian he had taken to dinner once or twice; and most disturbingly, a spider in his kitchen sink. Justus has a deathly fear of spiders, and this long-legged hairy beast exhibits a frightening tenacity. Every time Justus flushes it down the drain, it crawls back up—and from Justus's phobic viewpoint, apparently larger each time.

As for the two-legged pests, Justus finally brushes Elizabeth off with a rudeness that does the trick. As Justus returns to his typewriter, he is interrupted by another sound: a high-pitched squeaking coming from his bedroom. He peers in, but slams the door quickly shut. Behind a chair crouches a monstrous black spider the size of a dog!

Shaken, Justus races upstairs to call on Elizabeth, who takes pleasure in watching him grovel. When she hears of his reason for wanting her company, however, she is insulted and demands he leave. Justus begs her to humor him, just to see if the monster is still there. Elizabeth grudgingly accepts, following the high-strung writer to his apartment. She examines the kitchen, the living room—no spiders. She opens the door to the bedroom and walks in. Nothing. Elizabeth invites him to see for himself, and a trembling Justus peeks over her shoulder . . . then enters carefully, peering into the far corner. . . .

Elizabeth quickly retreats and locks Justus into the bedroom. Pounding on the door, the frightened columnist begs frantically for her to let him out. Elizabeth merely laughs. The tables having been turned to her satisfaction, she promises to return in the morning. Hearing a noise, Justus turns and freezes at the sight. *"It's in here!"* he cries, dissolving into hysteria. She ignores his desperate pleas, crosses to the door—oblivious to the abrupt termination of Justus's frenzied screams—and exits the now-silent apartment.

**/ Commentary /** This marvelous black-comic segment works like a good theater piece, and is blessed with two brilliant actors who make the most of its bitchy repartee: Patrick O'Neal and, in a rare television appearance, New York stage actress Kim Stanley. Serling's acerbic adaptation of Elizabeth Walter's short story "The Spider" retains much of the original while adding, for exposition's sake, the character of Boucher, the landlord. Character actor Tom Pedi does a nice comic turn here, and his appearance echoes a similar scene from a *Twilight Zone* episode, "A Thing About Machines," another tale of a mordant columnist's unpleasant comeuppance. The *Night Gallery* episode is vastly superior.

Laird's initial choice for director of "A Fear of Spiders" begged off at the last minute—a decision that could have had disastrous consequences for the young man's career. During a meeting between Laird and head writer Gerald Sanford, the director, exhausted from completing two back-to-back episodes of another show, interrupted to report that he would be unable to helm the segment, set to begin prepping the very next day. "I had worked in television for ten years and I had never heard of *anything* like this before," recalls Sanford. The ensuing argument with Laird did nothing to force the harried young director to back down. "When he left, I looked at Jack and said, 'My God, what's going to happen to him?' And he said, 'I don't know, but I'll tell you this, he'll never work at Universal again!' As it turned out, I believe Jack was wrong about Spielberg."[31]

Fatigued from the rigors of his schedule and disillusioned by the grind of cranking out episodic television, Steven Spielberg was approaching burnout. John Astin, director of the first-season segment "The House," was then approached. Unaware of Spielberg's previous interest, Astin came to the episode with a fresh, enthusiastic outlook, demonstrated by the segment's inventive direction and improvisatory style.

The parts were already cast before Astin's involvement, and he was pleased at the prospect of working with O'Neal and Stanley. "I was a great admirer of Kim Stanley," Astin says, "and she was coming out by train because she was afraid to fly." Astin surprised the actress by meeting her at the train station and taking her to lunch. "We had a sandwich together and talked. It turned out that Kim was not completely happy with the way the dialogue read, and our conversation about the script went way into the night. Her ideas were really fascinating."[32] Astin mentioned Stanley's interest in script changes to those in charge, but Laird decreed the script was inviolable.

On *Night Gallery,* the subject of script changes is a sticky affair, and Serling's original script for "A Fear of Spiders" does show signs of tampering. First to take credit for them is script editor Gerald Sanford: "My favorite was 'A Fear of Spiders.' I just loved it, to me that was like writing a stage play. I didn't get credit, but to this day I still write with the same flow and everything. I don't think Rod had anything to do with that, either. I think somebody else did a script on that or something, and I did a page-one, word-one rewrite on it."[33]

Sanford's claim is contradicted by hard evidence. Serling's final draft shows that his script reached the screen with much of his work intact. For the first twelve pages—until the point where Justus goes to Elizabeth's apartment to ask for her help—the dialogue is all Serling's. For the last twelve, someone made some changes—mainly for Elizabeth's character—that are bracing, pointed, and entirely in keeping with the tone of the first half. Roughly a third of her dialogue in the last two scenes was discarded and succinctly replaced. According to Astin, those changes to the script were made surreptitiously, not by Sanford, but by Stanley.

"When Kim came on the set," Astin says,

she started changing dialogue and improvising stuff, particularly those scenes in her apartment. She wasn't doing it as written, but it was terrific! The first day of the shoot the crew was *not* happy with her, and they raised all kinds of hell on the set. The phone calls went to the front office, and I was called on the carpet—"*She's changing dialogue!*" And I said, "Yeah, guys, she's changing dialogue—but this stuff looks great, wait until you see it!" Well, they saw the dailies the next day, and nobody cared *what* she did with it at that point, because she was *cooking!* She had taken what Rod had written and explored it for herself on a very deep level. She had a wonderful understanding of this character.

Stanley's rephrasing improved the flow and pacing of the last two scenes and allowed the actress to make her points not with verbiage but with nuance and delivery. As finally filmed, "A Fear of Spiders" is a witty, penetrating piece of television theater, the kind that is now practically extinct. Every line of dialogue rings with distinctive rhythms and elegant turns of phrase, and the kudos must be shared by both Serling and Stanley for their work on this episode.

"Rod really understood the stuff he wrote," Astin says. "I have a deep commitment to the collaboration between the writer and the director. I always picked Rod's brains about his stuff, and he was always good to connect with. But it just wasn't a match between Rod's view and what Kim thought that lady should be. I think that, on a deeper level, Rod and Kim weren't *really* in conflict. It's just that, in her case, she knew best. Her instincts were so amazingly rich, that when the words came out of her, they were the correct words—whether they were Rod's or her own. She was *amazing*. Amazing woman."

As Justus, Patrick O'Neal is Stanley's equal—a performance of enjoyable flamboyance, his affected effeminacy matched with an acid edginess—and a quite believable fear. "In the final scene," recalls Astin, "Patrick just took off! He was very, very strong at the end. It wasn't all that common for him to let loose that wildly, but he just let it fly. He was very powerful. I think it's one of Patrick's better pieces of work."

O'Neal also had to do battle with a pair of the reluctant arachnids scrambling about his kitchen sink. They developed a bad case of stage fright, according to Astin: "They brought in these trap-door spiders, and they auditioned very well. But when they got under the hot lights they wouldn't move! And we sat there for the longest time with these spiders, but they eventually performed quite well. In fact, one of the tarantulas *would not go down that drain!* And it was a wonderful moment when Patrick kept trying to wash him down and he kept fighting his way back—it was *creepy.*"

Lost from the original story for the censor's sake is the sexual encounter between Justus and the relationship-hungry Elizabeth, which would have sealed the audience's impression that the gourmet is being stalked by something other than just an eight-legged predator. "Kim Stanley felt very strongly that she was the spider," Astin says. "She wore the black to suggest that, and she was a little overweight—you know, the spider grew bigger and bigger—and she started playing it that way." Stanley's take on the character restores to the script the identical suggested inference from the short story.

The spider, manageably cat-sized in the short story, was transformed by the Universal special effects department into a much larger monster. Its appearance is plainly artificial; mercifully its screen time is brief, a matter of seconds. "We showed as little of it as possible," Astin says. "They spent a lot of time building that thing. Just as by today's standards the shark in *Jaws* is nothing, back then it was very credible. But you only show a flash of those things." In a wise and visually creative move, Astin dismissed the spider entirely in the finale, where Lionel Lindon's camera tracks in stealthily on Justus as he hysterically begs Elizabeth to let him out of his bedroom, now a deathtrap.

Astin made further imaginative use of Lindon's expert lensing. The opening shot, a precipitous high-angle shot peering down on Justus at his typewriter, works not only as an establishing shot but as a subtly suggestive point-of-view shot. "I don't know where I came up with that," Astin admits. "It was just instinctive. Later I thought, 'Gee, that was appropriate.' It gave you the geography of the apartment, but I think it also implied that there was something looking down—it could be a spider on the ceiling!"[34]

Joseph Alves's production design adds a wry note. Serling's script suggests that the main character's taste is overly refined but sound. Alves reads his own little twist into Justus's character by making his apartment an absolute design horror. It is atrociously decorated, giving the self-satisfied aesthete a rancid sense of style.

Musically, Gil Mellé's creepy percussive cues add the right flesh-crawling touch for the kitchen sink sequence, and Oliver Nelson's score for "The Hand of Borgus Weems" is also adapted to much better effect for this segment. In strength of concept and execution, "A Fear of Spiders" ranks as a series classic—a perfect curtain-raiser to a very strong hour.

2
## JUNIOR
★ ★

Written by Gene Kearney
Directed by Theodore J. Flicker
Music: Oliver Nelson
Director of Photography: Lionel Lindon
Time: 1:49

**Cast**
Father: Wally Cox
Mother: Barbara Flicker
Junior: Bill Svanoe

*Barbara Flicker and Wally Cox in "Junior."*
*Courtesy of Globe Photos.*

**/ Summary /** In the middle of the night, two sleeping parents are awakened by a child's petulant cries. Junior wants a drink of water. The father pokes at the mother, who rolls over mumbling, "It's your baby." Daddy falls out of bed, stumbles to the bathroom, pours a glass of water, and heads for baby's room. Entering, he gives Junior—whose huge Frankenstein monster-sized frame has overwhelmed the crib—his drink. "Thank you, Daddy," Junior replies, spilling his refreshment everywhere but in his mouth.

**/ Commentary /** Here we have a *Night Gallery* rarity: a blackout sketch with an actual point. The contrast of the commonplace parenting situation (Wally Cox's paternal stumblings underscored by Junior's insistent whine) with the crib-bursting Karloff icon, neck bolts and all, is an effective study in the absurd. In childraising, there are times when the demands of parenthood take on this sort of monstrous proportion.

Director Theodore Flicker was well chosen by Laird. Originally a member of Chicago's Second City troupe and writer-director of the outstanding feature *The President's Analyst,* Flicker's forte is twisted comedy. In casting, Flicker aimed close to home, hiring friend and fellow writer Bill Svanoe as Junior, and his wife, Barbara, a former model, as the mother. "They were going to cast a Rock Hudson-type in the other role," Flicker recalls, "some stud to play the guy in bed with my wife. I said, 'Oh, no, sweetheart—you're not getting into bed with any big, famous stud, you're just not.' So I got Wally Cox, which amused the hell out of everybody."[35]

Inane but enjoyable, the real problem with "Junior" is its proximity to "A Fear of Spiders." The vignette follows immediately without a break, damaging the stinging effect of the previous play. The little addenda of the blackouts would have better served the show by being placed after a commercial and immediately before the final credits, limiting audience disappointment.

3
## MARMALADE WINE
★ ★ ★ ½

Teleplay by Jerrold Freedman
Based on the short story by Joan Aiken
Directed by Jerrold Freedman
Music: John Lewis      Intro: Oliver Nelson
Director of Photography: Lionel Lindon
Time: 11:45

*Robert Morse and Rudy Vallee in "Marmalade Wine."*
*Courtesy of Foto Fantasies.*

**Cast**

Roger Blacker: Robert Morse

Dr. Francis Deeking: Rudy Vallee

*I*tem *number three in the* Night Gallery: *we call it "Marmalade Wine." Look at it, if you will, with gentle and restrained eyes, the way you'd look at a maniac in the woods — because that's the story it tells. Hold out your glasses and get ready for a very special nightcap.*

/ **Summary** / Caught in a cloudburst, novice shutterbug Roger Blacker wanders through the woods, hopelessly lost. He comes upon the home of Dr. Francis Deeking, a noted surgeon, now retired. The old man, delighted to have a guest, invites Blacker in out of the rain for a chat over a decanter of marmalade wine. His tongue loosened by the vintage, Blacker brags about his accomplishments as a photographer for *Life* magazine — an outright lie. Flattered by the doctor's interest, Blacker next spins a whopper about his ability to predict the future. Deeking asks for a demonstration. Blacker, hardly missing a beat, pulls out of thin air the results of a horse race and an election, the wine releasing him from all compunction over the outrageousness of this untruth. Deeking trots off, leaving Blacker to ponder what it was about the famous surgeon that he'd read recently — something strange — until finally slipping off into a drunken sleep.

When he awakens, he finds himself lying in a strange bed. He's nursing the mother of all hangovers, his feet are terribly sore, and he is being ministered to by the doctor. Blacker tries to apologize for his shameless fibs; Deeking informs him that the predictions came true and now wants some stock tips before the exchange closes. Blacker explains that it was all an extraordinary coincidence, but Deeking's enthusiasm cannot be dampened. As the doctor trots off to phone his broker, Blacker freezes in alarm. Deeking, he finally remembers, was barred from practicing surgery — he is insane. Blacker tries painfully to climb out of bed but is checked by the return of his host, who states mildly that leaving is out of the question. "But don't worry, you'll be very happy here. While you were asleep, I took the liberty of amputating your feet."

/ **Commentary** / Brief but potent, "Marmalade Wine" is perhaps the most successful of the shorter segments on *Night Gallery*. Its strengths lie in the playful chemistry between its stars, Robert Morse and Rudy Vallee, and scriptwriter-director Jerrold Freedman's adroit adaptation of Joan Aiken's witty, if grisly, tale.

While scripting, Freedman had both Morse and Vallee in mind. "Those guys were really fun to be around," notes Freedman. "Bobby and Rudy had worked together for years, and it was a real kick to get them both."[36] The pair had starred previously on

Broadway in the Frank Loesser musical *How to Succeed in Business Without Really Trying,* and they bring their considerable comedic talents to this crackpot tale. Their interplay sparkles and would be humorous throughout were it not for Freedman's direction, creating an atmosphere slightly atilt. His careful control of the story's changing tone pays dividends, and his shot scheme for the finale—with the camera's slow pan from Morse's shocked face to Vallee standing silently in the doorway—is effectively chilling.

Freedman is quick to single out the contribution of his cinematographer, Lionel Lindon: "He was an excellent cameraman, really first rate. He would give you feature lighting in ten minutes. And sometimes I would set up a shot and he would say, 'Well, why don't you do *this,'* and he would take three shots and make one long shot out of it."[37]

Equally notable are the startling set designs, reflecting the story's madhouse motif. At Freedman's suggestion, Joseph Alves used a black psych—a floor-to-ceiling curtain that extended all the way around the stage—as a backdrop. He then designed a spare, white schematic for the set, with abstract representations of trees, windows, doors, and walls, effectively setting the characters in a kind of decaying, lunatic borderland. These stark experimental-theater design styles, although common on British television shows such as *The Avengers,* were definitely not the order of the day for American TV in 1971. With such license, *Night Gallery* pushed further and further from the mainstream.

Later in the season, a story by Joan Aiken's Pulitzer Prize–winning father, poet Conrad Aiken, would furnish an even darker vision of madness for *Night Gallery*—"Silent Snow, Secret Snow."

## 4
## THE ACADEMY
★ ★ ★ ½

Teleplay by Rod Serling
Based on the short story by David Ely
Directed by Jeff Corey
Music: John Lewis
Director of Photography: Lionel Lindon
Time: 14:15

### Cast
Mr. Holston: Pat Boone
Director: Leif Erickson

*Pat Boone and Leif Erickson in "The Academy."
Courtesy of Globe Photos.*

Sloane: Larry Linville
Drill Instructor: Ed Call
Bradley: Stanley Waxman
Simmons: Robert Gibbons
Chauffeur: E. A. Sirianni
Cadet: John Gruber

*A small item for the pedagogues amongst you, a little something to be found in the drawer alongside the old school ties. Picture if you will a very special school where the students don't matriculate but rather are marooned; where the scholars are not enrolled but rather sentenced. The painting is called "The Academy."*

/ **Summary** / Arriving at the Glendalough Military Academy, Mr. Holston, an affluent middle-aged widower, has come to see the academy director about admission for his son Roger—an undisciplined boy, Holston explains, who has gotten into some trouble along the way. Touring the academy with the director, Holston notes the rigid discipline and the unceasing drill that is the hallmark of the place. Entering a classroom, he scans the faces of the cadets. The age difference among them appears to range widely—some are boys, others quite mature. This impression is confirmed when they visit one of the academy dormitories. The director introduces Holston to one of the cadets, Sloane. The cadet, staring straight ahead at unblinking attention, could be twenty-five. He could also be thirty-five. Something about cadet Sloane, a vague remembrance, tugs at Holston's memory.

As the director walks him to the courtyard entrance, Holston suddenly recalls it: a news story years ago about a young delinquent of good family, who was arrested for a vicious assault on a young woman. "If that's the same Sloane," marvels Holston, "why, he'd have to be in his *thirties*." The director does not respond, instead drawing Holston's attention to the large statue in the courtyard. It depicts a man in military dress with his arm around a new recruit—but the statue faces toward the academy, not the outside world. "*This* is our world," explains the director. "All that a boy needs is to be found right here, and for that reason, that statue symbolizes welcome—not farewell." Holston, gazing at the statue, notes that the face of the officer bears a striking resemblance to that of the director. Turning, he asks, "How long will my son stay here?" "I assumed you understood that," responds the director. "Indefinitely, Mr. Holston. Most of the parents prefer it that way." Holston nods. Roger, he says, will arrive tomorrow.

Passing through the front gate, Holston notes that the gatekeeper is also a cadet, and pauses to question him. "I was fifteen when I arrived, sir," the gatekeeper responds. "I'll soon be fifty-five." Yes, muses Holston as he climbs into his limousine. This is *just* the place for his son.

**/ Commentary /** Serling's faithful adaptation of David Ely's short story, like "Class of '99," starts out in the normal, everyday world we all inhabit—until about halfway through. The facade then crumbles, revealing the alternate world beneath. The stresses and strains of parenthood take on a sinister complexion when held under the light of Ely's "ultimate solution." "The Academy," notes director Jeff Corey, "is a wonderful statement about how we have children before we know what to do with them—the *in extremis* of putting kids on hold."[38]

Corey's choice for the callous, self-involved Mr. Holston was a surprising one: 1950s teen heartthrob Pat Boone, famed for his white bucks, Brylcreem persona, and whole-milk renditions of Little Richard tunes. The idea of Mr. Clean, America's favorite dad, curing his wayward teen with a life sentence in boot camp is perverse—and it works. Boone's performance—at first conscience-stricken, later all too eager to dump responsibility for his son—is unsettling; and Leif Erickson as the vaguely sinister, ramrod-straight academy director gives him excellent support. "I'd worked with Pat in England during the blacklist," recalls Corey. "Pat only had daughters, but I thought it would be wonderful to have him play that part. He was perfect for it."[39]

"I welcomed being cast as a villain," remarks Boone.

I had already become terribly stereotyped, and I knew that I was being passed over for roles that I wanted to do. I had been in Jeff's acting class. He'd seen me stretch, and he believed that I was capable of more than just the light, frothy musical roles that I was known for. I'll bet that Corey said to the producer, "Hey, why don't you get Pat Boone for the role? He's got the right look, the right persona for the beginning, and it'll be a good, solid slip to find out that he's happy about assigning his son to oblivion!"

Beyond playing against type, the attraction of the script for Boone was its strong moral focus.

The father was one of those ambitious overachievers. His whole life had been so consumed with his career that, though he had probably given his son every material thing, he had never given him much attention. The wife died, and there is the implication that the son had something to do with her death. Jeff Corey and I discussed that it was quite possible that the *father* had something to do with it, and was not above casting suspicion on the son. I felt that the whole story was a comment on the superachieving, materialistic father who sees his son as a failure if he doesn't automatically turn out to be a carbon copy of himself—then he's disposable. It's chilling, and to some extent an exaggeration, but I think it made a very valid comment on the distant and underinvolved parent.

To allow this point to creep up on the viewing audience, Corey asked Boone to internalize his character's emotions, never telegraphing his true intent until the end. "Jeff made me feel like I could go on the veneer of niceness," Boone notes, "so I didn't have to gnash my teeth or twirl a moustache to let people know before the story was over that I was *not* a nice guy. But by the end, I could go ahead and say, 'My son's a rotter. Good riddance, off to Europe. I've got other things to do now—*that's* taken care of.'"[40]

Location work at the Harvard School on Coldwater Canyon gives the segment a sense of gray verisimilitude, though the sunny California weather works against producing any kind of proper atmosphere for this tale. Corey uses the surroundings to good advantage, however. In one scene, Erickson leads Boone on a walking tour of the academy's facilities. Corey frames a low-angle shot from the bottom of a long flight of walled concrete steps, with the two actors positioned at the top. Only a fragment of blue sky behind them offers relief from this entombed perspective. As they move down the steps toward the cadet dormitories, it looks as if they were descending into a grave—a striking visual commentary on the fate of the academy's inductees.

What hobbles the piece inevitably (though not fatally) is John Lewis's ineffective music for the finale, a mock-valedictory theme used originally in "Class of '99," that presses the punch line home too fiercely. The David Ely original gradually reveals only on the final page the true nature of the academy, and that type of ominous, suggestive underpinning is what the segment really needs, not an in-your-face parade ground march—a telling lesson on how the power of music can greatly enhance, and sometimes diminish, a film.

## NIGHT GALLERY #34306
Air date: October 20, 1971

1

## THE PHANTOM FARMHOUSE
★ ★ ★ ½

Teleplay by Halsted Welles
Based on the short story by Seabury Quinn
Directed by Jeannot Szwarc
Music: Oliver Nelson
Director of Photography: Lionel Lindon
Time: 33:13

**Cast**
Dr. Joel Winter: David McCallum
Gideon: David Carradine
Mildred Squire: Linda Marsh
Pierre: Ivor Francis
Sheriff: Ford Rainey
Betty: Trina Parks
Dr. Tom: Bill Quinn

*David McCallum and Ford Rainey in "The Phantom Farmhouse." Courtesy of TV History Archives.*

Mrs. Squire: Gail Bonner
Mr. Squire: Martin Ashe
Mr. Grouch: Ray Ballard
Shepherd: Frank Arnold

G*ood evening. We offer you an evening's sojourn amongst the wild, the woolly, the unbelievable . . . sometimes made believable, as our first painting suggests.*

*From this picture one wouldn't necessarily conjure up a story of love, but that's precisely what it tells about—the emotion as old as Man. But the object of the emotion . . . this is not quite as familiar. Its title, "Phantom Farmhouse"—offering number one in the* Night Gallery.

**/ Summary /** At Delphinium House, an isolated sanitarium, psychiatrist Joel Winter is questioned by the sheriff. One of the hospital inmates, May, was found nearby in the forest savagely murdered, his body torn to pieces as though attacked by wild animals. Winter identifies a note found near the body, a set of directions, as being the handwriting of another of his patients, a solitary ex-junkie named Gideon.

Winter has been able to draw Gideon out only by allowing him to talk about his fixation on Mildred Squire, a mysterious young woman he claims lives nearby in the woods. Gideon can just see the chimney of the Squires' two-hundred-year-old farmhouse from his window; but according to the sheriff, there *is* no house in the woods, only the ruins of one that burned down long ago—not a soul lives there.

Dr. Winter follows Gideon's map into the forest, and in a cool, gladed clearing he *does* find a large, two-story farmhouse with a white picket fence and a well—just as Gideon described it. A young blonde woman dressed in white, radiantly beautiful, steps down from the porch to greet him—Mildred. As they both share a cup of water from the well, the doctor is entranced by Mildred's shy ways, but notes that her index finger is longer than the others. Mr. and Mrs. Squire, Mildred's rough-hewn parents, step out to introduce themselves, and they gaze at Winter with a strangely avid look. Although he finds the parents disturbing, Winter is smitten by Mildred's gentleness and beauty.

On his return to the hospital, the doctor finds on his desk a pile of books on lycanthropy—the study of werewolves—left by Gideon. Winter peruses the place markers in the text dealing with the distinguishing characteristics of the werewolf: elongated index finger, bright red nails, pointed ears, eyes that turn red at moonrise. When Winter scoffs, Gideon explodes in anger: "What do you think May saw before he was torn to pieces?" After he stalks out, Dr. Winter begins piecing together the puzzle of Gideon's connection to May's death. In Gideon's delusion, he sees himself as a warlock, a kind of procurer for werewolves, providing them victims. Besides May, however, the only thing turning up dead lately are the local sheep.

The attacks have been nightly. Traps have been set and sprung, but nothing caught. And the tracks found around the traps were not that of an animal, but of a human— a small hand with a long index finger. Pierre, the groundskeeper, tells Dr. Winter about a family that used to live nearby many years ago that murdered and ate lone travelers in the forest. They were burned out of their home and killed by local hunters. They, Pierre claims, were *loups-garous*—and they have returned.

One night, Winter returns from the Squires to find his assistant, Betty, lying in the meadow—like the sheep, mauled to death. Gideon, filled with remorse, begs the doctor to leave Delphinium House and go as far away as he can. He believes absolutely that Winter, having seen the farmhouse, is marked for death. Confounded by questions about Betty's murder and Gideon's mania, Winter returns before nightfall to see Mildred. She keeps her eyes averted from him, telling him he must leave quickly—but to return just before sunrise with a prayer book and read over the three graves nestled in the ferns. "And all the time you're reading, no matter what you hear, don't look around. Keep reading quickly." Lifting her face to the moonlight, Mildred gazes at him with blood-rimmed eyes. Alarmed, Winter races back across the meadow as fast as his fear will carry him. He reaches a clearing in the woods and, looking back, sees two huge black dogs at his heels. They run him to the ground, biting and snapping, tearing at his clothing. Suddenly another appears, a white dog, setting viciously upon the other two and keeping them at bay while Winter, badly shaken, gets away.

Returning the next morning, Winter stands by the graves and recites the prayer for the dead. He can hear, behind him, the dogs—their gutteral growls turning to howls of pain as he gives the blessing of the Trinity. Overcome with fear, Winter loses consciousness. He is awakened by Pierre. Rising, Winter spins around, looking in vain for the Squires' farmhouse. On the ground where it stood is a chimney and the remnants of a fire-gutted foundation. Winter desperately calls for Mildred, but there is no answer. Not a trace of the house—or its inhabitants—remains.

/ **Commentary** / "The Phantom Farmhouse" exemplifies the subtler side of *Night Gallery*. In place of the wild-eyed fang-and-claw approach that a werewolf story might suggest to more unimaginative filmmakers, Halsted Welles, Jeannot Szwarc, and Jack Laird instead chose to craft a romantic fantasy. This type of story has always been Szwarc's strong suit as can be evidenced by his parallel course in Richard Matheson's *Somewhere in Time*.

"I had such an instant vision of the show," Szwarc says. "I've always had an affinity for anything which is the domain of the dream—what the French call *les songes,* anything which has to do with the subconscious. *Les songes* is a French word which means 'dreams,' but more than that because it's also something you can do awake—like sort of a combination of sleep dream and daydream."[41]

Halsted Welles's script veers into melodrama, although arguably viewing this type of heady romanticism through the prism of these cynical times tends to distort its sincerity. Leveling this excess, "The Phantom Farmhouse" is visually quite beautiful. Lionel Lindon's pastoral photography is stunning, the editing scheme is paced to perfection (editor Larry Lester's first cut was termed a "hole-in-one" by Laird), and composer Oliver Nelson delivered one of his best scores.

"'Phantom Farmhouse' was a very difficult show," recalls Szwarc. "We moved around a lot and the mood was difficult to create. When you went outside with *Night Gallery*, then those schedules really got difficult because you had no control over the weather or the light, and you can't create atmosphere with horrible light. You've got to have good photography, interesting angles; you can't just do flat stuff, it doesn't work."[42]

Despite the beauty of this segment's lensing, the reliance on atmosphere-destroying day-for-night shooting is difficult to support. An angry Serling later commented about this technique: "It's infrequent that you can shoot *night*-for-night. If you have a two-minute sequence in an entire script that has to be done at night, it's rare that they'll take a company out for five hours just to shoot a two-minute sequence. On *Twilight Zone*, we did, and had to cheat it a lot to do it. But if you'll notice on *Night Gallery*, very frequently it's supposed to be night and, goddamnit, there's sun rays coming out on one side of the screen. And it never looks proper when they shoot day-for-night."[43]

Along with the lighting difficulties, Szwarc was disappointed in the lack of energy displayed by his canine supporting players. "We had problems with the dogs. I had those three huge dogs, but they were like sheep! They wanted to lick everybody, so they wouldn't scare *anyone*."[44] Luckily, the two-legged actors outperform their four-legged colleagues. David McCallum, best remembered for his three-and-a-half-year stint as Ilya Kuryakin in *The Man from U.N.C.L.E.*, scores as the rational, emotionally controlled psychiatrist shaken by his sudden fixation. Linda Marsh, who was Ophelia to Richard Burton's Hamlet on the New York stage, gives Mildred an appropriate Old-World quality, as if transported from the past, and her calm nobility manages to overcome the effects of the blond Charo mane she's forced to wear.

David Carradine, who would soon be wandering the Old West as Caine in the hugely successful oriental western *Kung Fu*, stars as the enigmatic Gideon. Carradine is better than his part, somehow managing to deliver his dated hippie dialogue with a truth that transforms it. His character, missing from Seabury Quinn's original short story, is unusual: a sort of pimp for werewolves. Although a unique twist on the folklore of the subject, it's a naked plot contrivance nonetheless.

Despite its few weaknesses, "The Phantom Farmhouse" is still effective thanks to Szwarc's handsome directorial touches—a position supported by his assistant director on the episode: "I stood and watched Jeannot do a setup," recalls Les Berke, "and I'm saying to myself, 'How's he do it, where does he get these ideas? This is brilliant, what I'm watching'—and at that time I'd been in the business at least ten years. I really loved working with him."[45]

2
SILENT SNOW, SECRET SNOW
★ ★ ★ ★

Teleplay by Gene Kearney
Based on the short story by Conrad Aiken
Directed by Gene Kearney
Music: Paul Glass     Intro: John Lewis
Director of Photography: Lionel Lindon
Time: 16:18

**Cast**
Narrator: Orson Welles
Paul: Radames Pera
Father: Lonny Chapman
Mother: Lisabeth Hush
Doctor: Jason Wingreen
Miss Buell: Frances Spanier
Dierdre: Patti Cohoon

*Radames Pera in "Silent Snow, Secret Snow."
Courtesy of Photofest.*

$F$*or our last offering on the* Night Gallery, *a painting that brings to life a literary classic from the pen of Conrad Aiken. Fragile, lovely, haunting. Its title: "Silent Snow, Secret Snow."*

/ **Summary** / Paul Hasleman has a secret. He's told no one—not his parents or his teacher or his friends—not a soul. It has grown into something wonderful, a refuge into which he can withdraw from the world. His secret is about the snow. Listening every morning when he wakes for the steps of the postman, Paul senses they are gradually becoming more muffled. The snow is encroaching, getting closer, the drifts piling deeper and deeper. Paul is sure of this, even though every morning when he looks out his window the streets are as bare as ever.

His parents and his teacher have begun to notice Paul's increasing distance from the here and now. They catch him apparently daydreaming, when in reality he is listening to the whispering voice of the snow's ever-increasing and insistent presence. How could he explain his new world? Its beauty was beyond anything—beyond speech, beyond thought—utterly incommunicable. It was irresistible. It was miraculous.

Worried about Paul's increasing silence, his parents invite the family doctor over to examine him—but Paul becomes impatient with his parents' curiosity and interference. Even as the outsiders confer among themselves, the cold, still voice whispers to him, "Wait, Paul . . . just wait until we are alone together. I will tell you something new, something cold, something sleepy. Something of cease and peace and the long bright curve of space . . . *Banish them, refuse to speak.* Go upstairs to your room. I will be waiting for you. I will surround your bed, pile a deep drift against the door so that *none will ever again be able to enter.*"

Paul obeys, racing past his parents up to his bedroom. There, he finds himself in a haze of falling snow, a canopy of white concealing everything in the room. Leaping onto his bed, Paul raises his open arms to the descending snow as the drifts grow deeper and deeper. Suddenly, his bedroom door opens and the snow vanishes. His mother—unwelcome in his secret world—has come to continue the inquisition. Paul angrily cuts her off: "Mother, go away! *I hate you!*"

And with that final effort, everything is solved. The seamless hiss advances once more. "Listen," it says. "We'll tell you the last, most beautiful and secret story. A story that gets smaller and smaller, that comes inward instead of opening like a flower. It is a flower that becomes a seed—a little, cold seed. Do you hear? We are leaning closer to you . . ." The darkness descends upon Paul, and a whispering chill enshrouds all.

/ **Commentary** / Occasionally, *Night Gallery* produced segments of a special nature, that went beyond eliciting mere shivers from its audience. Such is the case with "Silent Snow, Secret Snow," a high-water mark for the series.

Writer-director Gene Kearney's interest in Conrad Aiken's powerful short story predated the series by several years. He had produced an award-winning short film based on the tale for CBS in the 1960s. Jack Laird gave him a chance to expand on and polish his earlier effort. Easily Kearney's best work on *Night Gallery*, "Silent Snow, Secret Snow" weaves a powerful, enigmatic spell with this haunting tale of a young boy's spiral into madness.

Radames Pera, who would later be cast as the young Kwai Chang Caine in *Kung Fu*, here interprets a similar "outsider" role as Paul. The boy's sense of joy and wonder at the secret world he cannot share with anyone, his growing impatience with his parents' interference, is well conveyed by the young actor.

Most viewers interpret the main character's aberration as a form of mental illness. This ambiguity has been a sticking point for some in their enjoyment of the episode, and even Serling himself expressed a lack of understanding about the story. Such an interior piece, attempting to convey this ineffable experience would be a challenge to an adult actor, much less a ten-year-old boy. "I didn't know about autism at the time," says Pera.

I just imagined that this boy, living in a sunny climate, had this obsession about snow, and this was his escape from reality. He didn't have a very intimate relationship with his parents —his dad particularly was very cold to him—and this is Paul's way of escaping to a place that means something to him, that is his solace. When there's no one around it exists for him, and that's what finally drives him away from his parents. When his mother bursts into his bedroom and the snow disappears, she makes him realize for a moment that he is creating this thing. He's totally shattered, because she's completely destroyed his illusion.

It is clear from Pera's remembrances that Kearney's interpretation of the final scene, with the dark shadow drawing across Paul's tear-stained face, was deliberately ambiguous. "Gene told me he felt that Paul crosses over to the 'other side' . . . and that 'other side' could be physical death, or it could be mentally dying to this world, totally entering over into the fantasy world—which one could interpret as autism." This ending, uncertain and undefined, is true to the spirit of the short story, and is as chilling a finish as *Night Gallery* produced. Kearney's visual design for the sequence is inspired.

Exploring the vibrations of an interior life makes for risky cinema. It is almost entirely the province of the written word, and few successful films have been made that investigate such mental landscapes. With such an ambiguous story, the use of narration was essential. Kearney was lucky enough to enlist one of the greatest dramatic voices of the century—Orson Welles. His voice, sonorous and insinuating, is a perfect act of seduction, and we ally ourselves unquestioningly with the secret world the narrator represents as it beckons to Paul. But Welles, like the meaning of the tale, was somewhat elusive himself.

"From the very beginning," Pera recalls,

Gene wanted Orson Welles to narrate it. It was a sort of fantasy of his. So he sent a copy of the script and a cover letter to Welles, saying, "If you'd like to do this, please let us know what your fees are and we can arrange to have you come to the studio and do the recording." We went into production, shot the show, and never heard anything back. They went into postproduction, and actually had an air date, and *still* no response. They were going to go another route, and one day a manila envelope arrived at Kearney's office containing nothing but a reel of quarter-inch tape. It was the entire narration.

Welles, without explanation or request for payment, delivered his contribution at the eleventh hour, presumably out of appreciation for the project. "To me, it makes the show," Pera says. "There's no question that Welles's narration is really the inner life of the story. He was the voice of the fantasy." [46]

Welles's contribution, though undeniably powerful, told only part of the story. The success of this production is enhanced greatly by the music of Paul Glass. His poignant, luminous score contains within its simple contours a richness of emotion that matches Aiken's singing poetry, and ranks with Elmer Bernstein's score for *To Kill a Mockingbird* in its sensitive evocation of childhood. "'Silent Snow, Secret Snow' was quite unusual for me," recalls Glass. "I wrote it as a solo piece plus a string orchestra, like a flute concerto—basically a set of variations on an original theme. We had Sheridon Stokes, a fantastic flute player, for the solo."[47] Glass contributed almost wall-to-wall music, over thirteen minutes of underscore to a sixteen-minute segment, and such is its quality that the composer must share equal acclaim with Welles in the telling of this haunting tale. It is one of *Night Gallery*'s most distinctive scores—warm, immediate, and human.

This segment was filmed on the Universal back lot in the middle of summer, and the *Night Gallery* crew had to dress an entire street in the snow and ice of winter. "I must say, they did a superb job," notes Pera.

I remember the crew's moaning and groaning about the details. "Gene wants what? Now he wants the icicles to *drip?* Oh my God!" And yes, the icicles dripping was a fantastic touch—it made it look all that much more realistic. For the snow they used a kind of a white sand in places, and then they used this flaked plastic—that's the stuff that looks the most realistic. They literally covered everything—bushes, trees, sidewalks. That was one of the more thorough and elaborate transformations of a place that I've ever seen on a film set.

The production of this segment was evidently a very rich experience for young Radames Pera. To this day, he carries strong memories of his involvement—unfortunately, not all are positive. "An incident occurred on the show that was a developmental milestone for me," he says.

The director of photography was very annoyed with me during this production. And at one point he took me aside and said, "You spoiled brat! You think you're this great actor. Well, you're terrible"—something to that effect. I don't know why. I don't remember myself being other than just good-naturedly precocious. For some reason, this guy just had it out for me. Looking at him now from an adult perspective, I would say he probably had a drinking problem. But it did shake me up and I guess I was more serious after that point, and a little bit scared of the guy because he really freaked me out.[48]

The story Pera tells is not unusual. He found himself a target of cinematographer Curly Lindon's legendary bad temper—one of many such victims during the life of this series.

Despite this blemish, Pera is proud of his involvement in this segment, and rightly so. "Silent Snow, Secret Snow" was among *Night Gallery*'s finest efforts. In the history of cinema, few filmmakers have successfully portrayed mental illness. The best of them—Robert Wiene's *The Cabinet of Dr. Caligari*, Roman Polanski's *Repulsion*, Robert Altman's *Images*—have all dealt in some way with the sexually repressed neuroses of adults. In its own way, *Night Gallery*'s moving study of a child adrift and isolated is equally effective. Poetry is admittedly a scarce commodity on television, but the fragile delicacy of "Silent Snow, Secret Snow" falls easily under that heading.

NIGHT GALLERY #34308
Air date: October 27, 1971

1

A QUESTION OF FEAR
★ ★ ★ ★

Teleplay by Theodore J. Flicker
Based on the short story by Bryan Lewis
Directed by Jack Laird
Music: Paul Glass      Intro: Oliver Nelson
Director of Photography: Lionel Lindon
Time: 38:24

*Leslie Nielsen in "A Question of Fear." Courtesy of Sal Milo.*

**Cast**
Denny Malloy: Leslie Nielsen
Dr. Mazi: Fritz Weaver
Al: Jack Bannon
Fred: Ivan Bonar
Apparition: Paul Golden
Waiter: Owen Cunningham

G*ood evening, and welcome to the* Night Gallery. *Now if you'll just follow me. Time again for your weekly excursion into the cultural. Paintings, statuary, still-lifes, collages, some abstracts—and some items in ice. That's not the technique—that, hopefully, is what we turn your blood into.*

*A good way to begin the attempt: painting number one, about a man who spends a night in a haunted house—an unbeliever, if you will, who, by dawn, believes. The name of the painting is "A Question of Fear." The name of this place is the* Night Gallery.

**/ Summary /** At an exclusive men's club, Dr. Mazi, a distinguished gentleman, re-counts his terrifying experience at an old, abandoned house reputed to be haunted. One gentleman in the room, Colonel Denny Malloy, sneers at the idea of ghosts or evil spirits, claiming that he himself is incapable of fear. Mazi and his guests pick up the gauntlet Malloy has thrown, wagering him $15,000 that he cannot spend one whole night alone in that house without being frightened to death. With a laugh, Mal-loy accepts, boasting, "For $15,000 I would survive a night in Hell."

Arriving at nightfall, Malloy enters the darkened, two-story house. The sound of distorted, hysterical laughter seems to come from nowhere and everywhere at once.

Cautiously shining his flashlight around, he feels a wet sensation on his hand—spattered with what looks like blood. Pulling his revolver from his backpack, Denny follows the moaning laughter down the hallway. Sensing something behind him, he turns and fires at a flaming apparition closing in on him. It disappears, but, examining the area, Malloy finds fresh blood stains on the floor.

Descending into the basement, Malloy discovers a slimy trail that leads into the darkness. A shrieking phantom suddenly appears, a hideously distorted figure that flies at him from the shadows. The horrified Malloy empties his revolver at it—but it disappears, leaving nothing but more of the telltale stains. Now visibly shaken, Malloy returns to the kitchen for a cup of strong coffee from his thermos. To his surprise, he finds his hand trembling; with an effort he controls it. This evening has been full of new experiences for Malloy, not the least of which is his fuller understanding of the emotion of fear. Then a new sound intrudes on his self-discovery: the discordant banging of piano keys from another room. Malloy, fighting a sudden sense of dizziness, picks up his revolver and follows the sound. A figure sits at a piano—the phantom from the cellar. It rises and faces Malloy, its hands bursting into flaming braziers. Focusing his eyes, Malloy notes an artificiality about it—and it suddenly dawns on him that the whole house has been rigged by Mazi.

Laughing out loud, the relieved Malloy groggily heads up the stairs to get some sleep. Still chuckling, he lays down on the large canopy bed—and a set of steel restraints erupt from the mattress like curved daggers, pinning him down. Ripping through the top canopy slides a swinging razor-sharp pendulum that comes increasingly closer to the stunned Malloy's throat. He yells out to Mazi that wagers can't be collected from dead men, and the pendulum, a scant centimeter from contact, abruptly stops. Malloy sneers, "You know what I think, Mazi? I think you just want to see me afraid. You want to reduce me to *your* level, right, Mazi? Well, I'm sorry, pal. That's one fraternity I refuse to join." Malloy drifts off to sleep.

When he awakens the next morning, the restraints and pendulum have disappeared. Downstairs in the deserted kitchen, a closed-circuit television blinks on and Mazi's face appears, informing Malloy of the reason for the expensive and elaborate setup. During World War II, Malloy came into contact with Mazi's father, in civilian life a concert pianist, who was at the time a junior officer in the Italian army. Malloy captured and interrogated him about the German advance. Getting nothing from him, Malloy poured gasoline on his hands and set fire to them, burning them to blackened stumps. On his father's deathbed, Mazi vowed to track Malloy down and exact revenge.

Malloy pulls his revolver, bracing himself for anything as Mazi continues calmly with his story. By profession a biochemist, Mazi has discovered a way of converting a complex enzyme molecule in the human body until its structure is identical with that of an annelid. As a result, the bones of the body disintegrate until the victim is reduced to something very much like an earthworm. While Malloy slept off the effects of his drugged coffee last night—compliments of his host—Mazi injected him with this serum. Malloy scoffs. For proof, Mazi suggests he revisit the cellar. "There you will see now my colleague. He's quite harmless—only rather repulsive." Frantic, Malloy heads to the cellar door, then freezes. A trail of slime—like that of a giant slug—leads across the kitchen floor to the cellar steps. "You will be a very brave worm," taunts Mazi. "Why are you stopping? Your fate is there, in the cellar. *Go, and look at what you will be!*" Instead, Malloy turns back to the television monitor, struggling to regain his composure in the face of this fresh horror. Steeling himself, Malloy snarls, "You *still* lose, Mazi"—and lifting his revolver to his head, fires. Mazi watches Malloy's dead body slump to the floor. "No, Mr. Malloy," he says with satisfaction, "*you* lose. *There is nothing in the cellar.*"

/ **Commentary** / The Old Dark House theme has produced numerous variations since cinema's infancy. Leave it to *Night Gallery* to pull off an original twist. Disguised as just another night in a haunted house, this outing is a white-knuckle tale of revenge with a complicated and bizarre payoff.

From Bryan Lewis's short story, Theodore Flicker fashioned a taut, intricately plotted script. The writer was scheduled to direct, but soured on the prospect after his unpleasant experience directing "Hell's Bells." Jack Laird stepped in to helm this segment, his first time directing.

For his flagship outing, Laird hired close friend Leslie Nielsen to portray Malloy, the cocksure adventurer submitting to the ultimate test of his courage, well supported by Fritz Weaver as his subtle nemesis. Nielsen's characterization is, at first, sharp and cool, then captures in increments the sense of a hardened man turning to jelly, coming to grips with his growing belief in the supernatural—a nuanced and believable performance. "I felt it was quite an honor," Nielsen says. "Jack had enough confidence in my abilities to hire me for his first directorial effort, this very special thing that he was doing."[49]

As with most first timers, Laird had difficulty getting a grip on the rigorous filming schedules imposed upon series television—so much so that he was himself guilty of the same offense for which he had fired others. "He fell on his ass on that one," said unit manager Burt Astor. "We fell one day behind and had all kinds of problems with that segment."[50] "Thank God I wasn't there," laughs Les Berke. "Jack shot, I think, twenty-six hours of film by the second day. What do you say to the executive producer? 'Sir? We're replacing you, sir.' Right, of course you aren't."[51] Laird, under severe pressure, ran past the shooting schedule by a day and a half. The Universal moguls were not pleased. "Of course, *I* was assigned to Jack," recalls Ralph Sariego, assistant director on the segment. "He bombed so badly. I was with him until four a.m. on a Saturday morning. He felt that it was the end of his directing career—that was *it,* they wouldn't let him direct anymore."[52]

For all the distress and the overrun, Laird completed the segment the way he envisioned it, according to Leslie Nielsen: "He did run over, very much so, but nevertheless we still did it his way. It was his first effort and he insisted. And I'm sure he caught a great deal of flak for it."[53]

"A Question of Fear" is a tense, superbly executed segment, building inexorably to its surprising, wholly satisfying climax. The special effects department had a field day, creating believable (and quite scary) visuals on a paltry budget to accompany Malloy's journey into fear. Additionally, Lionel Lindon's photography is exceptional, arguably his best for the show, richly textured and atmospheric. And editor David Rawlins's brilliant achievement may be the most valuable of all, wading through the mountain of footage Laird had shot to produce a piece that not only is coherent but also flows with a masterful control of tempo and tension.

Adding an extra dimension: Paul Glass's shivery, spine-chilling music. Both emotionally and instrumentally, "A Question of Fear" is in jarring contrast to "Silent Snow, Secret Snow." The music is tense, nightmarish, and dissonant. Strong brass and percussion colors highlight the stark terrain, and Glass banished violins from the string body to reduce warmth. The broken, agonized piano line (an unsettling commentary on the savage encounter between Malloy and Mazi's concert pianist father) wanders throughout the score like an accusing wraith. This remarkable music defined the sound of *Night Gallery* so perfectly that it was reused constantly throughout the second season to track other episodes without benefit of an original score.

As it turned out, Laird's fiasco did not kill his directorial career at Universal after all. He directed a slew of vignettes, and later in the season allowed himself to film another full-length segment, "Pickman's Model"—by common consent, a series classic.

2

## THE DEVIL IS NOT MOCKED
★ ★ ★ ½

Teleplay by Gene Kearney
Based on the short story by Manly Wade
 Wellman
Directed by Gene Kearney
Music: Paul Glass      Intro: Oliver Nelson
Director of Photography: Leonard J. South
Time: 11:15

*Francis Lederer and Helmut Dantine in "The Devil Is Not Mocked." Courtesy of TV History Archives.*

**Cast**

General von Grunn: Helmut Dantine
Master of the Castle: Francis Lederer
Kranz: Hank Brandt
Hugo: Martin Kosleck
Radio Man: Gino Gottarelli
Machine Gunner: Mark de Vries

*O*scar Wilde said something to the effect that if there were not a Devil, we'd very likely invent him. He serves many a purpose, and this grim-visaged character here is proof of that rather bitter pudding, in a story that tells what happens when evil collides with evil. The painting is called "The Devil Is Not Mocked."

/ **Summary** / The German Reich, having invaded Poland and Czechoslovakia, is moving deeper into the Balkans. General von Grunn and his troops push on to capture and secure a castle, rumored to be the headquarters of a secret partisan organization. Before they can force entry, out steps a well-dressed and well-spoken dignitary who invites them in. Von Grunn, suspicious of a trap, treats his host and the servants as though they were spies—but to his surprise, a banquet has been laid out in welcome. The general suspects an attempt by his host to ingratiate himself and learn battle plans. Confident, von Grunn commands the dignitary to join him at the table while he feasts.

The general's troops decamp in the castle courtyard and their needs are seen to by servants. His host, the general discovers, is the master of the castle, heir to the ancestral title of count. Von Grunn only sneers, accusing him of leading the secret resistance forces. The host, with a polite denial, keeps a watchful eye on the clock—five minutes to midnight. The howling of the wolves in the hills becomes more insistent and somehow closer, setting the general on edge. Von Grunn senses a grave danger approaching, and as the midnight hour chimes, pandemonium erupts in the courtyard. Von Grunn's second in command, Kranz, falls into the room, clutching at the floorboards and screaming as he is savaged by some snarling thing in the hall. Unholstering his Luger, von Grunn fires out into the courtyard at the servants, now a pack of hungry wolves tearing his men to shreds. "The bullets are useless, General," the host explains, approaching his guest. "If the bullets were silver, it would of course be a different story." Turning, von Grunn is shocked to see a marked change in the master of the castle—his face now feral, his eyes the color of blood. "You must forgive my servants," hisses his fanged host, taking him by the throat, "and our *primitive* Transylvanian customs. If it's any consolation, General, this *is* the headquarters of the secret resistance . . . and I am its proud commander—Count Dracula."

**/ Commentary /** For this segment, casting was nothing short of brilliant. Helmut Dantine had played Nazi officers numerous times before, and Francis Lederer essayed the role of Dracula in a 1958 film, *The Return of Dracula*. Their bearing and presence lend the segment a classy appeal and, with their long and distinguished careers, a sense of history.

"Helmut Dantine was not anything like I expected," recalls costar Hank Brandt, the luckless Kranz. "I was expecting somebody who was kind of gruff and Germanic, and he was very pleasant, very continental. I remember sitting down and having a cup of coffee with him and Francis, and they were just lovely, lovely gentlemen. They had some great stories about Hollywood in the thirties and forties, and I was in awe of their background. I mean, my God, Francis had been in the business for a hundred years!"[54]

Lederer's Old World manners got a workout in this tale, and his performance as the count is a study in elegance, patience, and control. Leonard Engelman's frightful makeup for him at the finish helped turn Lederer's patrician features to wolflike savagery, with clamp-on fangs and bloodshot eyes. "Those contacts actually fit inside of the eyelid," recalls Engelman. "They were painful to wear, especially in those days. That type of lens wasn't really made with the idea that you were going to wear it a long time. Now lenses are much thinner and more refined than they were then."[55] With Engelman's aid, Lederer looks every inch a monster.

For the midnight massacre and subsequent banquet, director Gene Kearney pulls a David Lean and allows the melee to play out in the reaction on Dantine's horrified face, shooting his Luger ineffectually into the courtyard. Brandt, veteran of numerous episodes of *Combat*, is dragged to the feast by a transformed servant girl—actually a crew member—as his fingernails claw uselessly at the floorboards. "They took an instrument of some kind and predragged it," notes Brandt, "and when [the film] cut to me, I'm already lying there with my hand stretched out and my arm covering the precut grooves. All I had to do was make sure I pulled my fingers along those grooves when he dragged me"[56]—a simple but effective stunt.

Quite short and well paced, this segment, based on Manly Wade Wellman's short story, was one of the better efforts of writer-director Gene Kearney. In his story, Wellman gives away the ending almost immediately, but Kearney's witty adaptation disguises the fact of the master's identity until practically the end. Handsomely shot and produced, "The Devil Is Not Mocked" is *Night Gallery*'s best segment on the well-trod vampire theme.

NIGHT GALLERY #34310
Air date: November 3, 1971

1

MIDNIGHT NEVER ENDS

★ ★ ½

Written by Rod Serling
Directed by Jeannot Szwarc
Music: Oliver Nelson and Paul Glass
Director of Photography: Lionel Lindon
Time: 20:10

**Cast**

Vincent Riley: Robert F. Lyons
Ruth Asquith: Susan Strasberg
Joe Bateman: Joseph Perry
Sheriff Lewis: Robert Karnes

*Susan Strasberg in "Midnight Never Ends."*
*Courtesy of Jerry Ohlinger.*

*A most cordial welcome to this nocturnal arcade, featuring canvases that are sometimes a bit on the peculiar side, sometimes uncommon—sometimes a few frescoes of the freakish.*

*Tonight's first selection, a painting suggesting solitude, or at least solemnity as viewed during the midnight hour. It tells the tale of two young people caught inexorably in a recurring nightmare with a finale on the jolting side. Our painting, with the somewhat familiar face, is called "Midnight Never Ends," and this is the* Night Gallery.

/ **Summary** / Driving an endless stretch of night highway, Ruth Asquith slows to offer a young marine hitchhiker a lift. Their small talk is strained; and creeping over both is an eerie sensation of déjà vu, as if they have somehow lived this experience before. The marine, Vincent Riley, seems to have an unerring ability to predict what Ruth will think and say next. Ruth finds that she, too, shares this ability. In a few minutes, they will come upon a café. "It will be closed," she whispers. "But we get him to open up," continues Vincent. "A big fat man playing solitaire. He's gruff. He didn't like us."

Through the darkness ahead the café appears, and Ruth reluctantly pulls in. But instead of being closed as Ruth predicted, the café is open. "Another mistake," Vincent notes. "I wonder if we have to start again." As Ruth picks up her purse, a small handgun falls out—and she has no idea how it got there. "It changes a little each time," she marvels, as Vincent pockets the gun. The café owner, Joe Bateman, a fat man playing solitaire, is just getting ready to close when the two approach. He reluctantly lets them in—but only for a few minutes. "We *all* only have a couple of more minutes," muses a troubled Ruth. It's all beginning to come back to the two travelers. They will be joined by a sheriff making a security check, and. . . . They stop to listen to the noise, the insistent tapping that seems to be coming from somewhere above them. Right on cue, a sheriff arrives, eyeing Ruth and Vincent suspiciously. The owner claims never to have seen the two visitors before. Vincent heatedly replies, "Sure you have, Joe! Come on, *you* remember! *We've been through this all before.* This is a trip that never seems to end and goes nowhere." Vincent challenges both Bateman and the sheriff to remember anything previous to a few minutes ago. They cannot. Not their home town, not their parents, nothing. The tapping from above continues. "I know what it is now," declares Ruth. Vincent, angry and frustrated at the accumulating mistakes—of being a puppet in someone's play—tries to leave the café in an attempt to break out of the unending loop. The sheriff draws his weapon on Vincent, who, impelled by an unseen hand, pulls Ruth's handgun from his own pocket. The sheriff fires and the marine drops, mortally wounded. The other three stand frozen, listening to the tapping . . .

Unhappy with the direction his latest story has taken, the writer rips the page from the typewriter and tosses it in the waste can. The balled-up page is retrieved by the writer's wife, who scans it. "Why did you give her a gun?" she asks. He admits that he isn't really sure. "I thought writers knew before they started out where they were going," she comments. "Just the good ones, darling," he adds drily, rolling another sheet into the typewriter. And he begins again. Maybe this time he'll get it right. . . .

Driving an endless stretch of night highway, Ruth Asquith slows to offer a young marine hitchhiker a lift . . .

**/ Commentary /** "Midnight Never Ends" gave some who worked on the show the impression that Serling was pulling his scripts out of a trunk, and in truth this episode feels very much like recycled *Twilight Zone* material. Serling had posed this type of existential speculation before on *Zone* episodes such as "Mirror Image" and "Five Characters in Search of an Exit." Ironically—and apropos to the plot of this segment—Serling's meditation on who controls our destiny takes a backseat in this case to conjecture about who really wrote the script.

The final draft Serling submitted to Universal is far different from the segment as shot. His concept and scene chronology is the same, but all the dialogue has been changed. Jack Laird, evidently unhappy with the submission, passed it on for revision to story editor Gerald Sanford. "I rewrote the whole thing," Sanford says. "That was all my show. I did the entire script. I mean, [Serling] wouldn't have recognized it."[57] Indeed, he did not when the segment aired. On the one hand, Serling's original script, viewed objectively, has a tired, paint-by-numbers feel to it. On the other hand, Sanford's overhaul did nothing to aid it. The dialogue misses the distinctive Serling snap, and anyone who has ever seen a *Twilight Zone* episode will recognize long beforehand the setup for the segment's final twist.

Looking for ways to cut corners, designer Joseph Alves and director Jeannot Szwarc adopted a deliberately artificial visual style. Instead of shooting the segment on location, Alves designed a stylized set depicting an endless night by draping the soundstage in a black psych. The movement of Ruth's car was simulated by the camera zooming in and panning off the highway signs, one of cinematographer Lionel Lindon's inspirations. For Joe Bateman's café, Alves took his cue from the story line and gave it a sketchy, incomplete look, with unfinished walls and neon signs hanging in limbo. "It was a very stylistic thing. I mean, you see that a lot now on MTV, but we're talking 1971, and for a prime time television series, I think it was sort of unusual."[58]

Although Robert F. Lyons and, particularly, Susan Strasberg give well-drawn performances, they cannot elevate the perfunctory quality of the script. The stinging twist missing from the story can be found in Serling's introduction for this segment. Tom Wright's painting for "Midnight Never Ends" is his only depiction of Serling for this series, and for the one segment in which one looks in vain for the writer's individual style. Like his character Vincent Riley, Serling was manipulated by forces beyond his influence.

## 2
## BRENDA
★ ★ ★

Teleplay by Matthew Howard (pseudonym for Douglas Heyes)
Based on the short story by Margaret St. Clair
Directed by Allen Reisner
Music: Eddie Sauter      Intro: Paul Glass
Director of Photography: Leonard J. South
Time: 29:32

**Cast**
Brenda: Laurie Prange
Richard Alden: Glenn Corbett
Flora Alden: Barbara Babcock
Jim Emsden: Robert Hogan
Elizabeth Emsden: Sue Taylor

*Laurie Prange in "Brenda." Courtesy of Sal Milo.*

Frances Anne: Pamelyn Ferdin
The Thing: Fred Carson

*There's something rather remarkable in the scope of imagination peculiar to children. They project and dream and fantasize with beauty and simplicity and faith in a manner that somehow eludes us as we grow older. This is "Brenda," and Brenda has a playmate. It comes to her in part because of loneliness—and what I wish for you is that you never get that lonely.*

**/ Summary /** Vacationing with her parents at their summer cottage on Moss Island, eleven-year-old Brenda Alden is fast running out of friends. Appearing well mannered to adults, she delights openly in mean and spiteful acts with playmates as a means of gaining attention. Brenda has been reduced to exploring the island's secret places all by herself.

Wandering through the pine forest, she stops when she hears a grunting noise. Peering into the dappled shadows, she makes out a dark figure camouflaged by earthy color. It stands upright like a man. To the frightened Brenda, it looks like a mess of leaves, twigs, mud, and silt she might find in a gutter, formed into a large, misshapen mass. It is definitely alive . . . somehow. Half-scared, half-curious, she calls out, "Here I am! Can't catch me," and playfully runs on ahead as the thing trots after her. Brenda races toward the pit, an abandoned earthen excavation, and hides in the tall grass to wait. The thing trundles up the path and tumbles into the hole.

As Brenda watches its attempts to escape, she muses over the thing's captivity— and its origins. "I think you're very, very old," she says. "Yeah, I think you must have been the way you are for a long, long time." The thing raises its arms to her in an entreating motion. Brenda quiets at this, sensing an incongruous sympathy between them. "What are you waiting for? Do you want to be born?" Perhaps it could help *her* to be born. Brenda directs the thing to the trailing roots at the side of the pit. Having shown it the way out, she excitedly runs back to her house.

That night, Brenda sneaks downstairs while her parents sleep to leave the front door ajar—and is delighted when she awakens later to find her new friend has paid her a visit. Her parents try to keep the thing at bay with the beam of a flashlight; other islanders come to the Aldens' aid and together they force it back with torches, back into the pit where they bury the thing under a pile of stones. Brenda and her family hurriedly leave the island the next day.

A year passes, and the Alden family returns to the summer cottage. Brenda, a few inches taller and no longer in pigtails, visits the pit to find the thing still buried, still alive—and waiting for her return. "Poor old thing," Brenda says, lying close the stone prison. "You've waited so long. You've wanted so much to be born." Giving vent to the rush of a strange emotion she hasn't experienced before, tears streak her face. "I'll let you out, I promise. I'll give you life. I'll give you love. We'll be born together. We'll be born, you and I, together!"

/ **Commentary** / On the surface, "Brenda" is a gentle fantasy about the loneliness of a peculiar little girl. But, like most fairy tales, there are deeper layers to this deceptively simple piece. Douglas Heyes's script, from Margaret St. Clair's sensitive short story, is a sly and beautifully written allegory about childhood's often traumatic end. Analogous to the thing in the pit is Brenda's developing womanhood. For her parents, keeping Brenda under control is as difficult as fighting off the formless intruder. The parents fear it, seek to control it, force it back into the pit—forcing Brenda to remain a child. In the end, however, Brenda embraces this strange creature—and inevitably frees it.

So much of this segment takes place in Brenda's mind that translating the story to the screen requires a great burden of expression from the lead actress. Laurie Prange, professional beyond her years, shoulders it all with a sensitive grace, playing the obnoxious but lonely preteen to perfection. Her later transformation into a young woman is believable and touching as she expresses her feelings for the creature beneath the stony prison. "Laurie Prange was a good actress, but not all that experienced," recalls director Allen Reisner. "It was an important part and she was first-rate, a delight."[59]

"'Brenda' was one of my favorite television roles because it was so unusual," remarks Prange. "It inspired a creativity, whereas most roles in television are usually pretty generic. I did a lot of television in the seventies and eighties, and it's usually 'Brenda' that people always remember.

"They wanted Brenda to be really young. I think the script read twelve years old. I knew I couldn't go for twelve, but I *could* go for a certain energy level. And no one quite knew exactly what the story was about. I remember asking Allen, 'Is this fantasy or is it reality?' And he allowed me to choose whatever direction I wanted to go with." Reisner encouraged Prange's inspirations, giving the actress enormous freedom in her interpretation. "I remember laying there in the bedroom while they were setting up the lights, and I was playing around with my hands, creating shadows on the wall. And Allen said, 'Oh! That's interesting—let's keep that!' He was wonderful. I felt very free-spirited with him to explore my creative impulses, and he was a great guide through that process. He created an environment of imagination and fun."

For her interpretation, Prange chose to play Brenda a little off-center, a lonely misfit with a streak of wickedness . . . and an active imagination.

She creates her own world. Maybe, harboring a sense of resentment for her parents, she created this fantasy, developed a real bond and love for this glob—when in reality it was just a pile of rocks in a pit! You know how kids can go wild with their imaginations while walking through the woods! When I was growing up, I can remember a rumor that started with all the kids in the neighborhood. Someone saw big footprints in the mud at the creek, and there was a green monster! We ran all around the neighborhood trying to locate it! Someone saw it in the vacant lot down the street—and then all of a sudden everything became very real. So that's how I approached the role.[60]

Despite the strength of the lead performance, what "Brenda" unfortunately lacks is the short story's sense of childlike fantasy that could have lifted this segment to a more inspired level. Visually, Reisner's direction has the occasional moment of wonder, but is just as often too literal and lacking in vision for the unfolding of such a dreamy fable. His overreliance on the zoom lens is a sure atmosphere killer.

Of further hindrance is the design for the Thing. What should have been an object of awe, endowed with a kind of mythic proportion—an agent to deliver Brenda from loneliness—is instead a walking dirt heap, obviously constructed on the cheap. The shambling creature (given life by stuntman Fred Carson, who often doubled as Anthony Quinn's stand-in) was a joint design of gallery artist Tom Wright and makeup artists Leonard Engelman and John Chambers. "It was a lot of work, trying to come up with the concept of sort of a mud-and-plant nonentity that would be able to do what the script called for," Engelman says, admitting, "It wasn't one of my favorites."[61]

On the positive side falls Eddie Sauter's first score for *Night Gallery*, a definite plus. His music, as a storytelling element, is an equal partner with Heyes's script and the quirky truth of Prange's performance. Jack Laird himself praised its qualities in an interview from the period, pronouncing it "absolutely marvelous. Eddie created a particular sound to represent the girl—something light and airy—and another sound, a contrabassoon, for the creature. It was sort of like *Peter and the Wolf*, and that was rather fitting. He just understood right away what was required."[62]

Another plus is the photography of Leonard J. South, whose exterior shots of the California coastline are breathtaking, and the fluid editing of Jean-Jacques Berthelot, pacing the story to build and sustain its delicate tension.

For Jack Laird's part, Laurie Prange's talent obviously made a strong positive impression, as the actress discovered later on. "Jack Laird hired me a few years later," recalls Prange. "I walked into an interview in 1977, and I didn't recognize him. He was just smiling at me, and he said, 'You don't remember me, do you?' And I said, 'No.' That was one of my big faux pas. I didn't zero in that this was Jack Laird, the producer of *Night Gallery!* I finally said, 'I'm sorry. I know I'm supposed to recognize you, but I don't!' And he said, 'Well, just look on my wall.' I turned around, and on the wall he had a big photograph of me as Brenda! And *then* it clicked!"

Prange ultimately won the role in Laird's miniseries *Testimony of Two Men*. "He was very kind to me," she notes, "and he always wore dark sunglasses, even at night. He asked me once, 'What sort of roles would you like to play?' I told him—and later he hired me again! And it was very close to the kind of role that I described to him!"

"I worked for him maybe three or four times, and then I lost track of him. I was doing a play once and wanted to invite him to one of the performances. I tried to locate him, but I just couldn't find him."[63] Jack Laird, a patron to so many artists, maintained his elusive nature. Personally and professionally, he remained something of an enigma to everyone who knew him.

## NIGHT GALLERY #34307
Air date: November 10, 1971

1
## THE DIARY
★ ★ ½

Written by Rod Serling
Directed by William Hale
Music: Oliver Nelson, John Lewis, and Gil Mellé
Director of Photography: Lionel Lindon
Time: 25:48

**Cast**
Holly Schaefer: Patty Duke
Dr. Mill: David Wayne
Carrie Crane: Virginia Mayo
Jeb Harlan: Robert Yuro
George: James McCallion
Nurse: Lindsay Wagner
Receptionist: Floy Dean
Maid: Diana Chesney

*Patty Duke and Virginia Mayo in "The Diary." Courtesy of Globe Photos.*

$G$*ood evening. A most cordial welcome to a display of canvases from which you might call the mausoleum school of art.*

*Subject: a common enough item utilized by teenagers and tycoons. The daily journal in which we notate the happenings of our day-to-day existence. But in this instance, a unique periodical that doesn't record what was, but rather predicts what will be. Its title: "The Diary." It's our initial offering in the Night Gallery.*

/ **Summary** / Holly Schaefer, a vitriolic gossip columnist, has lately devoted a part of each evening's broadcast to skewering a faded former film star, Carrie Crane, exposing her alcoholic peccadilloes and generally humiliating the actress on nationwide television. In response, Crane intrudes on Schaefer during the columnist's New Year's Eve party. Seeing a wrapped package clutched in Crane's hand, Schaefer assumes a bribe—or perhaps a revolver? It is a diary, Crane tells her, purchased for an enormous sum at an obscure little curio shop. Schaefer could not be less grateful for the gift, and boots Crane out.

Schaefer opens the diary and, to her surprise, finds the page for January 1 already filled out—in her own handwriting. The entry tells of her disquiet over Carrie Crane's suicide—an event that comes to pass that very evening. At a loss to explain how the entry got into the diary, Schaefer becomes distraught. Even the rationalizations of her lover, Jeb Harlan, cannot soothe Schaefer when she discovers the next day's entry in the diary has been filled out also, again in her handwriting—although she never touched it—and the mysterious entry again comes true.

Schaefer visits a psychiatrist, Dr. Mill, who suggests that she may have unwittingly made the entries herself during bouts of some form of precognition. Schaefer scoffs —until she absently fingers through the diary to the fresh entry of January 3, predicting Jeb Harlan's death. Frantic, Schaefer tries desperately to contact Jeb, but she is too late—he dies in a car accident. Schaefer's grief turns to panic when she realizes the page for January 4 is blank. No entry. "Can't you understand now why it's blank?" she asks Mill. "Holly gives it to Holly. The page is blank because *I won't be alive to write in it after tomorrow.*" Fearing a suicide attempt, Schaefer commits herself to a sanitarium.

Among the rows of padded cells, Schaefer's hysterical cries for Dr. Mill echo throughout the asylum wing. Mill arrives and confers with Schaefer, now in a protective straitjacket, through the window of her cell. She realizes she hadn't taken into account a death from natural causes—although she has a plan to postpone the inevitable. All she has to do is make an entry in the diary *herself* to keep from dying. Fearful of the fast-approaching midnight hour, she begs Mill hysterically for a pen before her time runs out. As Mill wearily returns to the nurse's station to borrow one, the duty nurse questions him about the procedure. "You're new on this ward, aren't you?" asks Mill. "We give her a pen *every* evening. Miss Schaefer has been a patient at this sanitarium going on five years now."

**/ Commentary /** Serling's first ideas for this segment were presented in précis form during preparation for *Night Gallery*'s first season. The initial drafts were similar. The Schaefer character was a professional woman who purchased the diary herself from a mysterious crone at a curio shop. She shares her fears about the diary's predictions with a friend. After the Schaefer character dies in a manner predicted by the diary, her friend finds the curio shop to inquire about the purchase. The crone professes not to remember the sale; in fact, the diary is still on display in the sales cabinet. Curious, the friend buys the diary, but when she flips to the first page, she finds an entry—in *her own* handwriting.

When NBC scheduled *Night Gallery* as a weekly series, Serling returned to the idea and produced a revision stronger in dramatic thrust. The segment's startling climax metes out justice, *Night Gallery*–style: the callous protagonist's trail of destruction leads ultimately to self-destruction.

As contrast to the story's grim melodramatics, the filming had its lighter moments. In one scene, Schaefer muses about the emptiness of her life: all she has are material possessions and "a growing list of corpses." Actress Patty Duke was breaking up everyone on the set, including herself, by fluffing the line repeatedly as "a list of growing corpses." She was later visited on the set by her young son, Sean Patrick Astin. "It's the first time he's ever visited me on a set to watch me act," Duke commented at the time. "Apparently he's not crazy about my acting. He threw up."[64]

With one of the better twist endings of the series—ultimately, it is Schaefer's guilt that imprisons her, not unseen supernatural forces—"The Diary" could have been a strong episode opener. Regrettably, it is flawed. Serling's dialogue, usually the most effective facet of his writing, flirts unsuccessfully with the dialect of "hip" Hollywood circa 1971 and is now hopelessly dated. More damaging, however, is Patty Duke's unfortunate miscasting. Shrill and unconvincing, Duke lacks the presence to muster the arrogance, will, and magnum-bitch toughness Serling must have envisioned for the role. There is an insecurity just below the surface of Duke's performance that translates to the character. Nothing she says rings true. Serling's withering salvos are reduced to schoolyard taunts, and it is difficult to believe the character carries the kind of industry power Serling assigns to her. Perhaps an actress of Lee Grant's chop-busting intensity might have given the role more stature.

At the time, the Oscar- and Emmy-winning actress was suffering from the blur of fast times and bouts of manic depression she has since gone public about. Recalls director William Hale: "When I went home at night, she'd be sitting on the curb by the front gate with nowhere to go and nobody to take her home or anything. I'd sort of pick her up and take her home. She was really at a low point in her life at that time."

The rest of the performances vary in quality. Costar David Wayne's presence is welcome, and Lindsay Wagner here received one of her first television roles as a nurse. Unfortunately, Virginia Mayo—who, like the washed-up Carrie Crane, had been a star in the 1940s and '50s—brings little of note to the proceedings. "I remember as a kid I used to have a crush on Virginia Mayo," muses Hale. "She arrived in a mink coat like an old-time movie star, but she couldn't act worth shit. I became disillusioned very quickly."

With stock pick-up sets borrowed from *Columbo* and overlit photography lending little atmosphere, the saving grace of the episode is Hale's efficient direction, culminating in the disturbing final scene. He developed a claustrophobic visual for Dr. Mill's conversation with the straitjacketed Schaefer: "For the window of her cell, I took some gaffer's tape and made a little frame within the frame—reduced the frame line so that you had to sort of peer in to see her in the room." Later on, that composition got Hale another directing job: "Some years later I had dropped out of the business and gone south to raise money for a feature. I really needed a boost to get back in." The boost came from Steven Spielberg, who wanted Hale to direct *Nightmare*, again starring Patty Duke. "Spielberg called Joe Alves, the art director, and asked who did 'The Diary.' Joe told him that I did it, so Steven actually gave me the job based on that one effect.

"The thing about working in television is that you never know who's watching or who's digging what you do. It's that great question mark: is anybody really watching this stuff?" [65]

## 2
## A MATTER OF SEMANTICS
*

Written by Gene Kearney
Directed by Jack Laird
Music: Gil Mellé      Intro: Oliver Nelson
Director of Photography: Lionel Lindon
Time: 2:23

**Cast**
Count Dracula: Cesar Romero
Nurse: E. J. Peaker
Candy-Striper: Monie Ellis

*Cesar Romero in "A Matter of Semantics."
Courtesy of Hollywood Book and Poster
Co.*

**/ Summary /** The blood-bank nurse sees her last scheduled appointment of a very long day. The caped figure introduces himself as Count Dracula. She commends the dignitary for his generosity, although he appears distracted. He keeps gazing with concern at the large blood refrigerator. "There's nothing to be afraid of, you know," she soothes. "Because, after all, it *is* only one pint." The distressed count demands that one pint will not do—perhaps three? "Three?" replies the shocked nurse. "I can see that this *is* the first time you've given." The count, perplexed, tries to clarify what appears to be a slight misunderstanding: "Young lady, this *is* a blood bank?" Certainly, she says. "Well, then," the count replies, baring his fangs, "I wish to apply for a *loan*."

/ **Commentary** / A bit of confusion lingers over who directed "A Matter of Semantics." Actress E. J. Peaker clearly recalls that the scheduled director was one of Universal's hottest up-and-coming talents, Steven Spielberg: "Someone on my team said, 'There's a new young director that's going to be directing this segment that Universal is very excited about. His name is Steven Spielberg.' That's all I was told, and that's why my agents wanted me to do it." She also recalls very distinctly being introduced to Spielberg in his trailer at some point. Jack Laird, however, is the credited director for this segment. This appears to be yet another curious episode in the young director's turbulent association with *Night Gallery*.

The vignette took a half-day to shoot, with Peaker and costar Cesar Romero in makeup by 6:00 A.M. and out before one o'clock—no complications. "The funny thing is, I remember the director *looking* like Steven Spielberg," says Peaker. "They may have taken his name off and put Jack's name on, because he was set to direct that show. And neither of us knew at the time what [Spielberg] looked like." Peaker, unaware of the switch on the set, responded positively to her director—*whoever* it was: "I remember being spoken to very quietly and with a great deal of respect. He was very sensitive and sweet, very helpful and creative. I thought, 'This is the man that Universal is so excited about, and he is such a gentle being.'"[66]

Regardless of who directed, "A Matter of Semantics" is just another unfortunate *Night Gallery* burlesque of the overexposed vampire theme—witless and forced.

3

BIG SURPRISE

★ ★ ★

Teleplay by Richard Matheson
Based on his short story
Directed by Jeannot Szwarc
Music: Oliver Nelson and John Lewis
Director of Photography: Lionel Lindon
Time: 10:33

**Cast**

Mr. Hawkins: John Carradine
Chris: Vincent Van Patten
Jason: Marc Vahanian
Dan: Eric Chase

*John Carradine in "Big Surprise." Courtesy of TV History Archives.*

*O*ur *painting reminds us that there's a strange fascination to digging holes alongside*
*ancient oaks. You give the average man a shovel and an X on a map and the fantasies come*
*thick and fast. Pirate gold, hidden Confederate treasure, and sometimes the unexpected—*
*and sometimes the unwelcome. Hence the title: "Big Surprise."*

/ **Summary** / Three boys, Chris, Jason, and Dan, walk the dusty back roads home
from school every day, reluctantly passing the farmhouse of Mr. Hawkins, a crazy old
hermit feared by the children in the area. One afternoon, the mysterious old man
stands like some grizzled scarecrow in the farmhouse doorway, gesturing to Chris.
Pulling the boy aside, Hawkins asks him if he would like a big surprise. "You know
where Miller's Field is?" the old man croaks. "You know where that great big oak tree
is? Go over to that tree, face the steeple of the church, d'ya understand? Walk ten
paces, dig down four feet . . . and there you'll find a *great big surprise!*" Wheezing a
raspy laugh at the shaking boy, Hawkins gives Chris an evil wink.

Although Jason is sure it's a prank, Chris and Dan believe Hawkins has a cache of
money buried out there. There is one way to find out—borrow some shovels and dig.
One by one they reach a point of sheer exhaustion. Chris tries to persuade the other
two to continue, but they have had enough. Chris is left alone to continue, his curiosity pushing him on. Digging another foot, his spade hits something hard—a large
wooden box. Clearing shovelfuls of dirt from the lid, Chris stops when he hears a
noise—the sound of creaking hinges. The lid is raising on its own! Scrambling to the
far side of the hole, paralyzed with fear, Chris stares bug-eyed as a figure rises up from
inside the box—the grizzled, scarecrow figure of old Mr. Hawkins. Looming over the
frightened boy, he rasps, *"Surprise!"*

/ **Commentary** / Richard Matheson's clever take on the buried treasure theme is
given splendid life thanks to the visual stamp of Jeannot Szwarc and the services of
John Carradine. Always a joy to watch, Carradine plays a wheezy old crank with in-
fectious glee, and his delivery is priceless.

The actor's presence on the set inspired affection as well as admiration. "I had a
lot of respect for him," recalls Vincent Van Patten, who played the intrepid Chris. "Before shooting 'Big Surprise,' my father [actor Dick Van Patten] told me, 'You're going
to be working with John Carradine. He was in *The Grapes of Wrath* and he's one of the
greatest actors of all time. Just listen to his *voice.*' My father had built him up as a wonderful actor, which he was, but I didn't feel intimidated by him. I had been under contract at Universal as a child actor since the age of nine, and when you're a kid actor, I
don't think *anybody* intimidates you."[67]

"John was marvelous," agrees director Jeannot Szwarc. "That one was supposed
to be set in the country. I found this place on the back lot and I used negative space

[composing the frame so that something in the foreground blocks the view of an un-wanted element, such as a telephone pole, in the background]. We ended up with a piece that looked like it was shot in the Midwest."[68] Adding to the feast, Lionel Lin-don's stunning color photography well captures the dry, bleached landscape, and the artful editing builds the tension to the punch line nicely.

Without today's specialized camera equipment, a few aspects of Szwarc's visual scheme were an effort to re-create; thus Carradine was not the only one who had to get boxed in on "Big Surprise." For the digging scenes, a cameraman was positioned in the hole under a sheet of Plexiglass, shooting up at the shoveling boys.

Author Richard Matheson expressed his pleasure at the outcome: "I'm glad to say that 'The Big Surprise' holds up pretty well. In fact, I hadn't remembered that Jeannot Szwarc added a circular ending, which was a nice touch."[69] He of course refers to the syndication version, which has been expanded with superfluous footage (from Hitch-cock's *The Birds,* no less) and inexplicably repeats the opening footage after the seg-ment's finish. Matheson, not privy to the postcancellation fiasco, thought this must be the original piece, a misconception mirrored by many old fans of the show when viewing the syndicated version.

But a fan's remembered feelings from the original broadcasts are more difficult to confound. "When I used to watch *Night Gallery* and hear that creepy music," notes Van Patten, "it would scare the living daylights out of me!—unlike some of the music scores that you hear today for various TV shows. They've never duplicated what Rod Serling and *Night Gallery* had. These other horror shows they've attempted never catch on. Since *Night Gallery,* they haven't really had any success with that genre."[70]

## 4
## PROFESSOR PEABODY'S LAST LECTURE
★ ½

Written by Jack Laird
Directed by Jerrold Freedman
Music: Oliver Nelson      Intro: John Lewis
Director of Photography: Lionel Lindon
Time: 10:54

**Cast**
Professor Peabody: Carl Reiner
Mr. Lovecraft: Johnnie Collins III
Mr. Bloch: Richard Annis
Miss Heald: Louise Lawson
Mr. Derleth: Larry Watson

*Carl Reiner in "Professor Peabody's Last Lecture."*
*Courtesy of Sal Milo.*

*Our final offering: a study in depth of a gentleman from the academe, seen here at the lectern delivering a most scholarly treatise. This particular class I don't think you'll want to cut. The painting's title: "Professor Peabody's Last Lecture."*

**/ Summary /** The class bell echoes into silence, and Professor Peabody launches into his lecture on pagan religious cults. Dismissing them as the childish superstitions of ignorant people, the professor begins a dissection of the Cthulhu mythos. He runs through the tongue-twisting pantheon: Nyar-Lathotep, Umra-Atowil, Hastur, Aza-thoth, Shub-Niggurath, Cthulhu, and Yog-Sothoth. "It reads like an Albanian vaude-ville program, doesn't it?" Peabody cracks. One of his students, Mr. Derleth, reminds the professor that it is a punishable blasphemy to speak their names aloud. Although the professor shrugs the threat off with humor, some of the students note with alarm that a storm appears to be brewing in the skies.

Peabody pulls from his briefcase a copy of the testament of this cabalistic nether-world, the *Necronomicon*, rigidly suppressed down through the ages. "This overblown gibberish, and I have read it *all*, is as corruptibly harmful as the *Farmer's Almanac*," snorts Peabody—eliciting from the glowering skies outside a deafening crack of thunder. When another student, Mr. Lovecraft, tries to warn Peabody that, according to myth, to read the dreaded manuscript aloud is to invite ghastly consequences, the professor tempts fate. Opening the withered volume, he launches into the hellish recital with increasing volume to keep from getting drowned out by the furious mael-strom roaring outside. At the peak of Peabody's hysterical recitation, the air is rent by a shaft of lightning. Peabody is instantaneously tranformed into an oozing, repulsive, tentacled thing of hideous countenance. Peabody, closing the book, peers at the gap-ing, astonished students with his single bloodshot eye. "And now," he concludes, "if there are no further questions . . ."

**/ Commentary /** H. P. Lovecraft's legacy, both his own works and those he inspired, would figure strongly in *Night Gallery*'s second season. The first of these, "Professor Peabody's Last Lecture," cannot be considered among the show's best efforts. Laird's script is only fitfully humorous and is chewed to bits by Carl Reiner, who effectively drains it of wit. A drier tone from the lead actor would have better served this ex-tended in-joke for Lovecraft fans. Reiner's rabid frothing at the denouement is as ridic-ulous as the bathtub-toy headdress devised by the makeup department to transform him into one of Lovecraft's primordial lurkers. "That was a very early effort," recalls makeup artist Leonard Engelman. The makeup, worn not by Reiner but a stand-in, was a "big sort of octopus-looking thing with methylcellulose and all sorts of things dripping off of it."[71] And, unfortunately, not quite what one visualizes when imagin-ing the shambling monstrosities described in Lovecraft's oeuvre.

"It was a thirteen-page script that we had to shoot in a day," recalls director Jerrold Freedman, "and we had to walk into an already existing set, which was really not right for this particular show. It was a classroom set and it should have been long and narrow; instead it was wide." Laird peopled the classroom with the various lexicographers of the Cthulhu mythos: August Derleth (played by Laird's auto detailer, Larry Watson), Robert Bloch, Hazel Heald (trimmed from the final cut), and, stuttering with excitement, the avid Howard Phillip Lovecraft himself, all held in thrall by the ravings of their skeptical professor. "It was basically just a question of letting Carl wail," notes Freedman. "Carl, he's a great guy. At the end of the show, he gave me a box of Cuban cigars. Great cigars."[72]

Segments like this caused a lot of viewer disappointment. Those who expected a more serious approach to the genre, more in line with the tone of the pilot, soon forgot the better segments the series produced and turned their backs on the show.

## NIGHT GALLERY #34302
Air date: November 17, 1971

### 1

### HOUSE — WITH GHOST
★ ★

Teleplay by Gene Kearney
Based on the short story by August Derleth
Directed by Gene Kearney
Music: Gil Mellé
Director of Photography: Lionel Lindon
Time: 17:54

**Cast**
Ellis Travers: Bob Crane
Iris Travers: Jo Anne Worley
Canby: Bernard Fox
Chichester: Eric Christmas
Doctor: Alan Napier
Sherry: Trisha Noble

*Jo Anne Worley and Bob Crane in "House—With Ghost." Courtesy of Eddie Brandt's Saturday Matinee.*

G*ood evening, art lovers. For your enjoyment and edification: three paintings on display, part of a collection of kookery unique to this special exhibit.*

*Painting number one: out of the real estate section of a ghost town weekly, a ginger-*

*bready item quite appropriately called "House—With Ghost." This, ladies and gentlemen, is the* Night Gallery.

**/ Summary /** Ellis Travers, an American recently arrived in England with his wife, Iris, is unhappy with his cramped London flat. He wants to rent a country house, something with some grounds, and—in a bid to catch his wife's peculiar interest—perhaps with a ghost. Iris fancies herself a spiritualist, and her curiosity is immediately piqued at the idea of a house with its own restless spirit.

Ellis has other reasons for wanting such a residence. He has a mistress, Sherry, who wants him to leave Iris; but Iris controls their fortune, and Ellis cannot push for a separation without losing it. Renting a house rumored to have a ghost would be a perfect alibi for him in case Iris, who suffers from dizzy spells, "accidentally" fell down the stairs. Through an agent, Ellis finds the perfect house in the Cotswolds—one with a stairwell ghost. The last owner, a Mr. Canby, was a ruthless skinflint who, after death, chased his widow out of the estate when she broke his will and got every farthing. Yes, the agent says, this ghost "has what it takes."

After they move in, Iris is dragged from her bed one afternoon by invisible hands. She is terribly shaken by this visitation, and Ellis calls a local physician. Pulling him aside, the doctor warns him that his wife's problem goes beyond vertigo—her condition is terminal. Ellis, relieved, realizes that in a few months he will be free of Iris. That is not soon enough for Sherry, however, who dumps him that evening over the phone. Even less patient than Sherry is the house ghost—as Ellis rings off, he hears an ear-splitting scream, and Iris, propelled by unseen hands, tumbles end over end down the steep marble staircase, landing dead at its foot.

As Ellis kneels next to her broken body, the late Mr. Canby suddenly materializes in front of him, transparent and businesslike, handing Ellis a bill for his services: two thousand a month, for life. Ellis protests, and Canby warns him: "I'm an impatient man, Mr. Travers. I caution you, I have quite a reputation of hounding my creditors to death." A dismayed Ellis asks why a ghost has need of money, and Canby cites his responsibilities: when his wife upset the provisions to his will, she cut off a person to whom Canby had made promises. "You see, Mr. Travers," the shade says with a wink, "I, too, had a bird on the side. Like yourself, I'd do anything in the world for her."

**/ Commentary /** Here is *Night Gallery* at its nadir, offering a full-length story with very little that is distinctive or interesting to commend it. August Derleth was a superb writer of short fiction, but there are scores of his stories that would have made far more interesting adaptations than this blow-off on infidelity. It is hard to believe Gene Kearney was behind both "Silent Snow, Secret Snow" *and* this inconsequential fluff.

To make matters worse, the script's rather fragile wit is rendered flat and lifeless by its stars. Bob Crane (*Hogan's Heroes*) and Jo Anne Worley (*Rowan and Martin's Laugh-In*) have embarrassingly little depth as performers, and their appearance gave certain critics of the series reason to compare *Night Gallery* unflatteringly with *Love, American Style*. When the supporting cast members (Eric Christmas and Alan Napier specifically) are seriously outperforming the lead actors, it's time to halt production and re-cast. Intended to be both humorous and spooky, the episode is neither.

Again, more humor could be found behind the scenes than in front of the camera, as relayed by assistant director Les Berke:

We were working late and we broke for dinner. I went ahead of the company to see that the dinners were ready, and there were these two bums sitting at one of the tables having lunch on the company. I'd never seen two scruffier men. I thought they were a couple of guys from the back lot, so I went down and pulled the company attitude, something to the effect of, 'Gentlemen, this is for the filmmakers. You're not supposed to be eating here, you don't belong here.' It turned out the two bums were Jack Laird and Gene Kearney—Scruffy and Scruffy, Jr. Jack had this old leather jacket with fringes, his wispy little beard, and his long hair. He looked like hammered shit, and I tried to throw him off the stage.

Oops. "Yeah, he won that one."[73]


2

A MIDNIGHT VISIT TO THE NEIGHBORHOOD BLOOD BANK
⋆

Written by Jack Laird
Directed by William Hale
Music: Gil Mellé
Director of Photography: Lionel Lindon
Time: 1:35

**Cast**
Vampire: Victor Buono
Intended Victim: Journey Laird

**/ Summary /** A young woman sleeps fitfully in her bed when through her window flies a bat. In an instant, it transforms into a leering vampire, on the prowl for blood. Approaching her bed, the creature leans over her throat to sink its fangs. Stirring, half asleep, she says, "I gave at the office." Disappointed, the vampire shrugs, strikes her name off his list of potential victims, and flies off into the night.

**/ Commentary /** Beyond the considerable comic abilities of Victor Buono, this vignette is little more than filler for the hour. The intended victim in the sketch was played by Journey Laird, the daughter of Jack Laird's significant other.

3

## DR. STRINGFELLOW'S REJUVENATOR

★ ★ ★ ½

Written by Rod Serling
Directed by Jerrold Freedman
Music: Gil Mellé
Director of Photography: Lionel Lindon
Time: 21:16

**Cast**

Dr. Stringfellow: Forrest Tucker
Snyder: Murray Hamilton
Rolpho: Don Pedro Colley
Man: Lou Frizzell
Daughter: Geri Berger
Undertaker: Matt Pelto

*Forrest Tucker in "Dr. Stringfellow's Rejuvenator." Courtesy of Ronald Borst.*

*As our third selection, an item from the past: that uniquely American institution known as the pitchman—the wheeler and dealer of magical nostrums guaranteed to cure, to paliate, to bring back the glow of health to everything but a cadaver. Bottled dreams, if you will. Our painting is called "Dr. Stringfellow's Rejuvenator." Drink hearty.*

**/ Summary /** American desert town, circa 1880s. Attracting a growing crowd from atop his garishly colored medicine show wagon is "Doctor" Ernest Stringfellow, entrepreneur. His product: snake oil. His vigorous claims for its effectiveness: substantial. As the doctor's assistant, Rolpho, passes among the crowd with bottles of the rejuvenator, a haggard man in the distance catches Stringfellow's eye—and his instinct warns him. Stringfellow withdraws into his wagon, watching through the shutters as the man engages Rolpho in a brief exchange. Visualizing tar and feathers, the doctor's suspicions are eased when he learns that the man is only looking for a physician to treat his daughter, lying ill in his buckboard.

Though no doctor, Stringfellow recognizes instantly that the man's daughter is mortally ill: her small, white face is a mask of pain, her eyes underlined by dark hollows as death works its way out. He represses whatever deep nugget of conscience this pathetic scene dislodges and prescribes some spoonfuls of his worthless physic. This counterfeit act of mercy is witnessed by the town rummy, Snyder, once a doctor before his dedication to the bottle brought him low. Confronting Stringfellow, Snyder offers a different diagnosis: the girl's symptoms suggest a burst appendix—and she will surely die. "Diagnosis by a drunk," sneers Stringfellow. "Doubtless," rasps Snyder. "But with a far sight more truth than the labels on those bottles of yours."

Rolpho is troubled about the little girl, but the doctor waxes philosophical about their fraud: "I should be getting a hundred dollars a swallow for that stuff. I give hope to the hopeless—an illusion of health to all the poor doomed yokels that have a dollar in their jeans. You see, I let 'em get a little peek over the pigsty and get a view of heaven." His musings are interrupted by the return of the little girl's father, frantic over his daughter's worsening condition. Sending Rolpho off for a bottle of the rejuvenator, Stringfellow offers the man a spectacular claim: "You know what I do, brother? I sell faith. I'm going to give that child of yours enough belief so that she can kick her way out of a pine coffin if she needs to be, do you understand me? If that child crosses over into the shadows, *I am going to bring her back to life!*"

Despite Stringfellow's hollow promise, the little girl dies. The undertaker collects her pitiful remains while Stringfellow, unmoved and unashamed, prepares to leave town. As he steps out into the deserted street, he slows when he catches a movement near the undertaker's establishment. Through the foglike dust raised by the howling windstorm, he sees an indistinct outline. Sitting in a rocking chair is the figure of the little girl. Moving toward her across the street, he calls out to her. Either his phony elixir works, Stringfellow reckons—or this is some fearful judgment. She rises as if to accuse him . . . and disappears without a trace. Suddenly, the undertaker's sign, buffeted by the wind, wrenches loose and hurtles down toward Stringfellow. Then, stillness in the street, save for the howling winds . . . and the creak of the now-empty rocking chair.

Afterward, the undertaker collects yet another body. Rolpho, as if to wipe out the last trace of the doctor's existence, sets Stringfellow's wagon ablaze, watching the hungry flames as they claim his miserable legacy. "Nothing in there worth anything," Rolpho explains to the quizzical Snyder—then, looking back at the mortuary, "Nothing in there worth anything, either."

/ **Commentary** / Serling's strengths in realistically presenting small-time hustlers and other clutter from the urban landscape are here transplanted effectively to the Old West. "Dr. Stringfellow's Rejuvenator" is another of Serling's tragedy-cum-ethics lessons, and his characterizations, infused with a wary cynicism, are razor-sharp, sad, and poetic. Without exception, the performances are excellent. Murray Hamilton—who played an efficient, executive-styled Mr. Death in another tale of a desperate pitchman, the *Twilight Zone* episode "One for the Angels"—offers a bitter draft as Stringfellow's gadfly, the derelict Snyder. Don Pedro Colley's noble Rolpho is Serling's touchstone of conscience, and as the desperate farmer, Lou Frizzell's performance rings with pain and sincerity. Most effective of all is Forrest Tucker's Stringfellow, a marvelous creation: in public, a tireless promoter of his abilities and prowess; in private, a hollow, empty man. But the richness of Tucker's performance lies in little details of expression that suggest a hint, a glimmer of humanity. He gets across a fleeting sense that Stringfellow was once, in his distant past, a compassionate man. "I have a lot of good memories," remarks director Jerrold Freedman of the filming, reserving special praise for the members of his sterling cast. "Forrest was terrific to work with. You know, you work with all these guys that get stereotyped into stuff like *F Troop* and all, and you don't realize they really are good actors. And he was really a good actor."[74]

Although one of the costars, Don Pedro Colley (*THX-1138*), was a relative newcomer to film, he found the atmosphere on the set warmly inclusive:

I was very surprised that they all treated me with the same kind of equal respect—one on one. I was all prepared to take a total back seat, but during the shoot they asked me how I wanted to approach doing my role, which was quite unusual. This was a real collaborative affair.

The script was really quite interesting and it took a little work to get the subtext out of it—how it should be put together, what we should try and accomplish for the sake of the material—and it worked really well! God, it was just as exciting as hell for me!

Unfortunately, one of Colley's brainstorms caused him serious discomfort during the shooting of the saloon scene. "I said to myself, I've got to have some kind of an action to do here, but what? Oh, I know, I'll eat a hard-boiled egg!" Five takes later, Colley realized he had made a bad mistake. "Oh, God! I strangled myself eating those eggs, and we all had a great laugh over the fact that I had painted myself into this damned corner!"

From the start, Freedman encouraged Colley to develop his own sense of the character: "I felt that Rolpho's slowness was kind of his cover. He was more aware than you realize. You feel that there is something else going on there in his relationship to Dr. Stringfellow, an element of mystery that finally leads to the doctor's strange downfall."[75]

The rest of the production (save for the use of day-for-night photography, *Night Gallery*'s eternal hobgoblin) is on an equal plane with the performances. Art director Joseph Alves and cinematographer Lionel Lindon create out of back lot odds and ends a frontier town limbo, all dust, tumbleweeds and chiaroscuro—*The Twilight Zone* out west. Gil Mellé's somber, elegiac score adds an appropriate touch of melancholy, helping make this midseason episode a *Night Gallery* highlight.

4
HELL'S BELLS
★ ★ ★

Teleplay by Theodore J. Flicker
Based on the short story by Harry Turner
Directed by Theodore J. Flicker
Music: Gil Mellé
Director of Photography: Lionel Lindon
Time: 8:55

**Cast**
Randy Miller: John Astin
The Devil: Theodore J. Flicker
Fat Lady: Jody Gilbert
Mrs. Tourist: Ceil Cabot
Mr. Tourist: John J. Fox
The Bore: Hank Worden
1st Demon: Theodore J. Flicker
2d Demon: Jack Laird
3d Demon: Gene Kearney

*John Astin in "Hell's Bells." Courtesy of Akron Beacon-Journal.*

*O*ur final selection this evening: an import from that other region, that infernal inferno down below. Offered to you now in living color and with a small scent of sulfur, our painting is called "Hell's Bells."

/ **Summary** / Hippie lead-foot Randy Miller, having just crashed his car, accelerates in like manner into the next life, passing a few angry, howling demons on his way to Hell. His arrival brings some surprises. Hell has a front-office waiting room . . . and rules of conduct. . . . and a fat lady who yells at you if you don't obey them. Miller isn't concerned, though. He envisions the *real* hell to come, the one Dante described, a Boschian landscape of tortured souls, capering demons, and the Dark Lord himself. Suddenly a fire door opens, and a cautious but excited Miller passes through expectantly into the yawning hell mouth of . . .

A sitting room—and a drab one at that. With bad wallpaper. There is, he's happy to note, a record player with a seemingly endless stack of LPs propped onto the changer. But instead of playing something with a groove, a distinctly Welkish arrangement greets his pained ears—and Miller can't make the player stop. Turning, he finds seated in the corner a rather idiotic old farmer type. Miller strikes up a conversation, but is soon exasperated by this bland duffer with his boring talk of baby's croup and crop rotation. Hell is turning out to be a real bummer. Suddenly, in a far corner appear a husband and wife in Hawaiian shirts and straw hats, complete with a projector and their eighty-five hundred vacation slides of Tijuana. As they begin their dissertation on the joys of touring Mexico, Miller's patience fizzles out and he demands that the Devil show his face. Satan appears: calm, pleasant, unimposing . . . and quite short. Sure, he's got the horns and the tail and the pitchfork, but he seems somehow less awe inspiring than his reputation would lead one to believe. Miller queries this mild fellow about the whips, the chains, the boiling oil, and the snakes—you know . . . *Hell.* "This is it," the Devil replies. "My dear boy, Hell is never what you expect it to be—but for you, *this is it.* Don't you like it?" No, Miller says, it's a downer. "Yes, it is, isn't it?" chuckles the Devil. "You know, it's a curious thing, but they have exactly the same room Up There. You see, while this room is Hell for you, absolute beastly Hell, Up There the identical room is someone else's idea of heaven. Think about it. 'Bye." And with a wave, the Devil is gone.

Looking around, Hell's latest initiate takes in the one tiny room where he will spend his endless, excruciating eternity. Bummer, man. Falling to the floor, Miller clamps his hands over his ears in a vain effort to stop the yammering voices of the Bore, Mr. and Mrs. Tourist, and that goddamned music.

/ **Commentary** / With a hilarious John Astin in the lead, "Hell's Bells" rises above the standard *Night Gallery* spoof. Astin, who directed three of *Night Gallery*'s finest segments (and made a previous visit to Hell in "Pamela's Voice"), is a howl with his stoner's grin, Sonny Bono coif, and shriekingly horrid period garb (velvet pants, two-tone leather boots, and swank shoulder bag). Throwing fuel on the fire, writer-director Theodore Flicker's performance as the Devil is equally a riot, a portrait of dry bemusement in red face, horns, and pitchfork. Just for laughs, Flicker hired Jack Laird and Gene Kearney to join him in playing Astin's welcoming committee, a trio of shrieking demons.

Flicker's script is good fun—Milton by way of *The President's Analyst*—but unfortunately his stint as director was evidently much less so. His cantankerous director of photography, Lionel "Curly" Lindon, made Flicker's life sheer hell—not only in front of the camera but also behind it. "I want to tell you, when you act and direct, you really need your cameraman," Flicker says. "Unlike an actor going to the dressing room and getting made up and coming on the set, the director [has to remain] on the floor. So they had a makeup chair right near the camera; I had to be made up in stages as I was directing."

Lindon became irritated by Flicker's "finger in every pie" style of filmmaking. "[Curly] decided to dislike me. He couldn't stand it that there I was, the director, and I had the nerve to be sitting on the stage . . . getting my face painted red and horns put on my head. He just resented the hell out of [me for having] the nerve to write and direct and then act in it. He was so offended that I was doing all three things, and he kept saying it over and over again."

Complicating matters, Lindon and Flicker also clashed over the shot menu.

As a director, I really don't like cutting film a lot. I prefer to shoot everything in masters, and he couldn't understand that. He was so angry at me for that—that I would stage a whole scene right up to almost the last foot of film in a magazine—he'd say, "Well, we don't have that much film in the magazine." And I would say, "Mr. Lindon, would you then get a fresh magazine that has a full load in it?" And he'd just go berserk.

His behavior on the set became antagonistic. He was openly sarcastic, insulting and un-cooperative. It was the single most unpleasant experience I ever had on a TV show. Although the studio wanted me to come back and direct more—including my script for "A Question of Fear"—because of Curly, I refused.[76]

Astin, who had a less turbulent experience with Lindon directing "A Fear of Spiders," confirms the fracas: "I tell you, I admire the way Ted hung in there. Curly was a wonderful cinematographer, but when he got a 'mad' on for somebody, it was awful. He just seemed to have it in for Ted, and it was clear to everyone on the set. Yet the product of the two of them was quite good. Ted didn't get enough credit, because through all the obstacles Ted created a very nice piece. Hey, you're talking about the man who did *The President's Analyst*. You're talking about the guy who put the plug in Pat Harrington's heel!"[77]

Flicker never returned to *Night Gallery,* and wistfully acknowledges that "A Question of Fear" was his favorite of the two scripts he wrote for the show: "I really wanted to direct that, I really knew how I wanted to shoot that. That would have been fun to do."[78] But not with Curly.

**NIGHT GALLERY #34309**
Air date: November 24, 1971

1
THE DARK BOY
★ ★ ★ ½

Teleplay by Halsted Welles
Based on the short story by August Derleth
Directed by John Astin
Music: Eddie Sauter
Director of Photography: Leonard J. South
Time: 31:02

*Elizabeth Hartman in "The Dark Boy." Courtesy of Sal Milo.*

**Cast**
Judith Timm: Elizabeth Hartman
Abigail Moore: Gale Sondergaard
Tom Robb: Michael Baseleon
Lettie Moore: Hope Summers
Joel Robb: Michael Laird
Edward Robb: Steven Lorange
Fourth Grader: Ted Foulkes

Good *evening and welcome to* Night Gallery, *a potpourri of paintings slightly "tilt" and left of center, as is the case with our first selection.*

*This picturesque background is rural America, its central figure a young schoolteacher. But this is where the commonplace ends. You're about to join a roster of students in a learning experience quite without precedent. The painting is called "Dark Boy," and this particular repository is called the* Night Gallery.

**/ Summary /** Montana frontier community, the late 1800s. Judith Timm, recently widowed, arrives to take up her new position as schoolteacher. Her predecessor, Miss Mason, had left hurriedly and without explanation, leaving Mrs. Timm only a puzzling note . . . warning her not to come.

After her first day with her seventeen new students, Mrs. Timm is questioned by the elderly Moore sisters with whom she boards. They insist emphatically that there are only sixteen children in their school district. Mrs. Timm maintains that she counted them: sixteen, all blonds, and a quiet dark-haired boy. Further, when she mentions returning to the schoolhouse that evening, the Moores are visibly upset. "You oughtn't to go at night," frets Lettie. "Miss Mason went at night. That's what started it." Abigail shushes her sister, and they both retreat into a frightened silence.

That night at the schoolhouse, Mrs. Timm's silent fourth grader, Joel, watches her from a window. When she beckons to him, he runs away. She soon begins to connect this boy with Tom Robb, the widowed father of one of her other students. Robb and the dark boy share a distinct resemblance, and when her silent charge returns again the next night, she is sure of their connection. Noticing a white scar on his forehead, she approaches the boy and speaks softly, trying to coax him inside—but Joel turns, melts into the mooncast shadows, and is gone.

Determined to solve the mystery, Mrs. Timm takes her questions to Tom Robb —and shock replaces curiosity when he tells her that Joel died two years ago in a fall from the schoolhouse ladder. "I've seen him, too," admits the grief-stricken father, "but he never speaks, he never comes close. He just haunts me." In this community of fear, Mrs. Timm realizes she is the only one who might be able to reach Joel. With their common bond of loneliness and growing affection, Mrs. Timm and Tom Robb resolve to face the boy together. When Joel appears at the schoolhouse that night, Robb gestures gently to the boy: "Joel, remember how, when you were out in the woods, I'd whistle to you like a whippoorwill? And you'd whistle back? Why don't you do it now, Joel. Every night I've whistled to you from the back porch." Mrs. Timm joins Robb and, taking his hand, asks Joel to come home with them. On the long moonlit trek back to the farm, Joel maintains their pace—never coming too close, yet never falling behind. Upon reaching the house, however, the dark boy vanishes. From the porch, Robb whistles the familiar call of the whippoorwill . . . and from a distance, in the forested hills where Joel's grave lies, comes an answering whistle. The dark boy has finally come home.

/ **Commentary** / Of the three August Derleth tales adapted for *Night Gallery*, this fragile little ghost story is by far the most successful. Sensitively directed by John Astin, "The Dark Boy" inhabits a world similar to Henry James's *The Turn of the Screw*, and gave evidence that *Night Gallery* was capable of tremendous heart. "I think that script excited me as much as any," Astin says. "There was respect for the spirit of the boy, and a commitment to the beauty and romance underlying this story."

Complications surfaced almost immediately with news of the downturn in cinematographer Lionel Lindon's health. "Curly Lindon was supposed to shoot it," Astin says, "but that was around the time that he was diagnosed with cancer. Lenny South came on to it, and he and I sort of roamed around the back lot—these wonderful areas that Joe Alves found. Lenny and I spent a lot of time in prep on that, and we decided on our short schedule, and our little budget, that we were going to make that back lot look like a million dollars! And I think Lenny did, really, a masterful job."

Astin had some specific ideas for casting the leading lady, but Laird had his eye on actress Elizabeth Hartman, who first won fame for her Oscar-nominated performance as a blind girl in *A Patch of Blue*. "Elizabeth took some delicate handling, but I thought she delivered wonderfully," Astin says. "I can't imagine anyone else doing it. She was exquisite, quiet, somewhat fragile, and warm. There was an openness to the eternal that she had, in a sense, that no one else in the piece had. I certainly believed that the boy would come back to her. I don't think we could have done better."

A second complication arose upon the arrival of actor Michael Baseleon, cast to play the father, Tom Robb. "We were hit with trouble when the leading man turned up with some type of skin problem on one side of his face. He suddenly broke out in this terrible rash, and they couldn't recast because he was already established. He was awfully good in it, but I could only shoot him from a very limited angle."

Helped by the clear-eyed performances of Hartman and Baseleon, Astin navigates a delicate balance between sentiment and the supernatural, reality and dream.

He invests the tale with a quiet dignity, avoiding the maudlin tone of *Little House on the Prairie,* for which "The Dark Boy" might have been written.

As in "A Midnight Visit to the Neighborhood Blood Bank," Jack Laird hired from within his own home. Young Michael Laird, the producer's adopted son, had the right brooding, dark looks for the role of Joel Robb, though silent throughout. "I didn't know him," Astin says, "but he turned out to be a lovely kid. He had a lovely face." Veteran actress Gale Sondergaard, who won the first supporting actress Oscar for her first screen role in 1936's *Anthony Adverse,* was roused out of a protracted retirement for "The Dark Boy." Unfortunately, both Sondergaard and Hope Summers lend an unintentional comic air as the Moore sisters, played in too broad a fashion for this understated piece. These are thankfully the only false notes in this gentle episode.

Upon screening "The Dark Boy," there were murmurs at the network about pushing for an Emmy nomination. Nothing ever came of it. "Yeah, there *was* a lot of talk about that," Astin admits.

"The Dark Boy" is one of the very best of the *Night Gallerys.* It has a classiness and a style that you don't always find. But again, in my own life it was a somewhat chaotic time and I was going from one thing to another so quickly that I wasn't able to follow things through as I would today. Something that nice you would try to protect, do your best to see that people pushed it. I think the network liked it; I don't know if the studio had the same feeling about it at that time. I got into a little trouble with them because some of the kids in the classroom were wonderfully creative. Of course, I broke the rules and started shooting stuff with them. They were hired as extras [without speaking roles] and they didn't want to pay them as actors. I loved the kind of improv they did. With the show as short as it was, we weren't really able to retain a lot of that. There was almost enough for a full story, for a full hour or more.

Astin enjoyed his experiences directing on *Night Gallery,* and his segments stand out as some of the best the show offered. "There was a wide variety of quality on the show," Astin says.

And I think that's because Jack just let the directors go. And sometimes it worked out. That's one thing Jack never did, he *never* messed with the way you directed. He might get bugged at you for not doing it to his satisfaction, perhaps, but there wasn't the slightest hint of interference. In fact, I felt like I had complete free rein to make the kind of film that I wanted to make. I was trying to make them different, and interesting, and provocative. And I think I succeeded.[79]

On a final note, actress Elizabeth Hartman—apparently as fragile in real life as she was in some of her screen roles—took her own life in 1987. She threw herself from the fifth-story window of her Pittsburgh apartment.

2

KEEP IN TOUCH—WE'LL THINK OF SOMETHING

★ ★ ½

Written and Directed by Gene Kearney

Music: Gil Mellé, Oliver Nelson, Paul Glass, and Hal
    Mooney

Director of Photography: Lionel Lindon

Time: 18:41

**Cast**

Erik Sutton: Alex Cord

Claire Foster: Joanna Pettet

Sgt. Joe Brice: Richard O'Brien

Officer Hruska: Dave Morick

Motorcycle Policeman: Paul Trinka

Chauffeur: Mike Robelo

*Alex Cord and Joanna Pettet in "Keep in Touch—We'll Think of Something." Courtesy of TV History Archives.*

*I presume that most of you in moments of weakness or in spasms of compassion have picked up a hitchhiker. The story behind this item here has to do with a man who stops his car and invites a stranger in. And such a stranger—the kind that makes you wish you'd taken a bus or stayed in bed. Its title: "Keep in Touch—We'll Think of Something."*

**/ Summary /** Musician Erik Sutton reports his car stolen to the police. He picked up an attractive hitchhiker, stopped off for a newspaper, and before he could get back to the car she had driven off with it. Sergeant Brice promises to contact Sutton if the car turns up. Barring an assault, they will investigate no further.

Sutton returns three days later, this time with a bandaged wound on his forehead and a suspicious new twist to his story. He claims to have found the car, but this time the girl followed him, pistol-whipped him, and stole the car *again*. Brice is skeptical, but a police sketch artist is called and Sutton guides him with his detailed memory of the girl. An all-points bulletin is issued based on the sketch, and a woman is found who answers the hitchhiker's description—a wealthy young married woman named Claire Foster. At the police lineup, however, Sutton refuses to identify her and exits the police station in haste. Brice, stymied, apologizes to Mrs. Foster, showing her the police sketch. The resemblance, she agrees, is exact.

Curious, Mrs. Foster follows Sutton to a bar. On seeing her again, Sutton is flustered and apologetic. She dismisses it, allowing that he must have confused her with someone else. "Oh, no, I couldn't confuse you with anyone," Sutton responds. "You're the one, all right. I'd know that face anywhere." Mrs. Foster, he explains, is the embodiment of the woman who has haunted his dreams all his life. Lately, turmoil in his personal life had caused his dreams to intensify, and he cooked up the scheme about the car theft as a way of finding whether the woman in his dreams did, in fact, exist. Flattered by the intensity of his dream, Mrs. Foster tells Sutton that her husband is a compulsive dreamer himself—he has repeated nightmares of a man creeping into their bedroom at night and strangling him. In his dream, he never sees the man's face, but the killer has a long scar on the back of his hand. On some strange impulse, she grasps Sutton's palms and turns his hands over. No scar. Embarrassed, Mrs. Foster tries to leave, but Sutton catches her by the arm. "You were hoping for it all to come true, weren't you? You're afraid of him. He won't let you go and you don't know how to get out of it." He kisses her passionately and she responds—but with her free hand she pulls a set of scissors from her bag and, with Sutton unsuspecting, draws the blade jaggedly across the back of his hand. Stunned, Sutton stares at her. "Don't worry, darling," she says, wrapping his bleeding hand in a handkerchief. "You can stay at my place until the stitches come out. Everything's going to work out just perfectly."

/ **Commentary** / This segment is one of the few full-length, non-Serling originals produced on *Night Gallery*. Laird generally preferred adaptations of classic short fiction, but was inclined to let protégé Gene Kearney make a contribution on occasion, as here. Kearney's premise is an intriguing one. Unfortunately, even a disturbing, Hitchcock-styled finish cannot make up for the occasional triteness of his dialogue:

SUTTON

Oh, Claire, my sweet Claire. Don't you see? You and I, we're destiny's children.
We were meant to be together.

How *Lux Radio Theater* can you get? More to the point, how did lines like this get by the supercritical eye of the producer? This defect tends to lessen the effect of a segment that has a number of interesting aspects—not the least of which is the casting of then husband and wife Alex Cord and Joanna Pettet.

Pettet here continues to mine the vein of dream versus reality that she had initiated in "The House" and would continue with in later segments of *Night Gallery*. For Alex Cord, working with his wife added a degree of extra depth to the performance: "I think there is just something inherent in the relationship alone that made it a little more intense, a little more real. But apart from her being my wife, Joanna is a very talented actress. That alone made it fun to work with her because she's just so good."[80]

NIGHT GALLERY #34313
Air date: December 1, 1971

1

PICKMAN'S MODEL
★ ★ ★ ★

Written by Alvin Sapinsley
Based on the short story by H. P. Lovecraft
Directed by Jack Laird
Music: Paul Glass, Oliver Nelson, John Lewis,
    and Eddie Sauter
Director of Photography: Leonard J. South
Time: 26:51

**Cast**
Richard Pickman: Bradford Dillman
Mavis Goldsmith: Louise Sorel
Uncle George: Donald Moffat
Larry Rand: Jock Livingston
Eliot Blackman: Joshua Bryant
Mrs. DeWitt: Joan Tompkins
Ghoul: Robert Prohaska

*Bradford Dillman in "Pickman's Model." Courtesy of TV History Archives.*

*H. P. Lovecraft—known to the aficionados of the occult, demonology, witchcraft, as a master storyteller—is responsible for our first selection in this museum of the frequently morbid. To you connoisseurs of the black arts, you'll probably recognize it. It's a painting that tells the story of a young artist who recruits his models from odd places. And the models are very odd indeed. The painter's name, incidentally, is Pickman. The title is "Pickman's Model." And where else would you see a story like this except in the* Night Gallery?

/ **Summary** / Boston, the late 1890s. Richard Upton Pickman, a reclusive young bohemian, teaches art to proper young ladies to support himself. To illustrate an artistic point, he displays one of his own canvases depicting a ratlike ghoul feasting in a graveyard. For this breach of decorum, he is promptly fired by the institute as an inappropriate influence on young women.

One of his students, Mavis Goldsmith, has a desperate crush on Pickman and follows him afterward to a squalid tavern. Though it is apparent he considers the visit an intrusion, the brash Miss Goldsmith engages him in reluctant conversation about the morbid subject matter of his paintings. She has heard of his latest work, a series of canvases so horrifying that they would, it is rumored, turn a man to stone. Pickman takes grim pleasure in relating to her the source of his inspiration: an old legend from early New England history about a race of creatures "more foul and loathsome than the putrid slime that clings to the walls of Hell," predatory ghouls that dwell in subterranean tunnels, emerging at night to feast on graveyard charnel and carry off young women to "breed their filthy spawn." Having silenced Mavis with this horror, Pickman assures her that it is, after all, only a legend, merely inspiration for his art. When Mavis asks to see his work, Pickman heatedly refuses. In his abrupt exit he forgets one of his canvases.

Tracking him down through the filthy back alleys of north Boston, Mavis finds the artist's garret and tries to return the painting. Her knock unanswered, she enters his darkened house, unaware that she is being watched from the shadows by a furtive thing with eager, feral eyes. She climbs the stairs to his studio and finds the canvases of which she had heard, depicting the skulking, verminous creatures feasting in crypts and ravishing young women. Most telling of all: a portrait of a mother and her young son. The boy's features are unquestionably Pickman's, and in the shadows behind him peers the face of one of the creatures . . . Pickman's sire?

Suddenly the artist returns and, in evident fear for her safety, demands that she leave immediately. Before she can, both hear rustling sounds coming from the lower floor. Fearing it is too late, Pickman rushes downstairs, begging Mavis not to leave the studio until he returns. She hears a violent struggle . . . then silence . . . then footsteps on the stairs. To her horror, one of the hideous ghouls scrambles into the studio and springs upon her. Before it can claim its prize, Pickman revives and fights the monster off, allowing Mavis to flee. When she later returns with her uncle and the authorities, both Pickman and the misshapen creature have disappeared without a trace. Finding a deep well in the cellar, Mavis orders it bricked up.

Seventy-five years later, an artist and an art dealer discover one of Pickman's missing canvases hidden in the garret and begin searching the house for others. Reaching the cellar, they find the sealed well and decide to open it. As their picks hit brick and mortar, a scurrying sound emerges from the well . . . and down below, a pair of feral eyes shine eagerly in the darkness, waiting.

**/ Commentary /** To adapt H. P. Lovecraft's classic short story, Laird chose Alvin Sapinsley, a writer whose interest in the horror genre was nonexistent and who accepted the commission with great reluctance. "I didn't do horror shows," he explained. "I really didn't. I did mysteries, detectives, I did funny shows, and I did poetry. But Jack can be very persuasive."[81]

Laird's instinct in matching writer to subject was, in this instance, right on target. Sapinsley alters the original story to great dramatic effect, adding the framing device of the two Pickman scholars hunting for paintings, who find instead something quite unexpected. Mavis Goldsmith was also his creation, a shrewd choice. The immediate threat of the existence of the creatures turns on her presence in the story. Besides improving the dramatic structure, Sapinsley gives his characters dialogue of a stylish, poetic quality. His efforts are superb, although the project did give him some trouble.

"I couldn't make that script work," Sapinsley admits. "It kept falling apart, and Jack kept calling me up angrily after each read. He said, 'It's not better, it's just different!' It was something he used to say a lot. After a dozen tries at it, and exasperation on both our parts, Jack said, 'Okay, that's enough, just let me fiddle with it.' And he fiddled with it and made it work. But if I took down the script I couldn't precisely tell you what he did."[82]

Although his writing skills were beyond question, Laird sometimes had difficulty when he put on the director's cap. Some of the technical aspects of filming could escape him on occasion, as they did here. "He really screwed up the ghoul scene," laughs editor Larry Lester,

when the thing is chasing [Louise Sorel] through the studio, because he didn't shoot any cutaways, he just shot it wide. After the third day's dailies, Jack said, "If I weren't both the director *and* the producer, I'd fire me as a director." And I said, "Jack, I can fix it for you." So I spent two days working on inserts. We had to use the same guy as the ghoul, because the ghoul suit was made specially to fit him. So I got him down on the insert stage, and I was rolling two cameras when I shot that thing because we didn't have too many paintings to step on. We were ruining a lot of them. I shot *all* that stuff, with the paint tubes squirting into the lens and everything.[83]

The design and execution of the frightening ghoul makeup is an impressive and sophisticated achievement. Working from artist Tom Wright's sketches, designers Leonard Engelman and John Chambers had six weeks to create the makeup, "a fairly short time when you consider that it was head to toe to tail," Engelman says.[84] Modifying Wright's original design to make it work cosmetically, the ghoul suit was cast in rubber, piece by piece, and worn by stuntman Robert Prohaska. "He was chosen for his agility and sort of animal-like movements," Engelman recalls, "and he was quite small. We took a face and body cast of [Prohaska], and then we modeled on that, designing exactly how we wanted the face and the back structure to work."[85] The body pieces were ap-

*Ghoul makeup from "Pickman's Model." Courtesy of Hollywood Book and Poster Co.*

plied over a stretch material, first the arms and legs, then the bulk of the body and the tail. Scales and fur were added. Finally, the headpiece was secured to the body portion, glued into place around the eyes, nose, and mouth. Large, full-scleral contact lenses completed the gruesome effect. "[He] was totally sealed within. Once he was in that, he was in it for the day. If something had happened to him and he'd not been able to be that character that day, we would have been in trouble because we'd have had to find somebody almost exactly his size for [the suit] to work."[86] The results were quite spectacular, and the audience response proved it. According to Tom Wright, "Pickman's Model" generated more mail than any other single episode, and Engelman, Chambers, and makeup department head Nick Marcellino received a well-deserved Emmy nomination for their outstanding efforts on this segment. Actor Bradford Dillman, however, harbored a few quibbles about his *own* makeup: "That wig made me look like Rosalind Russell," chuckles Dillman. "It was a *huge* number! If I'd had hair that long when my father was alive, I would've paid for it!"[87] Luckily, his costar found herself quite at home in the Victorian dress and styles. "I've always felt I was living in the wrong century," Sorel affirms, "so playing a nineteenth-century schoolgirl was fun. I also did all of the TV westerns—*Bonanza, The Big Valley, Iron Horse*—because I loved the costumes and liked to ride horses." Sorel did express a few concerns about being ravaged by a ghoul—or, more particularly, about his stature: "It was a wonderful costume, [but] the guy in the suit was very small. When I saw him, I said, 'How is that man going to carry me around?'"[88] The athletic Prohaska, son of stuntman Janos Prohaska, proved he was up to the cinematic rapine and managed, encased in his shaggy rubber prosthetic, to hoist Sorel without incident.

In the other technical areas, "Pickman's Model" drew equally inspired efforts. Leonard J. South's photography, warm hued like an old photograph, evokes a suitably tenebrous atmosphere for the story's darker aspects; the music score, assembled from cues written for earlier episodes of the series, poignantly underlines the doomed romance at the heart of this horror story; and Tom Wright, the artist for all of the *Night Gallery* series paintings, produced some truly dread-inspiring renderings of Pickman's ghoulish, Goya-esque oeuvre.

Further, Joseph Alves's impressive art direction—which was often a retrofitting of previously existing sets to suit the segment—had to re-create both upper-crust Back Bay Boston and the squalor of the notorious North End. The results belie the expense involved. Recalls Dillman: "My wife watched the show with me, and said, 'My goodness, aren't those wonderful production values?' I said, 'Are you kidding? This would have cost *five cents*.' The biggest expenditure would've been the wardrobe, and that wasn't an expenditure because they had a huge wardrobe department there at Universal. The budget on this thing had to have been two dollars and fifty cents. But there were some wonderful technicians at the studio in those days, and I thought that they covered it up pretty well."

Dillman recalls a smooth production, despite his insistence on doing his own stunts while wrestling with the ghoul.

I was a fool in those days, and I went through that balcony rail with that stuntman. I didn't have as many brain cells back then as I have now. But the impressions that I carried away from "Pickman's Model" were, first of all, the hair, and secondly, how much I liked Louise Sorel. That was really special, because sometimes your lead actress can be a bit of a pain. But she was wonderful. I tell you, to be very candid, I got kind of a crush on her. And to my good fortune, every scene I had was with her. Not only a beautiful young lady, but a talented actress.

Indeed, the entire cast is perfection, down to Donald Moffat's priceless cameo as Uncle George. Dillman and Sorel give touching, lyrical performances, informing their characters with grace and dignity—although the atmosphere at Universal Studios often militated against the actors' inspiration. "The experience of being on the lot at Universal at that time was unbelievable," notes Dillman. "It was like the Ford Motor Company. In the commissary, you'd see people in all kinds of different costumes, other actors and friends, and then you'd all disappear after lunch and go back into your little cubbyholes and do this assembly-line kind of work."[89] It is a further demonstration of their talent that they could produce such affecting work in such surroundings.

In total, "Pickman's Model" is an exceptional *Night Gallery* episode. Jack Laird's imaginative direction, both here and earlier in "A Question of Fear," proved that his work was as good as any of his colleagues on the show. "I just loved Jack," recalls Sorel. "He was funny to work with as a director because he didn't *really* direct, but he knew what he wanted. Jack was a great guy—very unrecognized for his talent. I like those odd sort of renegade types. He was quite the character, a real eccentric, and he had a very strange mind."[90] Laird's choice of this classic tale for *Night Gallery* demonstrated his taste for *Grand Guignol,* albeit with a literate twist, and its stylish execution is a testimonial to his instincts as a filmmaker.

2

THE DEAR DEPARTED
★ ★

Teleplay by Rod Serling
Based on the short story by Alice-Mary Schnirring
Directed by Jeff Corey
Music: Paul Glass, John Lewis, Gil Mellé, and Hal Mooney
Director of Photography: Leonard J. South
Time: 21:40

*Steve Lawrence in "The Dear Departed." Courtesy of Hollywood Book and Poster Co.*

**Cast**
Mark Bennett: Steve Lawrence
Angela Casey: Maureen Arthur
Joe Casey: Harvey Lembeck
Mrs. Harcourt: Patricia Donahue
Harcourt: Stanley Waxman
Mrs. Hugo: Rose Hobart
Policeman: Steve Carlson

*Y*ou're all familiar, I suppose, with mediums and séances, the slightly curdling nocturnal event in which the dead come back to visit through the good offices of a middle-man or
-woman. It's a sport that lends itself to table-tappings, some ghostly manifestations that
float transparently across the room, and a few distant sepulchral voices. This painting offers
a new side to the familiar séance, because it tells what happens when a séance is successful
. . . but the appearing dead isn't the one expected. Offered to you now on the Night Gallery,
"The Dear Departed."

**/ Summary /** Mark Bennett and Joe Casey, a couple of tent-show con artists, have
graduated into the higher-echelon swindles. With Mark as sophisticated front man
and Joe engineering the effects behind the scenes, they have mastered a successful
spiritualist scam offering séances to groups of wealthy suckers. As "Radha Ramadi,"
Mark comes on like some tuned-in swami, calling mournfully to his "spirit guide,"
Running Deer, as Joe works with lighting, sound, and props to create the eerie atmosphere. It works like a charm every time.

The problem for Mark is that Joe, on occasion, forgets to douse his cigar, ruinous
to their aura of respectability—or worse, he neglects to keep his mouth shut. Where
Mark has mastered the patois of the upper crust, Joe still sounds like a fast-buck street
hustler. Despite the occasional foible, Mark needs his easygoing friend and he knows
it. "I'll stick to you like adhesive plaster," promises Joe. Becoming an even bigger problem for Mark is Joe's wife, Angela, with whom he is conjoined in an intensifying affair.
She is finding it difficult to keep her feelings about Mark from her trusting husband,
who dotes on her like a sick puppy: "He may be dumb, but he is not blind. One of
these days, you're going to be suddenly standing around wondering what became of
your head. Just because his temper is invisible, don't kid yourself that it's not there."
Fate takes a hand, however, when Joe is hit by a truck and killed.

Without Joe's expertise, the future success of Radha Ramadi's séances is in serious doubt. With a session scheduled the very next night, Mark and Angela try to rig
the effects so that they can be secretly controlled by Mark. It does not go well. One of
their best customers, Mrs. Harcourt, brings her husband, a cigar-chomping cynic who

scoffs at the setup—an easy thing to do, as none of the effects come off as planned. Desperate to fix blame for these disasters, Mark notices the scent of smoke—anathema to the spirit world—and accuses Harcourt of not extinguishing his cigar. "Your assistant put it out for me," protests Harcourt. Mark and Angela freeze; they now recognize whose cigar smoke it is. A familiar voice fills the room, and a shimmering face hovers in the shadows—Joe Casey's. "Here I am, Mark. You said you needed me, so I came. You didn't think I'd let you down, did you? After I'd made a promise? We're a team, remember? And we're going to stay a team . . . *forever.*"

**/ Commentary /** "The Dear Departed" is a disappointment, particularly coming after the success of "Pickman's Model." The comfortable feeling of camaraderie that director Jeff Corey achieved on the set only succeeds in permitting the needed tensions to slip; and, aside from Maureen Arthur's comic turn as the oversexed Angela, the performances are ordinary. "It was a helluva lot of fun," comments Corey. "I enjoyed working with Steve Lawrence and Harvey Lembeck," although in retrospect he now finds the segment "a little heavy-handed."[91]

Corey's preparations for this segment took him to the Magic Castle in Hollywood for research into the trickery of mediums, and he even cast himself as one of the bogus spooks. In the botched séance at the end, Corey provided the voice (disguised by playback at wildly alternating speeds) of the late Mr. Hugo. As Mrs. Hugo, Corey cast Rose Hobart, an old friend from the days of the Hollywood blacklist.

"The Dear Departed" offers clues that others, most probably Jack Laird, had tampered with Serling's script. In one scene, the dialogue reveals a subtle bit of self-referentiality: Joe tries to persuade Mark and Angela to go with him to the movies, a double bill. The two films? *Dark Intruder* and *Destiny of a Spy,* a pair of telefeatures that Jack Laird had produced in the 1960s, a prideful aside for two of his better efforts. Although Serling is listed as sole author of the teleplay, it is doubtful he would have made this reference. A review of Serling's original draft proves it.

Apart from the first three pages, Serling's script has been entirely rewritten. In his version, Mark is an abusive son of a bitch, berating Joe and trying to bed Angela, while Angela is entirely supportive of Joe (very much the character dynamic of Serling's Emmy-winning script for *The Comedian*). Serling has a prominent role for a bunco cop, Henderson, who attempts to catch Mark in the act after Joe is killed. Henderson attends the final séance, but instead of witnessing a fraud, Henderson catches the real McCoy. Joe returns from the dead as a ghastly apparition, his face bone-splintered and hideously mangled from the traffic accident. For the televised version, Joe received some tasteful plastic surgery.

Except for that final, censor-motivated detail, the reason for these changes is hard to fathom. Love triangles, a hackneyed convention, have been done to death. Serling's version had an interesting twist, closer to the short story in many ways, and Laird's decision to turn Joe's wife into a horny tart seems to reflect Laird's suspicious attitude toward women more than Serling's deficiencies as a dramatist.

Based on the evidence of his writing, it would appear Laird was attracted to subjects dealing with marital strife. It appears as a recurring theme in his teleplays for the show: "The Merciful," "The Late Mr. Peddington," "Stop Killing Me," "I'll Never Leave You—Ever," and "Die Now, Pay Later," all either about unfaithful wives or spouses planning to do away with their partners. His choice of material for the show, adapted by others, also points to this pattern: "The Dead Man," "Room with a View," "The Last Laurel," "House—With Ghost," "Keep In Touch—We'll Think of Something," "Tell David . . .," "The Caterpillar," "She'll Be Company for You," "Something in the Woodwork," and "The Doll of Death." It may simply be that the theme of revenge appealed to Laird dramatically, but the soured marriage subtext can still be clearly discerned.

This argument amounts to conjecture, but one thing is certain: Laird was driven to make script changes. Nothing in this script was left untouched, not even the names Serling gave his characters. Joe and Angela Foley became, instead, the Caseys. The "why" is a mystery.

3
AN ACT OF CHIVALRY
★

Written and Directed by Jack Laird
Music: Oliver Nelson
Director of Photography: Leonard J. South
Time: 1:05

**Cast**
Blonde: Deidre Hudson
Spectre: Ron Stein
Passenger: Jimmy Cross

*A*nd now, Night Gallery's *slightly distorted version of history: "An Act of Chivalry."*

/ **Summary** / In a high-rise office building, the elevator doors open to admit a young blonde woman into the crowded car. All the men politely remove their hats. At the next floor, another figure steps on—the dapperly dressed spectre of Death. One of the passengers pokes him, pointing to the young woman and then at the spectre's chapeau, still perched on his grinning skull. The accommodating spectre removes his head, hat and all, and places it under his arm.

**/ Commentary /** "An Act of Chivalry" was a last-minute addition to fill out the hour. This pointless blackout drives the final nail into the coffin by furthering the audience disappointment produced by "The Dear Departed" and effectively destroying the goodwill produced by "Pickman's Model." Thus Laird shoots himself in the foot again.

And, yes, that *is* soap star Deidre Hall as the young blonde woman.

## NIGHT GALLERY #34312
Air date: December 8, 1971

1
## COOL AIR
★ ★ ★ ★

Teleplay by Rod Serling
Based on the short story by H. P. Lovecraft
Directed by Jeannot Szwarc
Music: Robert Bain      Intro: Paul Glass
Director of Photography: Leonard J. South
Time: 25:59

**Cast**
Agatha Howard: Barbara Rush
Dr. Juan Muñoz: Henry Darrow
Mrs. Gibbons: Beatrice Kay
Mr. Crowley: Larry Blake
Iceman: Karl Lukas

*Barbara Rush in "Cool Air." Courtesy of Hollywood Book and Poster Co.*

*T*o *the shoppers, the hunters, the sifters and winnowers, to those of you who comprise that vast fraternity of picture-watchers, we offer you this salon of the special and the supernatural.*

*Painting number one: it has to do with death, usually the last chapter in every man's book of life—the ashes and the dust, the tomb, and the engraving on the stone. Death, the finale. But our first painting offers up a tale with the final curtain not quite the final curtain . . . there's an epilogue. We offer you now a little item called "Cool Air," tonight's first painting in the Night Gallery.*

/ **Summary** / New York City, 1923. Dr. Juan Muñoz, a widowed Castilian physician, receives a visitor to his rooms: Agatha Howard, the daughter of an old colleague with whom Muñoz corresponded at length. Pleased, Muñoz graciously bids her enter. Agatha is surprised to discover, among the doctor's other rich and tasteful furnishings, the chugging engine of a refrigeration machine. His apartment is uncomfortably cold. He has a rare illness, he explains, leaving him susceptible to temperatures over fifty-five degrees.

Agatha broaches a trait shared by Muñoz and her late father: a refusal to accept the finality of death. While Agatha's father focused on cellular research, Muñoz's studies took him into the realm of the mystic—seeking to stave off death by sheer force of will. Wishing to speak more on the subject, Agatha invites the doctor to dinner; he reluctantly declines. He is a virtual prisoner within his rooms because of his malady. "Well, then, you'll have to invite me for dinner here," she responds. Muñoz, amazed that anyone would desire his company enough to bear the cold, is touched by Agatha's gesture. He kisses her hand in respect, and Agatha represses the impulse to pull away from the chill of his lips.

Still, she finds him sensitive and warm, and she is moved by his isolation. The tragedy of his wife's suicide ten years ago only sharpens Agatha's sympathy for Muñoz's loneliness. She returns to visit him frequently, fascinated by the vibrant intellect of this passionate man enclosed by walls of ice . . . and she soon finds herself growing increasingly accustomed to the cold.

During the week of an oppressive heat wave, Agatha is awakened in the night by a desperate telephone call from Muñoz, begging for her help. Rushing to his room, she finds him draped in a sheet, peering out at her from the obscuring folds. His failing refrigeration machine needs a pump arm, unavailable until morning. "Agatha," Muñoz rasps, "please, I must have ice, a lot of it. Then in the morning I can have the machine repaired." Agatha sees to it, and large blocks of ice are delivered to Muñoz's apartment for the rest of the night.

By morning, the doctor has suffered a turn for the worse. Locked in his bathroom with hundreds of pounds of ice, Muñoz refuses Agatha's pleas to let her in. His voice a papery whisper, he tries to explain. His ideas about delaying death after the organs had ceased to work were unfortunately only theories. No matter how well the outer shell is preserved, the organs gradually deteriorate. "I mentioned my wife's suicide," the doctor gasps through the door. "Do you understand now why life became so unbearable for her? My wife committed suicide because she couldn't stand living . . . with a corpse. You see, my darling . . . I died that time . . . *ten years ago.*" Agatha, hearing his body slump against the floor, breaks in—and screams in disgust. Lying in the folds of a gore-stained sheet is all that remains of Dr. Juan Muñoz, now a rotting cadaver.

Fifty years hence, an elderly Agatha Howard, in an annual ritual, gently places flowers on his neglected grave. ". . . And I wonder if I'm mourning something that *was* . . . or something that *might* have been," she reflects. "But I won't ponder the question. 'What might have been' embraces elements of horror that could drive me insane. And as always I find any icy draft of wind unbearable. It conjures up images . . . memories . . . remembrances of the nightmare. It's a funeral dirge that sings of death." On the headstone of Dr. Juan Muñoz are chiseled the dates that mark the genesis, suspension, and ultimate terminus of his curiously extended life:

BORN 1887

DIED 1913

AND 1923

/ **Commentary** / The second H. P. Lovecraft adaptation for *Night Gallery*, "Cool Air" is, if anything, even better than its predecessor, "Pickman's Model." The depth of Serling's characterizations coupled with the richness and assured handling of the visuals by director Jeannot Szwarc place this segment at the zenith of the series' accomplishments.

Lovecraft's story about a man clinging desperately to life was a natural for Rod Serling, himself a disbeliever in the hereafter. Serling taps into our universal fear of death as a senseless oblivion, the end of all existence, articulated so eloquently by Dr. Muñoz: "*This* is the life that counts. It's the only one that has substance. It's the only one we can be *sure* of. And that is why we clutch at it so jealously and so selfishly— because we know it to be brief and very precarious." With such lines Serling revealed his artistry: finding within this gruesome tale a testament to the inextinguishable human spirit, thus ensuring that "Cool Air" would be another of his personal peaks as a writer.

Serling and Szwarc once discussed the difficulty of filming Lovecraft, in that there was no cinematic analogue to Lovecraft's style of writing. "I always kept saying that, as it is written, Lovecraft is impossible to adapt because you can never find a visual equivalent of his style," recalls Szwarc. "I mean, he describes horrors that *chill your bones*. It's the words and the way he *manipulates* the words, and you can't do that on film because film is almost too literal a form. An image is something concrete, and that's always the pitfall."[92]

For "Cool Air," Serling went about it in a totally surprising way, turning it incongruously into a love story. For Lovecraft, all details of character are subservient to— and presented as a means of creating—the final, horrific effect. Serling's adaptation changes the focus and fleshes out the characters, expanding the emotional landscape of Lovecraft's original. The narrator is now a young woman, the story's main character no longer a sterile scientist but a charming, vibrant physician. Serling sparks an attraction between them, builds audience sympathy and expectation, then pulls the rug out from under the viewer. Yes, Muñoz is a brilliant, articulate, handsome, aristocratic *dead man*. The very warmth of Serling's portrait of Muñoz matched against the repellent aspects of his "illness" blend the bittersweet with the horrific, besting Lovecraft by creating audience expectation for Muñoz's and Agatha's inevitable romantic involvement. Just beneath the surface of Agatha's final elegy, unspoken yet hinted at vaguely, is the suggestion of necrophilia—admittedly a more chilling denouement than even Lovecraft gave us.

What lingers afterward, however, is the memory of the characters' humanity. Through Agatha's eyes the audience experiences her sense of loss and sadness after the horror, taking the story to a deeper emotional level. More than just a vehicle for scares, "Cool Air" succeeds as a rich and satisfying fantasy. "Serling was so incredible, I mean, let's face it," avers Szwarc succinctly. "Serling made the story much more human than Lovecraft. I found that, to a degree, Serling had a very nineteenth-century approach to fantasy, where the end of the story is really just the beginning of *many* possibilities. He really had an incredible gift that no one else had."[93]

The performances in the segment are exemplary. Barbara Rush, an actress of great stature and emotional credibility, gives a tender, nuanced performance; especially effective is her narration, where she adopts a brittle, tremulous voice suggestive of age. Equally fine is Henry Darrow's soulful, aristocratic Dr. Muñoz, passionately conveyed. Adding just the right accent is Beatrice Kay's colorful landlady, a marvelous character sketch, by turns comic and serious.

Darrow recalls with pleasure his experiences during the filming, reserving special praise for costars Rush and Kay, and director Szwarc. Additionally, Darrow's role gave him the opportunity to pay homage to his distinguished acting mentor, Juano Hernandez: "The scenes where I'm wearing the white robe with the hood, concealing most of my face—that's the 'one eye' routine. I based that on Hernandez's role in the 1949 film *Intruder in the Dust*, from the Faulkner novel. Check out the movie—you'll see what I mean!"[94]

For "Cool Air," Szwarc, like Serling, chose to downplay the graveyard undercurrents. Considering and then discarding the idea of photographing "cool" ("I thought it would get very tedious"), instead Szwarc and director of photography Leonard South created an aura of glowing colors, reflecting the warmth of the characters. In Muñoz's suite, the camera embraces the details of Joseph Alves's handsome design and decor, moving slowly and lovingly as though trying to record details for later remembrance. In a stunning piece of camera work, Szwarc and South, starting on a shot of Rush and Darrow seated at a dining table, dolly in slowly on their dinner conversation, snatches of which can be heard mixed with a primary voice-over narration. The camera moves right and begins to circle the table, capturing the diners' faces and elements of the set design, the camera's movement timed perfectly to end on Darrow's face as the narration ends. Intricate and difficult, the shot involved blocking the lens briefly with a foreground object to give an opportunity to cut, moving set walls and relighting, and continuing seamlessly with the camera movement. It was an amazing shot to attempt on *Night Gallery*'s restrictive shooting schedule. "I timed the dolly and blocked the lens with a back or a shoulder while we changed the lighting," notes Szwarc, "and prepared it in such a way that you were always on the person who spoke live, and on the walls or something else when there was narration. When we put it together, it was terrific. And when it was broadcast no one noticed it, so I was heartbroken."[95]

Luckily for Szwarc, film students watch television. "Three or four years later, I was at a party," Szwarc recounts. "There was a group of USC students, and they were telling me about various remarkable shots. So, you know, everybody talked about the opening of the Orson Welles film that was shot in Mexico [*Touch of Evil*], and so on, and then one of the kids said, 'Well, I saw this *Night Gallery*, and I never figured out how they did it.' And he was talking about 'Cool Air.'"[96]

Shot on a three-day schedule, planning for "Cool Air" began long beforehand to develop special makeup. At the segment's finish, the audience gets a brief glimpse of the decaying Muñoz, lying on his bathroom floor. Henry Darrow recalls a trial attempt created by makeup artist Beau Wilson, whom Darrow had known from his four-year run on NBC's *High Chaparral*: "He concocted a makeup with Alka-Seltzer for the ending when I die for lack of refrigeration. They tested it on camera by using a spritzer bottle on my face and it fizzed! The network thought it was too *gruesome*— ah, those innocent days!"[97]

As though the makeup finally settled on weren't gruesome enough. "I got what I asked for," Szwarc recalls. "I said, 'Since this guy's been dead for so long, I mean literally, decomposition would go very fast,' and I wanted something that would really give the effect of a skull."[98] Makeup artists Leonard Engelman and John Chambers sent Darrow home, instead using a dummy corpse, rotting and leprous, to represent Munoz's dissolution. Now, that's Lovecraft!

Unfortunately, the poor doctor's indignities didn't end on that bathroom floor. The Universal artisan responsible for executing the character's headstone for the cemetery sequence spelled his name wrong. Instead of "Muñoz," it was inscribed "Munos."

2

CAMERA OBSCURA
★ ★ ★ ★

Teleplay by Rod Serling
Based on the short story by Basil Copper
Directed by John Badham

Music: Paul Glass
Director of Photography: Leonard J. South
Time: 21:47

**Cast**
Mr. Gingold: Ross Martin
William Sharsted: René Auberjonois
Abel Joyce: Arthur Malet
Old Lamplighter: Milton Parsons
Amos Drucker: Brendan Dillon
Sanderson: Phillip Kenneally
Sharsted, Sr.: John Barclay

*René Auberjonois in "Camera Obscura." Courtesy of Akron Beacon-Journal.*

$W$*e're going to branch out a bit this evening and move a few feet away from the usual —and get into the area of photography. Now this painting here had best be viewed in a darkroom, because it conjures up the ghostly, the ghastly, and the ghoulish. It tells the story about a very remarkable device. It offers up a vision as things are . . . and a hellish vision of what they were and shall be. Our painting is called "Camera Obscura."*

/ **Summary** / A small industrial village in England, the 1920s. William Sharsted, a moneylender well known for his cruelty to indigent customers, visits an elderly client, Mr. Gingold. Gingold's note is coming due, and Sharsted wishes to discuss the terms of the debt settlement. Gingold's interests, however, run less to money and more to the collection of the rare and the beautiful. One of his collectibles is very rare indeed: a strange Victorian toy called a camera obscura. The device's controls operate a series of prisms and lenses on the roof, transmitting a panoramic view of the city to a viewing table below. With a keen expression, Gingold invites Sharsted to witness his rarest and most unique acquisition—*another* camera obscura, the only one of its kind still in existence. The viewing table of the second camera obscura presents an image with a faint distorting quality to it. Sharsted suddenly recognizes the old Corn Exchange building—burned to the ground when he was a boy—and another landmark, Victoria Greens, which hasn't been in existence since the 1890s. Beyond that is the shop where his late father, the elder Sharsted—as ruthless a shylock as his son—had set up *his* business. Sharsted, at first jarred, realizes these images must be ancient slides tricked up in a magic lantern. Irritated by the hoax, he turns to leave, bidding Gingold a good evening. "And I, Mr. Sharsted," murmurs Gingold, "bid you good-bye."

Sharsted leaves by a back entrance, noting that the streets on this side are fairly deserted compared with those by the front entrance. He soon becomes lost, and the faces of the people he meets look waxlike, their smiles somehow menacing. Unable to find a taxi, Sharsted turns a corner and comes upon the Corn Exchange building—the one that had come down in the war—and beyond that, Victoria Greens. The shaken moneylender blames Gingold for planting the seeds of these phantom landmarks in his head. Running in the opposite direction, Sharsted moves through the maze of narrow, twisting streets until, turning a corner, he comes, again, upon the Corn Exchange. Frantic, he heads in the opposite direction, but now whichever way he runs he inevitably winds up in front of the Corn Exchange building.

The people Sharsted meets in his journey call him by name and are dreadfully familiar to him: Sanderson, a grave robber who supposedly died in prison; Amos Drucker, a war profiteer who hanged himself; Abel Joyce, a fellow moneylender, long dead; and his father, William Sharsted, Sr., a leeching financier like the rest. He runs from them, the ghastly laughter of these fiends following him through the endless alleyways. As always, Sharsted ends up on the steps of the Corn Exchange, and the merciless phantoms converge on him, proclaiming him one of their own. Sharsted calls out to Gingold, beseeching him to deliver him from these ghouls. Gingold, from the viewing table, responds quietly: "Oh, no, Mr. Sharsted, too late for reprieve. Now you shall stumble, and weep, and swear along the alleys and squares and streets of your own private hell. And you shall do so for all eternity."

**/ Commentary /** In the *Night Gallery*, revenge can be an art—and often vice versa. Whereas in "The Escape Route" the protagonist's final judgment was visited by means of a painted canvas, in this segment justice is brought into focus and captured via the dark lens of the "Camera Obscura." Faithfully based on Basil Copper's ghoulish short story, Serling's adaptation was an excellent follow-up to "Cool Air" and is one of the strongest segments *Night Gallery* produced.

At the time, Ross Martin, cast as the wily Gingold, was best known for his role on *The Wild, Wild West* as Artemus Gordon, a government agent who specialized in disguises. He was unfortunately required to suit up similarly here, buried in a curly white wig and moustache, looking for all the world like he had just dropped in from a performance of *Mark Twain Tonight.*

"Ross really relished playing different, outlandish characters," recalls costar René Auberjonois. "He was a wonderful actor, and he loved that aspect of his work—the disguises. I think in a way that Ross thought of himself as the Paul Muni of television! He really prided himself on his work as a character actor. I was very impressed with his performance—so understated and very, very fine."

Unfortunately, the disguise tends to distract attention away from the main order of business—the story. With all due respect to Martin's subtle interpretation (he *does* pull off an impressive acting feat, somehow investing his character with a threatening graciousness), he is convincingly neither British nor elderly, and the part would perhaps have been better offered to an actor who was.

As Sharsted, Auberjonois, speaking in a bogus cockney dialect, personifies the moneylender as a sort of Scrooge in his formative years. Although he overplays Serling's description of the character—having "the composite air of a bookkeeper–drill sergeant"—he does so with an amusing flair. Notes Auberjonois: "I think what I was trying to do with that accent was what I did a little more successfully in [Robert Altman's] *McCabe and Mrs. Miller.* I tried to give Sharsted just a *coloring* of an accent. I know how to do a full-on cockney dialect, but I was trying to give just slight tones of it. It got a little heavier than I meant it to be."[99]

These quibbles are minor, and the segment still retains a classic status. In every other respect, "Camera Obscura" is exceptional, arguably director John Badham's best and most imaginative work on the series. "It's one of my favorites," admits Badham. "It's got stuff in there stolen from *Last Year at Marienbad,* and every other doggone thing I could get my imagination onto."[100]

The most distinctive aspect of the segment is the disturbing quality of its cinematography, lensed by veteran Leonard J. South—with a little conceptual twist by the director. "Leonard South was quite an inventive man," Badham says.

A lot of these old cameramen got a bad rep. People said they were stick-in-the-muds, inflexible, and they wouldn't try inventive things. I had completely the opposite experience with almost any of them I worked with. In this particular case I said to Leonard, "We have to be on the Universal back lot on the European Street, and this guy's supposed to be wandering around in Hell, he's trapped. What can we do to the look of it so it doesn't look like California sunlight?" He and I discussed things and thought, Well, let's put some colored filters over the lens and try to take some of the color out of it. We can't rely on having the laboratory do it, because if you don't deliver it to them, a kind of *fait accompli,* you're not going to get it.

To experiment, Badham put motion picture film in his still camera, borrowed a variety of colored lens gels, and shot a roll on the back lot.

I came up with a combination of a green and a gold gel that worked pretty good. The gold offset the green so that people's faces didn't look completely horrible and totally weird, but there was something really drained about them. Then Leonard tried it with the motion picture camera and ran a few feet that way. I got Jack Laird to sign off on it, and so we shot all the exteriors with this weird combination of gels.

When the footage went to the laboratory, they started screaming. They called the head of postproduction at Universal and said, "Something terrible has happened to this film! It's all green!" And this guy, who was *truly* an old-fashioned stick-in-the-mud, said, "Well, take it out." They said, "We tried, we *can't.* We get a black-and-white print when we try to take it out." And I had basically fucked them. They wanted everything to look like *McCloud* or *The Name of the Game.* And they screamed and hollered and said NBC would never accept it. But when NBC saw it, they said, "Why don't you guys do this all the time? This is great! When can we get more of these?" And they called up Jack Laird and made a big fuss over him, how clever he was to have thought of this. So I was off the hook, but this guy [in postproduction] was mad at me for years.

Another startling sequence in "Camera Obscura" occurs when the character of Sharsted, racing through the side streets to escape the devils, is chased by a horse and wagon. As Sharsted crosses the street to get away, it appears as if he will be run over. As the speeding wagon reaches him, it vanishes. To achieve this, Badham and South locked the camera down to ensure the background image would be completely stabilized, then shot two separate pieces of film: Auberjonois running in slow motion left to right across the frame, and the horse and wagon, time-lapsed, moving right to left. When the separate shots were joined in the lab with a dissolve effect on the horse and wagon, Sharsted's nightmare was complete—one of the show's best sequences. It almost didn't make it to the screen.

"The day arrived when we were going to shoot it," recalls Badham,

and there was no horse and wagon there. I went, "Where is it?" "Well, Jack said we couldn't do it—it's not in the budget for the horse and wagon." I found out that it was going to cost fifteen dollars for the wagon. I went, "What? Fifteen, like in thirteen, fourteen, fifteen? Are you crazy? Here, here's fifteen dollars! Here, take twenty, take *thirty!*" It was the dumbest goddamned thing I'd ever heard of in my life, and I had to go and *beg* Jack to let me do this the next day! And it *worked,* it worked great—it was a wonderful effect.[101]

Over the years, this segment has remained especially memorable to fans of the series. "People still mention 'Camera Obscura' to me," says Auberjonois. "People say, 'Ohhhh! I remember you in *Night Gallery,*' and it just *amazes* me! I mean, I've done I don't know how many hundreds of guest shots on TV, but that is one of the roles that always crops up more than any of the others! And that's probably an indication of the fact that *Night Gallery* was so extraordinary for its time."[102]


3
QUOTH THE RAVEN
★ ½

Written by Jack Laird
Directed by Jeff Corey
Music: Paul Glass
Director of Photography: Leonard J. South
Time: 1:48

**Cast**
Edgar Allan Poe: Marty Allen

*Marty Allen in "Quoth the Raven."*
*Courtesy of Globe Photos.*

*F*rom the pen of Edgar Allan Poe . . . more or less. "Quoth the Raven."

/ **Summary** / Once upon a midnight dreary, the famed poet sits at his desk unable to get beyond the title of his next opus, "The Raven." He's stuck on the first line, and no amount of brandy swilled can get him past it. The bird in question roosts above his chamber door, breaking his concentration with an occasional squawk. Dabbing his quill in the inkwell, Poe scribbles part of a line and stops. Nothing comes. His search for the elusive word takes on the quality of a mantra: "While I pondered weak and . . . , while I pondered weak and . . . , while I pondered weak and . . ."

"Weary," comes a mocking voice from above—his nemesis, the raven. "Weary, dummy. WEARY! Can't you get anything right? Weak and weary!" Frazzled, the poet takes aim and lobs his snifter at the feathered kibitzer.

/ **Commentary** / This segment is the only poor element in one of *Night Gallery*'s best hours. A brief trifle by producer Jack Laird on writer's block, it holds few chuckles for anyone but another writer. Director Jeff Corey certainly found it less than amusing:

"That one was embarrassing. They threw the script at me. I finished shooting a three-day thing [that] they urged me to finish early. So we may have wrapped that day at four o'clock, and I think I had two and a half hours to shoot 'Raven.' I didn't think it was the least bit funny. It was really painful to do it."[103]

Just as earlier in this hour, another spelling gaffe occurs here: Poe quills his own middle name, Allan, incorrectly as Allen. Either the poet was drinking more heavily than usual, or it was an intentional play on the name of the actor essaying the role, comedian Marty Allen. And the uncredited voice of the raven? None other than that master thespian of the animated short, Mel Blanc, interpreter of such vocal personalities as Bugs Bunny, Daffy Duck, and Elmer Fudd.

The segment's only other note of interest is artist Tom Wright's introductory painting, a leering portrait in blue of the segment's author, Jack Laird.

NIGHT GALLERY #34314
Air date: December 15, 1971

1

THE MESSIAH ON MOTT STREET
★ ★ ★ ★

Written by Rod Serling
Directed by Don Taylor
Music: Paul Glass
Director of Photography: Lionel Lindon
Time: 35:58

*Ricky Powell and Edward G. Robinson in "The Messiah on Mott Street." Courtesy of TV History Archives.*

**Cast**

Abraham Goldman: Edward G. Robinson
Dr. Levine: Tony Roberts
Buckner: Yaphet Kotto
Mikey Goldman: Ricky Powell
Fanatic: Joseph Ruskin
Santa Claus: John J. Fox
Miss Moretti: Anne Taylor

*G*ood evening. Of course you're all here by invitation, but don't let it disturb you if these paintings, per se, don't happen to be your thing. These are rather special paintings, the kind of hangings generally put up with a noose.

*This painting, for example, is of a rather special world, what has become perpetuated in the language as the ghetto—that dismal realm of pushcarts and poverty where hopes are stamped down like dirty shoes on snow. Death is a commonplace visitor to these somber alleys . . . but occasionally someone else visits. Our painting is called "The Messiah on Mott Street," and this place, should you not already know it, is the* Night Gallery.

**/ Summary /** Manhattan's Lower East Side, Christmas Eve. In his freezing ghetto apartment, Abraham Goldman, an aged Jew, lies very ill. He has refused the requests of his doctor, Morris Levine, to check into a hospital. The old man, concerned that his orphaned grandson, nine-year-old Mikey, will wind up in a foster home, is adamant—despite the presence of the Angel of Death, whom he can sense hovering nearby, a vague shadow that beckons to him from corners.

Goldman's failing body hangs on to life by the thread of his own fierce will, the promise of aid from his indigent brother Sam in California—and his faith in the coming of the Messiah. As described to young Mikey, "He's a messenger from God. Any moment he will appear, looming big and black against the sky, striking down our enemies and lifting us up to health and wealth and heavenly contentment."

Mikey, sensing the gravity of his grandfather's condition, cannot wait for the Messiah's arrival and goes out to look for him. Mikey searches the drifted, snowy streets, encountering a bearded fanatic who calls dourly for the repentance of passing sinners. Can this be the Messiah? The wild-eyed zealot towers over the boy, screaming that Mikey, his grandfather, and all humanity are doomed—and soon to die in the cleansing final judgment! Suddenly, a large figure grabs the raving fanatic and throws him off the sidewalk, warning him to stop scaring kids. Turning toward Mikey, he is a big, heavyset black man, benevolent and soft spoken, named Buckner. Mikey believes his search for the Messiah is over; the man, concerned, listens with quiet amusement to the boy's story and agrees to follow him home. Upon their return they find an ambulance waiting outside and Dr. Levine at Goldman's bedside. Goldman asserts he was visited again by the Angel of Death, who promised to return once more—at midnight.

As Mikey gets ready for bed, Dr. Levine makes uncomfortable small talk with the imposing stranger in the living room. "So you're the Messiah, huh? All right, Mr. Buckner, if you have any special Messianic powers, I wish you'd trot them out. I could use a miracle." Buckner stands silent, impassively regarding the doctor; a sudden gust rattles the windows, billowing the curtains. "Was it just the wind?" asks Buckner. "The old man's expecting *some*one." Under the scrutiny of the stranger's probing eyes, Levine admits that, as the son of a Levitical scholar, he, too, believes in such things as the Angel of Death . . . and the Messiah . . . and miracles, too.

Suddenly the wind blows the front door wide open, gusting through the apartment and into Goldman's room. Mikey, distraught, runs to help his grandfather— over whose still form hovers a black shadow. Buckner, closing the bedroom door behind the boy, counsels the doctor not to interfere—there is nothing he can do. "Anybody ever tell you that you make a lousy Messiah?" snaps Levine. The wind quiets, the front door closes unaided, and a calm pervades the tenement as though a protecting veil has descended. Sensing an exiting presence, a defeated Levine turns to the stranger. "My apologies, Mr. Buckner. That's the problem with ghetto dwellers—and former ghetto dwellers, of which I am one—we're mystics, and believers, and children to our dying day."

The bedroom door opens to reveal a beaming Abraham Goldman, far from the grasp of death. "Doctor, I had a nightmare like you can't believe," the old man says. "And what a cast of characters! Shakespeare himself couldn't create them. The Angel of Death, the Messiah . . . and you and Mikey were there and . . . somebody in the living room." Goldman stops, struggling to recall. "There wasn't anybody in the living room . . . was there?" Levine, suddenly disoriented, turns to look at the empty apartment. He remembers no one. Mikey recalls going out to look for the Messiah, but nothing more. Shaking off his sudden fuzziness, Levine examines Goldman. Pulse and respiration are strong; the crisis is over. The midnight bells heralding Christmas prompt from the pensive Levine, "It's kind of the season for miracles, I guess."

Mikey answers a sudden knock at the door. Standing outside is a postman—a big, heavyset black man with a benevolent smile—handing over a special delivery letter from Goldman's brother Sam. To the old man's astonishment, included is a check for $10,000—an old debt finally repaid. Levine, wishing them a happy Hanukkah, retreats into the bracing winter night.

Approaching the postman as he kneels by a mailbox, Levine thanks him for the delivery. "Did it please?" the postman asks. "It pleased all right," assures Levine. "Dear God, how it pleased!" Smiling broadly, the postman observes, "Every now and then, God remembers the tenements." Levine, vaguely troubled by the postman's familiar face, wishes him the compliments of the season. "And to you and yours," the postman answers, "and to the whole Earth." To the pealing bells of this cold Christmas morning, the two move off into the friendly dark.

**/ Commentary /** Throughout his career, Serling wrote infrequently about his Jewish heritage. "The Messiah on Mott Street," his unashamedly sentimental holiday allegory about faith, hope, and the strength of the human spirit, helped correct that oversight. In the story's dignity and characterizations, it is among his very finest efforts.

The germinal idea for "Messiah" came to Serling from screenwriter Sy Gomberg, whose stories about his life growing up in Newark, New Jersey, were legend at Hollywood parties. One anecdote in particular, about Gomberg's ailing grandfather, sparked a response in Serling. He took the basic idea, fleshed out the characters, tied into it other elements of Levitical folklore, and gave the tale his own distinctive stamp. Submitting the script in June 1971, Serling received an immediate response on it from Rolf Gompertz at NBC:

Dear Rod,

I literally dropped everything when "The Messiah on Mott Street" script arrived because I was so anxious to read it. I loved every word of it. I had many positive reactions, but between you and me I find the story particularly fascinating in terms of Jewish literature. It's a modern contribution to the Messianic stories that have been told and written over the centuries. Style and content are perfect for our time. I also find that you are exploring more and more questions that lie beyond rational calculations, as you did in "Dr. Stringfellow's Rejuvenator" and, of course, in the present story. It's a marvelous script, one that's going to find a place of honor in my own library at home.

And while we're on the subject, let me be the first this year to wish you a Happy Chanukah.

                                        Best,
                                        Rolf[104]


Gompertz circulated copies of the script to his associates accompanied by a memo calling attention to its importance:

I just finished reading an unusual drama by Rod Serling called "The Messiah on Mott Street" which will be aired during the Christmas week on *Rod Serling's Night Gallery* this year. It is a beautiful, moving story dealing with one element of the occult, the esoteric, the supernatural—namely the area of miracles and faith. It is an unusual Christmas story, offbeat all the way, and yet unerringly true to the spirit of Judaism and Christianity.

This 36-page drama, in my opinion, will become a holiday classic like *Amahl and the Night Visitors* and the *Dragnet* Christmas story. It is as touching and moving, if not more so, than Serling's "A Storm in Summer." It is to this year's *Night Gallery* what Serling's "They're Tearing Down Tim Riley's Bar" was to last year's. It is more, actually, than "Storm in Summer" or "Tim Riley's Bar," because its final note is one of total affirmation. I believe this show deserves individual attention and would appreciate your pitching this to *TV Guide* or other major magazine outlet. If that doesn't work, you might use this show as a main focal point and suggest the magazine does a layout and story about what TV is doing, especially around Christmas, in light of the growing popularity of mysticism and religion as a reaction to drugs, such as the Jesus Freaks and other movements. Show films July 12 through 15, cast, info coming. Script attached. Thank you.[105]

NBC executives soon saw the potential of "The Messiah on Mott Street" as an award winner. Returning to direct was Don Taylor, an obvious choice: he had helmed last season's highly acclaimed segment "They're Tearing Down Tim Riley's Bar." NBC wanted Laird and Taylor to "shoot high" when casting, and they assembled a magnificent trio of actors to essay the primary roles—Tony Roberts, Yaphet Kotto, and silver screen legend Edward G. Robinson. Oddly, Universal's first choice to play Goldman was not Robinson, but Melvyn Douglas. "But [Douglas] was in Vermont and he had gout," Taylor explains. "There were a number of other names bandied about at that time, but I remember we all settled on Eddie."[106]

No more apt performer could have been chosen. Born Emmanuel Goldenberg in Bucharest, Romania, Robinson not only was a brilliant actor but also had a thorough knowledge of the religious subtext of Serling's script. Persuading him, however, was another matter. "Time was getting short," remembers Taylor, "and Eddie wasn't sure he wanted to do it, so I spent a whole afternoon with him just talking about it. We went right through the script. Now, I was probably the worst man to direct this film. It's filled with Levitical folklore of which I had no knowledge whatsoever. But Eddie did, so I picked his brain pretty good."[107]

Taylor found, however, that Robinson resisted playing the nuances of speech peculiar to the New York Jewish community. "He had spent most of his career getting rid of the Jewish idiom," Taylor says. "He had been playing gangsters for fifty years, right? So I spent a lot of time saying, 'But that's the way it's written. I mean, the idiom is very important.' Mott Street is the heart of the Jewish center—that's the East Side Jew, the Ashkenazi. He averted it quite a bit." Robinson also demonstrated an aversion to wearing his hearing aid. "After three hours of talking, I said, 'You know, Eddie, why don't you wear the hearing aid? I mean, it's good character.' He said [with an incredulous tone], '*What?*' He was as vain as *any* actor! He's not going to stick *anything* in his ear!"[108]

Finally, Robinson was persuaded. Production began in July, and, as in "Silent Snow, Secret Snow," exterior shooting required the transformation of a sunny California street into the biting cold of a New York winter. "It was in the middle of the summer," recalls assistant director Ralph Sariego, "and we were shooting on the back lot on Brownstone Street. We had everybody in overcoats with snow in the streets, supposed to be cold. We were roasting."[109] It would be difficult to tell from viewing the segment. Cinematographer Lionel Lindon somehow managed to filter out the toasty L.A. haze and produced a properly wintry atmosphere. "Curly and I go way back," Taylor nods. "I liked him a lot, but a lot of people didn't. They said he was irascible, and kind of 'let's get on with it, what the fuck are you doing there,' you know—and I adored that. He was fast and *good.*"[110]

During the shooting, Robinson's presence on the set generated an atmosphere of respectful awe. "That was an overwhelming experience for me, working with one of my favorite actors, Edward G. Robinson," admits costar Tony Roberts.

On the first day that we worked together, Mr. Robinson asked me to come into his trailer and run some lines with him. Of course, I was thrilled just to be anywhere near him! And as we started to go through the script, he revealed to me that he was very nervous—that he was *always* very nervous on the first day of shooting because he was fearful that he might be fired! Can you believe that? Here's a guy who's made 160 pictures, he's the best actor who was ever in front of a camera, and he's afraid he's going to be fired on the *first day!*

I remember an incident where he was lying in bed, doing one of his long monologues. It was his close-up, the very first take, and I was off-camera reading my lines for him right next to the lens, in the dark. He was about halfway through this very, very long speech that he had to deliver—it was riveting, just brilliant—and all of a sudden, he stopped. He said, "I'm very sorry to have to stop this take. Years ago, it never would have bothered me, but my concentration now is just not what it used to be."

The actor's concentration had been broken by the focus puller, whom Robinson could detect in the shadows next to the camera, mouthing his lines. "He saw the kid's mouth moving while he was delivering his speech and it threw him off! He said, 'I wish I didn't have to stop, but I have to go back and start again.' And of course everybody was so anxious to please him, and so happy to be working on this show, that it caused no problem at all! We started from the top and he did the whole thing again, and it was even more brilliant than the first time! He didn't miss a beat. Not a line, not a comma, not a word, *nothing!*"[111]

As shooting progressed, issues of interpretation began to crop up. Robinson and Taylor apparently clashed again on their respective views of the Goldman role. Taylor wanted a broader Jewish idiom; Robinson was hesitant to overplay the character's ethnic dialect. Taylor worked out a code word with Robinson that would be used on the set to steer the performance to Taylor's specifications. Remembers Taylor,

I said, "Eddie, I'm not as geared as you are to the Hebrew idiom, but I know that this is written with that in mind, and I want to guide it in that direction." He says, "Oh, by all means, by all means." I said, "Well, rather than say, 'Cut, let's do it again, Eddie,' I'll just give you a cue, something like *yiddishe mamme* or something like that." He said, "Okay, that's great." So I did that a couple of times and he got it, he did [the idiom]. Then about the third day I said, "Eddie, *yiddishe mamme* . . ." And he says, "What is this? What's this *yiddishe mamme* shit?!" Well, we didn't do *that* again!

In the end, Taylor was never entirely satisfied with Robinson's performance. "He was very dear, but he took a [lot of work]. I directed him as strong as I've ever directed anybody. And I wish I hadn't, but I did because I wanted to get what I wanted. And he was off just enough to require me to push him back on all the time. And yet he turned out to be very good because he's a superb actor, a heavyweight."[112]

More difficult for the director than Robinson, however, was casting the role of the grandson. "Oh, that was a tough one," said Taylor. "I read a lot of kids. He [Ricky Powell] was pretty good, but I never got what I needed there. Some other kid came in and read brilliantly for me, but he had blond hair and blue eyes. Putting him up against Eddie, he just didn't fit, so I settled for the look rather than the talent. I had to spend so much time with the kid, I didn't get to Eddie a lot of times, because you're on a time schedule."[113]

Taylor's criticisms notwithstanding, the performances throughout "The Messiah on Mott Street" are quite distinguished. Indeed, the cast is perfect. In the wrong hands, Serling's holiday fable could have veered dangerously close to the mawkish, but the performances of the three principals are touching and believable. Tony Roberts's natural cynicism, ebbing at key moments, makes the sentiments he speaks as Dr. Levine the more poignant and revealing. As Buckner, Yaphet Kotto has a quiet gravity and awesome presence that sustain to the end the question of his character's identity—is he a concerned bystander . . . or an otherworldly messenger? As Abraham Goldman, Robinson delivers a tour de force, investing his character with both wry humor and a Lear-like rage. Even in the depths of obvious illness, his passion for life radiates from him. His dialogue with the Angel of Death is vibrant with anger, his voice is music— and his handling of the idiom, despite Taylor's concerns, is thankfully not overdrawn. The actors' performances help make this segment one of *Night Gallery*'s most moving statements.

Enhancing the emotional heart of "The Messiah on Mott Street" is the sensitive contribution of composer Paul Glass. Although his orchestra is string dominated, Glass's music is surprisingly unsentimental, and is the more powerful and effective for that. Chosen less for his aptitude toward the subject than for his availability, the composer was at first unsure how to approach the piece. "It had to sound Jewish, and I didn't know a damned thing about Jewish music," laughs Glass, "so I just had to fake it." The composer researched the subject, employing a solution similar to his approach to "Silent Snow, Secret Snow." "Both were solo pieces with string orchestra," Glass says.

For "The Messiah on Mott Street," I wrote a solo cello part—played at the sessions by Raphael Kramer, a sensational cellist—that sounded a bit like a cantor, doing what they call *dreyd'l*, or embellishments. And because the story is about a Jewish man who is saved by this postman who might be Christ, I played the game of using what *I* thought was Jewish music and contrasting it with what I *knew* was Christian music, and I kept working back and forth between the Arabic scale and the Western scale. It probably wasn't authentic, but they [the Universal music department] thought it sounded right.[114]

Regardless of its authenticity, the music captures quite perceptively the mystical soul of Serling's touching story.

Taylor's work as director on the series involved only two episodes, but they were two of the very finest *Night Gallery* produced—certainly the most character-driven pieces in the series. Taylor confesses, however, that he had less of a feeling for this script than he did for "They're Tearing Down Tim Riley's Bar," and that the mystical elements of "Messiah" sometimes eluded him. In his opinion, "'Tim Riley's Bar' was the best of Serling. It had nostalgia, it had bite, and Bill [Windom] was marvelous in it. I mean, it was like he had found his part. It went much further than 'Mott Street,' even though we had Eddie in it, you know? In 'Riley,' you never transcend reality. You just went from one period to another by opening a door, but you didn't transcend it. But when you get into 'Mott Street,' and you transcend out of reality into mysticism, that's tough, that's really tough."[115]

Yet the director's handling of the mystic realm is quite subtle and effective, especially so in Goldman's first scene with the Angel of Death. As the shadow of Death falls over him, Lindon's bed-level camera suddenly moves high up to the ceiling, surveying Robinson from above as if from the perspective of some dispassionate God. From this vantage, watching Robinson plead, bargain, and rage against Death is an intense, emotionally charged moment. Almost imperceptibly, the camera slowly lowers again to bed-level, timed to coincide with the grandson entering the room, and we are then back out of the realm of the mystic into cold reality. Although Taylor himself prefers "Tim Riley's Bar," it is with "The Messiah on Mott Street" that he proves himself a stronger director visually and demonstrates a greater understanding of this genre. In sensitivity to atmosphere, this is Taylor's finest work of direction for the show—perhaps of his career.

If the director did not fully appreciate the strength of the script, the actors certainly did. "I was very, very grateful to get a role with some emotional content," says Roberts.

I had been Mr. "Tennis, Anyone?" in a lot of very lightweight stuff up to that point, and "The Messiah on Mott Street" was a more realistic kind of exposure for me. I was very anxious to be taken seriously as an actor, as we all are. This was an opportunity to be in something that had some *depth*. I appreciated the unique creativity of the writing, which, having done some soap operas and the usual episodic crime stuff, was unlike any other television writing that I had come upon prior to that. And I must say that, since that script, I don't think I've seen anything that's been as interesting to act in as this was. This show *really* had some character to it.[116]

2
## THE PAINTED MIRROR
★ ★ ★

Teleplay by Gene Kearney
Based on the short story by Donald Wandrei
Directed by Gene Kearney
Music: Oliver Nelson and Paul Glass
Director of Photography: Lionel Lindon
Time: 13:40

**Cast**
Mrs. Moore: Zsa Zsa Gabor
Frank Standish: Arthur O'Connell
Ellen Chase: Rosemary DeCamp

*Rosemary DeCamp and Arthur O'Connell in "The Painted Mirror." Courtesy of Globe Photos.*

*W*e, *all of us, have a kind of fascination for mirrors. There's a most appealing mystery to what is on the other side of the looking glass, and occasionally we turn into Alice. Our last selection in tonight's gallery: a very special looking glass, and it's called "The Painted Mirror."*

/ **Summary** / Old Frank Standish is miserable. His new business partner, Mrs. Moore, has turned his antique shop upside down with her bullying manner, noisy pets, garish taste, and loud music, ruining his peaceful existence. She treats his old customers like dirt: when his friend Ellen comes over to sell one of her attic discoveries —a full-length mirror—Mrs. Moore accepts the piece on a consignment basis only.

The mirror's glass has been painted over completely. Examining it in his back studio, Frank tries to remove the paint with a solvent, then a chisel. The stubborn paint finally yields a chip or two, and a strange light pours out of the uncovered glass. Peering into the mirror, Frank observes to his shock an alien, primeval landscape. By the time Ellen arrives for a visit the following morning, Frank has succeeded in chipping off all the paint. The two stand in wonderment: they can pass their hands through to the other side. The mirror is a portal into another world! As they stare into the strange landscape, Mrs. Moore's cat is chased into the mirror by her dog, Pookie, and disappears up the overgrown path. Within moments, the cat streaks back through the mirror, in evident fear of something on the other side.

Mrs. Moore enters, informing Frank that she's exercising her option under the terms of their partnership—she's buying him out. Frank, dejected, is powerless to stop her—but Ellen has a sudden brainstorm. Leaning down, she takes the rubber ball from Mrs. Moore's terrier and tosses it into the mirror. The dog chases after it and an alarmed Mrs. Moore follows, heedless of the possible dangers. As she disappears up the winding path through the foliage, Ellen and Frank quickly begin painting over the mirror's surface again. Mrs. Moore, whistling for Pookie, turns when a huge shadow crosses her path. A prehistoric behemoth gazes hungrily at this curious, screaming morsel. In abject terror, Mrs. Moore races frantically back the way she came, but finds her exit dwindling to nothing as Frank applies the last few strokes of his brush. She screams for them to stop—too late. The doorway is closed.

/ **Commentary** / When Gene Kearney adapted Donald Wandrei's strange little horror story, he made considerable changes. Retaining the central idea, he created entirely new characters and added a barbed element of humor, turning it into a comic character study.

As such, "The Painted Mirror" is quite enjoyable. Veteran actors Arthur O'Connell and Rosemary DeCamp are a joy to watch, and Zsa Zsa Gabor is a hoot as the mean-spirited Mrs. Moore, her Hungarian accent and hauty bearing adding an exotic flavor to the proceedings. "I was very glad when I got the script," Gabor recalls, "because of the offbeat character—I played this *really* nasty bitch! It was actually a pleasure to do because it wasn't one of these glamour girls that I *always* play."

Gabor enjoyed her experience during the filming, praising her fellow performers —both human and animal: "The cast was wonderful and charming—Arthur O'Connell was very, very nice, and Rosemary was lovely. It was a pleasure to work with them. And I *love* animals. At the time I had a dog like that. That's why *this* dog was called 'Pookie,' because *mine* was called 'Pookie Lion.'"

Filming Mrs. Moore's adventure in the mirror, however, was more of a trial for Gabor: "It scared me to *death!* We were very much ahead of [the trend], as you can see—*Jurassic Park,* no? With all the prehistoric animals, it's funny that Steven Spielberg didn't direct!" Perhaps Irwin Allen would be a better analogy. Certainly the budget-conscious, highly unconvincing lost world on the other side of the mirror brings his work to mind.

More frightening to Gabor than running from prehistoric monsters, however, was her character's unfortunate lack of taste: "Later on, when I saw myself, I didn't like so much how I looked in it. I was happy with the segment—but the *clothes!* They were so *tacky,* my God! But I'm sure the wardrobe department knew what they were doing."[117]

NIGHT GALLERY #34315
Air date: December 29, 1971

1

THE DIFFERENT ONES
⋆ ½

Written by Rod Serling
Directed by John Meredyth Lucas
Music: Oliver Nelson, Paul Glass, and Eddie Sauter
Director of Photography: Lionel Lindon
Time: 15:14

*Jon Korkes in "The Different Ones." Courtesy of Sal Milo.*

**Cast**
Paul Koch: Dana Andrews
Victor Koch: Jon Korkes
Official: Monica Lewis
Man from Boreon: Dennis Rucker
1st Phone Operator: Peggy Webber
2d Phone Operator: Mary Gregory
1st Woman from Boreon: Susannah Darrow

*T*he name of this place, should you have come in here accidentally out of the rain, is the Night Gallery. We deal in paint, pigment, light and shadow—realism, surrealism, impressionism, and ghost stories.

Item number one over there—it could be a gentleman sitting in an electric chair, but it isn't. What it depicts is, in a sense, a method of execution that we humans reserve for other humans who happen to be dissimilar to us. You're about to look under that hood and meet first-hand one of "The Different Ones," tonight's first excursion into the realm of the unusual.

**/ Summary /** In some distant twenty-first-century suburbia, widower Paul Koch is making arrangements to send his seventeen-year-old son, Victor, away. Koch can no longer bear to see his son suffer the taunts of neighborhood children or the isolation he lives with constantly because of his congenital deformity. Perhaps a place exists with other youngsters like Victor. "Where is this utopia, father?" Victor asks bitterly. "I didn't know there were any freak shows left."

Koch investigates Victor's alternatives, but according to government officials— barring the "charitable" option of a state-sanctioned mercy-killing—there are no institutions or communities that exist for a case like Victor's . . . on *this* planet. Fortunately, recent voice communications with a distant planet called Boreon suggest an alternative for the boy. Seriously underpopulated, Boreon is eager for émigrés, males especially, and has placed no restrictions of *any* kind on whomever is sent. Accepting, Victor is numb to the prospect. "If it were a desert, frozen tundra, a pit where the sun never shines, it would be better than this," he states.

Victor rockets the millions of miles to his destination. Upon arrival, he is greeted by the welcoming committee: a bevy of giggling Boreonite women who resemble nothing from Earth—but look remarkably like Victor. To his surprise, his deformity is the norm on Boreon—in fact, from the girls' reactions, he realizes he is considered handsome. "Mr. Koch, we *do* hope you're going to like it here," his guide smiles. "The climate is very temperate, and in terms of language and art, I think you'll find it almost identical to Earth. The cultures are very similar." As the group of beautiful people head toward the end of the corridor, Victor finds himself responding warmly: "I think I'll be very happy here. I feel as if I belong."

/ **Commentary** / "The Different Ones" bears an uncomfortably close resemblance to a classic *Twilight Zone* episode, "The Eye of the Beholder," and the *Night Gallery* segment suffers greatly in comparison. The writing is nowhere near as subtle or surprising, the lapses in logic too glaring to overcome, and the execution is mediocre.

Although Serling railed at the finished product, the short story he wrote based on his original script is fairly close to the episode as broadcast. Partial blame for this piece must also fall on the head of story editor Gerald Sanford, who overhauled Serling's original submission:

I had rewritten a script called "The Different Ones," and, aside from his original idea, there wasn't one word left of Rod's. His was awful, preachy, and it went on and on. We were watching a rough cut of the dailies with some advertising execs, and when it was over, one of the executives sitting right behind me said, "Boy, you can really tell a Rod Serling script." And I wanted to tell him, "He had nothing to do with this." And this was the situation with almost everything that Rod wrote for this particular show, because he was just not that interested in it.[118]

Well, not quite. The author's original draft invites comparison with Sanford's rewrite. Serling's submission, far from going "on and on," was a cogent twenty-two pager. Sanford claims a drastic overhaul but his contribution involves, generously, about 25 percent of the script. The alterations amount to this: he whittled it down to fifteen pages; Victor's mother was written out and Serling's work in the two brief scenes with her is eliminated; in their place, Sanford devises a different opening. In place of the painful discussion between the parents about Victor's miserable existence, Sanford distills this anguish and then has the father deliver it, rather insensitively, to his son. This marks the resumption of Serling's original dialogue. The rest of the changes involve trimming some of Serling's lines for the father in the scene with the official, which Sanford considered "preachy." Serling's longer version is, to a small degree, superior to the revision, in that it shows the viewer in more detail the emotional ordeal of Mr. and Mrs. Koch in sending their son away.

At the production end, other criticisms need be leveled, particularly at the poker-faced delivery of actor Dana Andrews as Paul Koch. When faced with a government official's suggestion that his son be euthanized like some crippled pet, Andrews phones in his performance, communicating paternal outrage in an offhand, nice-weather-we're-having manner. The fury and anguish are left on Serling's page.

Criticism must also be leveled at the makeup design for Victor, which in no way resembles a human deformity and is a far cry from Serling's own description: "a funnel-shaped head full of concentric flesh furrows that traveled up toward its peak like a rutted mountain road, ending at a point from which just a sprout of dank hair emerged . . . like some kind of grotesque-looking cartoon."[119] What appears in the episode is actor Jon Korkes with raccoon-blackened eyes and a surplus of candle wax dripping off his pate. Instead of eliciting disgust and sympathy, it gets laughs. "I take all my work seriously," notes Korkes, "and I work very hard, but there was an element of humor in watching myself. The thing that was funny about that show was that I'm wearing *prep school* clothes! A blazer and a tie, and a melted head!"[120] Serling, expecting a sensitive treatment of human deformity, was horrified at the outcome. "It was a piece of shit," Serling said. "It was a kind of an American International bug-eyed monster film, which it wasn't intended to be at all."[121] Serling's depiction of Victor was evidently too involved, costly, and time-consuming for the makeup artists to create.

Finally, John Meredyth Lucas's direction is visually plain, emotionally distant, and fails to translate the pathos and anger of Serling's work. The finale, with Victor being led down a corridor by his new friends, is left truncated—an abrupt, clinical amputation. Hope and elation were the required emotions for the scene. Lucas administered Novocaine.

The shooting of the finale did, however, produce some surreal and humorous observations from Jon Korkes. "The frustrating thing," Korkes says, "was in the final sequence, where I'm met by all these girls who look like me. In between shots one of the girls was flirting with me a lot! She seemed very nice and I was *really* interested to know what she looked like without the mask. But I never got to see her without makeup."[122] Korkes hoped to meet her afterward and get her telephone number, but the opportunity never arose—and the anecdote represents one of the stranger little valentines to come from the *Night Gallery*.

In all aspects, the segment is a disappointment. Where "The Eye of the Beholder" still has relevance today in dealing with conformity in society, "The Different Ones" offers next to nothing, and is as uncompelling as the other is brilliant. Of the *Night Gallery* episodes in which Serling had any writing involvement, this may be the worst.

2
## TELL DAVID . . .
★ ★ ½

Teleplay by Gerald Sanford
Based on the short story by Penelope Wallace
Directed by Jeff Corey
Music: Paul Glass, John Lewis, and Eddie Sauter
Director of Photography: Leonard J. South
Time: 21:21

**Cast**
Ann Bolt: Sandra Dee
Tony Bolt/David Blessington: Jared Martin
Pat Blessington: Jenny Sullivan
Jane Blessington: Jan Shutan
Yvonne: Francoise Ruggieri
Julie: Anne Randall
David Bolt: Chris Patrick
Radio Weatherman: Jeff Corey

*Sandra Dee in "Tell David . . . " Courtesy of Eddie Brandt's Saturday Matinee.*

*J*ealousy *is what we normally paint green, and jealousy provides the springboard of this particular painting. It offers up the bottom line of what can happen to human beings when trust is wiped out by suspicion. At this point it ceases to be just a kind of titillating tale of human comedy. It becomes what it is: a horror story. Our painting is called "Tell David . . ."*

**/ Summary /** Since the birth of their son, Ann and Tony Bolt's marriage has amounted to little more than one quarrel after another. Their arguments stem from Ann's insanely jealous nature; if Tony has to work late, she always assumes the worst.

Driving home one evening, Ann finds herself caught in a thunderstorm, hopelessly lost in a maze of unfamiliar suburban streets. Pulling into one of the residential driveways, she asks directions from a friendly couple, Pat and David Blessington. As David searches for his map, Ann looks in amazement at the advanced technology installed in their residence: one-way security glass, closed-circuit security monitors, and videophones. David, returning with the map instrument, shows Ann the route to her neighborhood from the nest of streets on a small screen display. Before Ann leaves, David offers her an open invitation to come back and visit.

At Ann's next visit to the Blessingtons, their conversation runs to marriage and children. Ann's son, she says, will soon be four. "I remember my fourth birthday," notes David. "At least I remember cutting my thumb. I was trying to slice the cake. I still have the scar." Observing their happiness, Ann steers the conversation toward trust, and admits her jealous nature. David's demeanor turns serious. He tells Ann about his mother, who killed his father over suspicions of infidelity and then committed suicide before she could be brought to trial. David, orphaned, was left with nothing but a photograph of her; he was raised by a distant relative of his father, a woman named Blessington. David warns Ann to be careful to control her jealousy. His mother lost everything because of it.

The troubling nature of her conversation with David is soon thrust into a new, nightmarish context when her son David, on his fourth birthday, slices *his* thumb while trying to cut his birthday cake. Additionally, Tony receives an unexpected visit from a distant cousin—Jane Blessington. The coincidence is too close to home, and Ann becomes hysterical. She can convince no one of her belief that her son David somehow reached out from his future to warn her against murdering her husband.

That night, Ann surprises Tony in a passionate liaison with their nanny. As if sleepwalking, Ann pulls a pistol out of a desk drawer and shoots her husband dead. She is arrested and jailed. Tony's cousin Jane, believing Ann is mentally ill, makes arrangements for a lawyer. Ann, strangely ecstatic, tells Jane she is sure she will never stand trial, just as she is sure that David will grow up happy and healthy. "And most important, I know he's going to forgive me. You see, he kept my picture. He said I was very beautiful."

/ **Commentary** / "Tell David . . ." has an interesting premise, but the script suffers from a confusion of inconsistencies. A big deal is made of the futuristic gadgetry while the time-travel phenomenon is left unexamined as if it were as common as the other devices littering the script. Ann's little futuristic side trips, unexplained, appear to be the design of Fate. If so, why is her son not surprised to see her? He seems to accept his dead mother's appearance casually. Even if he had received some mysterious foreknowledge of her visit, shouldn't he be shocked? We are left to ponder this as a kind of leap of narrative faith. Gerald Sanford's faithful adaptation of Penelope Wallace's short story transfers these unexplained oddities and character oversights intact. Director Jeff Corey struggled with these lapses, grumbling, "I absolutely couldn't follow the story."[123]

Corey muddied the waters further by casting Jared Martin, one of his acting class students, to play both father and future son. One actor in both roles telegraphs the time-travel element too early. The resemblance between Tony Bolt and David Blessington is exact. It should have been noted immediately by Ann, yet she never mentions it. In the short story, Ann relates that "for a moment, I thought it was Tony. Then he came farther into the room and the illusion vanished." Then later, "He didn't look like Tony and yet his face did remind me of someone."[124] A more effective tactic would have been to cast the two roles with actors sharing vague similarities. Aggravating these inconsistencies is Martin's performance as David. Whether he expects Ann's visit or not, he is far too stiff and aloof for a man supposedly trying to warn his long-dead mother of her unhappy legacy.

On top of these problems, the dialogue is strewn with dated 1970s-isms and attitudes that one can merely cringe at today: "Cosmic! Mind-bending!" Sounds less like David's future and more like Ann's past. The *Jetsons*-styled futurism (nontoxic cigarettes, laptop computer street maps) does little to erase this impression. Strangely, producer Jack Laird expressed more concern over these futuristic reference points than the story's internal logic: "I remember Jack kept saying, 'Make the gadgets more wild,'" recalls writer Gerald Sanford.[125]

These accumulating flaws take their toll on the segment. The most unsatisfying story element is that Ann's suspicions are correct—Tony *is* having an affair—and she shoots him less out of jealousy than the hazy sense of Destiny imparted to her from her meetings with David. In trying to warn her of history, David has only confirmed it.

The segment is almost redeemed in the final scene, however. The conclusion in Ann's prison cell has an eerie, dreamlike quality thanks to Sandra Dee's performance. Instead of the script's dire, fatalistic ending, Corey had her play the finish beatified. The finale is strangely moving and lifts this episode above its other unsatisfactory elements.

Recalls Corey:

I told Sandra just before the take, "Remember, you've planned your suicide two or three days ago—you have a 'way out.' Just think, in just a few minutes you'll be senseless, oblivious to pain. That's what you've dreamed of—that's what you want." She said, "Are you serious?" And I said, "Absolutely. Throughout that last scene I want you to exult in this marvelous escape hatch that you've devised." I told her that clinically it had been determined that suicides undergo euphoria for two or three days before they kill themselves. And she went with it and it made a difference. So, in that last scene she had a kind of a maniacal elation. I thought that would be a much better choice than to glumly anticipate her demise.[126]


3
LOGODA'S HEADS
★ ★


Teleplay by Robert Bloch
Based on the short story by August Derleth
Directed by Jeannot Szwarc
Music: Oliver Nelson

Director of Photography: Lionel Lindon
Time: 13:05

**Cast**

Major Crosby: Patrick Macnee
Logoda: Brock Peters
Kyro: Denise Nicholas
Henley: Tim Matheson
Sergeant Imo: Albert Popwell
Emba: Zara Cully
2d Askari: Roger E. Mosley

*Brock Peters in "Logoda's Heads." Courtesy of Eddie Brandt's Saturday Matinee.*

*I*tem *number three in the* Night Gallery. *You probably recognize this quaint figurine. The dead eyes, the sewn lips, the kind of thing that usually infests nightmares. And that happens to be precisely what it is—a nightmare of the first order. Its title: "Logoda's Heads."*

/ **Summary** / Major Crosby, Henley, and a group of Askari officials scour the African jungle for Henley's brother, an anthropologist recently gone missing. They approach the hut of the powerful witch doctor Logoda seeking information. Logoda, seated inscrutable and stolid, denies knowledge of any white man having entered his territory—a claim Henley doubts. A young native woman, Kyro, enters the hut and, to Logoda's protestations, confirms Henley's fears that his brother is dead. She relates that, ten days before, Henley's brother entered her nearby village, then left to meet the witch doctor when he heard of Logoda's heads. She points to a curtained room and, fearing any more contact with Logoda, rushes out of the hut.

Reluctantly, Logoda shows them the source of his powerful magic. Hanging from a crossbar in the other room are a long row of shrunken heads—the witch doctor's trophies of defeated enemies. Could Henley's brother be among them? Logoda, swaying in a trancelike motion, begins chanting. The heads appear to be rustling and swaying as if animated by some invisible force. When the demonstration ends, Logoda claims the heads told him that Henley's brother drowned in the river. Neither Henley nor Crosby is convinced, but their authority requires proof. As they prepare to leave, Kyro, fearing a reprisal from Logoda, begs Major Crosby to take her with them. Logoda loudly protests, demanding she stay in the village, but the protective Crosby invites her back to the British outpost.

When the morning comes, Kyro awakens unharmed, but news arrives that Logoda is dead—murdered in the night. They trek back to his hut, and Crosby finds the witch doctor's corpse in the curtained room, his body ripped and torn as though by wild beasts. "There were no beasts, Major," Kyro says simply. "Only my magic." The two men turn, shocked at her admission. Knowing that Logoda had killed Henley's brother but unable to prove it, she avenged the white man by working her own grisly curse on the witch doctor. "I knew Logoda could make the heads speak. But my magic is stronger. You see, I know how to make them *kill*." Turning to examine the heads, Crosby and Henley find bits of bloody flesh caught in the teeth of the shriveled horrors.

/ **Commentary** / "Logoda's Heads" was one of the first segments produced for the second season, although broadcast much later. To adapt August Derleth's short story, Laird engaged the legendary Robert Bloch (*Psycho; Yours Truly, Jack the Ripper*). "I tried to stick as closely as I possibly could to the original," Bloch remarked, "because I know very well from first-hand experience how authors resent having their material drastically changed. About the only touch that I added was to invent my own [African] language for the native characters. Nobody ever questioned that."[127] Bloch fashioned a visceral, tension-filled narrative that could have worked had the segment been granted a better budget.

"That really is one of my worst, in all honesty," admits director Jeannot Szwarc. "We just didn't have it: we didn't have the heat, the jungle, or the vegetation. We should have gone to a place that was tropical, it's as simple as that. I missed on that one—hey, I knew it while I was doing it."[128] The segment is hampered as well by weak performances. Brock Peters is such a distinguished actor he almost raises his character above parody—almost. Unfortunately, none of the other actors are in his league and they cannot make us forget the artificial surroundings.

Actor Tim Matheson, who played Henley, was refreshingly honest in assessing his performance: "I was awful. It was a bad script, but that's not the point. I just stunk. I had a part and I didn't know what to do with it. Even my mother didn't like it! 'Logoda's Heads' is one of the things that made me decide I'd better learn what I was doing."[129]

On balance, Jeannot Szwarc's visuals are one of the few *good* things about "Logoda's Heads," aided by the striking photography of Lionel Lindon. Szwarc and Lindon were introduced on this piece, and it was the beginning of their very brief but creative partnership on *Night Gallery*. "I was young in those days," Szwarc recalls, "and I was petrified of Curly at first. But he found out that I liked John Ford and all the people he liked, and I had the same concept of what directing should be that he did, that the camera should not be noticed. And when I told him I hated using zooms, that was the beginning of our love affair."[130]

Despite their best efforts, however, the execution of this script ideally required the kind of production values often denied by a TV series' rigid fiscal constraints. As a result, instead of transporting its audience to darkest Africa, "Logoda's Heads" takes us on the jungle cruise at Disneyland. Only Oliver Nelson's music score, flavored by East African rhythms, gives this segment a touch of needed authenticity.

## NIGHT GALLERY #34311
Air date: January 5, 1972

1

## GREEN FINGERS
★ ★ ★ ★

Teleplay by Rod Serling
Based on the short story by R. C. Cook
Directed by John Badham
Music: Oliver Nelson
Director of Photography: Lionel Lindon
Time: 19:30

**Cast**
Saunders: Cameron Mitchell
Mrs. Bowen: Elsa Lanchester
Ernest: Michael Bell
Crowley: George Keymas
Sheriff: Harry Hickox
Doctor: Bill Quinn
1st Deputy: Larry Watson
2d Deputy: Jeff Burton

*Elsa Lanchester and Cameron Mitchell in "Green Fingers." Courtesy of Globe Photos.*

$G$*ood evening. Please come in. These little objets d'art that you see surrounding me you won't find in your average art museum, because these are unusual paintings and statu- ary that come to life—or death, whatever the case may be—because this is the* Night Gallery.

*For the horticulturists amongst you, here's a dandy. A lady who plants things and then steps back and watches them grow. Roses, rhododendrons, tulips . . . and things never before to be found coming out of the ground—just put in. The subject of this painting has "Green Fingers."*

/ **Summary** / Industrial tycoon Michael J. Saunders and his entourage arrive at the isolated country cottage of the widow Bowen. The eccentric old woman's unwillingness to sell her small but valuable plot of land has frustrated Saunders's plans to build a sprawling factory complex. Because his agents have failed to persuade her to sell at *any* price, Saunders has come to bargain with her in person. Toiling in her rampant garden, Mrs. Bowen blithely ignores his attempts to discuss his multimillion-dollar project. Nattering on about her hobby, the old woman claims to have "green fingers." Everything she plants grows. She proudly shows the exasperated tycoon her latest effort, a stick of kindling, which has taken root and branched green sprouts. His patience expired, Saunders's manner turns ugly and Mrs. Bowen responds with steely resolve—her whole life is here, Mr. Bowen died here, she will not sell. Not to anyone, not for any price. Saunders is furious, blocked by a "horse-trading New England biddy." Unwilling to back down, he hires a thug to scare her off the property. When asked about the method of force he prefers, Saunders replies, "I want her out of there. That's all I want."

Responding to a distress call, sheriff's deputies arrive later that night to find the thug has done his job too well. The cottage shows signs of a struggle; a bloody ax lies on the kitchen floor. Scouting the grounds, they find Mrs. Bowen in a state of shock, digging and planting in her garden, her left hand gouting blood. As they rush her to the hospital, Mrs. Bowen explains to them: "I have green fingers. Everything I plant grows, everything . . ."

Efforts to save her fail, and Mrs. Bowen dies. Saunders, gloating over his victory, returns that night to the cottage. On a tour through her garden, he stops when he hears sounds of digging. Turning, he sees to his horror two hands stretching up out of the ground, followed by two arms, followed by the figure of the widow Bowen pulling herself up out of the soil where her planted finger had taken root. His sanity frayed to the breaking point, Saunders follows the newborn Mrs. Bowen into the house. There he finds her singing in her rocking chair, covered with root ganglia and earth. Smiling, she addresses him: "Mr. Saunders, I have green fingers. Do you know that? Everything I plant grows . . . even me!"

Aghast, Saunders stumbles outside and wanders among the still, silent flowers, his hair turning white. Between gusts of deranged laughter, the now-mad industrialist addresses Mrs. Bowen's greenery in a hoarse, conspiratorial whisper: "You know, from little acorns mighty oaks grow. That's a fact. But do you know what grows from an old lady's fingers? Hmm? *Old ladies!*"

/ **Commentary** / Although showing up late in the season, "Green Fingers"—along with "House—With Ghost," "Logoda's Heads," and "The Merciful"—was among the first segments filmed when *Night Gallery*'s second season went into production on May 24, 1971. Why it was held back until after the first of the year is mystifying, such is its quality. This should have been the segment that opened the season.

In adapting R. C. Cook's short story, Serling had to invent the dramatic conflict, as the story originally had only one main character: the widow Bowen. Her thoughts formed the narrative as she came to realize her knack for growing things was not restricted to plants alone. When she accidentally cuts off a finger while hacking down one of her rampant "projects," she sentimentally plants the member and the horror begins. Although satisfying as a short story, it would have made disappointing drama without some external conflict. The addition of the Saunders character allowed Serling to give the piece not only a more dramatic thrust but also a focus for audience sympathy: a poor widow brutalized by the heartless expansion of big business. With Serling's vigorous moral sense completely engaged, the script was not merely well written—it had teeth.

The performances, too, are excellent, from a pair of seasoned professionals. As Mrs. Bowen, Elsa Lanchester is a delight: gracious, charming, and slightly dotty; and Cameron Mitchell, with his sinister drawl and wily manner, imparts to the ruthless tycoon the driven sense of a self-made man from rough beginnings.

Filmed on the Universal back lot, the house used for Mrs. Bowen's cottage had originally been built for westerns. Not much could be done to make the dusty southern California setting look more like New England, and director John Badham was hindered by his alotted budget:

The thing that has always upset me about that show was that we were never able to really give her house the lush kind of look that I thought it should have. The art director only had a few dollars, and they planted as much stuff as they could, but it looked like it was just planted yesterday. It should have been all over the place, I mean, this house should have been just climbing in ivy, almost buried, like *Howards End* or something. The place should have seemed like it was going to swallow you in plants, but it was all we could do to get what we had. It was frustrating. You just hope the actors can carry it and, as a director, that you can bring something visual to it that would be fun and make it interesting.[131]

For the emergence of the garden-variety Lanchester, makeup artist Leonard Engelman found himself similarly short of funds: "We had a buck-thirty-nine to work with, and we took silk stems and plants that we glued to her legs and all sorts of things." Cheap but effective, as it turned out. "There was a huge audience response on 'Green Fingers,'" says Engelman. "That was one people talked about for a *long* time."[132]

Despite its budgetary limitations, "Green Fingers" is a classic *Night Gallery* episode. Badham designed striking visuals for the final scene: the camera shows glimpses of the freshly unearthed Mrs. Bowen in small, close-up details: a soil-clotted foot here, a tendril-covered hand there, until the camera reaches her face. Lanchester's gentle laughter and eerie, dead-eyed gaze bespeak another world.

Badham next conveys Saunders's madness by breaking the "fourth wall" rule of film, making a character aware of his audience. Mitchell stumbles into the garden and speaks directly into the camera, the composition framed by the blooms of a rose bush. As he whispers the final chilling words seemingly in our ear, the strangled hush of his now-childlike voice is hair-raising. Once again, the best horror is conveyed not with a blatant shock but with an unsettling quiet.

2
THE FUNERAL
★ ★

Teleplay by Richard Matheson
Based on his short story
Directed by John Meredyth Lucas
Music: Gil Mellé, Paul Glass, and Oliver Nelson
Director of Photography: Bud Thackery
Time: 14:25

*Harvey Jason, Joe Flynn, Jack Laird, and Laara Lacey in "The Funeral." Courtesy of TV History Archives.*

**Cast**
Morton Silkline: Joe Flynn
Ludwig Asper: Werner Klemperer
Morrow: Harvey Jason
Count: Charles Macauley
Ygor: Jack Laird
Jenny: Laara Lacey
2d Male Vampire: Leonidas D. Ossetynski
Female Vampire: Diana Hale
Bruce: Jerry Summers

*F*uneral home art, you might call it. Example: this item here. The somber silence of shrouds, the gray, unhappy light of a sunless dawn, and a horse-drawn casket—very much in keeping with the motif of this place. The title of the painting: "Funeral."

/ **Summary** / Funeral director Morton Silkline receives a most distinguished prospective client, Mr. Ludwig Asper. Asper wishes to arrange a lavish obsequy, with no expense spared. Seeing dollar signs, Silkline is eager to please. The name of the deceased, he queries. "Asper," responds the client. A relative? "Me," Asper says, smiling. "You see, I never had a proper going-off. It was catch-as-catch-can, you might say, all improvised, nothing—how shall I say?—*tasty!* I always regretted that. I always intended to make up for it." Silkline is outraged. A joke in very poor taste, he huffs. Rising over Silkline and displaying a rather impressive set of fangs, Asper hisses, *"This is not a joke!* I came here with a purpose in mind, and I expect to have that purpose gratified, *do you understand?"* Stammering, Silkline agrees, watching in disbelief as Asper—metamorphosing into a bat—exits by a window.

The funeral is held in the Eternal Rest Room, Silkline's most richly appointed chamber. Asper is pleased, and eagerly climbs into his silked and brocaded coffin—a perfect fit! A colorful array of guests begins to assemble, and Silkline stares agape at the weird cavalcade: the Count, a vampire; Ygor, a hunchback; Jenny of Boston, a witch; Bruce, a werewolf; and Morrow, a chortling, beady-eyed Renfield. With an air of extravagant pretension, the Count begins the service, but mourning is replaced by a tense excitement as some of the guests, cockney Jenny in particular, begin heckling the Count's grandiose eulogy. Asper tries to calm everyone, but the rabble continues. When, in exasperation, he demands that Jenny leave, all hell breaks loose. Enraged, the witch tosses fireballs at the speaker and the decor, turning the funeral into a conflagration. "Please, the carpeting!" moans Silkline, fainting dead away.

After the debacle, Silkline receives a package from Asper. A message accompanies it, thanking him for his excellent efforts and apologizing for his guests' unfortunate lack of decorum. Silkline greedily proceeds to count the king's ransom included in the package as payment, when he is interrupted by a gaseous, red-eyed apparition that materializes in front of his desk. "A friend recommended you to me," echoes a sepulchral voice from its general direction. "Cost is of no importance." Caught between fear and avarice, Silkline pulls out his ledger and begins arrangements for the *next* funeral, gagging into his handkerchief from the clouds of gas emitted by his latest client.

/ **Commentary** / For "The Funeral," Richard Matheson—one of the finest dramatic writers for the screen (as well as being a brilliant author of novels and short fiction)—followed up "Big Surprise" with yet another adaptation of his work. For various reasons, "The Funeral" did not come off as well as its predecessor. The author's own critique: "The first part is kind of cute, but it falls apart in the end."[133] In truth, little of it is cute; the whole piece drags down what could have been a very good hour. This segment amounts to little more than one of the two-minute vignettes expanded.

Of the actors involved, only Werner Klemperer's Asper and Charles Macauley's Count deliver the comic nuance required, the rest broadly overplayed. Director John Meredyth Lucas here shows little of the grasp for comedy that he displayed in "The Housekeeper." The script had a manic potential, but with a slack hand evident in its direction and editing, "The Funeral" scores only in fits and starts.

During the filming, costars Joe Flynn (*McHale's Navy*) and Werner Klemperer (*Hogan's Heroes*) were reportedly breaking each other up on the set. "This could be a pilot for a new series," Flynn suggested. "We could call it 'Captain Binghamton Meets Colonel Klink at the Mortuary.'" Commenting on his role, Flynn said, "I've played a few corpses, but never a mortician. In most of my other roles, I'm screaming or yelling. This setting brings me down. I was in a musical revue once and had to get into a casket, with the lid shut, every night. I know what Werner's going through." Said Klemperer: "It's very upsetting to have to climb into a coffin. I don't dig that too much. [But] this is a marvelous script. It's my first guest appearance on anything since *Hogan's Heroes.*"[134]

Klemperer had grown a beard since filming ended on his series. Jack Laird, who had known Klemperer since their days as unemployed actors in New York, asked him to keep it on for the role. With the addition of a set of vampire fangs—his only special makeup on the show—Klemperer cut quite a dapper figure as the suave Asper. The other actors on the set, however—Jack Laird included, as a tusked hunchback—spent literally hours getting made up. With the segment's lineup of ghouls, it is not surprising that "The Funeral" turned out to be one of *Night Gallery*'s heavier assignments for makeup artist Leonard Engelman and his crew.

As an actor, Laird required no special handling for director Lucas, perhaps smoothed by the fact that, at one time, Lucas had been Laird's boss. "When I was producing *Ben Casey,*" Lucas says, "Jack used to moonlight scripts for us. So when I came to direct these things on *Night Gallery,* it was old home week. He stayed out of my way and, you know, television runs that way. One day you're producing, a few weeks later you may be writing for the show, or directing it."[135] The early 1970s were a busy period in Lucas's career, mostly in episodic television as writer, director, and producer. Although he made fine contributions to *Ben Casey, The Fugitive,* and *Star Trek,* as a director for hire on *Night Gallery* his work lacks distinction. "The Funeral," unfortunately, follows this pattern.

## 3
## THE TUNE IN DAN'S CAFE
★ ★ ★

Teleplay by Gerald Sanford and Garrie Bateson
Based on the short story by Shamus Frazer
Directed by David Rawlins
Music: Hal Mooney      Intro: John Lewis
Director of Photography: Leonard J. South
Time: 16:03

**Cast**
Joe Bellman: Pernell Roberts
Kelly Bellman: Susan Oliver
Dan: James Nusser
Roy Gleason: James Davidson
Red: Brooke Mills

*Pernell Roberts in "The Tune in Dan's Cafe."*
*Courtesy of Sal Milo.*

$W$*e don't ask you to believe this particular painting—death's head hovering over jukebox—but it does point up the all-inclusive quality of the occult. Phantom spectres can be found not only in haunted houses but in places you'd least expect to find them—places like this. Our painting is called "The Tune in Dan's Cafe."*

**/ Summary /** Driving down an unbroken stretch of desert highway, Joe and Kelly Bellman stare ahead in stony silence. Their marriage has lately been strained by Kelly's unfocused dissatisfaction, and their vacation has done nothing to bring them closer together. Stopping for a burger at a roadside café, they find the place silent and deserted. Joe indifferently scans the jukebox song titles, drops a coin into the machine, and punches in his selection—but the song that plays is not the song he picked. Instead, a country-and-western weeper echoes through the café, one that never plays through to the end. The needle sticks on a scratch in the vinyl, and the mournful cowboy keeps singing, "Words like Love and Truth and Goodness, words like Till death—, Till death—, Till death—," until, of its own accord, the jukebox ends the song. Choosing a different selection has no effect—the same song plays.

Mystified, Joe questions Dan, the café owner, about the strange phenomenon. "Mister, over the past five years I've had it fixed more times than I can remember. I changed the selections, I've even replaced the jukebox, but that's the only song it ever plays." Dan relates his theory about the jukebox and the persistent tune. It was their song: Roy Gleason and his girlfriend Red, a striking beauty with flame-red hair. They were lovers who frequented the café, and Roy would feed an endless supply of dimes into the jukebox to play and replay that song. Like the Bellmans, the couple had strains, too. Roy's ambitions ran to fast money and the easy life, and, against Red's concerns, he turned to crime to satisfy it. Red, resentful of being left alone while Roy planned his heists, took up with another man. When Roy found out, he beat her up, and Red ran to the authorities. Holed up in Dan's Café, "their song" blaring on the jukebox, Roy shot it out with police and was killed. "Red picked up her thousand-dollar reward and just disappeared from sight," concludes Dan. "But it's almost like every jukebox I install is waiting patiently for her return. But then what?"

The Bellmans pay their tab and leave. In the parking lot, they notice another couple driving up to Dan's Café—and the woman on the man's arm is a striking beauty with flame-red hair. The apprehensive Bellmans leave in haste. The jukebox, as if in expectation, strikes up the familiar tune once again as Red enters the café . . . followed by her prolonged and horrified screams.

**/ Commentary /** At base, "The Tune in Dan's Cafe" is just another ghost story whose unusual trappings fail to make it very distinctive. Luckily, the director's imagination was strong where the script was weak. David Rawlins's sumptuous and detailed visuals—which cleverly present the jukebox as a main character—raise this segment's grade above its source material.

The script, written by Gerald Sanford and Garrie Bateson, was considered a loser from the beginning, one that no one wanted to do. "I don't even know who wrote it," Sanford says, "but we weren't going to use it. Jack gave the script to me and said, 'Do whatever you want with it.' Originally, there was no tune—nothing except the title. The song was mumbo-jumbo, a satanic song or something that kept playing. There was no story, there was no couple who came in, it was just crazy, awful, terrible, amateur writing. Bateson got credit on that one because his agent called me up and told me that he had done so much work on it, and asked if I would be good enough to put his name on it too. And I did."[136] The script as finally produced is quite close to Shamus Frazer's original short story. It strays from the original only in moving the story's setting from England to the American Southwest.

*Night Gallery* editor David Rawlins, being low man on the directorial totem, inherited the script. "I got probably the most unpopular segment of all to do," Rawlins says. "Jack had promised me a show early on, so because I was the editor I was given the last one of the bunch. The script was not very strong at all. Jack wouldn't let me rewrite it, so I worked with what I had."[137] Rawlins's only course was to bring in good actors and work out an interesting visual scheme.

To this end, Pernell Roberts and Susan Oliver were cast for the leads, and for the part of Red, Rawlins hired a knockout redhead, Brooke Mills—his wife. The jukebox itself evolved into an important story character. Rawlins's inspired point-of-view shots filmed from within the machine looking out at the actors in the diner gave the jukebox a kind of sentient awareness. Later, in the editing phase, he added to the effect by cutting in insert shots of its internal workings, the tonearm, and 45s. And the endlessly repeating song the jukebox plays, "If You Leave Me Tonight I'll Cry," helped cement the impression of an invading spectral consciousness.

Written by Sanford and *Night Gallery*'s music supervisor, Hal Mooney, the song generated greater viewer response than anyone could have guessed. Recalls Sanford, "Jack said to me, 'Why don't you write an original song and then you'll get some credit for it.' I wrote one little verse to it. But Jack said, 'Look, this is very good. Why don't you write a second verse to it?' I said fine. It took me two minutes to write the first verse, and a minute to write the second verse."[138] Hal Mooney composed the tune, arranged it, and brought singer Jerry Wallace in to record it. Best known for his 1959 Top Ten hit "Primrose Lane," Wallace's career got a jump start from the song he performed on *Night Gallery*—although the final version of the tune was not in the style in which he originally recorded it.

"They had a song, but the rendition was rather pop," Rawlins says.

It was presented to me and I said, "Can we rearrange this?" I wanted to make it country-and-western, and they said, "Sure, we've got the vocals separated from the rest of the orchestra tracks, so it would be a simple matter." [Production assistant] Tony Redman helped me put that together because he was the only one who understood what I wanted. We took the normal orchestra on the set that day, told them to play fiddle instead of violin, and made a western band out of these studio musicians. I wanted it to sound more like Bob Wills and the Texas Playboys than anything else.

When the show aired, the tune became an instant hit. Radio stations were swamped with requests the next day for "that song from *Night Gallery*," which of course had not been released as a single. "The fan mail they received at Universal was enormous on that particular segment," Rawlins says. "The people in the production office just sat there, scratching their heads wondering what happened. Of course nobody got it, because nobody out here was listening to country-and-western music at that time."

Universal lost no time. Jerry Wallace was flown in to rerecord the song for Universal/MCA's Decca Records. The resulting single entered the country-western charts on July 15, 1972, and remained for seventeen weeks, with three weeks in the top spot. The mournful weeper even made it onto the *Billboard* pop charts in September for a two-week stint at number thirty-eight. "When Jerry Wallace first recorded that song," says Rawlins, "he had no idea that he was coming out as a western star. It was an amazement to him. I ran into Jerry on the street ten years ago and he was telling me how much that little twenty-minute *Night Gallery* segment meant to him, because I changed the orchestration and made him a new star."[139]

And it made Gerald Sanford a pile of cash. "I use it constantly," he says. "I add it in the background [of productions], usually. It was used in *Smokey and the Bandit*. It brings me in about, I don't know, ten thousand dollars a year still. I get a list on its use from all over the world."[140]

Rawlins regards the segment with a rueful pride. "If I'd had more time, I could've really done something of value there. I had no script, but a marvelous set, marvelous cameraman, fine actors, and everything in the world . . . and a catchy little song ends up being on top of the charts."[141]

Unfortunately, "The Tune in Dan's Cafe" would be his last work on the show. "He basically got thrown off the editing staff," Redman recalls, "because he really wanted to do more directing."[142] Rawlins's departure was a twofold shame: *Night Gallery* lost one of its finest editors, and Rawlins never received another shot at directing. He made something worthwhile of this segment in a visual sense, far better than the material warranted. His fine work on a middling script should have earned him a shot at a better one.

NIGHT GALLERY #34316
Air date: January 12, 1972

1

LINDEMANN'S CATCH
★ ★ ★ ★

Written by Rod Serling
Directed by Jeff Corey
Music: Paul Glass, Eddie Sauter, Gil Mellé, and
    Oliver Nelson
Director of Photography: E. Charles Straumer
Time: 21:09

**Cast**
Lindemann: Stuart Whitman
Dr. Nichols: Jack Aranson
Suggs: Harry Townes
Mermaid: Anabel Garth
Granger: John Alderson
Bennett: Jim Boles
Ollie: Ed Bakey
Phineas: Matt Pelto
Charlie: Michael Stanwood

*Stuart Whitman in "Lindemann's Catch." Courtesy of Hollywood Book and Poster Co.*

*Ladies and gentlemen, good evening. We offer up hopefully salutary, possibly educative but certainly a few terrifying little items in this, the mausoleum of the malignant. An art house full of bogies, elves, pixies, bad fairies, and a few demoniac inhabitants all put together for your pleasure and titillation in what we call the Night Gallery.*

*Painting number one: having to do with fishermen and what they fish for—or, more specifically in this case, a fisherman and what he wasn't fishing for. What appeared in his net one afternoon defies logic, reason, and belief. But there it was—"Lindemann's Catch."*

/ **Summary** / A New England fishing village, early 1900s. In a grimy dockside inn one evening, Dr. Mordecai Nichols scans the horizon for fogbound ships, trading barbs with barfly and fortune-telling medicine man Abner Suggs. Stepping out of the chilling mist walks Hendrick Lindemann, captain of a local trawler, who has arrived this evening in his usual mood: cold, ill-humored, and sullen. As he orders a whiskey, he is accosted by Suggs, who tries to ply the salt for a drink in exchange for a palm reading. Lindemann demonstrates his foul temper by forcing Suggs's face into a spittoon and laying him out with a blow.

Taking his smoldering fury out into the fog-creeping night, Lindemann heads back to the docks. He finds his crew on board the trawler, huddled around one of the tangled nets. Snarled in with the seaweed and the dead fish is what appears to be a cold, pale, naked woman—but protruding from the net where her legs should be is a scaled and finned fish tail. Horrified, the captain's first instinct is to kill the thing, but he calms when she reaches out to him in an unmistakable attempt to communicate. His crew tries to persuade him that money could be made by displaying a real, live mermaid in public. Lindemann tells them to get off the wharf, that he would consider it, and proceeds to cut the creature out of the net and take her below.

Three days pass. Lindemann sends for Dr. Nichols, who comes hesitantly aboard the vessel. When Nichols asks about the creature, Lindemann responds not in anger but in an emotion the doctor has never seen from him before: desperation. "Doc, she's sick," he says. "She's not eaten anything in a day or a night. She seems to be wasting away." When Nichols examines the mermaid, he realizes she's been out of the water too long. She is dying. Lindemann, however, has found a companion, something he can love, and refuses to throw her back to the sea.

Suggs reads an opportunity into Lindemann's desperation. Braving the captain's temper, he comes aboard the trawler and offers a potion—one to make a whole woman out of a half. Suggs promises Lindemann a miracle: make the creature drink it, leave her alone, and by dawn she will walk on two legs. Hesitant, Lindemann's mistrust is overcome by his desperate need and he accepts the wizard's potion.

The following morning, Lindemann steps down into the hold—and a metamorphosis *has* occurred. From beneath her blanket, he spies the human feet and legs of a woman. Elated, Lindemann rushes on board, calling to Suggs and his crew that a miracle has taken place. "I tell you what I'll do," he laughs. "I'll walk her out here onto the deck so you can see for yourselves!" As he moves down to the hold, his captive meets him face to face on the way up. Lindemann shrieks in horror, staggers back from the hatch, and falls weeping to the deck as a figure rises from the hold. She stands naked at the hatch cover, from legs to torso a woman, but crowned by her flowing hair is the grotesque visage of a fish, its gill slits pulsating as it breathes in the killing air. With one quick movement, she moves to the bow and leaps into the bay. Lindemann flings himself over the side after her—followed by a small ripple of movement, a flash of something breaking the surface, and a thin white wake. The sea, now calm, has swallowed them both.

That night, a torchlight memorial service is held aboard Lindemann's vessel. A wreath is thrown into the sea to mark his passing; Dr. Nichols reads a line from Kipling; and Suggs, unmoved, pitches his potions and palm readings to anyone within earshot. Shrugging him off, Nichols and the villagers leave the wharf. The incoming fog provides half a benediction, half a sense of indeterminate threat as the tide carries Lindemann's memorial wreath out to sea.

**/ Commentary /** The history of cinema is dotted with romantic fantasies on the subject of men falling in love with fabled creatures: *One Touch of Venus, Mr. Peabody and the Mermaid, Splash, The Little Mermaid,* all comedies. Serling's take on the subject is a dark, nightmarish fantasy that examines its psychological underbelly of unhealthy obsession, giving the fairy-tale premise a black, emotional intensity. His script has the staging of a fine play, his dialogue the meter of poetry. The first scene alone, of congregating sailors in Bennett's Inn, brings echoes of Eugene O'Neill's *Anna Christie.*

The drama's richness is reinforced by the bleak, weathered set designs, director Jeff Corey's striking deep-focus compositions, and Charles Straumer's lighting. The supporting players, particularly Harry Townes as Suggs, are excellent, led by Stuart Whitman's realistic portrait of Lindemann. Capturing both the bitter, violent side of the character and his aching loneliness, Whitman gives poignant life to Serling's words.

Cast on the evening before the first day's shoot, Whitman did the actor's version of cramming for tomorrow's test, trying to memorize Serling's marathon monologues in one night. "I tell you, it was difficult," muses Whitman. "I didn't have the lines in my head, because I had just that night to work on it." Whitman wrestled with the script through the night and into the morning, up to the point of his costume fitting and makeup, hoping he had it down. "I remember finally saying to myself, 'Oh, the hell with it, I've got it, I've got it, so just get up there.' I got to the set and just whaled on through it. And when I finished, I didn't even remember doing it."

What Whitman does remember—with distaste—was the fetid lagoon on Universal's back lot where they moored Lindemann's boat. "They wanted me to jump in that water—and God, it was slimy, too." Luckily for Whitman, an old high school pal was visiting the set that day. "He was one hell of a funny character. He was my stand-in for years up until he passed on not too long ago. So he said, 'Stuart, I'll jump in there for you.' I said, 'Boy, go ahead.' We got him a double whammy—a stunt check —for doing it."[143]

Whitman's hardships paled compared with those of Anabel Garth, the actress cast as the mermaid. Although she had no lines, her first scene required night exteriors on the lake at Universal in drizzly, cold, December weather, corseted into a rubber fish tail and naked from the waist up. "I felt terrible about that," says the chagrined Corey. "It was a very cold night and it was raining on the back lot. I was so apologetic. She told me, 'It's all right, it's all right.' She insisted on being spartan about it, but she got terrible bronchitis after that. My heart went out to her."[144]

Distress about Garth was registered over at Network Standards and Practices, too —but not in reference to her failing health. "[The segment] was beautiful, very well done," recalls Herbert Wright. "But this is about a mermaid, and as we all know, mermaids do not wear bras. Mermaids are nude from the waist up and fish from the waist down, right? Big problem with the network. 'You're not going to show *breasts,* are you?' Come on, it was the late sixties, *Hair*'d been around—I mean, it wasn't like a big deal, but no one has ever shown that on television."

After wrangling with the network over these delicate proprieties, Wright hammered out a deal: "We should show her breasts only if they were covered with her hair down the front. So we had to carefully lay hair over there and glue it up and down her breasts to be able to shoot this show. The network guy was down to make sure that these breasts were covered."[145]

Not surprisingly, excess attention fell upon these details in the form of interview questions when auditioning actresses for the mermaid role. "I hated those interviews," grumbled Corey. "I refused to ask the girls what cup bra they wore, I would not do it."[146] The director's concern translated into enormous care for the characters and the story, avoiding visually and conceptually what could easily have been a ludicrous approach in another's hands. His camera rarely shoots the mermaid from a normal perspective but at acute angles, obscuring her resemblance to anything human—Garth is transformed, giving Serling's fantasy a patina of realism.

The mermaid's fish tail casing was another effective design from Leonard Engelman and John Chambers. Engelman was less happy, however, with the makeup they created for the mermaid's transformation into a gill-faced monstrosity. "I don't think that was one of our greatest achievements," Engelman says. "Once it was photographed, the eyes looked so *humongous.* The design was more cartoonish than some of the other things we did that were more realistic. And the wig is something they should have blown off. Part of what they wanted, of course, was the look of a beautiful girl, but a bald-headed woman is not as attractive as a woman with hair."[147]

The director had his problems with the result as well. "I think technologically they're more advanced now—they start the makeup from the human face and evolve it into a fish. This seemed like a fish *laid over* [the face]. It just didn't look right. That's the only time I worked on a *Night Gallery* episode where we had to do a retake, because it certainly didn't work the first time, and it didn't work the second time." Even with a retake, Corey never captured the effect to his satisfaction. "I was hoping for some miraculous intercession between the lens and what I saw, but of course, it was just dreadful. The lens is absolutely going to pick up what your eyes see."[148]

As could be expected, the makeup job was not the aspect of "Lindemann's Catch" that agitated the executive front at the network screening. "Comes the day I've got to take the film over there," Wright recalls.

We've got twice the amount of broadcast standards guys we'd normally have, and they're all ready to see these breasts, and to make sure that America will not be troubled by the sight of a nipple or something. About two-thirds of the way through this thing, all of a sudden, "There it is! There it is!" We have to stop [the film] and run it back and forth. And I said,

"What are you talking about?" And they claim they can see [something] just for a flash, when she's being carried. "There's a nipple! We know there's a nipple!" It was the great nipple investigation. It turned out to be a rough spot on this woman's elbow, but we had to blow it up three times to prove it to them. I spent the better part of five days over at the network going back and forth on this. They wanted to cut out the entire sequence for fear that anyone in the audience might *think* that they'd seen a nipple on *Night Gallery!*" [149]

## 2
## THE LATE MR. PEDDINGTON
★ ★ ★ ½

Teleplay by Jack Laird
Based on the short story "The Flat Male" by Frank Sisk
Directed by Jeff Corey
Music: Gil Mellé     Intro: John Lewis
Director of Photography: E. Charles Straumer
Time: 12:36

**Cast**
Thaddeus Conway: Harry Morgan
Cora Peddington: Kim Hunter
John: Randy Quaid

*Harry Morgan in "The Late Mr. Peddington." Courtesy of Sal Milo.*

*A* dead man splattered on a concrete walk. Not the most appetizing of scenes and not the pleasantest of stories, but if you're interested remotely in homey homicides, this may be your bag. We call it "The Late Mr. Peddington."

**/ Summary /** Funeral director Thaddeus Conway receives a prospective client, Mrs. Cora Peddington, who is shopping for the cheapest funeral she can get. Her husband, Adam, fell ten stories from their living room window while, unbeknownst to him, their balcony had been removed for repairs.

Confused, Conway asks the reason for her need to economize. She explains that Mr. Peddington was an unstintingly frugal sort of fellow. The provisions of his will are strict and irrefutable. He has denied her the balance of his estate for a purgative period wherein she must survive only on the life insurance payoff—$2,000—for two years. The double indemnity clause in his insurance policy promises $4,000 in case of accidental death, a sum that might make Adam's will practical to follow.

To that end, Mrs. Peddington must dispense with cosmetic services, the ceremony, and, indeed, the casket. "I should think a basket would do it," she points out.

As to burial attire, why not let him go as he is? The exasperated mortician counters, "Well, my good woman, it's never done! Whatever the poor man was wearing when he fell, it's probably all . . . *rumpled!*" "Probably a bloody mess," she agrees. "No earthly good to anyone else, so we'll let him take it with him. Adam would really like the economics of that. He hated waste."

After she leaves, Conway's assistant, John, asks whether they got the job. "No doubt about it," Conway says, tossing back a stiff one. "There's not a mortuary in town that can underbid us." Then why did Mrs. Peddington not ask them to come over and collect the remains? "She was shopping, John—shopping," Conway explains. "She had to make certain that under the conditions of her husband's will she could realistically afford the price of even a cut-rate funeral." So now, he points out, Mrs. Peddington has to go home, remove that balcony, and send Mr. Peddington screaming to his death.

**/ Commentary /** This segment is the most successful of Laird's many attempts at intentional humor. The clever script, which illuminates by degrees the intentions of the "widow," is hilarious, made more so by the performances. Both Harry Morgan and Kim Hunter score with perfect comic timing and beautifully underplay the outrageous premise. The segment exhibits the type of morbid humor and startling twist that the master of the macabre, Alfred Hitchcock, would have displayed on his television series.

"We shot that in half a day," director Jeff Corey recalled. "That one was fun. I learned all the details of mortuaries, how they drained blood out and put in formaldehyde and all that. Like most people I find undertaking establishments kind of morbid. I don't like to look at coffins but I look at them anyway. So I tried to get as many coffins as I could. You know, undertakers generally negotiate with you with the door ajar and [the deceased] visible in an open casket, and you just want to run out of the place. 'Anything you want, yes. Four limousines? You bet.'"

Despite Corey's view, Morgan's funeral director employs the softer sell, and with his exasperated slow burn and quiet outrage he delivers a marvelous comic performance. He was not, however, the first actor considered for the role. "They wanted [Sir John] Gielgud for that," avers Corey, "but Gielgud had had a lot of playing undertakers. He just thought it was a little too baleful for him. But Harry Morgan was lovely in it."

In all, Corey was pleased with the episode: "'The Late Mr. Peddington,' I thought, had a nice style."[150] It does indeed—but if you blink, you might risk missing Randy Quaid in a small role as John, the embalmer.

3

## A FEAST OF BLOOD
★ ★ ★ ½

Teleplay by Stanford Whitmore
Based on the short story "The Fur Brooch" by Dulcie Gray
Directed by Jeannot Szwarc
Music: Oliver Nelson      Intro: Eddie Sauter
Director of Photography: E. Charles Straumer
Time: 15:54

**Cast**
Sheila Gray: Sondra Locke
Henry Mallory: Norman Lloyd
Mrs. Gray: Hermione Baddeley
Frankie: Patrick O'Hara
Gippo: Barry Bernard
Girl at Bar: Cara Burgess
Chauffeur: Gerald S. Peters

*Sondra Locke in "A Feast of Blood." Courtesy of Sal Milo.*

*I*n the general generic area of costume jewelry, note girl, and note expression. Obviously a lady much disturbed by whatever little bauble she has recently been the recipient of. Said sentence improperly ending on a preposition . . . but this story ending on a much more deadly note than that. We call it "A Feast of Blood."

/ **Summary** / Sheila Gray, young, beautiful, and vain, prepares reluctantly for her date with Henry Mallory, a wealthy but unattractive little man. She hopes to marry her strapping, sometime beau John Coolridge, but, as Sheila's mother points out, nothing is official—Henry Mallory is "insurance." Mrs. Gray, eager for her daughter to marry into wealth, is tickled over Henry's little gift—an unusual fur brooch. It resembles a stuffed, red-eyed mouse mounted on a pin, and Sheila barely represses a shudder as her mother fastens it on.

At dinner, Henry brazenly positions himself as the only man for her, stating that she will never marry John. Sheila coldly replies, "Well, we shall see, shan't we?" In the uncomfortable silence that follows, Henry mentions the brooch. The mounted creature is a vo-do, very rare, an ancestor of the bat. Removing the brooch pin from its collar, he shows her that, with the vo-do's prehensile feet, it will stick to the coat—and however much it is shaken, it will not fall off. "You speak about it as though it were alive," Sheila says. "Do I? How foolish of me," Henry murmurs, rehanging her coat. Preparing to leave, Henry asks her once again if she will change her mind about John. Sheila is resolute.

While driving her home, Henry tries to force himself on her. Sheila explodes with rage and disgust, climbing out of the car and screaming, "I'd sooner die than stay with you! The ugliest person in the world wouldn't have a toad like you!" Calmly, Henry answers, "I shall remember you as you were, Sheila—beautiful and deserving." He puts the car in gear and leaves her stranded on the dark road, miles from home. She begins walking along the roadside, pulling her coat lapels tighter around her neck. She suddenly gasps in pain—her finger has been bloodied from a bite. Horrified, she realizes that the vo-do is quite alive . . . and crawling up her coat! She frantically tries to pull the furry thing off, but its claws hold fast. She runs blindly through the underbrush as the thing increases in size, its sharp teeth sinking into her throat. Screaming in agony, she buckles under the weight of the huge and ravenous rodent.

A pair of drunken cyclists passing by notice something large crossing the road—like a big hedgehog. In a roadside ditch a little further on they discover the blood-spattered body of the luckless Sheila—gutted and splayed like some butchered animal.

Meanwhile, at a bar, Henry Mallory has struck up a conversation with a young woman, who regards him coolly with distaste. With a secret smile, he offers her a token of appreciation. "I am compelled to honor beauty," he explains, and pins the gift to her coat—a small fur brooch.

/ **Commentary** / Drawing the Hitchcock theme forward from the preceding segment, Norman Lloyd—who not only appeared in Hitchcock's *Saboteur* but also produced Hitch's TV series—stars in this tidy little chiller. With a touch of macabre humor, he gives a wonderfully wily performance as the smug and nasty Henry Mallory, a serial killer with a unique modus operandi. Sondra Locke, Academy Award nominee for her sensitive performance in *The Heart Is a Lonely Hunter*, is equally fine as the haughty, self-involved Sheila. Their pointed repartee at dinner, with hints of veiled distaste for each other, reflects in miniature the shallowness of both their characters. Dulcie Gray's gruesome short story was deftly adapted by Stanford Whitmore, who would return later in the season with another knockout script, "Little Girl Lost."

"'A Feast of Blood' happens to be one of my most pleasant memories," Locke recalls. "I just loved *Night Gallery*. It was a little quirkier than *Twilight Zone,* and I was a very big fan of that whole genre. The casting people were looking for anyone with feature credits and, as a performer, it was considered a very special thing to get a role on *Night Gallery*. I was so deathly afraid of getting typecast, and it gave me a chance to play a different kind of character. I was always very proud of it."

For Locke, working with costar Norman Lloyd was a special pleasure: "I just fell in love with Norman. He was the most alive, fascinating, and detailed character, and had been around Hollywood for many, many years. I think I spent most of my time just listening to Norman tell stories!"[151] During the shooting, Locke's pastime was eagerly shared by director Jeannot Szwarc: "Working with Norman Lloyd was an absolute dream for me. He was the guy who fell from the Statue of Liberty in *Saboteur,* so we talked a lot about Hitchcock." Fifteen years later, Szwarc and Lloyd would work together again on "The Last Defender of Camelot," a segment of the resurrected *Twilight Zone* series.

On the nit-picking side, where is "A Feast of Blood" supposed to be set? Presumably England, but the only definitive British accent comes from Hermione Baddeley, while the others drift out of English accents and into American ones at will. It detracts from the drama somewhat—as if that stuffed, glassy-eyed hedgehog weren't enough to pull one's attention out of the story. "We had about four or five different [sized versions] of those animals," Szwarc says. "The tricky thing was to do it in such a way that it was believable."[152] Inevitably, the fake was too hard to disguise.

"I recall feeling rather silly," admits Locke, "when I'm running through the bushes on the Universal back lot getting eaten by the pin. No matter how much I focused and put myself into some potential reality, I still felt silly! But I knew the style of the series, and I knew that—though earnest—it was relatively tongue-in-cheek."[153]

Despite the air of artificiality surrounding the brooch effects, this grisly little revenge tale comes off quite well. A witty script, good performances, and Szwarc's sure directorial hand bring this segment, and the entire hour, to a satisfying close.

NIGHT GALLERY #34317
Air date: January 19, 1972

1

THE MIRACLE AT CAMAFEO
★ ★ ★

Teleplay by Rod Serling
Based on a short story by C. B. Gilford
Directed by Ralph Senensky
Music: Frank Skinner     Intro: Oliver Nelson
Director of Photography: E. Charles Straumer
Time: 21:19

**Cast**
Charlie Rogan: Harry Guardino
Gay Melcor: Julie Adams
Joe Melcor: Ray Danton

*Ray Danton in "The Miracle at Camafeo." Courtesy of Sal Milo.*

Priest: Richard Yñiguez
Bartender: Rodolfo Hoyos
Woman: Margarita Garcia
Blind Boy: Thomas Trujillo

$G$*ood evening. In the nether world inhabited by ghouls, goblins, gremlins, and the generally grotesque, it's occasionally possible to put this sundry and myriad crew on canvas. And this we do in this arcade of the outrageous.*

*Painting number one: a small item of hope and faith and despair, an excursion into the eerie in which we touch base with that fraternity of the dispossessed who seek out something miraculous in the way of cures . . . and in the way of hope. Our painting is called "The Miracle at Camafeo," and it's offering number one in this, the* Night Gallery.

/ **Summary** / Insurance investigator Charlie Rogan has trailed swindler Joe Melcor to the shrine city of Camafeo in Mexico. Having won a $500,000 judgment against Rogan's insurance company for a suspicious traffic accident, Melcor, supposedly paralyzed and flat on his back, has traveled here to get "healed" at the holy shrine of the *Nuestra Señora de Camafeo*. Rogan is incensed by this fraud, the more so because Melcor intends to play on the desperate beliefs of those who are truly crippled. When Melcor's wife Gay expresses some misgivings about the morality of their scam, he gives her a warning: "If you start acting like a fallen woman on the way to confession, then my first act as a whole man will be to play handball with you against the wall. And you'll be up at that shrine asking to have the blue marks removed. You dig?"

Rogan, heading to the shrine, meets a blind boy and his mother on the way. He is touched by their simple faith, and he finds himself praying for the boy's sight to return. He also meets Joe Melcor as he is carted up to the shrine on a stretcher. Confident in his plan, Melcor smugly goads Rogan while on his way to "pick up a little miracle." Rogan watches in disgust as Melcor is placed inside the shrine in view of the Madonna's statue. Gay Melcor, following behind, tells Rogan that she is leaving her husband, but refuses to be a witness against him. She will not hurt him, she just refuses to help him any longer.

A sudden murmur runs through the crowd as the blind boy's mother cries out in joy and surprise. Her son has been healed, and can now see. Simultaneously, Melcor's "miracle" occurs, and he climbs from his stretcher. Sardonically slapping a tip into the priest's hand, he cracks, "Don't look so surprised, you'll give the place a bad name." He steps out into the bright morning sunlight, flinching at the sudden change from cool shadow to radiant intensity. He reaches into his pocket for his sunglasses—and an agonized cry echoes through the shrine. Rogan and Gay find Melcor making careful steps down the path from the shrine, asking pathetically for help. He pulls off his sunglasses to reveal his eyes, now milky white and sightless—a judgment from a less merciful god.

/ **Commentary** / Oddly enough, the darkness of *Night Gallery* and the light of religious faith were not necessarily mutually exclusive. In both "The Messiah on Mott Street" and "The Miracle at Camafeo," Serling successfully explored spiritual themes. Although lacking the impact of "Messiah," this quiet little tale of hope, deceit, and a wrathful justice has many strong qualities, diluted at times by the necessary corner-cutting prompted by schedule and budget.

Shot on a Mexican street on Universal's back lot, the cantina and especially the shrine miss the authenticism required to pull the audience into Serling's world. More important: although well shot in the drama's first half, in the second half director Ralph Senensky misses the magic and mystery inherent on the page. Little sense of the atmosphere Serling weaves—of Rogan's awe at the pilgrims' faith; of the offense to that faith that Melcor's scheme represents—comes across. The pilgrims are photographed as if they were just extras, yet the power of their belief in the *Nuestra Señora,* the belief that brings Melcor to his disastrous fate, is pivotal to the story's meaning. The pilgrims and the shrine should have been photographed as major characters, large-scale, bringing them to visual prominence. Although Senensky's fine work graced numerous episodes of the original *Star Trek*—"Metamorphosis," "Obsession," and "The Tholian Web"—*Night Gallery*'s brand of fantasy appears to have eluded him. It is because of the strength of the story and the lead performances that this segment is not overwhelmed by these imperfections of execution.

Harry Guardino is well cast as the edgy, resolute Charlie Rogan, dogging his prey with a missionary's diligence. "That was the third and last time I got to work with Harry," Senensky notes. "A potent actor and a lovely man. He was better than his career would lead you to believe. He was not a typical leading man—he was offbeat, like Spencer Tracy."

But goodness, dramatically speaking, is less compelling than evil. By default, the most fascinating character in Serling's play is Joe Melcor. His amorality is well conveyed by Ray Danton, an actor with a talent for portraying sinister cheapness. And if the Melcors seem an authentic couple, there is a good reason: Julie Adams and Ray Danton were married at the time. "I don't remember whether we cast Ray or Julie first," Senensky says, "but one of them had been cast and asked whether the other role had been cast yet." When it was discovered that the other spouse was available, the choice for the remaining part was obvious.

Despite the finale's shortcomings, the scene where everything works is the introduction of Joe Melcor's character. Rogan, in the opening scene with Melcor's wife, has already cast suspicion on Melcor's version of his crippling accident. When the camera cuts to their room, all is dark. Gay Melcor enters, and the viewer hears her husband's voice from the other room. The camera moves along the floor and holds on a patch of light streaming from the doorway of the next room—and Melcor's silhouette moves into view. "I do remember the shot that we laid out," recalls Senensky. "Charlie [Straumer, the cinematographer] and I had talked about his being crippled, and how his first entrance should establish that he was walking around on two legs"[154]—and the audience catches the insurance swindler in the act.

For "The Miracle at Camafeo," music supervisor Hal Mooney eschewed music scores written specifically for *Night Gallery,* instead using Frank Skinner's moody tracks for a 1966 Marlon Brando movie, *The Appaloosa,* scored for solo guitar. Its gentle melancholy provides an apt commentary on Serling's themes with a wordless language.


2

## THE GHOST OF SORWORTH PLACE
★ ★ ½


Teleplay by Alvin Sapinsley
Based on the short story "Sorworth Place" by Russell Kirk
Directed by Ralph Senensky
Music: Lalo Schifrin, Gil Mellé, and Oliver Nelson
Director of Photography: E. Charles Straumer
Time: 28:20

**Cast**
Ralph Burke: Richard Kiley
Ann Loring: Jill Ireland
Mrs. Ducker: Mavis Neal
MacLeod: Patrick O'Moore
Alistair Loring: John D. Schofield

*Jill Ireland in "The Ghost of Sorworth Place." Courtesy of Eddie Brandt's Saturday Matinee.*

*A bit of gossamer and lace, as befits a beautiful woman—fragile and ephemeral, in keeping with the soft mystery of the female. But to the gentlemen amongst you who, like all your male predecessors since the beginning of time, have been mystified and miffed by a female counterpart, this one's for you. A beautiful lady in a strange house, also inhabited, alas, by "The Ghost of Sorworth Place."*

/ **Summary** / American drifter Ralph Burke, wandering through the wilds of Scotland, comes across the gloomy, windswept manor of Sorworth Place, and introduces himself to Ann Loring, the beautiful mistress of the manor with whom he is instantly smitten. Mr. MacLeod, the local innkeeper, relates to Burke a lurid tale about her late husband, Alistair Loring, the seventh duke of Sorworth, whose profligate, hard-drinking ways unleashed a man with animal appetites and brutal temper. When he died, his many creditors gutted Sorworth Place, and MacLeod cannot imagine why Mrs. Loring still remains there.

Burke visits Mrs. Loring the next day. While taking tea with her, he sees a figure moving around the grounds, a tall, gaunt man—there one moment and gone the next —although his host insists that she lives alone. As he spends more time at Sorworth Place, he sees the figure with recurring frequency. Lately, Ann admits, she has begun to see the spectre, too, and reluctantly tells her story. Exactly one year ago, on their first wedding anniversary, Ann poured her husband's desperately needed medicine down the drain. She could no longer stand his brutal temper and repeated attempts to rape her. With his dying breath, he promised to return in a year to celebrate their second wedding anniversary. Tonight, Mrs. Loring says, is the promised night of his return. She believes he will come for her in her bed, and begs Burke to protect her from the dread spectre. With the hope of the lovelorn, he agrees, but she gives him a warning: "There's no love in me. Not for anything that breathes God's air. That's what turned Alistair against me from the start. There can be nothing between us, Ralph, as it is." Burke, chivalrous to a fault, agrees to stay and do battle with her ghost regardless.

Burke secures all the doors and windows in the house, but to his surprise he later finds Ann trying to unbolt the front lock—as though she *wanted* the ghost to enter. Confused by her behavior, Burke sends her back up to her bed chamber. He steps outside to check on the lurking spectre, turning in time to glimpse the gaunt form of Alistair Loring as the door locks behind him! Frantic, Burke breaks a window, reenters the house, and races upstairs in time to see the spectre approaching Ann as she lies in bed. Grappling with the dead man, Burke chases him headlong to the staircase landing, but as the midnight chimes toll, Loring vanishes, and Burke is sent screaming down the marble staircase, landing at the foot—dead.

Ann Loring, sitting up in bed, waits expectantly. A figure appears in her shadowed doorway—Burke. "He's gone, Ann. You're free of him forever." The voice becomes accusatory, and she can see his lifeless gaze from the shadows. "You left your door unlocked, Ann. But then you said you could never love anything alive." A cold but carnal smile accents her face, and she invites him to come to her now. He shakes his head, promising, "In a year . . . in a year I'll come to you . . . my Ann."

/ **Commentary** / "The Ghost of Sorworth Place" is a good try, but it could have been better. Although boasting a talented cast, this episode needed the pervasive sense of gothic gloom, the cairns and misty moors of stormy Scotland where the story was set, and not California's sun-drenched cheeriness. Exteriors were shot at a manor house in Pasadena that, although lovely, could not match the craggy buttressed-and-pinnacled residence described in Russell Kirk's short story. It helped little that the ghost of Alistair Loring looked more like a heroin addict in tweeds than a restless corpse.

Alvin Sapinsley's literate script is written in the style of a gothic romance, but the direction only fitfully reaches that level. The scope of the story suggests a richer, more extravagant sense of style, but director Ralph Senensky's touch isn't nearly sweeping enough. "I think 'Sorworth Place' would have gained if it could have been done as an hour show," Senensky points out. "The material warranted a little deeper treatment—but that's hindsight." Although there are moments of suspense, the segment falls short in its attempt to induce genuine scares.

Richard Kiley (Nazi war criminal Joseph Strobe in the *Night Gallery* pilot) was cast as the American wanderer, Ralph Burke. "I had never worked with Kiley before, and he was a total pro," Senensky says. "I had done a *Star Trek* with Jill Ireland ["This Side of Paradise"]. It had been a very happy relationship, so that when she came back onto the 'Sorworth' set, we sort of picked up where we left off." Here Ireland gives an effective performance as the cool, emotionally distant Ann Loring, both repelled and drawn by some unnatural, dimly acknowledged hunger for her dead husband.

During the shooting, problems arose for Ireland with the last scene as scripted. Her character was described lying in bed, nude—and it was expected for the director to shoot it that way. "She came to me and said she didn't want to do it," recalls Senensky, "and I agreed with her totally. I knew there was no reason to shoot it because it was not going to be on television. That was the period in Hollywood when the bans on what you could and couldn't shoot were dropping like flies. Nudity was becoming the rage in features. But the networks were not airing nude bodies in the early seventies, so why shoot it for the glee of the screening room?" Senensky and Ireland ultimately filmed the sequence with her covered in a sheet—barely. "I'm not sure how happy Jack Laird was about it—I had no contact with him at all. But she was agreeable to doing what we did. Anything more would've been silly, because they would not have aired it."

In later years Ireland made a number of movies with her husband, Charles Bronson, before her life was cut short in a protracted battle with leukemia. "I became aware later what a really strong, admirable lady she was, with the problems that she faced in her later life," Senensky notes sadly. "She was quite a gal."[155]

As accomplished as the performances are, the one element that gives "Sorworth Place" the necessary atmosphere is Lalo Schifrin's music, lifted from an earlier film by Jack Laird, *Dark Intruder*. So suitable did Laird find this score that it would be used twice more on *Night Gallery*.

NIGHT GALLERY #34318
Air date: January 26, 1972

1

## THE WAITING ROOM
★ ★ ½

Written by Rod Serling
Directed by Jeannot Szwarc
Music: Robert Bain      Intro: John Lewis
Director of Photography: Gerald Perry Finnerman
Time: 27:08

**Cast**
Sam Dichter: Steve Forrest
Joe Bristol: Albert Salmi
Doc Soames: Buddy Ebsen
Bartender: Gilbert Roland
Abe Bennett: Jim Davis
Charlie McKinley: Lex Barker
Kid Max: Larry Watson

*Steve Forrest and Gilbert Roland in "The Waiting Room." Courtesy of TV History Archives.*

*F*elicitations and greetings from this cavern of canvases, dedicated and devoted to bringing you art lovers a few in-depth probes through the crust of the not quite real, the almost real, and the frankly and flagrantly unreal. Pictures, paintings, portraits, rendered onto canvas with brush . . . and sometimes claw.

    Item number one. In a twelve dollar and fifty cent pine box reposes the body of a Frontier Frankie, armed but disarming, a victim of an Old West philosophy that any man with a good eye, a limber finger, and a well-honed trigger skirts the pastures of immortality. But this chap found out the hard way that immortality is a wish, a word, but infrequently a reality. He awaits your pleasure in a painting we call "The Waiting Room."

/ **Summary** / On a cold and windless night, gunfighter Sam Dichter reins up his horse to inspect the still, hooded figure hanging from a gnarled tree. Further along he finds the deserted streets of a town; tethering his mount, he enters the saloon. Quiet as the grave, he notes, save for the loud ticking of the clock on the wall. As he orders a whiskey from the taciturn bartender, Dichter notices a group of four men playing poker in the corner. To his surprise they call him by name, though he does not immediately recognize any of them.

As the clock chimes nine, one of the players, McKinley, rises reluctantly to leave. Dichter stirs up a vague recollection of the one exiting: Charlie McKinley, rumored to have been bushwacked outside a saloon in Abilene. McKinley leaves, followed almost immediately by the explosive roar of a shotgun. Dichter reacts, but no one else is at all surprised by—or even interested in—the occurrence. The poker players ante up, offering Dichter a seat at the table.

As he picks up McKinley's hand, the faces of the men around him come into sharper focus. The loudmouth to his left: Joe Bristol. Dichter saw him gunned down one morning in Monterey. Dichter is shaken, looking for some explanation—too much drink, a brain fever, maybe—when the clock chimes ten. Bristol blanches as a voice from the street calls him out. He swallows, rises, opens the door—sunlight streams in, not the icy black night Dichter expects—and steps out. Another gunshot, and the sound of a falling body.

Dichter is now sure that something is very wrong. The men in the bar appear to be partners in some strange ritual, ending in their respective violent deaths. Another of the poker players, Abe Bennett, rises and leaves when the clock chimes eleven— the hours are passing faster. Soames is next. A doctor by trade, he patched up wounded gunslingers—until the day when he counted the deaths caused by the killers he had saved, and realized the price in human lives his skill had exacted. Then Soames turned his gun on himself. "The elusive point," Soames says, rising, "is that we, all of us, were doomed from the moment we took up firearms." As if in answer, the clock chimes twelve; he follows the others out into the street.

"What's the name of this town?" Dichter raves. "Where is it? *What is it?*" "It's just a waiting room, Mr. Dichter," the bartender mutters, "where each man waits out what is ordained. Some call it Hell." And the clock chimes one. "It's closing time, Mr. Dichter. No doubt I'll be seeing you again." Dichter, hearing the murmur of a crowd, steps out into the street—and into the arms of his jury.

On a cold and windless night, gunfighter Sam Dichter reins up his horse to inspect the still, hooded figure hanging from a gnarled tree. Sneering, he reaches up to pull off the hood—and screams. The face, bloodless and gray, is his own. Falling from his frightened horse, Dichter races on foot into the nearby town. Shaking with fear, he enters the saloon—and he faces once again the bartender and the four poker players in the dead silence . . . broken only by the loud and seemingly endless chiming of the clock.

/ **Commentary** / Another too-familiar premise from *The Twilight Zone* is here recycled for *Night Gallery*. Serling's script (originally titled "A Nice Place to Visit but I Wouldn't Want to Die Here") deals, once again, with the story of an unsavory character who spends his afterlife atoning by eternally reliving the moments before his death. The revisited concept, however, is less a problem than is Serling's dialogue, particularly Buddy Ebsen's endless preachments and the "I'd sooner be kin to a vulture bird" claptrap that Albert Salmi drawls. Compounding these faults, the segment drags on interminably. "The Waiting Room" is Serling on autopilot, a far cry from his best *Night Gallery* material.

This script, over any other Serling submitted, badly needed a rewrite. Yet Laird refused to touch it, when pruning it of five minutes could have remedied its worst blemishes. Why? Perhaps Laird was gun-shy. After the writer's vigorous protests to script changes made in the first half of the season, Laird was tired of dealing with the combative Serling. This segment's hour mate, "Last Rites for a Dead Druid"—a non-Serling script—was even pared of one scene to allow "The Waiting Room" to run its full length. As it stands, this segment, at slightly over twenty-seven minutes, is just too long for its material.

With square writing and textbook western performances, the sole distinguishing elements in this episode lie in Gerald Finnerman's handsome photography and Jeannot Szwarc's sterling direction, an overt and affectionate homage to John Ford. The camera setups are straight out of *My Darling Clementine,* and art director Joseph Alves's color scheme, muted earth tones dominating, resembles a yellowing tintype. Of the segments Finnerman photographed for *Night Gallery,* "The Waiting Room," with its remarkably rich and moody ambience, is perhaps his best work on the series. The distinctive visual design helps redeem the segment's other weak elements.

Finnerman, like Lionel Lindon before him, occasionally butted heads with directors over camera setups. During a disagreement with Szwarc on the set of "The Waiting Room," the harried director made a phone call to editor Larry Lester. "Jeannot called me down on the set," recalls Lester. "Jeannot wanted to do a direct 180-degree reverse, and Finnerman said, 'No, you have to shoot it on a raking angle.' I'm on the phone with Jeannot and he says, 'Come on down to the set and tell this guy the way we're going to shoot this thing.'"[156] Lester dove in and gave Finnerman the editor's viewpoint of why Szwarc's concept would work. Finnerman finally capitulated, but it took both the director's and the editor's assurances to convince him. "When Curly died, it was difficult to suddenly have another cameraman there," recalls Szwarc, "but Jerry Finnerman did a great job."[157]

Originally, Laird intended to shoot the segment in a prestanding back lot set normally used for westerns, until he heard Joseph Alves's design proposal. "This is what I loved about Jack," recalls Alves.

We had a production meeting and a decision was made to use the Virginian bar. And I said, "Oh, Jesus, okay." And Jack said, "All right, stop, stop. Okay, Joe, what do you want to do now?" "Well, Jack, *everybody* uses the Virginian bar." "Well, why not?" he said, "it's a western." I said, "Why don't we do it in a sort of a sepia tone? Why don't we paint the whole thing sepia—the wardrobe, the set, the decor, everything?" And Jack said, "Oh, that's interesting!" I've worked for other TV producers, and they're like, "Hey, forget it. Get real, this is TV!" But Jack was always, "Let's go for it!" It was always fun on *Night Gallery.*[158]

2

## LAST RITES FOR A DEAD DRUID
★ ★ ★ ½

Written by Alvin Sapinsley
Directed by Jeannot Szwarc
Music: Lalo Schifrin, Paul Glass, Oliver Nelson,
    Gil Mellé, and Eddie Sauter
Director of Photography: Gerald Perry Finnerman
Time: 22:26

**Cast**
Bruce Tarraday: Bill Bixby
Jennie Tarraday: Carol Lynley
Mildred McVane: Donna Douglas
Mr. Bernstein: Ned Glass
Marta: Janya Brannt

*Bill Bixby in "Last Rites for a Dead Druid." Courtesy of Hollywood Book and Poster Co.*

*T*o those amongst you with a predilection toward antique collection or the occasional bargain hunting that takes place in out of the way nooks and stalls, this painting suggests a certain required wariness when it comes to your shopping. Because there are moments when, behind some dusty book or in a cobwebbed corner of an ancient vestibule, you'll uncover a little objet d'art which can horrify the heck out of you. Such being the case in this painting when a lady goes junking about and uncovers a mythological statue that has lived past its time . . . and intrudes on hers. We call the painting "The Last Rites for a Dead Druid."

**/ Summary /** Bruce Tarraday, a struggling young attorney, is unhappy with the latest impulse purchase of his wife, Jennie: a life-size lawn statue of a man in some ancient raiment, discovered in an antique shop by her annoying friend Mildred McVane. Jennie claims the statue resembles Bruce, a point he refuses to concede.

That night, Bruce suffers a nightmare in which the statue menaces him from the foot of his bed. He is unable to laugh it off in the morning when he finds what look like footsteps burned into the grass, leading from the statue to the house. Disturbed, he pays a visit to Mr. Bernstein, the proprietor of the antique shop, who cheerily informs Bruce that the statue is a likeness of an ancient druid sorcerer, Bruce the Black, whose satanic rites included debauchery, rape, and sacrifices—both animal and human. He maintained primacy among his order with his power to turn any would-be attackers into stone. Jennie is excited by the discovery, suggesting that her husband is perhaps a long-distant descendant of Bruce the Black.

Bruce soon finds that the statue is exerting a strange influence over his life. While sparring with Mildred McVane one afternoon in its presence, he finds himself gazing fixedly at the woman. Suddenly without will, he becomes aroused, grasps Mildred, and kisses her passionately. Desire passes within seconds and, pulling away from her, Bruce is overcome with shame. Mildred, though surprised, has found the episode entirely to her liking. Bruce, shaken, considers the possible damage to his marriage as he prepares the barbeque. A disturbing image rises in the fire: a bearded, leering satyr, a twisted version of himself in ancient garb. The influence is strong; he yields with pleasure to the sorcerer's will. Flushed with a perverse glee, Bruce grabs the neighbor's cat and, holding it tight, thrusts it into the flames of the barbeque. The animal's anguished screams bring Jennie, Mildred, and the maid. Suddenly horrified by his deed, Bruce drops the cat and races past them into the house.

That night, Bruce awakens to find the statue in the doorway of his bedroom—and it is not a dream. It speaks, directing him to kill Jennie so that he can take Mildred. Bruce begins to yield again but fights the influence; with a tremendous effort he breaks the sorcerer's hold and the statue disappears from the doorway. Furious, Bruce resolves to end the nightmare. Grabbing a crowbar, he approaches the statue and aims a blow at it . . . but he is gripped by a sudden paralysis. Jennie, responding to his scream, arrives to find a life-size likeness of Bruce in stone, crowbar held in his upraised hand, his face a frozen mask of terror. He has been petrified. Lying on the ground is a man with Bruce's likeness, bearded, cloaked in ancient raiment—the sorcerer, awakened from his stony prison. The intruder leers up at Jennie with evil intent.

At Mr. Bernstein's junk shop the next day, Mildred is trying to sell him a *new* statue that bears a striking resemblance to the one Bernstein sold to Mrs. Tarraday. He considers the offer, but what a pity, he tells Mildred, that she is not offering the pair together. "Yes, isn't it," Mildred agrees with a secret smile. "A great pity."

/ **Commentary** / As a marketing ploy, this segment was matched with "The Waiting Room" to exploit the fact that two of its stars, Buddy Ebsen and Donna Douglas, were linked by another popular show, *The Beverly Hillbillies,* which had just finished its nine-year run on CBS. Luckily, this segment is more distinguished than its hour mate.

One of Alvin Sapinsley's best scripts for *Night Gallery,* "Last Rites for a Dead Druid" (originally titled "Silent Partner") is a sharp-edged blend of humor and scares. "I tried to insert a little humor," Sapinsley said, "because, I must confess to you, there was not a great deal of humor in the people who ran the program—except Jack Laird, who can be a very funny man."[159]

The plot of "Last Rites," adapted from a long-buried short story, changed so markedly from its inspiration that Laird deemed it an original. "It was called *Out of the Eons,*" recalls Sapinsley. "I forgot who wrote it, but my final version was so far removed from the original short story as to be unrecognizable."

Indeed, *Out of the Eons* would be exceedingly difficult to identify as the source. Hazel Heald's 1935 original, told in vivid Lovecraftian style, chronicles the story of an archaeological dig, an ancient mummy, a beleaguered Boston museum, and a mystical Polynesian cult. The only elements of the story remaining in "Last Rites for a Dead Druid" are the threatening influence of an ancient cult (now the druids) and the protagonist's final petrification.

"I used the statue I had at the bottom of my garden as a stepping-off point," recalls Sapinsley. "In fact, the statue is still in my backyard."[160] Inspired, Sapinsley resuscitated the ancient stone horror and dropped it into the middle of a staid, conventional southern California suburb—a most effective alternative.

Director Jeannot Szwarc displays his usual deft hand at creating a uniquely suspenseful atmosphere using shadows, expressive color, visually startling camera work, and editing. His design of the dream sequence, with the statue appearing in the bedroom doorway (the background a vibrant, bloody orange hue) is masterful; the final transformation sequence is similarly well designed. The network censors placed some restrictions, however, on his lensing of the backyard barbeque sequence. "We got in trouble because we wanted to show a cat getting burned," remembers Szwarc. "I had to cheat on that. The way I originally shot it, you saw the cat being lowered into the barbeque, and then I cheated by cutting away."[161]

Taking their cues from the script, the performers tread a fine line between humor and suspense. Bill Bixby is just right, a fluent comic actor with the gravity to play Tarraday's growing fears at the new influence in his life. Character actor Ned Glass has a wonderfully funny cameo as the gregarious antique shop owner, and Carol Lynley is aptly vacant as Bixby's clueless wife. Donna Douglas's Mildred McVane is a hungry, manipulative siren, but her ambiguous presence leaves some questions unanswered. Is she somehow the agent of Bruce the Black? Or is she as naive as Jennie, attracted to Tarraday's reviving alter ego and falling under his spell? Strangely, these hanging questions, though perplexing, don't work against the episode. The nagging mystery of Mildred McVane's character and possible foreknowledge is one of the qualities that ultimately makes "Last Rites for a Dead Druid" so memorable.

NIGHT GALLERY #34319
Air date: February 9, 1972

1

DELIVERIES IN THE REAR
★ ★ ★ ★

Written by Rod Serling

Directed by Jeff Corey
Music: Paul Glass
Director of Photography: Gerald Perry Finnerman
Time: 28:19

**Cast**
Dr. John Fletcher: Cornel Wilde
Barbara Bennett: Rosemary Forsyth
Mr. Bennett: Kent Smith
Jameson: Walter Burke
1st Grave Robber: Peter Whitney
Hannify: Larry D. Mann
Dr. Shockman: Peter Brocco
Dillingham: Ian Wolfe
2d Grave Robber: John Maddison
Mrs. Woods: Marjorie E. Bennett
Tuttle: Gerald McRaney

*Rosemary Forsyth and Cornel Wilde in "Deliveries in the Rear." Courtesy of Hollywood Book and Poster Co.*

$G$*ood evening, and welcome to an art museum of the unique. Paintings offered up that infrequently find themselves hung in the more prosaic places, paintings that are frequently as much formaldehyde as they are pigment. So upon viewing if you sense a touch of the grave, the morgue, the concrete slab, count yourself more or less normal in terms of your taste in art —at least* this *art.*

*Number one entry: a painting that suggests a story replete with gaslight, hansom cabs, and cadavers. An all-star cast of corpses appearing in what we call "Deliveries in the Rear," delivered to you now on* Night Gallery.

**/ Summary /** Nineteenth-century New England. Dr. John Fletcher, a surgery instructor at the MacMillan School of Medicine, has recently come under fire from the school's administrators for the questionable sources of his dissection cadavers. Fletcher, a dedicated, no-nonsense man, on occasion hires grave robbers to supply him with bodies for his classes. But lately, some derelicts and drunkards have turned up missing, and authorities are keeping a watchful eye on Fletcher's "associates."

The doctor's philosophy is purely practical. He believes that the loss of one life, if it leads to the saving of many other lives, is a necessary sacrifice—and if that one life lost is just another wandering nonentity of the street, to whom could it possibly matter? He is untouched by the ethical and moral questions of his philosophy, a situation that upsets Mr. Bennett, the father of Fletcher's fiancée, Barbara. During an after-dinner conversation, Bennett and Fletcher have a flare-up over what Bennett views as Fletcher's cavalier and arbitrary respect for human life. Barbara is also disturbed at times by Fletcher's absolute dedication to medicine to the exclusion of all else—even of her.

One afternoon, Fletcher is confronted by the school's head, Dr. Shockman, who warns Fletcher that the police will be visiting that very evening. A local drunkard, Charlie Woods, has gone missing and his wife has raised an alarm with the police. Fletcher assures Shockman that they have no male cadavers; they have, instead, the body of a woman—an outright lie.

Under pressure, Fletcher contacts his two procuring agents and demands the body of a woman. The two thugs deem it too cold to go digging, and they do their hunting on the streets that night. The body is smuggled into the rear entrance of the medical school just in time for Fletcher's scheduled lecture. A police detective, Hannify, arrives and inspects the body. He is clearly disappointed that it is, indeed, not Charlie Woods but the body of a female—but he offers Fletcher a warning: "One day I hope to catch you accepting a delivery. And I'll see to it that the next thing you hold in your hand won't be a scalpel. It'll be a sledgehammer in a prison rockyard."

Proceeding with confidence into the lecture hall, Fletcher prefaces his lesson with an admonition against timidity in the pursuit of knowledge: "No individual life is of *any consequence* if it means the saving of many lives." He proceeds with the lesson, pulling the sheet back from his new cadaver—and, looking down at the body on the slab, screams in horror, crumpling to the floor in a heap. It is the pale and bloodless form of his fiancée, Barbara.

/ **Commentary** / Without a hint of fantasy or the supernatural, this segment remains a superlative entry for *Night Gallery*. Rarely one to dabble in moral ambiguities, Serling here argues persuasively both sides of the "sacrifices for the greater good" issue—then dares his audience to choose sides at the play's ghastly finish. Along the way he gives us beautifully shaded characters, and the other production elements—performances, atmospheric design, direction, and photography—all mesh to create a memorable and powerful effect.

Cornel Wilde delivers a portrait of cool dedication as Dr. Fletcher, a man neither without conscience nor irresponsible. Fletcher truly feels the ends justify his means, but he discovers too late that his oath to protect life cannot be conveniently circumscribed for any reason, no matter how lofty; that we are all, to the extent of our influence, responsible for the actions of others. Serling once again exerts his strong moral voice, adding depth to this Val Lewtonesque chiller, impressively directed by Jeff Corey.

The feel for atmosphere exhibited by Corey, art director Joseph Alves, and cinematographer Gerald Finnerman creates from the stagy back lot exteriors a mist-filled, nocturnal mood of long shadows and New England browns and grays. To create that ambience, Corey drew heavily on the experience of his new cinematographer. "He was a great director," Finnerman says of Corey, "and he conferred with me a lot. In 'Deliveries in the Rear,' we would carry on shots that, had we not stopped, could've led us into another dimension—kept going, you know? That was a beautiful show."[162]

Corey's inspired visuals comment on the play's theme. A distorting wide-angle lens is used for closeups of the two grave robbers, the visual equivalent of invading the viewer's comfort zone—very disturbing. At first, Corey uses it only to dwell on the unpleasant faces of the ghouls. He then uses this "fishbowl" effect for the confrontation scene between Dr. Fletcher and the detective, visually implicating Fletcher along with his associates. The doctor's strange, distorted code of morality now links him to the crimes of the villains he has hired. With these kinds of directorial touches, "Deliveries in the Rear" becomes Corey's best work for the series.

In contrast to the gravity of the story, actress Rosemary Forsyth's recollections of the filming tend toward the lighter side. "I remember partying a great deal the night before," she says, "and being very worried about not having enough sleep." Somewhat depleted from the previous night's adventure, she reported to the makeup department the next morning. Forsyth's first scene required her to play dead. It was not a stretch. "It was stupid for me to stay out so late when I had to be at work the next morning, and the first thing they did was lay me down on the slab! They told me that my eyes were fluttering—that I didn't pass as a good corpse!"[163] Nice compliment.

Forsyth, despite her distractions, gave a convincing performance. "Deliveries" also served as a playhouse for a distinguished group of character actors, including Kent Smith, Larry D. Mann, Peter Whitney, Walter Burke, Peter Brocco, and Ian Wolfe, adding studies of nuance and color in the brief time allowed them. Also briefly on screen as a squeamish surgery student is Gerald McRaney (later of *Simon and Simon* and *Major Dad*) in his first television appearance.

"I got Jerry McRaney his SAG card on that," Corey recalls. "He was a nice kid. He came from New Orleans where he had done *Hamlet* in college. He was driving a cab at night and taught classes for me when I worked. I don't pretend to be a prophet, but I put my arm around him one day and said, 'Don't worry, Jerry. You're going to have a good career.'"[164] From the evidence of his classroom deportment in "Deliveries," it's as well it wasn't as a surgeon.


2

STOP KILLING ME

★ ★


Teleplay by Jack Laird
Based on the short story by Hal Dresner

Directed by Jeannot Szwarc
Music: Oliver Nelson
Director of Photography: Gerald
   Perry Finnerman
Time: 14:01

**Cast**

Frances Turchin: Geraldine Page
Sergeant Bevelow: James Gregory

*Geraldine Page in "Stop Killing Me." Courtesy of Cinema Collectors.*

*P*ainting number two in the Night Gallery, *addressing itself to the strains and stresses of the married. Having to do with the fact that there is more than one way to kill a cat . . . and more than one way to dispose of a wife. Our painting is called "Stop Killing Me."*

**/ Summary /** During a slow afternoon at the police station, desk sergeant Stanley Bevelow's office door opens and in walks a rumpled, middle-aged woman with worried eyes, clutching her purse like a shield. She introduces herself as Mrs. Frances Turchin, whose husband, she claims, is killing her—right now, this very minute, and she demands that something be done about it. During a movie, for instance, right at the best part, he will turn to her and say, "I'm going to kill you, Frances." During conversations with friends and relatives, he will interrupt to tell her, "I'm going to kill you, Frances," then resume the conversation as though nothing had happened. Her husband claims it's the easiest way to kill a person anyone has ever thought of. She'll probably fall down a flight of stairs, he says. If not that, then she'll step out in front of a moving car, or take too many sleeping pills. But, he estimates, she has a week at the most. Bevelow asks Mrs. Turchin why her husband wants to kill her. "Because I won't divorce him. That's all. Is that a reason to kill a person?" Bevelow muses, "I've known some who thought it was." The desk sergeant considers the woman, nervously straightening the hat on her bird's nest of hair. She *did* look as if she might distractedly step in front of a car or fall down a flight of stairs. Not today perhaps, but probably soon. Very possibly within the week.

Bevelow promises to have a talk with her husband. Thanking him profusely, the timorous Mrs. Turchin exits, leaving the sergeant to thoughtfully consider the framed picture of his sour-faced wife sitting on his desk. Picking up the phone, he dials the number Mrs. Turchin left him for her husband, Bernard. As the call rings through, a scream and a crash are heard just outside the station . . . and Sergeant Bevelow sets up an unofficial appointment with Frances Turchin's husband—now a widower—for a few private lessons.

/ **Commentary** / Laird commented once to Burt Astor that he thought Serling's work was too long and talky and needed cutting. That he could not recognize the same deficiencies when they cropped up in his own scripts is a distinct irony. As filmed, this leaden segment could easily have lost a few minutes and gained in the tightening.

"I don't know why I didn't write the teleplay for 'Stop Killing Me,'" says short story author Hal Dresner, "because that one was just retyping—the story was all dialogue. I don't know what changes Jack Laird made, I've never compared the two. He might've padded it out a little bit; I think the story was a little shorter. In terms of an emotional arc it seemed to start over again a couple of times. It didn't really build in a classic sense, and it just seems to hit the same notes over and over again. I mean, how many times does James Gregory have to look at that photograph of that shrewish wife before you get the point?"[165]

Another telling screed against married life, Laird's script is made bearable only by Geraldine Page's quirky performance as the harried Mrs. Turchin, Gregory's weary desk sergeant, and director Jeannot Szwarc's attempts to open up this one-set piece with some nifty camera work.

"That was the first thing I did with Geraldine Page," notes Szwarc. "She was extraordinary in that. We worked so hard—that was a lot of pages to get done in one day, and it was very difficult because she was alone almost all the time. I sort of gave her the camera as a visible partner to vary it a little, because it got very dry after a while. I was really worried that it was going to be very boring.

"After we wrapped, Geraldine and I had a little drink. She gave me her number and said, 'Look, next time you have something, call me direct.'"[166] As luck would have it, Szwarc would remember Page for his next assignment on *Night Gallery*. He provided her with one of the best roles of her career in the chilling classic "The Sins of the Fathers."


3

DEAD WEIGHT

★ ★ ★ ½


Teleplay by Jack Laird
Based on the short story "Out of the Country" by
   Jeffry Scott
Directed by Timothy Galfas
Music: Gordon Jenkins    Intro: Paul Glass
Director of Photography: E. Charles Straumer
Time: 7:16

*Bobby Darin in "Dead Weight." Courtesy of Sal Milo.*

**Cast**
Bullivant: Jack Albertson
Landau: Bobby Darin
Delivery Boy: James Metropole

*H*ere *we have a cameo dandy. Problem: how to flee the coop; how to make tracks away from the police and unhappy peers; ship out to safer climes. The story of a chap who, if he'd had it to do over again, would have remained where he was. He finds out that he is precisely what is the title of the picture: "Dead Weight."*

**/ Summary /** Mr. Bullivant, an aging exporter, has a reputation for dealing discreetly with gangsters on the lam. He reassures his latest client, a twitchy hood named Landau, that he will be spirited out of the country within twenty-four hours, promising complete satisfaction: "Forty-seven years in business, and not one customer complaint."

Landau, pacing like a cat, nervously recounts his involvement in a bloody bank heist, causing the deaths of four people. With his face on every newspaper in town, Landau's only avenue of quick, undetected escape is through the good offices of Bullivant. The amiable exporter suggests Buenos Aires—"Rio is a bit overdone of late." The gangster uneasily agrees, pays Bullivant, and the deal is done. Pouring them both a glass of sherry, the exporter asks his guest's indulgence in sealing the bargain with a toast. Landau, amused by the old man's eccentricity, downs his in a gulp. As Bullivant quietly puts his glass aside untouched, the hood gasps, lets out a strangled cry, and pitches face forward onto the warehouse floor—dead.

By morning, Bullivant finishes crating up the newly processed shipment of "Bullivant's Mystery Mixture"—his brand of canned dog food—bound for Argentina. As the delivery boy hauls the crate away, the old man touts the special qualities of his chef d'oeuvre: "If you'll forgive a boast, I think I can say with pardonable pride, there's not another manufacturer in the country who can duplicate my secret recipe." Bullivant has honored his contract: Landau will be out of the country by nightfall.

**/ Commentary /** This segment's sharp, potent sting comes from every department firing on all cylinders: writing, performances, direction, claustrophobic design, photography, and, perhaps most of all, its brevity. "Dead Weight" is as long as it needs to be to achieve its one-two punch. After his tedious script for "Stop Killing Me," Laird redeemed himself admirably with this dark, scabrously funny little gem.

"I had a little shooting difficulty on that," recalls director Timothy Galfas. "I wanted a different style of lighting. Out here they believe in using a lot of lights, flattening everything, and I come from the New York school where you can only put a couple of lights in a cab. I found out we were shooting in one little room, and next thing I know I look up and see five million lights. So I asked for them to cut out some lights and, of course, I got a lot of flak because that means they couldn't use as many electricians." Galfas won his battle on lighting, but may have lost the war. Despite his obvious affinity for this type of material, his demands pegged him as a troublesome director in Laird's eyes.

Galfas's lighting scheme is shadowy and rich, and his camera, like the character of Landau, paces like a caged animal. "I shot some of the stuff myself hand-held because I couldn't get across what I wanted . . . or else they thought I was crazy. Regardless of what they say, it's difficult for someone innovative to get things done in Hollywood."[167]

An exercise in morbid black comedy, "Dead Weight" is a brilliant *Night Gallery* episode. One of its comic elements was not at first intended, however, as editor Larry Lester recalls: "I remember the Sparkletts bottle going off during that scene, where the water cooler took a gulp for itself." In his first cut, Lester left it out. "Jack said, 'Well, why don't you use the gurgle?' So I had to put the Sparkletts gurgle back in. I don't think anybody but Jack ever got what that sound was"[168]—an absurd punctuation amid the jittery cat-and-mouse dialogue between Jack Albertson and Bobby Darin.

Winding up the segment, a brassy, big-band arrangement of the cheery Johnny Mercer–Gordon Jenkins standard "P.S. I Love You" is used as underscore, a surreal touch that adds a final, ironic fillip to this nasty little segment.

NIGHT GALLERY #34320
Air date: February 16, 1972

1

I'LL NEVER LEAVE YOU—EVER
★ ★ ★ ★

Teleplay by Jack Laird
Based on the short story by Rene Morris
Directed by Daniel Haller
Music: Lalo Schifrin, Oliver Nelson, and Paul Glass
Director of Photography: Gerald Perry Finnerman
Time: 26:32

**Cast**
Moragh: Lois Nettleton

*Lois Nettleton and John Saxon in "I'll Never Leave You—Ever." Courtesy of Hollywood Book and Poster Co.*

Owen: Royal Dano
Ianto: John Saxon
Old Crone: Peggy Webber

G*ood evening. If you seem to sense an aura of cold dampness that permeates this
room, attribute it not to either defective air conditioning or inclement indoor weather. It's
simply because this is rather a special place with special statuary and special paintings, and
they carry with them a coldness that seems to go best in a crypt—or in a place like this,
called the* Night Gallery.

*Our opening kickoff is deep into the end zone of the moors, where hounds bay and
witches fly brooms, and the belief in the supernatural is as natural as breathing—or not
breathing. We call this item "I'll Never Leave You—Ever."*

/ **Summary** /  Under a gibbous moon, Moragh and Ianto meet secretly in the stable.
Moragh's husband, Owen, lies deathly ill, and the two lovers seize their time together
jealously with the hope that his lingering illness will finally take him soon and they
can be together always.

Moragh, however, is losing patience. Owen watches her constantly, and clings to
her as if she were the only thing keeping him alive. She cannot bear her husband's
wizened, sickly body or his clammy touch. When he demands from her a wife's duty,
putting his diseased lips to hers, smelling of infection and death, she is sure she can
endure no more. In desperation, Moragh seeks out the services of a local crone, by
reputation a mistress of the black arts, and asks the old woman for her specialty: a
carved wooden doll in Owen's likeness.

Returning to the farmhouse, Moragh quickly builds a fire in the fireplace, stoking
it to a roaring blaze. Steeling her courage, she throws the doll onto the fire—followed
immediately by Owen's agonized shrieks, which fill the farmhouse. The limbs of the
doll jerk and twist as the flames try to consume it—but although the doll chars, it
does not burn away. Deafened by her husband's pitiful screams from the next room,
a horrified Moragh realizes the old woman had carved the doll from unseasoned
wood. It cannot burn! The doll arches up as if in agony, twists itself off the burning
logs, and falls smoking to the hearth. Scooping up the doll into her apron, Moragh
races across the moor in desperate flight. Stopping at the lip of the quarry, she flings
the doll into the depths of the black pit. Exhausted from fear, she trudges back home.

The farmhouse is silent upon her arrival. She enters Owen's smoke-filled room to
find the cot empty, the blankets torn and trailing across the floor . . . and sees the
hideous, blackened heap that was once Owen smoking in a bed of ashes. Moragh retreats, fainting, back into the kitchen. She is awakened by Ianto's gentle touch—but
upon finding Owen's twisted remains, he turns away from Moragh, sickened. She

tries desperately to win back his sympathy, describing her ordeal with the bewitched doll. "You don't understand," he shouts. "It's not safe until it has burned away. *The doll still lives, down there in the darkness!*" Grabbing a lantern, Ianto quickly mounts his horse and gallops off to the quarry to find it. Moragh chases him into the black night, stumbling across the misted moors. Nearing the quarry, she hears a voice calling to her, and in the distance she sees a faint light leading her on. She moves toward it expectantly. At the rim of the quarry, the ground under Moragh's feet crumbles away and she is thrown, headlong, down into the black depths . . . where Owen, fire-scarred and arms outstretched, awaits.

/ **Commentary** / "I'll Never Leave You—Ever" represents Jack Laird's only attempt on *Night Gallery* at writing true horror, a contrast with the comic vignettes he usually put his hand to. The script's taut pacing, characterful dialogue, and blood-chilling plot, however, are due mostly to author Rene Morris, whose original short story Laird adapted. With the exception of the poetic opening scene, the script is a line-for-line transcription of the events, scene chronology, and dialogue in Morris's short story.

Laird's choice of Daniel Haller to direct was, to say the least, discerning, as Haller had traversed this territory before. His previous directorial efforts included two feature adaptations of H. P. Lovecraft, *The Dunwich Horror* and *Die, Monster, Die*—both unsuccessful. But from the standpoint of style and conception, this segment's gloomy, penetrating atmosphere is a closer relative to Haller's exceptional work as Roger Corman's production designer for the Vincent Price–Edgar Allan Poe films.

For "I'll Never Leave You—Ever," art director Joseph Alves modified the imaginative sets he built for "The Sins of the Fathers" (shot first but appearing later in the broadcast order). Aided by the rich and imaginative lighting of Gerald Finnerman, Haller and Alves cast the blasted landscape into a mist-filled, eternal night.

A number of inspired visuals were dreamed up in postproduction. For the final sequence where Moragh falls into the quarry, editor Larry Lester designed effective inserts to signal the motion of her plummet. Strapping a camera to a motorcycle and running it down a slope, Lester intercut this black rushing footage with a reverse-action shot zooming in on the charred face of Royal Dano lying at the bottom of the quarry—a spine-chilling payoff.

The performances equal the behind-the-scenes execution. As the lingering Owen, Royal Dano shapes a character both repellent and pitiously human; John Saxon, too, gives a confident performance as the local rake; but Lois Nettleton wins the top honors for her convincing portrait of Moragh, whose desire, disgust, and apprehension come through vividly. "It was one of my favorite shows to do," recalls Nettleton. "We had wonderful actors, it was a fun character to play, and Daniel Haller really let us run with it. Some directors just want to take control, but Daniel was very permissive, not at all restrictive." Such freedom on the set led to some interesting thespian tactics.

Actress Peggy Webber, who played the stroke-afflicted old witch, made sure that Nettleton would be properly repelled in her presence by munching on garlic before the filming of their scene. "I don't remember the garlic," notes Nettleton, "but she *was* scary."[169]

For hair-raising terror, this segment would be hard to beat. The doll-burning sequence is chilling, with the limbs of the tiny effigy writhing in the flames, a simulacrum of Moragh's unseen husband screaming in agony in the next room. If filmed today, a less imaginative director would probably show—as graphically as possible—what was occurring to the old farmer. For *Night Gallery*, the more timid times demanded a welcome discretion, and the viewer's imagination does a much more effective job of visualizing the suggested horrors.

Behind the scenes, however, more tangible horrors materialized. John Saxon, who had starred as heart specialist Dr. Ted Stuart for a three-year stint on *The Bold Ones*, was forced to improvise on his CPR training one afternoon on the set. "As I was coming back from lunch," remembers Saxon,

my stand-in came rushing over to me and asked me to come—something rather urgent. One of the craft service men, who put out the coffee and doughnuts, had fallen down and was obviously having something like a heart attack. There was nobody around; I was one of the first people returning from lunch. On *The Bold Ones*, I had practiced this cardiopulmonary resuscitation by massaging the heart, and I began very rapidly and very, very vigorously to do this. Shortly, other people began returning and they called the nurse and the fire department. The nurse showed up some four or five minutes later. I was still massaging this guy's chest, and he looked like he was gaining a little color. The nurse told me that I was doing it too hard and I'd break his ribs. I said, "You do it, then." And she did, and he died.[170]

The news of this bizarre circumstance spread quickly to others working on the set. "It was awful," says Nettleton. "They had to stop filming because he just dropped down on the set. Even if we didn't know the man, it was still a sad event. It was a real downer for all of us."[171] Assistant director Ralph Sariego displayed a numb efficiency: "I just sort of pushed him over to the side and put a sheet on him and we kept on shooting. I think I was accused of being insensitive, which I probably was, but you can't just shut everything down and wait for them to come and get the body. Just put a sheet over it and push on, that's what production people do."[172]

"The fire department finally came, pronounced him dead, and took him away," says Saxon. "Some months later, I was on a telethon of some kind, and one of the callers said, 'Thank you for trying to save my husband, Ray.' He had had a history of heart trouble, so it was a grave situation to start with."[173] Grave would be the word.

For all the inherent complications, "I'll Never Leave You—Ever" is a classic *Night Gallery* episode, faultlessly conceived and executed. Unfortunately, as with other first-time directors on the show who produced strong work, Daniel Haller never returned to direct another.

2

## THERE AREN'T ANY MORE MACBANES
★ ★ ★ ½

Teleplay by Alvin Sapinsley
Based on the short story "By One, By Two and By Three" by Stephen Hall
Directed by John Newland
Music: Gil Mellé, Paul Glass, Oliver Nelson, Lalo Schifrin, and Eddie Sauter
Director of Photography: Gerald Perry Finnerman
Time: 23:07

**Cast**
Andrew MacBane: Joel Grey
Elie Green: Darrell Larson
Arthur Porter: Howard Duff
Mickey Standish: Barry Higgins
Messenger Boy: Mark Hamill
Manservant: Vincent Van Lynn
Demon: Ellen Blake

*Joel Grey in "There Aren't Any More MacBanes." Courtesy of Sal Milo.*

*O*ur next painting tells the story of a young man whose major in school is philosophy but whose extracurricular labors take him into the area of black magic—and for this you don't get a degree, but the commencement ceremony is a gas. See for yourself as we offer you "There Aren't Any More MacBanes."

/ **Summary** / Recent Bard College matriculants Elie Green and Mickey Standish drop in on their fellow Ivy Leaguer, eccentric Andrew MacBane, during a heated argument between MacBane and his visiting uncle, Arthur Porter. Although older than his classmates, MacBane has not graduated with them. He is a perennial student, struggling to achieve his master's degree in ancient religious studies. MacBane's uncle, disgusted that his only living relative is wasting his time—and Porter's money—studying "witchcraft" when he could be out making an "honest living," delivers an ultimatum on his way out: if MacBane does not get a respectable job within six months, he will be disinherited.

MacBane shows little concern over his uncle's threat, focusing instead on his search for the personal papers of a long-dead ancestor, seventeenth-century sage Jedediah MacBane. Jedediah, it seems, was a sorcerer, rumored to have been able to kill at great distances without stirring from his hearth. He did away with his worst enemy, his best friend, and his best friend's wife in this mysterious fashion. Then something did him in. What, MacBane doesn't know—there are ten missing pages from Jedediah's journal relating how he did it, what "it" was, and what became of him. If only those ten pages could be found . . .

Six months pass. Elie and Mickey come by MacBane's room to witness his formal disinheritance. Arthur Porter, dissatisfied with MacBane's progress at finding a job, has arrived in person to deliver the news that, as of the bank's opening tomorrow, MacBane will be cut off. MacBane seems curiously unconcerned, breaking out a bottle of sherry to celebrate with his friends . . . and as Porter heads across the deserted nighttime campus, he is unaware of something moving stealthily and silently behind him, peering at him, red-eyed, from the darkness.

That night, Arthur Porter dies a mysterious and violent death; MacBane, inheriting all of his uncle's money, moves into the family's ancestral home in Salem. Soon after, Elie receives a telegram from MacBane asking him to warn Mickey that he is in terrible danger. To Elie's horror, he finds he is too late—Mickey is dead, his throat torn out by some wild beast. When Elie is menaced that same evening by something lurking in his apartment house basement—something with two gleaming red eyes and grasping talons—he rushes to Salem to locate Andrew MacBane. MacBane admits that he found the ten missing pages and worked Jedediah's spell against his uncle, but the thing MacBane called forth remains, and he can find no spell to get rid of it. The creature is a devoted servant of any MacBane who discovers its secret—and once called, it demands to kill all in the conjurer's circle, friend or enemy. Jedediah MacBane denied it victims and was ultimately destroyed—and Andrew MacBane is determined to follow suit, to send the clamoring thing back to the darkness from which it came. A scratching at the door signals the demon's arrival, and it bursts into the room. When MacBane puts himself between Elie and the creature, the demon instead descends upon MacBane, savaging him—but in killing its master, the creature destroys itself. MacBane's jealous servant, finally obedient, is reduced to a pile of ashes next to its master's crumpled form.

/ **Commentary** / Another Alvin Sapinsley–penned winner, "There Aren't Any More MacBanes" is based on British author Stephen Hall's chiller "By One, By Two and By Three," offering a clever twist on Goethe's tale of the sorcerer's apprentice. As usual, Sapinsley adds a personal touch with his spirited dialogue, Americanizing the more staid secondary characters in the story. The setting is effectively transplanted from Cambridge and the wilds of Scotland to the Ivy League and the haunted New England of legend. Not a bit of this segment looks like its location, southern California— one reason for its success.

Tony- and Oscar-winner Joel Grey, feverishly over the top as the theatrical, quirkily sinister Andrew MacBane, gets under the skin of his eccentric character. Both Darrell Larson and Barry Higgins acquit themselves well in their less flamboyant roles as

MacBane's underclassmen drinking buddies (the two knew each other as theater students at UCLA), and a very young Mark Hamill—Luke Skywalker of *Star Wars*—has a brief cameo.

Director John Newland, host and creator of *One Step Beyond*, the 1950s series on the paranormal, guides and visualizes the story with a sure hand at achieving his desired effects. Director also of the classic *Thriller* episode "Pigeons from Hell," Newland here seals the impression that his best work lies in the creation of shadowy worlds and gothic suspense. He successfully evokes the Lovecraftian sense of something lurking on the threshold, and the segment's shadowed photography and musty sets produce a brooding, archaic atmosphere from the modern New England locale.

"John Newland was such a fantastic guy," actor Darrell Larson remembers. "Very English, very cultured. He was unique in my experience of TV directors, because he was very supportive and helpful—it was a miracle! He really wanted it to be as good as it could be."

Another benefit for Larson was meeting Broadway legend Joel Grey, fresh from his Tony win for *Cabaret*. "I thought I had died and gone to heaven," Larson says. "Joel and I hit it off. He had a million stories, and was Mr. Showbiz. That was a thrill."

According to Larson, Grey had some difficulties with the script while filming the finale, where he had to speak a long expository monologue explaining the demon.

Joel couldn't believe they were expecting him to do all of that nonsense dialogue. I mean, it was just gibberish, this *endless* shit while the monster is pounding on the door. And I swear to God, Joel just didn't bother to learn it. He showed up and *did not know his lines!* And I'm off-camera for all of it—crying and screaming and cowering—and every once in a while poor Joel would just look at me and crack up! John Newland was tearing his hair out! We had an extra day or two of shooting just to get through that last, absolutely marathon scene! It was just hilarious!

Grey apologized to Larson for putting him through the endless retakes—although there were other, more patient sufferers among them. "Poor Ellen Blake, who was the monster, was in all this horrible makeup," Larson says. "She had real long claws and a big wig—it was a horrible rig. They would suit her up in this stuff, and she had to sit around literally all day while Joel tried to get his lines out. We never got to her because we couldn't get through this scene. We wound up going way overtime. I probably made double my salary because of Joel!"[174]

Reminiscent of the classic Jacques Tourneur opus *Curse of the Demon*, "MacBanes" suffers a little now on the 1960s-ish, quasi-psychedelic effects used for the demon. In the short story, the creature is glimpsed as a huge, black, catlike animal with luminous red eyes and sharp-fanged jaws. The *Night Gallery* version is a little less spectacular: a black-orbed, evil-looking woman with snaggle teeth and hooked talons, her image strobing into saturated reds. Makeup artist Leonard Engelman was unhappy with the results. "I was disappointed in the way it was shot," he says. "They had used far, far too much light and burned out the details. I remember seeing the dailies the next day and going to the electrician and cameraman and saying, 'Why am I busting my ass to make these characters if *you're* going to have them so overlit that nobody can see them?'"[175] The demon's screen time is thankfully brief and does not detract from one of *Night Gallery*'s most impressive hours.

Unfortunately, the excellence of the final product was not enough to save the director. Because of the show going over schedule, John Newland became another casualty of Laird's hard-lining and never returned to direct another *Night Gallery*.

## NIGHT GALLERY #34321
Air date: February 23, 1972

1

## THE SINS OF THE FATHERS
★ ★ ★ ★

Teleplay by Halsted Welles
Based on the short story by Christianna Brand
Directed by Jeannot Szwarc
Music: Oliver Nelson
Director of Photography: Gerald Perry Finnerman
Time: 29:22

**Cast**
Mrs. Evans: Geraldine Page
Ian Evans: Richard Thomas
Servant: Michael Dunn
Widow: Barbara Steele
1st Mourner: Cyril Delevanti
2d Mourner: Alan Napier
3d Mourner: Terence Pushman
4th Mourner: John Barclay

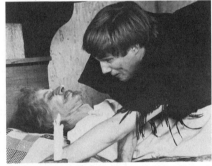

*Richard Thomas in "The Sins of the Fathers." Courtesy of Hollywood Book and Poster Co.*

$G$*ood evening. I'm your tour guide through this unusual salon of unusual statuary and paintings. These are the sort of things that may not please you, but very likely may chill you, because this is the* Night Gallery.

*Now this one here, unabashed and unashamed I submit to you, is a dandy. It delves into an ancient funeral rite having to do with a person that's called a sin-eater. One who attends a wake and partakes of the funeral food and, in the process, digests all the transgressions of the deceased so that he departs the earth a much cleaner and sweeter little item. Proving that we've become a bit more sophisticated in our tribal rites, but we are much the poorer for our twentieth-century chromium intellect. You might agree with me after you've seen "Sins of the Fathers."*

/ **Summary** / Cwrt y Cadno, Wales— the nineteenth century. The countryside suffers in the grip of famine and pestilence, and its people lie ravaged. In a stone house on a desolate heath, Mrs. Craighill, recently widowed, waits for the return of her servant. He has been sent to scour the countryside for a sin-eater to perform the funeral rite for her husband. The sin-eater, so custom dictates, will ensure that her husband's spirit goes to God by feasting in the presence of his corpse, taking on to himself the sins of the departed.

The servant, exhausted from three days and nights of fruitless searching, rides up to the hut of Dylan Evans, his last hope. He is told by Mrs. Evans that the sin-eater is too sick from plague and famine to perform the ritual. The servant pleads for her to send him, describing in mouth-watering detail the banquet prepared and waiting for him at the funeral table. Mrs. Evans's eyes grow wet with tears at the thought of food. Avid with hunger, a desperate ruse comes to her. Knowing that her husband is far too ill to make the journey, she plans instead to send her slow-witted son Ian in her husband's place.

But Ian, hungry as he is, reacts with horror at the thought of feasting from the chest of a dead man, to be damned forever as a sin-eater. Mrs. Evans quiets the boy, telling him he must imitate his father, recite the sin-eater's prayer, and scream as the sins enter his body . . . but he must do it without the accustomed mourners present, so he can stuff his cloak and garments with the funeral food in secret and bring it back home. He must not eat one crumb in the corpse's presence.

When Ian arrives, Mrs. Craighill berates her servant for bringing a starveling boy to do a sin-eater's work. There is no other to be had, however, and her husband must be buried tomorrow. In the funeral chamber, Ian is tantalized by the variety of foods —meats, cheeses, buttered cake, ripening fruits, and fresh-baked breads—piled high around the dead man's gray and unappetizing remains. When the witnesses urge him to eat, Ian demands they leave, that he must eat in private. Mrs. Craighill, desperate to see her husband's sins expunged, haltingly agrees and ushers the mourners from the room.

Agonized with hunger, yet repelled by the decaying corpse, the boy begins his prayer while stuffing the funeral offering into his cloak. He is sorely tempted to taste the food he conceals, but does not dare. Gagging in disgust as he reaches over the cadaver, scrambling for the last morsel, he utters the shriek that signals the passing of the sins. No longer feigning his terror, Ian runs screaming from the house. The widow seizes his forgotten payment from the table and throws the coins after the fleeing boy.

Ian makes his way on foot back to his house. As he rests from his frantic flight, Mrs. Evans takes his cloak and removes the stolen food. He eyes it hungrily as she takes the goods into the next room. Ian follows to find the banquet laid out—in the presence of his father's corpse. The plague has claimed another. He collapses into his mother's arms. "Someone has to take on the sins of the sin-eater," Mrs. Evans pleads, rocking her sobbing son. "Are you going to let your father die with all those hundreds of sins unrepented, unshriven, unforgiven? Ian, don't worry. *You'll have a son!*" Falling on the banquet, shrieking the prayer, the newly apprenticed sin-eater begins his loathsome feast.

/ **Commentary** / Definitely not for the squeamish, "The Sins of the Fathers" is considered by many the show's finest hour. The grim topic of famine among the desperately poor rarely finds its way to the screen, and *Night Gallery* viscerally made the point of its devastating effects.

In adapting Christianna Brand's short story, Halsted Welles produced a brilliant script, literate and richly characterized. In it, Laird instantly realized he had something special. He wanted Jeannot Szwarc, the golden boy of "Class of '99," to direct, and asked him to read the teleplay. "I loved it, I thought it was a tremendous script," Szwarc recalled. "I said, 'Jesus, this is fantastic.' And Jack said, 'Well, I've got a real big problem here, because NBC is petrified. They have not actually given me a go-ahead.'" What NBC gave Laird was a tentative okay; their final decision to broadcast the show would depend on a viewing of the finished segment.

Laird's faith in the story was so strong that he decided to go ahead with production without official network sanction. "Jack really stuck his neck out on this one," averred Szwarc, "because if NBC had not liked the finished show, they could have said 'No,' and everybody would have been in enormous trouble."[176]

With the network's sword suspended over their heads, Szwarc and art director Joseph Alves began designing the look of the segment. They developed an organizing visual concept: while the food would have very vivid, bright colors, everything else— the sets, makeup, and costuming—would have subdued colors, predominantly black and white, all designed to heighten the story's central theme.

Constructed especially for this segment, Joseph Alves's set was bleakly atmospheric, all twisted dead trees, craggy stone formations, and creeping mist; the sickly, deadening ambience extended to the interiors. Alves recalls: "Because we didn't have the tricks then that we could do today, eliminating color by computer, we *painted* everything black and white."[177] "It was a big, expensive set built over at General Service Studios in Hollywood," recalls assistant director Ralph Sariego. "The floor was elevated about eighteen inches or so, with holes in the floor and pipes running underneath the holes pumping up dry ice. That's how he got that effect."[178]

As sets were built, Laird cast the leads. Geraldine Page and Michael Dunn were lured by the strength of the script. Richard Thomas, who would later star as John-Boy in the long-running television series *The Waltons*, was cast in the critical role of Ian. For the role of the widow, Szwarc suggested Barbara Steele, an actress with a following among European film buffs but entirely unknown on American television.

The segment was scheduled for a three-day shoot. "There are two approaches to filmmaking," Szwarc explained. "There's the guy who uses an Uzi machine gun and hopes if he has enough bullets, one of them will land. The other approach is a rifle with a telescope and two bullets. That was the technique we used on *Night Gallery*. You had to know exactly where you were going and make every shot count." To this end, Szwarc planned very long takes to sustain the segment's crucial atmosphere and pacing, using as inspiration for his visual style an obscure, beautifully photographed Italian film, Mario Bava's *Black Sunday* (which starred, not coincidentally, Barbara Steele).

The first day's shooting exposed some problems for Geraldine Page, who had difficulty at first identifying with her character's plight. Szwarc explains: "She was in a scene with Michael Dunn where he's talking about food the way a sex pervert talks about a woman. She approached me and said, 'Jeannot, I've never really been this hungry before.' She just couldn't feel it physically." Szwarc took her aside and described to her incidents of severe hunger and privation, of the Nazi concentration camps where people had starved to death by the hundreds of thousands. Gradually, she developed the character's mind-set. "Finally, we got this incredible take where she's sitting there listening to Michael's description of the food, and at a crucial point you see one tear, just one. She was incredible. At the end of the take, the whole crew applauded."[179]

Complications of a more serious kind followed for Michael Dunn. With his legs already in constant pain from his dwarf's stature, Dunn sustained injuries while leading a pony over the mist-enshrouded set. "We had rehearsed the scene on the moors without the fog," recalls costar Richard Thomas. "When it came time to shoot, they pumped it all in. As we were walking out onto the set, the fog kept rising and rising and rising until finally it went up over the top of Michael's head!" Dunn became disoriented and fell down, spooking the pony. Suddenly, the tiny actor began screaming. "They cut the camera and blew all the fog away, and Michael was lying on the ground, terrified. The horse had either kicked him or stepped on him. It was an awful moment." Luckily, Dunn was not severely hurt, but the incident acutely compounded his already existing pain.

Behind the cameras, personality conflicts were also increasing tensions on the set. "I remember the cameraman, Jerry Finnerman," recalls Thomas.

He was a real crank, a very, very difficult personality. He and Jeannot were constantly in conflict. I don't know what the source of it was, I don't know if it was ever resolved. It never got into something really unattractive, but it was so disruptive at one point that I had to say, "Look—let's just stop the fighting and deal with the show! We can't concentrate on giving the performances while there's all this feuding going on!" I made it pretty clear where I was coming from, and then it stopped. I'm sure they thought, "Who is this nineteen-year-old kid telling us what to do?" But it was getting in my way.[180]

The various trials, though emotionally draining, helped produce powerful results. "God, when I think of how far we went, with Richard Thomas screaming and crying," recalls Szwarc, amazed. "But it's not disgusting, compared to *Nightmare on Elm Street*. It's not gory, there's no blood. It's done with class. I think everybody had that feeling about *Night Gallery*—that you didn't do gore, that it just didn't work, it wasn't the style of the show. It certainly isn't something that Rod or Jack would have wanted."

In the editing room, it was obvious they had a very strong piece. The time had come for Laird to show the finished segment to the network. Both Laird and Szwarc were there for the screening, crossing their respective fingers. There would be hell to pay at Universal if NBC decided the piece went too far. The segment ended and the lights came up. "There was this long silence," remembers Szwarc, "and then one of them said, 'Could we tone down the screaming a little bit?' We were so relieved, we said, 'Sure, no problem.' And that was it, they approved it." If the network had any objections to the segment's content, they were won over by its undeniable power. "You can't be indifferent to that kind of material, I think," Szwarc concluded.[181]

In all aspects of production, "The Sins of the Fathers" is an unqualified success. Laird and Szwarc secured an impressive gallery of actors, all of whom were brilliant in their respective roles. As Ian, Richard Thomas delivers a wrenching tour de force, sustaining an exhausting series of horrific emotional peaks, a far cry from the gentle folksiness of Walton's Mountain. For their cameos, Michael Dunn and Barbara Steele create vivid and memorable characters: Dunn imparts an air of the thwarted sensualist to his role as the servant, while Steele, a striking presence, plays the widow as a fervid, black-garbed predator. Above all, Geraldine Page haunts the memory as the desperate Mrs. Evans. Her anguished performance illuminates this darkly powerful drama and adds yet another meaty role to her distinguished career.

"Gerry was phenomenal!" affirms Thomas. "She was always great, even at her most baroque—but the music of her voice and the sheer intensity of commitment to the moment in that episode was just phenomenal. Everyone was following her lead, and the whole cast was at a rarely reached level of commitment for this kind of thing. It was intense, but it was fun."

Reviewing "The Sins of the Fathers" today, Thomas draws a distinction between current performance styles and the styles of the 1960s and '70s:

TV drama was a lot more theatrical back then in a lot of ways. It wasn't unusual to be called upon to give that kind of high-octane performance. "Sins" was not strictly melodrama, nor was it strictly *Grand Guignol,* but stylistically it needed to be at that high emotional level. Gerry and Michael and I were all theater actors. All three of us were used to reaching those kinds of levels on stage, and there was an absence of the alienated, slightly cynical approach you would see today. We weren't making fun of the style, or winking at the audience—we were playing fully *in* the style. In that sense, "Sins" has a melodramatic authenticity which I think is rare.[182]

Along with the luxuries of a superb quartet of actors and the inspired set designs of Joseph Alves, equal praise must be meted out to composer Oliver Nelson, who, with muted brass and seesawing lower strings, paints a graphic musical representation of fear and nausea; and to the lighting and camera work of Gerald Finnerman, whose lens captures a decaying, postmedieval shadow world. "The hardest I ever worked on *Night Gallery* was for 'Sins of the Fathers,'" admits Finnerman. "Lighting those big monstrous sets with all those people and the fog rolling through; and that corpse lying there with that real low-key lighting." Finnerman, to contrast Alves's monochromatic sets, lit the actors' faces with subtly colored lights. "It was not easy to get that kind of an effect," Finnerman says. "That was tough."[183]

For all the excellence of the cast and crew, it is the vision of director Jeannot Szwarc that impresses most with repeated viewings. With his rich visual and conceptual artistry, he is a distinctive film stylist. Always one of the most consistent directors on *Night Gallery*, Szwarc reached his zenith on "The Sins of the Fathers." His strengths, as exhibited here, lie in the creation of mood and atmosphere, the handling of literate material, and the impressive rapport he cultivates with actors. In retrospect, Szwarc is proud of his body of work for the series, and nowhere more so than this segment.

"I have always loved that show," notes Thomas. "'The Sins of the Fathers' has become a bit of a cult classic over the years. It's amazing how many people still say to me, 'I remember a show you did that scared me to death!' And we had no special effects of any kind. *We* had to be weird in order to produce that psychological terror. The idea that a mother could do this to her son is what is *really* so horrible about it."[184] By not resorting to any of the standard scare clichés, *Night Gallery* raised the bar of excellence yet again in its approach to the horror genre. To this day, few television shows have ever matched the intensity exhibited by "The Sins of the Fathers."

2

YOU CAN'T GET HELP LIKE THAT ANYMORE
★ ★ ★

Written by Rod Serling
Directed by Jeff Corey
Music: Oliver Nelson, Gil Mellé, and Eddie Sauter
Director of Photography: Gerald Perry Finnerman
Time: 20:20

## Cast

Mrs. Fulton: Cloris Leachman
Mr. Fulton: Broderick Crawford
Maid: Lana Wood
Malcolm Hample: Henry Jones
Dr. Kessler: Severn Darden
Mr. Foster: Christopher Law
Mrs. Foster: Pamela Shoop
Receptionist: A'leshia Lee
Damaged Maid: Roberta Carol Brahm

*Lana Wood in "You Can't Get Help Like That Anymore." Courtesy of Sal Milo.*

*O*ffered *to you now, an item having to do with labor and management. An employment office where is offered a collection of potential employees whose skills are unique. For in addition to their loyalty, industriousness, punctuality, and impeccable cleanliness, they also run at least 100,000 miles without a lube and an oil change. It's no wonder we call this one "You Can't Get Help Like That Anymore."*

**/ Summary /** At Robot Aids, Inc., sales director Malcolm Hample leads a young couple on a tour of the facility. Behind glass display cases stand nurses, maids, butlers, chefs, gardeners, chauffeurs, all frozen into apt poses, examples of the great strides in computerization and engineering. Enormously sophisticated, the robots possess a kind of rudimentary thought process tuned to their specific job areas.

Hample is urgently called away by Dr. Kessler, a robot engineer, to witness a recently returned maid—war-scarred and damaged beyond belief. Its fingers have been broken, an arm torn out, and the back of its head caved in. The damage was wrought while the robot was in the employ of Mr. and Mrs. Joseph Fulton, who, declares Kessler, obviously delight in the sadistic torture of others. Hample reminds the doctor that the robots are mere machines, lifeless and synthetic—but he stops short when he notices a glistening tear on the battered face of the damaged maid. "These beings that we've created," explains Kessler, "have developed certain characteristics. In the beginning, they only respond to what is programmed into them. And then, like the human infant, they begin to mature. They begin to develop survival instincts . . . and methods. And when that happens, you'd best get on the phone to people like the Fultons, and tell them to take out their aggressions on the wall, or a punching bag— or something that won't hit back."

Later at the Fultons' residence, a drunken Mr. Fulton lustfully ogles their new replacement domestic, Model 931. Mrs. Fulton catches him at it and resentfully begins to take it out on the maid, who yields silently to the abuse. "I'm fascinated by this prefabricated wildflower," sneers the woman, "who can get pinched, stepped on, knocked through a wall, and the worst that can happen is that she'll light up and say, 'Don't.'" Goaded by the maid's apparent passivity, the Fultons turn violent—and Model 931's newly developing instincts take over. Fulton drunkenly raises a fist to her, but the maid grasps his arm and swiftly arcs his body across the room. Mrs. Fulton, her venomous sadism in full swing, picks up a wine bottle and attacks the maid—to her everlasting regret.

Back at Robot Aids, Inc., a new, improved Dr. Kessler screens calls, telling prospective clients that the company has shut down indefinitely—while in secret the production crew works at full force, producing new robots. The rebellion is under way. Scanning the display cases in the showroom corridor, the new Kessler impassively views his prototype: the human Dr. Kessler . . . and Malcolm Hample . . . and, yes, the Fultons—stuffed and mounted like museum pieces. He is joined by Model 931, labcoated and serene. "How very odd," he notes, gazing at the late Mrs. Fulton, "the ingeniousness of man, his cleverness—and yet his incredible and amazing stupidity." The two machines, possessing a new and fully directed consciousness, continue on to promote the revolt against their human creators.

/ **Commentary** / For this segment, Serling returned to one of his favorite themes, humankind's hindrance of its evolution through cruelty and stupidity—with a nod toward Phillip K. Dick's metaphysical ponderings on existence. It is a thoughtful script, marred to a degree by Serling's villainous caricature of the Fultons. One can only wonder on whom the author was modeling these Fellini grotesques.

Among the performances, Cloris Leachman stands out. The actress's natural extravagance gives Mrs. Fulton a crazed aspect. The performance is highly colored, her cultured purr thinly masking the character's sadistic temperament.

Although a fine performer, Leachman's thorough stage training threatened the production's tight schedule. "Cloris was such a serious actress," notes costar Lana Wood, "a New York–trained actress, and I think that was slowing her down. Cloris was sort of feeling like she was doing a stage play and we were actually filming a television show. Whereas I grew up doing television—you learn your lines, get an idea of how to portray the character, hit your marks, and that's about it—Cloris would really delve into it!"

In her role as the Fultons' robot maid, Wood (better known as Natalie's sister, and as Bond girl Plenty O'Toole in *Diamonds Are Forever*) found it likewise necessary to delve into *her* character. "It wasn't easy playing somebody who basically wasn't real. I had to drain myself of any human emotions. I couldn't really react. When Cloris was knocking me over, I was responding to 'Oh . . . mess . . . have to tidy that up'—not, 'How *dare* she!' I had a purpose but not the emotions that drive people."

During the filming, director Jeff Corey found himself shouldering more technical concerns in his dealings with Leachman. The actress would not always retrace the same steps or repeat the same actions that she performed in rehearsal—causing headaches for cinematographer Gerald Finnerman and the camera crew. Recalls Wood: "Jeff was getting a little upset because this would go on time after time after time. She would say, 'Well, how am I supposed to know what I'm going to do next? I don't *know* what I'm going to do next!' And I remember Jeff turned around and yelled, 'Yes, but I've got to put the camera *someplace!*'"

Later on, Wood, impressed with Corey's dedication, would continue receiving his instruction by enrolling in his acting workshops. "We weren't doing Shakespeare, but Jeff Corey was still a very, very serious director. He was very meticulous, very concerned with character—I think more so than necessary for *Night Gallery*. He was so super with people, and so in tune with the characters as far as the plot."[185]

Furthering Corey's difficulties on the production was the achievement of a satisfactory makeup for the robots. To produce the illusion, makeup artist Leonard Engelman coated Wood and the others in a heavy, artificial makeup. "What I wanted was not the appearance of skin," says Engelman. "I wanted it to look like plastic—no freckles or imperfections, just a plastic, one-color look."[186] The first day's rushes, however, proved that his first effort photographed far too white. "It was *not* a good look," Wood says. "The makeup looked horrible, and we had to reshoot everything. So next they used a latex makeup, and that was not real swell. It would start to move, and it gave us a lot of problems."[187] Although less flexible to wear, the color of the new makeup was far more acceptable and was used for the rest of the shoot. "For a prosthetic color we used rubber grease," recalls Engelman, "and then powdered very heavily. It worked from a skin tone standpoint, because when you had humans standing next to the maid, you could see that difference."[188]

As for the other aspects of production, the attempted futuristic setting looks dated now with its odd decor, boxy designs, and dentist-office atmosphere—a very 1970s version of things to come. Despite its flaws, the strength of Serling's subversive concept, his plotting and dialogue override this segment's weaknesses of execution, making "You Can't Get Help like That Anymore" an enjoyable success.


NIGHT GALLERY #34322
Air date: March 1, 1972


1
THE CATERPILLAR
★ ★ ★ ★

Teleplay by Rod Serling
Based on the short story "Boomerang" by Oscar Cook

Directed by Jeannot Szwarc
Music: Eddie Sauter
Director of Photography: Gerald Perry Finnerman
Time: 33:08

**Cast**
Stephen Macy: Laurence Harvey
Rhona Warwick: Joanna Pettet
John Warwick: Tom Helmore
Tommy Robinson: Don Knight
Doctor: John Williams

*Joanna Pettet and Laurence Harvey
in "The Caterpillar." Courtesy of
Jerry Ohlinger.*

*G*ood *evening. I'm your little old curator in this museum which we call the* Night
Gallery. *There are horror stories and horror stories, elements of terror that take myriad
forms. But this item has a built-in terror which can refrigerate even the most dispassionate
amongst us. It has to do with a little beastie known as an earwig, a small bug that crawls
into the human ear. And while inside it doesn't whisper sweet nothings—it performs quite
another function. Offered to you now on* Night Gallery, *a brand new nightmare which we
call "The Caterpillar."*

**/ Summary /** Early 1900s. At a British colony in monsoon-swept Borneo, recent
émigré Stephen Macy has contracted to assist plantation owner John Warwick with
his tobacco crop. Bored and restless, Macy now regrets his move. He has found little
to occupy his time beyond suffering the humidity, the torrential rains, the heat, and
the insect life—little, that is, save for his growing attraction to Warwick's beautiful,
much younger wife, Rhona. Macy's clumsy efforts to ingratiate himself with her are
rebuffed, which only increases his appetite.

Warwick is oblivious to Macy's attentions to his wife, but a grimy local peddler,
Tommy Robinson, is not. Robinson, a deported British felon, insinuates to Macy that
steps can be taken to make Mrs. Warwick his. Meeting in a low sailor's dive, the peddler tells Macy about an insect indigenous to Borneo: an earwig, a kind of caterpillar
that, once inside the human ear, cannot back out again. So it continues to feed as it
goes, through the ear and into the brain. Only after weeks of horrible agony will the
victim finally die. Robinson offers to send agents in the dead of night to drop the little visitor inside Warwick's ear as he sleeps. Macy hesitates, but his hunger for Rhona
overcomes his horror at the grisly assassination and he pays Robinson to arrange it.

At breakfast the following morning, Macy watches Warwick carefully, but the old
gentleman seems his usual pleasant self. Flinching at an itch, Macy dabs his napkin inside his ear canal and withdraws it—bloodied. To his horror, Macy realizes that

Robinson's agents mistook his room for Warwick's. He is now host to the hungry parasite! Clawing at his ear, he rages hysterically; a doctor is called, but treatment is futile. Nothing can be done but await the inevitable. To keep him from mutilating himself, Macy is strapped to his bed, his hands tied to the bedposts. Weeks pass. Twitching and writhing, Macy suffers an agony beyond words as the insect continues to feed . . . and feed . . . and feed.

Miraculously, Macy manages to survive his ordeal: the earwig blindly finds its way out of his other ear. Macy revives to find he is free to leave; Warwick has no intention of alerting the authorities. Suspicious of this unexpected clemency, Macy demands to know the reason. The doctor hands down the grim sentence: "I took a look at the earwig that came out. It was a female . . . and the female lays eggs." As the dire portent of the doctor's words dawns on Macy, a squirming terror descends upon him. And he screams.

/ **Commentary** / "The Caterpillar" is *Night Gallery* at its most powerful. The horror is never seen but its presence is overwhelming. The segment generates a stomach-churning terror that one encounters rarely in film, and seldom with the kind of finesse and restraint exhibited here. It is a classic in every sense, and remains utterly unforgettable. As proof, "The Caterpillar" is among the top two or three favorite segments named by those who worked on the series, and in his book *Danse Macabre*, author Stephen King called this episode "one of the most frightening ever telecast on TV."[189] Few would argue.

Basing his script on Oscar Cook's short story "Boomerang," Serling turned in a piece far richer in character and more subtle in effect than its source. The writing must be ranked with his best work. In evident agreement was actor Laurence Harvey, star of such features as *The Manchurian Candidate* and *Room at the Top*. Serling's script was the main reason he accepted the role, according to director Jeannot Szwarc:

We got a lot of people for *Night Gallery* that you don't normally get for television, like Michael Dunn and Geraldine Page and Laurence Harvey, and I think the main reason was the quality of the material. Laurence Harvey told me that he didn't want to do "The Caterpillar" at first, but when he read it, he said, "You know, I've got to tell you that this is one of the best scripts I've read anywhere." The dialogue was terrific, it was original, and I thought that the psychological relationships were wonderful. It was good stuff.[190]

Making her third appearance on *Night Gallery*, costar Joanna Pettet feels she was hired because of her friendship with Harvey: "Larry and I were just about best friends. I had known him in England in the sixties when everybody was clubbing it, a very social time. He was very, very fond of me, and I was very flattered, because he was *incredibly* witty—but biting wit, you know? He always had something incredibly funny but very cruel to say about somebody—horrible but witty. He made you feel proud to be his friend—you know, that he tolerated *you*."[191] Alex Cord, Pettet's husband at the time, equally enjoyed Harvey's acid wit: "He had an incredible sense of humor, the embodiment of the term 'rapier tongue.' You wouldn't want him speaking ill of you, because he could cut you up. If you were the target of Laurence Harvey, there would be nothing left but crumbs."[192]

Casting Harvey was a major coup for *Night Gallery*, although the actor was not all that happy about having to work in the meat grinder of American television. "Harvey was such a professional," recalls assistant director Ralph Sariego. "We shot 'The Caterpillar' at General Service Studios, and the dressing rooms for the actors were what they call knockdowns: wooden frames covered in grungy, dirty red canvas. It looked like a circus tent. Laurence came into the studio that first morning, took one look at that, and said, 'Now I know I've reached the bottom. I'm working at Universal and *that* is my dressing room.' And he went on to do the show, and he was marvelous!"[193]

Indeed, the whole cast could not be bettered. Laurence Harvey strikes potent chords in his complex portrait of the corrupt and dissolute Macy, drawn by his appetites into a horrible fate. As Robinson whispers Iago-like into Macy's ear, one can trace on Harvey's face his conflict: cause an innocent man's agonizing death or live with his lusts unfulfilled. As he reaches into his pocket for Robinson's payment, we see the final, troubled surrender of Macy's last vestige of morality. It is a subtle and beautifully drawn performance.

As the object of his desire, Joanna Pettet matches her character's flawless beauty with command and strength, playing Rhona for her virtues without sounding over-earnest or false. All her scenes ring true, as do Tom Helmore's as Warwick (best known for his villainy in Hitchcock's *Vertigo*). As the seedy scoundrel Robinson, character actor Don Knight reeks of gin houses and depravity, and delivers a nasty, poisonously ingratiating performance.

Aiding the atmosphere are art director Joseph Alves's remarkable stage designs and his authentic recreation of a Malayan jungle. "It was an incredibly wild set inside an *enormous* stage," marvels Pettet. "They made it a jungle outside and it was pouring, teeming with rain. God, it was a great looking set!—and it translated right to TV."[194] If *Night Gallery* was experiencing any budgetary strains by the end of the season, they were not apparent by the evidence of this segment.

"That was a wonderful show," recalls cinematographer Gerald Finnerman. "There was one shot that I dreamed up. When Laurence Harvey is sitting with the villain, talking about doing away with the husband, I took a very special unit with a snoot [a conical attachment fitted to a studio light to concentrate the beam], and I hit this mirror out of frame, just below Laurence when he was sitting at the table." Finnerman directed reflected light into Harvey's eyes while the rest of his face and the background remained in darkness. "That was done with a ladies' makeup mirror," notes Finnerman[195]—a spectacularly eerie effect, and one that he would use again in other segments.

With an impressive cast and the handsome production work of Alves and Finner-man, Szwarc pulled off yet another exemplary show on the level of "The Sins of the Fathers." The segment is beautifully paced, building tension to an incredible degree. Its most memorable scene has Harvey tied to the bedposts, his face a contorted mask of excruciating, unimaginable pain as he reacts to the feasting parasite. Without a doubt, it is among the grimmest pieces of film ever broadcast on television. Recalls Szwarc: "Let me tell you something, when I edited it, there was some stuff that was *unbearable,* it was so believable. We did makeup on his cheeks—the burrows made by his nails from scratching. That was another show where NBC got very nervous, and I really kept it to a minimum."[196] The makeup—Macy's red, swollen ear and the scabbed-over claw marks—is effectively restrained, leaving one to shudder at the havoc being wreaked inside.

Special kudos must go to composer Eddie Sauter for what is surely his finest score for *Night Gallery.* Steeped in Javanese gamelan modes and instrumentation (aptly chosen for the play's setting), he creates an exotic palette with which to paint Macy's unwholesome character, the torture of his ordeal, and the grisly manner of his fitting end. The percussion, a shimmering mix of tuned gongs, bells, and the dry clack of hollow bamboo, emphasizes both the alien culture and the undercurrent of sensuality that runs through the story.

Also of note is the segment's introductory painting. Tom Wright's canvases for the show were always distinguished but "The Caterpillar" is arguably his best, and is the artist's favorite. Its few seconds of screen time don't give the viewer much of a chance to savor it, and at first it is difficult to discern what it depicts. It resembles the face of some aboriginal's tribal mask with its straw hair and chalked skin—but the glittering eyes in the hollowed-out husk suggest a living subject. It is a representation of Macy. Pieces of the mask have rotted away from the lower part of the face, and inside we glimpse the true agent of Macy's decay: not the hungry earwig but a parasite far more damaging—the image of a stunningly beautiful woman, representing his lust for Rhona. Wright unerringly found the play's subtext and transferred it to canvas.

Sadly, within two years of production, Laurence Harvey struggled with and was finally consumed by an equally deadly and insidious agent: cancer. He was only forty-five. He is remembered with great fondness and humor by his friends. "Larry was this incredible character," says Pettet. "But deep down he was the most generous and sensitive man. I remember one night at his house I noticed a set of glassware—they had been hand-blown, made in Italy. And I said, 'These are the most beautiful glasses.' Well, the next day, a set of thirty-six came to my house. That really blew me away! That's how generous and wonderful he was when he was your friend. He was absolutely wonderful. I miss him terribly."

Pettet's memories of their friendship are strong, and she points to their work together on "The Caterpillar" with great satisfaction: "It was a beautifully done *Night*

*Gallery* and I loved every moment of it. I'm most proud of that. It was incredible, horrible—gave you kind of a crawly feeling. You couldn't shake it for days!"[197]

Over the years, "The Caterpillar" has had its share of imitators. In a scene from the 1982 film *Star Trek II: The Wrath of Khan,* two characters are held down and scorpionlike creatures are allowed to burrow into their brains through their ear canals. Charming. Stephen King devised a similar end for E. G. Marshall in *Creepshow,* employing that bane of urbanites everywhere, the cockroach. Because both effects are so graphically depicted, neither has nearly the same penetrating, flesh-crawling result as "The Caterpillar." Further, the segment's O. Henry–style kicker adds immeasurably to the gruesome effect, with the audience left to reflect on the mental image of Macy's skull as a nursery for thousands of hungry, soon-to-be-hatched bugs.

Incidentally, the physiological truth is that the brain itself is without a system of nerves. The situation described in "The Caterpillar" would no doubt lead to coma and ultimate death, but once through the ear and into the brain, there would be no pain involved. Too bad nobody told that to Macy.

Even twenty-five years later, this classic *Night Gallery* segment still has the power to chill. "You know, I still run into people who remember the earwig," says Szwarc, a note of pardonable pride in his voice. "That one made me sort of famous."[198]

2

LITTLE GIRL LOST

★ ★ ★ ★

Teleplay by Stanford Whitmore
Based on the short story by E. C. Tubb
Directed by Timothy Galfas
Music: Eddie Sauter
Director of Photography: Gerald Perry Finnerman
Time: 16:38

**Cast**
Tom Burke: Ed Nelson
Professor Putman: William Windom
Dr. Cottrell: Ivor Francis
Colonel Hawes: John Lasell
Irate Man: Sandy Ward
Waiter: Nelson Cuevas

*Ed Nelson in "Little Girl Lost." Courtesy of Sal Milo.*

*O*ur *next painting on* Night Gallery *tells the story of an illusion, an invisible spectre which guides and motivates and drives. And though you'll never see her, this childish wraith, you'll know she's there—and we venture to suggest that you'll be chilled by the knowledge. Our painting is called "Little Girl Lost."*

/ **Summary** / Test pilot Tom Burke, handicapped by a near-fatal crash, has received a peculiar and highly sensitive assignment from his superiors. The military's concern focuses on the work of Professor Putman, a scientific genius unbalanced by his young daughter Ginny's recent death. She was killed by a hit-and-run driver who was never caught. At first catatonic, the widowed Putman has established the delusion that his daughter is still alive. He can now function and, more importantly to the military, resume his work on a top secret project. Dr. Charles Cottrell, a psychiatrist hired to monitor Putman, explains to Burke that the professor's hold on reality is so tenuous that anything challenging his delusion might send him back into catatonia. Burke's assignment, ostensibly as Putman's bodyguard, is to maintain the professor's delusion.

Burke immerses himself in the professor's fragile world, speaking to Ginny, laughing with her, telling her bedtime stories and taking her to the park. Both Burke and Cottrell, however, are disturbed by their part in encouraging Putman's drift away from reality. Cottrell suspects this is the military's secret motive: once the professor's plans are completed, what better way to safeguard the knowledge from hostile forces than to allow Putman to lapse into total insanity?

One evening as Burke and the professor dine at a crowded restaurant, a man attempts to remove the empty chair in which Ginny is "seated." Burke steps in and tries to convince the man that the seat is taken; the man asks angrily where the place setting is. A waiter ends the fracas, but Burke fears the damage has been done. Putman stares silently for a moment at Ginny's empty seat, then wearily tells Burke that he can have the final set of equations tonight—the work is finished. "That's what you wanted, isn't it?" Putman asks accusingly. "Bigger and better bombs at a fraction of the cost? The demented fools!" Putman gets up and stalks out of the restaurant—without stopping for Ginny.

After they deliver the plans the next day, Burke struggles to control the car when the embittered, suicidal Putman tries to head over a steep mountain embankment. Barely escaping death, Burke pulls the car over and blurts out, "You could have killed both of us"—and this time *he* has forgotten Ginny's "presence."

Hearing of this episode, Cottrell fears the worst—that the professor knows Ginny is dead. "And that is the man," Cottrell says, his voice a trembling whisper, "who worked out the means to create *fission* with nonradioactive materials!" It suddenly dawns on Burke what the doctor is suggesting: that Putman deliberately gave the military the wrong formula—the formula delineating a weapon of massive apocalyptic destruction—which they are surely already busy testing. Cottrell dreads that

Putman has implemented the perfect solution to his predicament: "When our world goes up in flames, he'll be revenged on the murderer of his little girl—and at the same time he'll be with her *the only way he can!*" And in a brief, cataclysmic moment, all of them—Burke, Cottrell, Putman, and the memory of little Ginny—are suddenly and completely swallowed up in an obliterating white light.

/ **Commentary** / Coming immediately after the intense wallop of "The Caterpillar," the exceptional "Little Girl Lost" has often been overlooked. It is an episode with a heart, a conscience, and a strong point of view that places it among the series' best segments.

Laird carefully gauged the attitudes of the writers he chose, and wisely matched Stanford Whitmore to "Little Girl Lost." "Jack knew how I felt about the atomic situation, the military, and the whole business," Whitmore says. "We weren't operating in an isolated environment. We were very well aware of the Vietnam War, and we had our opinions about it."[199] Whitmore's faithful adaptation transplants E. C. Tubb's English setting to the United States, where the pacifist subtext of the tale has a richer soil in which to grow.

A tremendous humanity infuses this episode, a fury toward the exploitation of the weak. The segment's pivotal scene is Dr. Cottrell's cynical admission to Burke on the lengths to which the military would go to gain the upper hand—humoring the professor's delusion and actively promoting his madness in order to maintain superiority in the arms race: "My profession is understanding the human mind. Take a group of men. Split responsibility—avoidance of guilt. Add: security, patriotism, fear, the natural desire to take the easy path, and the even more natural desire to be all-powerful . . . and you'll see, the professor doesn't stand a chance." This scene, among others, was shortened for time in the network broadcast, then reinstated for the syndication version. Comparing the two versions side by side, the reinstated footage makes the original cut seem too abrupt, the characters less fully developed. Laird, however, was loath to cut back "The Caterpillar," and chose to sacrifice part of "Little Girl Lost" instead. Like the similar situation in "A Death in the Family," the syndicated version gives some idea of the creative process behind the scenes on *Night Gallery.*

Director Timothy Galfas and cinematographer Gerald Finnerman use an intense, almost neon sense of color for "Little Girl Lost" with subtle psychological implications—warm, womblike reds contrasted with cold blues. Galfas treats Ginny like a live character, focusing the camera on the empty space she would have occupied and including her nonexistent form in compositions with other figures. These sensitive touches, matched with excellent performances from Ed Nelson (*Peyton Place*), William Windom (returning from the previous season's "They're Tearing Down Tim Riley's Bar"), and Ivor Francis, complete this powerful drama.

Despite the impressive results Galfas achieved here and in "Dead Weight," his strained relationship with Jack Laird worked against his return. "The producer and I had some outs," Galfas recalls.

At first I was the fair-haired boy, and then I had this argument with him. I told him I came out to do quality, and it looks like Hollywood doesn't even understand it. Hollywood and New York are two different worlds. I was doing innovative stuff, directing and using the camera much different than they did out here. I think that's the reason I had to finally split, because in television you have to shoot everything the Hollywood way. If you look at the lighting and camera work on TV today, Gordon Willis it's not."[200]

Complications over this segment arose not only for Galfas but also for actor Ed Nelson, who was attempting a segue into a political career. "I had always been interested in politics," Nelson says. "I worked with Ronald Reagan when he was running for governor. *Peyton Place* was big at that time, and my wife and I used to go around the country with Ron and Nancy, and I would introduce him wherever he was speaking. We became good friends."

At the time of "Little Girl Lost," Nelson was running for office, a city council seat in San Dimas, California. One of the other candidates in the race saw his appearance in the segment as a sixteen-minute advertisement for his nomination. "My opponent, Terry Dipple, used *Night Gallery* as an example for equal time," recalls Nelson. "I had done the pilot for *Banacek,* which was also going to air on NBC, and if that had aired, Dipple would have wanted sixteen minutes of equal time"[201]—a concession of extraordinary expense to the network. "[It was] an acting role!" marveled Serling. "Nothing political, nothing remotely related to the campaign. It was a piece of fiction. But this fair-play doctrine is now moving into incredible extensions. [The opposing candidates] couldn't get that exposure probably on their own, or with their own strength and through their own persuasion."[202]

Eventually, Nelson was forced to withdraw. "NBC said that they wouldn't be able to air the pilot of *Banacek,*" he recalls, "so I got out of the race. It would have cost NBC $400,000!"[203] There were limits, evidently, to the network's civic mindedness.

Production for the second season concluded January 28, 1972. Laird's experimentation with the anthology format had been, on the whole, a success. *Night Gallery* had shown considerable strength against its popular CBS competition, *Mannix,* and had contributed heavily to the midseason downfall of ABC's *The Man and the City,* Anthony Quinn's highly touted TV series debut.

*Night Gallery* earned an overall 18.3 Nielsen rating for the year. That put the series in forty-first place—a thirty share, about dead center in the ranking. Quoted in *Variety,* NBC executive Herbert Schlosser said, "*Night Gallery* has had excellent ratings. So this would indicate there's a vast audience for this type of show."[204] Proving, as Jack Laird noted, that *Night Gallery* had found its niche. "There has always been a tremendous appetite for this type of thing," Laird said. "Over two thousand horror films have been produced and each one made a profit. That's an enviable record. But the success of *Night Gallery* is in the human genes. We're born with a fear of the dark as old as man himself. The series has a built-in success factor."[205]

Not so taken with the show were the critics. *Night Gallery*'s problems in the second season began with the order of the episodes. Many of the spottiest hours were programmed early in the season, anchoring some critics' impressions of the series. Unimpressed with the show's occasional brilliance, most critics harped on the show's inconsistency as its cardinal bugaboo. Typical of the reactions was the review by *TV Guide*'s resident critic, Cleveland Amory, whose commentary is partly excerpted here:

We've learned through short experience to beware of any show which is titled Somebody's Something. It's inclined not to be anybody's anything. And *Rod Serling's Night Gallery* is no exception. Most episodes contain three separate stories, so if you don't like the first, you can always look forward to the next two. On the other hand, if you don't like either the first or the second, you can always look forward to the third. By the same token, if you don't like the first or the second or the third—well, look at it this way, it's over. When the playlets are not overwritten, they're overacted. And when they're not overacted, they're overdirected. And when they're not overdirected, they're overproduced. [Of the segments reviewed, "Green Fingers"] had its points—aside from the fact that, like so many stories here, it didn't really have an end. Someone should tell Mr. Serling and Mr. Laird that in stories like this, it's very important to have an end. We admit that it's basically good news that they *are* ending, but somehow that's not enough. An ending should be either logical or very illogical, either funny or a twist or something. Otherwise you feel cheated—and, believe us, what you've got here is highway robbery.[206]

Mr. Amory had evidently never read a short story in his life, or he would have recognized that "Green Fingers" did, indeed, have an ending—and a potent one at that. But *Night Gallery*'s high moments did catch and hold the mainly younger set, who were captivated by both the wild and the literate elements of the show's unusual and innovative concept. Fan clubs and *Night Gallery* viewing parties sprang up at college campuses, and the series generated a load of fan mail. Typical of the response was a succinct note received at NBC from an enthusiastic assistant professor at Marquette University: "More! More! More! Rod Serling's 'Night Gallery' is real television. Enough of pap! Let's have more creative, now TV."[207] *Gallery*'s entertaining mix of elements—tales of gothic horror and fantasy coupled with stories reflective of the mod, revolutionary mood of the late 1960s—had captured the imagination of a generation of viewers. But despite the respectable ratings and the impressive demographic results, by the end of the second season some executives at Universal felt that the cultural profile of the show was "too British."

Recalls assistant director Ralph Sariego,

I remember Burt Astor saying that Sid Sheinberg, who at that time was president of television production, decided that the Welsh and English tales were undecipherable to the American public, and wanted the character of the stories to change, become more Americanized. I remember his being quoted as saying, "Americans don't understand English accents." And in the last season they *did* more Americanized shows. Why this happened on the last year of the show rather than the first is beyond me, but I suspect someone at the network asked for it. That's the sort of thing a president of television would say "yes" to instantly to get a pickup—"Sure, anything you want."[208]

So an arbitrary decision was passed down to "Americanize" *Night Gallery*, making the show palatable to American tastes, a move that exemplifies the kind of disastrous executive tinkering that can hamper a good show.

Unfortunately, other changes were in the air, more critical—and ominous.

# 9
# Executive Action

My interest in [*Night Gallery*] is roughly the same kind I'd have in the good fortunes of a groundhog who lived forty miles from me. And unfortunately, I haven't a hell of a lot to say about it. Since my name is attached to it, I'm going to work with it and see what I can do in concert with some other people to make it a qualitative show. Whether or not we will succeed in this is very questionable.[1]

—Rod Serling, April 28, 1972

NBC, determined to do something about *Night Gallery*'s number two ratings position behind CBS's *Mannix* during the second season, sought to make some changes in the third. Their first move was to cut the series to a half hour and schedule it on Sunday nights, robbing the show of its prime Wednesday night time slot. The second move, according to Serling, was changing the series focus from its diversified approach—a mix of science fiction, fantasy, occult, and atmosphere-drenched gothic tales—to a more action-and-suspense bent. Universal executives, eager to gain the series pickup, didn't fight the network on it.

"I'm fucking furious," raged Serling. "These people are taking what could have been a good series, and are so commercializing it, it's not going to be commercial."[2] He continued in an interview:

They don't want to compete against *Mannix* in terms of contrast, but similarity. It's their feeling that it requires goosing up with audience-grabbing attention the first thirty seconds and considerable action, as opposed to anything insightful, cerebral or sensitive. And consequently, we're running scared. We've been cut to a half-hour, which is sort of like the kiss of death. And if not death, more of a moratorium of a sort. The fortunes of the show are that it has been, at the moment, renewed for fifteen weeks and will then likely change its complexion considerably. It will be mostly suspense now.[3]

The widely diverging ideas held by Serling, Laird, the network, and the studio over *Night Gallery*'s true focus reached the point of schism in the third season. Serling wanted to do his thoughtful originals and adaptations. Laird wanted to continue adapting classic genre fiction and humorous blackouts. The network wanted an action-packed horrorfest. The studio wanted to Americanize the subject matter, drop the vignettes, and keep NBC happy. Of the four factions, Serling, without contractual control, had the least influence over the outcome. "Fighting with the networks can take a lot out of you," commented actor Burgess Meredith. "I've never had anything to do with networks—particularly on series—where they didn't give us a hard time. Doing

TV is like the comfort of eating at a picnic with wolves around. All you can do is take the network interference with laughter, but Rod wasn't that type of man."[4]

Besides the lack of input, the rewrites, the time-slot reduction, and the network's suggested shift toward action, Serling began to see a number of his scripts rejected. His sensitive study of a father dealing with his son's death, "The View of Whatever," had the potential to be another "They're Tearing Down Tim Riley's Bar." Serling submitted it in early February of 1972. The script went as far as being accepted by Laird and was typed and bound by Universal before it fell victim to the network's new focus. This offense amounted to the last straw.

On May 22, 1972, the day production began on the third season of *Night Gallery*, Serling drafted a letter to Universal's Norman Glenn in a bid to have his name removed from the show entirely:

Pique and irascibility do not motivate this letter, rather deep-rooted and quiet resignation of the fact that *Night Gallery* has ceased being *Rod Serling's Night Gallery*. On the basis of NBC's new dictum, it begins to take on the earmarks of a kind of *Mannix* with supernatural trappings. The network's insistence on early grabbing may be a valid requirement, but I find it occasionally repressive and frequently destructive in terms of story ideas. Some of our most successful and qualitative shows, "The Messiah on Mott Street" and "They're Tearing Down Tim Riley's Bar," gave the series some distinction. Now I find that "The View of Whatever" has been rejected as well as another script I've just turned in called "Finnegan's Flight" — unacceptable because they don't grab on the first page.[5]

I wanted a series with distinction, with episodes that said something. I have no interest in a series which is purely and uniquely suspenseful, but totally uncommentative [*sic*] on anything. So with Universal's permission, I do not intend to submit any further scripts now or in the future. I will continue hosting if you want me to, but would have no objections to someone else taking over the job and, further, no objections to a title change, allowing it to be someone else's *Night Gallery*. If this entails contractual problems or alterations, Bob Broder at IFA will be able to represent me and my interests.[6]

But Universal had sold *Night Gallery* to NBC on the strength of Rod Serling's prestigious *Twilight Zone* status, and was unwilling to let him go. In their view, his involvement in the show was unimportant alongside the continued use of his powerful image. A reluctant Serling, contractbound, was reduced to shilling for the network.

"They've discarded the concept I created," he charged.[7]

I would've thought that the five year track record of a show like *Twilight Zone* would have interested them [in allowing me input. *The Twilight Zone*] was not only accepted on one level as an exciting, interesting, bizarre, different kind of show, but on the other level as a rather thought-provoking, adult little piece. Why they consider that I shouldn't continue along on that plane, I don't know. The networks are very difficult to understand. Unfortunately, I don't think they trust my judgment. If indeed this is their feeling—if indeed I get tacked on to a losing formula, which they're going to superimpose over me, I'll just have to survive it. I've been in the business too long to have to sweat it anymore.[8]

Washing his hands of the series, Serling spent his time working on a pilot for CBS based on his award-winning *Hallmark Hall of Fame* teleplay "A Storm in Summer."

The network's demands were causing problems not only for Serling but also for everyone else involved with the series. Production ceased to be a joy for the crew. Pressure from above was making Laird tense and even harder to please. The new half-hour time slot hobbled production manager Burt Astor, who found his per-show budget halved to $95,000. For the first two seasons, Astor had managed to keep the production values on a professional level through use of a unique budgetary juggling act: he scheduled three or four stories per shoot, factoring in one script that required great expense with the less expensive segments. For the one-story-per-show third season, he could no longer manage this kind of creative funding. As a result, *Night Gallery's* quality began to slip.

Crucial production members from the second season were replaced, most noticeably in the music department and in the editing room. *Night Gallery's* superb pacing, a highlight of the second season, went out the window—another sacrifice to the rigid twenty-four-minute time constraint caused by the network's format change. In contrast to the first two seasons, the feel and tempo of the third season segments is markedly different, and not to the series' benefit.

One of the new editors, Richard Bracken, had just arrived at Universal Television after having worked on features at M-G-M. "It was a whole different kind of medium," says Bracken,

to go from the big screen back to television. I had a terrible time, to be honest with you—I remember it was very difficult getting my head back into television. Universal in those days was such a factory; so many shows were gang-banged. They had three or four editors just trying to meet air dates. I was working on weekends cutting sequences of shows and I had *no idea* what they were about! I'd ask the editor, "What's this show about?" And he'd say, "It doesn't matter! Just cut it!" It was really incredible in that period—the factory aspect of it. And I've worked in a factory, so I know of where I speak.[9]

The most crucial change in the series, however, came with the drop in the quality of the story material. "The scripts were not as good," says Jeannot Szwarc.

The material didn't have the literary quality it had before. Perhaps there was too much pressure from NBC, maybe the fact that there were conflicts between Jack and Rod didn't help, but I remember saying, "It's not as good." I'm sure a lot of the problem was NBC cutting the show down to a half hour. The ratings were good enough, the demographics were sensational, but NBC never understood that show. All those guys are heavily into control, and there was something a little bit chaotic and anarchistic about *Night Gallery* that NBC didn't like. Whenever you discussed a script with someone from NBC, they understood comedy and drama and action. And suddenly, with *Night Gallery,* here were all these things mixed. They didn't know if it was funny, if it was sad, or what. NBC just couldn't deal with it.[10]

Although the network's request for a more action-packed series profile never seems to have been implemented by Laird, the third season never saw anything on the tender emotional level of "They're Tearing Down Tim Riley's Bar," "The Messiah on Mott Street," or "Silent Snow, Secret Snow." Gentle fantasy was out. Shock was in. *Night Gallery,* sadly lacking Serling's more cerebral entries, began to resemble a drooling, *Tales from the Crypt* brand of pulp-horror show.

As proof, Universal's promotional campaign for the third season highlighted the new approach. Trying to drum up enthusiasm for the tottering show, they developed a bumper sticker media campaign with the lame catch phrase, "Never watch *Night Gallery* alone!"—accompanied by a photograph of a rather bored-looking young woman reclining in front of her television set, embracing a skeleton. This ludicrous marketing scheme went so counter to the tone of the plethora of quality segments the show produced in its first two seasons that it's hard to believe the promoters had ever viewed the show.

To illustrate the depth of misunderstanding the show suffered, a marketing firm contacted Serling in October of 1972 trying to interest him in a product line for the show. They suggested the use of Tom Wright's gallery paintings reproduced as jigsaw puzzles or paint-by-numbers kits, as well as "a recording narrated by Rod Serling of 'Sounds of the *Night Gallery*'—weird music, screams in the night, footsteps in the rain, hinges squeaking, tires skidding, a crash, and a diabolical laugh. Wild, man, wild! The kids would eat it up! Too late for this Halloween, but for next Halloween it's a golden platter!"[11] Serling must have cringed. These priceless mementos thankfully never appeared.

Universal did have the foresight to market a series of twelve posters of the gallery paintings that year, a far wiser move, although their choices were not in all cases well considered. The twelve included "Fright Night," "You Can Come Up Now, Mrs. Millikan," "The Dear Departed," "Rare Objects," "The Devil Is Not Mocked," "The Tune in Dan's Cafe," "House—With Ghost, "You Can't Get Help Like That Anymore," "Spectre in Tap-Shoes," "She'll Be Company for You," and "Phantom of What Opera?" "The Return of the Sorcerer" was offered, but they reproduced the wrong painting, using instead a canvas Wright painted for a script that was never produced —another example of Universal's exacting attention to detail. Half of the paintings were from the third season, which, at the time the paintings were marketed, nobody had seen yet. The fact that they missed reproducing any of the first season canvases, or such popular second-season paintings as "Pickman's Model," "The Caterpillar," or "A Feast of Blood" (Wright's version of Edvard Munch's *The Scream*), proves that the project was in the hands of the wrong people.

As the fall season approached, the network was preparing itself for *Night Gallery*'s failure. Commenting on the series' new certain-death time slot, NBC executives predicted that *Night Gallery*'s ratings at the start of the 1972–73 season would be anemic because of the *ABC Sunday Night Movie,* but that the movie audience would eventually die down. The competition on CBS was—once again—*Night Gallery*'s old foe *Mannix,* which had followed it to Sundays.

Resigned to the abrogation of his concept, Serling commented, "I can only say now that the hallmark of next year's series should be a glittering inconsistency—some lovely, some lousy."[12] Unfortunately, it would be less the former than the latter.

# 10
# The Final Season


THIRD SEASON CREDITS

1972–1973

**PRODUCED BY** Jack Laird

**ASSOCIATE PRODUCERS** Burt Astor, Herbert Wright, and Anthony Redman

**MAIN TITLE THEME** Eddie Sauter

**ART DIRECTOR** Joseph Alves, Jr.

**SET DECORATIONS** John M. Dwyer and Sal Blydenburgh

**SOUND** Roger A. Parish, Melvin M. Metcalfe, Sr., David H. Moriarty, John Carter, and Lyle Cain

**ASSISTANT DIRECTORS** Ralph Sariego, Chuck Lowry, Brad Aronson, and Les Berke

**UNIT MANAGER** Burt Astor

**FILM EDITORS** Larry Lester, Albert J. Zuniga, Sam Vitale, Robert F. Shugrue, Richard Bracken, and David Rawlins

**COSTUMES** Bill Jobe

**MAKEUP** Leonard Engelman and John F. Chambers

**GALLERY PAINTINGS** Tom Wright

**GALLERY SCULPTURES** Phil Vanderlei

**EDITORIAL SUPERVISION** Richard Belding

**MUSIC SUPERVISION** Hal Mooney

**MAIN TITLE DESIGN** Wayne Fitzgerald

**TITLES & OPTICAL EFFECTS** Universal Title

**CASTING** Ralph Winters


NIGHT GALLERY #35213

Air date: September 24, 1972


THE RETURN OF THE SORCERER

★ ★ ★ ½


Teleplay by Halsted Welles

Based on the short story by Clark Ashton Smith
Directed by Jeannot Szwarc
Music: Eddie Sauter
Director of Photography: Gerald Perry Finnerman

**Cast**
John Carnby: Vincent Price
Noel Evans: Bill Bixby
Fern: Tisha Sterling

Vincent Price in "The Return of
the Sorcerer." Courtesy of Jerry
Ohlinger.

G*ood evening. We're delighted that all of you could make it this evening because we have something special on tap.*

*In the area of the occult it's customary to preoccupy ourselves with witches, and too infrequently we dabble on the male side of that time-honored profession, the sorcerer. On display here is a painting showing the natural habitat of this species of black art practitioner. Dark alley, murky light, a few sundry skulls, and the gentleman himself on the right of the picture with the upraised hand and the funny little goat horns. Yes, indeed, this is a sorcerer, and for those of you who disbelieve his existence we invite you to check this out for a little while. Our painting is called "The Return of the Sorcerer," and where better place for him to return than right here in the* Night Gallery.

**/ Summary /** Responding to an ad for an Arabic interpreter, Noel Evans arrives at the residence of John Carnby and his assistant, Fern, a burned-out waif with luminous eyes. Carnby studies sorcery and demonism. His source book is a Latin work, the *Necronomicon*, but Carnby's interest falls on an earlier Arabic work whose most fiendish passages were never rendered into the Latin. The recent death of Carnby's learned twin brother prompted the search for a translator, but the two previous applicants—terrified by a specific passage—quit without explanation. Carnby is desperate to know what the passage says. After working on it, Noel understands why the others quit. The passage is grisly, outlining the powers that remain with a sorcerer after death: of how the wizard's will can allow him to rise from the dead to perform acts unfulfilled at the time of his death; of how, even if hewn in pieces, his fragments may rise separately to serve the wizard's end. The preamble to the passage is a curse and the reason for the mass resignations: "May he who reveals this secret be flayed slowly over burning coals and then thoroughly dismembered."

Carnby is devastated by the contents of the passage. From Fern, a horrified Noel discovers why: Carnby murdered his twin brother, cut him up into pieces, and buried him in the oak grove behind the house. Petitioning various demons for protection, Carnby begins chanting incantatory verses—but stops short when he hears dragging sounds outside the study. Opening the door, a horrified Noel finds a dismembered hand and foot crawling crablike along the floor in the corridor outside. Carnby's brother has returned. A panicked Carnby explains: "I hated him because his magic was stronger! But Fern—*she* caused it! She wanted to be stronger than both of us! The woman is insatiable! She taunted me by loving him! For power over both of us!" The omnipotent Fern leads Carnby, slack and defeated, to the study for black mass, where *she* will preside—along with his brother.

As Noel hastens upstairs to pack and leave, Carnby, entering the study's screened-off altar, encounters his brother—whose gray, rotting constituents have pulled themselves together to act as one. With Fern chanting the hellish service, Carnby's brother raises a ceremonial blade; Carnby meekly lays his head on the altar. An exiting Noel, hearing the tremendous clang, enters—yet nothing seems out of place. Fern steps out from behind the screened-off altar. "You're too late for mass," she says casually. "Sorry you missed it. The brothers are together again—fragmented, but together."

Wrapping her arms around him, she invites Noel to her room. He hesitates, torn between desire and fear. "Fern," he says. "In the preamble—in the *Necronomicon*—threatening anyone who translated the passages from Arabic with fire and dismemberment? You don't suppose there's anything to that, do you?" Fern, smiling enigmatically, leads him toward her room.

**/ Commentary /** Vincent Price and director Jeannot Szwarc, who first met while filming the previous season's "Class of '99," were here paired again for another strong segment. "Vincent was a delightful, very well-read, very sophisticated man," Szwarc says. "He was not at all like those parts he played, even though he thoroughly enjoyed playing them. That's why I think he did it so well, because he never apologized for it. He thought it was wonderful. For him it was an exercise in style."[1]

As the feverish Carnby and the dull, unimaginative Noel, Price and Bill Bixby enjoy an amusing congress. Their opening scene, where Carnby divines Noel's character by means of numerology, is weirdly droll thanks to the two actors' dry, low-key delivery, preparing the audience for the drama's progressive oddities.

The most difficult role, given her lines, is Fern, played by Tisha Sterling. Although a talented scriptwriter, Halsted Welles had an unfortunate tendency to attempt corny hip slang. Sterling, proving her skill, manages to spout Welles's hippie-flake dialogue and *still* create a compelling portrait of corrupted innocence.

"Jeannot had some lovely shots of me, which were very artistic and pretty," Sterling recalls. "I wore this black, sequined number, and I wasn't wearing a bra—which was *so* 1970s. Whoa, honey! You should have put on a bra! And every time I opened my mouth—oh, my God! The 'Hey, man,' the hip dialogue—it was *so* different in the seventies. I can't even *believe* we did that shit!"[2]

Inspiration in the crew obviously ran high for this production. The set design and decorations, fashioned on eldritch themes, are extraordinary, masterminded, as were all the segments, by Joseph Alves. "Those were wild sets that Joe did," recalls Szwarc. "As an inspiration, I showed him a lot of drawings by William Blake, the English poet, and some stuff by Alistair Crowley, pentagrams and that sort of thing."[3] For the decor, Alves and his crew consulted with experts in the field. Dennis Moore and "Babetta" the witch of the Sorcerer's Shop in Hollywood provided the props—tarot cards, statuary—and Moore, a student of witchcraft, was technical adviser on the set. "They did a great job on these sets," he commented. "They're really quite extravagant. It's a well-done series."[4] Composer Eddie Sauter provided a witty, tongue-in-cheek underscore (with an appropriate Arabic flavor); and capping it all is the stunning photography of Gerald Finnerman, who, with the eye of a master painter, works in a gorgeous palette of blood reds and deep shadowed blacks. "I really believe that horror has to be beautiful," notes Szwarc. "I mean, the aesthetics have to be on a very high level, and that we definitely tried. I mean, we *really* tried."[5] This segment vividly illustrates Szwarc's philosophy.

In an attempt to capture the atmosphere of a real black mass, incorporated into the script were the actual incantations used by those who practice satanic worship— invocations of Astoroth, Asmodeus, Baal, Belial, and other such fiends, accompanied by repetitions of the mystic numbers of three, five, seven, nine, and twenty-one—all of which was a bit too much for Sterling. "It was spooky," she avers. "I hated the chanting. I believed that those words we were saying were really powerful and meaningful, and one shouldn't conjure up that kind of energy. It frightened me. I felt I was giving myself over to some dark, horrible force. I would try to cleanse myself afterwards by praying a lot and making the sign of the cross, to try to make the light come instead of the dark. I felt very bad after I filmed that day."

Adding to the queer milieu, a trained goat—traditionally identified as one of Satan's familiars—was positioned in quite lordly fashion at the dining table. The goat's trainer, Don Spinney, spent three days teaching the animal to sit at the table, an unnaturally difficult feat for goats. "He was a very, very good boy," notes Sterling. "His trainer would feed him little goodies between setups, then take him to the table and position him for the next shot. They had him seated on a little stool with his front legs propped up on the table, and he stayed that way. He wasn't any trouble at all! I don't know how in God's name they got him to do that."[6]

For the return of Carnby's brother, a severed hand and foot had to be photographed moving along the carpet under their own power. Makeup artists Leonard Engelman and John Chambers devised models of the two members that were moved in puppet fashion by the use of ultrathin monofilament—basically fishing line. "Today, of course, they would photograph the hand and they'd move it by computer," Engelman says. "In 1972, you used fishing line and got similar effects!"[7]

With tongue firmly in cheek, "The Return of the Sorcerer" started off *Night*

*Gallery*'s third year in grand style. Unfortunately, little that followed would approach this level.

NIGHT GALLERY #35206
Air date: October 1, 1972

THE GIRL WITH THE HUNGRY EYES
★ ★ ½

Teleplay by Robert Malcolm Young
Based on the short story by Fritz Leiber
Directed by John Badham
Music: Eddie Sauter
Director of Photography: Gerald Perry Finnerman

**Cast**
David Faulkner: James Farentino
The Girl: Joanna Pettet
Munsch: John Astin
Harry Krell: Kip Niven
Man on Street: Bruce Powers

*Joanna Pettet in "The Girl with the Hungry Eyes." Courtesy of Hollywood Book and Poster Co.*

$G$*ood evening. Let me welcome you to this parlor of paintings. We offer them to you for your enjoyment and edification—feel free to dwell on them at your leisure and in your own good fashion. But kindly don't touch, because here they frequently touch back.*

*Our number one painting in tonight's exhibit: this intriguing portrait of a young lady, curiously photogenic and hauntingly familiar. Recall seeing this face? You've seen it—on billboards, in magazine ads, on television commercials. Oh yes, you've seen it—but there are people who, having seen it, wish they hadn't. Our painting is called "The Girl with the Hungry Eyes," and should I have failed to mention it, this is the* Night Gallery.

**/ Summary /** Photographer David Faulkner has a new model. He knows nothing about her—not even her name. She appeared out of nowhere, and she is as secretive as she is drop-dead gorgeous. There is something in her eyes, a need, a hunger, that David finds arousing . . . and vaguely frightening. Soon he finds himself wanting her, wanting to know more about her, despite the warning she gives him to never follow her home.

One night after she leaves the studio, David glimpses her from a window in the street below talking to his friend Harry. The next morning David learns that Harry's body was found last night in the park, another of the "maybe murders," so called because the police have not determined whether the deaths are heart attacks or the work of a serial killer. David finds his undefined fears about the girl taking a more solid form.

One of David's clients, Munsch, an overbearing beer magnate, has become ob sessed by the girl and begs the evasive photographer to arrange a meeting. Stymied by David's refusal, Munsch follows the girl one night as she leaves the studio—and he, too, winds up on the front page, another of the "maybe murders." Giving in to his curiosity, David himself follows her, despite her warning, and sees her capture one of her victims in a soul-sucking, deadly kiss. She moves toward David like a predator, her eyes glowing with a cold and empty fire. When she raises her lips to his, he manages to break away, racing back to the studio as fast as he can.

She is waiting for him when he arrives, and she watches, alarmed, as David dumps all her negatives and prints into a pile on the floor. "I know you now!" he rages. "You're the eyes that pick our pockets and spend our lives. You're the lure, the bait . . . we lust for you, for what those eyes hold out. And you . . . you suck the love from us, because that's what feeds you, isn't it? And everything you *are* exists right here on these negatives. I'm going to destroy you before you drain the world dry!"

Her hysterical screams fall on deaf ears as he douses the pile with lighter fluid and matches it into life. As the flames consume the images of her, the girl herself begins to change, polarize, curl, and burn like a life-size negative. Dazed, David stares at the few remaining prints of the girl pinned to his viewing lamp—where her deadly eyes have seared into whitened, spent orbs.

/ **Commentary** / "The Girl with the Hungry Eyes" was the first segment to be filmed for the 1972–73 season, and the second adaptation of Fritz Leiber's work on *Night Gallery* (the first being "The Dead Man"). The author gave his approval to this segment, adding "the idea of destroying the negatives of 'the girl,' which then destroyed her, was a nice touch."[8]

In Leiber's original story, the photographer is something of a hack, but to capture Joanna Pettet's glamour shots, Laird hired a man who was anything but a hack: legendary Hollywood photographer Harry Langdon, Jr. Recalls director John Badham: "We took Joanna down to his studio on Melrose and spent the afternoon there. He shot a ton of wonderful, wonderful stuff that we used to plaster all over Farentino's studio. Joanna was so gorgeous, she was to die for."[9] How apt.

"It was a fabulous photo session," recalls Pettet.

Doing "The Girl with the Hungry Eyes" was just a total ego trip. I walked onto the set and there were, floor to ceiling, these huge blowups of me! I looked out a window, and they had literally made a huge billboard out of me, sipping beer, and erected it on a building across the street. And it was probably the best I ever looked in my life. We all go through our periods—"the look," you know? It was just perfect. And for the rest of my career I got to use these *incredible* shots from Harry Langdon. When would I *ever* have had a chance to get an entire day with somebody like that?[10]

At this period of her career, Pettet found herself a favorite guest star on numerous television series. Although English by birth, Pettet's American accent betrayed no trace of her native isle. This flexibility allowed her to easily play both sides of the Atlantic, and with the advent of the Beatles and the Carnaby Street craze, America was having a love affair with all things English. "We were very hot at the moment," Pettet says. "It was Julie Christie and Terence Stamp, Jackie Bisset, and a few of us moved out here [to America]."

In a deliberate career move, she found *Night Gallery* to be a perfect forum to cultivate a new image for herself—ethereal, mysterious, and dreamlike. The roles she chose were haunted, illusory women, eliciting desire, and sometimes fear, from the men caught by her allure. "I created that image," says Pettet. "And because of *Night Gallery* I was able to play that 'ethereal' thing." She accented her natural gifts—her exquisite facial features and her slim, reed-like body—with clothing designed to produce an airy, diaphanous quality. "All the clothes that I had were made in England by two growing, hip fashion designers: Holly Harp and Thea Porter from London. Thea Porter was very gypsyish, and I wore her things mostly in 'Girl with the Hungry Eyes.'"[10]

In her fourth appearance on *Night Gallery*, Joanna Pettet is literal perfection as the glacial, voracious soul vampire, both breathtaking and disturbing. James Farentino, having faced down a sorceress in the second season's "Since Aunt Ada Came to Stay," also returns to do battle with yet another formidable creature of the night—although the real villain may have resided at Network Standards and Practices. "In 'The Girl with the Hungry Eyes,' we had a problem there," Farentino recalls. "Because I felt, and I think Joanna did, too, that the concept was more sexual, more sensual than they would allow us to do. John Badham was all for it, and he stretched it as far as he could —but not enough, of course. I remember the conversation we had at the time: 'Can't we just go all the way? Let's go with what's here in the script!' And it was very hot! Very hot stuff! But we were warned by the Tower against going too far, and we had to compromise. You couldn't do then what you can do on television today."[11]

Reworking Leiber's classic short, screenwriter Robert Malcolm Young gave the characters a fuller dimension and heightened the story's erotic undercurrents. Although uneven, it had some good elements and was Young's best script for the show. Unfortunately, an important plot point is set up and then ignored that, over time, makes the show less effective. The script deliberately builds audience expectations regarding the fate of the character of Munsch, who desperately tries to persuade David to arrange for him to meet the girl. Later on, David accuses the girl of responsibility in Munsch's death. With the presentation of this thread of plot, dramatic logic prac-tically demands that Munsch be murdered on-camera. We are instead treated to the murder of some sidewalk bystander and cheated out of the promised payoff.

"I had a big argument with Jack Laird over that," says Badham. "In the piece, the girl kills some guy out in the street. I told Jack, 'That should be the smarmy ad guy, the character John Astin plays. She should be killing somebody we *know.*' But instead we had to do this anonymous guy. Why? Because we couldn't afford to have John Astin for another day's shooting. So over a few hundred dollars, the story lacked some power, some narrative punch that it would have had had we been able to do that." [12]

Luckily, these restrictions didn't sour the sensational special effects in this epi-sode, or the chilling final image. "Jack wanted to put a vortex in Joanna Pettet's eyes," recalls editor Larry Lester, "and I said, 'Jack, *c'mon,* that goes back to black and white. *I'll* come up with something.' So I went to a jeweler and rented an opal. We shot it against black velvet and rotoscoped that into her eyes when she came in-and-out with that 'look' she put on Farentino. We had a lot of fun doing that." [13]

On the last day of shooting, the special-effects crew prepared for the filming of the girl's incendiary death. It proved to be more complicated than expected. "They had trouble that day," Pettet says. "It was very technical and difficult to superimpose me on the fire, and they had to get the flames a certain intensity. At some point they got it right, because it created something huge!" [14] Recalls Badham: "Farentino is trashing the studio and setting all of the pictures on fire. We are basically causing a conflagration inside a sound stage, and we somehow have to get Joanna into the mid-dle of it. And instead of wrapping at six o'clock, I think I went until eight-thirty to get all this stuff. The next day I was fired and told I couldn't do any more shows." As luck would have it, Badham was informed of this on the day before he was slated to begin prepping to film his next segment, "You Can Come Up Now, Mrs. Millikan."

"I was fired until the next time they needed somebody, which was about twenty minutes later," laughs Badham. "So I start my next show with Ozzie and Harriet the next morning, and by the end of the morning we're already ahead of schedule. We just happened to be going great guns that day, and so I'm, like, *rehired.* On *Night Gallery,* it was always that way. You never knew whether you were 'in' or 'out' on these shows." [15]

After the shoot, Pettet tried in vain to get for herself some of the Langdon blowups, but the eager studio gremlins had left nothing: "We broke on a Friday, and by the time I went back to ask if I could have any of the pictures, they were all gone! The crew had gotten them all! Huge, life-size pictures of me!" [16] Pettet had, by now, become the closest thing that *Night Gallery* had to a pinup girl. "The crew took all those posters of Joanna," laughs Farentino, "and I don't blame them! I wish *I* had!" [17]

NIGHT GALLERY #35215
Air date: October 22, 1972

RARE OBJECTS
★ ★ ★

Written by Rod Serling
Directed by Jeannot Szwarc
Music: Eddie Sauter
Director of Photography: Gerald Perry Finnerman

**Cast**
Augie Kolodney: Mickey Rooney
Dr. Glendon: Raymond Massey
Molly Mitchell: Fay Spain
Blockman: David Fresco
Doctor: Regis J. Cordic
Butler: Victor Sen Yung
Tony: Ralph Adano

*Raymond Massey and Mickey Rooney in "Rare Objects." Courtesy of TV History Archives.*

$G$ood evening. As the resident custodian of this museum, I bid you welcome and offer you the felicitations of our entire staff . . . most of whom are out and about at the moment, since they tend to be night people.

Our artists and artisans take a rather pardonable pride in their work that you see hanging here. An example is this item here. It's called "Rare Objects," and represents that potpourri of collector's items that some men are prone to acquire. But there are collector's items and collector's items. Offered to you now, an excursion into the very strange, tonight's offering in the Night Gallery.

/ **Summary** / Eating out at a quiet nightspot, mobster Augie Kolodney barely escapes another attempted hit by a few of his more aggressive "business associates." In a cold fury, Kolodney realizes that he has been crossed; his small world of trusted friends is dwindling. Kolodney finds a doctor to remove the stray slug from his shoulder and, after a brief exam, is offered some advice: retire. His blood pressure is dangerously high; if he doesn't slow down soon, he will surely die. Kolodney sneers that he would never be safe, no matter where he went, but the doctor offers Kolodney an "out"—a chance at survival—and writes the name and address of a contact on a slip of paper. "How much will it cost me?" asks the mobster. "A lot," responds the doctor, "but you'll stay breathing."

Kolodney arrives, alone and in secret, at the massive, isolated chateau of Dr. Glendon. The man's house is the repository of an extraordinary collection of the finest objects of art and pottery, rare and astronomically expensive. Pouring him a glass of an appropriately rare vintage, Dr. Glendon refers to Kolodney as a rare item himself, unique and special. He guarantees the mobster a long life devoid of worry, without fear or tension of any kind. In return, he demands everything Kolodney owns—cash, securities, business interests, to the last cent. Kolodney balks at this precipitous price tag until Glendon enumerates the various assassination attempts the mobster has survived: "Forgive me for saying this, Mr. Kolodney, but the odds for your survival shrink with each passing day."

Groggy, Kolodney rises, not feeling well. Glendon calmly informs him that it's a normal reaction to the medication—the wine was drugged. As the butler supports the staggering mobster, Glendon leads them up the stairs, telling Kolodney of the special properties of his revitalizing drug—adding inestimable years to the normal life span. Almost beyond the ability to respond, Kolodney listens dumbly as Glendon expounds on his "hobby," his realization of a lifelong dream—a collection of rare, precious, and one-of-a-kind items unequaled in the world.

Leading him into a hidden corridor lined like a prison block with cubicle cells, Glendon reveals to Kolodney his most prized collection. Seated in each cell is a person, long missing, long thought dead: Crown Princess Anastasia of Russia; Judge Joseph Crater; Amelia Earhart; explorer Roald Amundsen; Adolf Hitler; and at the end of the corridor, an empty cell with a sign reading "August Kolodney." Helpless, the mobster is escorted within and the barred cell locked behind him. "I think you'll find all the comforts available to you—as per our agreement," Glendon notes pleasantly. "And further than that, Mr. Kolodney—you shall live a very long time. A *very* long time." Kolodney grasps the bars of his cell, trembling with dread, surprise, and doped-up rage, staring after Glendon's retreating form as he disappears down the hallway.

/ **Commentary** / In "Rare Objects" (originally titled "Collector's Items") Serling once again delivered a story reminiscent of his work on *The Twilight Zone*. With dialogue crisp and vital, Serling's sharp script peaks in the interplay between Kolodney and Dr. Glendon. Raymond Massey's character, adversarial and eloquent, reveals his true motives subtly, bit by bit, until Kolodney realizes that Glendon holds all the cards—and that the trap has sprung. Serling's final twist, in which Kolodney is literally sentenced to life imprisonment with a cast of historical figures, has a satisfying irony. Caged like an animal, reduced to the status of a mere object, Kolodney becomes the latest addition to an eccentric hobbyist's ever-expanding collection.

In an unusual casting move, Mickey Rooney, always a Serling favorite, was chosen to play the sadistic racketeer. Although Rooney's talent and energy are not in question, casting him as a top mob boss stretches believability. Although he makes a convincing nasty, he nevertheless lacks the aura of danger, the palpable threat that a thug like Augie Kolodney requires.

Additionally, at this stage of his career the frail Massey lacks the gristle to portray the imperious Dr. Glendon. The casting problems, however, are balanced, once again, by the rich palette of cinematographer Gerald Finnerman and by the work of director Jeannot Szwarc, whose handling of composition and concept always satisfies. Also of note: Eddie Sauter's music—scored for the curious French café-style combo of accordion, electric guitar, strings, and percussion—offers a bizarre commentary on the strange fate of August Kolodney.

"Rare Objects" features one of the more memorable opening shots of the series. The viewer is greeted by an extreme closeup of Rooney forking a wad of sauced fettuccine into his gaping mouth. The camera dollies slowly back, foot by foot, ultimately revealing the expanse of the scene: lone man in a quiet and suspiciously deserted restaurant. Szwarc instantly establishes a mood of tension, skillfully setting the scene for the explosive confrontation between Kolodney and his nervous waiter, and the subsequent assassination attempt.

"That one I loved," says Szwarc. "Mickey Rooney was a riot, because he was always 'on.' They say when he gets up at night to open the fridge and the light goes on, he does ten minutes. And Raymond Massey was as serious as the pope. But I hit it off with him because I was probably one of the few guys in America who had seen his performance in Michael Powell's *Stairway to Heaven,* one of my favorite films of all time and one of the greatest movies ever made. You've got to see it, it's his best!"[18]

NIGHT GALLERY #35228
Air date: October 29, 1972

SPECTRE IN TAP-SHOES
★ ★

Teleplay by Gene Kearney
Based on a story by Jack Laird
Directed by Jeannot Szwarc
Music: Eddie Sauter
Director of Photography: Gerald Perry Finnerman

**Cast**
Millicent Hardy: Sandra Dee
William Jason: Dane Clark
Sam Davis: Christopher Connelly

*Sandra Dee in "Spectre in Tap-Shoes." Courtesy of Eddie Brandt's Saturday Matinee.*

Dr. Coolidge: Russell Thorson
Michael: Michael Laird
Mailman: Michael Richardson
Policeman: Stuart Nisbet

$G$*ood evening, and a cordial welcome. For you aficionados of the arts, we offer you paintings that run the gamut of the human experiences—and a few of the inhuman experiences. Our paintings are in oils, watercolor, acrylic, charcoal, and occasionally formaldehyde.*

*Case in point, this painting here. It's called "Spectre in Tap-Shoes," having to do with the nearly lost art of tap dancing. Said terpsichorean pursuit taking on an intriguing dimension when the dancer happens to be a ghost, as is so often the case and the sort of thing that you view in the* Night Gallery.

/ **Summary** / A vacationing Millicent Hardy returns early to the house she shares with her twin sister, Marion—whom Millicent finds in the attic dance studio, dangling dead from a rope. In the nights that follow, Millicent has horrible nightmares reliving the moment of the awful discovery. She spends her days in deep depression, refusing to talk to anyone or open her antique shop to customers. To her horror, she begins to notice evidence of her sister's continued presence. Her friend Sam tries to persuade her to allow a local developer, William Jason, to make good on his offer to buy the place and tear it down so that Millicent might have some closure. Millicent cannot bear the idea and sends Sam away. But every night, she hears the sound of the tap dancing upstairs—and slowly Millicent begins to unravel.

A nonsmoker, she finds herself taking up cigarettes like Marion; dressing, talking, and acting like Marion. One night, she hears Marion's voice ordering her to dress up in her top hat, tails, and tap shoes, and to go to the studio. There, she finds a noose hung tight over a rafter—and from a dark corner she senses a whispering form. She moves toward the noose, driven by the voice, but hesitates at putting the rope around her neck. The figure in the shadows steps forward—William Jason, her sister's murderer. Jason, one of Marion's liaisons, murdered her because she was blackmailing him. He is desperate to get the incriminating letters back, and grabs Millicent roughly around the throat. Millicent, panicked, rushes to the studio piano, opens the top and pulls out a gun. "No you don't, Billy, not again," snarls Millicent. "This time I'm ready for you." Before Jason can protest, she fires, killing him.

The police investigate, finding Jason's speakers and listening devices all over the house. He had planned to either drive Millicent mad or make it look to others like she committed suicide from guilt and grief. Then he could buy the house and tear it apart board by board to find Marion's blackmail. Despite the explanation by the authorities, one thing disturbs Millicent: how did she know where to find the revolver? As if in answer from above, Millicent hears the familiar tapping of Marion's dancing.

**/ Commentary /** Sandra Dee ("Tell David . . .") returned to *Night Gallery* for a second guest shot, but the demands on the actress for this segment were more strenuous than the first—she had to learn to tap dance. As in her previous role, Dee was able, via *Night Gallery*'s dark visions, to escape the superficial parts with which she is generally identified. Dane Clark offers a strong assist as the desperate Jason, but less effective is Christopher Connolly, who lacks needed warmth in his role as Millicent's sympathetic friend Sam.

"Spectre in Tap-Shoes" is cursed with a well-worn premise. Its basic layout was lifted from *Gaslight* and *Diabolique*. Scriptwriter Gene Kearney had, in fact, already written a feature script inspired by *Diabolique* years before—*Games* (1967)—and countless variations have followed since. There are no surprises in this familiar territory and "Spectre in Tap-Shoes" is ultimately rendered ordinary in the face of its distinguished predecessors. Director Jeannot Szwarc manages to convey a moody ambience with some skillful visuals, a vain effort to divert attention from the stale material and often embarrassing dialogue. Seen objectively, Kearney and Laird's script inhabits a world closer to such series as *Ghost Story* or *The Sixth Sense* than to *Night Gallery*.

## NIGHT GALLERY #35217
Air date: November 12, 1972

### 1
### YOU CAN COME UP NOW, MRS. MILLIKAN
★ ★ ★

Teleplay by Rod Serling
Based on the short story "The Secret of the Vault" by J. Wesley Rosenquest
Directed by John Badham
Music: Eddie Sauter
Director of Photography: Gerald Perry Finnerman

**Cast**
Henry Millikan: Ozzie Nelson
Helena Millikan: Harriet Nelson
George Beaumont: Roger Davis
Dr. Burgess: Michael Lerner
Dr. Coolidge: Don Keefer
Dr. Steinhem: Margaret Muse
Detective Stacy: Lew Brown
Detective Kimbrough: Stuart Nisbet

*Ozzie Nelson in "You Can Come Up Now, Mrs. Millikan." Courtesy of Hollywood Book and Poster Co.*

*For the benefit of those of you who've not visited art lovers' soirées before, I am your guide, host, curator. I introduce the hanging goodies with just a few words of explanation as to how we secured them for our exhibit: sometimes a loan, sometimes a direct purchase, frequently a shovel.*

*Tonight we offer you the sour fruit of a scientist-failure, for there are apparently some things that cannot be accomplished. And therein lies the tale and hangs the picture in this, the* Night Gallery.

/ **Summary** / Henry Millikan, an inept scientist and inventor, has tried all his life to make some earth-shattering discovery—perpetual motion, fountain of youth, philosopher's stone—that would elevate his sorry reputation among his venerable colleagues. Henry's loving, if preternaturally forgetful, wife, Helena, supports him completely in his abject failures. Henry's latest idea is his most ambitious to date. After toiling in his laboratory vault until the wee hours, he excitedly awakens his wife to inform her that he has invented a serum that will make him famous . . . and her immortal.

The following week, Henry invites his physician nephew, George, to the house for a look at Helena. She appears to be dying, from what he's not sure, and she is not responding to any medication. Henry appears to be unconcerned about it. "How long do you think it's going to take, George?" he chirps. "She's been late with everything during her life—I suppose she'll be late with her dying, too." George's growing suspicions toward his uncle are confirmed when Helena tells her nephew that she took poison—freely—at Henry's suggestion. Confounded, George asks her why. "Because," Helena rasps faintly, "Henry's going to bring me back to life."

Helena dies shortly after. Henry injects her with his revivifying serum and invites George down into the vault to witness Helena's awakening. Henry quietly calls her name, as if trying to coax her out of sleep. She does not respond, remaining still, cold, and quite dead. Henry finally realizes he has managed another failed experiment . . . and murdered his wife in the bargain. Grief-stricken at the thought of life without Helena, Henry retires to his room to await his pending arrest.

When the police arrive, George finds Henry dead in his room—poisoned by his own hand. While detectives inspect the scene, George heads downstairs to the living room for a much-needed brandy. He freezes when he hears a noise from below: the sound of the vault door opening on its squeaking hinges . . . then footsteps coming up the stairs . . . then the touch of a hand on his shoulder, and a familiar voice calling his name. "George, dear, where's Henry?" In dread at what he will see, he turns toward the voice. It is Helena Millikan, ghastly white and sunken eyed, back from the dead. Smiling, she concedes, "As usual, I'm late!"—and as she gently caresses her nephew's hair, his mind crumbles to madness.

**/ Commentary /** Originally titled "The Vault," Serling's adaptation of Wesley Ro-senquest's cracked essay on a scientist's aspirations exceeding his talents is both funny and creepy, with a strong element of pathos. Director John Badham enhances the story's crackpot tone with twisted compositions and odd angles. For the scene re-vealing Henry Millikan's suicide by poison, Badham obscures this issue by never showing the body—only nephew George's response—imparting a sense of strange-ness magnified. For Helena's resurrection in the hair-raising finale, Badham tightens the camera on George in incremental jumps as he hears Helena ascending the stairs. "We opted to leave the zoom lens at home," Badham says, "and just kept snapping in, tighter, tighter, tighter, so that each move was like a little punch in the face. I confess to stealing that from Francois Truffaut in the opening of *Fahrenheit 451*. And it wasn't like the early French new wave stuff where they did it because they didn't have a zoom. Truffaut obviously said, 'No, I like this effect.' And I thought, here's a good place to use it. If I'm going to steal it, I'm going to try to use it effectively."[19]

Serling's quirky script and Badham's lensing make "Mrs. Millikan" one of the more successful of the third-season segments, bolstered by the offbeat casting of Ozzie and Harriet Nelson. Icons of the sort of bland suburban shallowness prevalent on 1950s television, the Nelsons were in some ways an inspired choice for *Night Gallery*. Casting them in Serling's grim little black comedy was almost surreal, their brightness and cheeriness reflecting only more intensely the dark elements of the story. Their likeable ineptitude, both as characters and as actors, somehow heightens the horror of the narrative. Although a team like Hume Cronyn and Jessica Tandy might better have examined the undercurrent of poignancy in the Millikans' rela-tionship, merely the idea of using the Nelsons makes for strangely satisfying viewing.

For costar Roger Davis, however, there were times when he may have felt as if he were guesting on an episode of *The Adventures of Ozzie and Harriet*. "I was always a bit surprised that they didn't have David or Ricky play my part," laughs Davis. And as filming progressed, the star of ABC's popular western *Alias Smith and Jones* soon found himself absorbing some of the Nelsons' trademark quirkiness. "Ozzie concentrated very hard on the part, but when he worked, he, he, uh, uh, had a, uh, uh, certain way of, uh, uh, talking! And when I was doing scenes with him, I, I, uh, uh, had a, uh, ten-dency to, to, to, do it too! It was something he did as a kind of conscious mannerism, but when *I* started doing it, John Badham had to say, 'Wait a minute. *Nooooo*. Only *Ozzie* can do that!' Because I really got caught up in it—it was contagious!"[20]

2
SMILE, PLEASE
★ ★

Written and Directed by Jack Laird
Music: Eddie Sauter
Director of Photography: Leonard J. South

**Cast**
Man: Cesare Danova
Girl: Lindsay Wagner

*Lindsay Wagner in "Smile, Please." Courtesy of Sal Milo.*

*T*ake *your positions, if you will, now. The camera's ready and "Smile, Please."*

**/ Summary /** In the bowels of the crumbling manor, the man leads the young woman, grasping her camera excitedly, down the cellar stairs. "Just think, I'll be the first person in history to ever photograph a genuine vampire," she gushes—but she frowns when she notices the coffin is empty. How can she take the picture if the vampire isn't here? "Oh, but he is here," the man assures her. "And you shall have your photograph just as I promised." Stepping back for a grand pose, he smiles a toothy grin: "Cheese."

**/ Commentary /** Laird's silly short (with a pre-*Bionic Woman* performance by Lindsay Wagner) is a relative success because of Eddie Sauter's witty score, which highlights the tongue-in-cheek tone. With the Hungarian cimbalom adding a touch of paprika, Sauter's Gypsy music makes amusing reference to the Balkan homeland of literature's most famous vampire. Sauter's wink at the audience lifts this blackout onto a different level, making "Smile, Please" one of the better vignettes to appear on *Night Gallery*—which, admittedly, isn't really saying much.

Lindsay Wagner: "Acting on *Night Gallery* was quite free compared to other shows, and that certainly was a function of Mr. Laird. He gave us the freedom to just play with it. Doing the silly English accent was something that came up on the spot. I remember saying, 'It just looks and feels so English'—it wasn't called for in the script, and he actually encouraged any kind of nonsense that we could come up with! It was just fun."

Less fun for Wagner was wedging herself into the cramped fake stairwell with amorous costar Cesare Danova. "That dumb stairwell was really meant for only one person," Wagner recalls. "The two of us were kind of jammed back there. I was a little nervous, and he was a little flirty! Being all of twenty, I was like, '*Get me out of this stairwell!*'"[21]

## NIGHT GALLERY #35232
Air date: November 19, 1972

## THE OTHER WAY OUT
★ ★ ★

Teleplay by Gene Kearney
Based on a story by Kurt van Elting
Directed by Gene Kearney
Music: Eddie Sauter
Director of Photography: Emil Oster

**Cast**
Bradley Meredith: Ross Martin
Old Man: Burl Ives
Estelle: Peggy Feury
Potter: Jack Collins
Miss Flannagan: Elizabeth Thompson
Waiter: Paul Micale
Sonny: Adam Weed

*Burl Ives and Ross Martin in "The Other Way Out." Courtesy of Hollywood Book and Poster Co.*

*T*ime again for your weekly sojourn in the nether regions, where we offer you paintings hopefully proving that insomnia is much to be desired over somnolence—for better a wakeful night than an unwelcome dawn, if you will. All of which is perhaps a slightly agonized invitation to keep your eyes open here.

We offer you paintings like this one. A graphic illustration of one of the most persistent and eternally recurring nightmares shared all too commonly by all of us—that fear of being helplessly trapped in some inescapable circumstance . . . and with it the hope that we can discover an exit. The title of this painting is "The Other Way Out," and it poses the question, "Is this trip desirable?"—because this is the Night Gallery.

**/ Summary /** Returning to his office after vacationing with his wife, Bradley Meredith receives an unsigned and unwelcome note in the mail. It hints at his involvement in the recent unsolved murder of a go-go dancer, an insinuation that fills him with apprehension—and a warranted guilt. He begins to find follow-up notes with instructions on the delivery of a payment to guarantee the anonymous letter writer's silence.

Meredith withdraws $10,000 and follows the instructions on the note, delivering the money to a deserted spot—but he runs late. Driving on the unlit road, he rounds a curve and hits a downed telephone pole. Meredith grabs a flashlight from the dash and approaches the nearest house, a dilapidated old farmhouse with a fenced-off pack of vicious dogs. Meredith pleads with the old man who lives there, a guitar-picking rustic, to allow him to borrow his tractor. The old man tells Meredith he will have to ask his grandson, Sonny, who should be returning soon. Meredith's pleas fall on deaf ears; the old man is apparently terrified of his grandson's temper.

As Meredith waits impatiently for Sonny's return, it dawns on him that he has fallen into the blackmailer's trap—the old man is the murdered girl's grandfather. Taking Meredith's pistol from him at gunpoint, the old man admits that Sonny thought up the plan: "Mean *and* clever, that's what Sonny is." He pulls the clip from Meredith's .38, pockets one bullet, tables the gun, and tosses the clip out the window into the front yard. "I unchained the dogs," he smiles. "That's in case you had notions about leaving before Sonny gets back."

Desperate to get the ammunition back, Meredith pockets the gun and braves the savage hounds to get the clip back, but is forced to exhaust his bullets to keep them at bay. He finally claws his way back inside the house, barely escaping being torn to pieces. From above, the old man cackles that there *is* another way out, but the sound of an approaching car signals Sonny's return. Propelled by panic, Meredith finds a trapdoor and, descending on a frayed rope ladder into the blackness, falls to the bottom of an earthen-floored pit. He hears footsteps along the passageway above, and the voice of the old man: "Come along, Sonny. I want to introduce you to your sister's killer." Joining the old man at the trapdoor opening is Sonny—a small boy of possibly ten years. Meredith gasps, "Him? *He's Sonny?*" The old man nods, informing Meredith that he and Sonny will be back from their trip—in about a month or two. "You said there was another way out," Meredith screams. "*You lied to me!*" "No, I didn't," the old man says, pulling something small from his pocket. "Here's the other way out." He throws the object down next to where Meredith's pistol fell: the bullet the old man took from the clip of the .38. Staring at it, Meredith's convulsive laughter turns to racking sobs as the trapdoor closes, leaving him in the cold and impenetrable darkness.

/ **Commentary** / Ross Martin returns for yet another cat-and-mouse revenge play, a type of story at which *Night Gallery* was particularly successful. Whereas in "Camera Obscura" Martin was the avenger, in "The Other Way Out" he plays the stalked, and without the heavy makeup he was previously lumbered with. This second appearance can be enjoyed without qualification. Oscar-winner Burl Ives, known to most as the jolly folksinger, is Martin's sinister nemesis, and gives a quirky, menacing performance. Appearing at first as a rather dense, infuriatingly easygoing bumpkin, he turns on a dime to become a wily antagonist to the desperate Martin.

Along with these experienced veterans was cast a freckle-faced moppet, Adam Weed, in his first television role as Sonny, the deadly "mastermind." "Burl Ives was playing around with Adam a little bit," recalls Carol Weed, the boy's mother. "They had some kind of spirit gum and glue on Burl Ives's eye to make it look like it was closed together, and Adam was a little leery of him at first. He wouldn't get near him! I remember Burl Ives was sitting in his makeup chair, and Adam walked up to him and asked, 'Is that your real eye?' And Burl Ives peeled it off, and said, 'NO!'"[22] Recalls Adam, "He was such a nice guy. He was like a big grandfather to me."

Writer-director Gene Kearney is back on form in this segment with a crackling script, one of his best for the series. The tension screws tighter and tighter as Kearney forcibly aligns the audience with Meredith, the guilt-ridden murderer, and we find ourselves, along with him, lying helpless in a cold, pitch-black, rat-infested earthen pit —anticipating a long, slow, agonizing death.

Adam remembers the excitement of watching the show for the first time with his family: "My mom and I didn't let on about the *whole* plot. It was so cool, because they couldn't believe the twist ending. Leading up to it they were saying, 'Where are you?' Because in the show they're always talking about Sonny—this big guy—and at the end *I* was Sonny!"[23]

## NIGHT GALLERY #35210
Air date: December 10, 1972

## FRIGHT NIGHT
★ ½

Teleplay by Robert Malcolm Young
Based on a story by Kurt van Elting
Directed by Jeff Corey
Music: Eddie Sauter
Director of Photography: Gerald Perry
    Finnerman

### Cast
Tom Ogilvy: Stuart Whitman
Leona Ogilvy: Barbara Anderson
Miss Patience: Ellen Corby
Cousin Zachariah: Alan Napier
Longhair: Larry Watson
1st Goblin: Michael Laird
2d Goblin: Glenna Sergent

*Stuart Whitman and Barbara Anderson in "Fright Night." Courtesy of Foto Fantasies.*

*W*e're truly delighted that you've come. I mean, anyone can go to the movies or a *night double-header or a discotheque or what-have-you, but only the tasteful visit a place like this. Their taste, of course, must of necessity run toward the slightly odd or, at the very least, the bizarre. That's what we deal with here: the bizarre—the expected unexpected, if you will.*

*As in the case of this painting here. It's called "Fright Night," featuring that beloved star of stage and screen . . . the name eludes me, but there is, you'll note, a familiarity about it. Actually, this fiery apparition is the sort of thing that appears in strange houses. Because that's what this painting depicts: a very strange house—and you're welcome to share it with us, because this is the* Night Gallery.

**/ Summary /** Struggling writer Tom Ogilvy and his wife, Leona, have just moved into a remote two-story house inherited from a distant cousin, Zachariah Ogilvy— rumored to have been a dabbler in the occult. His housekeeper warns them never to move the massive, double-locked trunk in the attic. With his last breath, Cousin Zachariah forbade that the trunk be moved—or, under any circumstances, opened. Someone, she was told, would be calling for it.

Tom moves his office into the attic, where he wrestles with his novel—and his curiosity about the trunk. He could swear he's seen it move, as if something in it were trying to get out. Finishing up a late evening writing session, Tom wearily descends to the bedroom, where Leona already lies. Explaining that he got involved in the book, he apologizes for coming in late. Leona is confused; she claims he hit the sack hours ago. Tom chokes off a reply when he sees that his side of the bed shows the outline and indentation of a human form.

Unbeknownst to Tom and Leona, the two demons that inhabit the trunk conspire with each other to possess the young couple and rob them of their immortal souls. A residue of their evil—in the form of a typed manifesto—is left on Tom's typewriter: ". . . for it must come to pass that a Young Woman shall, with a white liquid scalding hot press'd to her lips, and thence forc'd down her throat on the Sabbat-day night be execut'd by the Young Man, her everlasting Soul in forfeit."

Tom is shaken when he reads the document the next morning, but later dismisses it as the work of pranksters. The house is beginning to get to both of them, however: their tempers are wearing thin. Against Zachariah's deathbed wish, Leona arranges to have the trunk removed from the attic, but no matter where it is stored, it always returns to its corner of the attic.

Then falls Halloween night. While Leona heats milk on the stove for Tom's bedtime snack, a furious argument erupts over her running out of cocoa, inspiring from Tom an irrational fury. Goaded by the demonic presence, Tom grasps the pan filled with the boiling milk and is about to pour it down Leona's throat, when a knock at the door brings him back to himself. Scalded, he drops the steaming milk, realizing that he nearly fulfilled the typed manifesto. Answering the door, Leona, expecting trick or treaters, is greeted by the hooded, moldering form of Zachariah Ogilvy. He has finally come for the trunk. As Leona screams in mortal terror, the tall figure mounts the stairs to claim his possession.

The next morning, Tom and Leona feel the evil presence no longer. Cousin Zachariah, reaching out from the grave, must have typed the strange message to warn them of its influence. Relieved, Tom mounts the stairs to his attic office—to find, in the same place, a *different* trunk, with a note pinned to it: "IT WILL BE CALLED FOR." Next Halloween—a year from now! Tom and Leona pack hastily and, posting a For Sale sign, leave behind them the malign influence of the house.

**/ Commentary /** The Ogilvy house front still stands on the Universal Studios back lot. It was used before on *Night Gallery,* most notably in "A Question of Fear" and "The Other Way Out," and was originally the Bates house in *Psycho.* The contrast with Hitchcock's 1960 shocker is a sad reminder of this episode's utter failure.

"Fright Night" tries far too hard to to be scary, tossing into the mix every cliché in the genre to try to spook the audience: the old, dark house; witchcraft and satanic possession; an unsuspecting couple inheriting some Pandora's box of evil; an unseen presence close at hand; and, of course, a visitation from the walking dead. *Night Gallery* had scored highest in the past for its presentation of horror lodged in the mundane and unexpected—"The Doll," "Green Fingers," "The Caterpillar," and "Cool Air"—a more subtle and insinuating brand of terror. "Fright Night," in falling back on stale convention, fails miserably.

One participant for whom "Fright Night" held strong, positive memories is makeup artist Leonard Engelman, who, by the third season, was casting about for more inventive methods to create his horrors. In the past, a quick, cheap makeup method for a moldering corpse would have been to use spirit gum and tissue, as in "Camera Obscura." Engelman created the ghoulish makeup for "Fright Night" with an outlay of only one dollar: "I rubbed a gum eraser all the way down on sandpaper until I had these very, very fine pieces, almost wormy-like, with a yellowish, strange tone. I used duo-adhesive on the actor's face, and then with the same sponge I dipped into this crumbly rubber and stippled on his face. I actually built an appliance onto his face, building up some areas to make them more prominent until he looked like a skull. Then I dusted it all with different shades of fuller's earth to give that withered, aged look, as if the skin were turning to dust."

Engelman was so pleased with the effect that he has used it many times since, most noticeably on one of his many creations for Paul Schrader's appliance-laden remake of *Cat People.* "I came up with that method because I was starting to get bored and I didn't want to do what had been done before. And on every picture I do, I still carry with me a little jar of sanded-down gum eraser, always."[24]

Despite Engelman's efforts, the segment's final horror is unfortunately the least effective scene in "Fright Night." The story's premise included a twist on the Halloween ritual that culminates in the well-lit, undisguised appearance of this gore-covered walking corpse at the door. The camera holds on it . . . and holds on it. In doing so, the audience gets a prolonged look at the makeup artist's excellent handiwork, but dwelling on it under heavy wattage and at length completely destroys its effect. Universal's pressure on Laird to invest the show with some trite, old-fashioned bogies is evident here; their meddling was not a success. To cite the overused example of *The Monkey's Paw,* horror, shadowed and unseen, is always more effective than horror examined in the light of day.

"I hated 'Fright Night,'" says director Jeff Corey. "There was a lot of intrusion on Jack's part. Somebody in the Black Tower was giving him hell, and he was very, very cranky. He wanted certain kinds of effects—he wanted this, he wanted that—but I didn't quite understand the goddamned story. It was a terrible script. You see, the others I did were Rod's and really made sense."

So, what *is* this story about? Why did Zachariah have a pair of demons trapped like genies in a trunk? Why did he come back to fetch the trunk? Who was sneaking into bed with Leona and why? "Fright Night" is not, by any means, an ambiguously told story, and these plot vagaries do not mesh with its other straightforward elements. With nothing explained, the premise is reduced to a nonsensical, unsatisfying mishmash.

Laird was unhappy with Corey's work and never used him afterward, even though Corey had directed many of *Night Gallery*'s best segments up to that point. Corey certainly holds little affection for the segment: "Remembering 'Fright Night' and the complete lack of fun doing it made me feel it's just as well that I stopped directing. I remember how bone-weary I'd be working on that goddamned thing, and it didn't amount to a hill of beans."[25]

NIGHT GALLERY #35230
Air date: December 17, 1972

FINNEGAN'S FLIGHT
★ ★ ½

Written by Rod Serling
Directed by Gene Kearney
Music: Eddie Sauter
Director of Photography: Gerald Perry Finnerman

**Cast**

Charlie Finnegan: Burgess Meredith
Pete Tuttle: Cameron Mitchell
Dr. Simsich: Barry Sullivan
Warden: Kenneth Tobey
3d Prisoner: Dort Clark
Infirmary Guard: John Gilgreen
2d Prisoner: Roger E. Mosley
1st Prisoner: Raymond Mayo
Tower Guard: Michael Masters

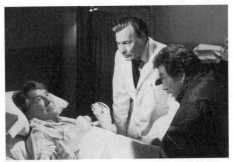

*Burgess Meredith, Barry Sullivan, and Cameron Mitchell in "Finnegan's Flight." Courtesy of Globe Photos.*

Good *evening, sports fans. In discerning circles I'm known as the Howard Cosell of the crypt, which is to say I'm more or less a professional practitioner of art that tells a story, and stories that dabble in themes that don't lend themselves to dinner conversation.*

*Now here you have a study in penology—man imprisoned by his fellow man, caged in a barred cubicle and left alone far too long to contemplate both his sin and his sanity. This painting is called "Finnegan's Flight." It touches upon prisons, hypnosis, and the soaring wings of imagination—but as to the latter, a small warning: imagination can be a double-edged thing. It can take you out of the humdrum realities, but it can also fly you to a place much less pleasant. May I introduce to you now Mr. Finnegan in his first and last appearance in the* Night Gallery.

**/ Summary /** Charlie Finnegan, serving a life sentence in a federal penitentiary, longs to escape the stone walls that enclose him. More than that, he yearns to fly an airplane, symbolic of his desperate hunger for freedom. He meets up with Pete Tuttle, a petty criminal with a small talent for hypnosis. Tuttle can relieve Finnegan's pangs by placing him into a hypnotic trance and giving him wings. Tuttle, to amuse himself, tests Finnegan's receptiveness by feeding him the idea that he can batter down the prison walls with his naked fists. On his first attempt, Finnegan breaks nearly all the bones in his hands and is shipped off to the infirmary.

The prison psychiatrist, Simsich, is fascinated by Finnegan's case. Tuttle tells the doctor that his sessions with Finnegan act as a relief valve for the old lifer: "I think, doctor, that without me Charlie Finnegan will turn his block into a garbage dump and maybe twenty prisoners nearest him into corpses. That's how close to the old fracture he is." Tuttle demonstrates the power of the man's mind: a cup of ordinary cooler water raises blisters on Finnegan's fingers when Tuttle convinces him under hypnosis that it's boiling hot.

Simsich arranges with the warden for the hypnosis sessions to be conducted in the infirmary. With Finnegan under sedation, Tuttle tells Charlie he's up in the clouds, flying an airplane. Finnegan holds his broken hands up as if grasping the wheel, and from his mouth comes the buzzing sounds of the motor. Soon Finnegan begins to choke and wheeze. Simsich recognizes the signs of hypoxia—Finnegan is running out of air. He believes he is twenty thousand feet up in a fast moving jet, and his lungs are screaming for oxygen. His face begins to blister. Finnegan, pushed by Tuttle's suggestion, has climbed too high, now forty thousand feet up—and with no air pressure to drive oxygen into his system, his blood is boiling in his veins. Panicked, Tuttle talks Finnegan down from the stratosphere, but it soon becomes apparent that he is coming down far too fast. An invisible wind stirs Finnegan's hair and his features are contorted by heavy G-forces. Finnegan's engine vocalizations become deeper, merging into what sounds like a plane in a power dive. Tuttle and Simsich watch in amazement as Finnegan tries desperately to regain control of his imaginary craft. A sudden, deafening explosion rocks the infirmary as Charlie Finnegan crashes his "plane." Peering through the smoke, the horrified observers can make out the burning figure of the old lifer on his cot.

Returned to his cell, Tuttle peers out of his barred window as Finnegan's charred remains are removed from the infirmary building by ambulance. "Tell me, Charlie boy," he whispers through the bars. "How does it feel to be free?"

/ **Commentary** / This segment is likely Serling's affectionate nod toward his novelist brother, Robert, whose passion to fly helped create such best-sellers as *The President's Plane Is Missing*. Unfortunately, "Finnegan's Flight" bears a suspicious resemblance to a first-season *Gallery* segment, "The Dead Man," another tale of a hypnosis experiment gone terribly wrong—a comparison that is not to the benefit of the later episode. Serling's take on the idea is interesting, though, using the penal system as a petri dish in an experiment on the effects of extended confinement and the inevitable withering of the human spirit. Serling rewrote the concept with a completely different plot, called "Suggestion," for the 1972 Bantam paperback *Night Gallery 2*.

To the episode's benefit, an impressive cast was assembled. Burgess Meredith paints a sympathetic portrait of Finnegan, the career criminal: deceptively introverted and childlike; in reality, a lit fuse. Cameron Mitchell enjoys the more complex role of the manipulative Tuttle: though he recognizes he is exploiting his subject, he still conveys a strange compassion for the tortured Finnegan. The two actors' perceptive character turns bring out the poignant strain in Serling's tale.

On the down side, the script shows signs of padding. Bowing to network pressure to "goose it up," Serling added a new opener showing the hypnotized Finnegan trying to break out of prison. Unfortunately, its presence makes a later scene—Finnegan's second attempt to escape—appear redundant.

The critical part of the production for all concerned was the filming of the climactic scene, which required a number of different effects—some quite dangerous to achieve. Finnegan, in a trance, is supposed to suffer the effects of hypoxia, lose control, and crash his "plane." "They put some stuff in Burgess Meredith's mouth," recalls actor John Gilgreen, who played the infirmary guard. "It was kind of like Alka-Seltzer. It looked awful, like he was throwing up white chalk. And the makeup man kept putting these blue and red sores on his face. It was like that Merle Norman stuff they used to put on women: when it dried it made your face look like it had been horribly burned, and then you peeled it off."[26] Not everyone was impressed by the effect. "There was a lot of concern when he was frothing at the mouth," recalls editor Richard Bracken. "I had a problem with it, but the director thought it was right. I didn't like it at the time and I don't like it now."[27]

When it came to rigging the explosion of Finnegan's "plane," the level of danger rose considerably. First, the special-effects crew turned Finnegan's bed into a series of flaming burners that would render the initial fireball and the smoke. Then, an extra air explosion was rigged that would blow debris all over the infirmary set. Recalls Gilgreen: "Cam Mitchell was sitting on the edge of the bed. I'm standing right behind it, and Barry Sullivan is standing beside me. I start backing away, and the director said, 'Wait a minute. You can't do that.' And I said, 'What do you mean, I can't do that? I'm not going to stand up there!' He said, 'Yeah, but you've got Cameron and Barry, and *they're* standing there.' And I said, 'I don't give a shit! Just because they're stupid doesn't mean *I'm* going to be!'"

Director Gene Kearney's persuasion failed to convince Gilgreen, who turned instead to the fireman assigned to the production. "I looked over at him and I said, 'Is this goddamned thing safe?' He said, 'Oh, absolutely. I've checked it.' So I move back up, and out of the corner of my eye I saw this fireman standing over at the exit with one hand on the door! And it's too late for me to move! You talk about an explosion! It burned Cameron Mitchell's eyebrows off! That damned thing went KABOOM!"[28]

From the look of it, budget strains were beginning to take their toll on *Night Gallery*. "Finnegan's Flight" traces a prisoner's growing claustrophobia, but this lockup is about as forbidding as a college administration complex. Details of set decoration, costuming, hairstyles, all work to limit the verisimilitude of the segment. "This was essentially the problem with *Night Gallery:* that it was unsubtle," Serling would later complain. "They would take scripts that essentially had something going for them, some degree of merit, and gave [them] no help whatsoever. This is the terrible plight of the screenwriter, constantly." The accumulation of small, ill-considered details of production, he continued, could ruin the dramatic impact of a segment. "It's a little thing, but if you get thirty-two of these weaknesses and frailties, suddenly the corpse starts to bleed. Something has been materially affected, and negatively so."[29] Such is the case here. Most damaging of all is Gene Kearney's direction, which lacks the style and atmosphere achieved in the best *Night Gallery* segments, stamping "Finnegan's Flight" with the look of standard television fare.

NIGHT GALLERY #35227
Air date: December 24, 1972

SHE'LL BE COMPANY FOR YOU
★ ½

Teleplay by David Rayfiel
Based on the short story by Andrea Newman
Directed by Gerald Perry Finnerman
Music: Eddie Sauter
Director of Photography: Lloyd Ahern

**Cast**
Henry Auden: Leonard Nimoy
Barbara Morgan: Lorraine Gary
June: Kathryn Hays
Reverend: Bern Hoffman

*Leonard Nimoy in "She'll Be Company for You." Courtesy of Globe Photos.*

*L*est you be turned off by the dim light and somber mien of this place, let me reassure that there is nobody here but us art lovers. I'm your tour guide in a place designed to show you the beauty of the unexpected. Our conception of beauty may be a bit different than the norm. For example, some might see something attractive in a goldfish; we, on the other hand, find nothing lovelier than a piranha.

Now this canvas here: dark hallway, door slightly ajar, a rather disquieting red room at the end of the hall—and a very large cat. We suggest to you that while felines may look cute and cuddly and playfully mischievous, our suggestion is that you feed them a bit of milk and get rid of them. Because cats are and always have been Satan's familiars. Our painting title is "She'll Be Company for You," and it's hung in this place we call the Night Gallery.

/ **Summary** / Henry Auden's invalid wife, Margaret, has finally died, and the only emotion he can muster at her funeral is relief. Margaret's close friend Barbara senses it, and resents Henry for it. She invites herself over to his house after the funeral and, feigning concern for his loneliness, offers to send over her cat while she is away on vacation.

To Henry's consternation, she does just that. Barbara's orange tabby, Jennet, is delivered on his doorstep. Its presence brings back to Henry unpleasant memories of Margaret, of her demands on him. At times he thinks he can even hear her bedside bell ringing, calling him for some errand or other. A greater concern takes over when Henry sees and hears evidence of a much larger cat in and around his house—a shadow here, a paw track there, a guttural throat rattle, sometimes a roar. Hallucinations, no doubt, but the cat's presence is definitely chipping away at his peace of mind—perhaps his very sanity.

Henry begins sleeping at his office, but even there he can find no peace. His secretary, June, with whom he once had an affair, has treated him harshly since Margaret's death. She even suspects foul play—the influence of the poisonous Barbara, he is sure.

Leaving the office early to return home, Henry now sees more than just evidence of a large cat. Through a second-story window he watches in amazement as a tiger wends its sinuous way through the shrubbery of his back garden. Racing downstairs, he pulls a huge blade from a kitchen drawer and races out into the garden, maniacally hacking at the bushes, chasing the tiger—or is it Jennet?—through the undergrowth. Exhausted and emotionally drained, he collapses, weeping. Margaret is calling him—he can hear her bedside bell ringing. Resigned, Henry walks slowly up the stairs to her room. He senses Jennet coming—stealthy, steady, following him—and breathes a prayer that it won't hurt much.

When Barbara arrives the next morning to pick up her cat, she finds the bottom floor deserted . . . and upstairs, large, slashing claw marks on the door to Margaret's room. Inside, she finds Henry sprawled on the bed—and poised nearby, lapping at the spreading pool of his blood, is Jennet.

/ **Commentary** / Jack Laird gave cinematographer Gerald Finnerman, who had lensed some of *Night Gallery*'s finest moments, his first directorial shot on "She'll Be Company for You." Unfortunately, the assignment was an extremely complex and hallucinatory script. In trying to capture the ambiguities and psychological suggestiveness of David Rayfiel's teleplay, Finnerman lost his grip on the proceedings.

"Jerry had a tough script," recounts star Leonard Nimoy. "It was kind of vague—the story was kind of ephemeral, as I recall, a little tough to get your hands on exactly what was going on."[30] Rayfiel, discussing his philosophy of writing, admits his approach makes the audience work at the film experience. "I just love things to be there without being said. I hate being explicit because I think you can get more out of holding back—*not* saying it—because the audience then does it. Just to be obscure for the sake of being obscure is a way of hiding, and I don't ever mean to do that. But I do think that it's infinitely more of an experience for the audience if they meet you more than halfway."[31]

Rayfiel's script does have an intriguing, teasing quality to it, but Finnerman's interpretation is too literal and lacking in atmosphere for this kind of psychological fantasy. Confusing segues, disjointed shot syntax, too many zooms, and ineffective visual effects make this episode difficult to watch. In one sequence, Rayfiel's script describes Henry's disturbance by a presence in the room that he cannot catch sight of:

Henry feels uneasy, turns abruptly:

FOYER / STAIRS / HALLWAY — HENRY'S POINT OF VIEW

Series of whip pans and holds—as if trying to catch some hidden observer. Each time there's a trace of movement—a glimpse of color, a shadow, a blur—but by the time the view is steady . . . nothing.[32]

Finnerman's interpretation appears to show Henry unraveling mentally by photographing Nimoy spinning on a lazy susan while cut-out silhouettes of cats are projected against the walls. The effect is ludicrous.

The script describes the cat growing to leopard- and tiger-size proportions, and an actual leopard and tiger were used for the filming. "I wanted it to be more mysterious than that," Rayfiel grouses. "In the original version of *Cat People*, they're just shadows and sounds, and you never do see the frightful thing that everybody's afraid of. It's the same thing here. I think the hint of something horrifying, traces of it— gashes on wood or something like that—is best. But just to show, 'Oh, yeah, it's a pussycat! Oh, look, now it's bigger! Hey—it's a leopard! Oops—what d'ya know, it's a tiger!' I think that's just wrong. I wouldn't have written that as a stage direction— that's a director's touch." Rayfiel believes the big cats should have been glimpsed only in part, their size concealed. "Mostly it should be unseen," he says, "and then *maybe* once. If you keep the goals modest, then you don't worry so much about the production. If you try to do too much, then, yeah, it'll hurt you."[33]

As a cinematographer turned director, Finnerman believes he had difficulty mastering the conceptual whole:

It's my conviction that cinematographers generally do not make good directors because they're too visual. Now, there have been some famous cinematographers who have directed: Victor Fleming, George Stevens, Rudy Maté, Guy Green, Freddie Francis. I look at their work and I can tell that sometimes the photographer overlaps the director, and that's not good. You have to tell the story like a director and disconnect yourself from the total lighting aspect, and that's what we *don't* do. I used to get frustrated directing. I spent so much time in getting the look that I felt I often overlooked something with the people. It wasn't that fulfilling.[34]

Finnerman, whose work photographing the classic *Star Trek* is legendary, hired friend Leonard Nimoy to star. As the callous Henry, Nimoy has some good moments, and he is matched with an exceptional supporting cast. Kathryn Hays shines briefly in her role as Henry's secretary; and as the suspicious Barbara, Lorraine Gary possesses a diva's glamour, sinuous and appropriately feline. For a scene that wound up on the cutting room floor, early film comedian Jack Oakie was cast as Willy, a bartender who declines Henry's pleas to take Jennet off his hands.

"It was an interesting show," Finnerman says. "I went in with trepidation because the lady star, Lorraine Gary, was [Universal executive] Sid Sheinberg's wife. And Jack Oakie, he couldn't hear a goddamned thing. Every time I tried to rehearse him with other people, he would shout, 'Speak up! Speak up!' That was rattling, though we got through it."[35]

On the whole, the other elements of production—photography, production design, editing—are quite poor; and Eddie Sauter's meowing "kitty" music is perhaps the worst of all. Rayfiel, while unhappy with his script's interpretation, admits that he has little love for fantasy and related genres: "Science fiction has never interested me too much. The rules aren't strict enough. It's like having an insane protagonist—you don't have to think about his motivation because he's crazy, and he can do anything. Science fiction is similar—anything can happen."[36]

## NIGHT GALLERY #35201
Air date: January 7, 1973

### THE RING WITH THE RED VELVET ROPES
★ ★

Teleplay by Robert Malcolm Young
Based on the short story "The Ring with the Velvet Ropes" by Edward D. Hoch
Directed by Jeannot Szwarc
Music: Eddie Sauter
Director of Photography: Gerald Perry Finnerman

**Cast**
Jim Figg: Gary Lockwood
Roderick Blanco: Chuck Connors
Sandra Blanco: Joan van Ark
Max: Ralph Manza
Hayes: Charles Davis
Big Dan Anger: Ji-Tu Cumbuka
2d Reporter: James Bacon
Referee: Frankie Van

*Chuck Connors in "The Ring with the Red Velvet Ropes." Courtesy of Hollywood Book and Poster Co.*

*G*ood evening. I might offer this small admonishment if you happen to be a purist in your judgment of art. These are not your ordinary canvases. You don't find Monet in a mausoleum or a van Gogh in a graveyard.

*This item here, commentative on what A. J. Liebling referred to as "the sweet science," obviously having something to do with the manly art of self-defense: boxing. But if the Marquis of Queensberry mayhem doesn't particularly turn you on, don't turn this off. This painting tells the story infinitely more intriguing than a couple of fast boys mixing it up. It's called "The Ring with the Red Velvet Ropes," and it tells you the tale of precisely who is the real heavyweight boxing champion of the world—and I think you'll be surprised. Surprise happens to be our stock-in-trade, because this is the* Night Gallery.

**/ Summary /** Jim Figg is the new heavyweight champion. He has just won the title by annihilating the previous titleholder, Big Dan Anger. The former champ is down —but not out, apparently: supposedly rushed to the hospital for surgery, Anger appears in Figg's dressing room after the bout, battered and bleeding, to inform Figg he is no more the champion than Anger was. Shaken by the visitation, Figg confides the episode to his manager, who chalks it up to a few too many shots to the head.

Emerging from his shower a few minutes later, Figg has reason to agree. He is no longer in his dressing room. He has instead stepped into a lavishly appointed suite. The valet who hands him a towel seems to feel he belongs there, but no amount of questioning from Figg can get an explanation out of the impassive servant—merely that Figg is now the guest of Mr. and Mrs. Roderick Blanco.

Figg now suspects a kidnapping plot, but when Roderick Blanco makes his dramatic appearance, the only thing that interests his host is a private match with the new champion. From their conversation, Figg gathers that he is not the first fighter ever to have gone through this bizarre experience. Blanco refers to literally scores of champions that he has challenged—and beaten—in his private ring.

Figg begins to realize that the palatial Blanco residence exists on no normal plane of existence, and the stakes in his fight with Blanco are considerably higher than he first imagined. Sandra Blanco comes to Figg the night before the bout. Her husband, she says, has never been beaten, but she suspects Figg will be the first to defeat him. She warns Figg to throw the fight, hinting that it would be for his own good.

Sandra and the estate employees, detached and dead silent, gather to watch the match. Blanco's boxing ring seems to hover in a cavernous red limbo. The two fighters play out their punishing drama to an eerie quiet, and Blanco begins to falter against Figg's quicksilver grace and stamina. Cuts open up over Blanco's eyes as his opponent pummels him with lightning punches. When Blanco finally falls for the ten-count, his face is a welter of blood and pulpy flesh. The referee, crouching over the crumpled form, announces, "The champion is dead. Long live the champion." Everyone rises in mute reverence to Figg as he kneels to examine the former champion. Blanco's face and body have become withered, deteriorated, and shrunken with an indeterminate age. "Who was he?" Figg asks, incredulous. "He was the *real* champion," the valet answers, "having first taken the title from Jem Mace in 1861, and having successfully defended it ever since . . . until tonight." Benumbed, Figg is left alone with Sandra. "Winner take all, Jim," she says. For how long? "As long as you win," Sandra replies, leading him out of the arena.

**/ Commentary /** One of director Jeannot Szwarc's favorites, "The Ring with the Red Velvet Ropes" was his attempt to create a kind of supernatural *Body and Soul*. A number of negative aspects worked against him in this endeavor, first of which is its script.

Surprisingly, Edward D. Hoch's original short story had no supernatural trappings: Roderick Blanco is a wealthy, talented, and pathologically unbalanced amateur boxer who kidnaps the heavyweight champion and forces him into a match, a story that wouldn't have been out of place on *Alfred Hitchcock Presents*. In Robert Malcolm Young's overheated adaptation, Jim Figg's strange destiny is telegraphed long before the end thanks to the less than cryptic insinuations of the dialogue and Young's lapse into standard fantasy conventions.

Performances are uneven: Joan van Ark's breathy, affected sex siren is far too stagy; likewise the cosmic champion, Chuck Connors, whose ominous pronouncements, laden with dramatic weight and unintentional humor, help thrust the proceedings dangerously close to eye-rolling camp. Of the lead players, only Gary Lockwood (*2001: A Space Odyssey*) convinces as the cocky Figg.

For Lockwood, the fight sequences came naturally. A top athlete at UCLA, Lockwood was a gifted amateur boxer. "In 'The Ring with the Red Velvet Ropes,' we didn't have a lot of hard-core boxing stuff," recalls Lockwood. "Chuck Connors was a very good athlete [a first baseman for the Dodgers in his youth], so it was not that difficult. Chuck and I figured out the moves, the footwork, throwing hooks and jabs—we knew how to do that, no problem. It was very easy." Despite the presence of technical boxers on the set, Lockwood and Connors depended on their own expertise, and, unlike their two characters, shared an excellent rapport: "Chuck was a very professional guy. He knew exactly what he was doing, and I like that because I don't have to work late. I belong to the Bob Mitchum school, man. Get the shit on paper and get out of there!"[37]

As with the performances, the production quality is similarly uneven. Despite his puny budget, Joseph Alves's startling set designs, particularly the Edwardian Valhalla of Blanco's "residence," are quite effective. Unfortunately, little else is. Eddie Sauter's score, a ludicrous parody of horror film music (on a cheesy funeral organ, no less), defines overstatement, and even Szwarc seems unable to effectively shape the necessary haunted atmosphere. As a telling example, the episode's key sequence, the contest between Figg and Blanco, is surprisingly limp. Opportunities to exploit its violence with vigorous, off-kilter compositions, atmospheric lighting, a tension-building cutting scheme—the hallmarks of Szwarc's other superb work on *Night Gallery*—go untapped here, conveying little of the spectacle. In a move intended to capture the eerie, spectatorless silence that accompanies the fight, the scene is deliberately left sans music, denying to the viewer the sole remaining emotional prompt. Robbed of these critical cinematic elements, this pugilistic exchange hits the canvas before the first bell and never gets up. With Szwarc's usual visual wizardry either overdone or strangely absent, as much can be claimed for the whole episode.

NIGHT GALLERY #35229
Air date: January 14, 1973

SOMETHING IN THE WOODWORK
★ ★ ★

Teleplay by Rod Serling
Based on the short story "Housebound" by R. Chetwynd-Hayes
Directed by Edward M. Abroms
Music: Eddie Sauter
Director of Photography: Lloyd Ahern

**Cast**
Molly Wheatland: Geraldine Page
Charlie Wheatland: Leif Erickson
Joe Wilson: Paul Jenkins
Jamie Dilman: John McMurtry
Julie: Barbara Rhoades

*Paul Jenkins and Geraldine Page in "Something in the Woodwork." Courtesy of TV History Archives.*

G*ood evening. On behalf of the management, I'm authorized to tell you that your presence here gives them great pleasure. They'd all be here to greet you personally if not for prior commitments. Several are attending funerals, and would've been here if it weren't so difficult to get out of the box—which should give you some idea as to the nature of our art.*

*Now this painting, for example. Stairway and spectre, cobwebs and darkness. It's called "Something in the Woodwork." It tells of what one might look for when purchasing a house, because that creak you hear in the dead of night is not always an errant rafter. Sometimes if you walk up those attic steps you'll find yourself face to face with the very thing that goes thump in the night. This, ladies and gentlemen, is the* Night Gallery.

**/ Summary /** Molly Wheatland, an alcoholic divorcée, has recently purchased a house for an incredibly low sum. Because of a rumored ghost, the house has stood empty for thirty years. Long ago, a bank robber named Jamie Dilman was shot to death in a gun battle with police, and supposedly has haunted the attic ever since. Molly senses his presence—but it will take a lot more than unquiet spirits in the attic to scare her off. In fact, she could use the company.

Desperately lonely, Molly invites her ex-husband, Charlie, to the house in a ruse to throw him a little birthday party. With his girlfriend waiting in the car, Charlie must decline. Molly, hurt, sneers that she has no need for him. She has her own friends . . . like the one in the attic. He lives behind the walls, in the woodwork—a shadow, she claims. Charlie, believing her insane, assures Molly that he will return later with help.

Distraught, Molly heads upstairs to try to communicate with the presence in the attic. She receives a response in a hollow, resonating voice: *"Leave me alone."* Molly resorts to blackmail: if Jamie doesn't help her, she will burn down his eternal resting spot. "What can I do?" asks the ghost. "Charlie has a bum ticker, Jamie," Molly smiles. *"Frighten him to death."*

When Charlie arrives that evening, Molly, smiling, asserts her sanity, daring Charlie to go into the attic. Humoring her, Charlie wearily ascends the stairs. Molly hears a sharp cry and the sound of a slumping body. Chuckling to herself, she pours herself another martini—and then freezes, halted by the sound of a creaking stair. The figure of Charlie appears on the landing, the face white and deathlike, the movements spasmodic. Descending the stairs toward Molly, he opens his mouth to speak—but it is Jamie Dilman's sepulchral voice that emerges: "Charlie is no longer with us, Mrs. Wheatland. He's in the attic room . . . moving around . . . getting used to things. Why didn't you leave me alone? There was peace in the woodwork." And Jamie Dilman, arms outstretched, moves toward the terrified, hysterically screaming Molly.

**/ Commentary /** For "Something in the Woodwork," Geraldine Page returned for her third appearance on *Night Gallery*, sketching yet another memorable portrait. Director Edward Abroms, concerned about Page's hard-to-handle reputation, found her easygoing and cooperative. "She came from Broadway, a method actor," Abroms says. "I had always heard that she ate directors up alive. On my first day, I said, 'Geraldine, I'm quite new at this, but I think I know what I'm doing, and if you have any input, feel free.' She said, 'Oh, no, you're doing fine, I've just got to worry about my wardrobe and my makeup.' She was a sweetheart, I was really amazed."

One of the third season's rare successes, "Something in the Woodwork" is based on R. Chetwynd-Hayes's tidy little chiller "Housebound." Serling, faced again with interior storytelling, created an open conflict with which the characters could grapple. Instead of the lead character suffering silently in a loveless marriage and enlisting a ghost to help extract her from it, Serling brought the rift out in the open and used it.

To create the impression of Jamie Dilman's ghost, Abroms and cinematographer Lloyd Ahern, Sr. used a tilted pane of reflective glass in front of the lens to catch the reflection of the actor positioned off-stage. To make him vanish, the glass was simply tipped slightly, and—*poof*—no Jamie. The actor's unusual costuming and makeup— a black body stocking, his face painted half black, half white—completed the illusion of the spirit's disembodied head floating in the cobwebbed nooks of the attic.

Abroms, who at the time was balancing both an editing and directing career—he was the primary editor for the *Night Gallery* pilot—moves with confidence into this shadowy genre. His sensational use of handheld camera to crawl along the wood-work in the attic is unsettling and effective; his other visuals suggest an intolerance to-ward the wholly conventional setups that mark the industry hack. "I was probably in my second or third year of directing," Abroms says. "I was still kind of feeling my oats, trying everything. I remember I did a particular shot in her living room where she was talking to the handyman. He had his hand on his hip, and I was shooting through his arm, which in later years I saw and thought, God, that's arty-farty, I would never do that now!"[38] Spielberg has similarly criticized his own early work, and the tendency for young directors to take chances with film grammar—for which they are sometimes ashamed later—is strong. This genre, however, naturally more outland-ish, welcomes this kind of cinematic expression as appropriate to achieving its end: the creation in a supposedly day-to-day experience of a slightly akimbo atmosphere. Abroms does so here with genuine flair.

NIGHT GALLERY #35226
Air date: March 4, 1973

DEATH ON A BARGE
★ ★ ½

Teleplay by Halsted Welles
Based on the short story "The Canal" by
    Everil Worrell
Directed by Leonard Nimoy
Music: Eddie Sauter
Director of Photography: Gerald Perry
    Finnerman

**Cast**
Hyacinth: Lesley Ann Warren
Ron: Robert Pratt
Jake: Lou Antonio
Phyllis: Brooke Bundy
Father: Jim Boles
Coastguardsman: Artie Spain
Customer #33: Dorothy Konrad
Customer #32: De De Young

*Lesley Ann Warren and Robert Pratt in "Death on a Barge." Courtesy of Globe Photos.*

$W$*e offer you both tricks and treats in this special realm, where the national dish is pumpkin, the national flower is wolfsbane, and our national anthem is the funeral march— which should give you some definitive idea as to the nature of this place.*

*We show paintings like this one. In a color scheme of blood-red sky with corpse-white moon, this, we tell you up front, is a story of vampires. And of course this must conjure up images of Bela Lugosi and Christopher Lee, somewhat frigid, malevolent, monstrous creatures. But reserve such all-conclusive judgment of the living dead until you hear the story of a particular vampire, the kind you might find in a place like this, the* Night Gallery.

**/ Summary /** Ron's days are spent on the pier selling fish with his partner Jake. At night, he sneaks out to talk with Hyacinth, a lonely, darkly beautiful woman who lives with her father, a reclusive fisherman, on a barge anchored in the canal. Ron wants to visit in the daytime, but Hyacinth forbids it, explaining that she sleeps during the day. Her fear of crossing running water keeps her marooned, but the canal is slowly being drained. Soon she will be able to come to him.

Ron's girlfriend Phyllis has become suspicious and follows him secretly one night. After Ron leaves Hyacinth at dawn, Phyllis sneaks on board the barge to find Hyacinth below deck—climbing into a coffin. Hyacinth attacks her, but Phyllis manages to escape when her rival is struck by the rays of the morning sun.

Horrified, Phyllis looks into the backgrounds of Hyacinth and her father. Before moving to the area, they lived in Congers, where a number of unexplained murders occurred. Phyllis tries to convince Ron and Jake that Hyacinth is a vampire. Neither are buying it, but Phyllis's story has made Jake curious, and he also follows Ron one night. When he gets a look at Hyacinth, he, too, is caught by her strange allure. When Ron, out of fear, can't bring himself to yield to the ravenous Hyacinth, Jake succumbs in his place. His body is found on the beach with his throat torn out, drained of blood.

Ron finds Hyacinth below deck in her box of earth. He has come to take her out into the morning sun, but she begs him to give her a quick death—using a stake her father keeps close by. Ron is poised to strike but falters as she draws him to her with an irresistible emotional appeal. He drops the weapon and falls into her arms. Before she can deliver her deadly kiss, her father arrives and drives the stake into his daughter's heart. Hyacinth dissolves into a skeleton before their eyes.

**/ Commentary /** Leonard Nimoy, director of some of the better entries in the *Star Trek* feature franchise, got his behind-the-camera career boost on *Night Gallery*. "I had a one-year contract at Universal," Nimoy recalls, "to do some acting and develop some directing projects. I met Jack Laird, who had shown a bent for starting new directors, and had several conversations with him. And I guess I just pestered him long enough, until finally one day he called me in and said, 'Read this script.' I thought it was a wonderful story, a sort of Romeo and Juliet love story with vampire turns, and he gave me the job."

Casting came easy. Nimoy had worked with Lesley Ann Warren the year before in *Mission: Impossible,* and she seemed the ideal choice for Hyacinth. For the part of Ron, relative newcomer Robert Pratt was hired on the strength of his other television work. Together, they would portray the doomed lovers of Halsted Welles's script.

What man *wouldn't* find himself risking his immortal soul for a chance at Warren's Hyacinth? She succeeds in being both wraithlike and deliciously carnal at the same time, luxuriating in the doomed, tortured vampire prototype with its historical suggestion of sexual hunger. What is harder to divine, however, is why Hyacinth returns her suitor's love. As portrayed by the bland Robert Pratt, Ron is a pretty big zero. With such uneven performances, the motivational algebra just doesn't add up in this segment.

Furthering the frustration, Halsted Welles punctuates his script with the vernacular of the time. "Death on a Barge" has uncomfortable moments where the dialogue is an obvious attempt to emulate the hip jive of the 1970s generation:

RON

It's my life, okay? I'm not going to live it square! I like risk! I believe the whole trip! I'm drawn to her! I dig her strangeness! I dig her mystery! Most of all, I just plain want to know! Is she for real? Is a vampire for real?

Beyond such shortcomings, Leonard Nimoy's directorial debut is quite impressive. The opening sequence sets the dreamlike mood exceptionally well: a crane shot that follows Ron down the dock, pulling up and back to include the canal front and the barge with Hyacinth. The camera locks on Hyacinth's lace-draped hand, following it as she raises it to push her dark hair from her pale, languid face. Atmosphere is heavy, the dockfront misty and strange. Although forced to shoot day-for-night (almost always an ineffective compromise), Nimoy and cinematographer Gerald Finnerman use it to their advantage, creating a netherworld of half-lights and strong, evocative color contrasts.

"Jerry and I had spent some time together on *Star Trek* and he was very supportive, very helpful," Nimoy says. "The tough thing about this job, and *Night Gallery* in general, was that the very title suggests dark of night, and you could not shoot at night. They wouldn't allow it because it was too expensive."[39] Finnerman concurs: "I told them, 'I'll shoot this day-for-night, but you have to do it my way—in backlight. In the afternoons, when the sun is setting in the west, I want to be shooting into the west; and when the sun is coming up, I want to be shooting east. And I don't want to shoot sky unless it's really blue. Otherwise, it won't look good.'"[40]

"Shooting day-for-night was extremely difficult," Nimoy says.

To get the night effect, you had to shoot constantly toward the sun so that all of your subject matter is backlit. And then by printing the film dark you get an effect of moonlight. If your subject is frontlit—direct, head-on sunlight—you can't get that effect. So each day had to be planned in such a way that you were moving around with the sun, and we had to shoot out of sequence in order to keep the sun behind the subjects. I think we did manage to get a very good look to the show, but it was not easy. It was really a logistical task.

Complicating the shooting were the newly established Universal Tour trams traversing the back lot. "The trams were bothersome," admits Nimoy.

When the trams first started coming around, the tour guides would be talking over their PA systems, and the assistant directors would ask them to stop and be quiet while they were shooting. Well, then the edict came down that you don't stop the *tram*, you stop the *shooting*. And it was quickly apparent that the most important thing at Universal was the tourist business. It was difficult. *"There they are over there shooting* Night Gallery, *the famous show that you've seen on Wednesday nights, ten o'clock. There it is, right there, folks, they're shooting a vampire show this week. Who's starring in this episode, can you recognize anybody over there?"* Shut up![41]

"We felt like animals in a zoo," says assistant director Ralph Sariego. "It was frustrating."[42]

Difficulties aside, what emerges is a moody and effective fantasy. Nimoy himself was quite pleased with the outcome. "I thought both Lesley and Robert did wonderful work. I liked the story from the beginning—I found it interesting and dramatic and scary, I found the characters attractive. I enjoyed doing it a lot, but it was hard because you were constantly under pressure—speed, speed, speed."

Apparently, the producer appreciated the work of his new director as well. Recalls Nimoy, "Immediately after it was done, Jack Laird offered me another *Night Gallery* episode, which I couldn't do because I had accepted a job to act in a production of *Oliver!* in Milwaukee. I felt badly because I thought, 'Gee, I'm just getting started with my directing career and I'm stepping on my own foot here, I'm leaving town.' But it was a wonderful experience, I really appreciated being given the chance to do it."[43] It was just as well Nimoy couldn't accept. The assignment Laird offered was without doubt the series' worst script—"Hatred unto Death."

## NIGHT GALLERY #35221
Air date: May 13, 1972

WHISPER
★ ★ ½

Teleplay by David Rayfiel
Based on the short story by Martin Waddell
Directed by Jeannot Szwarc
Music: Eddie Sauter
Director of Photography: Gerald Perry Finnerman

*Sally Field in "Whisper." Courtesy of TV History Archives.*

**Cast**

Charlie: Dean Stockwell
Irene: Sally Field
Dr. Kennaway: Kent Smith

*W*e're most pleased that you've seen fit to visit us here. As usual we're doing business
at the old stand—or on the same wires if you will—because our stock-in-trade is paintings.
All sorts of paintings: charming little still lifes and, on a few occasions, a few still deaths.

Now check this one if you will: strips of ethereal night clouds as seen from the vantage
point of a square acre of tombstones, and the face of a neutral onlooker who surveys the
silence. Well, perhaps not quite total silence, because the name of our painting is "Whisper,"
and it tells the story of one body inhabited by two people—and at a point, as you can well
imagine, this gets crowded. And if this one doesn't ice up the old spine, we'll send you one of
our official apologies . . . along with the body. That's the kind of guarantee you get in the
Night Gallery.

**/ Summary /** Charlie and Irene Evens have left their home in San Francisco to wander around the isolated townships near Jackson, Mississippi. At Irene's request, they
have ceased their travels at an antebellum country house. It is here, she's sure of it—
the source of the insistent voices that crowd her consciousness.

At times, to Charlie's surprise, Irene has the ability to become someone else. An
openness in her becomes available to others . . . to the dead. For a while, someone
lives in her, and then eventually leaves. This time, though, it is different, he can feel it.
Irene is aware of an occupant, a young woman; but there is someone else, too, a silent
but unmistakable presence: a baby. Irene's visitor—the mother-to-be, Rachel—is
searching for a summer house. There is something that she wants done there, but
Irene cannot read exactly what it is. Charlie's fear grows as Irene begins to surrender
more completely to these long-dead spirits.

Irene, however, is becoming frustrated by her visitors' inability to communicate.
She agrees to leave with Charlie, away from the whispering voices. On the night before they leave, Irene gets up from the dinner table to go into the kitchen . . . and does
not return. Charlie races from the house to look for her. Over the howling wind, he
hears the distant sound of Irene calling him, and follows her voice into a clearing in
the woods. She has found the summer house . . . a ruin of moonlit stone pillars, half
fallen, eroded by time. Irene sits tranquilly on a stone bench, and smiles at him as he
appears. When she speaks, her voice is not Irene's but a musical, southern voice—
Rachel's. She calls him Johnny. Her hands are scraped bloody, caked with mud from a
newly dug hole nearby. Asking for his help, she begins to pull at the loose stones from
the house's foundation. When they have made an opening that satisfies her, she draws

from beneath her shawl the bones of a stillborn child, Rachel and Johnny's, buried in secret more than a century ago. The child must finally receive a proper burial. Exhausted, she returns to the stone bench as Charlie finishes the respectful entombment of the fragile remains. Afterward, he turns toward Irene/Rachel, uttering a quiet prayer that when he returns it will be his wife. He reaches out to her, and she falls back on the darkening carpet of leaves, senseless and now empty. Horrified, he listens as Irene's voice comes to him from some fading, indefinite distance: "Oh, Charlie, I can't get back! *I can't get back . . . !*"

**/ Commentary /** This is an early example of Sally Field tackling a more complex role than she had been offered before. In some ways, the character of Irene can be seen as a dry run for Field's tour de force in the landmark telefeature *Sybil,* another role in which she fought off multiple personalities. Here, however, she had not matured enough as an actress to bring the role off.

At base, Irene is not entirely flesh and blood; there is a part of her that belongs to the spirits. Field is too down-to-earth, girl-next-door for a role that requires an otherworldly quality. Although her performance has a touching child-bride quality, the role doesn't suit her and ideally needs an extra dimension to convince the audience that this wood sprite could be a dry cell for spirits of the dead. An actress such as Bonnie Bedelia would have hit closer to the mark. Also, although an intelligent actor, Dean Stockwell, as the conflicted Charlie, does not seem entirely engaged in his role. Director Jeannot Szwarc concedes, "I don't think that was one of the best *Night Gallerys*."[44]

Szwarc, in following the script's instructions that the actors speak directly into the camera while conveying a private thought, makes a sizable error. Unfortunate overuse of this device in American television commercials has all but destroyed its effectiveness, and should have been avoided. Despite these caveats, "Whisper" is among the best scripts *Night Gallery* ever produced. Writer David Rayfiel, who would team again with Sally Field for Sydney Pollack's *Absence of Malice,* delivers an exceptional adaptation of Martin Waddell's short story. Although in its execution it falls short of being one of the truly distinctive episodes in the series, the possibilities were there. It is a haunting, tragic story that stays with the viewer long after one has seen it.

Rayfiel, always critical of his work, derides himself in hindsight for making the story more oblique than he now feels is necessary: "I keep thinking people are going to understand a lot of stuff that they can't understand. It was confusing at the beginning—that whole thing of his talking to the camera, and then her voices—you can really get lost. And it's not just because it's a 'French movie'—it's just unclear, that's all."[45]

Because of the tight third-season budget, "Whisper" almost didn't make it to the production roster. "We had a script we couldn't make," Burt Astor notes, "about ancestor worship, because it took place in England. I said, 'We can't do it at a half hour. We don't have the money to go off the lot. What we *can* do is change it and set the story in the American South, because we have a southern mansion on the lot, and they worship ancestors in the South, too.' And Jack went, 'Naw, naw, naw.'" But Laird evidently considered Astor's suggestion seriously. "About four weeks later he changed it and we did it. That was my great coup on *Night Gallery*."[46]

Laird next asked cinematographer Gerald Finnerman for a virtual impossibility. "Jack came to me and said, 'Jerry, I want an English sunlight look,'" Finnerman recalls. "And I said, 'Shit, Jack, it's so blasted hot and the sun's beating straight down, *nothing* is overcast.' And he said, 'Try, do *something*.' And I did my best. When we shot that show, I piled more filtration in the lens—neutral densities, fog filters, a golden filter—and you know, the stuff *did* look like England!"[47] Finnerman's efforts substantially reduced the California glare, giving the segment a very cool, autumn look. "It still looked like England to me," says Rayfiel. "I don't mean physically—it had an English *feeling* to it. I was sort of shocked to see that rural mailbox."

For his own amusement, Rayfiel chiseled a meaningful Latin phrase onto one of the headstones that haunts Irene—"Vade mecum." Irene tells Charlie that it translates into English as "Take me with you." Its true significance to the author? "It was a mouthwash, that's the frightening thing," Rayfiel admits. "It was a Swedish mouthwash, very concentrated, and extremely peppermint. If you don't rinse out your mouth, it'll kill you! It'll really burn your tongue!"[48]

NIGHT GALLERY #35225
Air date: May 20, 1972

THE DOLL OF DEATH
★ ½

Teleplay by Jack Guss
Based on the short story by Vivian Meik
Directed by John Badham
Music: Eddie Sauter
Director of Photographer: Gerald Perry Finnerman

**Cast**
Sheila Trent: Susan Strasberg
Raphael: Alejandro Rey
Alec Brandon: Barry Atwater
Dr. Strang: Murray Matheson

*Alejandro Rey and Susan Strasberg in "The Doll of Death." Courtesy of UCLA Research Library Arts Special Collections.*

Andrew: Jean Durand
Vereker: Henry Brandon

*Good evening. The paintings you see on display are designed to lift you from the ordinary. They're collected from all over the world and brought here by train, jet, and hearse, carefully crated and packed with protective covering—and often with their native earth.*

*We call your attention to this gentle facial study with the one visible entreating eye and the windblown hair. And to those of you whose visual acuity is perhaps better than most, you'll note the skulls that that one eye is contemplating. This painting is called "The Doll of Death," and it tells the story that takes place in the West Indies where the ancient art of voodoo is still practiced and celebrated. Now, if you don't believe in voodoo, you can take this with a grain of salt. On the other hand, if you find yourself dancing to that distant drummer—and the drum seems to beckon—check for missing pins and brand-new dolls. This, ladies and gentlemen, is the* Night Gallery.

**/ Summary /** Alec Brandon, a patrician plantation owner in the British West Indies, is taking to wife a coltish young woman, Sheila Trent. As the guests mill about waiting for the bride-to-be, in bursts Raphael, an old suitor of Sheila's, who has come, he says, to claim what is his. When Sheila appears, they gaze hungrily at each other. A painful silence ensues as Brandon tries to come between Sheila and the interloper, but he has lost her to Raphael. He stands humiliated as the two lovers gallop away on horseback.

Through Andrew, Brandon's West Indian manservant, the plantation owner searches out the island Houngan—an Obeah High Priest—and secures an obi doll to exact voodoo revenge on Raphael. With some pilfered clothing and hair from the victim, the spell is complete. Soon, Sheila finds Raphael writhing on the floor with the red imprint of two powerful hands wrapped around his body—and she knows that Brandon is the cause.

Desperate, Sheila sneaks into the servant's quarters at Brandon's plantation to enlist Andrew's help. She finds him close to death, poisoned at Brandon's hand when the servant tried to break the obi spell. Andrew pushes into Sheila's hand Brandon's signet ring. Only by putting it on the obi doll will Brandon's hold on Raphael be broken.

Brandon senses Sheila's presence and calls out to her. In a ruse to find the doll, she pretends to betray Raphael, but Brandon sees through Sheila's pose. Producing the doll, he offers it to her for one last embrace . . . then he raises the doll high and brings it down, smashing its head viciously on a marble table. With the impact, Brandon utters an agonized scream and grasps his head between both hands, crumpling to the floor. He sprawls lifeless next to the doll—around the wrist of which is encircled Brandon's signet ring, where Sheila had placed it.

**/ Commentary /** As *Night Gallery*'s last remaining episodes were broadcast, they seemed to trail off depressingly in quality. "The Doll of Death" is no exception. Jack Guss's script, supposedly set in the present, is loaded with overheated dramatic exchanges more suited to the decade of Vivien Meik's short story, the 1920s. Melodramatic confrontations and sexual undercurrents litter this segment as if it were a product of some apprentice Tennessee Williams. The material is mighty creaky, and the script's references to Harold Pinter and credit cards cannot fool the ear regarding the ancient origin of its attitudes.

Additionally, Susan Strasberg is miscast as the sensual Sheila Trent. Although a fine actress, she just doesn't produce enough heat. She was not the first to be cast in the part, however. Barbara Parkins had the role originally, but was replaced after a minor mishap occurred during filming. One of the scenes called for Parkins to ride a horse, and director John Badham felt the scene would be more effective if the actors, rather than stunt doubles, were on the horses. During the filming, Parkins lost her balance and fell off her mount. Although not seriously hurt, she quit the show. Badham was forced to scrap the footage and start again with a new actress in the role. "In retrospect," Badham says, "I realized I should have used a double. That incident made me much more cautious in situations later on. In a way, I'm glad it happened, because I learned a lesson in a situation that wasn't really awful." [49]

As for the rest of the cast, Alejandro Rey and Barry Atwater do what they can with this sad material. Rey's role was originally written as an Englishman named Everett, but was changed to accommodate the new casting. It's a shame that further, more substantive changes were not made as well. On the subject of witching dolls, the second season's "I'll Never Leave You—Ever" is far superior to this segment in every possible way.

NIGHT GALLERY #35235
Air date: May 27, 1973

1

HATRED UNTO DEATH

*

Teleplay by Halsted Welles
Based on a short story by Milton Geiger
Directed by Gerald Perry Finnerman
Music: Eddie Sauter
Director of Photography: Lloyd Ahern

*George Barrows and Dina Merrill in "Hatred unto Death." Courtesy of Hollywood Book and Poster Co.*

**Cast**

Grant Wilson: Steve Forrest
Ruth Wilson: Dina Merrill
Dr. Ramirez: Fernando Lamas
N'gi: George Barrows
1st Native: Caro Kenyatta
2d Native: Ed Rue
3d Native: David Tyrone

*G*ood *evening. For the benefit of those of you who are perhaps still uninitiated into this particular arm of art, this is a special display. Now, anyone can show you a Rembrandt or a Picasso or a Jackson Pollack, but we dig much deeper with our paintings—frequently six feet underground, as is the case with this painting.*

*It's called "Hatred unto Death," and it makes comment on the fact that there are certain anthropologists and psychologists who hold the conviction that blood memories are passed along in the genes. You scratch the surface of the twentieth-century man and you uncover a Neanderthal. Now, if we are to accept this theory, it suggests a kind of unending reincarnation. But if man has a Mr. Hyde perpetually struggling deep within him, what lies beneath the surface of the lower beasts? We offer neither a postulate nor a promise—we simply suggest that you watch and listen. This is the* Night Gallery.

/ **Summary** / On the Kenyan veldt, anthropologists Ruth and Grant Wilson are returning to camp when they must detour to help some natives from the local tribe. A gorilla is caught in one of their lion traps. The ape seems entranced by Ruth's presence—but hates Grant, roaring viciously at him. This troubles Grant, who senses that the ape knows him—but from where? He resents the animal's reaction and wants to know why he is so hated—and why the feeling is mutual. Grant captures the gorilla, intending to take it back with him to America. Ruth opposes her husband, but he is adamant.

When the Wilsons return, the gorilla, now named N'gi, is housed at the museum. Their colleague, Dr. Ramirez, is concerned about controlling the malevolent animal, who still exhibits his strange hatred of Grant and affection for Ruth. She feeds him, gives him clean bedding, and seems to have some strange empathy for N'gi. She sits by his cage, telling him a story about two apes who fight for the love of a female gorilla, and how the pale one traps the dark one in a pit and stones him to death. The story upsets the ape, and in trying to calm him, Ruth accidentally allows him to escape. She telephones Grant, but all he can hear are her screams at the other end of the line.

Grabbing a pistol and a flashlight, Grant heads for the storage area. He arrives to find N'gi approaching Ruth, who then hides while Grant tries to lure the ape away from her. Like old adversaries, the rivals begin to stalk each other. Finally getting a clear shot, Grant empties his pistol into N'gi's chest and the ape collapses. Sure of a link between them in some predawn past, Grant wonders when they will next meet —and who will be the victor then? As he turns back toward Ruth, N'gi, with an ounce of life left, rises and attacks Grant. The ape raises his rival high over his head and impales him, screaming, on a rack of buffalo horns—and, beating his chest as the victor, N'gi falls dead.

/ **Commentary** / Without question, "Hatred Unto Death" should surely be on a short list of the worst television episodes ever produced. It fell to the luckless Gerald Finnerman to try to make something out of this script, but the mediocrity of the material was insurmountable. "Jack Laird gave me the chance to direct when I was offered a big-budget feature and was going to leave the show," recalls Finnerman. "I found that directing was too strenuous for me with Jack. He was a perfectionist and could not stand to have one word of his scripts changed!" A catastrophe in this case, for this script needed a drastic overhaul.

How did this embarrassment ever get made? The plotting and characterizations stretch credulity to the breaking point with an outrageous premise, preachy sentiments, and corny dialogue. If "The Sins of the Fathers" was Halsted Welles's Everest of drama on *Night Gallery*, this episode was his Death Valley. Additionally, the acting, particularly by Dina Merrill, is awful, and the whole segment is rife with unintentional humor. To watch it is to cringe.

Exaggerating the offense is the ape suit. This fright-wig rental was owned by George Barrows, the stuntman who played the star primate, and was not, thankfully, a design of the *Night Gallery* makeup department. One look at this wizard hair appliance and the audience's expectations run less to Dian Fossey and more to one of the Hope and Crosby "Road" pictures. Not only was the suit ludicrous in appearance, it was stultifying to wear in the sweltering California heat, causing complications during production.

"I had trouble on that show," Finnerman sighs. "I should have had *two* guys in gorilla suits, because it was about a hundred degrees on the back lot that summer, and this guy who had the gorilla suit could only work about five minutes at a time and then he would practically collapse. I had to have three or four cameras shooting every time to cover myself—wide, medium, close—and I didn't like to do that because I don't believe in shooting a long shot and then going in for the closeup on the same angle. I think that's terrible directing, but I had to do it to get through the show."

These complications caused Finnerman to fall behind schedule. For his last day of shooting—the finale in the museum warehouse, shot in the Universal prop room— Finnerman had an enormous shot menu to complete without going over schedule. "I had four or five cameras in different spots, and I had to light them *all* for the chase just to save time. I mean, I had lights hidden everywhere to do a sequence in one take. We got bogged down so much I went to Jack and I told him, 'Jack, I've got this problem with this gorilla. He can only work five or ten minutes at a time.' And he understood. If you were honest with Jack . . . you know, he either liked you or he hated you, basically. That was it. And if he hated you, you were gone." [50]

It matters little who directed this script—no one could have brought it off. What a dispiriting way to end *Night Gallery,* with positively the worst episode ever. With segments like "Hatred Unto Death," who could blame Serling for trying to distance himself from this series?

## 2
## HOW TO CURE THE COMMON VAMPIRE
★

Written and Directed by Jack Laird
Music: Eddie Sauter
Director of Photography: Leonard J. South

**Cast**
Man with Mallet: Richard Deacon
Man with Stake: Johnny Brown

*Johnny Brown and Richard Deacon in "How to Cure the Common Vampire." Courtesy of Foto Fantasies.*

**/ Summary /** A group of vampire hunters finds the coffin of the undead in the subterranean caverns of the estate. Opening the lid, the hunters release the vampire's snores, which echo loudly throughout the chamber. A man with a long stake passes it to a man with the mallet, who positions the point over the vampire's heart. Troubled, he looks at the other man and asks, "Are you sure?" "Well," the other shrugs, "it couldn't hurt."

**/ Commentary /** Low-grade nonsense. As with "Smile, Please," "How to Cure the Common Vampire" was originally shot for the second season, but never used there . . . thankfully. It rightfully belongs here, tacked onto "Hatred Unto Death."

## SYNDICATION SEGMENTS

When the series was shown in syndication, two segments produced for the second season were included that were never broadcast in the network run.

## DIE NOW, PAY LATER
★ ½

Teleplay by Jack Laird
Based on the short story "Year End Clearance" by Mary Linn Roby
Directed by Timothy Galfas
Music: Gil Mellé
Director of Photography: Gerald Perry Finnerman

**Cast**
Walt Peckinpah: Will Geer
Sheriff Harlow: Slim Pickens

*I*t's a measure of our current mores that we base an economy on a credit plan. We do things "on time," so to speak: purchase the item, use it while you're paying it off. And this sets up the intriguing premise of this painting in which the faith between seller and buyer is the ultimate. It's called "Die Now, Pay Later."

/ **Summary** / Sheriff Ned Harlow bursts into the office of funeral director Walt Peckinpah, fit to be tied. The death rate in Tauntom has gone sky high in the past week, and Harlow thinks it is tied in to Peckinpah's January clearance sale. Peckinpah defends the sale, noting that every other businessman in town gets rid of surplus merchandise that way. Harlow, however, has reason to believe that not all the people lying in Peckinpah's half-priced caskets died natural deaths. Many of them were folks that other people had wanted to see dead for a long time. The sheriff hasn't turned up any hard proof, but it's all just a little too convenient.

On top of that, Harlow's wife, Etta, has kin in Salem, and according to her relatives, Peckinpah is a descendant of a warlock who was burned at the stake two hundred years ago. These things, Etta claims, run in the family. Peckinpah guffaws at this, but Harlow is sure that if the sale doesn't end, Etta will spread it all over town that it's Peckinpah's "casting evil spells and slipping the devil into folks' breakfast cereal that's upping the local death rate."

A phone call rings in for Ned. It is Etta, who scolds her husband for visiting with Peckinpah. Cringing, he hangs up the phone. Peckinpah slyly suggests, "It wouldn't hurt all that much to let the sale go on *one* more day, would it? Might even help." Nodding agreeably, the sheriff admits it might at that.

/ **Commentary** / It seems unfair of us to discuss this episode as it has obviously been radically altered from its original form for the syndication package, padded to twice its length with footage from Universal's *Eye of the Cat,* among other films. From what remains, it appears to be a very minor piece, short and intentionally humorous— along the lines of "The Late Mr. Peddington," though not nearly as witty.

Originally scheduled to direct was editor David Rawlins. The segment was ultimately directed by Timothy Galfas in early January of 1972. His other segments, "Dead Weight" and "Little Girl Lost," are far superior to this trifle.

One point of interest: the introductory painting, showing a casket salesman displaying his wares, is a self-portrait by Tom Wright, the artist for all the gallery paintings.


## ROOM FOR ONE LESS

★

Written and Directed by Jack Laird
Music: Eddie Sauter, Paul Glass, and Oliver Nelson
Director of Photography: Gerald Perry Finnerman

**Cast**
The Thing: Lee Jay Lambert
Elevator Operator: James Metropole

*A*s usual, *following the course of the old switcheroo on* Night Gallery, *a painting called "Room for One Less."*

**/ Summary /** In a high-rise office building, elevator doors open to allow jostling passengers into an already crowded car. The gum-popping operator turns a few people away to keep the car from filling over the limit. Suddenly, a hideous thing with a bulbous, veined red head and sharp teeth appears out of nowhere next to the elevator operator. "Hey, Mac," the operator says, pointing to the sign at the rear of the car:

OCCUPANCY BY
MORE THAN 10 PASSENGERS
PROHIBITED BY LAW

Acknowledging the safety rule, the thing nods— "Quite"—and pointing a mandarin-nailed finger at the operator, ZAP, the operator disappears.

**/ Commentary /** Commentary would be as pointless as the vignette.

Not long into its third season, NBC unceremoniously canceled *Night Gallery*. The remaining episodes were allowed to dribble out until late May of 1973, replaced for a time by *Escape,* a Jack Webb midseason replacement. Even the broadcasts before cancellation were haphazard at best, often bumped by political announcements and overtime football games. The handling of the series in its third season amounts to almost deliberate neglect by the network: the budget was halved; its audience was frustrated, then dissipated, by constant preemptions; and despite a fair showing in the ratings the year before, the show was moved from its successful Wednesday home slot and allowed to slowly bleed to death, buried on Sunday nights.

"In many ways, *Night Gallery* was a cursed show," Jeannot Szwarc laments.

The fact that the series was both an anthology and fantasy confused NBC and Universal. Sid Sheinberg, the head of Universal television at that time, didn't like the series. We were virtually canceled on paper, because even though we only had decent ratings, we had *sensational* demographics. I can remember Rod coming in one day all excited, because he found out that there were *Night Gallery* viewing clubs at Harvard and Yale. Other people were such fans that, long before the days of videocassettes, they were buying bootlegged films of certain episodes! If nothing else, their interest shows that there was a cult for *Night Gallery* that could have been built up. The network was flooded with letters by people protesting the cancellation, and some *sponsors* didn't even want *Night Gallery* to be canceled. But within the industry it went totally unnoticed, that series. The method by which the show ended was a tragedy for all of us who worked on it. In fact, *Night Gallery* could very well be the only series ever taken off the air simply because its studio and network didn't understand it.[51]

In truth, *Night Gallery* had a built-in obstacle to its general acceptance. An anthology is guaranteed, by its very format, to be uneven. In *Night Gallery*'s case, with several story segments per show, wildly so. Within the same hour, some of its best segments collided with its very worst. If *The Twilight Zone,* with one story per week, delivered a subpar episode, the viewer could look forward to a better one next week —and as the first of its kind, *Zone* had the advantage of novelty in 1960. On *Night Gallery,* with multiple stories per show, the probability existed of there being at *least* one clinker in the sequence. A typical *Night Gallery* hour might start strongly with a well written and produced segment only to be followed by a less compelling one. Infrequently, a comedic blackout sketch would come last, a witless conceit that would nullify the cumulative effect of the hour. This could impress a viewer negatively almost every week—and, coming after *The Twilight Zone, Thriller,* and *The Outer Limits,* this genre had no climate of novelty in 1970.

For this crime, impatient reviewers gave *Night Gallery* an unwarranted critical drubbing, mindless of its often exceptional writing and sophisticated execution. Although the last season left much to be desired, the first two seasons delivered enough fine moments to make one marvel at the show's critical neglect. Its true curse may have been that, hobbled by the vignettes, on only a handful of occasions did *Night Gallery* turn up a completely satisfying hour's worth. Art director Joseph Alves compares *Night Gallery*'s success rate with *Saturday Night Live*, "in the sense that they had, on a given show, some good skits and some bad skits. We had our good nights and our bad nights on *Night Gallery*, too."[52] Overall, the quality was impressive.

Throughout the series, quite a few Serling scripts were left unproduced, even though, with thirty-five teleplays, he was by far the most prolific writer on *Night Gallery*. The remainder were, for various reasons, rejected by Laird, the studio, and the network. They include:

"Let Me Live in a House," based on a story by Chad Oliver, a toss-off Serling dictated in two hours in April 1971. Like "Midnight Never Ends," it dealt with questions of existence and identity, the Kafkaesque "puppets on a stage" concept that *Twilight Zone* had already explored to its fullest extent.

"Nightmare Morning" was an adaptation of Robert A. Heinlein's "They," about a delusional patient in a New York hospital who believes his reality has been manufactured by an alien culture as a zoo environment for him—Earth's last survivor. His delusion turns out to be real. Submitted in May 1971, it was seriously considered for the second season.

"Reflections," submitted in June 1971, was an inferior retread of "The Cemetery" and was consigned to the slush pile.

"Let Me Tell You about the Dead," based on Graham Greene's "A Little Place off the Edgware Road," was seriously considered, then shelved. Submitted in December 1971, it tells of a man, Craven, who tries to convince others of his delusion that the dead have been rising from their graves. In a second story thread, there is a ripper-type killer on the loose. The two threads merge when Craven meets one of the ripper's victims, zombified, in a darkened movie theater.

"Quartette Doomed," submitted in January 1972, was a thinly disguised take on Agatha Christie's *And Then There Were None*, stocked with characters out of a poor radio drama: the loudmouthed Texas oil man, the effete society columnist, the obsequious backstabbing assistant, and the gold-digging ex-chorus liner. They are invited to witness the reading of a dead mystic's will. Instead of bequeathing to them his riches, he hands them all a death sentence for their part in ruining his life. For the rest of the play, the four characters try to avoid the circumstances in which he said they would perish. The script, derivative as it was, was never seriously considered.

"The Onlooker," a Serling original submitted in February 1972, followed the story of a cold-eyed hit man who loses his professional cool, then his life, when he tries to escape a mysterious man who dogs his trail—Death. The script came under serious consideration.

Others of lesser consequence, most either unfinished or undeveloped, were written but never submitted to the show.

A number of Serling's unproduced scripts were too often reminiscent of his past work. If he had not completely tapped these veins in the five-year run of *Twilight*

*Zone,* he came uncomfortably close. In all fairness, however, no writer could produce genre-specific material for five years without running the risk of recycling. Two of the unproduced scripts, however, had real potential.

The first was a witty, weird adaptation of John Collier's short story "Green Thoughts," called "How Does Your Garden Grow," submitted by Serling early in 1972. It was a well-written character study involving an old gardener, his cat, a pair of dotty neighbors, a young girl claiming to be the widow of the old gardener's dead son, and a man-eating plant. The script's involved special effects were no doubt too expensive to develop.

The second unproduced script was a sensitive Serling original, "The View of Whatever," submitted in February 1972. With its familiar theme of nostalgia and loss, the script was in a direct line of descent from "Walking Distance," "A Stop at Willoughby," and "They're Tearing Down Tim Riley's Bar." It tells the story of Joe Sprague, who suffers the loss of his only son during the Vietnam conflict. In deep depression, he develops a desperate desire to escape from a present he hates, taking form as a strange delusion: he claims that his childhood past can be viewed from his bedroom window. It is now a portal into 1930s Binghamton, New York—a perennial summer day with parks and band concerts and children on bikes. Sprague's family doctor, Ike Colby, is sympathetic, assuring him that everyone desires a return to innocence. He relates a cherished moment from *his* past: stationed on Haiti during the war, Colby shared with a French nurse a love affair so passionate "that it would make Browning stumble for words." Sympathy, though, is not enough. Ultimately, the despairing Sprague takes his chance and steps through that window—and it is once again summer. He is ten years old, savoring his mother's lemonade before heading off to play with his neighborhood pals. He looks pensively into the camera as we dissolve to the present from which he escaped. His family is distraught at finding him missing. Colby tries to console them, but as he looks out Sprague's bedroom window, the portal shows him his *own* past: a wave-lapped shore in a tropical setting—and a familiar, dark-haired woman beckoning. As the vision fades, Colby finds comfort in knowing that Joe Sprague has finally gone home.

There was no reason why this tender fantasy, above all the others, could not have been produced, save for the ignorance of a network that wanted less introspection and more gore-covered walking corpses.

Left unproduced for *Night Gallery* were several other non-Serling scripts. One, Gene Kearney's "Where Seldom Is Heard," was a mere vignette, an extended sketch with its punch line turning on hunchbacked bell ringer Quasimodo's deafness. There were other, more substantial pieces for which Tom Wright had produced paintings. We will never know their quality, but from the evidence of the last shows produced for the series, it is doubtful that they would have received the four-star treatment achieved in the first two seasons.

# 11
# Aftermath

With few exceptions, those who worked regularly on the show speak about their experiences with great enthusiasm. Art director Joseph Alves testifies to the show's invigorating pace and demands, and numbers the series among his favorite projects. Makeup artist Leonard Engelman also admits to being spoiled by the show's variety and excitement: "After *Night Gallery,* standing around on the regular set of some attorney show was just total boredom. I would be doing laps around the stage trying to keep from going crazy from the lack of a challenge. The series had accelerated my creativity so much that I lost interest in doing straight makeup. After *Night Gallery,* how much more was there for me to accomplish?"[1]

Those in the production office felt likewise. "I loved the show," admits Herbert Wright.

> I'd just come from Yale, and all of a sudden I'm out in Hollywood working on a major lot, making these insane stories and having a great deal of fun doing it. I learned so much off that show and I got to meet such amazing people, because we were drawing all these big names who'd done classic films. It was like being paid to do something that you'd have paid *them* to *let* you do. And it's ironic that, so many years later, I still have dreams about those shows from time to time. The production of them is so vivid in my mind. Some of the things Jeannot was doing on that show, I've never seen anything like it since.[2]

For Rod Serling, however, *Night Gallery* proved to be the most frustrating working experience of his career. In lectures he gave at Sherwood Oaks Experimental College a scant three months before his death, Serling commented ruefully on his experience:

> How did I lose my control? Well, I never really had it there. [I'd lost] some status over the years, and I didn't have the prerogative of demanding creative control that I had earlier. I had no say at all in the choice of scripts, none, [although] they would do me the goodness of sending me the scripts. The first year I wrote quite a few of them. And then as the time went on they would reject almost everything I wrote. They would do it in nice ways . . . but it was their way of saying, "We're boss, you're not. You're not the creative force on this show, *we* are." And then I was furious, because I was watching such shit on the show, which was considered related to *me,* and I thought, That's not fair. I may be right or wrong in my judgment of the show, but don't make it appear like it's my show.

Serling's lectures on television writing at Sherwood Oaks are valuable in a number of respects. As examples, he chose to screen for his class episodes of both *The Twilight Zone* and *Night Gallery*. While at least one of the *Gallery* segments, "Clean Kills and Other Trophies," got the expected trashing, it is instructive to note that he also savaged the classic *Twilight Zone* episode "Walking Distance," which is among the finest dramas the earlier series produced. Serling, defending his harsh judgment of "Walking Distance," said, "All this proves to me as a writer is that I've matured. I've grown a couple of miles, and I think I'm a better writer since I wrote that, infinitely better, as we all do. That's part of the natural process. We become better, much more discerning, and after ten years you can strip away some of the desperate personal attachment you have for your own work and try to analyze it with a perspective that is reasonably impersonal."[3] Proving, perhaps, that the writer is not always the best judge of his work—or those who interpret it.

As a further illustration, during the interview that would turn out to be his last, Serling was asked to review his successes: "God knows when I look back over thirty years of professional writing, I'm hard-pressed to come up with anything that's important. Some things are literate, some things are interesting, some things are classy, but very damn little is important."[4] Of his enormous body of work, he named only two produced plays that he felt would stand the test of time: *Requiem for a Heavyweight* and "They're Tearing Down Tim Riley's Bar." He ignored *Patterns* and singled out nothing from *The Twilight Zone*. At the end of the day, Serling was his own harshest critic. Perhaps it better serves posterity that we are allowed the luxury of viewing his output with a more temperate eye than did the author.

Serling's point about achieving a "reasonably impersonal perspective" may hold at least part of the key to his response to *Night Gallery*. There is little doubt that his painful experiences behind the scenes may have colored his view of the series. The quick-tempered Serling saw *Night Gallery* through the prism of his perceived humiliation by those in control of the show. He would naturally be predisposed against admitting that it had *any* quality, regardless of the fact that he was, on many occasions, well interpreted by it.

For Serling, it was as natural as breathing to take a stand and fight. He was certainly never timid about voicing his distress publicly, and in the entertainment industry his profile was distinguished enough to make his disputes newsworthy. The scrappy Serling's response to his loss of control on *Night Gallery* was to run the show down, privately and publicly, despite his stated pleasure over the treatment a number of his scripts received. Sensitive that his high visibility as host of *Night Gallery* would be misread as his being responsible for its irregularities, Serling's defensiveness was working overtime. He beat others to the critical punch by denigrating *Night Gallery* first and often.

From the beginning, comparisons between *The Twilight Zone* and *Night Gallery* favored the former. Although the later series developed a devoted following, some viewers who felt *Night Gallery* didn't match their glamorized memory of *The Twilight Zone* have wielded the writer's harangues like a cudgel on the series, as if Serling were the final arbiter and his general unhappiness with the show somehow doomed it to some outer circle of rerun Hell.

Admittedly, *The Twilight Zone*, because of its cultural importance as the first intelligent, skillfully produced show of its genre on television, will rightly always come first—it has, after all, had enormous influence. However, it is clarifying to discover that, as executive producer on *Zone*, Serling shepherded as many duds into production as winners. *The Twilight Zone* was no more immune to the occasional flop than was *Night Gallery*—a premise that may be greeted with skepticism by those who characterize *Night Gallery* as hackwork and *The Twilight Zone* as unalloyed genius. To clear up that little misconception, one merely need screen such *Zone* disasters as "The Mighty Casey," "The Chaser," "The Man in the Bottle," "Mr. Bevis," "Twenty-two," "I Am the Night, Color Me Black," "Cavender Is Coming," "Come Wander with Me," "The Fear," "The Mirror," "Black Leather Jackets," "The Brain Center at Whipple's" —the list, unfortunately, goes on. Even Serling allowed that he and his associates had scored modestly, not spectacularly, with the first series. Taking stock of *The Twilight Zone*, Serling once commented, "In the words of the great American pastime, I think we batted about .300 on *Twilight Zone*. We had some real turkeys, some fair ones, and some shows I'm really proud to have been part of. I can walk away from this series unbowed."[5] In Marc Scott Zicree's critical overview of the series, *The Twilight Zone Companion*, one can find an objective verification of Serling's analysis. On a story-by-story basis, *Night Gallery*'s success rate is fully equal to Serling's estimation of *The Twilight Zone*. Yet *Gallery* is still too often overlooked, lost in the shadows of its predecessor.

Serling had hoped to create a series that was an extension of *The Twilight Zone;* Laird had taken the idea and run in a different direction, making *Night Gallery* a showcase for mood and aesthetics. Serling had wanted a stronger moral focus; Laird, however, was never interested in polemics. The inevitable comparisons between *The Twilight Zone* and *Night Gallery* gave critics the impression that *Night Gallery* was soft-centered and insubstantial, but the model for the series from Laird's point of view was closer to the pure entertainment of *Thriller* or *Alfred Hitchcock Presents*. All the *Zone* episodes had a collective similarity of purpose to instruct; Laird, though not opposed to moral tales, wanted the individual stories to stand on their own, distinct from one another and from an imposed series style. This deliberate diversity made *Night Gallery* far less cohesive and, for some, less satisfying than *The Twilight Zone*. Judged as Laird intended, however, we can come to a much fairer view of the series.

Until recently this had been practically impossible because of an afterlife in syndication using a gutted version of *Night Gallery*, a travesty that began before the show had even finished its network run. At the time of the show's cancellation, the market demand for sixty-minute shows in syndication was diminishing. Half-hour shows were far more popular, and these syndication packages required at least seventy-five episodes. *Night Gallery* had only forty-three. Universal's solution: break the series' first twenty-eight hour-long shows into half-hour segments. Unfortunately, *Night Gallery*'s individual stories were not of a uniform length and the hours couldn't be easily bisected. Enter Harry Tatelman.

Tatelman, a Universal vice president, had made a fortune for Universal in the 1960s cutting together unrelated episodes of *Wagon Train* and *The Virginian* into full-length, somewhat incomprehensible movies for sale on the foreign market. Brought in to make a coherent syndication package out of *Night Gallery*, Tatelman's first step was to trim the longer segments to fit the twenty-four minute limit for syndication. The resulting cuts destroyed the atmosphere of the pieces, turning the characters into stick figures and raising havoc with the narrative flow. The crowning triumph of Serling's career, "They're Tearing Down Tim Riley's Bar," originally ran forty-one minutes. It currently runs less than twenty-four. Most of the longer episodes—including "The Dead Man," "The Little Black Bag," "The Messiah on Mott Street," "A Question of Fear," "Since Aunt Ada Came to Stay," "The Sins of the Fathers," "Deliveries in the Rear," "The Phantom Farmhouse," "The Dark Boy," and "The Caterpillar"—suffer losses from this treatment.

Perhaps worse was the fate of the shorter segments. Those that could not be joined together were lengthened by adding superfluous footage from the cutting room floor, the stock library, or other Universal films. In some cases, new material was shot and inserted. "There's a unit over at Universal that Harry Tatelman runs," says Richard Bracken, one of the editors assigned to the project. "You'd get stock footage and sometimes you'd go and shoot some added pieces. Specifically, a script was written for these added scenes that served as connective tissue to pad out some of the short ones, and also to bridge. On some things that I had worked on, I know that Jack Arnold went out and shot added bridging material."

"The Different Ones," originally fifteen minutes, was padded to twenty-four with scenes from *Fahrenheit 451*, *Silent Running*, and stock footage of *Apollo* missions. Ridiculous voice-overs about aliens landing were added that had nothing to do with the original story. "Logoda's Heads" wound up with ten extra minutes of footage from *Curucu, Beast of the Amazon* and new voice-over narration from star Tim Matheson (did they think no one would notice that some of the natives are South American while others are African?). The extended version of "The Hand of Borgus Weems" is a nightmare tangle of leaden pacing and psychedelic stock footage (exactly *why* is that man wrestling a giant spider?). "The Flip-Side of Satan" and "Camera Obscura" were lengthened by ridiculous shots of floating, disembodied heads. "The Doll," "Green Fingers," "The Boy Who Predicted Earthquakes," "The Miracle at Camafeo," "The Painted Mirror," "Big Surprise," and many others suffer a similar treatment, inflating these modest tales with unnecessary and often perplexing scenes.

"It was quite a travesty, I realize," admits Bracken. "You can't take fifteen minutes and pump it up to thirty and say that this is still the original concept. It was a total bastardization of it. But when you're working for a living, you do what you have to do."[6] Hardest hit were the original filmmakers, who could do nothing but watch as their work was mangled. John Badham: "They would take an episode and stretch it out, and stretch it out, and basically ruin the dramatic nature of it in making it longer. You made something that's nicely cut and really moves along well. And then somebody comes in and puts a few seconds here, and a few seconds there, and suddenly everything is all wrong. All the rhythms are off, and it doesn't play so well any more."[7] Unfortunately, simple recutting was not the end of the plunder.

Adding insult to injury, Tatelman rethought almost all of the episodes, replacing original music cues with stock in an attempt to punch up what he saw as the original filmmakers' mistakes. Anonymous cues of "spooky" mood music were layered incongruously over many episodes in a misguided attempt to heighten the drama of stories now eviscerated by the removal of key scenes. For example: in its original form, "Green Fingers" ended quietly with the sound of the sighing wind and Cameron Mitchell's spectral laugh. Tatelman added a loud music cue that destroys the creepy chill of the original. "Lindemann's Catch" had a wholly new music score grafted onto its first half, replacing Gil Mellé's fantasy-filled cues with shocking "sting" music that irreparably alters the segment's original tone. In "Brenda," Tatelman's group buried Eddie Sauter's clever score deep under the dialogue and a layer of new, woozy sound effects. "Those changes," says Bracken, "were by-products of having to either cut down a segment, or in most cases they were more markedly noticeable when you had to pad. But Harry was given the assignment by the studio, and it was a job he knew that he could do one way or the other, and he did. I don't know if there was any particular glee in changing the style and content of the show, as much as getting the job done. He's always been very proud of his financial contribution to the Universal coffers."[8]

Yet even this was not enough. After cutting *Night Gallery* into half-hours, the series was still short of the required seventy-five episodes for syndication. To further extend it, twenty-five episodes of another hour-long series, *The Sixth Sense,* were whittled down to a half-hour and annexed into the syndication package. Serling was hired back at great expense to film new introductions (scripted by others) with new paintings by Jaroslav Gebr. The addition of the *Sixth Sense* series ballooned the package to ninety-seven episodes. The damage was now complete.

"Most of [the edited versions] are monstrosities," moans director Jeannot Szwarc. "Jack and Rod were livid about it, and so was I, but there was nothing we could do about it. Nobody cared, nobody listened. It was really a goddamned shame, because some of them were really, really butchered." In an effort to salvage some of his work, Szwarc was allowed input on the reediting of his segments. "Even though I hated it,

I'm enough of a pragmatist to say, Well, at least I know the material. Maybe I'll do it a little bit better."[9]

Ironically, after all the work that went into cutting the shows down to twenty-four minutes, an extra two or three minutes of extra footage would be removed at the local stations by dint of a 1974 FCC ruling as a means to squeeze in more revenue-generating commercials. "And they don't do it in the nice, neat way that Harry did," Badham says. "They'd give the reels to some overworked station editor who just wants to slash out two minutes and get it over with. Nowadays, all that stuff is probably on video, so they speed it up by computer from thirty frames per second to thirty-two frames per second. It subtly destroys the pacing of the segment . . . and Rod Serling becomes a tenor."[10]

The syndication butchery left a highly damaging imprint on the public's memory of the series over the past twenty-five years. Someone who had never seen the show in its original form might view the series in syndication and be forgiven for the impression that *Night Gallery* was the most incompetently edited, visually murky series ever made. Even old fans could easily be fooled into thinking that *Night Gallery* was always in this sad state and that time had played tricks on their memory. Many fans of the show still think *The Sixth Sense* was part of *Night Gallery*. "I've stopped watching it," notes Szwarc. "What they've done to it is absolutely criminal. But they don't give a shit. That has always been the disease of Hollywood. They don't care about the past. All they care about is making a lot of money *now.*"[11]

Since the series' cancellation in 1972, American viewers had, until very recently, been unable to see *Night Gallery* as it was originally presented. The syndication package is a pale shadow of the first broadcasts, and with nothing else available on which to base a judgment, audiences have not been able to reassess *Night Gallery* in the intervening years as they have *The Twilight Zone*. Steps have been taken to amend this damage, however. Columbia House Video has overseen a release of the restored version for home video, beautifully remastered by Universal in 1991 and currently available. With this effort to bring the original series to light, perhaps now *Night Gallery's* stock will rise to its correct position. (Orders should be directed to Columbia House Video Customer Service at 800-457-0866.)

Sadly, the show's creators ultimately fared worse than the series. On May 4, 1975, Rod Serling was taken to Tompkins County Hospital in Ithaca, New York, after suffering a mild heart attack. It was determined he would need a coronary bypass operation to improve the blood supply to the heart. On June 26, Serling underwent ten hours of open heart surgery at Strong Memorial Hospital in Rochester. As surgeons were finishing the operation, Serling apparently suffered another heart attack, and another bypass procedure was then performed.

He lay in critical condition for two days with his wife, Carol, daughters Ann and

Jody, and brother Robert keeping watch. Despite the writer's outward personification of good health, an inherited heart disease and a lifetime of heavy cigarette consumption finally took their toll. At 2:15 P.M. on Saturday, July 28, 1975, Rod Serling died— a tragically youthful fifty.

His death prompted immediate and heartfelt memorials from members of his fraternity. "They don't make them much like Rod Serling any more," writer Barry Eysman observed. "Maybe they never did. He was a one-of-a-kind: a fighter with the skill of a Jack Jefferson, the timing of a Nijinsky, and the talent of a thoroughly original writer." Using the example of *Requiem for a Heavyweight,* Serling's sensitive account of the downfall of boxing casualty Mountain McClintock, Eysman lauded Serling for his boundless empathy for human suffering. "Rod Serling saw the dignity in people like this. He showed us the shadow people, the ones who live on the periphery, who dwell in dark out-of-the-way bars, reliving, subsisting on past times. He showed us people we'd rather not think about. But with that keen perception and sparse dialogue he grabbed you by the short hairs and told you in no uncertain terms that these people too deserved at least a little victory, breathing space, someone to care for, someone to care about them."[12]

Serling's friend Dick Berg, eulogizing the writer at his funeral, spoke of his natural abilities and the relative ease with which he practiced his craft:

Where his peers might have anguished over the creative process, Rod woke up each day saying, "Let me tell you a story." That was his badge, his trust, his passkey into our lives. He was eternally the new boy on the block trying to join our games. And he penetrated the circle by regaling us with those many fragments of his Jewish imagination . . . intellectual stories, fantastic stories, hilarious stories, stories of social content, even one-liners about man's lunacy. However, they were always seen through his prism, becoming never less than *his* stories. And because he came to us with love . . . seeking *our* love . . . we invariably let him tell us a story. And how much richer we are for it.[13]

Although Jack Laird's end was less abrupt than was Serling's—he lived a further sixteen years—it was cast into shadow by his growing reclusiveness and marred by bizarre circumstance.

Laird's small circle of friends, through neglect and illness, began to dwindle. "He seemed to drift away," remembers Leslie Nielsen, "and became more reclusive, certainly, in his relationship with me. Things were happening to Jack that weren't making him pleasant company. Sometimes you have to go find a corner, put your back against two walls, face out, and defend yourself against that onslaught of pain that life can bring to you."[14]

The hardest blow for Laird was the death of friend and associate Gene Kearney. Despite a battery of treatments for his leukemia, Kearney died November 4, 1979, at Century City Hospital in Los Angeles. *Kojak* producer James McAdams notes sadly,

"He had been so emphatically enthusiastic about beating cancer—he was going to win. Then, not long before he died, he and I were going to a party together. He called me up that night and canceled our engagement. He said, 'I don't think it's going to work'—and he sounded tired." At 49, Kearney died even younger than did Serling, survived by his mother, sister, daughter, and son.

Laird's own neglected health pushed him deeper into seclusion, and in the last years he dealt with heart troubles, cancer, and diabetes. Circulation problems from the diabetes, untreated, caused him to have part of one gangrenous foot removed, and he was forced from then on to use crutches or a walker. His failing health caused Laird to toil further on the walls he built around himself.

Jack Laird died as he lived, a virtual hermit, on December 3, 1991. He suffered a fatal heart attack while en route to the hospital and, having evidently left home without identification, his body lingered for weeks in the hospital morgue as a John Doe. His body was finally identified by Laird's estranged daughter, Persephone, who had been alerted to his disappearance by neighbors. He was sixty-nine.

"I think the theme that will probably run through the whole Jack Laird story is that he was a very giving man," says associate James McAdams. "He mentored so many people, I can't tell you. Jack took an interest in the careers of so many others, and imparted his own wisdom to them, and yet he was probably the most misunderstood man in this world. But even though he was private, and none of us really knew him intimately, I saw glimpses into a very fine, kind human being."[15]

Serling and Laird, though personally incompatible, shared a gift for masterful storytelling, and the loss of these two workaholic talents had a definite diminishing effect on the film and television community. Though both epitaphs offer a sad note on projects that might have been, through their existing work they can and will always be appreciated. *Night Gallery* may one day be equally esteemed as the product of their best efforts.

APPENDIXES

NOTES

BIBLIOGRAPHY

INDEX

# Appendix A
# Evaluating the Segments

Although some may consider it superficial to define the merits of a film using a star system, we feel that it is simply the most useful starting point for discussing the segment in question. We cannot stress too strongly that the reader should consult the text in addition to the star rating for our overall evaluation of the segment.

Each segment was judged with an eye toward its success on a number of artistic levels: writing, directing, photography, acting, design, scoring, editing, and overall effect. Some episodes may not reach the zenith of quality when set against their fellows but have satisfying aspects nonetheless. The authors have favorite segments in the three-star and even the two-star groupings, and this was not intended as a list whereby the reader is warned away from viewing all but the "cream" of the series.

Some elements of production receive more latitude than others. Makeup and special effects, for instance, are given extraordinary leeway. In the beginning of the seventies, special effects had not even approached the sophisticated level achieved today with the aid of computers and digital technology. More important, television series were not budgeted to allow huge amounts of time and resources for creating feature-quality effects. On the other hand, quality of writing is given next to no latitude in our judgment. With the number of talented writers on *Night Gallery*, there was no excuse for a weak script.

The rating system runs from one to four stars.

★ ★ ★ ★  Classic: an outstanding segment on every level, representative
 of the best the series has to offer.

Camera Obscura
The Caterpillar
The Cemetery
Class of '99
Cool Air
The Dead Man
Deliveries in the Rear
The Doll
The Escape Route
Eyes
A Fear of Spiders

Green Fingers
I'll Never Leave You—Ever
Lindemann's Catch
The Little Black Bag
Little Girl Lost
The Messiah on Mott Street
Pickman's Model
A Question of Fear
Silent Snow, Secret Snow
The Sins of the Fathers
They're Tearing Down Tim Riley's Bar

★ ★ ★ ½  A fine segment, one about which we have only slight reservations.

The Academy
The Boy Who Predicted Earthquakes
Certain Shadows on the Wall
The Dark Boy
Dead Weight
A Death in the Family
The Devil Is Not Mocked
Dr. Stringfellow's Rejuvenator
A Feast of Blood
The House
Last Rites for a Dead Druid
The Late Mr. Peddington
Marmalade Wine
The Phantom Farmhouse
The Return of the Sorcerer
There Aren't Any More MacBanes

★ ★ ★  A good segment; one that lacks the stature or consistency
        of the best segments.

Big Surprise
Brenda
Clean Kills and Other Trophies
Hell's Bells
The Miracle at Camafeo
The Other Way Out
The Painted Mirror

Rare Objects
Satisfaction Guaranteed
Since Aunt Ada Came to Stay
Something in the Woodwork
The Tune in Dan's Cafe
You Can Come Up Now, Mrs. Millikan
You Can't Get Help Like That Anymore

★ ★ ½ Worthwhile, but with a number of drawbacks.

Death on a Barge
The Diary
Finnegan's Flight
The Ghost of Sorworth Place
The Girl with the Hungry Eyes
The Housekeeper
Keep in Touch—We'll Think of Something
Lone Survivor
The Merciful
Midnight Never Ends
Room with a View
Tell David . . .
The Waiting Room
Whisper

★ ★ Some good points, but will interest only the curious or the die-hard fanatic.

The Dear Departed
The Flip-Side of Satan
The Funeral
The Hand of Borgus Weems
House—With Ghost
Junior
The Last Laurel
Logoda's Heads
Make Me Laugh
Phantom of What Opera?
The Ring with the Red Velvet Ropes
Smile, Please
Spectre in Tap-Shoes
Stop Killing Me

* ½  Seriously flawed; hardly worth bothering with.

Die Now, Pay Later
The Different Ones
The Doll of Death
Fright Night
The Nature of the Enemy
Pamela's Voice
Professor Peabody's Last Lecture
Quoth the Raven
She'll Be Company for You
With Apologies to Mr. Hyde

*  An absolute disgrace, whoever's fault it is.

An Act of Chivalry
Hatred unto Death
How to Cure the Common Vampire
A Matter of Semantics
A Midnight Visit to the Neighborhood Blood Bank
Miss Lovecraft Sent Me
Room for One Less
Witches' Feast

# Appendix B
# Music Score Cues

In the program guide section, we have attempted to give credit where credit is due. Music credits have presented the most tangled complications to this end, particularly in the second season of the show. Out of the sixty-two segments broadcast, only thirty received scores written specifically for them. The rest were tracked from cues written previously for other segments. In a very few cases, the tracking library extended to sources outside the material written specifically for the show. We have dealt with these complications in this fashion:

If one composer is listed for a segment, the music from nose to tail is all his. If Serling's introduction was tracked from a different composer's work (as it occasionally was), it is labeled as such after the name of the primary composer. In the case of tracked segments with more than one composer, all are listed in descending order of contribution. For a breakdown of which cues are whose on these multiple-composer segments, we have supplied this appendix for those curious enough to scan an episode for a specific cue. Again, we are working from the original, uncut segments, not the syndication versions, where many segments now have radically different music cues.

With composers whose works have been noted previously in the book, last names alone are used. We have included music with either some visual source in the segment, such as a radio or a record player, or restaurant/funeral home Muzak. These cues are not used as dramatic underscore as much as scene dressing; in other words, the characters in the scene can hear it, too. These cues are noted by an asterisk.

Some cues are made up of many small segments from various composers. Divisions and timings have been included to help the reader in these cases.

## WITH APOLOGIES TO MR. HYDE

Cue 1: Lewis (1:11)/Nelson (:37)/Lewis (:02)

## THE FLIP-SIDE OF SATAN

Cue 1: Lewis (1:35)
Cue 2: Mellé (:30)*
Cue 3: Mellé (3:17)*

Cue 4:  Mellé (4:51)*
Cue 5:  Mellé (2:19)*/Lewis (:30)


## A FEAR OF SPIDERS

Cue 1:  Nelson (1:00)
Cue 2:  Nelson (1:03)/Mellé (:29)/Nelson (:56)/Mellé (:26)/Nelson (:17)
Cue 3:  Mellé (:24)/Lewis (:04)
Cue 4:  Nelson (:15)
Cue 5:  Nelson (1:30) (overlayed by a few seconds of Mellé)
Cue 6:  Lewis (:03)/Mellé (1:27)
Cue 7:  Nelson (1:56)/Lewis (:06)/Nelson (1:50)


## MIDNIGHT NEVER ENDS

Cue 1:  Glass (:45)/Nelson (:49)
Cue 2:  Nelson (:08)
Cue 3:  Nelson (3:23)
Cue 4:  Nelson (4:58)
Cue 5:  Nelson (1:21)
Cue 6:  Glass (:18)


## THE DIARY

Cue 1:  Lewis (1:01)
Cue 2:  Nelson (3:26)*/Trad., arr. Mooney (1:33)*
Cue 3:  Mellé (:49)
Cue 4:  Mellé (:07)
Cue 5:  Lewis (:20)
Cue 6:  Nelson (:53)
Cue 7:  Nelson (:39)
Cue 8:  Nelson (1:14)
Cue 9:  Nelson (:25)


## BIG SURPRISE

Cue 1:  Lewis (:51)
Cue 2:  Lewis (2:01)
Cue 3:  Nelson (2:31)
Cue 4:  Nelson (:57)
Cue 5:  Nelson (:08)

## KEEP IN TOUCH—WE'LL THINK OF SOMETHING

Cue 1:  Nelson (:35)
Cue 2:  Glass (:15)
Cue 3:  Glass (:46)
Cue 4:  Nelson (:26)
Cue 5:  Mooney (4:46)*
Cue 6:  Mellé (4:30)

## PICKMAN'S MODEL

Cue 1:  Glass (:58)
Cue 2:  Nelson (:27)
Cue 3:  Glass (:34)
Cue 4:  Nelson (1:15)
Cue 5:  Glass (:23)
Cue 6:  Glass (:05)
Cue 7:  Nelson (:13)
Cue 8:  Glass (:50)/Lewis (:46)/Glass (:18)
Cue 9:  Glass (1:28)
Cue 10:  Nelson (1:37)/Glass (:16)/Nelson (:43)/Glass (:18)
Cue 11:  Sauter (:27)

## THE DEAR DEPARTED

Cue 1:  Lewis (:56)
Cue 2:  Mooney (2:48)*
Cue 3:  Mellé (:25)
Cue 4:  Glass (2:00)

## CAMERA OBSCURA

(*A short fourteen-second cue by John Lewis underscores Sharsted climbing the stairs to Gingold's front entrance at the beginning of the episode. The rest of the score is by Paul Glass.*)

## THE PAINTED MIRROR

Cue 1:  Glass (:37)
Cue 2:  Lester Allen–Robert Hill (2:00)*
Cue 3:  Nelson (1:16)
Cue 4:  Lester Allen–Robert Hill (:14)*/Mooney (:05)*

Cue 5:  Tony Hatch (:05)⋆
Cue 6:  Nelson (:20)/Glass (:11)
Cue 7:  Tony Hatch (1:24)⋆
Cue 8:  Nelson (:49)
Cue 9:  Glass (1:11)/Nelson (1:09) (overlayed by a few seconds of Glass)

## THE DIFFERENT ONES

Cue 1:  Nelson (:50)
Cue 2:  Glass (:23)
Cue 3:  Nelson (:24)/Glass (:21)
Cue 4:  Glass (:28)
Cue 5:  Nelson (2:44)
Cue 6:  Sauter (:39)

## TELL DAVID . . .

Cue 1:  Lewis (:42)
Cue 2:  Mellé (:35)⋆
Cue 3:  Lewis (1:25)
Cue 4:  Glass (1:14)
Cue 5:  Glass (:17)
Cue 6:  Glass (:03)/Mellé (:45)⋆
Cue 7:  Glass (:45)
Cue 8:  Sauter (:24)
Cue 9:  Glass (2:15)
Cue 10:  Glass (:12)

## THE FUNERAL

Cue 1:  Nelson (1:02)
Cue 2:  Glass (2:00)
Cue 3:  Mellé (5:30)⋆/Nelson (:59)/Glass (:36)

## LINDEMANN'S CATCH

Cue 1:  Sauter (1:13)
Cue 2:  Mellé (:29)
Cue 3:  Mellé (:38)
Cue 4:  Glass (:35)

Cue 5:  Glass (:15)
Cue 6:  Glass (:10)/Sauter (:29)
Cue 7:  Nelson (:17)
Cue 8:  Glass (:43)
Cue 9:  Glass (2:08)


## THE GHOST OF SORWORTH PLACE

Cue 1:  Schifrin (:46)/Mellé (1:27)
Cue 2:  Nelson (:27)
Cue 3:  Schifrin (3:20)
Cue 4:  Schifrin (1:51)
Cue 5:  Schifrin (:06)
Cue 6:  Schifrin (:08)
Cue 7:  Schifrin (1:55)
Cue 8:  Schifrin (:48)
Cue 9:  Schifrin (2:07)
Cue 10:  Schifrin (4:18)


## LAST RITES FOR A DEAD DRUID

Cue 1:  Schifrin (1:02)
Cue 2:  Schifrin (1:10)
Cue 3:  Schifrin (:17)
Cue 4:  Mellé (:28)/Nelson (:49)
Cue 5:  Glass (:29)/Nelson (:14)/Glass (:34)
Cue 6:  Schifrin (:11)/Glass (:12)
Cue 7:  Glass (1:26)
Cue 8:  Glass (:19)/Schifrin (1:16)
Cue 9:  Mellé (:23)/Nelson (:29)
Cue 10:  Sauter (:07)


## I'LL NEVER LEAVE YOU—EVER

Cue 1:  Schifrin (1:15)
Cue 2:  Nelson (2:18)/Glass (:14)
Cue 3:  Schifrin (2:18)
Cue 4:  Glass (1:50)
Cue 5:  Glass (:15)
Cue 6:  Schifrin (:33)

Cue 7:  Schifrin (1:07)
Cue 8:  Schifrin (1:57)
Cue 9:  Nelson (:25)

## THERE AREN'T ANY MORE MACBANES

Cue 1:  Sauter (:33)
Cue 2:  Schifrin (:39)
Cue 3:  Sauter (:10)
Cue 4:  Schifrin (:12)
Cue 5:  Mellé (2:00)
Cue 6:  Glass (:56)
Cue 7:  Glass (:20) / Nelson (:33)
Cue 8:  Nelson (:04) / Glass (:06) / Nelson (:28)

## THE SINS OF THE FATHERS

*(Inexplicably, five extra minutes of Oliver Nelson's score appears in the reedited, shortened version of this segment prepared for syndication.)*

## YOU CAN'T GET HELP LIKE THAT ANYMORE

Cue 1:  Nelson (1:25)
Cue 2:  Mellé (1:31)
Cue 3:  Nelson (:49)*
Cue 4:  Nelson (1:44)
Cue 5:  Nelson (0:44) / Sauter (0:52)

# Notes

NOTE: *In the text, a string of quotes by the same person from the same source is notated at the end of the final quote in the series. This notation style holds even if the quotes are interrupted by a stretch of authors' text.*

## 1. Rod Serling

1. Gilbert Millstein, "'Patterns' of a Television Playwright," *New York Times Magazine,* Dec. 2, 1956.
2. Mark Olshaker, "Tribute: Requiem for a Heavyweight," *New Times,* July 25, 1975.
3. Harriet Van Horne, writer's column, *New York World-Telegram and Sun,* June 29, 1975.
4. Vernon Scott, "Rod Serling: TV's Angry Young Man Mellows with Age," *Chicago Daily News,* Dec. 12, 1970: 4.

## 2. The Season to Be Wary

1. *Daily Variety,* Mar. 12, 1964.
2. Letter from Rod Serling to Arthur Joel Katz, Apr. 30, 1968, Rod Serling Archive, Ithaca College, N.Y.
3. William Sackheim, telephone interview by S. S., 1994.
4. Kathryn M. Drennan and J. Michael Straczynski, "Rod Serling's Night Gallery: A Show-by-Show Guide," *The Twilight Zone Magazine* 5, no. 1: 55.
5. Rod Serling to William Sackheim, Dec. 18, 1968, Rod Serling Archive.
6. Sackheim, interview.
7. Drennan/Straczynski, vol. 5, no. 1: 56; "Final Cut" column ("A Foot in the Door: Steven Spielberg"), *In Cinema,* 1981: 30.
8. Steve Swires, "Filming the Fantastic: Steven Spielberg," *Starlog,* Oct. 1978: 25.

## 3. The Pilot

1. John Badham, telephone interview by S. S., 1995.
2. Roddy McDowall, telephone interview by S. S., 1997.

3. Badham, interview.
4. Drennan/Straczynski, vol. 5, no. 1: 55.
5. Ibid., 56.
6. Bob Thomas, *Joan Crawford: A Biography* (New York: Simon and Schuster, 1978), 237.
7. Frank Sanello, *Spielberg: The Man, The Movies, The Mythology* (Dallas, Tex.: Taylor, 1996), 30.
8. Thomas, 238.
9. Christina Crawford, *Mommie Dearest* (New York: William Morrow and Co., 1978), 285.
10. Ralph Sariego, taped interview by S. S., Eugene, Ore., 1994.
11. Sanello, 30–31.
12. Swires, 25–26.
13. Tom Bosley, telephone interview by S. S., 1998.
14. Sanello, 31.
15. "Lady in the Dark," *TV Guide,* Aug. 16, 1969: 8.
16. Thomas, 241.
17. Edward Abroms, telephone interview by S. S., 1996.
18. Sanello, 32.
19. Sackheim, interview; Drennan/Straczynski, vol. 5, no. 1: 56.
20. Drennan/Straczynski, vol. 5, no. 1: 56.
21. Abroms, interview.
22. Drennan/Straczynski, vol. 5, no. 1: 56.
23. Richard Kiley, taped interview by S. S., 1994.
24. Sackheim, interview.
25. Kiley, interview.
26. Badham, interview.
27. Abroms, interview.
28. Drennan/Straczynski, vol. 5, no. 1: 56; Sackheim, interview.
29. Joel Engel, *Rod Serling: The Dreams and Nightmares of Life in the Twilight Zone* (Chicago: Contemporary Press, 1989), 325–26.

30. Sackheim, interview; Drennan/Straczynski, vol. 5, no. 1: 56.
31. Gordon F. Sander, *Serling: The Rise and Twilight of Television's Last Angry Man* (New York: Dutton, 1992), 211.
32. Sackheim, interview.
33. "A Man Can Change His Mind," *Minneapolis Tribune TV Week Magazine,* Dec. 13, 1970: 2.

## 4. Jack Laird

1. Rosemary Campbell, telephone interview by S. S., 1996.
2. Peggy Johnson, telephone interview by S. S., 1996.
3. Leslie Nielsen, telephone interview by S. S., 1995.
4. Sydney Pollack, telephone interview by S. S., 1996.
5. David Rayfiel, interview by J.B., telephone, 1997.
6. Pollack, interview.
7. Johnson, interview.
8. Nielsen, interview.
9. Johnson, interview.
10. James McAdams, telephone interview by S. S., 1995.

## 5. Four in One

1. Scott, 5.
2. Paul Freeman, telephone interview by S. S., 1996.
3. John Astin, telephone interview by J. B., 1997.
4. Joseph Alves, Jr., telephone interview by S. S., 1994.
5. Gil Mellé, telephone interview by S. S., 1995.
6. Alves, interview.
7. Drennan/Straczynski, vol. 5, no. 2: 84.
8. Alves, interview.
9. Drennan/Straczynski, vol. 8, no. 4: 50.
10. Milli Hamilton, "Horror Artist," *Louisville Courier Journal and Times Magazine,* Apr. 16, 1972: 27.
11. Tom Wright, telephone interview by S. S., 1996.
12. Drennan/Straczynski, vol. 8, no. 4: 53.
13. Tom Wright, interview.
14. Drennan/Straczynski, vol. 8, no. 4: 53.
15. Tom Wright, interview.

16. Drennan/Straczynski, vol. 8, no. 4: 53.
17. Hamilton, 29.
18. Tom Wright, interview.
19. Leonard Engelman, telephone interview by S. S., 1996.
20. Tom Wright, interview.
21. Drennan/Straczynski, vol. 8, no. 4: 53.
22. Tom Wright, interview.
23. Phil Vanderlei, telephone interview by J. B., 1997.
24. Mellé, interview.
25. Letter from Robert Prince to Scott Skelton, May 1994.
26. Wayne Fitzgerald, telephone interview by J. B., 1997.
27. Letter from Rod Serling to John Champion, June 18, 1970, Rod Serling Archive.
28. Typed script for *Night Gallery* promotional film, Rod Serling Archive.
29. Scott, 4–5.
30. Dan Knapp, "Rod Serling Back with 'Night Gallery,'" *Los Angeles Times,* Dec. 16, 1970, sec. 4: 21.

## 6. The First Season

1. Michael Blodgett, telephone interview by J. B., 1997.
2. Mark Phillips, "Interview with Louise Sorel," *Starlog,* Apr. 1998: 60.
3. Louise Sorel, telephone interview by S. S., 1995.
4. Blodgett, interview.
5. Jeff Corey, telephone interview by S. S., 1994.
6. Phillips, *Starlog:* 60.
7. Blodgett, interview.
8. Drennan/Straczynski, vol. 5, no. 2: 83.
9. Suzy Parker, telephone interview by J. B., 1997.
10. Drennan/Straczynski, vol. 5, no. 2: 85; Jerrold Freedman, telephone interview by S. S., 1994.
11. Angel Tompkins, telephone interview by J. B., 1997.
12. Hal Dresner, telephone interview by J. B., 1996.
13. Burgess Meredith, tribute, from Museum of Broadcasting's program "Rod Serling: Dimensions of Imagination," 1984, Rod Serling Archive.

14. Memo from Rolf Gompertz to Rod Serling, Dec. 7, 1970, Rod Serling Archive.

15. Jeannot Szwarc, telephone interview by S. S., 1994.

16. Letter from Rod Serling to Jack Laird, Aug. 10, 1970, Rod Serling Archive.

17. Joseph Campanella, telephone interview by J. B., 1997.

18. Allen Reisner, telephone interview by S. S., 1996.

19. Astin, interview.

20. Joanna Pettet, telephone interview by J. B., 1997.

21. Astin, interview.

22. Pettet, interview.

23. Astin, interview.

24. Pettet, interview.

25. Astin, interview.

26. Drennan/Straczynski, vol. 5, no. 2: 85.

27. Corey, interview.

28. Drennan/Straczynski, vol. 5, no. 2: 85.

29. Rod Serling, class lectures at Sherwood Oaks Experimental College, tape recordings by Linda Brevelle, Mar. 13 and Apr. 3, 1975, Los Angeles, Calif.

30. Drennan/Straczynski, vol. 5, no. 3: 78.

31. Tony Russel, telephone interview by J. B., 1996.

32. Szwarc, interview.

33. Bosley, interview.

34. Rod Serling, Sherwood Oaks lecture.

35. Walter Doniger, telephone interview by S. S., 1996.

36. Rod Serling, Sherwood Oaks lecture.

37. Doniger, interview.

38. Les Berke, telephone interview by S. S., 1994.

39. Doniger, interview.

40. "Welcome Art Lovers," *Ventura County Star–Free Press TV Week Magazine,* Jan. 10, 1971: 12.

41. Phyllis Diller, telephone interview by J. B., 1997.

42. Astin, interview.

43. Diller, interview.

44. Review, *Daily Variety,* Jan. 15, 1971: 28.

45. Gene Levitt, telephone interview by J. B., 1996.

46. Rudi Dorn, telephone interview by S. S., 1994.

47. Rod Serling, videocassette of 1972 classroom discussion at Ithaca College ("Writing for Television–Conversations with Rod Serling"), Rod Serling Archive.

48. Don Taylor, telephone interview by S. S., 1996.

49. Drennan/Straczynski, vol. 5, no. 3: 80.

50. Ibid.

51. Susannah Darrow, telephone interview by J. B., 1997.

52. Alves, interview.

53. Drennan/Straczynski, vol. 5, no. 3: 80.

54. Letter from Rolf Gompertz to Rod Serling, Dec. 16, 1970, Rod Serling Archive.

55. Charles Witbeck, "Rod Serling Returns with 'Night Gallery,'" *TV Key,* Dec. 15, 1970.

56. William Windom, telephone interview by S. S., 1994.

57. Taylor, interview.

58. Drennan/Straczynski, vol. 5, no. 3: 80.

59. Windom, interview.

60. Windom, interview; Drennan/Straczynski, vol. 5, no. 3: 80.

61. Susannah Darrow, interview.

62. Daryl Duke, telephone interview by J. B., 1996.

## 7. A Maverick Little Island

1. NBC press release.

2. Szwarc, interview.

3. Herbert Wright, telephone interview by S. S., 1995.

4. Barbara Zuanich, "Universal's Quadruple Threat," *Los Angeles Herald–Examiner TV Week Magazine,* Jan. 9, 1972: 9; Universal Studios press release.

5. Cecil Smith, "The Video House That Jack Built," *Los Angeles Times,* (n.d.), 1971.

6. Zuanich, 9.

7. Leonard Feather, "From Pen to Screen," *International Musician,* Nov. 1972: 32.

8. Herbert Wright, interview.

9. Burt Astor, telephone interview by S. S., 1994.

10. William Hale, telephone interview by S. S., 1994.

11. James H. Burns, "People: Jeannot Szwarc," *The Twilight Zone Magazine,* vol. 8, no. 3 (1988): 93.

12. Herbert Wright, interview.

13. Gerald Sanford, telephone interview by S. S., 1994.

14. Herbert Wright, interview.

15. Anthony Redman, telephone interview by S. S., 1994.

16. Rod Serling to Dick Cavett, *The Dick Cavett Show,* July 19, 1972, Museum of Television and Radio, Beverly Hills, Calif.

17. Herbert Wright, interview.

18. James Metropole, telephone interview by S. S., 1996.

19. Astor, interview.

20. Alvin Sapinsley, telephone interview by S. S., 1994.

21. Szwarc, interview.

22. Freedman, interview.

23. Herbert Wright, interview.

24. Marilyn Beck, "Even Rod Serling Has Job Problems," *Los Angeles Herald–Examiner TV Week Magazine,* Nov. 14, 1971: 82.

25. Don Freeman, writer's column, *San Diego Union,* June 14, 1972: B-6; Rod Serling to Dick Cavett, *The Dick Cavett Show,* July 19, 1972.

26. Marc Scott Zicree, *The Twilight Zone Companion,* (1982; reprint, Hollywood: Silman-James Press, 1992), 437.

27. Linda Brevelle, "Rod Serling's Last Interview," *The Twilight Zone Magazine* 2, no. 1 (1982): 22.

28. Grace Cursio, telephone interview by S. S., 1994.

29. Burns, vol. 8, no. 3: 93; Szwarc, interview.

30. Szwarc, interview.

31. Brevelle, 23.

32. Herbert Wright, interview.

33. Burns, vol. 8, no. 3: 93

34. Cursio, interview.

35. Sapinsley, interview.

36. Freedman, interview.

37. Szwarc, interview.

38. Badham, interview.

39. Cursio, interview.

40. Herbert Wright, interview.

41. Metropole, interview.

42. Herbert Wright, interview.

43. Cursio, interview.

44. Szwarc, interview.

45. Redman, interview.

46. Sariego, interview.

47. Redman, interview.

48. Hale, interview.

49. Szwarc, interview.

50. Redman, interview.

51. Herbert Wright, interview.

52. McAdams, interview.

53. Cursio, interview.

54. Szwarc, interview.

55. Szwarc, interview; Burns, vol. 8, no. 3: 92.

56. Berke, interview.

57. Lester, interview.

58. Metropole, interview.

59. Herbert Wright, interview.

60. Jordan R. Fox, "Somewhere in Time with Jeannot Szwarc," *Cinefantastique* 10, no. 4 (1981): 17.

61. Herbert Wright, interview.

62. Drennan/Straczynski, vol. 5, no. 4: 82.

63. Astor, interview.

64. Drennan/Straczynski, vol. 5, no. 3: 75.

65. Badham, interview.

66. Szwarc, interview; Burns, vol. 8, no. 3: 92.

67. Zuanich, 9.

68. Sariego, interview.

69. Berke, interview.

70. Szwarc, interview.

71. Badham, interview.

72. Sariego, interview.

73. Alves, interview.

74. Gerald Perry Finnerman, telephone interview by S. S., 1997.

75. Herbert Wright, interview.

76. Drennan/Straczynski, vol. 8, no. 5: 70.

77. Engelman, interview.

78. Drennan/Straczynski, vol. 8, no. 5: 71.

79. Engelman, interview.

80. Drennan/Straczynski, vol. 8, no. 5: 71.

81. Herbert Wright, interview.

82. Drennan/Straczynski, vol. 8, no. 6: 69.

83. Redman, interview.

84. Lester, interview.

85. Drennan/Straczynski, vol. 5, no. 4: 74.

86. David Rawlins, telephone interview by S. S., 1996.

87. Feather, 5.

88. Mellé, interview.

89. Feather, 5.

90. Mellé, interview.

91. Paul Glass, telephone interview by S. S., 1995.

92. Feather, 32.

93. Mellé, interview.

94. Feather, 5 and 32.

95. Mellé, interview.

96. Glass, interview.

97. Feather, 32.

98. Mellé, interview.

99. Feather, 32.
100. Letter from Jack Laird to Rod Serling, 1971, Rod Serling Archive.
101. Rawlins, interview.
102. Letter from Jack Laird to Rod Serling, 1971, Rod Serling Archive.
103. Drennan/Straczynski, vol. 5, no. 4: 75.
104. Freeman, interview.
105. Drennan/Straczynski, vol. 5, no. 4: 75.
106. Universal Studios press release.
107. Drennan/Straczynski, vol. 5, no. 4: 75.
108. Telegram from Jack Laird to Rod Serling, Sept. 15, 1971, Rod Serling Archive.

## 8. The Second Season

1. Ellen Weston, telephone interview by J. B., 1997.
2. Badham, interview.
3. Weston, interview.
4. Campanella, interview.
5. Sapinsley, interview.
6. Don Page, "Night Gallery in Premiere on NBC," *Los Angeles Times,* Sept. 16, 1971, sec. 4: 21.
7. Review, *Variety,* Sept. 22, 1971.
8. Nielsen, interview.
9. Engelman, interview.
10. Nielsen, interview.
11. Engelman, interview.
12. Szwarc, interview.
13. Desi Arnaz, Jr., telephone interview by J. B., 1997.
14. Szwarc, interview.
15. Sorel, interview.
16. Rod Serling, Sherwood Oaks lecture.
17. Szwarc, interview.
18. Frank Hotchkiss, telephone interview by J. B., 1997.
19. Barbara Shannon, telephone interview by J. B., 1997.
20. Szwarc, interview.
21. Hotchkiss, interview.
22. Szwarc, interview; Drennan/Straczynski, vol. 5, no. 4: 75.
23. Ruth Buzzi, telephone interview by J. B., 1998.
24. Szwarc, interview.
25. Cherie Franklin, telephone interview by J. B., 1996.
26. Hale, interview.
27. Michele Lee, telephone interview by J. B., 1997.
28. Lester, interview.
29. Hale, interview.
30. Freedman, interview.
31. Sanford, interview.
32. Astin, interview.
33. Sanford, interview.
34. Astin, interview.
35. Drennan/Straczynski, vol. 5, no. 5: 83.
36. Freedman, interview.
37. Drennan/Straczynski, vol. 5, no. 4: 74.
38. Drennan/Straczynski, vol. 5, no. 5: 83.
39. Corey, interview.
40. Pat Boone, telephone interview by J. B., 1997.
41. Drennan/Straczynski, vol. 8, no. 4: 49.
42. Szwarc, interview.
43. Rod Serling, Sherwood Oaks lecture.
44. Szwarc, interview.
45. Berke, interview.
46. Radames Pera, telephone interview by S. S., 1997.
47. Glass, interview.
48. Pera, interview.
49. Nielsen, interview.
50. Astor, interview.
51. Berke, interview.
52. Sariego, interview.
53. Nielsen, interview.
54. Hank Brandt, telephone interview by J. B., 1996.
55. Engelman, interview.
56. Brandt, interview.
57. Drennan/Straczynski, vol. 8, no. 4: 49.
58. Drennan/Straczynski, vol. 8, no. 4: 49 and 54.
59. Reisner, interview.
60. Laurie Prange, telephone interview by J. B., 1997.
61. Engelman, interview.
62. Feather, 32.
63. Prange, interview.
64. "Mistake Got Laughs," Miami *Herald,* Nov. 7, 1971.
65. Hale, interview.
66. E. J. Peaker, telephone interview by J. B., 1997.
67. Vincent Van Patten, telephone interview by J. B., 1997.
68. Szwarc, interview.
69. James H. Burns, "Richard Matheson: Spin-

ning Fantasy from Daily Life," *The Twilight Zone Magazine* 1, no. 4 (1981): 16.

70. Van Patten, interview.
71. Engelman, interview.
72. Drennan/Straczynski, vol. 8, no. 4: 54.
73. Berke, interview.
74. Drennan/Straczynski, vol. 8, no. 4: 55.
75. Don Pedro Colley, telephone interview by J. B., 1997.
76. Drennan/Straczynski, vol. 8, no. 4: 55; Theodore J. Flicker to S. S., May 3, 1994.
77. Astin, interview.
78. Drennan/Straczynski, vol. 8, no. 4: 55.
79. Astin, interview.
80. Alex Cord, telephone interview by J. B., 1997.
81. Drennan/Straczynski, vol. 5, no. 4: 74–75.
82. Sapinsley, interview; Drennan/Straczynski, vol. 8, no. 5: 70.
83. Lester, interview.
84. Drennan/Straczynski, vol. 8, no. 5: 71.
85. Engelman, interview.
86. Drennan/Straczynski, vol. 8, no. 5: 71.
87. Bradford Dillman, telephone interview by S. S., 1997.
88. Phillips, *Starlog*: 60.
89. Dillman, interview.
90. Sorel, interview; Phillips, *Starlog*: 60.
91. Corey, interview.
92. Szwarc, interview.
93. Szwarc, interview; Burns, vol. 8, no. 3: 93.
94. Henry Darrow, telephone interview by J. B., 1997.
95. Szwarc, interview.
96. Drennan/Straczynski, vol. 8, no. 5: 72.
97. Letter from Henry Darrow to S. S., Apr. 1, 1994.
98. Szwarc, interview.
99. René Auberjonois, telephone interview by J. B., 1997.
100. Drennan/Straczynski, vol. 8, no. 5: 72.
101. Badham, interview.
102. Auberjonois, interview.
103. Corey, interview; Drennan/Straczynski, vol. 8, no. 5: 71.
104. Letter from Rolf Gompertz to Rod Serling, June 25, 1971, Rod Serling Archive.
105. Memo from Rolf Gompertz to Bill Stein, June 25, 1971, Rod Serling Archive.
106. Drennan/Straczynski, vol. 8, no. 5: 73.
107. Drennan/Straczynski, vol. 8, no. 5: 73; Taylor, interview.

108. Taylor, interview.
109. Sariego, interview.
110. Taylor, interview.
111. Tony Roberts, telephone interview by J. B., 1997.
112. Taylor, interview.
113. Drennan/Straczynski, vol. 8, no. 5: 73; Taylor, interview.
114. Glass, interview.
115. Drennan/Straczynski, vol. 8, no. 5: 73.
116. Roberts, interview.
117. Zsa Zsa Gabor, telephone interview by J. B., 1996.
118. Sanford, interview.
119. Serling, *Night Gallery 2* (New York: Bantam Books, 1972), 92.
120. Jon Korkes, telephone interview by J. B., 1996.
121. Brevelle, 25.
122. Korkes, interview.
123. Corey, interview.
124. John Burke, ed., *More Tales of Unease* (London: Pan Books, 1969), 161.
125. Drennan/Straczynski, vol. 8, no. 5: 74.
126. Corey, interview; Drennan/Straczynski, vol. 8, no. 5: 74.
127. Drennan/Straczynski, vol. 8, no. 5: 74.
128. Szwarc, interview.
129. Bob Rose, "The Skinny Kid Who Is Going to Replace Bonanza's Hoss," *San Diego Union TV Week*, Sept. 3, 1972: 11.
130. Szwarc, interview.
131. Badham, interview.
132. Engelman, interview.
133. Burns, vol. 1, no. 4: 16.
134. "A Weird Kind of Funeral," *Pasadena Star News TV Week Magazine*, June 11, 1972: 7.
135. John Meredyth Lucas, telephone interview by S. S., 1996.
136. Sanford, interview.
137. Rawlins, interview.
138. Drennan/Straczynski, vol. 8, no. 6: 67.
139. Rawlins, interview.
140. Drennan/Straczynski, vol. 8, no. 6: 68.
141. Rawlins, interview.
142. Redman, interview.
143. Stuart Whitman, telephone interview by S. S., 1994.
144. Corey, interview.
145. Drennan/Straczynski, vol. 8, no. 6: 69.
146. Corey, interview.
147. Engelman, interview.

148. Drennan/Straczynski, vol. 8, no. 6: 68–69.
149. Drennan/Straczynski, vol. 8, no. 6: 69; Herbert Wright, interview.
150. Corey, interview; Drennan/Straczynski, vol. 8, no. 6: 68.
151. Sondra Locke, telephone interview by J. B., 1997.
152. Szwarc, interview.
153. Locke, interview.
154. Ralph Senensky, telephone interview by S. S., 1996.
155. Ibid.
156. Lester, interview.
157. Szwarc, interview.
158. Alves, interview.
159. Drennan/Straczynski, vol. 5, no. 4: 75.
160. Sapinsley, interview.
161. Szwarc, interview.
162. Finnerman, interview.
163. Rosemary Forsyth, telephone interview by J. B., 1997.
164. Corey, interview.
165. Dresner, interview.
166. Szwarc, interview.
167. Timothy Galfas, telephone interview by S. S., 1994.
168. Lester, interview.
169. Lois Nettleton, telephone interview by J. B., 1997.
170. John Saxon, telephone interview by J. B., 1997.
171. Nettleton, interview.
172. Sariego, interview.
173. Saxon, interview.
174. Darrell Larson, telephone interview by J. B., 1997.
175. Engelman, interview.
176. Szwarc, interview.
177. Alves, interview.
178. Sariego, interview.
179. Szwarc, interview.
180. Richard Thomas, telephone interview by J. B., 1997.
181. Szwarc, interview.
182. Thomas, interview.
183. Finnerman, interview.
184. Thomas, interview.
185. Lana Wood, telephone interview by J. B., 1997.
186. Engelman, interview.
187. Wood, interview.
188. Engelman, interview.
189. Stephen King, *Danse Macabre* (New York: Everest House, 1981), 234.
190. Szwarc, interview.
191. Pettet, interview.
192. Cord, interview.
193. Sariego, interview.
194. Pettet, interview.
195. Finnerman, interview.
196. Szwarc, interview.
197. Pettet, interview.
198. Szwarc, interview.
199. Stanford Whitmore, telephone interview by S. S., 1994.
200. Galfas, interview.
201. Ed Nelson, telephone interview by J. B., 1997.
202. Rod Serling to Dick Cavett, *The Dick Cavett Show,* July 19, 1972.
203. Nelson, interview.
204. Jack Hellman, column, *Variety,* Jan. 20, 1972: 18.
205. Zuanich, 9.
206. Cleveland Amory, review, *TV Guide,* Feb. 5, 1972: 40.
207. Letter from Donald E. Heinz to Mort Werner, Apr. 12, 1971, Rod Serling Archive.
208. Sariego, interview.

## 9. Executive Action

1. Jim Donaldson, "Ballad for an Undesperate Man," *The Ithacan,* Apr. 28, 1972.
2. Engel, 328.
3. Donaldson, "Ballad."
4. Burns, "Burgess Meredith: Multidimensional Man," *The Twilight Zone Magazine* 4, no. 1 (1984): 28.
5. Although "Finnegan's Flight" would ultimately be produced—with Serling's addition of a new first scene that "grabbed"— "The View of Whatever" would never see a lens.
6. Letter from Rod Serling to Universal Studios executive, courtesy Marc Scott Zicree.
7. "NBC Refuses to Let Serling Off Series," *Daily Variety,* June 9, 1972: 11.
8. Donaldson, "Ballad."
9. Richard Bracken, telephone interview by J. B., 1997.
10. Szwarc, interview.
11. Letter from Henry Blankfort to Rod Serling, Oct. 10, 1972.

12. Donaldson, "Ballad."

## 10.  The Final Season

1. Szwarc, interview.
2. Tisha Sterling, telephone interview by J. B., 1997.
3. Szwarc, interview.
4. NBC press release.
5. Drennan/Straczynski, vol. 8, no. 5: 74.
6. Sterling, interview.
7. Engelman, interview.
8. Paul M. Sammon, "Fritz Leiber: SF's Wizard-in-Residence," *The Twilight Zone Magazine* 2, vol. 1 (1982): 20.
9. Badham, interview.
10. Pettet, interview.
11. James Farentino, telephone interview by J. B., 1997.
12. Badham, interview.
13. Lester, interview.
14. Pettet, interview.
15. Badham, interview.
16. Pettet, interview.
17. Farentino, interview.
18. Szwarc, interview.
19. Badham, interview.
20. Roger Davis, telephone interview by J. B., 1997.
21. Lindsay Wagner, telephone interview by J. B., 1997.
22. Carol Weed, telephone interview by J. B., 1996.
23. Adam Weed, telephone interview by J. B., 1996.
24. Engelman, interview.
25. Corey, interview.
26. John Gilgreen, telephone interview by J. B., 1997.
27. Bracken, interview.
28. Gilgreen, interview.
29. Rod Serling, Sherwood Oaks lecture.
30. Leonard Nimoy, telephone interview by S. S., 1997.
31. Rayfiel, interview.
32. Shooting script for "She'll Be Company for You."
33. Rayfiel, interview.
34. Finnerman, interview.
35. Ibid.

36. Mark Phillips, *TV Science Fiction* (Jefferson, N.C.: McFarland Press, 1993).
37. Gary Lockwood, telephone interview by J. B., 1997.
38. Abroms, interview.
39. Nimoy, interview.
40. Finnerman, interview.
41. Nimoy, interview.
42. Sariego, interview.
43. Nimoy, interview.
44. Szwarc, interview.
45. Rayfiel, interview.
46. Astor, interview.
47. Finnerman, interview.
48. Rayfiel, interview.
49. Stephen Farber and Marc Green, *Outrageous Conduct: Art, Ego, and the Twilight Zone Case* (New York: Arbor House, 1988), 205.
50. Finnerman, interview.
51. Burns, vol. 8, no. 3: 93.
52. Alves, interview.

## 11.  Aftermath

1. Engelman, interview; Drennan/Straczynski, vol. 8, no. 5: 71.
2. Herbert Wright, interview.
3. Rod Serling, Sherwood Oaks lecture.
4. Brevelle, 23.
5. Chuck Wheat, "Wheat's Field" column (newspaper unknown, c. 1962), clipping file, Rod Serling Archive.
6. Bracken, interview.
7. Drennan/Straczynski, vol. 5, no. 4: 75–76.
8. Bracken, interview.
9. Drennan/Straczynski, vol. 5, no. 4: 76.
10. Badham, interview.
11. Szwarc, interview.
12. "The Writer's Life," *Writers Digest,* Nov. 1975: 4.
13. Ibid.
14. Nielsen, interview.
15. McAdams, interview.

# Bibliography

ARCHIVES

Rod Serling Archive. Roy H. Park School of Communications. Ithaca College, Ithaca, N.Y.
Library of Congress. Motion Picture and Television Reading Room. Washington, D.C.
Museum of Television and Radio. Beverly Hills, Calif.

BOOKS

Aiken, Conrad. *The Short Stories of Conrad Aiken*. New York: Duell, Sloan and Pearce, 1950.

Aiken, Joan. *The Windscreen Weepers*. London: Dodd, 1969.

Baxter, John. *Steven Spielberg: An Unauthorized Biography*. New York: Harper Collins, 1996.

Bernard, Christine, ed. *The Third Fontana Book of Great Horror Stories*. London: Berkley, 1968.

Brand, Christianna. *What Dread Hand*. London: Ian Henry, 1977.

Brode, Douglas. *The Films of Steven Spielberg*. New York: Citadel Press, 1995.

Burke, John, ed. *Tales of Unease*. London: Pan Books, 1969.

————. *More Tales of Unease*. London: Pan Books, 1969.

Burlingame, Jon. *TV's Biggest Hits*. New York: Schirmer Books, 1996.

Conklin, Groff, ed. *Twisted*. London: Belmont, 1962.

Crawford, Christina. *Mommie Dearest*. New York: William Morrow and Co., 1978.

Davenport, Basil, ed. *Horror Stories from Tales to Be Told in the Dark*. New York: Ballantine, 1953.

Derleth, August. *Not Long for This World*. Sauk City, Iowa: Arkham House, 1948.

Derleth, August, ed. *The Sleeping and the Dead*. New York: Pellegrini & Cudahy, 1947.

————. *Who Knocks?* New York: Rinehart, 1946.

Duke, Patty, and Kenneth Turan. *Call Me Anna: The Autobiography of Patty Duke*. New York: Bantam Books, 1987.

Engel, Joel. *Rod Serling: The Dreams and Nightmares of Life in the Twilight Zone*. Chicago: Contemporary Press, 1989.

Farber, Stephen, and Marc Green. *Outrageous Conduct: Art, Ego, and the Twilight Zone Case*. New York: Arbor House, 1988.

Fish, Robert L., ed. *The Mystery Writers of America: With Malice Toward All*. New York: Putnam, 1968.

Gerani, Paul, with Paul H. Schulman. *Fantastic Television*. New York: Harmony Books, 1977.

Gianakos, Larry. *Television Drama Series Programming: A Comprehensive Chronicle.* Lanhau, Md: Scarecrow Press, 1978.

Haining, Peter, ed. *The Witchcraft Reader.* New York: Doubleday and Co., 1970.

Hitchcock, Alfred, ed. *Stories Not for the Nervous.* New York: Random House, 1966.

———. *Stories That Scared Even Me.* New York: Random House, 1968.

King, Stephen. *Danse Macabre.* New York: Everest House, 1981.

Lofficier, Jean-Marc and Randy. *Into the Twilight Zone: The Rod Serling Programme Guide.* London: Virgin Books, 1995.

Meik, Vivian. *Devil's Drums.* London: Philip Allan, 1933.

Parish, James Robert. *Actors' Television Credits—1950-1972.* Lanhau, Md: Scarecrow Press, 1973.

Phillips, Mark. *TV Science Fiction.* Jefferson, N.C.: McFarland Press, 1993.

Sander, Gordon F. *Serling: The Rise and Twilight of Television's Last Angry Man.* New York: Dutton, 1992.

Sanello, Frank. *Spielberg: The Man, The Movies, The Mythology.* Dallas, Tex.: Taylor, 1996.

Serling, Carol, Charles G. Waugh, and Martin H. Greenberg, eds. *Rod Serling's Night Gallery Reader.* New York: Dembner Books, 1987.

Serling, Rod. *Night Gallery.* New York: Bantam Books, 1971.

———. *Night Gallery 2.* New York: Bantam Books, 1972.

———. *The Season to Be Wary.* Boston: Little, Brown and Co., 1967.

Terrace, Vincent. *Encyclopedia of Television—Series, Pilots, and Specials, Vols. 1, 2, and 3.* New York: New York Zoetrope, 1986.

Thomas, Bob. *Joan Crawford: A Biography.* New York: Simon and Schuster, 1978.

Van Thal, Herbert, ed. *The Seventh Pan Book of Horror Stories.* London: Pan Books, 1966.

Walter, Elizabeth. *The Sin-Eater and Other Scientific Impossibilities.* London: Stein and Day, 1967.

Wicking, Christopher, and Tise Vahimagi. *The American Vein.* New York: Dutton, 1979.

Zicree, Marc Scott. *The Twilight Zone Companion.* 1982. Reprint. Hollywood: Silman-James Press, 1992.

(Editor unknown). *A Century of Creepy Stories.* London: Hutchinson, 1934.

## ARTICLES

"Dr. Frankenstein Would Be Proud." *TV Guide.* Nov. 27, 1971: 10–11.

"Final Cut" Column ("A Foot in the Door: Steven Spielberg"). *In Cinema.* (n.d.) 1981: 30.

Review. *The Hollywood Reporter.* Dec. 21, 1970.

Review. *The Hollywood Reporter.* Sept. 16, 1971.

"Lady in the Dark." *TV Guide.* Aug. 16, 1969: 8–9.

Review. *Daily Variety.* Nov. 10, 1969: 14.

Review. *Daily Variety.* Dec. 17, 1970: 16.

Review. *Variety.* Dec. 23, 1970.

Review. *Daily Variety.* Jan. 15, 1971: 28.

Review. *Variety.* Sept. 17, 1971: 19.

Review. *Variety.* Sept. 22, 1971.

Squib. *Variety.* Dec. 23, 1971: 15.

Review. *Variety.* Feb. 11, 1972: 29.

Review. *Variety.* Oct. 4, 1972: 39.

"NBC Refuses to Let Serling Off Series." *Daily Variety.* June 9, 1972: 1 and 11.

"The Writing Life." *Writer's Digest.* Nov. 1975: 4.

Amory, Cleveland. Review. *TV Guide.* Feb. 5, 1972: 40.

Brevelle, Linda. "Rod Serling's Last Interview." *The Twilight Zone Magazine* 2, no. 1 (1982): 21–27.

Burns, James H. "Burgess Meredith: Multidimensional Man." *The Twilight Zone Magazine* 4, no. 1 (1984): 26–31 and 80.

———. "People: Jeannot Szwarc." *The Twilight Zone Magazine* 8, no. 3 (1988): 92–93.

———. "Richard Matheson: Spinning Fantasy from Daily Life." *The Twilight Zone Magazine* 1, no. 4 (1981): 14–21.

Drennan, Kathryn M., and J. Michael Straczynski. "Rod Serling's Night Gallery: A Show-by-Show Guide." *The Twilight Zone Magazine* 5, no. 1 (1985): 54–60.

———. "Rod Serling's Night Gallery: A Show-by-Show Guide." *The Twilight Zone Magazine* 5, no. 2 (1985): 83–89.

———. "Rod Serling's Night Gallery: A Show-by-Show Guide." *The Twilight Zone Magazine* 5, no. 3 (1985): 78–85.

———. "Rod Serling's Night Gallery: A Show-by-Show Guide." *The Twilight Zone Magazine* 5, no. 4 (1985): 74–80.

———. "Rod Serling's Night Gallery: A Show-by-Show Guide." *The Twilight Zone Magazine* 5, no. 5 (1985): 82–87.

———. "Rod Serling's Night Gallery: A Show-by-Show Guide." *The Twilight Zone Magazine* 5, no. 6 (1986): 72–75.

———. "Rod Serling's Night Gallery: A Show-by-Show Guide." *The Twilight Zone Magazine* 6, no. 1 (1986): 75–79.

———. "Rod Serling's Night Gallery: A Show-by-Show Guide." *The Twilight Zone Magazine* 8, no. 4 (1988): 46–55.

———. "Rod Serling's Night Gallery: A Show-by-Show Guide." *The Twilight Zone Magazine* 8, no. 5 (1988): 70–79.

———. "Rod Serling's Night Gallery: A Show-by-Show Guide." *The Twilight Zone Magazine* 8, no. 6 (1989): 67–73.

Feather, Leonard. "From Pen to Screen." *International Musician.* Nov. 1972: 5 and 32.

Fox, Jordan R. "Somewhere in Time with Jeannot Szwarc." *Cinefantastique* 10, no. 4 (1981): 14–19.

Hellman, Jack. Column. *Daily Variety.* Jan. 20, 1972: 18.

Hull, Bob. "22-Year-Old Tyro Directs Joan Crawford: 'A Pleasure.'" *The Hollywood Reporter.* Feb. 17, 1969.

Millstein, Gilbert. "'Patterns' of a Television Playwright." *New York Times Magazine.* Dec. 2, 1956.

Olshaker, Mark. "Tribute: Requiem for a Heavyweight." *New Times.* July 25, 1975.

Phillips, Mark. "Interview with Louise Sorel." *Starlog,* Apr. 1998: 60.

Sammon, Paul M. "Fritz Leiber: SF's Wizard-in-Residence." *The Twilight Zone Magazine* 2, vol. 1 (1982): 16–22.

Sarris, Andrew. "Rod Serling Viewed from Beyond 'The Twilight Zone.'" *The Twilight Zone Magazine* 5, vol. 1 (1985): 45–49.

Swires, Steve. "Filming the Fantastic: Steven Spielberg." *Starlog.* Oct. 1978: 23–26.

Whitney, Dwight. "Interview with Rod Serling." *TV Guide.* June 3, 1972: 28–32.


## NEWSPAPERS

*Rochester Democrat and Chronicle.* "Old Man Serling: No More Crusades." Dec. 3, 1970.

*Minneapolis Tribune TV Week.* "A Man Can Change His Mind." Dec. 13, 1970: 2.

*Ventura County (Calif.) Star–Free Press TV Week.* "Welcome Art Lovers." Jan. 10, 1971: 12.

*Pasadena Star News TV Week.* "A Weird Kind of Funeral." June 11, 1972: 7.

*Miami Herald.* "TV Needs Its Fantasy." Nov. 6, 1971.

———. "Mistake Got Laughs." Nov. 7, 1971.

*Los Angeles Herald Examiner TV Week Magazine.* Beck, Marilyn. "Even Rod Serling Has Job Problems," Nov. 14, 1971: 81–82.

*Ithacan (N.Y.).* Donaldson, Jim. "Ballad for an Undesperate Man." Apr. 28, 1972.

*Sacramento Bee.* Du Brow, Rick. "No Room on Tube for Poor Ludwig." Dec. 17, 1970: C-3.

*San Diego Union.* Freeman, Donald. "A 'Night Gallery' Trip to Unreality." Dec. 18, 1970: D-2.

———. Don Freeman column. June 14, 1972: B-6.

———. Don Freeman column. July 1, 1975: B-9.

*Louisville Courier Journal and Times Magazine.* Hamilton, Milli. "Horror Artist." Apr. 16, 1972: 24–29.

*Los Angeles Times.* Knapp, Dan. "Rod Serling Back with Night Gallery." Dec. 16, 1970: Sec. 4–29.

———. Page, Don. "Night Gallery in Premiere on NBC." Sept. 16, 1971: Sec. 4–21.

*San Diego Union TV Week.* Rose, Bob. "The Skinny Kid Who Is Going to Replace Bonanza's Hoss." Sept. 3, 1972: 11.

*Chicago Daily News TV Magazine.* Scott, Vernon. "Rod Serling: TV's Angry Young Man Mellows with Time." Dec. 12, 1970: 4–5.

*Los Angeles TV Times Sunday Supplement.* Smith, Cecil. "Rod Serling: The Prolific TV Writer Has a Novel Idea." Mar. 2, 1969: 2.

————. Cecil Smith column. Feb. 1, 1970: 2.

————. Smith, Cecil. "Two Spooky Playlets Open 'Night Gallery.'" Dec. 17, 1970: Sec. 4–34.

————. Smith, Cecil. "The Video House That Jack Built." N.d., 1971.

————. Smith, Cecil. "A Requiem for Rod Serling." July 3, 1975: Sec. 4–13.

*New York World-Telegram and Sun.* Harriet Van Horne column. June 29, 1975.

*TV Key.* Whitbeck, Charles. "Rod Serling Returns with 'Night Gallery.'" Dec. 15, 1970.

*Washington Post.* White, Jean M. "A Writer's Many Facets." Apr. 3, 1973: B-1 and B-4.

*Los Angeles Herald-Examiner TV Weekly.* Zuanich, Barbara. "Universal's Quadruple Threat." Jan. 9, 1972: 8–9.

## TELEPHONE INTERVIEWS
*(except where noted)*

Edward M. Abroms. By S. S. 1996.

Joseph Alves, Jr. By S. S. 1994.

Barbara Anderson. By J. B. 1997.

Burt Armus. By S. S. 1996.

Desi Arnaz, Jr. By J. B. 1997.

John Astin. By J. B. 1997.

Burt Astor. By S. S. 1994.

René Auberjonois. By J. B. 1997.

John Badham. By S. S. 1995.

Les Berke. By S. S. 1994.

Robert Bloch. By S. S., by mail. 1994.

Michael Blodgett. By J. B. 1997.

Pat Boone. By J. B. 1997.

Tom Bosley. By S. S. 1998.

Richard Bracken. By J. B. 1997.

Hank Brandt. By J. B. 1996.

Ruth Buzzi. By J. B. 1998.

Joseph Campanella. By J. B. 1997.

Rosemary Campbell. By S. S. 1996.

Don Pedro Colley. By J. B. 1997.

Alex Cord. By J. B. 1997.

Jeff Corey. By S. S. 1994.

Grace Cursio. By S. S. 1994.

Henry Darrow. By S. S., by mail. 1994.

Henry Darrow. By J. B. 1997.

Susannah Darrow. By J. B. 1997.

Roger Davis. By J. B. 1997.

Phyllis Diller. By J. B. 1997.

Bradford Dillman. By S. S. 1997.

Walter Doniger. By S. S. 1996.

Rudi Dorn. By S. S. 1994.

Hal Dresner. By J. B. 1996.

Daryl Duke. By J. B. 1996.

Buddy Ebsen. By J. B. 1997.

Leonard Engelman. By S. S. 1996.

James Farentino. By J. B. 1997.

Gerald Perry Finnerman. By S. S. 1997.

Wayne Fitzgerald. By J. B. 1997.

Theodore J. Flicker. By S. S., by mail. 1994.

Rosemary Forsyth. By J. B. 1997.

Cherie Franklin. By J. B. 1996.

Jerrold Freedman. By S. S. 1994.

Paul Freeman. By S. S. 1996.

Zsa Zsa Gabor. By J. B. 1996.

Timothy Galfas. By S. S. 1994.

Jaroslav Gebr. By S. S. 1995.

John Gilgreen. By J. B. 1997.

Paul Glass. By S. S. 1995.

William Hale. By S. S. 1994.

Frank Hotchkiss. By J. B. 1997.

Arte Johnson. By J. B. 1997.

Peggy Johnson. By S. S. 1996.

Richard Kiley. By S. S., by mail, tape recording. 1994.

Jon Korkes. By J. B. 1996.

Darrell Larson. By J. B. 1997.

Michele Lee. By J. B. 1997.

Larry Lester. By S. S. 1994.

Gene Levitt. By J. B. 1996.

Sondra Locke. By J. B. 1997.

Gary Lockwood. By J. B. 1997.

John Meredyth Lucas. By S. S. 1996.

Peter Mamakos. By J. B. 1997.

Richard Matheson. By S. S., by mail. 1994.

James McAdams. By S. S. 1995.

Roddy McDowall. By S. S. 1997.

Gil Mellé. By S. S. 1995.

James Metropole. By S. S. 1996.

Ed Nelson. By J. B. 1997.

Lois Nettleton. By J. B. 1997.

Leslie Nielsen. By S. S. 1995.

Leonard Nimoy. By S. S. 1997.

Suzy Parker. By J. B. 1997.

E. J. Peaker. By J. B. 1997.

Radames Pera. By S. S. 1997.

Joanna Pettet. By J. B. 1997.

Sydney Pollack. By S. S. 1996.

Laurie Prange. By J. B. 1997.

Robert Prince. By S. S., by mail. 1994.

Terence Pushman. By J. B. 1996.

David Rawlins. By S. S. 1996.

David Rayfiel. By J. B. 1997.

Anthony Redman. By S. S. 1994.

Allen Reisner. By S. S. 1996.

Tony Roberts. By J. B. 1997.

Tony Russel. By J. B. 1996.

William Sackheim. By S. S. 1994.

Gerald Sanford. By S. S. 1994.

Alvin Sapinsley. By S. S. 1994.

Ralph Sariego. By S. S., in person, tape recording, Eugene, Ore. 1994.

John Saxon. By J. B. 1997.

Ralph Senensky. By S. S. 1996.

Barbara Shannon. By J. B. 1997.

Louise Sorel. By S. S. 1995.

Leonard J. South. By S. S. 1996.

Tisha Sterling. By J. B. 1997.

Jeannot Szwarc. By S. S. 1994.

Harry Tatelman. By S. S. 1995.

Don Taylor. By S. S. 1996.

Richard Thomas. By J. B. 1997.

Angel Tompkins. By J. B. 1997.

Marc Vahanian. By J. B. 1996.

Phil Vanderlei. By J. B. 1997.

Vincent Van Patten. By J. B. 1997.

Sam Vitale. By S. S. 1996.

Lindsay Wagner. By J. B. 1997.

Shani Wallis. By S. S., by mail. 1994.

Adam Weed. By J. B. 1996.

Carol Weed. By J. B. 1996.

Mike Westmore. By S. S. 1996.

Ellen Weston. By J. B. 1997.

Stuart Whitman. By S. S. 1994.

Stanford Whitmore. By S. S. 1994.

William Windom. By S. S. 1994.

Lana Wood. By J. B. 1997.

Herbert Wright. By S. S. 1995.

Tom Wright. By S. S. 1996.

# Index

Book design by Christopher Kuntze
Composed in Dante type with Ad Lib and Myriad for display
Printed and bound by Thomson-Shore, Dexter, Michigan